Tolley's Capital Allowances 2017–18

Tolley's Capital Allowances 2017–18

30th Edition

by

Kevin Walton MA

David Smailes FCA

with a section on tax planning by Heather Britton of Francis Clark Tax Consultancy Limited

Tolley®

Members of the LexisNexis Group worldwide

United Kingdom	RELX (UK) Limited, trading as LexisNexis, Lexis House, 30 Farringdon Street, London, EC4A 4HH
Australia	LexisNexis Butterworths, Chatswood, New South Wales
Austria	LexisNexis Verlag ARD Orac GmbH & Co KG, Vienna
Benelux	LexisNexis Benelux, Amsterdam
Canada	LexisNexis Butterworths, Markham, Ontario
China	LexisNexis China, Beijing and Shanghai
France	LexisNexis SA, Paris
Germany	LexisNexis Deutschland GmbH, Munster
Hong Kong	LexisNexis Hong Kong, Hong Kong
India	LexisNexis India, New Delhi
Italy	Giuffrè Editore, Milan
Japan	LexisNexis Japan, Tokyo
Malaysia	Malayan Law Journal Sdn Bhd, Kuala Lumpur
Mexico	LexisNexis Mexico, Mexico
New Zealand	LexisNexis NZ Ltd, Wellington
Singapore	LexisNexis Singapore, Singapore
South Africa	LexisNexis Butterworths, Durban
USA	LexisNexis, Dayton, Ohio

Published by LexisNexis

A CIP Catalogue record for this book is available from the British Library.

ISBN for this volume: 9780754553670

Printed and bound by Hobbs the Printers Ltd, Totton, Hampshire

Visit LexisNexis at www.lexisnexis.co.uk

About This Book

This is the thirtieth edition of Tolley's Capital Allowances. It contains the legislation, relevant case law and other important information, including the provisions of the Finance Act 2017 and the Finance (No 2) Act 2017, to 1 September 2017 and later material where significant. Note that, at the time of writing, the Finance (No 2) Act 2017 had not completed its passage through Parliament. The provisions included in the Act and described in this edition are therefore subject to any changes made during the Parliamentary process.

As well as current information, the book includes, where appropriate, the law and practice relating to superseded provisions which still have effect for capital expenditure incurred when such provisions were in force.

All of the currently available allowance codes are included. The section on the most common allowance, that for expenditure on plant and machinery, has been broken up into a number of separate chapters and brought to the front of the book. It is introduced by a summary chapter which gives a concise outline of the code and cross references to where the detailed rules can be found. The other current capital allowances are described in the chapters following the plant and machinery section, together with a chapter dealing with allowances for capital expenditure which are not formally capital allowances.

Also included are two chapters on tax planning for capital allowances, written by Heather Britton of Francis Clark Tax Consultancy Limited. The first of these chapters, Chapter 18, provides general guidance on planning principles and the second, Chapter 19, focuses on plant and machinery in buildings and related issues.

The book includes worked examples to illustrate the effect of the legislation and discussion of problem areas. A comprehensive list of what may qualify as plant or machinery is included in Appendix 1.

Comments and suggestions for the improvement of future editions are always welcome. Please contact kevin.walton@lexisnexis.co.uk.

Contents

Abbreviations and References

Abbreviations

AIA	Annual invesment allowance
b/fwd	Brought forward
CA	Court of Appeal
CAA	Capital Allowances Act
CCAB	Consultative Committee of Accountancy Bodies
CES	Court of Exchequer (Scotland)
c/fwd	Carried forward
CGTA	Capital Gains Tax Act
ChD	Chancery Division
CIR	Commissioners of Inland Revenue
CRCA	Commissioners for Revenue and Customs Act
CS	Scottish Court of Session
CTA	Corporation Tax Act
EC	European Communities
EEC	European Economic Community
ESC	HMRC Extra-Statutory Concession
FA	Finance Act
FTT	First-tier Tribunal
FYA	First-year allowance
HC(I)	High Court (Irish Republic)
HL	House of Lords
HMRC	Her Majesty's Revenue and Customs
IBA	Industrial Buildings Allowance
ICAEW	Institute of Chartered Accountants in England and Wales
ICTA	Income and Corporation Taxes Act

ISA	Individual Savings Account
ITA	Income Tax Act
ITEPA	Income Tax (Earnings and Pensions) Act
ITTOIA	Income Tax (Trading and Other Income) Act
KB	King's Bench Division
LJ	Lord Justice
NI	Northern Ireland
PCA	Proceeds of Crime Act
Pt	Part
QB	Queen's Bench Division
s	Section
SpC	Special Commissioners
Sch	Schedule
SI	Statutory Instrument
SP	Inland Revenue Statement of Practice
SR	Statutory Rule
TCGA	Taxation of Chargeable Gains Act
TIOPA	Taxation (International and Other Provisions) Act
TMA	Taxes Management Act
UK	United Kingdom
UT	Upper Tribunal
VAT	Value Added Tax
WDA	Writing-down allowance
WDV	Written-down value

References

All ER	All England Reports
Ch	Law Reports, Chancery Division
IR	Irish Reports
QBD	Queen's Bench Division Reports
SLT	Scots Law Times
SFTD	Simon's First-tier Tax Decisions

SSCD	Simon's Special Commissioners' Decisions
STC	Simon's Tax Cases
TC	Official Reports of Tax Cases
TL	Tax Case Leaflets (Irish Republic)
TR	Taxation Reports

Table of Statutes

Table of Cases

E

F

G

H

J

K

L

T

U

V

W

Y

1

Introduction

Background

[1.1] It will be no surprise to those acquainted with the UK direct tax system that the present capital allowance legislation is an exception to the general principle that capital expenditure is not allowable in computing taxable income. That principle (see, for example, *ITTOIA 2005, s 33*) generally still holds good for expenditure incurred in circumstances where none of the forms of capital allowance is available (but see **2.3** below where the cash basis for small businesses applies). In the past, when no capital allowance system was in force, taxpayers had attempted to lift this prohibition but with no success. However, their failure did prompt the legislature to recognise the inequity this caused and slowly from 1878 the frontiers began to be rolled back so that increasingly capital expenditure incurred for a variety of purposes was admitted for allowances. The current situation is examined briefly in **1.2** below and throughout Chapters **3–14** of this book.

An examination of reported tax cases reveals that it is common for there to be a dispute as to the status of expenditure; 'No part of our law on taxation presents such almost insoluble conundrums as the decision whether a receipt or outgoing is capital or income for tax purposes' (Upjohn LJ in *Strick v Regent Oil Co Ltd* HL 1965, 43 TC 1). Obviously if a taxpayer can obtain relief for expenditure incurred as a deduction in arriving at the taxable income to be assessed, there will be no requirement to claim a capital allowance. This book is thus concerned with the allowances available for capital expenditure and the identification of such expenditure is examined in **1.3** and onwards below.

The Office for Tax Simplification is undertaking a review of the capital allowances regime, exploring the impact and challenges of replacing allowances with accounts depreciation for tangible assets. See www.gov.uk/government/publications/ots-starts-new-review-on-capital-allowances-and-depreciation.

Current legislation

[1.2] Some of the current codes of capital allowances have their origin in *ITA 1945* but these have been amended and added to by later capital allowance legislation to such an extent that over time three consolidating acts have had to be introduced. The first was *CAA 1968* and the second was *CAA 1990*. The third consolidating act was *CAA 2001*, which was enacted as part of the Tax Law Rewrite Project. As well being a consolidating Act, therefore, *CAA 2001* substantially rewrote the capital allowances legislation to make it clearer and easier to use. It also made some 66 minor changes to the law.

Allowances are currently available for expenditure within the following categories:

- plant and machinery (see CHAPTERS 3–7);
- mineral extraction (see CHAPTER 10);
- research and development (see CHAPTER 11);
- know-how (see CHAPTER 12);
- patents (see CHAPTER 12); and
- dredging (see CHAPTER 13).

[*CAA 2001, s 1(2); FA 2012, Sch 39 paras 38(2), 40*].

A further code of allowances provided relief for certain expenditure on flat conversion, but the code has been abolished for expenditure incurred on or after 6 April 2013 (1 April 2013 for corporation tax purposes). Despite the abolition of the code, balancing adjustments in respect of allowances already given may continue to arise (see CHAPTER 9). Similarly, the code of allowances for expenditure on business premises renovation in disadvantaged areas has now been abolished for expenditure incurred on or after 6 April 2017 (1 April 2017 for corporation tax purposes). Again, balancing adjustments in respect of allowances already given may continue to arise (see CHAPTER 8).

Before 6 April 2011 for income tax purposes or 1 April 2011 for corporation tax purposes, allowances were also available for expenditure on agricultural buildings and industrial buildings, but those allowances have been abolished, and any unrelieved qualifying expenditure incurred before those dates will receive no further relief. Agricultural buildings allowances and industrial buildings allowances are therefore no longer covered in this work. For a full account of the allowances see the 2010/11 or earlier edition.

The allowances, in the main, operate within a general legislative framework common to all the forms of allowance. Subjects such as the time expenditure is deemed to be incurred, the making of allowances and charges and the utilisation of allowances as reliefs are accordingly dealt with in CHAPTER 2 below.

Although capital allowances constitute the main exception to the rule prohibiting deduction of capital expenditure there are a number of other provisions which provide for such deductions. For completeness, these are covered in CHAPTER 14 below.

Partnerships, whether of individuals, companies or a mixture of the two, present many problems in tax law because of the need to recognise the tax status of individual partners (who may join, change their profit share in, or leave, the partnership) as well as that of the continuing business of the partnership. The effect on capital allowances generally is considered in CHAPTER 15 below. The interaction of capital gains tax (or corporation tax in respect of chargeable gains) with capital allowances is examined in CHAPTER 16 below.

Problems, whether of specific or general application, that commonly arise in practice are dealt with in CHAPTER 17 below.

CHAPTERS 18 and 19 below discuss tax planning approaches to ensuring that capital allowances are maximised. CHAPTER 18 considers planning generally and CHAPTER 19 looks at plant and machinery in buildings.

What is capital expenditure?

Introduction

[1.3] Capital allowances are due in respect of capital expenditure if it is also qualifying expenditure for the particular form of allowance being claimed. In the vast majority of cases, persons incurring expenditure would prefer it to be classed as revenue expenditure so that they obtain a deduction for it in arriving at their profits, and thus receive 100% tax relief for the period of account in which the expenditure is incurred. In many cases capital allowances do not provide for a 100% deduction in the first year, the exceptions being plant and machinery allowances (within certain limits — see **5.2** and **5.16** below), research and development allowances (see CHAPTER **11** below) and business premises renovation allowances (see CHAPTER **8** below).

Statutory provisions

[1.4] So what is capital expenditure? It is a difficult question to answer, as Lord Upjohn said in *Strick v Regent Oil Co Ltd* (see **1.1** above). Sir Wilfred Greene MR remarked in *CIR v British Salmson Aero Engines* CA 1938, 22 TC 29 that 'it is almost as true to say that the spin of a coin would decide the matter almost as satisfactorily as an attempt to find reasons'. The legislation is certainly not very helpful on this subject. It lists a number of items of expenditure which cannot be deducted in computing the profits of a trade, but this is by no means confined to capital expenditure, nor does it define such expenditure. For the purposes of capital allowances, the legislation goes some way towards defining capital expenditure but only by stating what it is not. Thus, capital expenditure cannot include:

(a) expenditure which may be deducted in computing the taxable profits or gains of a trade, profession, property business, or vocation carried on or held by the person incurring the expenditure,
(b) expenditure incurred (other than on the provision of a car) at a time when the profits of a trade, profession, property business, or vocation are calculated on the cash basis (see **17.1A** below),
(c) expenditure which may be allowed as a deduction from the taxable earnings from an office or employment, and
(d) payments which may be made after deduction of tax at source under *ITA 2007, Pt 15 Ch 6* (annual payments or patent royalties), *ITA 2007, s 906* (royalties etc. where usual place of abode of owner is abroad).

[*CAA 2001, s 4; F(No 2)A 2017, Sch 2 para 51*].

Case law

[1.5] An approach which has withstood the test of time is to be found in the judgment of Viscount Cave in the case of *Atherton v British Insulated and Helsby Cables Ltd* HL 1925, 10 TC 155. He said:

> . . . when an expenditure is made, not only once and for all, but with a view to bringing into existence an asset or an advantage for the enduring benefit of a trade

> . . . there is very good reason (in the absence of special circumstances leading to an opposite conclusion) for treating such an expenditure as properly attributable not to revenue but to capital.

The case concerned the creation of a pension fund; but obviously the test would apply to the purchase, as well as to the creation, of an asset. Expenditure incurred on the provision of an item of plant or machinery or the construction of a building would normally be classed as capital expenditure (other than, in both cases, by a person whose stock in trade would include the assets mentioned). However, the payment of a hire charge for a machine or rent for a building would not involve the acquisition of an asset or bring about a lasting benefit, and would normally be a revenue expense.

Repairs and renewals

[1.6] The distinction is probably most difficult when one considers expenditure on an existing asset, the question being whether it is a repair (revenue) or an improvement (capital). Another way of posing the question might be: is the expenditure for the purpose of maintaining the asset in its present state and/or at its present value, or is the effect to alter the very nature of the asset (so as virtually to bring into existence a new asset) and/or to increase its intrinsic value?

This problem has been before the courts on many occasions. Cases of particular interest include the following.

(i) *Ounsworth v Vickers Ltd* KB 1915, 6 TC 671. This case (dealt with more fully at **13.7** below) demonstrates that a partial restoration of an asset, perhaps when associated with the addition of new features to it and a change in its function, may be deemed to be treated as the creation of a new asset.

(ii) *Law Shipping Co Ltd v CIR* CS 1923, 12 TC 621. The cost of repairs to a newly acquired ship was capital to the extent that such repairs were already necessary when the ship was acquired; the cost of such repairs was part of the cost of acquiring the ship.

(iii) *Odeon Associated Theatres Ltd v Jones* CA 1971, 48 TC 257. The facts were similar to *Law Shipping* in that the expenditure in question was on repairs, in this case to cinemas, which were already necessary at the time of acquisition. However, their state of disrepair did not affect the purchase price of the cinemas nor did it restrict their use as such. The expenditure was therefore classed as revenue.

See also **18.3** below for further discussion of this issue.

[1.7] In the case of *Hinton v Maden and Ireland Ltd* HL 1959, 38 TC 391, expenditure on large numbers of knives and lasts, essential for the functioning of the company's machines, was held to be capital expenditure. The knives and lasts had an average life of three years and were held to be plant. The case is an important one, and the judgments are of particular interest not only in distinguishing between capital and revenue but also in defining 'plant' (for which see **4.10** below).

However, expenditure incurred before 6 April 2016 (1 April 2016 for corporation tax purposes) on replacing or altering any 'tool' used for the purposes of a trade etc. could be deducted as a revenue expense. For this purpose, a '*tool*' is any implement, utensil or article. [*ITTOIA 2005, s 68; CTA 2009, s 68; FA 2016, s 72(1)(4)(5)*]. For expenditure incurred before 6 April 2013 (1 April 2013 for corporation tax purposes) there was also a non-statutory renewals basis which allowed a deduction for expenditure on the replacement of items of plant and machinery where capital allowances were not claimed. Following the abolition of these reliefs, a more limited statutory relief for certain replacement expenditure incurred on or after 6 April 2016 (1 April 2016 for corporation tax purposes) has been introduced. It applies only to expenditure by a property business on the replacement of 'domestic items' for use in a dwelling-house by the lessee. Such expenditure does not qualify for capital allowances unless the property business is a furnished holiday lettings business (see **4.20**(b) below), but relief was previously available by way of the wear and tear allowance (see **4.20**(b) below). That allowance has also now been abolished with effect for 2016/17 onwards (for corporation tax, subject to transitional rules, for accounting periods beginning on or after 1 April 2016). For further discussion of the renewals basis and the property business replacement of domestic items relief see **7.15–7.16A** below.

Replacing part of an asset

[1.8] Where part of an asset is replaced, the replacement may be a separate asset in itself and the expenditure will therefore be capital expenditure. That each case must be judged on its merits is illustrated by the contrasting decisions in *O'Grady v Bullcroft Main Collieries Ltd* KB 1932, 17 TC 93 and *Samuel Jones and Co (Devonvale) Ltd v CIR* CS 1951, 32 TC 513, both of which concerned factory chimneys. In the former case, the cost of demolishing a factory chimney and building another was held to be capital, the chimney being regarded as a separate entity and the replacement being of an entirety. In the latter case, expenditure of a similar nature was held to be revenue, the chimney being regarded as an integral part of the factory and not as an asset in itself.

Miscellaneous points

[1.9] The following additional points should be noted.

(i) Certain expenditure which would otherwise be classed as capital may be treated as revenue by virtue of specific provisions of the tax legislation. One example is a premium on a short lease, part of which can be written off over the duration of the lease. [*ITTOIA 2005, s 61; CTA 2009, s 62*].
Further examples are:
- expenditure on the production or acquisition of the original master version of a sound recording (see *ITTOIA 2005, s 134, CTA 2009, s 150*);

- expenditure by a film production company that would otherwise be treated as capital only because it is incurred on the creation of an asset (the film) (see *CTA 2009, s 1191(3)*);
- expenditure by a TV production company that would otherwise be treated as capital only because it is incurred on the creation of an asset (the TV programme) (see *CTA 2009, s 1216BC(3)*);
- expenditure by a video games development company that would otherwise be treated as capital only because it is incurred on the creation of an asset (the video game) (see *CTA 2009, s 1217BC(3)*);
- expenditure by a theatrical production company that would otherwise by treated as capital only because it is incurred on the creation of an asset (the theatrical production) (see *CTA 2009, s 1217IC(3)*); and
- expenditure by an orchestral production company that would otherwise by treated as capital only because it is incurred on the creation of an asset (the concert or concert series) (see *CTA 2009, s 1217QD(3)*).

(ii) The question of whether expenditure could be said to have been 'incurred' by the claimant was considered by the House of Lords in *Ensign Tankers (Leasing) London Ltd v Stokes HL 1992, 64 TC 617*. This case concerned a company which had become a partner in two limited partnerships, each set up to finance the production and exploitation of a feature film. It claimed relief for losses incurred by the partnerships, which arose from claims for capital allowances in respect of the expenditure incurred on production of the films. The first of the films cost £14 million, of which the partnership contributed £3,250,000, the balance being financed through payments from the production company. These payments were described as 'non-recourse loans', and were repayable exclusively out of the receipts of the film. The claimant company contended that the partnership was entitled to a first-year allowance in respect of the whole cost of the film. However, the House of Lords held that it was only entitled to allowances in respect of expenditure of £3,250,000. The balance of the expenditure (£10,750,000) had been paid by the production company, and could not in any meaningful sense be categorised as a loan. The reason why it had been paid into a bank account in the partnership name was not to finance the production of the film, but to enable the partnership to indulge in a tax avoidance scheme.

See also *Tower Mcashback LLP1 v HMRC (and related appeal)* SC 2011; [2011] STC 1143. In this case, two limited liability partnerships claimed capital allowances in respect of capital expenditure on computer software. 75% of the purchase price of the software was funded by 'non-recourse loans', which were indirectly made available by the vendor of the software. The Supreme Court held that, on the facts found by the Special Commissioner, the partnerships were only entitled to 25% of the allowances which they had claimed, applying the decision in *Ensign Tankers* above. Lord Walker held that the composite transactions in this case 'did not, on a realistic appraisal of the facts, meet the test laid down by the Capital Allowances Act, which requires real expenditure for the real purpose of acquiring plant for use in a trade'.

In *Brain Disorders Research Partnership v HMRC* UT; [2017] STC 1170, a partnership unsuccessfully implemented a complex scheme designed to enhance capital allowances and interest relief. The scheme broadly worked as follows (using hypothetical simple numbers). The partnership paid 100 to a special purpose vehicle ('SPV') to undertake research and development work. 100 was verified by a third party as the amount required to undertake the research conventionally. The SPV then sub-contracted the work to a company which held the technology, expertise, systems and data bank to enable it to perform the work for a fraction of the price. The SPV therefore only paid 6 to its sub-contractor. As the partnership had paid 100 to the SPV, it hoped to claim research and development capital allowances for 100. A clause of the contract between the partnership and the SPV provided that the SPV 'shall by itself or through the Appointed Sub-Contractor undertake for the Partnership a programme of research work'. The Tribunal observed that there was no intention that the SPV would or could undertake the project itself so that the first limb of the clause was false and it was the foundation of the partnership's claim for vastly excessive capital allowances. That part of the transaction was therefore struck down as a sham. Furthermore, applying *CAA 2001, s 437* purposively, and analysing the facts realistically, it was 'absolutely impossible' to conclude that capital expenditure was incurred on any scientific research in any amount in excess of 6. Additionally, all the money movements were steps in a scheme designed to generate up-front tax savings so that no trading activity took place.

(iii) Where doubt may otherwise exist, the treatment of an item of expenditure in the relevant accounts, provided the item has been correctly accounted for, is likely to be followed. See, for example, **4.19** below with regard to computer software; *Heather v P-E Consulting Group Ltd* CA 1972, 48 TC 293 and the *Odeon Associated Theatres Ltd* case mentioned at **1.6** above.

(iv) The incidental costs of acquiring an asset and setting it up for use in a trade, e.g. legal fees, architects' fees, surveyors' fees, transport and installation costs, may themselves be capital expenditure, being part of the cost of the asset acquired. The question of whether such costs are qualifying expenditure for capital allowances purposes is discussed, where relevant, in the coverage of each form of allowance.

(v) Capital expenditure (including that in (iv) above) can be abortive in that no asset is acquired, provided or constructed, etc. In the absence of a qualifying asset, capital allowances will not usually be available, but see Chapter **10** below as regards abortive exploration expenditure incurred on mineral extraction.

(vi) The capital allowances legislation often makes specific provision for demolition costs to be treated as qualifying expenditure for capital allowances purposes. This is discussed, where relevant, in the appropriate chapter.

(vii) Interest on money borrowed to finance capital expenditure is normally allowed as revenue expenditure. In *Ben-Odeco Ltd v Powlson HL 1978, 52 TC 459*, such interest had been properly charged to capital, but was held not to be qualifying expenditure for capital allowances purposes because it had not been incurred 'on the provision of' plant or machinery.

(viii) Exchange losses linked to capital expenditure may themselves be part of the expenditure. See *Van Arkadie v Sterling Coated Materials Ltd* ChD 1982, 56 TC 479.

(ix) As regards the mineral extraction industry, the Revenue published in 1967 a decision made by the Special Commissioners in 1920 regarding capital expenditure. See **10.4** below.

2

General Scheme of Allowances

Introduction

[2.1] The different forms of allowances operate, in the main, within a general legislative framework common to all. The coverage below is therefore relevant, except where stated, to all the allowances covered by the legislation.

CAA 2001 provides that allowances and charges are given effect in calculating income (or, for corporation tax purposes, profits — i.e. income and chargeable gains) for a 'chargeable period'.

'*Chargeable period*' means an accounting period of a company or a period of account (see **2.22** below).

[*CAA 2001, ss 2, 6(1); FA 2012, Sch 39 para 38(3)*].

See **2.31** below for the interpretation of various other terms used in this chapter.

Exclusion of double relief

[2.2] Where an allowance is made to a person in respect of capital expenditure (including any contribution to capital expenditure) under one of the codes of allowances listed below, he cannot obtain an allowance under another of those codes, in respect of either that expenditure or the provision, construction or acquisition of an asset to which that expenditure related. The allowances in question are:

(a) business premises renovation allowances (now abolished);
(b) flat conversion allowances (now abolished);
(c) plant and machinery allowances;
(d) allowances for mineral extraction;
(e) research and development allowances; and
(f) allowances for expenditure on dredging.

Because of the requirement to pool expenditure on plant and machinery, it cannot be stated that an allowance has been made in respect of a particular item of expenditure; rather, allowances are made in respect of the pool to which the expenditure is allocated. Accordingly an additional provision is required to prevent double relief through pooling. Where an allowance has been made to a person in respect of capital expenditure (including any contribution to capital expenditure) under any of the above codes other than the plant and machinery code, the person to whom it has been made cannot allocate that expenditure (or any expenditure on the provision, construction or acquisition of an asset to which it related) to any plant and machinery pool.

Similarly, where capital expenditure has been allocated to a pool and an allowance or charge has been made in respect of that pool, the person to whom the allowance or charge has been made cannot obtain an allowance under any of the other codes listed above in respect of that expenditure (or the provision, construction or acquisition of an asset to which that expenditure related).

[*CAA 2001, ss 7, 8, 10*].

These provisions should not prevent the purchaser of an asset from claiming allowances on a different basis from the vendor, where alternative bases of claim are permissible.

There are special provisions preventing double allowances in relation to plant or machinery treated as fixtures (see CHAPTER 6).

Time when capital expenditure is incurred

[2.4] It will often be important to determine for allowances purposes the time when capital expenditure is incurred. For example, an allowance for all or part of the expenditure may only be available for a chargeable period if the expenditure is incurred in that period. The rate at which an allowance is granted may change by reference to expenditure incurred after a certain date. The rules described in **2.5** and **2.6** below determine the date on which capital expenditure is treated as having been incurred on all the types of expenditure mentioned in this book. Alternative rules apply as regards the incurring of an additional VAT liability or rebate (see **17.48** onwards below). [*CAA 2001, s 5(7)(b)*].

General rule

[2.5] Subject to the exceptions described in **2.6** below, an amount of capital expenditure is treated as incurred as soon as there is an unconditional obligation to pay it, regardless of whether there is a later date by which payment is required. [*CAA 2001, s 5(1)–(3)*].

The Revenue commented on an old wording of this rule in the Tax Bulletin, November 1993, at page 97. They stated that the date on which an obligation to pay becomes unconditional varies with the terms of the particular contract for the supply of the asset concerned. The point is not established by reference to the date of the contract for supply or of the issue of an invoice. In most cases, a legal obligation to pay for goods arises on or within a prescribed time of delivery. In such cases, the obligation to pay becomes unconditional when the asset is delivered.

Exceptions to general rule

[2.6] The general rule of **2.5** above is subject to the following exceptions.

(a) If, under any agreement,

(i) whether through the issue of a certificate or otherwise, an unconditional obligation to pay an amount of expenditure on the provision of an asset arises within one month after the end of a chargeable period (see **2.1** above), and

(ii) during that chargeable period, the asset becomes the property of, or otherwise under the agreement is attributed to, the person with that obligation,

the expenditure is treated as incurred immediately before the end of that chargeable period.

(b) If there is any agreement whereby any of the expenditure is not payable until a date more than four months after the date when the unconditional obligation to pay arises, the amount so payable is treated as incurred on the later date.

(c) If under an agreement,

(i) there is an unconditional obligation to pay an amount of expenditure on a date earlier than accords with normal commercial usage, and

(ii) the sole or main benefit to be expected from this would have been the expenditure being treated as incurred in an earlier period than otherwise would have been the case,

the expenditure is treated as incurred on the date by which payment is actually due.

(d) If any provision of *CAA 2001* would cause expenditure to be deemed to be incurred later than under the foregoing rules, that provision applies, notwithstanding these rules (see, for example, **8.3** below).

[*CAA 2001, s 5(4)–(6)(7)(a)*].

Subsidies and other capital contributions

[2.7] There are special provisions relating to subsidies and other contributions made by one person to another's capital expenditure. Broadly, a recipient cannot obtain capital allowances on expenditure to the extent that it is funded by a contribution (see **2.8** below), but the contributor can do so if the contribution is made for the purposes of his trade etc. (see **2.9** below). These provisions do not apply to dredging, but there are analogous provisions for that (see **13.2** below).

Sums received

[2.8] Expenditure is not treated as incurred by a person if it has been, or is to be, met, directly or indirectly by:

(a) the Crown, or

(b) any government or public or local authority, in the UK or elsewhere (see further *Cyril Lord Carpets Ltd v Schofield* CA (NI) 1966, 42 TC 637, and for the scope of 'public authority' see *Mckinney v Hagans Caravans (Manufacturing) Ltd* CA (NI), [1997] STC 1023), or

(c) any other person.

This is subject to the following exceptions.

(i) Insurance or other compensation money receivable in respect of an asset which has been demolished, destroyed or put out of use are disregarded.

(ii) Any amount written off a government investment in the recipient, if a company, is not treated as having been met by the Crown, any government or public or local authority. [*CTA 2010, s 96(2)(3)*].

(iii) The exclusion does not apply to expenditure met by a grant ('regional development grant') (except in the case of a grant for oil activities within *Oil Taxation Act 1975, Sch 3 para 8*) under:

  (A) *Industrial Development Act 1982, Pt II*, or a corresponding Northern Ireland grant (where the grant agreement is entered into before 1 April 2003), or

  (B) *Industry Act 1972, Pt I*, or a corresponding Northern Ireland grant.

  Note that *CAA 2001, s 534(1)* refers directly only to Northern Ireland grants within (A) above. The remaining grants within (A) and (B) above are incorporated indirectly within that provision by *CAA 2001, Sch 3 para 106* as they now have at most only transitional effect, with no applications being accepted after 31 March 1988.

(iv) Expenditure within (c) above which would not qualify for capital allowances under **2.9** below (e.g. because the contributor was not a trader etc.) is disregarded, provided that the expenditure is not deductible in computing the profits of a trade or 'relevant activity'. In determining whether expenditure would qualify for allowances by being pooled, or the subject of a claim made, on or after 29 May 2013, the changes at **2.9** below which apply by reference to that date are treated as having always had effect.

  Where:

  - a person has been treated as incurring expenditure by virtue of this exception, and the expenditure was pooled between 1 January 2013 and 28 May 2013 inclusive or was pooled before 1 January 2013 but no claim for allowances was made in respect of the expenditure before that date, and
  - if the changes made at **2.9** below by reference to 29 May 2013 had been in force at the time the expenditure was incurred, that person would not have been regarded as having incurred the expenditure,

  that person must bring into account a disposal value equal to the written-down value of the expenditure for the chargeable period in which 29 May 2013 falls. The written-down value is determined for this purpose as if the expenditure were the only expenditure qualifying for capital allowances.

  A '*relevant activity*' is, for the purposes of plant and machinery allowances, a property business within **4.4** below, a profession or vocation, any concern listed in *CTA 2009, s 39(4)* or *ITTOIA 2005, s 12(4)* or the management of an investment company. For other purposes, only a profession or vocation is a relevant activity.

  In determining whether expenditure would qualify for capital allowances under **2.9** below, it is to be assumed that the contributor is within the charge to tax, whether or not that is the case.

(v) Notwithstanding (iv) above, capital expenditure incurred before 6 April 2013 (1 April 2013 for corporation tax purposes) in improving the safety or comfort of spectators at a ground to be used for the playing of association football is not treated as met by another person insofar as it has been or is to be met, directly or indirectly, out of certain pools payments made in consequence of a reduction in pool betting duty, even though such payments are specifically deductible in computing the payer's trading profits. [*FA 1990, s 126(4); FA 2012, Sch 39 para 19*].

(vi) The incurring of 'reimbursement expenditure' to reimburse a contributing participator who has made a 'default payment' (within *Oil Taxation Act 1975, Sch 5 para 2A*) is not regarded as the meeting of the expenditure of the qualifying participator in making the default payment. [*CTA 2010, s 298(7)*].

(vii) If capital allowances have been restricted because the expenditure was met by a grant falling within (a) or (b) above, and that grant is later repaid in whole or in part, by concession HMRC will treat the repayment as expenditure on which capital allowances may be given. (Inland Revenue Press Release, 19 June 1996).

(viii) If capital allowances have been restricted because the expenditure was met by a person (other than the Crown or a public body) who is entitled to capital allowances or a trading deduction on the expenditure, and that grant is later repaid in whole or in part, by concession HMRC will treat the repayment as expenditure on which capital allowances may be given, provided the repayment falls to be taxed on the recipient through a balancing adjustment or as a trading receipt. (Inland Revenue Press Release, 19 June 1996).

[*CAA 2001, ss 532, 534–536; FA 2011, Sch 14 para 12(15); FA 2013, s 73(5)(7)–(10)*].

See also **8.1** below for the denial of business premises renovation where a 'relevant grant or payment' is made.

Sums paid — contribution allowances

[2.9] Capital allowances ('contribution allowances') are available in certain circumstances to a person who contributes a capital sum to expenditure on the provision of an asset, provided that the parties are not connected persons within **2.34** above. The expenditure on the asset must be such that, but for the provisions described in **2.8** above:

- it would have been treated as wholly incurred by another person, and
- except in the case of expenditure by the Crown or any UK public or local authority, it would have entitled that person to a plant and machinery allowance or a, mineral extraction allowance.

The contribution must be made for the purposes of a trade or a relevant activity (see **2.8** (iv) above) which is carried on (or to be carried on) by the contributor. There is an additional condition for plant and machinery allowances, that the contribution must be to expenditure on the provision of plant or machinery. This condition applies to expenditure pooled, and claims made, on or after 29 May 2013 but is intended to confirm HMRC's previous understanding of the legislation. See also **2.8**(iv) above.

Mineral extraction allowances are made to the contributor as if:

- the contribution had been expenditure on the provision of a similar asset for the purposes of the trade; and
- this asset were at all times in use for the purposes of the trade.

Plant and machinery allowances are made to the contributor as if:

(a) the contribution had been expenditure on the provision of the plant or machinery for the purposes of the trade or relevant activity;
(b) the plant or machinery were at all times plant or machinery in use for the purposes of the trade or relevant activity; and
(c) the contributor owned the plant or machinery at any time when the recipient of the contribution owns it (or is treated as owning it under *CAA 2001, Pt 2*).

For expenditure pooled, and claims made, before 29 May 2013, plant and machinery allowances were made to the contributor as if:

(a) the contribution had been expenditure on the provision of the actual asset for the purposes of the trade or relevant activity;
(b) this asset were at all times in use for the purposes of the trade or relevant activity; and
(c) the contributor owned the asset at any time when the recipient of the contribution owns it (or is treated as owning it under *CAA 2001, Pt 2*).

Note that the change in wording is intended to confirm HMRC's understanding of the old legislation.

The following further provisions apply to the calculation of the allowances.

(i) In the case of plant or machinery, the expenditure, if allocated to a pool, must be allocated to a single asset pool (see **5.48** below).
(ii) If the contribution was made for the purposes of the contributor's trade or relevant activity, and the trade etc. is subsequently transferred, writing-down allowances for chargeable periods ending after the date of transfer are made to the transferee. If only part of the trade is transferred, so much of the allowance as is properly referable to the part transferred is made to the transferee.

The changes made by reference to 29 May 2013 do not affect a contributor's entitlement to an allowance in respect of a contribution made before that date.

[*CAA 2001, ss 537–542, 575(1); FA 2013, s 73(1)–(4)(6)*].

An allowance for a contribution may be restricted under other provisions, e.g. under **5.53** below.

Methods of making allowances

[2.10] *CAA 2001* specifies separately for each type of allowance the method of making allowances for each eligible activity.

Trades

[2.11] Where a person carrying on a trade is entitled to an allowance, or is liable to a charge, for a chargeable period, in respect of the trade, the allowance or charge is given effect in calculating the profits of the trade by treating the allowance as an expense of the trade, and the charge as a receipt of the trade. The allowances to which this provision may apply are:

(a) business premises renovation allowances;
(b) plant and machinery allowances;
(c) mineral extraction allowances;
(d) research and development allowances (formerly scientific research allowances);
(e) allowances for patent rights;
(f) allowances for know-how; and
(g) dredging allowances.

[*CAA 2001, ss 247(1), 360Z, 432, 450, 463, 478, 489; FA 2010, Sch 4 para 4*].

See **17.1D** below for the general prohibition on allowances where profits of a trade are calculated on the cash basis.

Professions and vocations

[2.12] Where a person carrying on a profession or vocation is entitled to an allowance, or is liable to a charge, in respect of the profession or vocation, the allowance or charge is given effect by treating the allowance as an expense of, and the charge as a receipt of, the profession or vocation. The relevant allowances are:

- business premises renovation allowances; and
- plant and machinery allowances.

[*CAA 2001, ss 251, 360Z*].

See **17.1D** below for the general prohibition on allowances where profits of a profession or vocation are calculated on the cash basis.

Concerns within CTA 2009, s 39(4) or ITTOIA 2005, s 12(4)

[2.13] Plant and machinery allowances to which a person carrying on a concern listed in *CTA 2009, s 39(4)* or *ITTOIA 2005, s 12(4)* (mines, transport undertakings etc. — see **4.5** below) is entitled are given effect by treating the allowance as an expense of the concern. Charges are treated as a receipt of the concern. [*CAA 2001, s 252*].

Employments and offices

[2.14] A plant and machinery allowance or charge to which an employee or office-holder is entitled or liable is given effect by treating the allowance as a deduction from the taxable earnings from the employment or office and by treating the charge as earnings. [*CAA 2001, s 262*].

The above provision is considered to treat a balancing charge as earnings only for the limited purpose of giving effect to the charge, so that, for example, the charge is not taken into account in calculating earnings to determine whether the employment is lower-paid employment for the purposes of the benefits code (see *ITEPA 2003, ss 216–220*) (Revenue Explanatory Notes to the Capital Allowances Bill, Annex 2 Note 41).

Property businesses

[2.15] This paragraph considers the method of making:

(a) business premises renovation allowances to a person whose interest in the building is subject to a lease;
(b) flat conversion allowances; and
(c) plant and machinery allowances to a person whose qualifying activity is one of the property businesses within **4.4** below (i.e. an ordinary UK property business, a UK furnished holiday lettings business, an ordinary overseas property business, an EEA furnished holiday lettings business or, previously, an overseas property business).

Where the person entitled to the allowances is carrying on a UK property business (or where appropriate, one of the other types of property business within (c) above) allowances are treated as expenses of that business, and charges as receipts.

Where, in the case of (a) or (b) above, that person is not carrying on such a business, the allowance or charge is given effect by treating him as if he were carrying on a UK property business, so that allowances and charges are treated as expenses and receipts of that business.

[*CAA 2001, ss 248–250A, 360Z1, 393T; FA 2011, Sch 14 para 12(11)–(14)*].

Where an individual carries on an ordinary overseas property business or an EEA furnished holiday letting business in a tax year which is a 'split year' for the purposes of the statutory residence test for 2013/14 onwards, only the part of the profits arising in the UK part of the year are chargeable and allowances and charges within (c) above are treated as expenses and receipts in calculating the profits arising in that part only. For this purpose, the profits for the tax year, before adjustment for the allowances and charges, must be apportioned between the UK and overseas parts of the year on a just and reasonable basis. [*ITTOIA 2005, s 270(3)–(5); FA 2013, Sch 45 paras 81, 153(2)*].

See **17.1D** below for the general prohibition on allowances where profits of a property business are calculated on the cash basis.

Companies with investment business and life assurance companies

[2.16] For the method of making allowances for plant and machinery used, or provided for use in the management of the investment business of a company and for plant and machinery which is a management asset of a life assurance company, see **5.85** below.

Special leasing of plant and machinery

[2.17] Where a person is entitled to allowances in respect of special leasing of plant and machinery (see **4.7**, **5.87** and **6.19** below), the allowances are given effect by deducting them from (or setting them off against) the income (including a balancing charge) from special leasing for the tax year or accounting period. For income tax purposes, the deduction is given effect at Step 2 of the calculation in *ITA 2007, s 23*. For income tax purposes, a balancing charge is assessed directly to income tax. For corporation tax purposes, a balancing charge is treated as income from special leasing of plant and machinery. See **5.87** below for restrictions which apply where the lessee does not use the plant or machinery for the purposes of a qualifying activity.

Any excess of the allowance over the income is carried forward and set, at the first opportunity, against subsequent income from special leasing. Alternatively, a company can make a claim for an excess of allowances (excluding any allowances brought forward) to be set against any other profits or surrender the excess as group relief. See **2.43** and **2.44** below.

[*CAA 2001, ss 258–260*].

Where an amount of government investment in a company is written off, allowances carried forward under the above provision may be reduced by the amount written off. A claim to set excess allowances against other profits made before the write-off date is left undisturbed, but a claim made on or after that date is ignored in determining the amount of any allowances falling to be reduced. [*CTA 2010, ss 92–96; F(No 2)A 2017, Sch 4 para 156*].

An allowance given under the foregoing cannot be deducted from or set off against a company's ring fence profits arising from oil extraction activities or from oil rights except where in the accounting period for which an allowance is due, the asset to which it relates is used by an associated company in carrying on oil extraction activities. [*CTA 2010, s 306*].

Patent allowances for non-traders

[2.18] An allowance to which a person is entitled in respect of qualifying non-trade expenditure on patent rights (see **12.2** below) is given effect by deducting it or setting it off against the person's income from patents for the current tax year or accounting period. For income tax purposes, the deduction is given effect at Step 2 of the calculation in *ITA 2007, s 23*.

For income tax purposes, a charge is assessable directly to income tax. For corporation tax purposes a charge is treated as income from patents.

Where the allowance exceeds the income from patents for the tax year or accounting period, the excess is carried forward and set, at the first opportunity, against subsequent income from patents.

[*CAA 2001, ss 479, 480*].

Claims for allowances

[2.19] No capital allowance can be made or first-year tax credit paid (see **5.28** below) unless a claim for it is made. [*CAA 2001, s 3(1)*].

Income tax claims

[2.20] Subject to the exceptions noted below, a claim for allowances is to be made in the claimant's return of income, and the normal rules for claims in *TMA 1970, s 42* do not apply. [*CAA 2001, s 3(2)(3)*]. This means that the time limit for making the claim is the time limit for making or amending the return. Claims or amendments to claims must therefore be made within 12 months from 31 January following the end of the year of assessment. For example, the capital allowance claim for 2015/16 can be made or amended at any time up until 31 January 2018.

A claim to business premises renovation allowances must be separately identified as such in the return. [*CAA 2001, s 3(2A)*].

The above provisions do not apply to claims for

- allowances in respect of special leasing of plant or machinery (see **2.17** above); and
- patent allowances in respect of non-trade expenditure (see **2.18** above).

Relief for such allowances is obtainable by means of a claim made in accordance with *TMA 1970, s 42*.

[*CAA 2001, s 3(4)*].

If no assessment giving effect to an allowance is made, but the claimant and HMRC agree in writing as to the amount due for a year, an allowance of this amount is taken to have been made as if an assessment had been made. [*CAA 2001, s 565*].

See **15.2** to **15.5** below for partnership capital allowance claims.

Corporation tax claims

[2.21] Capital allowance claims and claims to first-year tax credit must, subject to the exceptions noted below, be included in the return for the relevant accounting period and the amount of the claim must be quantified when the claim is made and specified in the claim. The claim may be amended or withdrawn only by submitting an amended return. [*CAA 2001, s 3(2)(3); FA 1998, Sch 18 paras 79–81, 83ZA(1)*]. Claims to business premises renovation allowances or first-year tax credit (see **5.28** below) must be separately identified as such in the return. [*CAA 2001, s 3(2A)(2B))*]. Claims to first-year tax credit must also specify the plant or machinery to which the claim relates, the amount of the expenditure involved and the date on which it was incurred. Where the first-year allowances in respect of which the claim is made require that a certificate of energy efficiency (see **5.17** below) or of environmental benefit (see **5.21** below) must be in force, the certificate must be submitted with the return. [*FA 1998, Sch 18 para 83ZA(2)(3)*].

The time-limit for making, amending or withdrawing a claim is the last of:

(a) the first anniversary of the filing date for the return;
(b) 30 days after the completion of any enquiry into the return;
(c) if after the completion of an enquiry HMRC amend the return, 30 days after notice of the amendment is issued; or
(d) if the company appeals against such an amendment, 30 days after the date on which the appeal is finally determined.

References above to an enquiry do not include an enquiry which, being otherwise out of time, was commenced as a result of an amendment to a return by a company consisting of the making, amendment or withdrawing of a capital allowance claim and therefore limited in scope under *FA 1998, Sch 18 para 25(2)* to matters relating to that amendment or affected by it.

These time limits override the normal time limits for making or amending a return. HMRC have the power to admit claims outside these time limits.

[*FA 1998, Sch 18 para 82*].

HMRC's practice is only to admit late claims where the claim could not have been made within the statutory time limits for reasons beyond the company's control. This will include that situation where a claim is late as a result of the illness or absence of an officer of the company, provided that the illness or absence arose at a critical time preventing a timeous claim, there was good reason why the claim could not have been made before the absence or illness arose, there was no other person who could have made the claim timeously, and (in the case of absence) there was good reason for the officer's unavailability.

Late claims are not, for example, admitted where they result from:

- an oversight or negligence of the claimant company;
- failure, without good reason, to compute the necessary figure;
- the wish to avoid commitment pending clarification of the effects of the claim; or
- the illness or absence of an adviser to the company.

An application for admission of a late claim should explain why the claim could not have been made within the statutory time limit, and must be made as soon as possible. Delay in making a late claim after the circumstances causing the lateness cease to apply may result in the rejection of the claim.

(HMRC Statement of Practice, SP 5/01).

If the effect of the claim is to reduce the capital allowances available for another accounting period for which a return has already been made, the company has 30 days to make the necessary amendments to that return. If it fails to do so, HMRC may, by written notice and subject to a right of appeal within 30 days of the issue of the notice, amend the return to correct the position (notwithstanding any time limit otherwise applicable). [*FA 1998, Sch 18 para 83*].

The above provisions do not apply to claims to carry back an allowance in respect of special leasing of plant and machinery (see **2.17** above). Such claims are instead subject to *FA 1998, Sch 18 paras 54–60*. [*CAA 2001, s 3(5)*].

Inclusion of State aid information

[2.21A] A claim made on or after 1 July 2016 for business premises renovation allowances or plant and machinery first-year allowances for zero-emission goods vehicles or plant or machinery for use in a designated assisted area (see **5.16**(6) and (7) below) must include any information required by HMRC for the purpose of complying with certain EU State aid obligations. This may include information about the claimant (or its activities), information about the subject matter of the claim and other information relating to the grant of State aid through the provision of the allowances. [*FA 2016, s 180(1)–(4)(10), Sch 24 Pt 1*].

Meaning of 'period of account'

[2.22] Capital allowances are given by reference to chargeable periods (see **2.1** above). For income tax purposes, a chargeable period means a 'period of account'.

For a person entitled to an allowance in calculating the profits of a trade, profession or vocation, a period of account is, subject to the following, the period for which the accounts of the trade etc. are made up.

If two periods of account would otherwise overlap, the period common to both falls into the first period only. This means that assets qualifying for allowances are treated as being acquired in the first period of account rather than the second. References to the overlapping of two periods of account includes the coincidence of two periods and to the inclusion of one period in another.

If there is an interval between the periods of account for two consecutive accounting periods, the interval forms part of the first period. This means that acquisitions and disposals in the interval are treated as relating to the earlier period.

If the period of account exceeds 18 months, it is split into two or more periods of account, beginning on, or on an anniversary of, the date on which the actual period commences. This means allowances will be computed on the basis of one or more periods of account of 12 months plus a period of account covering the residue of the period. The allowances for the separate periods are then aggregated and deducted as an expense of the whole period.

[*CAA 2001, s 6(2)–(6)*].

Where a period of account is for less than or more than 12 months, writing-down allowances are adjusted in proportion to the length of that period (subject to the overriding rule above that a period of account cannot exceed 18 months). Thus, a long period of account of 15 months would produce a writing-down allowance in respect of a plant and machinery pool of (20% × $^{15}/_{12}$) 25%, whereas a short period of say eight months would result in a writing-down allowance of (20% × $^{8}/_{12}$) 13.33%.

For any person not carrying on a trade, profession or vocation who is subject to income tax and is eligible to claim capital allowances, 'period of account' means a year of assessment.

EXAMPLE 1

[2.23]

G commences in business on 1 September 2014, preparing accounts initially to 31 August 2015, but then changing his accounting date to prepare his next accounts for the 13-month period ended 30 September 2016 (the conditions in *ITTOIA 2005, s 217* for a valid accounting change not having to be met). He incurs qualifying expenditure on plant and machinery on 1 October 2014 of £3,600, on 5 January 2016 of £8,000 and on 19 March 2016 of £2,000. He disposes of an asset on 22 February 2016 for £450 which had originally cost £1,000. Tax adjusted profits, before capital allowances, were as follows:

	£
Year ended 31 August 2015	15,000
Period ended 30 September 2016	18,000
Year ended 30 September 2017	22,000

	Expenditure qualifying for AIA	*Main pool*	*Total allowances*
	£	£	£
Year ended 31.8.15			
Additions	3,600		
AIA (100%)	(3,600)		3,600
	3,600		
Transfer to pool	(—)		
WDV at 31.8.15		—	
Total allowances claimed			£3,600
Period ended 30.9.16			
Additions	8,000		
AIA (100%)	(8,000)		8,000
Transfer to pool	—	—	
Disposal value		(450)	
		(450)	
Balancing charge		450	(450)
WDV at 30.9.16		Nil	
Total allowances claimed			£7,550
Year ended 30.9.17			
Additions	2,000		
AIA (100%)	(2,000)		2,000
Transfer to pool	—	—	
WDV at 30.9.17		—	
Total allowances claimed			£2,000

The profits chargeable to tax will be as follows:

	Profits	*Capital Allowances*	*After Allowances*
	£	£	£
Year ended 31.8.15	15,000	3,600	11,400
Period ended 30.9.16	18,000	7,550	10,450
Year ended 30.9.17	22,000	2,000	20,000

The first four years' self-assessments will be as follows:

	£	£
2014/15 1.9.14–5.4.15 (£11,400 × 7/12)		6,650
2015/16 1.9.14–31.8.15		11,400
2016/17 1.9.15–30.9.16	10,450	
Less overlap relief £6,650 × 1/7	(950)	
		9,500
2017/18 1.10.16–30.9.17		20,000

The profits of the first year of £11,400 are taxed more than once. Consequently, the allowance of £3,600 deducted from the profits for the first year is given more than once. However, ignoring inflation, any advantage gained by this is later negated on cessation or, as can be seen here in 2016/17, either partly or fully negated on a change of accounting date to a date later in the tax year. As the overlap is for 7 months in this example and the basis period for 2016/17 is one month greater than one year, 1/7 of the overlap is relieved in 2016/17, the balance being carried forward to a later change of accounting date or to cessation as the case may be.

In fact, G ceases in business on 31 March 2019 and he prepares a final set of accounts for the 18-month period ending on cessation. He incurs qualifying expenditure on plant and machinery on 20 August 2018 of £2,308. On cessation, G disposes of all the plant and machinery previously purchased for the sum of £1,500. The tax adjusted profit for the final period is £13,900.

	Pool	*Allowances*
	£	£
Period ended 31.3.19		
WDV at 1.10.17	—	
Additions	2,308	
Disposal value	(1,500)	
	£838	£838

Profit after capital allowances is £13,900 - £838 = £13,062

The final self-assessment will be as follows:

		£
2018/19	1.10.17–31.3.19	13,062
	Less overlap relief b/fwd (£6,650 – £950)	(5,700)
Profit		£7,362

Overlap relief is always calculated on the profits after capital allowances.

EXAMPLE 2

[2.24]

H has been trading for many years and decides to change his accounting date by preparing a 30-month set of accounts to 30 April 2017. The periods of account for capital allowances will be as follows:

Period 1	1.11.14–31.10.15	12 months
Period 2	1.11.15–31.10.16	12 months
Period 3	1.11.16–30.4.17	6 months

Additions and disposals are dealt with in the relevant periods. The allowances for the three separate periods are then aggregated and deducted as an expense of the whole 30-month period.

Miscellaneous

Apportionment of consideration

[2.25] For the purposes of all the allowance codes, any reference to the sale of any property includes the sale of that property together with any other property. In the case of a sale of an item of property together with other property:

- so much of the net proceeds of sale of the whole property as, on a just and reasonable apportionment, is properly attributable to that item is deemed to be the net proceeds of that item; and
- the expenditure incurred on the provision or purchase of that item is treated as being so much of the consideration given for the whole property as, on a just and reasonable apportionment, is attributable to that item.

The term 'property' is used in its general sense and is not, for example, restricted to land and buildings. The term specifically includes, in relation to mineral extraction allowances, mineral assets and land outside the UK.

For the purposes of these provisions, all property which is sold as a result of a single bargain is deemed to be sold together, even if there are (or purport to be) separate prices for separate items, or separate sales of separate items.

The foregoing provisions apply, with the necessary adaptations, to any other proceeds (consisting of insurance money or other compensation) as they do to net sale proceeds.

[*CAA 2001, s 562*].

Exchanges and surrenders of leasehold interests

[2.26] Any reference to the sale of any property is deemed to include a reference to:

(a) the exchange of any property, and

(b) in the case of a leasehold interest (or in Scotland, the interest of the tenant in property subject to a lease), the surrender of it for valuable consideration.

The references have effect with the necessary adaptations. In particular,

(i) references to the net proceeds of sale and the price include the consideration for the exchange or surrender, and
(ii) references to capital sums included in the price include so much of the consideration as would have been a capital sum if it had been a money payment.

[*CAA 2001, s 572(1)–(3)*].

Successions to trades, etc.

[2.27] The following provisions apply for the purposes of allowances other than those relating to research and development and plant and machinery.

If:

(a) a person succeeds to any trade, profession, vocation or property business and the succession:
    (i) results in no person carrying on the activity immediately before the succession continuing to carry it on afterwards, or
    (ii) results in no company carrying on the activity in partnership immediately before the succession continuing to carry it on in partnership afterwards, and
(b) any property was immediately beforehand in use for the old trade, etc., and without being sold is immediately afterwards in use for the new one,

the property is treated as having been sold for net proceeds equal to open market value, but the successor is not entitled to any initial allowance.

See **7.17** below as regards plant and machinery allowances on successions to trades under *CAA 2001, s 265* and **7.18** below where such a succession is between connected persons under *CAA 2001, s 266*. See **17.43** for transfers of long-term business of insurance companies.

See **15.6** below for the effect of partnership changes on the making of allowances.

[*CAA 2001, ss 557, 559*].

Privatisation schemes

[2.28] It was common for the enabling legislation for privatisation schemes to contain specific provisions regarding capital allowances. See, for example, *Water Act 1989, s 95, Sch 2, Environmental Protection Act 1990, Sch 2 para 9* and the *Railways Act 1993* provisions of *FA 1994, Sch 24* for schemes whereby companies succeeded to the activities previously carried on by water and waste disposal and railway authorities. See also *FA 1991, s 78* for capital allowances provisions relating to plant and machinery where there are disposals between national broadcasting companies.

Proceeds of crime

[2.29] *Part 5* of the *Proceeds of Crime Act 2002* provides for the National Crime Agency to recover, in civil proceedings before the High Court (or, in Scotland, before the Court of Session), 'property' which is, or represents, property obtained through 'unlawful conduct' (as defined in the *Act*). If the Court is satisfied that any property is recoverable under the provisions it will make a '*recovery order*', vesting the property in an appointed trustee for civil recovery. [*PCA 2002, ss 240(1), 266(1)(2), 316(1)*]. Alternatively, the Court may make an order staying (or, in Scotland, sisting) proceedings for a recovery order on terms agreed by the parties. [*PCA 2002, s 276*]. In certain circumstances a recovery order, or the terms on which an order under *s 276* is made, may provide for the trustee to pay a compensating amount in respect of the transfer of the property. (See, for example, *PCA 2002, s 272(3)* which provides for such a payment to be made to the holder of 'associated property' (as defined, but including, where the property is a tenancy in common, the interest of the other tenant) or to a joint tenant who acquired his interest in the property in circumstances in which it would not be recoverable as against him.) For the purposes of these provisions, '*property*' is all property, wherever situated, and includes money, all forms of property, real or personal, heritable or moveable, things in action and other intangible or incorporeal property. [*PCA 2002, s 316(4)*].

Given the wide definition of property, it is possible for assets in respect of which capital allowances have been claimed to be recovered under the above provisions. Accordingly, provision is made in *Schedule 10* to the *Act* to determine the capital allowances (and other tax) consequences in the event of such a recovery. The capital allowances codes affected are those for flat conversion, plant and machinery and research and development.

Broadly, the vesting of property in the trustee for civil recovery or any other person by a recovery order made under *Part 5* or in pursuance of an order under *s 276* (a '*Part 5 transfer*') is treated as a disposal or balancing event. [*PCA 2002, s 448, Sch 10 paras 2(1), 12, 18, 22, 26*]. If a 'compensating payment' is made, the amount of the payment is treated as the disposal value or proceeds from the balancing event. Otherwise, the disposal value or proceeds will be the amount that will give rise to neither a balancing allowance nor a balancing charge. See **5.41**, **9.10**, **9.11**, **5.41** and **11.13** below for the detailed provisions. Where property belonged, immediately before the *Part 5* transfer, to joint tenants, and a compensating payment is made to one or more (but not all) of them, these provisions apply separately to each joint tenant. [*PCA 2002, Sch 10 para 2(5)*].

A '*compensating payment*' for these purposes is any amount paid in respect of a *Part 5* transfer, by the trustee for civil recovery or another, to a person who held the property in question immediately before the transfer. If a recovery order, or the terms on which an order under *s 276* is made, provide for the creation of any interest in favour of such a person, that person is treated as receiving (in addition to any actual compensating payment) a compensating payment equal to the value of the interest. [*PCA 2002, Sch 10 para 2(3)(4)*].

Procedure on apportionments, etc.

[2.30] The following provisions apply where the determination of a question is required in circumstances where that determination appears to be material to the tax liability, for any period, of one or more persons. The provisions apply to the determination of the following:

(a) any question about the way in which a sum is to be apportioned for the purposes of any allowance other than in respect of plant and machinery;
(b) the market value of property for the purposes of:
  (i) plant and machinery allowances;
  (ii) the provisions in *CAA 2001, s 423* relating to disposal values for mineral extraction allowances (see **10.27** below);
  (iii) the provisions in *CAA 2001, s 559* relating to successions (see **2.27** above);
  (iv) the provisions in *CAA 2001, ss 568, 569* relating to certain sales between persons who are under common control or connected, and certain sales apparently effected to secure a tax benefit (see **17.2** below); and
  (v) the provisions in *CAA 2001, s 573* relating to transfers treated as sales (see **8.10** and **9.10** below);
(c) any question of apportionment of expenditure under *CAA 2001, s 561(3)* (transfer of a UK trade to a company in another Member State — see **17.27** below).

Any question is decided, broadly as if it were an appeal, by the tribunal.

All the persons are entitled to be a party to the proceedings. The determination of the tribunal applies for the purposes of the tax of all the persons.

Note that the above provisions previously applied only to the determination of a question material to the tax liability of two or more persons. The change was made to enable the making of applications to the tribunal for a determination with respect to the 'fixed value requirement' in **6.17** below (see **6.17**(1)(I)).

[*CAA 2001, ss 563, 564; FA 2012, Sch 10 para 5*].

For cases in which the courts have upheld apportionments made by the appeal Commissioners, see *Fitton v Gilder & Heaton* ChD 1955, 36 TC 233 and *Alfred Wood & Co v Provan* CA 1968, 44 TC 701.

Interpretation provisions

[2.31] Except where the context otherwise requires, the following interpretation provisions apply for the purposes of all allowances except where otherwise stated. See **2.1** above for the meaning of 'chargeable period'.

'Capital sums' cannot include:

(a) amounts which:
- may be added in computing the taxable profits or gains of a trade, profession, property business, or vocation carried on by the recipient, or
- are earnings of an office or employment held by the recipient; and

(b) payments which may be made after deduction of tax at source under *ITA 2007, Pt 15 Ch 6* (annual payments or patent royalties), *ITA 2007, s 906* (royalties etc. where usual place of abode of owner is abroad).

'Control' has the following meanings.

(i) In relation to a body corporate: the power of a person to secure, through shares or voting power in that or any other body corporate, or through powers under the articles of association or other document regulating any body corporate, that the affairs of the first-mentioned body corporate are conducted in accordance with his wishes.

(ii) In relation to a partnership: the right to a share of more than half the assets or income.

'Dual resident investing company' means a company so designated for the purposes of *CTA 2010, s 949*.

'Market value' of an asset means the price the asset would fetch in the open market.

'Notice' means a notice in writing.

'Property business' means a UK property business, a Schedule A business or an overseas property business.

'Tax' means either 'corporation tax' or 'income tax' if neither is specified.

[*CAA 2001, ss 4, 574, 576, 577(1); CTA 2010, s 1119*].

[2.32] The following further rules apply to the interpretation of the provisions relating to allowances.

A source of income is 'within the charge to' corporation tax or income tax if that tax is chargeable on the income arising from it, or would be if there were any income. References to a person, or to income, being within the charge to tax are to be construed accordingly.

A reference to an asset of any kind, including a building, structure, machinery, plant or works, includes a reference to any part thereof, unless the reference is expressed to be to the whole of an asset.

A reference to the time of sale signifies the earlier of the time of completion and the time when possession is given. This provision does not apply for research and development allowances (but see **11.12** below for an equivalent rule).

A reference to the setting-up or permanent discontinuance of a trade, profession, vocation or property business includes, unless the contrary is expressly provided, a reference to any event treated as such by the Tax Acts.

A reference to an allowance made or a deduction allowed includes one which would be made or allowed but for an insufficiency of profits, etc.

A person obtains a tax advantage if he obtains an allowance or a greater allowance or avoids or reduces a charge.

[*CAA 2001, ss 571, 572(4), 577(2)–(4); ITA 2007, s 1009; CTA 2010, s 1167*].

Net proceeds of sale

[2.33] For capital allowances purposes, the 'net proceeds of sale' are what the seller actually receives, rather than the amount which he is entitled to receive. Any part of the agreed sale price which is ultimately irrecoverable is therefore excluded (HMRC Capital Allowances Manual, CA11540). This view is based on *Tyser v A-G* (1938) 1 Ch 426, in which the Court considered the meaning of the expression 'proceeds of sale' in the context of estate duty. The judge held that the expression meant 'the proceeds of sale which reached the vendor or any person on his behalf and for his use after payment of the proper expenses of sale'.

Connected persons

[2.34] The capital allowances legislation refers on a number of occasions to transactions between 'connected persons'. Except where otherwise extended, the term is defined as follows.

(a) A person is connected with an individual if he or she is the individual's spouse or civil partner, or is a 'relative', or the spouse or civil partner of a relative, of either the individual or his spouse or civil partner. '*Relative*' means brother, sister, ancestor or lineal descendant.

(b) A trustee of a 'settlement', in his capacity as such, is connected with the 'settlor' and with any person connected with the settlor (providing the settlor is an individual), and with any body corporate connected with the settlement. A trustee of a settlement which is the 'principal settlement' in relation to one or more 'sub-fund settlements', is also connected with the trustees of the sub-fund settlements. A trustee of a sub-fund settlement is connected with the trustees of the principal settlement's other sub-fund settlements. '*Settlement*' includes any disposition, trust, covenant, agreement or arrangement and '*settlor*' means any person by whom a settlement is made. [*ITTOIA 2005, s 620(1)*]. '*Principal settlement*' and '*sub-fund settlement*' have the meaning given by *TCGA 1992, Sch 4ZA para 1*. '*Close company*' has the meaning given by *CTA 2010, ss 439–454* and '*control*' is as defined by *CAA 2001, s 574*. Any person in whom settled property or its management is vested is a trustee for this purpose if there would otherwise be no trustees.

(c) A person is connected with any person with whom he is in partnership and with the spouse, civil partner or relative of any such person (if an individual). This does not, however, apply in relation to acquisitions or disposals of partnership assets pursuant to *bona fide* commercial arrangements.

(d) A 'company' is connected with another company if:
    (i) the same person has 'control' of both, or
    (ii) a person has control of one, and persons connected with him, or he and persons connected with him, have control of the other, or

(iii) the same group of persons controls both, or

(iv) the companies are controlled by different groups of persons which could be regarded as the same group of persons by treating any one or more members of either group as replaced by persons with whom they are connected.

'*Company*' includes any body corporate or unincorporated association, but does not include a partnership. A unit trust scheme is treated as if the scheme was a company and as if the rights of the unit holders were shares in the company. '*Control*' is as defined by *CTA 2010, ss 450, 451*.

(e) A company is connected with another person if that person, or that person and persons connected with him, have control (within *CTA 2010, ss 450, 451*) of it.

(f) Persons acting together to secure or exercise control of a company are treated in relation to that company as connected with one another and with any person acting on the directions of any of them to secure or exercise such control.

[*CAA 2001, ss 575, 575A*].

Interaction of allowances with losses

Introduction

[2.35] The following paragraphs deal with the various loss reliefs available only in so far as they affect or are affected by capital allowances. A general discussion of loss reliefs is beyond the scope of this book. Given the time limits applicable to loss claims, only the provisions applying for the current tax year and the four preceding years are covered.

For the limitations under *CTA 2010, ss 673–705* on the carry-forward of losses on a change of ownership of a company, and for the carry-forward of losses on a company reconstruction within *CTA 2010, ss 938–953*, see **17.22** and **17.29** below.

Trading losses

Individuals etc.

[2.36] An individual etc. who incurs a loss in a trade (or a profession or vocation) may, subject to the relevant conditions, claim relief for that loss under one or more of the following provisions.

(a) *ITA 2007, s 64*. Losses may be set off against general income for the tax year in which the loss is sustained and/or the preceding tax year.

(b) *TCGA 1992, s 261B*. A person making a claim under (a) above (or prevented from doing so only by a lack of income) may make a claim effectively converting any unrelieved trading loss into a capital loss.

(c) *ITA 2007, s 72*. Where an individual begins to carry on a trade, profession or vocation, either alone or in partnership, and sustains a loss in any of the first four tax years, he may claim loss relief against his income for the three tax years preceding that in which the loss is sustained, taking income for an earlier year before that for a later year.

(d) *ITA 2007, s 89*. Where a person has carried on a trade, profession or vocation, either alone or in partnership, and permanently ceases to do so, that person may make a claim for any terminal loss sustained to be relieved against profits of the same trade charged to income tax for the tax year in which the cessation occurs and the three tax years preceding it, taking later years before earlier years. For this purpose, the terminal loss is the aggregate of any loss sustained in the tax year in which the trade permanently ceases and so much of any loss sustained in the preceding tax year as relates to a period beginning twelve months before the date of cessation.

(e) *ITA 2007, s 83*. To the extent that no claim has been made under (a)–(d) above, a claim can be made to carry forward the loss to be set off against future profits of the same trade, profession or vocation at the first opportunity.

Relief under (a)–(c) above cannot be claimed for losses calculated using the cash basis (see **17.1A** below).

As indicated at **2.11** (and **2.12**) above, where an individual etc. is entitled to a capital allowance or is subject to a balancing charge in respect of a trade (or profession or vocation), the allowance or charge is given effect in calculating the profits of the trade etc. by treating the allowance as an expense of the trade, and the charge as a receipt of the trade. Accordingly, a claim for capital allowances will have the effect of automatically creating or increasing a loss and only a few special provisions are required to deal with the interaction of allowances and losses.

For the purposes of relief under (a) and (c) above ('*sideways relief*'), certain restrictions apply to limit the extent to which capital allowances may create or enhance a loss.

Sideways relief is not available to an individual for so much of a loss as derives from a 'trade leasing allowance' unless:

- the trade is carried on by him (alone or in partnership) for a continuous period of at least six months beginning or ending in the 'period of loss'; and
- he devotes substantially the whole of his time to carrying it on throughout that period or, if the trade begins or ceases (or both) during the tax year in which the loss is made, for a continuous period of at least six months beginning or ending in the period of loss.

For this purpose, a '*trade leasing allowance*' is a plant or machinery allowance in respect of:

- expenditure incurred on the provision of plant or machinery for leasing in the course of a trade; or

- expenditure incurred on the provision, for the purposes of a trade, of an asset which is not to be leased but where payments in the nature of royalties or licence fees are to arise from rights granted by the individual in connection with that asset.

The '*period of loss*' is the basis period (within *ITTOIA 2005, ss 196–202*) for the tax year in which the loss is sustained; for earlier years it is the tax year itself.

[*ITA 2007, s 75*].

Chartering of a yacht without a skipper was held to be 'provision of plant or machinery for leasing in the course of a trade' in *Johnson v HMRC* FTT, [2012] UKFTT 399 (TC); 2012 STI 2737.

Sideways relief is also denied to an individual where such relief would be by reference to a first-year allowance on plant or machinery for leasing (or letting a ship on charter) in the course of a qualifying activity (see **4.2** below) if:

(A) at the time the expenditure was incurred the activity was carried on by him in partnership with a company (with or without other partners); or

(B) a scheme has been effected or arrangements have been made (whether before or after the incurring of the expenditure) with a view to the activity being carried on as in (A) above.

Relief is similarly denied to an individual by reference to an annual investment allowance or a first-year allowance if the allowance is made in connection with either:

(i) a qualifying activity which, at the time the expenditure was incurred, was carried on by him in partnership or which has subsequently been carried on by him in partnership or has been transferred to a person connected with him (within **2.34** above); or

(ii) an asset which, after the incurring of the expenditure, has been transferred by him to a person connected with him (within **2.34** above) or, at a price lower than its market value, to any other person.

However, (i) and (ii) above only apply where a scheme has been effected or arrangements made (whether before or after the incurring of the expenditure) such that the sole or main benefit which might be expected to arise to the individual from the transaction under which the expenditure was incurred was the obtaining of a reduction in tax liability by means of sideways relief.

[*ITA 2007, ss 76–78*].

Where relief has been given and any of the above restrictions are subsequently found to apply, the relief is withdrawn by means of an income tax assessment. [*ITA 2007, s 79(1)*].

In *Vaccine Research Limited Partnership v HMRC* UT 2014, [2015] STC 179, a claim to sideways loss relief for a trade loss deriving mainly from a claim to research and development allowances failed in part. The members of a Jersey limited partnership claimed allowances for expenditure on vaccine research and development. They claimed loss relief totalling more than £192,000,000. HMRC rejected the claims, accepting that a Jersey company (N), which was a member of the partnership, had paid a subcontractor (P) £14,000,000 on research and development, but considering that the partnership had not been trading and that the other partners were not entitled to the allowances which they had claimed. The partners appealed, contending that N had been working for the partnership as a contractor. The First-tier Tribunal reviewed the evidence in detail and allowed their appeals in part but rejected the majority of the partners' claims for relief. The Tribunal held that only the £14,000,000 which N had paid to P could in law 'be regarded as incurred on research and development'. The other sums which the partners had contributed to the partnership had not been spent on research and development, and thus did not qualify for allowances. The Upper Tribunal upheld the First-tier decision as one of fact.

A claim for relief under (a) to (e) above cannot be made for only part of a loss, so that, for example, personal allowances may be wasted as a result of the claim. However, as capital allowances are treated as a trading expense it may be possible to restrict the amount of a loss by not claiming such allowances or claiming a reduced amount. See *Example 3* below. See **2.45** onwards below for a discussion of the possibility of making a claim for reduced allowances, and in particular see **2.51** below for further possible reasons for making a reduced claim.

EXAMPLE 3

[2.37]

C, a single woman aged 30, has been trading for many years making up accounts to 30 April. She has the following trading results:

Year ended 30.4.16	Profit £6,000
Year ended 30.4.17	Loss £15,000
Year ended 30.4.18	Profit £50,000

The above results are all after deduction of capital allowances. The allowances relate entirely to plant and machinery, and the loss for the year ended 30 April 2017 includes allowances of £5,000. C has the following other income: 2016/17, £8,000; 2017/18, £13,000; and 2018/19, £14,000.

There are a number of options C could take to obtain relief for the loss for the year ended 30 April 2017 and these are discussed below. A claim for relief under *ITA 2007, s 64* must be made by 31 January 2020, which is also the deadline for the 2018/19 tax return so that all the results for that year should be known by then.

(1) Assume C makes a *ITA 2007, s 64* claim for relief against income of 2017/18 in respect of the trading loss. £13,000 of the loss is set against the other income of 2017/18. The claim therefore wastes the 2017/18 personal allowance of £11,500. An *ITA 2007, s 64* claim could be made for 2016/17 in respect of the remaining £2,000 of the loss. Note that although such relief is calculated by reference to the liability for 2016/17 effect is given to the claim for 2017/18 by repayment or set-off against the liability of that year. [*TMA 1970, Sch 1B para 2*]. If no such claim is made the remaining £2,000 of the loss will be carried forward under *ITA 2007, s 83* to set against the profits of the year ended 30 April 2018.

(2) Alternatively, priority could be given to the claim for the preceding year, giving relief against the 2016/17 income of £14,000. The claim wastes the 2016/17 personal allowance of £11,000. The remaining £1,000 of the loss could be claimed against income of 2017/18 or carried forward to set against profits of the year ended 30 April 2018.

(3) C could make no claim at all under *s 64* with the result that the trading loss of £15,000 would be available to be carried forward for utilisation against trading profits of the year ended 30 April 2018. In view of the size of the profits for that year, and depending on the basic rate limit for 2018/19, the result would be that much of the relief for the loss would be at the higher rate.

(4) C could claim a reduced amount of capital allowance (including an amount of nil) with the result that the pool of expenditure would be increased when the allowances for the year ended 30 April 2018 and later years are computed. This could be done in all the situations in (1)–(3) above, and in particular, could prevent the wasting of personal allowances in (1) and (2). See **2.45** onwards below for a discussion of this point.

If C had chargeable gains for 2016/17 or 2017/18 the claims under *ITA 2007, s 64* within (1) or (2) above could be extended by a claim under *TCGA 1992, s 261B*.

Companies

[2.38] A company which incurs a loss in a trade may, subject to the relevant conditions, obtain corporation tax relief for that loss under one or more of the following provisions.

(a) *CTA 2010, s 37*. Claim for the loss be set off against its profits of any description of that accounting period, and if the company was then carrying on the trade and the claim so requires, of preceding accounting periods falling wholly or partly within the period of twelve months immediately preceding the accounting period in which the loss is incurred. The carry-back period is extended to three years to the extent that a loss in a ring fence trade is attributable to any capital allowances under *CAA 2001, s 164* (general decommissioning expenditure — see **5.40** below), *s 416ZA* (restoration expenditure — see **10.11** below) or, before *s 416ZA* took effect, under *s 403* (expenditure on acquiring mineral asset — see **10.6** below) in respect of decommissioning expenditure (as defined). For expenditure incurred in connection with decommissioning carried out before 21 March 2012, the extension applied only to the extent that such a loss was occasioned by allowances under *CAA 2001, s 164*. See *CTA 2010, s 40*. Where a company ceases to carry on a trade, a three-year carry back applies to the whole of any loss incurred in an accounting period beginning twelve months (or beginning within twelve months) before the date of cessation. Where that twelve-month period comprises more than one accounting period, the extended carry-back also applies to a proportion (on a time basis) of any loss incurred in a period beginning before and ending within that twelve-month period.

(b) *CTA 2010, ss 99, 100*. Surrender of loss as group relief.

(c) *CTA 2010, s 45*. If no claim is made under (a) or (b) above, losses arising before 1 April 2017 are carried forward and set-off against any trading income from the same trade in succeeding accounting periods.

(d) *CTA 2010, ss 45A, 45C.* If no claim is made under (a) or (b) above, claim for loss arising on or after 1 April 2017 to be carried forward and set-off against profits of any description in succeeding accounting periods.

(e) *CTA 2010, ss 45B, 45D, 45E.* If no claim is made under (a) or (b) above , losses arising on or after 1 April 2017 which do not qualify for relief under (d) above are carried forward and set-off against any trading income from the same trade in succeeding accounting periods.

(f) *CTA 2010, s 45F.* Claim for relief for loss carried forward to the accounting period in which the trade ceases under any of (c)–(e) above to be relieved against relevant profits of that accounting period and previous accounting periods falling within the three years ending with the cessation. Where the loss was carried forward under (d) above the relevant profits are profits of any description; otherwise they are the profits of the trade. The loss cannot be relieved in the loss-making period, any period before the loss-making period or any period beginning before 1 April 2017.

(g) *CTA 2010, s 188BB.* Surrender of loss as group relief for carried-forward losses.

For the purposes of (c)–(f) above, in determining whether a loss arises before, or on or after, 1 April 2017, accounting periods straddling that date are treated as two separate accounting periods, the second of which starts on 1 April 2017. Any necessary apportionments between the two notional periods must generally be made on a time basis. [*F(No 2)A 2017, Sch 4 para 190*].

As with non-corporate traders, for corporation tax purposes capital allowances made in relation to a trade are treated as trading expenses (and balancing charges as trading receipts), so that few special provisions for such allowances are needed.

A claim under (a) above must be made within two years from the end of the accounting period in which the loss is incurred or within such further period as HMRC may allow. This two-year period is increased to five years to the extent that the claim relates to the deemed incurring of expenditure under *CAA 2001, ss 416, 416ZA* (see **10.11** below). To the extent that the claim relates to an increase in qualifying expenditure under *CAA 2001, s 165* (see **5.40** below), the claim must be made within two years after the end of the post-cessation period (within the meaning of that section). A claim under (d) above must be made within two years from the end of the accounting period to which the loss is carried forward or within such further period as HMRC may allow. [*CTA 2010, ss 37(7), 43, 45A(7); FA 2013, s 92(9); F(No 2)A 2017, Sch 4 para 11*].

Because capital allowances are treated as trading expenses they can provide some flexibility in determining the amount of a loss. This may enable the loss to be utilised more tax-efficiently and can be done by making a claim for a reduced amount of allowances. See **2.45** onwards below for a discussion of the possibility of making such a claim and in particular see **2.51** below for possible reasons for making a reduced claim.

For restrictions on utilisation of losses from leasing partnerships see **15.11** below.

For payable tax credits for companies making losses which are attributable to first-year allowances for expenditure on energy-saving or environmentally beneficial plant or machinery, see **5.28** below.

Note that, at the time of writing, *F(No 2)A 2017* had not completed its passage through Parliament. The changes made to these provisions with effect from 1 April 2017 are therefore subject to any changes made during the Parliamentary process.

Restriction on utilisation of farming, etc. losses

[2.39] Where a trade of farming or market gardening, within the definition in *CTA 2010, s 1125* (but not restricted to activities in the UK) or *ITA 2007, s 996* is carried on either by a company or by an individual, partnership, etc., there are rules for restricting the setting off of losses against other income, or against general profits in the case of a company, where losses are incurred for more than five successive tax years or company accounting years (but see the extra-statutory concession below). A loss incurred in the tax year or company accounting period immediately following such a five-year period cannot be relieved against general income for individuals, etc., under *ITA 2007, s 64* (see **2.36** above) or against company profits under *CTA 2010, s 37* (see **2.38** above).

In ascertaining whether a loss was incurred in any of the years, capital allowances (and balancing charges) are disregarded, the loss being otherwise computed under the trading profits rules. This applies both to corporate and non-corporate farmers etc. Thus, a trade profit which is converted into a loss by the deduction of capital allowances is still regarded as a profit. It is therefore possible to incur a loss after capital allowances for more than five consecutive years and suffer no restriction of loss relief as long as there is never a period of more than five years of consecutive losses before capital allowances.

[*ITA 2007, s 67, Sch 1 para 74; CTA 2010, s 48*].

A trader can nevertheless claim the reliefs mentioned above if, broadly, he is able to show that the trade is being carried on in such a way as to justify a reasonable expectation of profit. [*ITA 2007, ss 67(3)(b), 68–70; CTA 2010, s 48(3)(b), 49*].

Where a company is denied relief for a loss under these provisions, it cannot make a claim to carry forward the loss for set off against general profits under *CTA 2010, s 45A*. [*CTA 2010, s 45A(1)(3); F(No 2)A 2017, Sch 4 para 11*].

It should be noted that where relief for a loss is denied only under the above provisions, the loss may still be carried forward under *ITA 2007, s 83* or *CTA 2010, s 45* or *s 45B* (see **2.36** and **2.38** above) against future profits of the same trade. Loss relief given or available for losses arising in the previous five years remain undisturbed.

Property business losses

Individuals etc.

[2.40] Allowances due in respect of a property business are deducted as expenses of the business in arriving at the profit or loss. Losses arising in a UK property business or overseas property business carried on by an individual solely or in partnership may be carried forward and set, at the first opportunity, against profits of the business.

Where, however, a loss is incurred in a tax year (the year of loss) and there are net capital allowances (i.e. allowances less balancing charges) relating to the business, a claim under *ITA 2007, s 120* may be made to set an amount of the loss against general income for the year of loss or the following year. This relief also applies to allowable agricultural expenses of an agricultural estate (as defined). The amount in respect of which relief can be claimed is restricted to the lower of:

(a) the loss; and
(b) the net capital allowances, the allowable agricultural expenses, or the sum of those two items.

Relief cannot normally be claimed in respect of both years in respect of the same loss, but where the relievable amount cannot be utilised in full in the year specified in the claim, a separate claim can be made to relieve the balance in the other year. Where a claim is made to relieve the loss against income of the following tax year, that relief is given effect in priority to any relief claimed under these provisions in respect of a loss incurred in that following year. The losses to be carried forward are reduced or extinguished by the relief given.

Relief against general income cannot be claimed for losses calculated using the cash basis (see **17.1A** below).

Relief against general income also cannot be claimed to the extent that the loss is attributable to an annual investment allowance (see **5.2** below) if the loss arises out of certain tax avoidance 'arrangements' to which the taxpayer is a party. This rule applies to arrangements entered into on or after 24 March 2010 and to any transaction forming part of arrangements entered into on or after that date, but it does not apply if the arrangements or transaction are entered into under an 'unconditional obligation' in a contract made before that date. An '*unconditional obligation*' is one which cannot be varied or extinguished by exercising a right (under the contract or otherwise).

The restriction applies where the loss arises directly or indirectly in consequence of, or otherwise in connection with, the arrangements. The main purpose (or one of the main purposes) of the arrangements must be to put the taxpayer in a position to use the annual investment allowance to reduce his tax liability by using the relief against general income. '*Arrangements*' for this purpose include any agreement, understanding, scheme, transaction or series of transactions. They do not need to be legally enforceable.

In applying this restriction, the amount in respect of which relief could otherwise be claimed is taken to be attributable first to capital allowances and to the annual investment allowance before other capital allowances.

A similar restriction applies where a loss is attributable to agricultural expenses arising out of tax avoidance arrangements. The restriction applies to arrangements entered into on or after 13 March 2012 and to any transaction forming part of arrangements entered into on or after that date, but it does not apply if the arrangements or transaction are entered into under an unconditional obligation (as above) in a contract made before that date.

A claim for loss relief against general income must be made within 12 months after 31 January following the year to which the claim relates.

[*ITA 2007, ss 118–124, 127A, 127B, 127BA; FA 2012, s 10; F(No 2)A 2017, Sch 2 para 62*].

EXAMPLE 4

[2.41]

X has the following income.

	Year 1	*Year 2*	*Year 3*
	£	£	£
UK property business profit/(loss)	(10,000)	(5,000)	4,000
Other income	7,000	11,000	5,000

X elects for each year not to calculate profits and losses of the UK property business on the cash basis and capital allowances of £9,000 for each year have been given.

X makes claims under *ITA 2007, s 120* in respect of the UK property business losses of both years 1 and 2, and in both cases opts to set the relievable part of the loss against other income of the current year first. The maximum claim in respect of the Year 1 loss is £9,000 (to be utilised in years 1 and 2) and the maximum for year 2 is £5,000. The computations are therefore as follows.

	£	£
Year 1		
Other income		7,000
Less: Year 1 UK property business loss (part)		(7,000)
		Nil
Year 2		
Other income		11,000
Less: Year 1 UK property business loss (part)		(2,000)
Year 2 UK property business loss		(5,000)
		4,000
Year 3		
UK property business profit	4,000	
Less: Year 1 UK property business loss (remainder)	(1,000)	3,000
Other income		5,000
		8,000

The UK property business losses have been utilised as follows:

	£
Year 1 loss	10,000
Used in year 1 under *ITA 2007, s 120*	(7,000)
Used in year 2 under *ITA 2007, s 120*	(2,000)
Used in year 3 under *ITA 2007, s 118*	(1,000)

Year 2 loss	5,000
Used in year 2 under *ITA 2007, s 120*	(5,000)

Companies

[2.42] As for individuals etc., capital allowances due to a company in connection with a UK property business are given in computing the profit or loss of the business. A loss of a UK property business is to be set off against the total profits of the same accounting period. No claim is required. Any unrelieved amount is carried forward and treated as a UK property business loss of succeeding accounting periods, for set-off against total profits, provided that the company continues to carry on the business in the period concerned. Where the company is a company with investment business and the UK property business ceases, unrelieved losses are treated as excess management expenses, provided that the company continues to be a company with investment business (or investment company). These reliefs are only available where the business is carried on on a commercial basis or in the exercise of statutory functions (as defined). For accounting periods beginning on or after 1 April 2017, relief for carried-forward losses must be claimed within two years from the end of the accounting period to which the losses are carried forward or within such further time as HMRC may allow (and partial claims are permitted). For this purpose, accounting periods straddling 1 April 2017 are treated as two separate accounting periods, the second of which starts on that date. Any necessary apportionments between the two notional periods must generally be made on a time basis. Previously, set-off of carried-forward losses was automatic and no claims were required. [*CTA 2010, ss 62–64; F(No 2)A 2017, Sch 4 paras 13, 14, 190*].

Alternatively, the loss may be surrendered as group relief. Only the loss actually arising in the period concerned qualifies for group relief, i.e. excluding any amounts carried forward to be treated for all other purposes as a loss of the period, but carried-forward amounts which originally arose in accounting periods beginning on or after 1 April 2017 (treating accounting periods straddling that date as two periods as above) may be surrendered as group relief for carried-forward losses. [*CTA 2010, ss 99(1)(2), 102, 188BB, 188BC; F(No 2)A 2017, Sch 4 paras 23, 190*].

There are no provisions specifically relating to capital allowances, but the comments at **2.38** above regarding the possibility of claiming reduced allowances apply equally to UK property businesses.

Losses of an overseas property business are carried forward to set against profits of the business for subsequent accounting periods, earliest first. Again, this relief is only available where the overseas property business is carried on on a commercial basis or in the exercise of statutory functions (as defined). No claims are required. [*CTA 2010, ss 66, 67*].

For restrictions on utilisation of losses from leasing partnerships see **15.11** below.

Note that, at the time of writing, *F(No 2)A 2017* had not completed its passage through Parliament. The changes made to these provisions from 1 April 2017 are therefore subject to any changes made during the Parliamentary process.

Capital allowances as losses

Individuals etc.

[2.43] The following allowances due to individuals etc. are deducted from, or set against, income of the particular class for the tax year.

(i) plant and machinery allowances in respect of special leasing (see **2.17** above); and
(ii) patent allowances for non-traders (see **2.18** above).

Any excess of such allowances is carried forward and must be set, at the first opportunity, against subsequent income from that class. Any amount carried forward is therefore effectively treated as a loss available for future use without time limit. There are no identification rules as regards allowances or excess allowances carried forward. [*CAA 2001, ss 258(5), 479(3)*].

Companies

[2.44] The allowances referred to at **2.43**(i)(ii) above are, for corporation tax purposes, as for income tax purposes, deducted from, or set against, income of the particular class for the accounting period. Any excess is carried forward and must be set, at the first opportunity, against subsequent income from that class, provided that the company is still within the charge to tax. Any amount carried forward is therefore effectively treated as a loss available for future use without time limit. There are no identification rules as regards amounts carried forward.

Alternatively, the company can make a claim for an excess of allowances (excluding any allowances brought forward) within **2.43**(i) above (see **4.7** and **6.19** below) to be set against any other profits of the accounting period in which the excess arose. If these profits are insufficient, further relief is given against earlier profits. These earlier profits are those attributable to a period of time equal to the length of the period in which the capital allowances arose. If an accounting period falls only partly within that period of time, its profits are apportioned on a time basis; and the total reliefs, under this provision and any other loss provision, given for the relevant part are limited to the profits attributable to that part on a time basis. If more than one accounting period is involved, relief is given first against the profits of a later period. A claim for relief must be made within two years of the end of the accounting period in which the excess allowances arose. The plant or machinery must be used for the purposes of a qualifying activity carried on by the lessee during the chargeable period for which the allowance arises. Where the item is so used during only part of that period, the allowance is proportionately reduced for the purpose of giving relief against profits.

See **15.11** below for circumstances in which excess allowances cannot be so set off against other profits where the company's leasing business is carried on in partnership.

[*CAA 2001, ss 259, 260, 480*].

No allowance in respect of special leasing (see **4.7** below) may be given to any extent by deduction from a company's oil contractor profits which are subject to the ring-fence under *CTA 2010, s 356M*. [*CTA 2010, s 356NG; FA 2014, Sch 16 para 4*].

An excess allowance (ignoring any losses attributable to income for any other period and capital allowances brought forward) within **2.43**(i) above (but not any part of it carried forward from an earlier period) arising in an accounting period may alternatively be surrendered as group relief. The requirement above for the plant or machinery to be used for the purposes of a qualifying activity carried on by the lessee applies also to allowances surrendered as group relief. [*CTA 2010, ss 99(1)(2), 101; CAA 2001, s 260(7), Sch 2 para 36*].

Where a company claims group relief under *CTA 2010, ss 130* or *135* in respect of a trading loss surrendered by another company in the group, that relief takes precedence over any capital allowances carried back from a subsequent period under the above provisions. [*CTA 2010, s 137(1)(4)(5)(b)*].

Where allowances made under *CAA 2001, s 253* (see **5.85** below) to a company with investment business exceed its income from the business, the excess may be treated as a management expense and thus deductible against total profits of the company of the accounting period in question and of succeeding periods. Excess management expenses (but not any part of them carried forward from an earlier period) may be surrendered as group relief. Carried-forward amounts which originally arose in accounting periods beginning on or after 1 April 2017 may be surrendered as group relief for carried-forward losses. For this purpose, accounting periods straddling 1 April 2017 are treated as two separate accounting periods, the second of which starts on that date. Any necessary apportionments between the two notional periods must generally be made on a time basis. [*CTA 2009, ss 1219, 1223, 1233; CTA 2010, ss 99, 188BB, 188BC; F(No 2)A 2017, Sch 4 paras 6, 23, 144, 190*].

Note that, at the time of writing, *F(No 2)A 2017* had not completed its passage through Parliament. The changes made to these provisions with effect from 1 April 2017 are therefore subject to any changes made during the Parliamentary process.

Allowances not claimed

Introduction

[2.45] In certain situations (see **2.51** below) it may be advantageous to a taxpayer to forgo capital allowances that would otherwise have been made to him for a particular chargeable period (see **2.1** above) if an equal amount of allowances can be obtained later instead (even though the amount might have to be spread over a number of chargeable periods). The effect of forgoing allowances (see **2.47–2.50** below) is not the same for each type of expenditure, but in most cases it is clear that if the full entitlement is not taken, there will be no overall loss.

Specific provision requires a claim to be made before capital allowances can be given (see **2.19** above). If allowances must be claimed it follows that they are not mandatory.

Provisions for reduction of allowances

[2.46] Prior to the enactment of *CAA 2001*, there were few statutory provisions permitting a taxpayer to claim a reduced allowance. *CAA 2001*, however, extended the right to make a claim to reduce allowances to a specified amount to all the allowances codes, for chargeable periods for which it has effect (see **1.2** above).

[*CAA 2001, ss 52(4), 56(5), 102, 109, 360G(3), 360I(4), 393H(3), 393J(4), 418(6), 441(3), 458(4), 472(4), 487(6), 507(2)*].

Of course, in practice it is unlikely to be to a trader's advantage to make a partial claim if the part of the allowance not claimed is simply lost (see **2.49** below).

There seems nothing to prevent a taxpayer claiming one type of allowance but not another. For example, a company incurring qualifying expenditure on mineral extraction and also plant or machinery might choose to claim, for any particular chargeable period, mineral extraction allowances but not plant and machinery allowances.

Consequences of not claiming allowances

[2.47] It seems unlikely that a trader would wish to forgo an allowance for any particular chargeable period unless he receives the benefit of that allowance or some other related benefit at some stage. See **2.51** below for some situations in which this position might arise. The effect of not claiming depends on the type of allowance, and the more common of these are considered below.

Allowances on a reducing balance basis

[2.48] Plant and machinery allowances are calculated on a reducing balance of qualifying expenditure. If an allowance is not claimed, or a partial claim is made, the balance of qualifying expenditure carried forward to the succeeding period, on which the allowance for that succeeding period will be based, will be higher than would have been the case if the full writing-down allowance had been claimed. Any balancing allowance or charge arising in the succeeding period will be greater or lower, respectively, than would otherwise have been the case. Therefore, the taxpayer does not lose the benefit of allowances not claimed. The same applies to other allowances calculated on this basis, i.e. mineral extraction, patent rights and know-how.

Dredging

[2.49] Allowances are given on a straight-line basis over a specific writing-down period. Therefore any allowances not claimed or not claimed in full cannot be claimed in later years. (See HMRC Capital Allowances Manual, CA81100.)

Research and development

[2.50] A research and development allowance of 100% is due for the chargeable period (see **2.1** above) in which the expenditure is incurred or, if it is incurred before the commencement of trading, the first chargeable period of the trade. There is no provision for the allowance to be deferred to a later period so if it is not taken when due, it will be forgone.

Reasons for not claiming allowances

[2.51] Some possible reasons for not claiming the full amount of capital allowances available are listed below. The list is not intended to be exhaustive.

(i) Where it is expected that an asset will be sold in the foreseeable future, resulting in a balancing allowance or charge arising, the non-claiming of allowances would increase the amount of unrelieved capital expenditure carried forward and thus increase a subsequent balancing allowance or reduce a balancing charge. This could be desirable if, for example, a large balancing charge would be likely to take a person into a higher rate of tax in a subsequent year.

(ii) For an individual, a claim to full capital allowances may result in the wasting of personal allowances.

(iii) There may be trading losses brought forward which it is thought desirable to utilise as far as possible in the current year. One way of preserving sufficient trading profits in the current year to cover those losses would be by not claiming full capital allowances.

(iv) It may be desirable to leave sufficient income within the charge to tax to obtain the full benefit of double taxation relief which can be carried neither forward nor back.

3

Plant and Machinery — Introduction

Introduction

[3.1] Plant and machinery allowances are by far the most commonly claimed of the remaining allowances. The current system has its origins in *ITA 1945*, which, as an incentive to industry to rebuild and expand following the Second World War, replaced the previous system of wear and tear allowances with a new, albeit rather complex, system of writing-down allowances, balancing allowances and balancing charges. As an entirely new concept, initial allowances, designed to encourage new investment by enabling a disproportionately high percentage of qualifying capital expenditure to be written off in the first year, were also introduced. Initial allowances varied between 20% and 40% of expenditure, and were replaced by first-year allowances (which were similar) by *FA 1971*. During the currency of initial allowances they were supplemented for a time by investment allowances, which were similar to initial allowances but were not deducted from the capital expenditure for the calculation of other allowances or balancing charges. *CAA 1968* consolidated the existing legislation relating to capital allowances; but its specific application to plant and machinery was made largely redundant by the introduction of a new scheme of calculating allowances in *FA 1971*. This simplified the calculation of writing-down allowances by introducing a pooling system. The general scheme of allowances introduced by *FA 1971* continues to operate in the consolidated *CAA 2001*. Writing-down allowances are now supplemented by the annual investment allowance and first-year allowances.

Summary of the plant and machinery code

[3.2] Allowances are available to a person carrying on a qualifying activity who incurs qualifying expenditure on plant or machinery. [*CAA 2001, s 11(1)*]. Allowances are not, however, available where the profits of a trade, profession, vocation or property business are calculated on the cash basis, except for allowances on the provision of a car. See **17.1D** below.

Qualifying activities

[3.3] Qualifying activities are widely defined to include almost all types of business. The activities are: trades, professions and vocations; employments and offices; property businesses; investment business of companies; mines, quarries, railways and similar concerns which do not amount to trades; and 'special leasing' (i.e. leasing assets otherwise than in the course of another qualifying activity). See **4.2** onwards below.

Qualifying expenditure

[3.4] Qualifying expenditure is capital expenditure on the provision of plant or machinery for the purposes of the qualifying activity carried on by the person incurring the expenditure. That person must as a consequence own the plant or machinery. Neither plant nor machinery are defined in the legislation so they take their ordinary meaning. Whilst what constitutes machinery is usually straightforward, plant is much more difficult to define and as a result there have been a number of tax cases in which the meaning has been considered. Particular difficulties arise in relation to assets which are attached to or become part of a building. The meaning of qualifying expenditure is discussed in detail at **4.9** onwards below.

Allowances, charges and pooling

[3.5] Three types of allowance are available for qualifying expenditure: annual investment allowance; first-year allowances and writing-down allowances. For the purpose of calculating writing-down allowances and balancing allowances and charges, expenditure is pooled. In addition to a main pool, there are requirements for certain types of expenditure to be allocated either to a single asset pool or to a class pool. In particular, expenditure on assets qualifying for writing-down allowances at only 8% must generally be allocated to the special rate class pool and, for non-corporate taxpayers, assets with partial non-business use must be allocated to a single asset pool. Allowances are generally given as a deduction in calculating the taxable profits of the qualifying activity, and balancing charges are treated as receipts of the activity.

Annual investment allowance

[3.6] The annual investment allowance currently provides for a 100% allowance for the first £200,000 of investment in plant and machinery each year. The annual limit has changed several times; most recently it was reduced from £500,000, the £200,000 limit applying for expenditure incurred on or after 1 January 2016. Complex transitional provisions apply to chargeable periods which include the date of each change. Companies are entitled to only one allowance no matter how many qualifying activities they carry on, and a single limit is divided between companies in a group or under common control.

The allowance is not available for expenditure on cars or in certain other circumstances — see **5.3** below.

See **5.2–5.12** below for full details of the allowance.

First-year allowances

[3.7] As their name suggests, first-year allowances are given in the chargeable period in which qualifying expenditure is incurred. They have been much tinkered with over the years, so that there have been universal allowances, temporary allowances, allowances for particular types of expenditure or businesses and allowances given at different rates. There was even a lengthy period in which first-year allowances were not available at all.

The first-year allowances which are currently available are as follows.

(1) Expenditure on the provision of specified 'energy-saving plant or machinery' qualifies for allowances at 100%.
(2) Expenditure on the provision of unused (not second-hand) cars with 'low carbon dioxide emissions' that is incurred before 1 April 2018 qualifies for allowances at 100%.
(3) Expenditure on the provision of unused (not second-hand) plant or machinery for gas refuelling stations that is incurred before 1 April 2018 qualifies for allowances at 100%.
(4) Expenditure by a company on the provision of plant or machinery for use wholly for the purposes of a ring fence trade qualifies for allowances at 100%.
(5) Expenditure on the provision of specified 'environmentally beneficial plant or machinery' qualifies for allowances at 100%.
(6) Expenditure on the provision of unused (not second-hand) registered 'zero-emission goods vehicles' that is incurred after 5 April 2010 and before 6 April 2018 (after 31 March 2010 and before 1 April 2018 for corporation tax purposes) qualifies for allowances at 100%. The allowances are subject to a maximum limit of 85 million euros per undertaking (as defined) over the five years.
(7) Expenditure by a company on the provision of unused (not second-hand) plant or machinery for use primarily in an area which (at the time the expenditure is incurred) is a 'designated assisted area' that is incurred after 31 March 2012 and in the period of eight years beginning with the date on which the area is (or is treated as) designated qualifies for allowances at 100%. The allowance is limited to expenditure of 125 million euros by any person in respect of any single investment project in a particular designated assisted area.
(8) Expenditure on the provision of unused (not second-hand) plant or machinery installed solely for the purpose of charging 'electric vehicles' that is incurred after 22 November 2016 and before 6 April 2019 (1 April 2019 for corporation tax purposes) qualifies for allowances at 100%.

There are a number of exclusions which deny first-year allowances, for details of which see **5.26** below. Companies making losses attributable to allowances within (1) or (5) above can claim payable tax credits — see **5.28** below.

Following the introduction of the annual investment allowance, first-year allowances are now of little consequence to businesses which incur less than £200,000 of qualifying expenditure each year. They continue to be of importance for larger businesses. Although it is not possible to claim both annual investment allowance and a first-year allowance in respect of the same expenditure, where the expenditure would qualify for both the taxpayer can choose which allowance to claim. Clearly it will usually be beneficial to claim a 100% first-year allowance where possible, as this leaves the annual investment allowance available for expenditure not attracting such allowances.

For full details of first-year allowances see **5.15–5.27** below.

Writing-down allowances and balancing adjustments

[3.8] As noted at 3.5 above, for the purpose of calculating writing-down allowances and balancing allowances and charges, expenditure is pooled. For each qualifying activity there is a main pool and there may also be one or more single asset pools and/or a class pool. For each pool, a writing-down allowance is available for each chargeable period (other than the final chargeable period) calculated by reference to the excess of the 'available qualifying expenditure' over any disposal values which are to be brought into account (see below). The amount of the allowance is either 18%, or for certain special rate expenditure 8%, per year, on the reducing balance basis. The allowance is proportionately increased or decreased where the chargeable period is more or less than a year. Special rate expenditure includes expenditure on long-life assets, cars with higher carbon dioxide emissions and integral features of buildings (see **5.49** below). The allowance rates were reduced from 20% and 10% from April 2012, with a hybrid rate applying for chargeable periods straddling those dates.

If no annual investment allowance of first-year allowance is claimed, an item of expenditure is usually allocated to the appropriate pool for the chargeable period in which it is incurred by adding the amount of it to any balance brought forward from the previous chargeable period. Expenditure in respect of which annual investment allowance is claimed must be allocated to a pool for the chargeable period in which it is incurred (but the balance in the pool is immediately reduced by the same amount). This allows a disposal value to be allocated to the pool on disposal etc. of the asset (see below). Similarly, where expenditure has been the subject of a first-year allowance, the balance of the expenditure, or at least part of it (even if this is nil) must be allocated to a pool for a chargeable period in which a disposal event occurs in respect of the asset, so that a disposal value can be brought into account. Such expenditure can be allocated to a pool in the chargeable period in which it is incurred only if a disposal event occurs in that period.

Expenditure on assets qualifying for writing-down allowances at 8% must generally be allocated to the special rate class pool and, for non-corporate taxpayers, assets with partial non-business use must be allocated to a single asset pool. Single asset pools are also used for assets in respect of which a short-life asset election has been made and for ships (except where an election to disapply the single ship pool rules is made). See **5.48–5.80** below. Some taxpayers may also have a class pool known as the overseas leasing pool for plant or machinery used for overseas leasing under leases finalised before 1 April 2006. See **6.45** below.

Where an item of plant or machinery in respect of which any of the above allowances have been given is disposed of, a disposal value must be brought into account by deducting it from the balance in the appropriate pool. Disposal values must also be deducted on the happening of any of a number of other disposal events, including where the qualifying activity ceases, the plant or machinery ceases to be used for that activity or ceases to exist (see **5.41** below for the complete list of such events).

For each pool for each chargeable period, if any disposal value to be brought into account exceeds the amount of unrelieved expenditure in the pool concerned then a balancing charge is made equal to the difference. If the chargeable period is the 'final chargeable period' for the pool and any disposal value is less than the unrelieved expenditure or is nil, a balancing allowance is made equal to the difference; otherwise, writing-down allowance is given on the balance as reduced by any disposal value at the appropriate rate. For the main pool and the special rate pool, the 'final chargeable period' is that in which the qualifying activity is permanently discontinued. The final chargeable period for a single asset pool is generally that in which a disposal event occurs. Short-life asset pools, however, have an eight-year cut off after which any remaining unrelieved expenditure is reallocated to the main pool. See **5.32–5.46** below.

Manner of making allowances and charges

[3.9] Where the qualifying activity is a trade, profession, vocation, property business or concern within *CTA 2009, s 39(4)* or *ITTOIA 2005, s 12(4)*, allowances for a chargeable period are treated as allowable expenses of, and balancing charges as receipts of, the activity for the period. See **5.85–5.88** for the manner of making allowances and charges for the remaining qualifying activities.

Fixtures under leases

[3.10] Special provisions apply to determine entitlement to capital allowances for expenditure on plant or machinery that is, or becomes, a 'fixture', i.e. plant or machinery 'that is so installed or otherwise fixed in or to a building or other description of land as to become, in law, part of that building or other land'. Also included in the definition are any boiler or water-filled radiator installed in a building as part of a space or water heating system. The provisions are complex and are described at **6.2–6.17** below.

Leasing

[3.11] Expenditure on plant or machinery used for leasing is subject to the general rules for capital allowances, as modified by the special provisions below.

Special leasing (see **4.7** below) is treated as a separate qualifying activity as in **6.19** below. For plant or machinery provided by a lessee, see **6.20** below.

For restrictions on first-year allowances, see **5.26**(v) below.

There is a special regime for certain 'long funding leases' under which it is the lessee who obtains capital allowances. See **6.21–6.40** below.

Writing-down allowances on plant or machinery used for certain overseas leasing were previously either restricted to 10% per annum or prohibited altogether. The restrictions are abolished for new leases finalised on or after 1 April 2006 (on the introduction of the long funding lease regime). See **6.21–6.55** below.

Miscellaneous matters

[3.12] The following further miscellaneous rules apply to plant and machinery allowances.

(1) **Anti-avoidance.** See **7.2** below for the effect of disposals to connected persons and **7.3–7.6** below for the restriction of allowances on certain sales, hire-purchase etc. arrangements. See also **17.2** onwards below for further anti-avoidance provisions.

(2) **Hire-purchase and leasing agreements.** Special provisions apply to expenditure incurred under a contract providing that the person incurring it may become the owner of the plant or machinery on the performance of the contract — see **7.7–7.10** below.

(3) **Abortive expenditure.** See **7.11** below.

(4) **Gifts.** Where plant or machinery is received by a person carrying on a qualifying activity as a gift for use in that activity it is treated as acquired at its market value. See **7.12** below.

(5) **Previous use outside qualifying activity.** Where plant or machinery previously used for other purposes begins to be used for the purposes of a qualifying activity, it is treated as acquired at that time, usually at its market value or actual cost if lower. See **7.13** below.

(6) **Partial depreciation subsidies.** Where such a subsidy is received in respect of plant or machinery allowances and charges are restricted. See **7.14** below.

(7) **Renewals basis.** Before 6 April 2016 (1 April 2016 for corporation tax purposes), the renewals basis could be used as an alternative to capital allowances, particularly for small items. A limited renewals basis for landlords of residential property continues to be available in the form of replacement domestic items relief. No allowance or deduction is given on the cost of an original item but the cost of replacement is allowed as a revenue deduction. See **7.15–7.16A** below.

(8) **Replacement domestic items relief.** A limited renewals basis for landlords of residential property continues to be available in the form of replacement domestic items relief. See **7.16A** below.

(9) **Successions to trades etc.** Special provisions apply to successions to qualifying activities. See **7.17–7.19** below.

(10) **Oil production sharing contracts.** See **7.20** below.

(11) **Co-ownership authorised contractual schemes.** See **7.21** below.

See also Chapter **17** for further miscellaneous matters affecting capital allowances generally, including plant and machinery allowances.

4

Plant and Machinery — Qualifying Activities and Expenditure

Introduction

[4.1] Plant and machinery capital allowances are available to a person carrying on a 'qualifying activity' who incurs 'qualifying expenditure' on plant or machinery. [*CAA 2001, s 11(1)*].

Qualifying activities are, broadly, trades, professions, vocations, property businesses, managing the investments of a company with investment business, certain industrial concerns not amounting to trades, and 'special leasing' of plant or machinery. See **4.2–4.8** below. See **17.1D** below for the general prohibition on allowances where profits of a trade, profession, vocation or property business are calculated on the cash basis.

Qualifying expenditure is capital expenditure on the provision of plant or machinery wholly or partly for the purposes of the qualifying activity carried on by the person incurring the expenditure. That person must also own the plant or machinery as a consequence of incurring the expenditure. The terms 'plant' and 'machinery' are not comprehensively defined, although some expenditure is deemed to be on plant or machinery (see **4.17** below) and certain types of expenditure are excluded from being qualifying expenditure (see **4.20** below). Complex rules apply to determine whether expenditure on plant and machinery in buildings, structures and land can be qualifying expenditure (see **4.21–4.30** below). The question of what constitutes 'plant' has been the subject of a considerable number of cases, and these are discussed at **4.10–4.15** below.

Qualifying activities

[4.2] Subject to what is said at **4.3** to **4.8** below, the following are '*qualifying activities*' for the purposes of plant and machinery allowances:

- (i) a trade;
- (ii) an ordinary UK property business;
- (iii) a UK furnished holiday lettings business;
- (iv) an ordinary overseas property business;
- (v) an EEA furnished holiday lettings business;
- (vi) a profession or vocation;
- (vii) a concern within *CTA 2009, s 39(4)* or *ITTOIA 2005, s 12(4)*;
- (viii) managing the investments of a company with investment business;
- (ix) special leasing of plant and machinery; and
- (x) an employment or office.

Allowances are to be calculated separately for each qualifying activity carried on by a person. A 'ring fence trade' (see **5.40** below) is, for this purpose, a separate qualifying activity.

For chargeable periods beginning before 6 April 2011 (1 April 2011 for corporation tax purposes), (v) above was not a separate qualifying activity; instead there was a single qualifying activity, an overseas property business, which included all overseas property letting. See further **4.4** below.

See **17.46A** onwards below for the treatment of an activity subject to the Northern Ireland rate of corporation tax (from a date to be fixed) as a separate activity.

[*CAA 2001, s 15(1)–(3), s 162(1); FA 2011, s 52, Sch 14 paras 12(3), 13; CTNIA 2015, Sch 1 para 4*].

See **17.1D** below for the general prohibition on allowances where profits of a trade, profession, vocation or property business are calculated on the cash basis.

For plant and machinery provided for mineral exploration and access, see **10.8** and **10.12** below. See **17.59** for plant and machinery provided for use in a tonnage tax trade.

See **5.81** onwards below for the method of giving effect to allowances and charges for each type of qualifying activity.

Non-residents etc.

[4.3] The activities within **4.2** are qualifying activities only to the extent that any profits or gains are (or would be, if there were any) chargeable to UK tax. [*CAA 2001, s 15(1)*].

This provision confirms that plant and machinery allowances are available only if the activity is taxable in the UK. Where only part of an activity is taxable, for example, the UK branch or permanent establishment of a non-resident, allowances are due in respect of that part as if it were a separate activity (Treasury Notes to the Finance Bill 2000).

Property businesses

[4.4] For the purposes of **4.2** above, an '*ordinary UK property business*' is a UK property business except insofar as it consists of the commercial letting of furnished holiday accommodation in the UK (within *CTA 2009, s 265* or *ITTOIA 2005, ss 323–326*). To the extent that it does consist of such letting, the relevant part of the business is referred to as a '*UK furnished holiday lettings business*' which is treated as a separate qualifying activity and all such lettings by a particular person, partnership or body of persons are treated as a single qualifying activity. Where property falls only partly within the scope of a furnished holiday lettings business, apportionments are to be made on a just and reasonable basis. [*CAA 2001, ss 16, 17; FA 2011, Sch 14 para 12(4)(5)*].

Similar provisions apply to separate an ordinary overseas property business from an EEA furnished holiday lettings business: an '*ordinary overseas property business*' is an overseas property business except insofar as it consists of the commercial letting of furnished holiday accommodation in one or more European Economic Area ('EEA') states. To the extent that it does consist of such lettings, the relevant part of the business is referred to as an '*EEA furnished holiday lettings business*' which is treated as a separate qualifying activity and all such lettings by a particular person, partnership or body of persons are treated as a single qualifying activity. Where property falls only partly within the scope of such a furnished holiday lettings business, apportionments are to be made on a just and reasonable basis. [*CAA 2001, ss 17A, 17B; FA 2011, Sch 14 para 12(6)*].

As noted at **4.2** above, for chargeable periods beginning before 6 April 2011 (1 April 2011 for corporation tax purposes), an EEA furnished holiday lettings business was not a separate qualifying activity; instead there was a single qualifying activity, an overseas property business, which included all overseas property letting. This was because furnished holiday lettings outside the UK did not qualify for the special tax treatment available for such lettings in the UK. In 2009 HMRC announced that this may have been contrary to EU law and that they would accept claims to apply the special treatment to the commercial letting of qualifying furnished holiday accommodation outside the UK but in the EEA for all open years up to and including 2010/11. This treatment was then given statutory force by *FA 2011* as above. Under the concessionary treatment, transitional rules apply to determine the capital allowances available. Taxpayers with EEA furnished holiday lettings are not treated as starting a new qualifying activity as a result of changing to the special treatment; there is no deemed disposal and reacquisition at market value and any existing pools continue. Plant and machinery in a dwelling house used as a furnished holiday letting, which would not previously have qualified for allowances (see **4.20**(b) below), is treated as being brought into use for the purposes of a qualifying activity on the latest of the date the property was first used as a qualifying furnished holiday letting; the date on which the country in which the property is situated joined the EEA; and 1 January 1994. As a result expenditure equal to the market value of the plant or machinery concerned is treated as incurred on the latest of those dates (see **7.13** below). Expenditure incurred after the latest of the three dates is qualifying expenditure in the normal way. (HMRC Technical Note, 22 April 2009).

The EEA consists of: Austria, Belgium, Bulgaria, Cyprus, Czech Republic, Denmark, Estonia, Finland, France, Germany, Gibraltar, Greece, Hungary, Iceland, Ireland, Italy, Latvia, Liechtenstein, Lithuania, Luxembourg, Malta, Netherlands, Norway, Poland, Portugal, Romania, Slovakia, Slovenia, Spain, Sweden, Switzerland and the UK.

For chargeable periods beginning on or after 6 April 2011 (1 April 2011 for corporation tax purposes), a special rule applies where a person carrying on any of the above four types of property business uses an item of plant or machinery in rotation between the different types whilst retaining ownership throughout.

The rule applies where the person acquired the item for the purposes of one business (Business A) and has begun to use it for the purposes of a second business (Business B). If he then ceases to use the item for the purposes of Business B and recommences using it for the purposes of Business A, he is treated as having incurred capital expenditure on the day after the cessation on the provision of the item of plant or machinery for the purposes of Business A. The amount of the deemed expenditure is the lower of the market value of the item on the date of cessation and the original expenditure on the item. The item is then regarded as a different item of plant or machinery from the original item.

It would appear that on the initial movement of the item from Business A to Business B, a full disposal value (see **5.41** below) is required to be brought into account. The above rule operates only where the item reverts to being used in Business A.

[*CAA 2001, s 13B; FA 2011, Sch 14 paras 12(2), 13*].

Concerns within CTA 2009, s 39(4) or ITTOIA 2005, s 12(4)

[4.5] The concerns are:

- mines and quarries (including gravel pits, sand pits and brickfields);
- ironworks, gasworks, salt springs or works, alum mines or works and waterworks and streams of water;
- canals, inland navigation, docks and drains or levels;
- fishings;
- rights of markets and fairs, tolls, bridges and ferries;
- railways and other ways; and
- other concerns of the like nature.

Companies with investment business

[4.6] For the purposes of **4.2** above, managing the investments of a company with investment business means the pursuit of purposes expenditure on which would be treated as expenses of management within *CTA 2009, s 1219*. [*CAA 2001, s 18; FA 2013, Sch 18 para 21(4)*]. 'Company with investment business' is defined by *CTA 2009, s 1218B(1)* as a company whose business consists wholly or partly in making investments.

A company with investment business may, of course, be entitled to allowances in respect of any other qualifying activities (such as a property business) which it carries on.

Special leasing

[4.7] Capital allowances are available to persons hiring out plant or machinery otherwise than in the course of any other qualifying activity, referred to in *CAA 2001* as '*special leasing*'. Each item of plant or machinery that is subject to special leasing is treated as leased in the course of a separate qualifying activity which commences when the item is first hired and is permanently discontinued when the lessor permanently ceases to hire it out. [*CAA 2001, s 19(1)–(4)*].

Employments and offices

[4.8] 'Employment' in **4.2** above does not include an employment treated as a trade by *ITTOIA 2005, s 15* (divers and diving supervisors in the North Sea etc.) nor an employment the earnings from which are chargeable on the remittance basis of *ITEPA 2003, s 22* or *s 26*. [*CAA 2001, s 20*].

Where the qualifying activity is an employment or office, qualifying expenditure is limited to expenditure incurred on plant or machinery *necessarily* provided for use in the performance of the duties of the employment or office. Expenditure on the provision of a mechanically propelled motor vehicle or cycle (as defined by *Road Traffic Act 1988, s 192(1)*) is not qualifying expenditure. [*CAA 2001, s 36*].

The 'necessarily' test is in keeping with the general rule that for expenditure to be allowable as a deduction from employment income, it must be incurred 'wholly, exclusively and necessarily in the performance of the duties'. [*ITEPA 2003, s 336(1)(b)*]. It is not a question of whether or not the employer requires such expenditure to be incurred, but of whether the duties could be performed without incurring the expenditure, in which case the expenditure cannot be said to have been necessarily incurred. This was the point at issue in *White v Higginbottom ChD 1982, 57 TC 283* in which a vicar claimed capital allowances in respect of a slide projector and an overhead projector which he had bought in order to provide visual sermons. It was held that the vicar would have been able to do his job without such equipment, as would any other vicar, and that the items were not 'necessarily provided' for use in the performance of his duties. The claim therefore failed. See also *Telfer v HMRC* FTT, [2016] UKFTT 614 (TC) in which caravans owned and occupied by an employed assistant warden at caravan sites satisfied the 'necessarily' test but were held not to qualify for allowances on other grounds (see **4.12** below).

It is clear that the test is a very restrictive one and that cases in which allowances can be successfully claimed by employees will be relatively few in number. However, HMRC do accept that capital allowances may be given to an employed insurance agent for a computer or word processor and their peripherals provided that the claimant

- is paid by, or largely by, results;
- although the objective of selling insurance is clear, the method by which the agent is to achieve sales is not clearly defined or stereotyped; and
- the agent is required to bear the cost of any equipment-performing functions or activities designed to achieve that objective (the employer neither providing nor paying for such equipment)

(HMRC Employment Income Manual, EIM64650).

Qualifying expenditure

[4.9] The basic rule is that '*qualifying expenditure*' for plant and machinery allowance purposes is capital expenditure (see **1.3** above) on the provision of plant or machinery wholly or partly for the purposes of the qualifying activity carried on by the person incurring the expenditure. That person must also own the plant or machinery as a consequence of incurring the expenditure. [*CAA 2001, s 11(4)*]. See also **17.1D** below for the prohibition on capital allowances (other than on the provision of a car) for businesses using the cash basis for 2013/14 or a subsequent year.

The question of whether expenditure was incurred 'on the provision of plant or machinery' was considered in *Barclays Mercantile Business Finance Ltd v Mawson* HL 2004, [2005] STC1. Expenditure incurred under a complex series of transactions involving a sale and finance leaseback of a gas pipeline was held by the ChD not to have been so incurred but to have been incurred on the creation of a network of agreements under which money flows would take place annually. However, the CA overturned this decision, holding that the legislation requires 'one to look only at what the taxpayer did . . . it is immaterial how the trader acquires the funds to incur the expenditure or what the vendor of the provided plant does with the consideration received'. The CA's decision was upheld by the House of Lords.

In *BMBF (No 24) Ltd v CIR* CA [2004] STC 97, the appellant company failed to establish its *legal* ownership of certain machinery, but its *equitable* ownership was held by the High Court (see [2002] STC 1450) sufficient for the purposes of these provisions (although its claim for capital allowances failed on other grounds — see **6.46** below). This point was not pursued in the Court of Appeal. See also the cases referred to at **1.9**(ii) above.

Where a person is carrying on a trade of mineral extraction, expenditure incurred by him in connection with that trade on the provision of plant or machinery for mineral exploration and access is taken to be incurred on the provision of the plant or machinery for the purposes of that trade. For claims to allowances made on or after 6 April 2014 (1 April 2014 for corporation tax purposes), this rule does not apply if:

(1) when the expenditure is incurred the trade is being carried on but is not then a mineral extraction trade (because, for example, the trade is not within the charge to UK tax; see **10.1** below); or
(2) the trade has not begun to be carried on when the expenditure is incurred and when it begins to be carried on it is not a mineral extraction trade.

An event treated by the Taxes Acts as a deemed commencement of a trade is not a commencement of a trade for the purposes of (2) above.

[*CAA 2001, s 160; FA 2014, s 67(4)(8)*].

The terms 'plant' and 'machinery' are not comprehensively defined anywhere in the *Taxes Acts*. However, whereas it is usually quite obvious whether something constitutes machinery in this context (as evidenced by an absence of case law), plant is infinitely more difficult to define and hence the situation has led to a profusion of judge-made law.

HMRC give 'machinery' its normal meaning, to include any machine or its working parts, mechanism or works. A machine is any apparatus which applies mechanical power (Revenue Tax Bulletin October 1994, p 166). By contrast, HMRC merely say that 'guidance about the meaning of plant has to be found in case law' (HMRC Capital Allowances Manual, CA21100). The case law on the meaning of 'plant' is discussed at **4.10** to **4.15** below.

Certain types of expenditure are specifically treated as qualifying expenditure where they would not otherwise be so, and these are considered at **4.17** to **4.19** below. There are also a number of specific exclusions, discussed at **4.20** below.

FA 1994, s 117 introduced restrictions on what can qualify as plant in buildings, structures and interests in land, but without overriding specific items which had been shown to be plant in previous court decisions. These restrictions are considered at **4.24** to **4.30** below.

For provisions deeming qualifying expenditure to be an amount other than the actual capital expenditure incurred, see **6.36** (lessee under long funding lease), **6.39** (previous use for long funding leasing), **7.3**, **7.4** (anti-avoidance provisions for connected persons), **7.12** (gifts) and **7.13** (previous use outside qualifying activity) below.

HMRC have issued specific guidance on plant and machinery allowances for the pig industry in HMRC Brief 3/10. The Brief is reproduced at **Appendix 2** below.

What is plant and machinery — case law consideration

[4.10] Interestingly, neither of the two cases which have provided the starting point for most subsequent rulings on the meaning of 'plant' was actually concerned with capital allowances. Still the most widely referred to definition of the word was contained in a worker's compensation case, *Yarmouth v France* CA 1887, 19 QBD 647, where Lindley LJ said the following, at page 658.

> In its ordinary sense, it includes whatever apparatus is used by a business man for carrying on his business — not his stock-in-trade, which he buys or makes for sale; but all goods and chattels, fixed or moveable, live or dead, which he keeps for permanent employment in his business.

Yarmouth v France was applied by Lord Reid in *Hinton v Maden & Ireland Ltd* HL 1959, 38 TC 391 in which it was held (by a three to two majority) that expenditure on large numbers of knives and lasts having an average life of three years and used by a shoe manufacturer on the machines of his business represented capital expenditure on plant or machinery. He regarded them as plant rather than machinery, and said that in relation to loose tools their durability was a test in determining whether they were also plant and the three-year life in the present case satisfied this test. The case also holds a useful discussion of what is now *ITTOIA 2005, s 68; CTA 2009, s 68* for which see **7.15** below. It is usually considered in practice that a useful, economic life of two years or more is sufficient to pass the test of durability.

The other case which has frequently been used as a starting point for later ones concerned war damage compensation: *J Lyons and Co Ltd v Attorney-General* ChD, [1944] 1 All E R 477, in which Uthwatt J said:

> The question at issue may, I think, be put thus: Are the lamps and fitments properly to be regarded as part of the setting in which the business is carried on or as part of the apparatus used for carrying on the business?

The scope of the phrase 'the setting in which the business is carried on' has been the subject of subsequent discussion, for example by Lord Wilberforce in *CIR v Scottish & Newcastle Breweries Ltd* (see **4.13** below).

In *Jarrold v John Good & Sons Ltd* CA 1962, 40 TC 681, movable partitioning in an office was held to be plant. The partitions were secured to the structure by screws only at the floor and ceiling. They were easily and quickly movable and were in fact frequently moved. Consequently they were apparatus which fulfilled a functional role in the business, rather than solely part of the setting in which the business was carried on. The necessity for apparatus to be functional, if it is to qualify as plant, has been borne out by subsequent cases.

The 'functional' test

[4.11] The principle that something which performs a functional role in a business is likely to qualify as plant was given weight by the House of Lords decision in *CIR v Barclay Curle & Co Ltd* HL 1969, 45 TC 221. A company of shipbuilders and repairers constructed a dry dock. When the dock was flooded, ships for repair could be towed into it from an adjacent river. The dock could be drained for hull repairs to take place, and afterwards flooded to allow ships to be towed out. The dock served the active function of transporting ships to and from the river, and was consequently held to be plant.

This case was applied in *Cooke v Beach Station Caravans Ltd* ChD 1974, 49 TC 514. Swimming pools were built at a caravan park and an elaborate system was provided for filtering, chlorinating and heating the water. The pools were held to be plant. The caravan park itself was the setting for the business; the pools were a specific amenity which provided the active function of 'pleasurable buoyancy' for the swimmers.

Barclay Curle & Co was also applied in a Northern Ireland case, *Schofield v R & H Hall Ltd* CA(NI) 1974, 49 TC 538. The dockside concrete silos of a grain importing company were held to be plant because they fulfilled the active function of holding the grain in a position from which it could be conveniently delivered to purchasers. They were not simply for storage.

John Good and Sons Ltd (see **4.10** above) was applied in *Leeds Permanent Building Society v Proctor* ChD 1982, 56 TC 293, where decorative screens used for window displays were held to be part of the apparatus employed in the commercial activities of the business, rather than the structure within which it was carried on.

Mezzanine storage platforms erected in warehouses were held to be plant in *Hunt v Henry Quick Ltd* ChD, [1992] STC 633 and *King v Bridisco Ltd* ChD, [1992] STC 633. The Commissioners held that the platforms constituted a 'movable temporary structure', and their decision on this issue was upheld as one of fact. (For another issue in this case, see **4.13** below.) A wooden gazebo placed in a public house garden for the use of smokers was held to be plant in *Andrew v HMRC* FTT 2010, [2011] SFTD 145. The gazebo was not something which simply performed the function of housing the business, but rather provided facilities for its customers to sit and eat and drink.

[4.12] Conversely, something which is primarily part of the premises is unlikely to have sufficient functional purpose to qualify as plant. In *St John's School v Ward* CA 1974, 49 TC 524, a gymnasium and laboratory were held to be buildings in which school activities were carried on and thus part of the setting rather than plant. The buildings in question contained plant, but they were not themselves plant. In *Dixon v Fitch's Garage Ltd* ChD 1975, 50 TC 509, a canopy covering a petrol filling station was held to be part of the setting rather than plant. Its function was merely to provide adequate lighting and protection from the weather.

The decision was doubted by Lord Hailsham in *Cole Bros v Philips* (see **4.13** below). (However, a canopy which was used for advertising purposes was held to constitute plant in the Irish case of *O'Culachain v McMullan Brothers* HC(I) 1991, 1 IR 363.)

A stand at a football ground was held not to be plant in *Brown v Burnley Football Club Ltd* ChD 1980, 53 TC 357. The stand was the place from which, rather than by means of which, spectators watched the matches.

In contrast, expenditure incurred on the provision of an improved racecourse stand with accommodation which provided shelter from the elements, with new and improved viewing steps, was considered to be part of the means to attract people to the racecourse for viewing horse races and thus constituted plant for capital allowance purposes in the Irish case of *O'Grady v Roscommon Race Committee* HC(I) 6 November 1992 unreported. The stand was considered to be very much akin to the function of the swimming pool provided by the caravan park owners in *Cooke v Beach Station Caravans Ltd* ChD 1974, 49 TC 514 (see **4.11** above) in that it was 'part of the means to get people to go to that racecourse for viewing horses'.

An old barge kept moored and used as a floating restaurant was held not to be plant in *Benson v Yard Arm Club Ltd* CA 1979, 53 TC 67. The barge was the structure within which the business was carried on, rather than functional apparatus used in carrying on the business. Had the meals been served on a motorboat which journeyed up and down the Thames while the diners were eating, such a boat would probably have been accepted as plant — and would probably have qualified for allowances anyway by reason of being a 'ship'.

False ceilings in a restaurant were held not to be plant in *Hampton v Fortes Autogrill Ltd* ChD 1979, 53 TC 691. Their only function was to conceal service pipes, wiring, etc. An inflatable cover protecting a tennis court was held not to be plant in *Thomas v Reynolds and Broomhead* ChD 1987, 59 TC 502 and putting greens on a golf course were held not to be a plant in *Family Golf Centres Ltd v Thorne*, (Sp C 150) [1998] SSCD 106.

Quarantine kennels were held not to be plant in *Carr v Sayer* ChD, [1992] STC 396. The kennels were clearly functional, but buildings which would not normally be regarded as plant did not cease to be buildings and become plant simply because they were purpose-built for a particular trading activity.

A 'planteria' with no mechanical controls was held not to be plant but simply the premises in which the final part of the taxpayers' trade as nurserymen was carried on in *Gray v Seymours Garden Centre (Horticulture)* ChD, [1993]

STC 354 and CA, [1995] STC 706. The 'planteria' was a form of greenhouse with special panes of glass in the glazed roof which could be opened and shut to control ventilation. It was merely used to protect plants already in a saleable condition and provide a suitable climate for their display for sale to the public. See further below and Revenue Tax Bulletin November 1992, p 46, for an outline of what glasshouses are accepted as qualifying as plant.

The *Seymours Garden Centre* case has been quoted in another recent case *Attwood v Anduff Car Wash* CA, [1997] STC 1167. In this case a special structure containing car automatic washing equipment was not plant for the purposes of claiming capital allowances. Although the design of the structure was crucial to the car washing system, allowing four cars to pass through simultaneously, it was held that the structure formed part of the premises in which the trade of car washing was carried on. It was not plant with which the trade was carried on.

In *Bradley v London Electricity plc* ChD, [1996] STC 1054, housing for an underground electricity sub-station was held not to be plant.

In *Shove v Lingfield Park 1991 Ltd* CA, [2004] STC 805, an all-weather track for horse racing was held not to be plant. Conversely, in *Anchor International Ltd v CIR* CS, [2005] STC 411 artificial football pitches were held to be plant.

In *Rogate Services Ltd v HMRC* FTT, [2014] UKFTT 312 (TC); 2014 STI 2092, a purpose-built building used to apply glasscoat finishes to cars was held not to be plant on general principles. The Tribunal observed that the building was 'a workshop designed to allow glasscoat to be applied advantageously', and was 'a place of work which does not amount to plant'.

In *Telfer v HMRC* FTT, [2016] UKFTT 614 (TC) caravans owned and occupied by an employed assistant warden at caravan sites were held not to qualify for allowances. Although the Tribunal accepted that the taxpayer could not legally or realistically have performed the duties of his employment as an assistant warden without the use of the caravans, 'the caravans were not something by means of which those duties were in part carried on, but were instead structures which played no part in the carrying on of those duties, but were merely the place within which they were carried on'.

[4.13] The question of whether electrical equipment is specifically functional, or merely part of the setting, was considered in *Cole Brothers Ltd v Phillips* HL 1982, 55 TC 188. The Special Commissioners found that the multiplicity of elements in the installation precluded it from being treated as a single whole, although they held that transformers constituted plant, as did window lighting specifically designed to attract customers. The Court of Appeal held that the switchboard was also plant and the House of Lords upheld this decision. The company's contention that the entire installation constituted plant was rejected at every stage. Thus the following items were held not to be plant: wiring to and on each floor, associated equipment, and indoor lighting.

The *Cole Brothers* case is helpful in a further respect in that the Case Stated contains an analysis of the electrical installation setting out the items which the Revenue accepted as plant.

(i) Wiring, etc. to heating and ventilation equipment.
(ii) Wiring, etc. to smoke detectors, fire alarm and burglar alarm.
(iii) Wiring, etc. to clocks.
(iv) Public address system and staff location.
(v) Wiring, etc. to TV workshop and cash registers.
(vi) Trunking for telephone system.
(vii) Wiring, etc. to lifts and escalators.
(viii) Wiring, etc. to Electrical Appliance Department, compactor room, etc.
(ix) Emergency lighting system.
(x) Standby supply system.
(xi) The fitments for the display of fittings for sale in the Lighting Department.
(xii) Additional sockets installed in the television sales area.

The argument that equipment which might be considered part of the setting actually had a specific function, and therefore constituted plant, was put forward in the case of *CIR v Scottish & Newcastle Breweries Ltd* HL 1982, 55 TC 252. This case illustrates the point that the nature of the business which is being carried on and the use to which an item is put have to be considered along with the nature of the item itself.

In the *Scottish & Newcastle* case the company had incurred expenditure on the provision of decor, murals, and electrical fittings and wiring in some hotels and public houses it ran, and claimed that the expenditure was on plant.

Included in the decor and murals were a number of items which were fixed to the walls, and in one instance, two sculptures entitled 'Seagulls in Flight' which were fixed to the ceiling and forecourt of a hotel. Each of these items was detachable, however. The evidence was that the lighting and decor were carefully designed according to the type of clientele the business wished to attract. The Special Commissioners took the view that the company's trade included the provision of accommodation in 'a situation which includes *atmosphere* — atmosphere judged in the light of the market' which particular premises were intended to serve, and that the fittings and decor had a functional purpose in the trade.

When the case reached the House of Lords, Lord Wilberforce considered a number of other cases which he felt had a bearing and, in doing so, provided a useful summary of what he considered to be the criteria for assessing what is 'plant'. He said:

> Later cases [following *Yarmouth v France*] have revealed that a permanent structure may be plant (*CIR v Barclay Curle & Co. Ltd* HL 1969, 45 TC 221) and argument has ranged over the question whether, to constitute plant, an item of property must fulfil an active role or whether a passive role will suffice — a distinction which led to some agreeable casuistry in relation to a swimming pool (*Cooke v Beach Station Caravans Ltd* ChD 1974, 49 TC 514). Perhaps the most useful discrimen, for present purposes, where we are concerned with something done to premises, is to be found in that of "setting": to provide a setting for the conduct of a trade or business is not to provide plant — *J Lyons & Co. Ltd v Attorney-General* ChD, [1944] 1 All ER 477, concerning electric lamps, sockets and cords for lighting a tea shop. But this, too, is not without difficulty. In the *Lyons* case itself Uthwatt J thought that different considerations (so that they might qualify as apparatus) might apply to

> certain specific lamps because they might "be connected with the needs of the particular trade carried on upon the premises".
>
> In *Jarrold v John Good & Sons Ltd* CA 1962, 40 TC 681, some fixed but movable partitions, although in a sense "setting", were thought capable of being also "apparatus". And in *Schofield v R & H Hall Ltd* CA(NI) 1974, 49 TC 538, the same argument was applied to the external walls of grain silos, as well as to the connected machinery.
>
> Another much used test word is "functional" — this is useful as expanding the notion of "apparatus"; it was used by Lord Reid in *Barclay, Curle* (above). But this, too, must be considered, in itself, as inconclusive. Functional for what? Does the item serve a functional purpose in providing a setting? Or one for use in the trade?
>
> It is easy, without excessive imagination, to devise perplexing cases. A false ceiling designed to hide unsightly pipes is not plant, though the pipes themselves may be (*Hampton v Fortes Autogrill Ltd* ChD 1979, 53 TC 691): is a tapestry hung on an unsightly wall any different from a painted mural? And does it make a difference whether there was a damp patch underneath? What limit can be placed on attractions, interior or exterior, designed to make premises more pleasing, to the eye or other senses? There is no universal formula which can solve these puzzles.
>
> In the end each case must be resolved, in my opinion, by considering carefully the nature of the particular trade being carried on, and the relation of the expenditure to the promotion of the trade. I do not think that the courts should shrink, as a backstop, from asking whether it can really be supposed that Parliament desired to encourage a particular expenditure out of, in effect, taxpayers' money, and perhaps ultimately, in extreme cases, to say that this is too much to stomach. It seems to me, on the Commissioners' findings, which are clear and emphatic, that the [taxpayer company's] trade includes, and is intended to be furthered by, the provision of what may be called "atmosphere" or "ambience", which (rightly or wrongly) they think may attract customers. Such intangibles may in a very real and concrete sense be part of what the trader sets out, and spends money, to achieve. A good example might be a private clinic or hospital, where quiet and seclusion are provided, and charged for accordingly. One can well apply the "setting" test to these situations. The amenities and decoration in such a case as the present are not, by contrast with the *Lyons* case, the setting in which the trader carries on his business, but the setting which he offers to his customers for them to resort to and enjoy. That it is setting in the latter and not the former sense for which the money was spent is proved beyond doubt by the Commissioners' findings.

It follows from the judgments in this case that items added to the premises can qualify as plant provided that they do not become part of the premises. A building must have a floor, walls and ceilings, so that floors, walls and ceilings do not constitute plant even if they are particularly attractive or decorative. However pictures, murals, tapestries, etc. are not an integral part of a building and can therefore qualify as plant.

It is also important to note that the provision of atmosphere was held to be part of the trade of a hotelier. Commissioners have rejected a claim by a firm of solicitors for capital allowances in respect of pictures on the firm's office walls, as the 'provision of atmosphere' forms no part of a solicitor's profession. Furniture at a surveyor's premises was held not to constitute plant in *Mason v Tyson* ChD 1980, 53 TC 333. Applying the test in *Fortes Autogrill* above, the furniture was not part of the profit-making apparatus of his business.

In the case of *Wimpy International Ltd v Warland* CA 1988, 61 TC 51 , Hoffman J in the High Court accepted that light fittings in a 'fast food' restaurant were not part of the premises but were plant because, on the finding of the Special Commissioners themselves, their object was to create an atmosphere of brightness and efficiency suitable to such activities that were carried on and to attract custom. The decision of the Special Commissioners that they were not plant was therefore inconsistent with their findings of fact, and was overruled. Their decision that decorative items such as murals, decorative brickwork and wall panels were plant was upheld, as was their decision that shop-fronts, floor and wall tiles, false ceilings, floors and stairs were not plant because they formed part of the premises. The Court of Appeal upheld this decision. Light fittings in public house toilets were also held to be plant in *J D Wetherspoon v HMRC (No 2)* FTT. [2009] UKFTT 374 (TC) because they created an attractive ambience in the toilets. However, light fittings were held not to constitute plant in *Hunt v Henry Quick Ltd* ChD, [1992] STC 633 and *King v Bridisco Ltd* ChD, [1992] STC 633. The lighting in question had been installed to provide 'a normal level of illumination', and was therefore part of the setting in which the business was carried on.

Likewise, decorative wall panelling in a public house was held not to constitute plant in *J D Wetherspoon plc v HMRC* UT, [2012] STC 1450. Although there were considerations pointing either way, the panelling was regarded as 'an unexceptional component which would not be an unusual feature of premises of the type to which the appellant is inviting the public', and therefore as having lost its separate identity and become part of the premises.

[4.14] The fact that something may not ordinarily be regarded as plant does not prevent it from being treated as plant for tax purposes. In *Munby v Furlong* CA 1977, 50 TC 491, a barrister's textbooks, being functional chattels of his profession, were held to be plant within the *Yarmouth v France* definition. This overturned the earlier decision of *Daphne v Shaw* KB 1926, 11 TC 256.

The Revenue have successfully resisted a claim for the licence-plate of a black taxicab to be treated as plant. The expenditure was not primarily laid out for the acquisition of the licence-plate as a physical item, but was for the purpose of obtaining a licence to operate as a black cab driver. For further discussion of taxicab licence-plates see '*Taxation*' magazine, 20 February 1992, pp 507, 508 and HMRC Capital Allowances Manual, CA21250.

HMRC consider the majority of glasshouse structures to be the setting in which a grower's business is carried on. On that basis, they do not qualify for plant and machinery allowances. However, HMRC do accept that, in some cases, a glasshouse unit and its attendant machinery are interdependent, forming a single entity which will function as apparatus within a grower's business and as such will be plant, although each case will depend on its precise facts. The type of unit which may qualify for plant and machinery allowances is one of an extremely sophisticated design, including extensive computer controlled equipment, without which the structure cannot operate to achieve the optimum artificial growing environment for the particular crops involved. The equipment will have been permanently installed during construction of the glasshouse unit, and will normally include a computer system which monitors and controls boiler and piped heating systems, temperature and humidity controls, automatic ventilation equipment and automatic thermal or shade screens. (Revenue Tax Bulletin November, 1992, p 46; HMRC Capital Allowances Manual, CA22090). See also **5.66** below. Where a glasshouse itself fails to qualify for plant and machinery allowances, it may of course contain equipment which does so qualify under general principles.

In the case of *Gray v Seymours Garden Centre (Horticulture)* ChD, [1993] STC 354 and CA, [1995] STC 706 (see **4.12** above) a form of greenhouse with no mechanical controls and which was used to display plants for sale to the public was held not to be plant. However, in his judgment in the High Court, Vinelott J stated that 'a specialised glasshouse with integral heating, temperature and humidity controls, automatic ventilation, shade screens and other equipment could be considered to be . . . apparatus for carrying on a trade and not the premises in which the trade is carried on'.

Sophisticated glasshouses are specifically exempted from the restrictions introduced by *FA 1994, s 117* on what may qualify as plant.

Similarly, HMRC now accept that polytunnels may in some cases qualify for plant and machinery allowances provided that they are not fixed structures (see **4.27** below) and are not part of the premises or setting in which the qualifying activity is carried on. This represents a change of view by HMRC in December 2012. Previously, they considered that most polytunnels were either fixed structures or premises/setting. Where a polytunnel is not used solely for growing plants HMRC still consider that its primary use will be to offer shelter and that it will therefore form part of the premises. HMRC accept, however, that in relation to the growing of plants a polytunnel does far more than just provide shelter; it can provide an enhanced growing environment, extend the crop growing season and protect plant from insect infestation. In such cases, qualification for allowances will be determined by whether or not the polytunnel is a fixed structure, which will depend on the circumstances of the particular case. HMRC give the example of growing strawberries. If strawberries are grown in the ground in a polytunnel it will usually be necessary to move the crops every four years and the polytunnel will not be a fixed structure and so qualify for allowances. If the strawberries are grown in raised beds, however, there is no need or expectation that the crops will ever need to be grown elsewhere and it is far more likely that the polytunnel will be a fixed structure. Where claims to allowances were settled on the basis of HMRC's previous view, taxpayers should contact the office which dealt with the claim to ask for it to be reconsidered. (HMRC Brief 32/12 and HMRC Capital Allowances Manual, CA22090).

[4.15] The difficulty of defining plant was recognised by Stephenson LJ in his judgment in *Cole Brothers Ltd v Phillips* (see **4.13** above):

> The philosopher-statesman, Balfour, is reported to have said that it was unnecessary to define a great power because, like an elephant, you recognised it when you met it. Unhappily plant in taxing and other statutes is no elephant (although I suppose an elephant might be plant).

Further cases on the question of what constitutes plant can be found in Tolley's Tax Cases. See also **Appendix 1** for a list of items which may qualify as plant or machinery.

Ancillary and preliminary expenditure

[4.16] Where a person carrying on a qualifying activity incurs capital expenditure on alterations to an existing building which is incidental to the installation of plant or machinery, such expenditure is treated as if it formed part of the cost of that plant or machinery and as if the works representing that expenditure formed part of that plant or machinery. [*CAA 2001, s 25*].

In *J D Wetherspoon plc v HMRC* UT, [2012] STC 1450 the Tribunal held that, 'viewed purposively, the focus of [section 25] is on the point that if plant is installed in an existing building rather than in a purpose-built new building, it is entirely possible that something will not fit, and this will lead to alterations having to be made to the existing building.' There would be no equivalent need for such expenditure in a purpose-built new building. In interpreting the section it was necessary, 'to start with a broad assessment of what is incidental to what'. Thus, the construction of tiled kitchen walls in a public house was not incidental to the installation of cookers or other kitchen equipment; it was part of the creation of a kitchen, in which the cookers and other equipment could function properly. Although the walls were in any event specifically excluded by the provisions at **4.26** below, the tiling was not. An exception was held to apply to 'splashbacks', i.e. tiling sufficient specifically to deal with splashing which may be expected to be caused by the usual functioning of an item of equipment. Where, however, an area of a wholly-tiled wall or floor in effect functioned as a splashback, this would not qualify as an alteration incidental to the installation of plant. Plastering of a wall prior to installation of a splashback would also not qualify as it was simply part of the finishing of the walls generally. See *J D Wetherspoon plc v HMRC (No 2)* FTT [2009] UKFTT 374 (TC). The strengthening of a kitchen floor was held to be incidental to the installation of plant in the kitchen. Similarly, the cost of installing an inclined floor in a cold store was incidental to the installation of a drain.

Installation costs and other costs ancillary to the provision of plant and machinery such as delivery charges are in practice also regarded as forming part of the cost of it. HMRC also accept that the costs of removing and reinstalling plant or machinery at a different site can be qualifying expenditure if a deduction is not otherwise available in computing profits from the qualifying activity (HMRC Capital Allowances Manual CA21190).

Much of the expenditure in the *Cole Brothers* case which was at no stage in dispute (see **4.13** above) was in respect of wiring to plant, etc., and thus ancillary to that plant. HMRC will not normally accept that electrical wiring for the purpose of general power distribution throughout a building constitutes plant. Wiring installed specifically to supply equipment that is plant or machinery does, however, qualify (see HMRC Capital Allowances Manual CA21180), and it can therefore be important in a claim to be able to give a very detailed breakdown of expenditure showing clearly the allocation of all ancillary expenditure to the appropriate items of plant.

This line of approach also applies to expenditure on other mains services. See, however, **4.23** below for electrical systems and cold water systems which now qualify as integral features of a building.

HMRC also accept that hot water, central heating, ventilation or air conditioning, alarm and sprinkler systems and, baths, wash basins, etc., are plant (HMRC Capital Allowances Manual CA21200).

Although correctly treated as capital expenditure, the costs of borrowing (e.g. commitment fees and interest) prior to trading to finance the purchase of plant and machinery put into use on the commencement of trading was held to have been incurred on obtaining funds and not on the provision of plant or machinery (*Ben-Odeco Ltd v Powlson* HL 1978, 52 TC 459).

HMRC consider that professional fees (for example, architects' fees, survey fees, quantity surveyors' fees, service engineers' fees and legal costs) and preliminaries can be qualifying expenditure only if they relate directly to the acquisition, transport and installation of plant or machinery. Where such fees etc. are paid in connection with a building project which includes the provision of machinery or plant, only that part which can be properly attributed or apportioned to plant or machinery can be qualifying expenditure. Where a combined fee is paid, the services to which it relates must be analysed to determine how much of it relates to such services. The HMRC view is that it is not appropriate simply to apportion the fee by reference to the building costs of the plant or machinery compared to the building cost of the other assets, as this may overstate the extent to which the services relate to the provision of plant and machinery (HMRC Capital Allowances Manual, CA20070). In the *Wetherspoon* case, however, the Special Commissioners adopted a pragmatic approach to apportionment, holding that, 'if the capital expenditure to which the preliminaries relate involves a multiplicity of items many of them relatively small we consider that a pro rata apportionment is in principle reasonable'. Conversely, where a substantial preliminary item can be allocated to a small number of works, it would be reasonable to do this rather than to include it in a general apportionment. The Upper Tribunal upheld this decision.

An exchange loss on repayment of a loan linked to the purchase of plant and machinery may be allowable depending on the facts of the case. In *Van Arkadie v Sterling Coated Materials Ltd* ChD 1982, 56 TC 479, the claimant company paid off loan finance (denominated in Swiss francs and used to finance the purchase price of plant which was also payable in that currency) early; but as a result of the fall in the sterling/Swiss franc exchange rate the total cost in sterling was in excess of what it would have been if the exchange rate had remained unchanged. The Special Commissioners found that the extra expenditure had been incurred in discharging the original liability and was thus part of the expenditure on the provision of the plant. The High Court upheld the Commissioners' decision.

A payment to cancel another person's option to buy plant belonging to the payer has been held to be an integral part of the cost to the payer of providing itself with the plant (*Bolton v International Drilling Co Ltd* ChD 1982, 56 TC 449).

In a Press Release dated 15 March 1984, the Revenue stated that the cost of the provision and installation of ducting in connection with the construction of cable television networks is regarded as expenditure on plant and machinery.

Other expenditure treated as being on plant and machinery

Expenditure deemed to be on plant or machinery

[4.17] Allowances are available in respect of certain expenditure under specific provisions where no plant or machinery allowance or deduction would otherwise be made in computing the profits of the qualifying activity concerned. The expenditure is treated as if it were capital expenditure on the provision of plant or machinery for the purposes of the qualifying activity, which in consequence of incurring it is owned by the person who incurred it (i.e. it is treated as qualifying expenditure). [*CAA 2001, s 27; FA 2012, Sch 39 para 34(3)*]. The theme of such expenditure is one of safety and the law is clearly intended to encourage such work to be carried out, although the requirements themselves are frequently statutory. The following types of expenditure are included.

(a) *Fire safety*. Expenditure incurred before 6 April 2008 (1 April 2008 for corporation tax purposes) by a person carrying on a qualifying activity in taking the following steps in respect of premises he uses for the purposes of that activity. The steps are:
   - those specified in a notice under the *Fire Precautions Act 1971, s 5(4)*;
   - those specified in a document issued by or on behalf of the fire and rescue authority identifying steps that might have been specified in a notice under *s 5(4)* of the *Act*; and
   - those taken to remedy matters specified in a prohibition notice under *s 10* of the *Act*.

   [*CAA 2001, s 29; Fire and Rescue Services Act 2004, Sch 1 para 96; FA 2008, s 72*].
   The *Fire Precautions Act 1971* applies by order to certain boarding houses and hotels [*SI 1972 No 238*] and to certain premises of factories, offices, shops and railways [*SI 1989 No 76*]. Lessors of such premises may claim allowances on contributions towards tenants' qualifying expenditure or on similar direct expenditure of their own as in **2.9** above. HMRC do not consider that similar expenditure by a nursing home, school or college qualifies under these provisions, on the grounds that they are not 'designated premises' within the *Fire Precautions Act 1971* (HMRC Capital Allowances Manual, CA22230).
   These provisions are repealed for expenditure incurred on or after 6 April 2008 (1 April 2008 for corporation tax purposes) as they provide relief only for the non-compliant and the Government accordingly considers them to be counter-productive (Treasury Explanatory Notes to the 2008 Finance Bill).

(b) *Thermal insulation of an existing building*. Expenditure incurred by a person carrying on a qualifying activity in adding insulation against heat loss to a building occupied or let by him in the course of the activity. Where the qualifying activity is an ordinary UK property business or an ordinary overseas property business (previously an overseas property business — see **4.4** above), this is subject to the exclusion for expenditure incurred on plant or machinery for use in a dwelling-house (see **4.20**(b) below). Expenditure which is allowable under *CTA 2009, s 251* or *ITTOIA 2005, s 312* (landlord's energy-saving allowance) is excluded.

For expenditure incurred before 6 April 2008 (1 April 2008 for corporation tax purposes), allowances can be claimed within this category only by a person carrying on a trade, an ordinary property business, or an overseas property business, and the building must be an industrial building. For this purpose, the meaning of 'industrial building' is limited to a building or structure in use for the purposes of a qualifying trade.

[*CAA 2001, s 28; FA 2011, Sch 14 para 12(7)*].

Expenditure within the above provision which is incurred on or after 6 April 2008 (1 April 2008 for corporation tax purposes) is special rate expenditure, qualifying for writing-down allowances at 10%. See **5.49** below.

(c) *Sports grounds*. Expenditure incurred before 6 April 2013 (1 April 2013 for corporation tax purposes) by a person carrying on a qualifying activity in taking required safety precautions in respect of:

  (A) a sports ground used by that person for the purposes of the activity and designated under the *Safety of Sports Grounds Act 1975, s 1* as requiring a safety certificate;

  (B) a stand at a sports ground used by that person for the purposes of the activity where the use requires a safety certificate under the *Fire Safety and Safety of Places of Sport Act 1987, Pt III*; or

  (C) a sports ground used by that person for the purposes of the activity which is of a kind mentioned in *Safety of Sports Ground Act 1975, s 1(1)* but in respect of which no designation order is in force.

For these purposes, required safety precautions are:

- steps necessary for compliance with the terms and conditions of a safety certificate previously issued under the relevant *Act*;
- steps specified in a document issued by or on behalf of the relevant local authority which identifies steps which, if taken, would be taken into account in determining the terms and conditions of, or would lead to the amendment or replacement of, a safety certificate under the relevant *Act*; or
- for the purposes of (C) above, steps which the relevant local authority certifies would have been necessary for compliance with such a certificate or specified in such a document if a designation order under *s 1* of the 1975 *Act* had been in force and a safety certificate had been issued or applied for.

[*CAA 2001, ss 30–32; FA 2012, Sch 39 paras 33, 35*].

(d) *Personal security*. Expenditure incurred on the provision of 'security assets' where it is incurred by an individual or partnership of individuals carrying on a trade, profession or vocation or any of the property businesses within **4.4** above to meet a special threat to the individual's personal physical security arising wholly or mainly because of the trade, etc.

Expenditure does not qualify for allowances unless the person incurring the expenditure has as his sole object in doing so the meeting of the threat and unless he intends the asset to be used solely to improve personal physical security. However, where an asset is intended to be partly used to improve such security, the appropriate part qualifies for allowances. Incidental use of an asset for other purposes is ignored provided that the intention of the person incurring the expenditure is that the asset is to be used solely to improve such security, and the fact that an asset also improves the personal physical security of any member of the individual's family or household, or becomes affixed to land (including a dwelling) does not prevent allowances being granted. A '*security asset*' is defined as an asset which improves personal security. It does not include a dwelling (or grounds appurtenant to a dwelling), a car, a ship, or an aircraft, but does include 'equipment' or a structure (such as a wall).
[*CAA 2001, s 33; FA 2011, Sch 14 para 12(8)*].

On a disposal of any of the property represented by the expenditure mentioned in (a)–(d) above, the disposal value (see **5.41** below) of the ancillary expenditure is taken as nil. [*CAA 2001, s 63(5)*].

See also **4.23** below for expenditure on integral features of a building or structure which is treated as expenditure on plant or machinery.

Parts of and shares in plant and machinery

[4.18] Two further statutory provisions assist in defining plant and machinery. A reference to any plant or machinery is to be construed as including a reference to a part of any plant or machinery. [*CAA 2001, s 571*]. A share in plant or machinery is treated as for a part of plant and machinery; and such a share is deemed to be used for the purposes of a qualifying activity so long as, and only so long as, the plant or machinery is used for those purposes. [*CAA 2001, s 270*].

Computer software and hardware

[4.19] Expenditure on computer software may be classed as capital expenditure on the provision of plant, or as revenue expenditure, depending on the facts of the case.

Where the corporation tax intangible assets regime does not apply (see below), capital expenditure by businesses on acquiring a right to use or otherwise deal with computer software qualifies for capital allowances. The software and the right are treated as plant provided for the purpose of the qualifying activity, and as owned by the person incurring the expenditure. Previously, such expenditure could not normally attract capital allowances, as ownership did not pass. [*CAA 2001, s 71, Sch 3 para 18*].

Where a person who has incurred qualifying expenditure on the provision of software or a right to use or otherwise deal with software grants to another a right to use or deal with the whole or part of that software, and the consideration for the grant consists of (or would if it were money consist of) a capital sum, a disposal value has to be brought into account (see **5.41** below). This does not apply where the software or rights have previously begun to be used wholly or partly for purposes other than those of the qualifying activity or where the qualifying activity has been permanently discontinued. The amount of the disposal value to be brought into account is normally the net consideration in money received for the grant, plus any insurance monies or other capital compensation received in respect of the software by reason of any event affecting that consideration. However, market value is substituted where the consideration for the grant was not, or not wholly, in money. Market value is also substituted where no consideration, or consideration of less than market value, was given for the grant, except where there is a charge to tax under *ITEPA 2003* in respect of the grant of the right, where the person to whom the right is granted can obtain plant or machinery allowances or research and development (formerly scientific research) allowances, for his expenditure, or where that person is a dual resident investing company connected with the grantor.

A chargeable period is not treated as the 'final chargeable period' in relation to a short-life asset pool (see **5.61** below) solely because a disposal value is brought into account under the above provision. A disposal event within *CAA 2001, s 61(1)* (see **5.41**(i)–(vi) below) is required to trigger the 'final chargeable period'.

Where a disposal value falls to be calculated in relation to software or rights over which a right has previously been granted as above, that disposal value is increased by the disposal value taken into account in relation to that grant in determining whether it is to be limited by reference to the capital expenditure incurred.

[*CAA 2001, ss 72, 73*].

'Computer software' is not specifically defined in the legislation. HMRC consider that computer programs and data of any kind are computer software, but that the information stored on the software, such as the contents of a spreadsheet, are not (HMRC Capital Allowances Manual, CA22280).

The incidental costs of installing computer hardware may, in line with the general principles mentioned in **4.16** above, also qualify as expenditure on plant or machinery, for example where an alteration has to be made to a building in order to maintain operating efficiency (e.g. ventilating ducts).

The Revenue have summarised their views on the treatment of expenditure on computer software, whether acquired under licence or owned outright. Regular payments for software akin to a rental are allowable revenue expenditure, the timing of the deductions being governed by correct accountancy practice. A lump sum payment is capital if the licence is of a sufficiently enduring nature to be considered a capital asset in the context of the licensee's trade, e.g. where it may be expected to function as a tool of the trade for several years. Equally the benefit may be transitory (and the expenditure revenue) even though the licence is for an indefinite period. The Inspector will in any event accept that expenditure is on revenue account where the software has a useful economic life of less than two years. Timing of the deduction in these circumstances will again depend on correct accountancy practice. Equipment acquired as a package containing both hardware and a licence to use software must be apportioned before the above principles are applied (Revenue Tax Bulletin November 1993, p 99).

Licences and rights over software will usually be within the meaning of 'intangible fixed assets' for the purposes of the corporation tax intangible assets regime of *CTA 2009, Pt 8*. That regime applies broadly to assets created after 31 March 2002 or acquired after that date other than, in certain circumstances, from a 'related party' (as defined). See **12.2** below for the detailed commencement provisions. Where the regime applies, capital allowances are not available as expenditure is relieved for tax purposes under the rules of the regime. Software is, however, specifically excluded from the regime in two cases. Where the exclusions have effect, the above rules will continue to apply. The first exclusion is for expenditure on software that falls for accounting purposes to be treated as part of the cost of related hardware. Such expenditure is excluded entirely from the regime (except as regards royalties). The second exclusion applies by election to exclude from the regime an asset representing capital expenditure on software. Where the election is made, those provisions of the regime which would otherwise override the above capital allowances rules are disapplied, and receipts from the realisation of software remain within the regime only to the extent that they exceed the disposal value for capital allowances purposes. The election must be made within two years after the end of the accounting period in which the expenditure is incurred and is irrevocable. The election would normally be beneficial if the rate at which the expenditure is relieved for tax purposes under the existing rules exceeds the rate under the intangible assets regime (which would normally follow the accounting treatment). [*CTA 2009, ss 813, 815, 816; FA 2002, Sch 29 paras 1(3), 81, 83, 117, 118; FA 2012, Sch 16 para 177*].

Also excluded from the regime is any asset treated in a company's accounts as an intangible asset but which in a previous accounting period was treated as a tangible asset and on which plant and machinery capital allowances were claimed. This provision applies in respect of periods for which companies draw up accounts beginning on or after 1 January 2005 and was introduced as part of a package of measures dealing with the tax consequences of the adoption of international accounting standards (IAS) by UK companies. [*CTA 2009, s 804*]. The provision is intended particularly to deal with the case of certain expenditure on websites classified under UK generally accepted accounting practice as a tangible asset, but under IAS as an intangible asset in principle within the regime. As capital allowances have been given on such expenditure in some cases, the exclusion from the regime was introduced as the simplest solution (Treasury Explanatory Notes to the Finance Bill 2004).

Exclusions from qualifying expenditure

[4.20] The following types of expenditure are not qualifying expenditure.

(a) Expenditure incurred by a member of the House of Commons, Scottish Parliament, National Assembly of Wales or Northern Ireland Assembly in connection with the provision or use of residential or overnight accommodation for the purpose of enabling the member to perform his duties in or about either the place the relevant body sits or his constituency or region. [*CAA 2001, s 34*].

(b) Expenditure incurred on providing plant or machinery for use in a dwelling-house, where the qualifying activity is an ordinary UK property business (i.e. *not* a UK furnished holiday lettings business), an ordinary overseas property business (i.e., for chargeable periods beginning on or after 6 April 2011 (1 April 2011 for corporation tax purposes), *not* an EEA furnished holiday lettings business) or a special leasing. If plant or machinery is provided partly for such use, the expenditure is apportioned on a just and reasonable basis. [*CAA 2001, s 35; FA 2011, Sch 14 paras 12(9), 13*].

Expenditure incurred on or after 6 April 2016 (1 April 2016 for corporation tax purposes) by a property business on the replacement of 'domestic items' for use in a dwelling-house by the lessee and which does not qualify for capital allowances does, however, qualify for a deduction in computing the business profits. See **7.16A** below.

Previously, an election could be made for a wear and tear deduction based on 10% of rents received to cover the costs of replacing furniture, furnishings etc. where capital allowances were not due. The deduction was calculated after first deducting any amounts included in rents but covering council tax and other expenditure which would normally be borne by a tenant. For income tax purposes, the wear and tear deduction is abolished for 2016/17 onwards. For corporation tax it is abolished for accounting periods beginning on or after 1 April 2016. For this purpose, accounting periods straddling 1 April 2016 are treated as two accounting periods, the second beginning on that date. Any apportionments required between the two deemed accounting periods must be made on a time basis or, if that method would produce an unjust or unreasonable result, on a just and reasonable basis. [*ITTOIA 2005, ss 308A–308C; CTA 2009, ss 248A–248C; FA 2016, s 74; SI 2011 No 1037*].

Alternatively, prior to its withdrawal for expenditure incurred before 6 April 2013 (1 April 2013 for corporation tax purposes), the non-statutory renewals basis (see **7.15** below) could be operated for furniture, furnishings and chattels.

HMRC accept that a lift, central heating system or fire alarm serving the communal parts of a block of residential flats can qualify for allowances, as the block of flats is not itself a dwelling-house (although clearly the individual flats are dwelling-houses) (HMRC Capital Allowances Manual, CA20020, CA23060). HMRC similarly accept that the communal areas of a university hall or residence or key worker accommodation, together with any areas to which the tenants do not have access, are not a dwelling-house. They do, however, consider that all other areas are dwelling-houses. This represents a change of view: previously HMRC accepted that halls of residence etc. were not dwelling-houses (HMRC Brief 66/08).

(c) Expenditure incurred on plant or machinery where it appears that sums are to be payable to the person incurring it in respect of, or to take account of, the whole of the depreciation of the plant or machinery resulting from its use in the qualifying activity. The exclusion does not apply where the sums are treated as income or receipts of the qualifying activity. [*CAA 2001, s 37*]. See **7.14** below for the position where the subsidy covers only part of the depreciation..

(d) Expenditure incurred on animals or other creatures to which *ITTOIA 2005, s 30* or *ss 111–129* or *CTA 2009, s 50* or *ss 109–127* apply (animals etc. kept for the purposes of farming or any other trade) or on shares in such animals etc. [*CAA 2001, s 38*].

(e) Where the qualifying activity is an employment or office, expenditure incurred on the provision of a mechanically propelled motor vehicle or cycle (as defined by *Road Traffic Act 1988, s 192(1)*). [*CAA 2001, s 36*].

(f) Expenditure incurred on plant or machinery for leasing under a long funding lease. [*CAA 2001, s 34A*]. See **6.21–6.40** below for long funding leases generally and in particular **6.23** below for commencement provisions and **6.39** below for lessors and capital allowances.

(g) For income tax purposes for 2013/14 onwards, expenditure which is incurred on a vehicle in a period of account is not qualifying expenditure if a fixed rate deduction under *ITTOIA 2005, s 94D* is made for the period in respect of the expenditure. [*CAA 2001, s 38ZA; FA 2013, Sch 5 paras 5(2), 6*]. Where capital allowances are initially claimed for such expenditure but in a later period of account the taxpayer switches to using the fixed rate deduction, the capital allowances consequences are as described at **5.34** below.

Plant and machinery in buildings, structures and land

[4.21] Most commercial buildings contain some items which constitute plant and machinery. When purchasing such a building, it is possible to claim capital allowances on a proportion of the consideration for the property in accordance with the provisions of *CAA 2001, s 562* (see **2.25** above). The following table, now somewhat dated, was prepared from an analysis of about 100 capital allowances claims and published in '*Taxation*' magazine, 11 June 1992, pp 262–265. It gives an approximate illustration of the relative proportions by cost of plant, based upon the total purchase price (including land) of different types of building.

Type of building	*% of purchase price attributable to plant or machinery*	
	Minimum	*Maximum*
Computer centres	25	37½
'Luxury' hotels	20	26
Air-conditioned offices	18	24
Standard hotels	13	21½
Modern offices (not air-conditioned)	12½	20
Covered shopping centres	12	18
Older-style offices	8	13
Business/retail	7½	14½
BI/high-tech development	7½	12

Type of building	*% of purchase price attributable to plant or machinery*	
	Minimum	*Maximum*
Industrial	5	10
Shop shells	2½	5

A more recent list, published in published in '*Taxation*' magazine, 21 September 2017, p 16, gave typical proportions of plant or machinery which are fixtures by building type, ranging upt o a maximum of 40% for hotels, care homes and offices.

As noted at **2.25** above, *s 562* requires the purchase consideration to be apportioned on a just and reasonable basis to arrive at the qualifying expenditure (Q), but there is no statutory formula for doing so. The Valuation Office Agency's preferred formula, however, is:

$$Q = P \times \frac{A}{B + C}$$

where:

P = purchase consideration;
A = replacement value of the plant or machinery;
B = replacement value of the building (including plant or machinery); and
C = value of the bare land.
(Valuation Office Agency Capital Gains Tax Manual, para 3.31).

The Agency consider that for these purposes, the value of the bare site is the open market value of the actual site as at the date of purchase and should reflect the effect of any reclamation works which have been carried out on the site which permanently enhance the value of the land. Replacement values should be taken as the estimated cost of replacing the item if work had commenced at the appropriate time so as to have the building available for occupation at the date of purchase. (Valuation Office Agency Capital Gains Tax Manual, paras 3.33, 3.34). See para 3.35 of the manual for adjustments to replacement values where the building is near the end of its life. See also **19.4** below for further discussion of this issue.

Where, in the case of a second-hand building, plant or machinery is a 'fixture' within the meaning of *CAA 2001, s 173* (see **6.2** onwards below), the amount in respect of which allowances can be claimed may be restricted. An election can be made in some circumstances to fix the amount to be treated as the expenditure by the purchaser on the fixtures. This overrides the apportionment above. See **6.15** and **6.17** below.

Although the above formula is not statutory, any attempt to inflate the proportion of the consideration which is reasonably attributable to plant and machinery is likely to lead to detailed questioning by HMRC. Professional valuations of land, building and plant and machinery will assist in achieving a successful optimum claim.

Claims for allowances using sampling

[4.22] Where a business undertakes large programmes of work on its properties and the nature of the work is very similar, HMRC will in certain circumstances accept claims for allowances for expenditure incurred on qualifying fixtures based on a detailed breakdown of expenditure in a sample of those properties. Sampling may be used, for example, where a company acquires a number of similar sized retail units and fits them out in their corporate style to create a standard type of shop. See HMRC Capital Allowances Manual, CA20075. Currently, HMRC's guidance requires only the use of 'statistically acceptable sampling methodologies', but proposed revised guidance has been published in HMRC Brief 24/2012 to include a stricter definition of that expression. Under the revised guidance HMRC will consider sampling where:

(i) the overall size of the population (i.e. the total number of properties or units) allows for a reasonable sample size;
(ii) there would be a considerable and demonstrable burden on the business in analysing the expenditure for the whole population; and
(iii) the nature of the works is reasonably similar across the whole population or appropriate stratified sampling (where the population is separated into different categories) is to be used.

HMRC do not consider that a sample size of less than 15 is reasonable for the purposes of (i) above. Under the revised guidance, sampling must be random and must achieve a specified confidence interval, depending on the amount of the expenditure. Detailed information must be included with the claim.

Integral features of a building or structure

[4.23] Allowances are available in respect of expenditure incurred on or after 6 April 2008 (1 April 2008 for corporation tax purposes) by a person carrying on a qualifying activity, on the provision or 'replacement' of an 'integral feature' of a building or structure used by him for the purposes of that activity. The expenditure is treated as if it were capital expenditure on the provision of plant or machinery for the purposes of the qualifying activity, which in consequence of incurring it is owned by the person who incurred it (i.e., unless subject to an exclusion, it is treated as qualifying expenditure). Expenditure treated as qualifying expenditure in this way cannot be deducted in computing the income of the qualifying activity.

The expenditure may qualify for annual investment allowance or, if it meets the necessary conditions, for first-year allowances within **5.16**(1) or (5) below. The expenditure is special rate expenditure and must normally be allocated to the special rate pool (see **5.49** below).

For these purposes, an '*integral feature*' is any of the following:

- an electrical system (including a lighting system);
- a cold water system;
- a space or water heating system, a powered system of ventilation, air cooling or air purification, and any floor or ceiling comprised in such a system;
- a lift, escalator or moving walkway; or

- external solar shading.

Any asset whose principal purpose is to insulate or enclose the interior of a building or to provide an interior wall, floor or ceiling which is intended to remain permanently in place is excluded.

The Treasury can by order exclude a specified feature from the above list if expenditure on it would be qualifying expenditure other than special rate expenditure and can so add a feature provided that expenditure on its provision would not otherwise be qualifying expenditure.

Expenditure incurred on an integral feature is treated for the above purposes as expenditure on its '*replacement*' if the amount of the expenditure is more than 50% of the cost of replacing the feature at the time it is incurred. Where expenditure fails the 50% test but further expenditure is incurred on the feature within the following twelve months, then, if the aggregate expenditure is more than 50% of the cost of replacing the feature at the time of the initial expenditure, all of the expenditure is treated as expenditure on the replacement of the feature. The initial expenditure and further expenditure do not have to be incurred in the same chargeable period; amendments can be made to tax returns as necessary.

[*CAA 2001, ss 33A, 33B; FA 2008, s 73(2)(6)*].

Restrictions on eligible expenditure

[4.24] As can be seen from **4.21** above, there is often a substantial amount of plant in buildings, particularly in computer centres and hotels. In response to a growing number of attempts by taxpayers to inflate the plant and machinery element of buildings and structures over and above what the Revenue perhaps regarded as reasonable (the more generous rate of allowance for plant over that for buildings undoubtedly being the prime motive for taxpayers), and to prevent further erosion of the distinction between plant and buildings, provisions, as described in **4.25** onwards below, were introduced by *FA 1994, s 117* to 'clarify' the boundaries between buildings, structures and land on the one hand and plant and machinery on the other.

A Revenue Press Release of 17 December 1993, which accompanied the publication of the draft provisions, stated that 'case law suggests that a "building" is anything with four walls and a roof provided that it is of a reasonably substantial size. Thus while a wooden hut large enough to contain people is likely to be a building, a small dog kennel is not'. It went on to say that the provisions introduced by *FA 1994, s 117* 'will not apply to certain parts of buildings (e.g. central heating) or to certain specialised buildings (e.g. sophisticated glasshouses) which have been accepted as plant in the past'.

[4.25] *CAA 2001, ss 21–25* restrict the range of expenditure on which plant and machinery allowances can be claimed by providing that buildings, structures, certain other assets and works involving the alteration of land, and interests in land cannot qualify as plant or machinery. References to the provision of any building, structure or other asset include references to its construction or acquisition. [*CAA 2001, ss 21(2), 22(2)*].

Assets which have been held to be plant under specific court decisions continue to qualify for plant and machinery allowances, but assets which have been held to be plant by common consent or under some past unappealed decisions of the Commissioners, for example, may no longer qualify as they are not law. The provisions in *CAA 2001, ss 21–24* only state what cannot be plant or machinery and make no attempt to clarify what exactly is within the scope of that phrase. Assets not covered by these provisions thus remain subject to prevailing plant case law as discussed in **4.9** onwards above; and the question of whether something is plant or not will depend on the facts of each particular case.

See Appendix **1** for a list of items which have been held to be plant in the past; not all by virtue of previous court decisions. The list should be read in the light of the *FA 1994* provisions.

Expenditure on buildings which does not qualify for allowances

[4.26] Subject to **4.28** below, expenditure on the provision of a building will not qualify for plant and machinery allowances. For these purposes the expression 'building' includes:

(a) any assets incorporated in the building;
(b) any assets not incorporated in the building, because they are movable or for some other reason, but are nevertheless of a kind which are normally incorporated into buildings; and
(c) any of the following:
  (A) walls, floors, ceilings, doors, gates, shutters, windows and stairs;
  (B) mains services, and systems, for water, electricity and gas;
  (C) waste disposal systems;
  (D) sewerage and drainage systems;
  (E) shafts or other structures in which lifts, hoists, escalators and moving walkways are installed; and
  (F) fire safety systems.

[*CAA 2001, s 21*].

It would appear that there is room for debate over the meaning of 'normally' in (b) above. What may be normal for one type of building may not be normal for another.

Whilst doors and gates in (A) above do not qualify, motors, machinery, etc. controlling or operating them do qualify (see **4.28**(1) below) ('*Taxation*' magazine 28 July 1994, p 417).

Expenditure on structures, assets and works not qualifying for allowances

[4.27] For the purposes of these provisions the word 'structure' means a fixed structure of any kind, other than a building. [*CAA 2001, s 22(3)(a)*]. 'A structure is any substantial man-made asset' (Inland Revenue Press Release 17 December 1993).

Subject to **4.28** below, expenditure on the provision of a structure or other asset listed in (a) to (g) below, or on any works involving the alteration of land, will not qualify for plant and machinery allowances.

(a) Any tunnel, bridge, viaduct, aqueduct, embankment or cutting.

(b) Any way or hard standing, such as a pavement, road, railway (see below) or tramway, a park for vehicles or containers, or an airstrip or runway.
(c) Any inland navigation, including a canal or basin or a navigable river.
(d) Any dam, reservoir or barrage (including any sluices, gates, generators and other equipment associated with it).
(e) Any dock, harbour, wharf, pier, marina or jetty, and any other structure in or at which vessels may be kept or merchandise or passengers may be shipped or unshipped.
(f) Any dike, sea wall, weir or drainage ditch.
(g) Any structure not in (a) to (f) above, with the exception of an industrial structure (other than a building) which is or is to be an industrial building within the meaning of *CAA 2001, Pt 3 Ch 2* (now repealed), a structure in use for the purposes of an undertaking for the extraction, production, processing or distribution of gas, or a structure in use for the purposes of a trade which consists in the provision of telecommunication, television or radio services.

For the purposes of these provisions, the alteration of land does not include the alteration of buildings or structures.

[*CAA 2001, s 22*].

The term 'railway' in (b) above means any structure which is part of the rail 'way' itself such as any concrete hardstanding ('*Taxation*' magazine 28 July 1994, p 417).

In *Andrew v HMRC* FTT 2010, [2011] SFTD 145 a wooden gazebo placed in a public house garden for the use of smokers was held not to be a fixed structure.

Expenditure on buildings not excluded from qualifying for allowances

[4.28] Expenditure incurred on the provision of any assets listed in (1) to (33) below is not excluded by the rules in **4.26** and **4.27** above from qualifying for plant and machinery allowances (and any question as to whether such expenditure listed below will qualify will depend on the particular facts of each case and prevailing plant case law). An asset does not, however, fall within (1) to (16) below (and is thus excluded from qualifying as plant or machinery) if its principal purpose is to insulate or enclose the interior of the building or to provide an interior wall, a floor or a ceiling which (in each case) is intended to remain permanently in place. This does not override ceilings or floors in (3) below where they form part of a system as opposed to just covering it ('*Taxation*' magazine 28 July 1994, p 417).

(1) Any machinery (including devices for providing motive power) not within (2) to (33) below.
(2) Gas and sewerage systems and, for expenditure incurred before 6 April 2008 (1 April 2008 for corporation tax purposes), electrical systems (including lighting systems) and cold water systems, provided mainly to meet the particular requirements of the qualifying activity, or provided mainly to serve particular plant or machinery used for the purposes of that activity.

(3) For expenditure incurred before 6 April 2008 (1 April 2008 for corporation tax purposes), space or water heating systems; powered systems of ventilation, air cooling or air purification; and any ceiling or floor comprised in such systems.
(4) Manufacturing or processing equipment; storage equipment, including cold rooms; display equipment; and counters, checkouts and similar equipment.
(5) Cookers, washing machines, dishwashers, refrigerators and similar equipment; washbasins, sinks, baths, showers, sanitary ware and similar equipment; and furniture and furnishings.
(6) Hoists and, for expenditure incurred before 6 April 2008 (1 April 2008 for corporation tax purposes), lifts, escalators and moving walkways.
(7) Sound insulation provided mainly to meet the particular requirements of the qualifying activity.
(8) Computer, telecommunication and surveillance systems (including their wiring or other links).
(9) Refrigeration or cooling equipment.
(10) Fire alarm systems; sprinkler equipment and other equipment for extinguishing or containing fire.
(11) Burglar alarm systems.
(12) Strong rooms in bank or building society premises; safes.
(13) Partition walls, where moveable and intended to be moved in the course of the qualifying activity.
(14) Decorative assets provided for the enjoyment of the public in the hotel, restaurant or similar trades.
(15) Advertising hoardings; and signs, displays and similar assets.
(16) Swimming pools (including diving boards, slides and structures on which such boards or slides are mounted).
(17) Any glasshouse constructed so that the required environment (i.e. air, heat, light, irrigation and temperature) is controlled automatically by devices forming an integral part of its structure. See also **4.12** and **4.14** above for further discussion on glasshouses.
(18) Any cold store.
(19) Any caravan provided mainly for holiday lettings. For this purpose, the wide definition of 'caravan' in *Caravan Sites and Control of Development Act 1960 s 29(1)* (or equivalent Northern Ireland provision) is used in relation to caravans on holiday caravan sites.
(20) Any building provided for testing aircraft engines run within the building (i.e. test beds).
(21) Any moveable building intended to be moved in the course of the qualifying activity.
(22) The alteration of land for the purpose only of installing plant or machinery (e.g. excavation costs incurred in the construction of a dry dock).
(23) The provision of dry docks.
(24) The provision of any jetty or similar structure provided mainly to carry plant or machinery.
(25) The provision of pipelines, or underground ducts or tunnels with a primary purpose of carrying utility conduits.
(26) The provision of towers to support floodlights.

(27) The provision of any reservoir incorporated into a water treatment works or the provision of any service reservoir of treated water for supply within any housing estate or other particular locality.
(28) The provision of silos provided for temporary storage or the provision of storage tanks.
(29) the provision of slurry pits or silage clamps.
(30) The provision of fish tanks or fish ponds.
(31) The provision of rails, sleepers and ballast for a railway or tramway.
(32) The provision of structures and other assets for providing the setting for any ride at an amusement park or exhibition.
(33) The provision of fixed zoo cages.

[*CAA 2001, s 23*].

The changes in the items listed at (1), (3) and (6) above in relation to expenditure incurred on or after 6 April 2008 (or 1 April 2008) is a result of the inclusion of the assets concerned in *CAA 2001, s 33A* (integral features of buildings and structures — see **4.23** above). Such assets are automatically excluded from the scope of *CAA 2001, ss 21, 22* — see **4.30** below.

Although it is the intention that all previous plant case decisions be fully taken into account, it is unclear whether the following decisions have been fully catered for.

(A) Mezzanine storage platforms, which were held to be plant in *Hunt v Henry Quick Ltd*ChD [1992] STC 633. These could be included in 'storage equipment' in item (4) above where they are in the form of large storage shelves, but as noted above, items in (1) to (16) above are precluded from qualifying as plant to the extent that they form interior walls which are intended to remain permanently in place (as could well be the case with mezzanine platforms which become part of the premises). HMRC do not accept that such platforms are, in general, plant ('*Taxation*' magazine 28 July 1994, p 417).
(B) The external brick plant house in *Wimpy International v Warland* CA 1988, 61 TC 51 used to enclose plant and machinery on the roof of a restaurant and which was considered to be integral with the plant.
(C) Petrol station canopies as in the Irish case of *O'Culachain v McMullan Brothers* HC(I) 1991, 1 IR 363. Although held not to be plant in *Dixon v Fitch's Garage Ltd* ChD 1975, 50 TC 509, that decision and the tests applied in reaching it were criticised by Lord Hailsham in the later case of *Cole Brothers Ltd v Philips* HL 1982, 55 TC 188, making it more likely that canopies would now be regarded as plant should a similar case be brought.

With regard to the interpretation of the above list (1) to (33) by the courts, it is likely that the *ejusdem generis* (of the same genus) rule may be used. Where particular words are followed by general words, the general words are to be read in relation to those particular words. The question may then arise as to whether something which is not one of the specified genus falls within the general words, i.e. whether the asset in question is *ejusdem generis* with the particular class. For example, the rule could be applied to see whether a type of cabinet would fall within 'similar equipment' in item (4) above. The court may have regard to the purposes of the provisions as a whole in reaching its conclusion. Regard may also be had, in certain circumstances, to any Parliamentary statements made in connection with the promotion of the provisions during their course through the legislative process (see HC, Official Report, Standing Committee A (Eleventh Sitting, 10 March 1994) *Parts I & II* Cols 601–638), following the case of *Pepper v Hart* HL, [1992] STC 898.

The Financial Secretary to the Treasury said during the debate on the provisions:

> . . . if the courts have ruled that an item which, on a commonsense interpretation would be buildings and structures is, in fact, plant and machinery, we do not want to unravel that decision.
>
> (Col 632 of the Standing Committee debate).

This ministerial statement would appear to safeguard the decisions mentioned in (A) to (C) above and may help to ensure that mezzanine floors, external plant housing and possibly petrol station canopies continue to be regarded as plant. Until a test case is taken before the courts, the position will remain unclear.

Interests in land

[4.29] The Inland Revenue Press Release of 17 December 1993 stated that 'existing law does not permit allowances to be claimed on expenditure on the acquisition of an interest in land except to the extent that the interest is in a machinery and plant fixture'.

The rules in *CAA 2001, s 24* are intended to reflect this treatment by providing that expenditure on the provision of plant or machinery does not include expenditure on the acquisition of any interest in land. But for this purpose 'land' does not include any asset which is so installed or otherwise fixed in or to any description of land as to become, in law, part of that land.

The definition of 'land' in *Interpretation Act 1978, Sch 1* 'includes buildings and other structures, land covered with water, and any estate, interest, easement, servitude or right in or over land', but for the purposes of the above provision, it is accordingly amended to omit the words 'buildings and other structures', but otherwise 'interest in land' for these purposes has the same meaning as that for fixtures under leases in *CAA 2001, s 175* (see **6.2** onwards below).

[*CAA 2001, s 24*].

General exemptions

[4.30] Expenditure incurred on any of the following do not fall within the scope of expenditure prohibited from qualifying for plant and machinery allowances under the provisions at **4.26** and **4.27** above and are regulated by specific rules:

(a) (for expenditure incurred before 6 April 2008 (1 April 2008 for corporation tax purposes)) fire safety within *CAA 2001, s 29* (see **4.17**(a) above);

(b) thermal insulation within *CAA 2001, s 28* (see **4.17**(b) above);

(c) (for expenditure incurred before 6 April 2013 (1 April 2013 for corporation tax purposes)) safety at sports grounds within *CAA 2001, ss 30–32* (see **4.17**(c) above);
(d) personal security assets within *CAA 2001, s 33* (see **4.17**(e) above);
(e) films, tapes and discs dealt with in accordance with an election under *ITTOIA 2005, s 143* or *F(No 2) A 1992, s 40D* (both now repealed);
(f) computer software within *CAA 2001, s 71* (see **4.19** above); or
(g) (for expenditure incurred on or after 6 April 2008 (1 April 2008 for corporation tax purposes)) integral features of a building or structure within *CAA 2001, s 33A* (see **4.23** above).

[*CAA 2001, s 23(1)(2); FA 2012, Sch 39 paras 34(2), 35*].

Where expenditure on building alterations which are incidental to the installation of plant and machinery falls within *CAA 2001, s 25* plant and machinery allowances may be claimed on that expenditure (see **4.16** above).

5

Plant and Machinery — Pooling, Allowances and Charges

Introduction

[5.1] Three types of allowance are available for qualifying expenditure on plant and machinery: annual investment allowance; first-year allowances and writing-down allowances. For the purpose of calculating writing-down allowances and balancing allowances and charges, expenditure is pooled. In addition to a main pool, there are requirements for certain types of expenditure to be allocated either to a single asset pool or to a class pool. In particular, expenditure on assets qualifying for writing-down allowances at only 8% must generally be allocated to a class pool known as the special rate pool and, for non-corporate taxpayers, assets with partial non-business use must be allocated to a single asset pool. See **5.48–5.80** below. Allowances are generally given as a deduction in calculating the taxable profits of the qualifying activity, and balancing charges are treated as receipts of the activity (see **5.81** onwards below).

The annual investment allowance currently provides for a 100% allowance for the first £200,000 of investment in plant and machinery each year. Companies are entitled to only one allowance no matter how many qualifying activities they carry on, and a single limit is divided between companies in a group or under common control. See **5.2–5.12** below for full details.

First-year allowances are also given in the chargeable period in which qualifying expenditure is incurred. Currently there are eight categories of allowance, each at 100%. Six of the categories are for particular types of asset, the others are for ring fence trades and plant and machinery for use in certain assisted areas. See **5.15–5.27** below. Writing-down allowances are given at 18% of the unrelieved balance in the particular pool per year, or for certain special rate expenditure 8% (but see **5.35** below for small balances on the main or special rate pool). See **5.32–5.40** below.

Where an item of plant or machinery in respect of which any of the above allowances have been given is disposed of. a disposal value must be brought into account. If the disposal value exceeds the amount of unrelieved expenditure in the pool concerned then a balancing charge is made. If the chargeable period is the final chargeable period for the pool and the disposal value is less than the unrelieved expenditure, a balancing allowance is made; otherwise, writing-down allowances continue to be made on the balance reduced by the disposal value. See **5.41–5.46** below.

Annual investment allowance

Introduction

[5.2] The annual investment allowance was introduced by *FA 2008* and currently provides a 100% allowance for the first £200,000 of investment in plant or machinery each year. The maximum amount has been changed several times since the introduction of the allowance, most recently being reduced to £200,000 (from £500,000) for expenditure incurred on or after 1 January 2016. Transitional rules apply to all of the changes in the maximum allowance for chargeable periods which straddle the dates of the changes.

The allowance is available in respect of '*AIA qualifying expenditure*', which is qualifying expenditure incurred on or after 6 April 2008 by an individual or a partnership made up entirely of individuals or incurred on or after 1 April 2008 by a company. Expenditure incurred by partnerships which include partners who are not individuals or by trusts does not qualify for the allowance (see *Hoardweel Farm Partnership v HMRC* FTT, [2012] UKFTT 402 (TC) and, for a case in which expenditure incurred by a limited liability partnership consisting of an individual and an unlimited company did not qualify, *Drilling Global Consultant LLP v HMRC* FTT, [2014] UKFTT 888 (TC)). See **5.3** below for expenditure excluded from being AIA qualifying expenditure.

In determining whether expenditure is AIA qualifying expenditure, *CAA 2001, s 12* (pre-trading expenditure to be treated as incurred on the first day of trading — see **5.36** below) is ignored. In other words, *CAA 2001, s 12* applies to determine the chargeable period for which an annual investment allowance or writing-down allowance is available, but expenditure incurred before whichever of the above dates applies cannot qualify for an annual investment allowance by virtue of the first day of trading falling on or after that date.

[*CAA 2001, s 38A*].

An annual investment allowance and a first-year allowance cannot be claimed in respect of the same expenditure. [*CAA 2001, s 52A*]. Where qualifying expenditure in a chargeable period exceeds the annual investment allowance limit, it will be beneficial to claim 100% first-year allowances in priority to annual investment allowance where possible, as this leaves the annual investment allowance available for expenditure not attracting such allowances. Likewise, it will generally be beneficial to claim annual investment allowance in respect of special rate expenditure in priority to other expenditure so as to maximise writing-down allowances in future years.

Exclusions

[5.3] Expenditure within any of the following categories is not AIA qualifying expenditure.

(i) Expenditure incurred in the chargeable period in which the qualifying activity is permanently discontinued (see *Keyl v HMRC* UT, [2015] STC 410).

(ii) Expenditure incurred on the provision of a car, as defined at **5.51** below).

(iii) Expenditure incurred wholly for the purposes of a ring fence trade (see **5.40** below) to which the supplementary charge in *CTA 2010, s 330(1)* applies.

(iv) Expenditure where the provision of the plant or machinery is connected with a change in the nature or conduct of a trade or business carried on by a person other than the person incurring the expenditure and the obtaining of an annual investment allowance is the main benefit, or one of the main benefits, which could reasonably be expected to arise from the making of the change.

(v) Expenditure where the provision of the plant or machinery is by way of gift (see **7.12** below).

(vi) Expenditure where the plant or machinery was previously used by the owner for purposes outside the qualifying activity (see **7.13** below) or for leasing under a long funding lease (see **6.39** below).

(vii) Expenditure where the plant or machinery is acquired in circumstances where the anti-avoidance provisions at **7.3**, **6.36** or **7.9** below apply.

The exclusions at (v) and (vi) above are subject to *CAA 2001, s 161* (pre-trading expenditure on mineral exploration and access — see **10.12** below).

[*CAA 2001, s 38B*].

Where an arrangement is entered into and a main purpose of it is to enable a person to obtain an annual investment allowance to which he would not otherwise be entitled, that allowance is not made, or, if already made, is withdrawn. [*CAA 2001, s 218A*].

Entitlement to allowance

[5.4] A person is entitled to an annual investment allowance for the chargeable period in which the AIA qualifying expenditure was incurred if he owns the plant or machinery at some time during that period. The amount of the allowance is the lower of the AIA qualifying expenditure incurred in the period and the 'maximum allowance'. A claim for an allowance can be made in respect of all or only part of the expenditure.

The '*maximum allowance*' has changed several times, with effect as shown in the table below. Transitional rules apply in relation to all of the changes for chargeable periods which straddle the affected dates. The allowance is proportionately increased or reduced where the chargeable period is more than or less than a year.

	Expenditure incurred after	*Expenditure incurred before*	*Maximum allowance*
Income tax	**31 December 2015**		**£200,000**
	5 April 2014	1 January 2016	£500,000
	31 December 2012	6 April 2014	£250,000

	5 April 2012	1 January 2013	£25,000
	5 April 2010	6 April 2012	£100,000
	5 April 2008	6 April 2010	£50,000
Corporation tax	**31 December 2015**		**£200,000**
	31 March 2014	1 January 2016	£500,000
	31 December 2012	1 April 2014	£250,000
	31 March 2012	1 January 2013	£25,000
	31 March 2010	1 April 2012	£100,000
	31 March 2008	1 April 2010	£50,000

The transitional rules operate as follows.

(1) *Chargeable periods beginning before, and ending on or after, 1 January 2016.* The chargeable period is divided into two separate chargeable periods, the first beginning on the first day of the actual chargeable period and ending on 31 December 2015, and the second beginning on the following day and ending on the last day of the actual period. The maximum amount for each of the two notional periods is then calculated and the sum of the two amounts is taken as the maximum amount for the actual chargeable period. This rule is subject to an overriding rule that, for expenditure incurred on or after 1 January 2016, the maximum allowance for the actual chargeable period is the maximum allowance for the second of the notional chargeable periods. See Example 1 at **5.4A** below.

(2) *Chargeable periods beginning before, and ending on or after, 6 April 2014 (1 April 2014 for corporation tax purposes).* The chargeable period is divided into two or, where the period begins before 1 January 2013, three separate chargeable periods. The notional chargeable periods are: the part of the actual chargeable period falling before 1 January 2013; the part of the actual chargeable period starting with the later of 1 January 2013 and the start of the actual period and ending on 5 April 2014 (31 March 2014 for corporation tax purposes); and the period beginning on 6 April 2014 (or 1 April 2014) and ending on the last day of the actual period. The maximum amount for each of the two (or three) notional periods is then calculated and the sum of the two (or three) amounts is taken as the maximum amount for the actual chargeable period. This rule is subject to the following overriding rules. If no part of the actual chargeable period falls before 1 January 2013, the overriding rule is that, for expenditure incurred before 6 April 2014 (or 1 April 2014), the maximum allowance for the actual chargeable period must be calculated as if the annual limit had remained at £250,000. See Example 2 at **5.5** below.

If the actual chargeable period begins before 1 January 2013, the following overriding rules apply.

- For expenditure incurred before 1 January 2013, the maximum allowance for the actual chargeable period must be calculated as if the annual limit had remained at £25,000.

- For expenditure incurred before 6 April 2014 (or 1 April 2014), the maximum allowance for the actual chargeable period must be calculated as if the annual limit had increased to £250,000 for expenditure incurred on or after 1 January 2013 but had remained at £250,000 for the remainder of the period.

See Example 3 at **5.6** below.

(3) *Chargeable periods beginning before, and ending on or after, 1 January 2013* . Except where (2) above applies, the chargeable period is divided into two or, where the period begins before 6 April 2012 (1 April 2012 for corporation tax purposes), three separate chargeable periods. The notional chargeable periods are: the part of the actual chargeable period falling before 6 April 2012 (or 1 April 2012); the part of the actual chargeable period starting with the later of 6 April 2012 (or 1 April 2012) and the start of the actual period and ending on 31 December 2012; and the period beginning on 1 January 2013 and ending on the last day of the actual period. The maximum amount for each of the two (or three) notional periods is then calculated and the sum of the two (or three) amounts is taken as the maximum amount for the actual chargeable period. This rule is subject to the following overriding rules.

If no part of the actual chargeable period falls before 6 April 2012 (or 1 April 2012), the overriding rule is that, for expenditure incurred before 1 January 2013, the maximum allowance for the actual chargeable period must be calculated as if the annual limit had remained at £25,000. See Example 4 at **5.7** below.

If the actual chargeable period begins before 6 April 2012 (or 1 April 2012), the following overriding rules apply.

- For expenditure incurred before 6 April 2012 (or 1 April 2012), the maximum allowance for the actual chargeable period must be calculated as if the annual limit had remained at £25,000 until the end of that period (i.e. by using the rule at (4) below).
- For expenditure incurred in the period starting on 6 April 2012 (or 1 April 2012) and ending on 31 December 2012, the maximum allowance for the actual chargeable period is: A – B, where:

  A = the amount that would have been the maximum allowance for the period 6 April 2012 (or 1 April 2012) to the end of the actual chargeable period if that period had been a separate chargeable period, calculated as if the annual limit had remained at £25,000; and

  B = the amount (if any) by which the expenditure incurred in the part of the actual chargeable period falling before 6 April 2012 (or 1 April 2012) in respect of which a claim for annual investment allowance is made exceeds what would be the maximum allowance for that period if it were treated as a separate chargeable period.
- For expenditure incurred on or after 1 January 2013, the maximum allowance for the actual chargeable period is the sum of each maximum allowance that would be found if the period

6 April 2012 (or 1 April 2012) to 31 December 2012 and the period 1 January 2013 to the end of the actual chargeable period were separate chargeable periods.

See Example 5 at **5.8** below.

(4) *Chargeable periods beginning before, and ending on or after, 6 April 2012 (1 April 2012 for corporation tax purposes).* Except where (3) above applies, the chargeable period is divided into two separate chargeable periods, the first beginning on the first day of the actual chargeable period and ending on 5 April 2012 (31 March 2012 for corporation tax purposes), and the second beginning on the following day and ending on the last day of the actual period. The maximum amount for each of the two notional periods is then calculated and the sum of the two amounts is taken as the maximum amount for the actual chargeable period. This rule is subject to an overriding rule that, for expenditure incurred on or after 6 April 2012 (or 1 April 2012), the maximum allowance for the actual chargeable period is the maximum allowance for the second of the notional chargeable periods. See Example 6 at **5.9** below.

(5) *Chargeable periods beginning before, and ending on or after, 6 April 2010 (1 April 2010 for corporation tax purposes).* The chargeable period is divided into two separate chargeable periods, the first beginning on the first day of the actual chargeable period and ending on 5 April 2010 (31 March 2010 for corporation tax purposes), and the second beginning on the following day and ending on the last day of the actual period. The maximum amount for each of the two notional periods is then calculated and the sum of the two amounts is taken as the maximum amount for the actual chargeable period. This rule is subject to an overriding rule that, for expenditure incurred before 6 April 2010 (or 1 April 2010) the maximum allowance for the actual chargeable period must be calculated as if the annual limit had remained at £50,000. See Example 7 at **5.10** below.

(6) *Chargeable periods beginning before, and ending on or after, 6 April 2008 (1 April 2008 for corporation tax purposes)* are deemed to begin on that date for annual investment allowance purposes.

See also **5.12** below for the application of, and modifications to, the transitional rules where restrictions apply to the allowance.

[*CAA 2001, s 51A; FA 2011, s 11(1)–(7)(13); FA 2013, s 7, Sch 1 paras 1–4; FA 2014, s 10, Sch 2 paras 1–4, 6, 7; F(No 2)A 2015, s 8*].

Additional VAT liabilities, whenever incurred, in respect of AIA qualifying expenditure are also AIA qualifying expenditure if the plant or machinery is still provided for the purposes of the qualifying activity. See **17.49** onwards below.

See **5.11** below for restrictions on the amount of annual investment allowance and **5.12** below for the operation of the allowance where a restriction applies.

See also **5.56** and **7.14** below for the reduction of annual investment allowance where, respectively, plant or machinery is provided partly for purposes other than a qualifying activity or a partial depreciation subsidy is payable.

EXAMPLE 1

[5.4A]

Eagle Ltd draws up accounts each year to 31 March. The company incurs AIA qualifying expenditure of £300,000 on 31 January 2016. As the period of account in which the expenditure is incurred, i.e. the year ended 31 March 2016, straddles 1 January 2016, the maximum allowance for the period is calculated using the transitional rules at 5.4(1) above.

The overall maximum allowance for the accounting period is £425,000 ((£500,000 × $^{9}/_{12}$ = £375,000) + (£200,000 × $^{3}/_{12}$ = £50,000)). However, for expenditure incurred after 31 December 2016, the maximum allowance for the actual chargeable period is the maximum allowance for the second of the notional chargeable periods (i.e. 1 January 2016 to 31 March 2016). Accordingly, only £50,000 of the £300,000 expenditure incurred on 31 January 2016 qualifies for annual investment allowance.

EXAMPLE 2

[5.5]

Swift Ltd draws up accounts each year to 31 December. The company incurs AIA qualifying expenditure of £300,000 on 31 January 2014 and £150,000 on 1 June 2014. As the period of account in which the expenditure is incurred, i.e. the year ended 31 December 2014, straddles 1 April 2014, the maximum allowance for the period is calculated using the transitional rules at 5.4(2) above.

The overall maximum allowance for the accounting period is £437,500 ((£250,000 × $^{3}/_{12}$ = £62,500) + (£500,000 × $^{9}/_{12}$ = £375,000)). However, for expenditure incurred before 1 April 2014 the maximum allowance must be calculated as if the limit had not been increased to £500,000, so that the maximum allowance for such expenditure is £250,000. Accordingly, only £250,000 of the £300,000 expenditure incurred on 31 January 2014 qualifies for annual investment allowance. Swift Ltd is therefore entitled to claim annual investment allowance of £400,000 for the year ended 31 December 2014.

EXAMPLE 3

[5.6]

Ben draws up accounts for the 16-month period to 30 April 2014. He incurs AIA qualifying expenditure of £100,000 on 1 December 2012, £400,000 on 1 December 2013 and £150,000 on 7 April 2014. As the period of account in which the expenditure is incurred, i.e. the 16 months ended 30 April 2014, straddles both 1 January 2013 and 6 April 2014, the maximum allowance for the period is calculated using the transitional rules at 5.4(2) above.

Period 1.12.12 to 31.12.13 (31 days)	
Maximum £25,000 × $^{31}/_{365}$	2,123
Period 1.1.13 to 5.4.14 (460 days)	
Maximum £250,000 × $^{460}/_{365}$	315,068
Period 6.4.14 to 30.4.14 (25 days)	
Maximum £500,000 × $^{25}/_{365}$	34,247
Maximum qualifying for AIAs for the period (subject to below)	£351,438

There are two overriding rules to be considered.

The first overriding rule is that, as regards expenditure incurred before 1.1.13, the maximum that can qualify for the AIA is calculated as if the increases from £25,000 to £250,000 and £500,000 had not taken place. Accordingly, only £35,342 (£25,000 × $^{516}/_{365}$) of the £100,000 expenditure incurred on 1 December 2012 qualifies for annual investment allowance.

The second overriding rule is that, as regards expenditure incurred before 6.4.14, the maximum that can qualify for the AIA is calculated as if the increase from £250,000 to £500,000 had not taken place, so that the £250,000 maximum applied throughout the period 1.1.13 to 30.4.14. This means that the maximum for expenditure incurred in the period 1.12.12 to 5.4.14 is (£25,000 × $^{31}/_{365}$) + (£250,000 × $^{485}/_{365}$) = £334,315. If Ben allocates £35,342 of this limit to the expenditure incurred on 1 December 2012 as above, then only £298,973 (£334,315 – £35,342) of the £400,000 expenditure incurred on 1.12.13 qualifies for annual investment allowance. Alternatively Ben may allocate the full £334,315 to the expenditure incurred on 1.12.13 (so that none of the expenditure incurred on 1.12.12 qualifies for annual investment allowance).

If Ben allocates the maximum £334,315 to the expenditure incurred before 6.4.14, then annual investment allowance of £17,123 (£351,438 – £334,315) remains available to be allocated to expenditure incurred after 5.4.14. As only £10,000 of expenditure was incurred after that date, however, only that amount can be so allocated. The maximum annual investment allowance for the entire period of account is therefore £344,315 (£334,315 + £10,000).

EXAMPLE 4

[5.7]

Robin has previously drawn up accounts each year to 30 June but changes his accounting date to 31 March, drawing up nine-month accounts to 31 March 2013. He incurs AIA qualifying expenditure of £45,000 on 31 October 2012 and £24,000 on 28 February 2013. As the period of account in which the expenditure is incurred, i.e. the nine months ended 31 March 2013, straddles 1 January 2013, the maximum allowance for the period is calculated using the transitional rules at **5.4**(3) above.

The overall maximum allowance for the accounting period is £75,000 ((£25,000 × $^{6}/_{12}$ = £12,500) + (£250,000 × $^{3}/_{12}$ = £62,500)). However, for expenditure incurred before 1 January 2013 the maximum allowance must be calculated as if the limit had not been increased to £250,000, so that the maximum allowance for such expenditure is £25,000. Accordingly, only £25,000 of the £45,000 expenditure incurred on 31 October 2012 qualifies for annual investment allowance. Robin is therefore entitled to claim annual investment allowance of £49,000 for the nine months ended 31 March 2013.

EXAMPLE 5

[5.8]

Kathryn prepares accounts for her trade to the end of January each year. For the year ended 31 January 2013, Kathryn incurs expenditure of £63,000 on plant and machinery. £20,000 of this amount was incurred before 6 April 2012, £21,000 in the period 6 April 2012 to 31 December 2012 and £22,000 in the month of January 2013. All the expenditure is AIA qualifying expenditure.

Kathryn's maximum annual investment allowance for the year ended 31 January 2013 is computed using the transitional rules at **5.4**(3) above as follows:

Period 1.2.12 to 5.4.12 (65 days)

Maximum $£100,000 \times \frac{65}{366}$	17,759
Period 6.4.12 to 31.12.12 (270 days)	
Maximum $£25,000 \times \frac{270}{366}$	18,443
Period 1.1.13 to 31.1.13 (31 days)	
Maximum $£250,000 \times \frac{31}{366}$	21,175
Maximum qualifying for AIAs for the year	£57,377

However, there are three overriding rules to be considered.

The first overriding rule is that, as regards expenditure incurred before 6.4.12, the maximum that can qualify for the AIA is calculated as if the increase from £25,000 to £250,000 had not taken place. This brings into account the rules for periods straddling 6 April 2012. For Kathryn, this maximum is: (£100,000 × 65/366) + (£25,000 × 301/366) = £38,319.

The second overriding rule is that, as regards expenditure incurred in the period 6.4.12 to 31.12.12, the maximum that can qualify for the AIA is: A – B (see **5.4**(2) above).

For Kathryn, A = (£25,000 × 301/366) = £20,560. On the assumption that Kathryn claims AIA for the full £20,000 of expenditure incurred before 6.4.12, B = (£20,000 – £17,759) = £2,241. (The maximum allowance for the period 1.2.12 to 5.4.12 if it were treated as a separate chargeable period is £17,759 (£100,000 × 65/366).) Therefore, A – B = (£20,560 – £2,241) = £18,319.

The third overriding rule is that, as regards expenditure incurred after 31.12.12, the maximum that can qualify for the AIA is the sum of each maximum allowance that would be found if the periods 6.4.12 to 31.12.12 and 1.1.13 to 31.1.13 were each treated as separate chargeable periods. For Kathryn, this sum is: (£25,000 × 270/366) + (£250,000 × 31/366) = £39,618.

So for Kathryn the maximum that can qualify for the AIA in respect of the three periods in question are, respectively, £38,319, £18,319 and £39,618. But this does not alter the fact that the maximum AIA that Kathryn can claim for the full 12-month period ending on 31 January 2013 is £57,377 as already calculated above before applying the overriding rules. As Kathryn has already claimed £20,000 for the first notional period and is limited to £18,319 for the second, she can claim a further £19,058, making £57,377 in all.

EXAMPLE 6

[5.9]

Blackbird Ltd draws up accounts each year to 30 September. The company incurs AIA qualifying expenditure of £40,000 on 30 January 2012 and £22,500 on 30 April 2012. As the accounting period in which the expenditure is incurred, i.e. the year ended 30 September 2012, straddles 1 April 2012, the maximum allowance for the period is calculated using the transitional rules at **5.4**(4) above.

The overall maximum allowance for the accounting period is £62,500 ((£100,000 × $^6/_{12}$ = £50,000) + (£25,000 × $^6/_{12}$ = £12,500)), the same amount as the total AIA qualifying expenditure. However, for expenditure incurred on or after 1 April 2012 the maximum allowance must be calculated as if the limit were that for the notional period 1 April 2012 to 30 September 2012, so that the maximum allowance for such expenditure is £12,500. Accordingly, only £12,500 of the £22,500 expenditure incurred on 30 April 2012 qualifies for annual investment allowance. Blackbird Ltd is therefore entitled to claim annual investment allowance of £52,500 for the year ended 30 September 2012.

EXAMPLE 7

[5.10]

Bluebird Ltd draws up accounts each year to 30 September. The company incurs AIA qualifying expenditure of £60,000 on 30 January 2010 and £15,000 on 30 April 2010. As the accounting period in which the expenditure is incurred, i.e. the year ended 30 September 2010, straddles 1 April 2010, the maximum allowance for the period is calculated using the transitional rules at **5.4**(5) above.

The overall maximum allowance for the accounting period is £75,000 ((£50,000 × $^{6}/_{12}$) + (£100,000 × $^{6}/_{12}$)), the same amount as the total AIA qualifying expenditure. However, for expenditure incurred before 1 April 2010 the maximum allowance must be calculated as if the limit had not been increased to £100,000, so that the maximum allowance for such expenditure is £50,000. Accordingly, only £50,000 of the £60,000 expenditure incurred on 30 January 2010 qualifies for annual investment allowance. Bluebird Ltd is therefore entitled to claim annual investment allowance of £65,000 for the year ended 30 September 2010.

Restrictions on allowance

[5.11] The following provisions apply to restrict the amount of annual investment allowance. See **5.12** below for the operation of the allowance where a restriction within (1)–(5) below applies.

(1) *Companies.* A company is entitled to only one annual investment allowance for a chargeable period, regardless of how many qualifying activities it carries on. It may allocate the allowance between qualifying activities as it thinks fit. [*CAA 2001, s 51B*]. This restriction is subject, however, to those at (2)–(4) below.

(2) *Groups of companies.* A company which is a 'parent undertaking' of one or more other companies in a financial year and those other companies are entitled to only one annual investment allowance between them for chargeable periods ending in that financial year. The companies can allocate the allowance between them as they think fit. This restriction is subject to that in (3) below.
A company is a '*parent undertaking*' of another company in a financial year only if it is a parent undertaking (within *Companies Act 2006, s 1162*) of the other company at the end of that company's chargeable period ending in that year.
[*CAA 2001, s 51C*].

(3) *Groups under common control.* Where in a financial year two or more 'groups of companies' are 'controlled' by the same person and are 'related' to one another, the members of those groups are entitled to only one annual investment allowance between them for chargeable periods ending in that financial year. The companies in the groups can allocate the allowance between them as they think fit.
For this purpose, a '*group of companies*' consists of a company which, in the financial year concerned, is a parent undertaking (as at (2) above) of one or more other companies and those other companies. A group of companies is '*controlled*' by a person in a financial year if the parent undertaking is controlled by that person at the end of its chargeable period ending in that year. 'Control' is defined for this purpose as at **2.31** above, but, where the company concerned is not a body corporate,

control means the power of a person to secure, through shares (as defined in *Companies Act 2006, s 1161(2)*) or voting power in the company or another body, or through powers conferred by the constitution of the company or another body, that the affairs of the company are conducted in accordance with his wishes.

A group of companies is '*related*' to another group in a financial year if in that year a member of the first group is related to a member of the other group. Where two groups are so related, each group is also related to any groups which are related to the other group in that financial year.

A company is related to another company in a financial year if either or both of the 'shared premises condition' and the 'similar activities condition' are met in that year. Where two companies are related in a financial year, each company is also related to any companies which are related to the other company in that year.

The '*shared premises condition*' is that, at the end of the chargeable period ending in the financial year concerned of one or both companies, the companies carry on qualifying activities from the same premises. The '*similar activities condition*' is that more than 50% of the turnover of each company for their chargeable period ending in the financial year concerned is derived from qualifying activities within the same 'NACE classification'. The '*NACE classification*' system is the first level of the common statistical classification of economic activities in the EU established by Regulation (EC) No. 1983/2006 of the European Parliament and the Council of 20 December 2006. The system divides industries into 17 main categories. Information can be obtained on the website of the Office of National Statistics (www.ons.gov.uk) and at HMRC Capital Allowances Manual CA 23090.

[*CAA 2001, ss 51D, 51F, 51G*].

(4) *Other companies under common control.* Where two or more companies are 'controlled' by the same person and are related (as in (2) above) to one another in a financial year, and neither (2) nor (3) above apply, the companies are entitled to only one annual investment allowance between them for chargeable periods ending in that financial year. The companies can allocate the allowance between them as they think fit.

For this purpose, a company is controlled by another person in a financial year if it is controlled (as in (2) above) by him at the end of its chargeable period ending in that year.

[*CAA 2001, ss 51E–51G*].

(5) *Qualifying activities under common control.* A restriction applies where, in a tax year, two or more qualifying activities are carried on by one or more persons other than companies and are 'controlled' by the same person and are 'related' to one another. If one person carries on all the qualifying activities, he is entitled to only one annual investment allowance for the chargeable periods for those activities which end in the tax year. If more than one person carries on the qualifying activity, they are between them entitled to only one annual investment allowance for the chargeable periods for those activities which end in the tax year. In either case, the allowance can be allocated as the person or persons think fit.

For the above purpose, a person is treated as carrying on a qualifying activity in a tax year only if he is carrying it on at the end of the chargeable period for that activity which ends in the tax year. A qualifying activity carried on by an individual is controlled by that individual. A qualifying activity carried on by a partnership is controlled by the person who controls (as at **2.31** above) the partnership. Where partners who between them control one partnership also control another partnership, the qualifying activities carried on by the partnerships are treated as controlled by the same person.

A qualifying activity is related to another such activity in a tax year if either or both of the 'shared premises condition' and the 'similar activities condition' are met in that year. Where two qualifying activities are related in a tax year, each is also related to any qualifying activities which are related to the other qualifying activity in that year.

The '*shared premises condition*' is that, at the end of the chargeable period of one or both activities ending in the tax year concerned, the activities are carried on from the same premises. The '*similar activities condition*' is that at the end of the chargeable period for one or both of the activities ending in the tax year concerned both activities are within the same 'NACE classification' (as in (3) above).

[*CAA 2001, ss 51H–51J*].

(6) *Allocation where profits chargeable at Northern Ireland rate of corporation tax*. A further restriction applies where any of the restrictions in (1) to (4) above apply and the relevant AIA qualifying expenditure under the restriction in question (see **5.12** below) includes expenditure incurred in respect of an NI rate activity (see **17.46B** below) in a financial year for which the Northern Ireland rate of corporation tax is lower than the main rate (a 'low rate year'). The maximum annual investment allowance that may be allocated under **5.12** below to AIA qualifying expenditure incurred in a low rate year in respect of qualifying activities other than NI rate activities is:

$$\frac{(T - NI)}{T} \times A$$

where:

A is the amount of the single annual investment allowance that would otherwise be available for allocation;

T is so much of the relevant AIA qualifying expenditure for the purposes of the restriction in question as is incurred in a low-rate year; and

NI is so much of the relevant AIA qualifying expenditure for the purposes of the restriction in question as is incurred in a low-rate year in respect of an NI rate activity.

Note that the Northern Ireland rate of corporation tax is not expected to come into force until 2017.

[*CAA 2001, s 51JA; CTNIA 2015, Sch 1 para 5*].

Where more than one chargeable period of a company ends in a financial year, whether (2), (3) or (4) apply to the company is determined in relation to each chargeable period as if it were the only chargeable period ending in that year.

Likewise, where more than one chargeable period for a qualifying activity ends in a tax year, whether (5) above applies is determined in relation to each chargeable period as if it were the only chargeable period ending in that year. [*CAA 2001, s 51L(1)(2)*].

Operation of allowance where restrictions apply

[5.12] Where one of the restrictions at **5.11**(1)–(5) above applies to limit a person to a single annual investment allowance or more than one person to a single allowance between them, the amount of the allowance is the lower of the 'relevant AIA qualifying expenditure' and the 'maximum allowance'. The person or persons can claim for the allowance to be made in respect of all or only part of the expenditure.

The amount of the annual investment allowance allocated to relevant AIA qualifying expenditure incurred in a chargeable period must not exceed the amount of the allowance to which a person would be entitled in respect of that expenditure if the restrictions did not apply. This means that, where, for example, a group of three companies incurs AIA qualifying expenditure of £500,000 in chargeable periods ending on 31 March 2015, but the chargeable period for one of those companies was only nine months long, a maximum of £375,000 (£500,000 × 9/12) of the allowance can be allocated to that company.

The '*relevant AIA qualifying expenditure*' is:

(a) where **5.11**(1) above applies, the AIA qualifying expenditure incurred in the chargeable period;
(b) where **5.11**(2), (3) or (4) above apply, the AIA qualifying expenditure incurred by the companies in chargeable periods ending in the financial year concerned; or
(c) where **5.11**(5) above applies, the AIA qualifying expenditure incurred for the purposes of the qualifying activities in the chargeable periods for those activities ending in the tax year concerned.

Where there is more than one chargeable period ending in the financial or tax year concerned, AIA qualifying expenditure incurred in a chargeable period to which **5.11**(2), (3) or (4) or **5.11**(5) above does not apply as a result of *CAA 2001, s 51L* (see **5.11** above), is not relevant AIA qualifying expenditure.

The 'maximum allowance' is currently £200,000 (but has changed frequently – see **5.4** above). Transitional rules apply to determine the maximum amount for chargeable periods straddling the dates of the changes and the following modifications to those rules apply where the allowance is subject to restriction. The modifications do not affect the operation of the rules for chargeable periods longer than a year below.

- Where the 2012 transitional rules at **5.4**(3) above apply, only chargeable periods of one year or less are taken into account in applying the rule, and for this purpose any chargeable period which is longer than a year and ends in 2012/13 is treated as a chargeable period of one year ending on the date on which the actual period ends. If there is more than one chargeable period which would otherwise be taken into account, only that which gives the greatest maximum allowance is taken into account. In relation to a chargeable period, the maximum amount that would have been available if no restriction had applied is to be treated as reduced (but not below nil) by the amount allocated to relevant AIA qualifying expenditure incurred in any other chargeable period which ends at the same time as, or later than, the chargeable period in question.

- Where the 2013 transitional rules at **5.4**(3) above apply, only chargeable periods of one year or less are taken into account in applying the rule, and, if there is more than one such period, only that period which gives the greatest maximum allowance. For this purpose only, a chargeable period of more than a year ending in 2012/13, 2013/14 or 2014/15 is to be treated as being a chargeable period of one year ending on the date the actual period ends.
- Where the 2014 or 2016 transitional rules at **5.4**(1) and (2) above apply, only chargeable periods of one year or less are taken into account in applying the rule, and, if there is more than one such period, only that period which gives the greatest maximum allowance. For this purpose only, a chargeable period of more than a year ending in 2013/14, 2014/15, 2015/16, 2016/17 or 2017/18 is to be treated as being a chargeable period of one year ending on the date the actual period ends.

Where **5.11**(5) above applies for a tax year to two or more qualifying activities controlled by a person ('P') and the chargeable period for one of those activities ('A1') is longer than one year, an additional amount of annual investment allowance can be allocated to relevant AIA qualifying expenditure. The amount to be allocated is the amount, or the aggregate amounts, of any 'relevant unused allowance' for each previous tax year in which part of the long chargeable period falls.

The amount of the '*relevant unused allowance*' for a previous tax year is:

$$MA - AM$$

where:

MA is the specified limit for the previous tax year in question (i.e. £500,000, £250,000, £200,000, £100,000, £50,000 or £25,000), and

AM is the amount of any annual investment allowance made in respect of expenditure incurred for the purposes of a 'relevant qualifying activity' in the chargeable period for that activity ending in the previous tax year in question.

For this purpose, any qualifying activities carried on by an individual or partnership of individuals which was both controlled by P and related to A1 in that year, together with A1 itself (if controlled by P in that year) are '*relevant qualifying activities*'. Where the above formula gives a negative result, the amount of the relevant unused allowance is nil.

The amount of the relevant unused allowance is reduced by so much of it, if any, as has already been allocated to expenditure incurred for the purposes of a qualifying activity controlled by P in a tax year before the year in question on a previous application of this provision. Where the amount of a relevant unused allowance would otherwise exceed the amount given by the following formula, it is restricted to that amount. The formula is:

$$\frac{DCPY}{DY} \times MA$$

where:

DCPY is the number of days in A1's chargeable period falling in the previous tax year in question,

DY is the number of days in that tax year, and

MA is the specified limit for the previous tax year in question (i.e. £500,000, £250,000, £200,000, £100,000, £50,000 or £25,000).

The addition of relevant unused allowance does not prevent the application of the rule that the amount of the annual investment allowance allocated to relevant AIA qualifying expenditure incurred in a chargeable period must not exceed the amount of the allowance to which a person would be entitled in respect of that expenditure if the restriction in **5.11**(5) did not apply.

Where the chargeable periods for more than one of the qualifying activities are more than one year long, the above provision applies in relation to each of those activities. But it applies in modified form where two or more of those activities were related in a previous tax year. The amount of the relevant unused allowance for that tax year is calculated without applying the (DCPY/DY × MA) formula limit, and the definition of 'relevant qualifying activity' applies as if the reference to A1 were a reference to any of the qualifying activities with a long chargeable period. The amount of the relevant unused allowance can then be allocated between those activities, but the amount allocated to any one activity cannot exceed the amount given by the formula (DCPY/DY × MA).

[*CAA 2001, ss 51B(3), 51C(4), 51D(4), 51E(4), 51H(6), ss 51K, 51L(3), 51M, 51N; FA 2011, s 11(8)–(12); FA 2013, Sch 1 para 5; FA 2014, Sch 2 para 5*].

EXAMPLE 8

[5.13]

X controls two related businesses, A1 and A2. A1 is a new business commenced on 1 July 2016. In 2017/18, accounts for A1 are prepared for the 18 months to 31 December 2017 and accounts for A2 are prepared as usual for the year ended on that date. For their chargeable periods ending in 2017/18, A1 and A2 have AIA qualifying expenditure of £300,000 and £100,000 respectively. In the absence of the special rule for long chargeable periods, X would be entitled to an AIA of only £200,000. For the year ended 31 December 2016, A2 had AIA qualifying expenditure of £25,000, so, in theory, there is unused AIA qualifying expenditure of £175,000 for 2016/17 (£200,000 – £25,000); however, this is capped at £150,000 (£200,000 × 3/4) as only 9 months of A1's long period of account falls within 2016/17. The unused amount of £150,000 is added to the amount of £200,000 for the chargeable periods ending on 31 December 2015 to give a theoretical AIA of £350,000. This must still be compared to the maximum available AIA for A1 for the period ended 31 December 2017, i.e. £300,000 (£200,000 × 18/12). X can allocate this between A1 and A2 as he likes, except that the AIA for each business cannot exceed what would have been the available AIA if the related activity restriction had not applied, i.e. £300,000 for A1 and £100,000 for A2.

EXAMPLE 9

[5.14]

A, B and C are companies related within **5.11**(4) above and draw up annual accounts to 30 April 2012, 31 December 2012 and 31 March 2013 respectively. The maximum annual investment allowance to be shared between the three companies for the chargeable periods ending in the year to 31 March 2013 is arrived at as follows. Applying the transitional rules at **5.4** above, the maximum amounts for A and B are £93,750 and £43,750 respectively. The maximum amount for C is £81,250 ((£25,000 × 9/12) + (£250,000 × 3/12)). The maximum amount to be shared between the three companies is therefore £93,750. If B claims AIA of £43,750, the maximum amount to be shared between A and C is then £50,000. Alternatively, if C claims £81,250, the maximum amount to be shared between A and B is only £12,500. Note that the actual AIA available to each company remains subject to the overriding rules for chargeable periods straddling 1 April 2012 and chargeable periods straddling 1 January 2013 (see **5.4** above).

First-year allowances

History

[5.15] First-year allowances were introduced at the rate of 60%, but in fact stood at the rate of 100% for approximately twelve years prior to 1984. This reduced the effect of the difference between revenue and capital expenditure. As part of a scheme to implement major reductions in tax rates, first-year allowances were gradually reduced and then abolished (with certain transitional exceptions) for expenditure after 31 March 1986. They were subsequently reintroduced on a temporary basis for a number of different periods, usually with restrictions on the type of business and expenditure qualifying. *FA 2000* made permanent the reintroduction of first-year allowances at 40% for expenditure incurred by small and medium-sized enterprises on or after 2 July 1998 (see **5.16** below), but these were in turn abolished for expenditure incurred on or after 6 April 2008 (1 April 2008 for corporation tax purposes), and replaced by the annual investment allowance (see **5.2** onwards above). Temporary 40% first-year allowances were then reintroduced for expenditure incurred by any business in the year ended 5 April 2010 (31 March 2010 for corporation tax purposes). Currently allowances are available under eight limited categories.

Current first-year allowances

[5.16] First-year allowances are currently available for the following qualifying expenditure, referred to in *CAA 2001* as '*first-year qualifying expenditure*'.

(1) Expenditure on the provision of 'energy-saving plant or machinery' (see **5.17** below) that is incurred after 31 March 2001 (and, for income tax purposes, in a period of account ending after 5 April 2001) qualifies for allowances at 100%. [*CAA 2001, ss 45A(1), 52(3)*].

(2) Expenditure on the provision of unused (not second-hand) cars with 'low carbon dioxide emissions' (see **5.18** below) that is incurred after 16 April 2002 and before 1 April 2021 qualifies for allowances at 100%. [*CAA 2001, ss 45D(1), 52(3); FA 2013, s 68(1); SI 2015 No 60, Art 4; SI 2016 No 984, Art 4*].

(3) Expenditure on the provision of unused (not second-hand) plant or machinery for gas refuelling stations that is incurred after 16 April 2002 and before 1 April 2018 qualifies for allowances at 100%. [*CAA 2001, ss 45E(1), 52(3); FA 2013, s 69; SI 2015 No 60, Art 5*]. See **5.19** below.

(4) Expenditure on the provision of plant or machinery for use wholly for the purposes of a ring fence trade that is incurred by a company after 16 April 2002 qualifies for allowances at 100% or, for expenditure incurred before 12 March 2008, 24% for long-life assets (see **5.66** below). [*CAA 2001, ss 45F(1), 52(3)*]. See **5.20** below.

(5) Expenditure on the provision of 'environmentally beneficial plant or machinery' (see **5.21** below) that is incurred after 31 March 2003 qualifies for allowances at 100%. [*CAA 2001, ss 45H(1), 52(3)*].

(6) Expenditure on the provision of unused (not second-hand) registered 'zero-emission goods vehicles' that is incurred after 5 April 2010 and before 6 April 2018 (after 31 March 2010 and before 1 April 2018 for corporation tax purposes) qualifies for allowances at 100%. The allowances are subject to a maximum limit of 85 million euros per undertaking (as defined) over the eight years. [*CAA 2001, ss 45DA(1), 52(3); F(No 3)A 2010, s 18, Sch 7 paras 3, 5, 7; FA 2015, s 45(2)*]. See **5.22** below.

(7) Expenditure by a company on the provision of unused (not second-hand) plant or machinery for use primarily in an area which (at the time the expenditure is incurred) is a 'designated assisted area' that is incurred after 31 March 2012 and in the period of eight years beginning with the date on which the area is (or is treated as) designated qualifies

for allowances at 100%. [*CAA 2001, ss 45K(1)(9), 52(3); FA 2012, s 44, Sch 11 paras 3, 5; FA 2014, s 64(5); FA 2016, s 69*]. See **5.23** below.

(8) Expenditure on the provision of unused (not second-hand) plant or machinery installed solely for the purpose of charging 'electric vehicles' that is incurred after 22 November 2016 and before 6 April 2019 (1 April 2019 for corporation tax purposes) qualifies for allowances at 100%. For this purpose, an '*electric vehicle*' is a road vehicle which can be propelled by electric power, whether or not it can also be propelled by another form of power. [*CAA 2001, ss 45EA(1)–(3)(5), 52(3); F(No 2)A 2017, s 38(3)(5)*].

First-year allowances are also available in respect of any 'additional VAT liability', whenever incurred, in respect of expenditure within the above categories. See **17.49** below.

The periods in which expenditure can qualify for allowances under (2), (3), (6), (7) and (8) can be extended by Treasury order. If the Treasury extends the qualifying period for allowances under (8) above it may also vary the rate of the allowance, but only with effect for expenditure incurred after the end of the existing period. [*CAA 2001, ss 45D(1A), 45DA(1A), 45E(1A), 45EA(4), 45K(1A), 52(3A)(3B); FA 2014, s 64; F(No 2)A 2017, s 38(3)(5)*].

The following temporary first-year allowances have also been available in recent years.

(a) Expenditure incurred after 5 April 2009 and before 6 April 2010 (after 31 March 2009 and before 1 April 2010 for corporation tax purposes) qualifies for allowances at a rate of 40%. [*FA 2009, s 24*].

(b) Expenditure incurred after 1 July 1998 and before 6 April 2008 (1 April 2008 for corporation tax purposes) by a 'small or medium-sized enterprise' (see **5.24** below) qualifies for allowances at a rate of
    (i) for expenditure incurred by a 'small enterprise' (see **5.24** below) in the year beginning 6 April 2004 (the year beginning 1 April 2004 for corporation tax purposes) or after 5 April 2006 and before 6 April 2008 (after 31 March 2006 and before 1 April 2008 for corporation tax purposes), 50%; or
    (ii) in all other cases, 40%.

    [*CAA 2001, ss 44(1), 52(3); FA 2004, s 142; FA 2006, s 30; FA 2007, s 37; FA 2008, s 75*].

As with the current first-year allowances, additional VAT liabilities, whenever incurred, in respect of such expenditure also qualify for first-year allowances. See **17.49** below.

See **5.26** below for various types of expenditure which are excluded from being first-year qualifying expenditure.

CAA 2001, s 5 (see **2.4** to **2.6** above) applies to determine the time when expenditure is incurred. In determining whether expenditure is incurred within the various time limits mentioned above, *CAA 2001, s 12* (pre-trading expenditure to be treated as incurred on the first day of trading — see **5.36** below) is ignored. [*CAA 2001, s 50; FA 2009, s 24(6)*]. In other words, *CAA*

2001, s 12 applies to determine the chargeable period for which a first-year or writing-down allowance is available, but expenditure incurred outside one of the above periods cannot qualify for a first-year allowance by virtue of the first day of trading falling within that period.

HMRC accept that a vehicle is unused and not second hand for the purposes of (2) and (6) above even if it has been driven a limited number of miles for the purposes of testing, delivery, test driven by a potential purchaser, or used as a demonstration car (HMRC Capital Allowances Manual, CA23145, CA23153).

A claim made on or after 1 July 2016 for first-year allowances under (6) or (7) above must include any information required by HMRC for the purpose of complying with certain EU State aid obligations. See **2.21A** above.

Energy-saving plant or machinery

[5.17] For the purposes of 5.16(1) above, '*energy-saving plant or machinery*' is plant or machinery which is unused and not second-hand, and which, at the time the expenditure is incurred or the contract for the provision of the plant or machinery is made:

(i) is of a description then specified by Treasury order; and
(ii) meets the energy-saving criteria specified by Treasury order for plant or machinery of that description.

The Treasury Order giving effect to these provisions (the *Capital Allowances (Energy-saving Plant and Machinery) Order 2001, SI 2001 No 2541*) operates by giving statutory authority to the energy technology lists issued by the Department for Business, Energy and Industrial Strategy (formerly the Department of Energy and Climate Change) and HMRC. Plant or machinery qualifies as energy-saving plant or machinery, therefore, if:

(a) it falls within a technology class specified in the Energy Technology Criteria List;
(b) it meets the energy-saving criteria set out in that List; and
(c) in the case of classes (4) to (17) below, it is of a type specified in (and not removed from) or which has been accepted for inclusion in, the Energy Technology Product List.

The Energy Technology Criteria List specifies the following technology classes:

(1) combined heat and power;
(2) lighting;
(3) pipework insulation;
(4) boilers;
(5) motors and drives;
(6) refrigeration;
(7) thermal screens (for expenditure incurred **before** 7 September 2006).
(8) (for expenditure incurred on or after 5 August 2002) heat pumps;
(9) (for expenditure incurred on or after 5 August 2002) radiant and warm air heaters;
(10) (for expenditure incurred on or after 5 August 2002) compressed air equipment;

(11) (for expenditure incurred on or after 5 August 2002) solar thermal systems;
(12) (for expenditure incurred on or after 5 August 2003) automatic monitoring and targeting equipment;
(13) (for expenditure incurred on or after 26 August 2004) air to air energy recovery equipment;
(14) (for expenditure incurred on or after 26 August 2004 and before 8 October 2010) compact heat exchangers;
(15) (for expenditure incurred on or after 26 August 2004) heating, ventilation and air conditioning equipment (for expenditure incurred before 4 August 2009, air conditioning zone controls);
(16) (for expenditure incurred on or after 4 August 2009) uninterruptible power supplies;
(17) (for expenditure incurred on or after 1 October 2011) high speed hand air dryers; and
(18) (for expenditure incurred on or after 2 July 2015) waste heat to electricity conversion equipment.

The Energy Technology Criteria and Product Lists can be viewed on the enhanced capital allowances website at www.gov.uk/guidance/energy-technology-list.

Where expenditure was incurred, or a contract entered into, on or after 1 April 2001 but before the date of the making of the Treasury Order, the plant or machinery concerned can nevertheless be energy-saving plant or machinery provided that, at the time the expenditure is incurred or the contract is entered into, it meets the conditions specified in the Order.

The Treasury have the power to provide that, in specified cases, a 100% first-year allowance cannot be made unless a 'certificate of energy efficiency' issued by, or by a person authorised by, the Secretary of State, the Scottish Ministers, the National Assembly for Wales, or the Department of Enterprise, Trade and Investment in Northern Ireland as appropriate, is in force. A '*certificate of energy efficiency*' certifies that particular plant or machinery, or plant or machinery of a particular design, meets the energy-saving criteria specified as in (ii) above. Currently, the Treasury Order requires a certificate of energy efficiency to be in force in the case only of plant and machinery:

- falling within the 'combined heat and power' technology class; and
- comprising a component based fixed system falling within the 'automatic monitoring and targeting equipment' technology class.

If such a certificate is revoked, it is treated as if it had never been issued and all such assessments and adjustments of assessments are made as necessary. If a person becomes aware that a tax return of his has become incorrect as a result of the revocation of a certificate, he must, subject to a penalty under *TMA 1970, s 98*, notify HMRC within three months specifying how the return needs to be amended.

If one or more components of plant or machinery, but not all of it, qualify as energy-saving plant or machinery, and an amount (the 'claim value') is specified in the Energy Technology Product List in respect of that component or components, the part of the expenditure which qualifies for the 100%

first-year allowance is limited to the amount, or the total of the amounts, specified. If the expenditure is treated for capital allowances purposes as incurred in instalments, the proportion of each instalment that qualifies for the allowance is the same as the proportion of the whole that qualifies. Where these provisions apply, the normal apportionment provisions in *CAA 2001, s 562(3)* (see **2.25** above) are disapplied.

[*CAA 2001, ss 45A(2)–(4), 45B, 45C; FA 2012, s 45(2); SI 2001 No 2541; SI 2011 No 2221; SI 2012 No 1832; SI 2013 No 1763; SI 2015 No 1508; SI 2016 No 927*].

Expenditure incurred on or after 6 April 2012 (1 April 2012 for corporation tax purposes) is treated as never having qualified for a first-year allowance under the above provisions if a payment or other incentive is received under the *Energy Act 2008, s 41* feed-in tariff scheme for electricity generated by the plant or machinery concerned or under the renewable heat incentive scheme (see *Energy Act 2008, s 100*) for heat generated, or gas or fuel produced, by the plant or machinery. This exclusion also applies to expenditure incurred on or after 6 April 2013 (1 April 2013 for corporation tax purposes) on plant or machinery used or for use in Northern Ireland where a payment or incentive is received under the renewable heat incentive scheme for Northern Ireland (see *Energy Act 2011, s 113*) or under a feed-in tariff scheme.

Where the expenditure is incurred on a combined heat and power system, the exclusion applies only to expenditure incurred on or after 6 April 2014 (1 April 2014 for corporation tax purposes) where the payment or incentive is under the renewable heat incentive scheme.

Where first-year allowances have been given in respect of expenditure and a payment or other incentive is subsequently received, an assessment or adjustment to an assessment can be made to withdraw the allowance. Where a taxpayer has made a return and subsequently becomes aware that it has become incorrect because of this provision, he must give notice to HMRC, within 3 months beginning with the day on which he first became so aware, specifying how the return needs to be amended.

[*CAA 2001, s 45AA; FA 2012, s 45(3); FA 2013, s 67*].

Cars with low carbon dioxide emissions

[5.18] To qualify as a car with '*low carbon dioxide emissions*' for the purposes of **5.16**(2) above, a car must be first registered after 16 April 2002 and must be either:

(a) an 'electrically-propelled' car, or
(b) a car which:
  (i) is first registered on the basis of either an 'EC certificate of conformity' or a 'UK approval certificate' specifying carbon dioxide emissions figures in terms of grams per kilometre driven, and
  (ii) has an 'applicable carbon dioxide emissions figure' not exceeding 75 grams per kilometre driven (50 grams per kilometre for expenditure incurred on or after 1 April 2018; 95 grams per

kilometre for expenditure incurred before 1 April 2015; 110 grams per kilometre for expenditure incurred before 1 April 2013; 120 grams for expenditure incurred before 1 April 2008).

An '*electrically-propelled*' car is one that is propelled solely by electrical power derived from a source external to the vehicle or from a storage battery which is not connected to a power source when the car is moving.

The '*applicable carbon dioxide emissions figure*' for the purposes of (b)(ii) above is the figure specified on the certificate mentioned in (b)(i) above. If the certificate specifies more than one emissions figure, the figure specified as the carbon dioxide emissions (combined) figure is taken to be the applicable figure. If the car is a bi-fuel car (i.e. one capable of being propelled by petrol and 'road fuel gas' (within the meaning of *ITEPA 2003, s 171(1)*), or by diesel and road fuel gas), the certificate will include emissions figures for each of the different fuels. In that case the lowest figure is taken to be the applicable figure, except that where the certificate specifies more than one figure in relation to each type of fuel, the lowest of the carbon dioxide emissions (combined) figures is taken.

An '*EC certificate of conformity*' is a certificate of conformity issued by a manufacturer under any law of a member State implementing Article 6 of Council Directive 70/156/EEC, as amended. A '*UK approval certificate*' is a certificate issued under the *Road Traffic Act 1988, s 58(1)* or *(4)*, or Northern Ireland equivalent.

For the purposes of these provisions, 'car' has the extended meaning given at **5.51** below, except that motorcycles are excluded in all cases. Hackney carriages are specifically included.

The Treasury has the power to amend the amount in (b)(ii) above by order.

[*CAA 2001, ss 45D, 268B, 268C; FA 2013, s 68(1)(5); FA 2014, s 64(2); SI 2015 No 60, Arts 2, 4; SI 2016 No 984, Arts 2, 4*].

The single asset pool provisions for old expenditure on cars costing more than £12,000 (see **5.53** below) did not apply to expenditure on cars qualifying for first-year allowances under these provisions. [*CAA 2001, s 74(2)(c); FA 2009, Sch 11 para 25*].

Gas refuelling stations

[5.19] To qualify for first-year allowances under **5.16**(3) above, plant or machinery must be installed at a 'gas refuelling station' for use solely for, or in connection with, the refuelling of mechanically propelled road vehicles with natural gas, 'hydrogen fuel' or, for expenditure incurred on or after 1 April 2008, 'biogas'. Such plant or machinery may include storage tanks, compressors, pumps, controls or meters and any equipment for dispensing fuel to the fuel tank of a vehicle.

A '*gas refuelling station*' for this purpose is any premises, or part of any premises, where vehicles are refuelled with natural gas, hydrogen fuel or, for expenditure incurred on or after 1 April 2008, biogas. '*Hydrogen fuel*' means a fuel consisting of gaseous or cryogenic liquid hydrogen which is used for propelling vehicles. '*Biogas*' means gas produced by the anaerobic conversion of organic matter which is used for propelling vehicles.

[*CAA 2001, s 45E; FA 2013, s 69; FA 2014, s 64(4)*].

Ring fence trades

[5.20] For the purposes of 5.16(4) above, a '*ring fence trade*' means a ring fence trade (see 5.40 below) to which the supplementary charge in *CTA 2010, s 330(1)* applies. [*CAA 2001, s 45F(3)*].

There are provisions for the withdrawal of first-year allowances in respect of a ring fence trade if, within the period of five years beginning with its acquisition, the plant or machinery is not used in a ring fence trade carried on by the company or a company connected with it (see 2.34 above) or is used for a purpose other than that of such a trade. Where the plant or machinery ceases to be owned by the company or any company connected with it at a time before the end of the five-year period, the provisions for withdrawal apply only up to that time. Any person whose return is rendered incorrect as a result of the provisions must (subject to a penalty under *TMA 1970, s 98*) give notice, specifying how the return needs to be amended, within three months of becoming aware that it has become incorrect. [*CAA 2001, ss 45F(2), 45G*].

Environmentally beneficial plant or machinery

[5.21] For the purposes of 5.16(5) above, 'environmentally beneficial plant or machinery' is plant or machinery which is unused and not second-hand, which is not long-life asset expenditure (see 5.66 below), and which, at the time the expenditure is incurred or the contract for the provision of the plant or machinery is made:

(i) is of a description then specified by Treasury order; and
(ii) meets the environmental criteria specified by Treasury order for plant or machinery of that description.

The Treasury may make orders for the above purposes as appears appropriate in order to promote the use of technologies or products designed to remedy or prevent damage to the physical environment or natural resources.

In practice, all the technologies and products currently qualifying as environmentally beneficial plant or machinery relate to sustainable water use, and the Treasury Order giving effect to the provisions (the *Capital Allowances (Environmentally Beneficial Plant and Machinery) Order 2003, SI 2003 No 2076*) operates by giving statutory authority to the water technology lists issued by the Department for Environment, Food and Rural Affairs and HMRC. Plant or machinery qualifies as environmentally beneficial plant or machinery, therefore, if:

(a) it falls within a technology class specified in the Water Technology Criteria List;
(b) it meets the environmental criteria set out in that List; and
(c) it is of a type specified in (and not removed from), or which has been accepted for inclusion in, the Water Technology Product List.

The Water Technology Criteria List specifies the following technology classes:

(1) meters and monitoring equipment;
(2) flow controllers;

(3) leakage detection equipment;
(4) efficient toilets;
(5) efficient taps;
(6) (for expenditure incurred on or after 26 August 2004) rainwater harvesting equipment;
(7) (for expenditure on or after 22 September 2005) water reuse systems (for expenditure before 11 August 2008, efficient membrane filtration systems for the treatment of wastewater for recovery and reuse only);
(8) for expenditure on or after 22 September 2005) cleaning in place equipment;
(9) for expenditure on or after 22 September 2005) efficient showers;
(10) (for expenditure incurred on or after 7 September 2006) efficient washing machines;
(11) (for expenditure incurred on or after 7 September 2006) small scale slurry and sludge dewatering equipment;
(12) (for expenditure incurred on or after 16 August 2007) vehicle wash waste reclaim units;
(13) (for expenditure incurred on or after 16 August 2007) water efficient industrial cleaning equipment;
(14) (for expenditure incurred on or after 16 August 2007) water management equipment for mechanical seals (for expenditure before 11 August 2008, waste management for mechanical seals); and
(15) (for expenditure incurred on or after 7 August 2013) greywater recovery and reuse equipment.

The Water Technology Criteria and Product Lists can be viewed at https://www.gov.uk/government/publications/water-efficient-enhanced-capital-a llowances.

Where expenditure was incurred, or a contract entered into, on or after 1 April 2003 but before the date of the making of the Treasury Order, the plant or machinery concerned can nevertheless be environmentally beneficial plant or machinery provided that, at the time the expenditure is incurred or the contract is entered into, it meets the conditions specified in the Order.

The Treasury have the power to provide that, in specified cases, a 100% first-year allowance cannot be made unless a 'certificate of environmental benefit' issued by, or by a person authorised by, the Secretary of State, the Scottish Ministers, the National Assembly for Wales, or the Department of Enterprise, Trade and Investment in Northern Ireland as appropriate, is in force. A '*certificate of environmental benefit*' certifies that particular plant or machinery, or plant or machinery of a particular design, meets the environmental criteria specified as in (ii) above. Currently, the Treasury Order requires a certificate of environmental benefit to be in force in the case only of efficient membrane filtration systems and (for expenditure incurred on or after 11 August 2008) efficient wastewater recovery and reuse systems within (7) above.

If such a certificate is revoked, it is treated as if it had never been issued and all such assessments and adjustments of assessments are made as necessary. If a person becomes aware that a tax return of his has become incorrect as a result of the revocation of a certificate, he must, subject to a penalty under *TMA 1970, s 98*, notify HMRC within three months specifying how the return needs to be amended.

If one or more components of plant or machinery, but not all of it, qualify as environmentally beneficial plant or machinery, and an amount is specified in the Water Technology Product List in respect of that component or components, the part of the expenditure which qualifies for the 100% first-year allowance is limited to the amount, or the total of the amounts, specified. If the expenditure is treated for capital allowances purposes as incurred in instalments, the proportion of each instalment that qualifies for the allowance is the same as the proportion of the whole that qualifies. Where these provisions apply, the normal apportionment provisions in *CAA 2001, s 562(3)* (see **2.25** above) are disapplied.

[*CAA 2001, ss 45H, 45I, 45J; SI 2011 No 2220; SI 2012 Nos 1838, 2602; SI 2013 No 1762; SI 2015 No 1509; SI 2016 No 952*].

Zero-emissions goods vehicles

[5.22] For the purposes of **5.16**(6) above a '*zero-emissions goods vehicle*' is a mechanically propelled road vehicle which cannot under any circumstances produce carbon dioxide by being driven and which is of a design primarily suited to the conveyance of goods or burden. The vehicle must be registered, but it does not matter whether it is first registered before or after the expenditure is incurred. The Treasury can by order provide for certain specified types of vehicles to be treated as (or not treated as) goods vehicles for this purpose.

The general exclusions at **5.26** below apply, along with the following additional exclusions. Allowances cannot be claimed where the person incurring the expenditure is, or forms part of, an 'undertaking' which is:

- in difficulty for the purposes of the General Block Exemption Regulation (651/2014) (previously the European Community Guidelines on State Aid for Rescuing and Restructuring Firms in Difficulty (2004/C244/02)); or
- subject to an outstanding recovery order following a European Commission decision declaring an aid illegal.

HMRC consider an undertaking to be in difficulty if its latest accounts are not prepared on a going concern basis (HMRC Capital Allowances Manual, CA23146).

Expenditure is also excluded if it is incurred for the purposes of a qualifying activity:

(a) in the fishery or aquaculture sectors as covered by EU Council Regulation No 1379/2013 (previously EC Council Regulation No 104/2000); or
(b) relating to the management of waste for other undertakings (such as a waste collector contracting with a local authority or large retail business to provide an integrated waste management service).

Expenditure is also excluded to the extent that it is taken into account for the purposes of a grant or payment made towards the expenditure which is either a State Aid or is of a type specified by Treasury order. If such a grant or payment is made after a first-year allowance has already been given, the allowance is withdrawn. An assessment or adjustment to an assessment withdrawing an allowance is not out of time if made within three years of the end of the chargeable period in which the grant or payment was made. For grants or payments made towards expenditure incurred before 6 April 2015 (1 April 2015 for corporation tax purposes), other than grants or payments made on or after that date towards expenditure incurred before that date, the exclusion is limited to State Aid which is required to be notified to and approved by the European Commission (and grants or payments specified by Treasury order).

For these purposes, an '*undertaking*' means an 'autonomous enterprise' or an enterprise and its 'partner enterprises' and 'linked enterprises', if any (all terms as defined in Annex 1 to the General Block Exemption Regulation (651/2014). In (b) above, 'management' and 'waste' have the meanings given in Article 1 of Directive 2006/12/EC.

Expenditure on which the allowance is available is limited to 85 million euros over the five years. The limit applies by aggregating the total expenditure of the person incurring the expenditure in question (the '*investor*') with:

- where the investor is a partnership, expenditure incurred by an enterprise which is a partner enterprise of the investor at the time the current expenditure is incurred; and
- where the investor and one or more others form, or have at any time formed, an undertaking, expenditure incurred by the undertaking, and expenditure incurred by any of those others at a time when they and the investor are part of the same undertaking or at a time before they both became part of the same undertaking (or, if they became part of the same undertaking more than once, before the last time).

Where the expenditure in question takes the total expenditure over the limit, that part of it which falls within the limit will qualify for allowances. Expenditure which is not incurred in euros is converted in order to apply the limit using the spot rate of exchange for the day on which it is incurred.

The Treasury may increase the limit by statutory instrument.

[*CAA 2001, ss 45DA, 45DB, 212T; F(No 3)A 2010, s 18, Sch 7 paras 3, 6, 7; FA 2014, s 64(3), Sch 13 paras 2, 6; FA 2015, s 45(3)–(9)*].

Designated assisted areas

[5.23] For the purposes of 5.16(7) above, '*designated assisted area*' means an area designated as such by Treasury order and falling wholly within an 'assisted area'. An area may be so designated only if, at the time the order is made, it falls wholly within an 'enterprise zone' and the Treasury and the responsible local authority have entered into a memorandum of understanding relating to the availability of the first-year allowances. The areas listed in the tables below have been so designated and are treated as having been designated on the date indicated in the table heading.

Areas treated as designated on 1 April 2012

Name of responsible authority	Date of memorandum of understanding	Area included in the map	Enterprise Zone within which area falls	Assisted area within which area falls
Welsh Ministers	19 April 2013	Deeside Enterprise Zone	Deeside Enterprise Zone	Sealand
		Ebbw Vale Enterprise Zone	Ebbw Vale Enterprise Zone	Rassau and Badminton
		Haven Waterway Enterprise Zone	Haven Waterway Enterprise Zone	Milford East and Neyland West
Scottish Ministers	5 June 2013	Dundee Port,	Low Carbon / Renewables East Enterprise Area	East Port
		Dundee Camperdown,	Low Carbon / Renewables East Enterprise Area	East Port
		Dundee Claverhouse	Low Carbon / Renewables East Enterprise Area	Longhaugh
		Nigg	Low Carbon / Renewables North Enterprise Area	Seaboard
		Irvine	Life Sciences Enterprise Area	Irvine Townhead
East Riding of Yorkshire Council	21 May 2014	Paull	Humber Green Port Corridor	South West Holderness
Hartlepool Borough Council	21 May 2014	Hartlepool Port Estates	Tees Valley	Headland and Harbour
Kingston upon Hull City Council	21 May 2014	Green Port Hull	Humber Renewable Energy Super Cluster	Marfleet
Kingston upon Hull City Council	21 May 2014	Queen Elizabeth Dock South	Humber Renewable Energy Super Cluster	Marfleet
Newcastle City Council	21 May 2014	Neptune Yard	North East	Walkergate
North Lincolnshire Council	21 May 2014	Able Marine Energy Park	Humber Renewable Energy Super Cluster	Ferry
Northumberland County Council	21 May 2014	Port of Blyth - Bates	North East	Cowpen
Northumberland County Council	21 May 2014	Port of Blyth - East Sleekburn	North East	Sleekburn
North Tyneside Council	21 May 2014	North Bank of the Tyne (Port of Tyne)	North East	Riverside
Stockton on Tees Borough Council	21 May 2014	New Energy and Technology Park	Tees Valley	Billingham South
Redcar and Cleveland Borough Council	16 July 2013	South Bank Wharf site	Tees Valley Enterprise Zone	North East

Areas treated as designated on 1 April 2012

Name of responsible authority	Date of memorandum of understanding	Area included in the map	Enterprise Zone within which area falls	Assisted area within which area falls
Redcar and Cleveland Borough Council	16 July 2013	Wilton site	Tees Valley Enterprise Zone	North East
Wirral Metropolitan Borough Council	9 March 2015	Wirral Waters site	Mersey Waters Enterprise Zone	North West
Walsall Metropolitan Borough Council	2 March 2015	George Dyke site	Black Country Enterprise Zone	West Midlands
Walsall Metropolitan Borough Council	2 March 2015	Gasholder site	Black Country Enterprise Zone	West Midlands
Walsall Metropolitan Borough Council	2 March 2015	Phoenix 10 site	Black Country Enterprise Zone	West Midlands

Areas treated as designated on 18 March 2015

Name of responsible authority	Date of memorandum of understanding	Area included in the map	Enterprise Zone within which area falls	Assisted area within which area falls
Leeds City Council	12 June 2015	Logic Leeds	Leeds City Region Enterprise Zone	Yorkshire and the Humber
East Riding of Yorkshire Council and North Lincolnshire Council and North East Lincolnshire Council	20 January 2016	Great Coates	Humber Enterprise Zone	North East
Wyre Borough Council	27 January 2016	Hillhouse	Hillhouse International Business Park Enterprise Zone	North West
Blackpool Council	28 January 2016	Blackpool Airport	Blackpool Airport Enterprise Zone	North West
Cumbria County Council and Carlisle City Council	29 January 2016	Kingmoor Park	Kingmoor Park Enterprise Zone	North West
Cheshire West and Chester Borough Council	29 January 2016	South Road Former Simms Recycling Ellesmere Port	Cheshire Science Corridor Enterprise Zone	North West
		Thornton Science Park	Cheshire Science Corridor Enterprise Zone	North West

Areas treated as designated on 18 March 2015

Name of responsible authority	Date of memorandum of understanding	Area included in the map	Enterprise Zone within which area falls	Assisted area within which area falls
		South Road Former Simms Recycling Ellesmere Port	Cheshire Science Corridor Enterprise Zone	North West
Cheshire West and Chester Borough Council	29 January 2016	Ince Park (Phase 1) Ellesmere Port	Cheshire Science Corridor Enterprise Zone	North West
Stoke-on-Trent City Council	29 January 2016	Chatterley Valley East	Ceramic Valley Enterprise Zone	West Midlands
		Etruria Valley	Ceramic Valley Enterprise Zone	West Midlands
		Temple Green	Ceramic Valley Enterprise Zone	West Midlands
Luton Borough Council	29 January 2016	Luton Airport Business Park	Luton Airport Enterprise Zone	East of England
Derby City Council	23 June 2016	Infinity Park	Nottingham and Derby Enterprise Zone	East Midlands
Cornwall Council	12 June 2015	Newquay	Aerohub Enterprise Zone	Cornwall and the Isles of Scilly
		Goonhilly Earth Station	Aerohub Enterprise Zone	Cornwall and the Isles of Scilly

Areas treated as designated on 1 April 2015

Name of responsible authority	Date of memorandum of understanding	Area included in the map	Enterprise Zone within which area falls	Assisted area within which area falls
Redcar and Cleveland Borough Council	16 June 2015	Prairie site	Tees Valley Enterprise Zone	North East

Areas treated as designated on 16 March 2016

Name of responsible authority	Date of memorandum of understanding	Area included in the map	Enterprise Zone within which area falls	Assisted area within which area falls
Department for the Economy (Northern Ireland)	23 June 2016	Coleraine Industrial Area	Coleraine	Northern Ireland
		Dundooan Road	Coleraine	Northern Ireland
Welsh Ministers	29 June 2016	Baglan Energy Park	Port Talbot	Wales
		Industrial Estate	Port Talbot	Wales

Areas treated as designated on 16 March 2016

Name of responsible authority	Date of memorandum of understanding	Area included in the map	Enterprise Zone within which area falls	Assisted area within which area falls
		Port Talbot Docks	Port Talbot	Wales

Each memorandum of understanding includes a map indicating the boundaries of the designated area and can be viewed without charge at HM Treasury, 1 Horse Guards Road, London SW1A 2HQ or at www.gov.uk/government/publications/enterprise-zones.

An '*assisted area*' is an area specified as a development area under *Industrial Development Act 1982, s 1* or Northern Ireland. An '*enterprise zone*' is an area recognised by the Treasury as an area in respect of which there is special focus on economic development and identified on a map published by the Treasury for the purposes of the first-year allowances. The responsible local authority is the local authority for all or part of the area or two or more such authorities or, where relevant, the Scottish Ministers, the Welsh Ministers or the Department of Enterprise, Trade and Investment in Northern Ireland. The Treasury may by order amend the definition of 'assisted area' in certain circumstances.

In order for expenditure to qualify for first-year allowances under **5.16**(7) above, the following further conditions must be met:

(I) the company must be within the charge to corporation tax;
(II) the expenditure must be incurred for the purposes of a trade or a concern within *CTA 2009, s 39(4)*;
(III) the expenditure must be incurred for the purposes of:
  - (i) a business of a kind not previously carried on by the company;
  - (ii) expanding a business carried on by the company; or
  - (iii) starting up an activity which relates to a fundamental change in a product or production process of, or service provided by, a business carried on by the company; and

(IV) the expenditure must not be 'replacement expenditure'.

For expenditure incurred on or after 17 July 2014, the condition in (III) above can be met by virtue of (III)(iii) above only if the expenditure exceeds the amount by which the 'relevant plant or machinery' has been depreciated in the three years ending immediately before the beginning of the chargeable period in which the expenditure is incurred. The '*relevant plant or machinery*' is the plant or machinery in use for the purposes of the product, process or service immediately before the beginning of the chargeable period in which the expenditure is incurred.

For this purpose, '*replacement expenditure*' is expenditure on providing plant or machinery intended to perform the same or a similar function as plant or machinery on which the company had previously incurred qualifying expenditure and which is superseded by the new plant or machinery. If the new plant or machinery is capable of and intended to perform a significant additional function which enhances the capacity or productivity of the qualifying activity, then to the extent that the expenditure is attributable to that function it is not replacement expenditure. The part of the expenditure attributable to the additional function must be determined on a just and reasonable basis.

The general exclusions at **5.26** below apply, along with the following additional exclusions. If, at the time the company incurs the expenditure, it intends the plant or machinery to be used partly in an area which is not a designated assisted area, no first-year allowance can be claimed if a main purpose for which any person is a party to the transaction under which the expenditure is incurred (or any scheme or arrangements of which that transaction is part) is to obtain a first-year allowance or a greater such allowance in respect of the part of the expenditure attributable (on a just and reasonable basis) to the intended use in the non-designated area.

Allowances also cannot be claimed where the person incurring the expenditure is, or forms part of, an 'undertaking' which is:

- in difficulty for the purposes of the General Block Exemption Regulation (651/2014) (previously the European Community Guidelines on State Aid for Rescuing and Restructuring Firms in Difficulty (2004/C244/02)); or
- subject to an outstanding recovery order following a European Commission decision declaring an aid illegal.

Expenditure is also excluded if it is incurred for the purposes of a qualifying activity:

(a) in the fishery or aquaculture sectors as covered by EU Council Regulation No 1379/2013 (previously EC Council Regulation No 104/2000);
(b) in the coal, steel, shipbuilding or synthetic fibres sectors;
(c) relating to the management of waste for other undertakings (such as a waste collector contracting with a local authority or large retail business to provide an integrated waste management service);
(d) relating to the primary production of agricultural products, on-farm activities necessary for preparing an animal or plant product for first sale or the first sale of agricultural products by a primary producer to wholesalers, retailers or processors, in circumstances where the sale does not take place on separate premises reserved for that purpose;
(e) (for expenditure incurred on or after 17 July 2014) in the transport sector or related infrastructure;
(f) (for expenditure incurred on or after 17 July 2014) relating to energy generation, distribution or infrastructure; or
(g) (for expenditure incurred on or after 17 July 2014) relating to the development of broadband networks.

Expenditure incurred before 17 July 2014 is also excluded if it is incurred on a means of transport or transport equipment for the purposes of a qualifying activity in the road freight or air transport sectors.

Expenditure is also excluded if a grant or payment is made towards the expenditure or any other expenditure incurred by any person in respect of the same designated assisted area and the same 'single investment project', if the grant or payment is either a State Aid (whether or not notified) or of a type specified by Treasury order. If such a grant or payment is made towards the expenditure after a first-year allowance has already been given, the allowance is withdrawn. An allowance is similarly withdrawn if such a grant or payment is made towards any other expenditure incurred by any person in respect of the same designated assisted area and on the same single investment project, but only if the grant or payment is made within three years of the incurring of the original expenditure. Expenditure incurred in respect of a designated assisted area includes, for this purpose, expenditure incurred on the provision of things for use primarily in that area or on services to be provided primarily in that area.

Expenditure incurred on or after 17 July 2014 is also excluded if the designated assisted area is not an area falling within Article 107(3)(a) of the Treaty on the Functioning of the EU (areas where the standard of living is abnormally low or where there is serious underemployment), the condition in (III)(i) above is not met and, at the time the expenditure is incurred, the company is not a small or medium enterprise for the purpose of the General Block Exemption Regulation.

Except in relation to the first exclusion noted above, if a person who has made a return becomes aware that anything in it has become incorrect because of the above exclusions, he must give notice to HMRC, within three months of first becoming aware of the incorrectness, specifying how the return needs to be amended.

For these purposes, an '*undertaking*' means an 'autonomous enterprise' or an enterprise and its 'partner enterprises' and 'linked enterprises', if any (all terms as defined in Annex 1 to EC Regulation 800/2008). 'Agricultural product', 'single investment project' and expressions used in (b) and (e)–(g) above have the same meanings as in the General Block Exemption Regulation. In (c) above, 'management' and 'waste' have the meanings given in Article 1 of Directive 2006/12/EC.

The Treasury may amend the above provisions by order to give effect to changes in the relevant EU Regulations.

There are provisions for the withdrawal of first-year allowances if, within the period of five years beginning with the day the plant of machinery is first brought into use for the purposes of a qualifying company or, if earlier, the day on which it is first held for such use, either:

(1) the primary use to which the plant or machinery is put is not in an area which was a designated assisted area at the time the expenditure was incurred; or
(2) the plant or machinery is held for use otherwise than primarily in an area which was a designated assisted area at that time.

For expenditure which would have fallen within the final exclusion above if the designated assisted area in question had not been an area falling within Article 107(3)(a) of the Treaty on the Functioning of the EU, the references in (1) and (2) above to a designated assisted area must be read as references to a designated assisted area which falls within Article 107(3)(a).

Where the plant or machinery ceases to be owned by the company or any person connected with it (see **2.34** above) at a time before the end of the five-year period, the provisions for withdrawal apply only up to that time. Any person whose return becomes incorrect as a result of the provisions must give notice to HMRC, specifying how the return needs to be amended, within three months of becoming aware that it has become incorrect.

The allowance is limited to expenditure of 125 million euros by any person in respect of any single investment project in a particular designated assisted area. In applying the limit, expenditure incurred in a different currency is to be converted into euros using the spot rate of exchange for the day on which it is incurred. Note that the limit is on allowances for expenditure incurred in respect of a single project and not expenditure incurred by a single company. The Treasury can increase the limit by statutory instrument.

[*CAA 2001, ss 45K–45N, 212U; FA 2012, Sch 11 paras 3, 7; FA 2014, s 64(5), Sch 13 paras 3–5, 7, 8; SI 2014 No 3183; SI 2015 No 2047*].

Small or medium-sized enterprises

[5.24] For the purposes of **5.16**(b) above, '*small or medium-sized enterprise*' is defined by reference to the *Companies Act 2006, ss 382, 465* (previously *Companies Act 1985, s 247* or Northern Ireland equivalent) definition of 'small or medium-sized company'. Subject to what is said below regarding changes in the qualifying status of a business, the requirement is broadly that two of the following three conditions are fulfilled in relation to the 'financial year' in which the expenditure is incurred: that annual turnover not exceed £22.8 million (£11.2 million for financial years ending before 30 January 2004); that the assets not exceed £11. 4 million (£5.6 million for financial years ending before 30 January 2004); and that there be not more than 250 employees. '*Financial year*' for this purpose is as defined in *Companies Act 2006, s 390* (previously *Companies Act 1985, Part VII*), being, broadly, a period for which the business makes up accounts. Note that the old limits apply to a financial year which ends on or after 30 January 2004 only because of a change in accounting date.

A business which is a small or medium-sized enterprise will cease to be one only if it fails to meet the qualifying conditions over two consecutive years. A business that is not a small or medium-sized enterprise will become one only if it satisfies the criteria over two successive years. Where a business was not a small or medium-sized enterprise for its last financial year ending before 30 January 2004 but meets the increased qualifying conditions in the first financial year ending on or after that date, it can qualify as a small or medium-sized enterprise for that later year if it met the increased conditions in the previous year.

In non-company cases, all the trades, businesses, professions or vocations carried on by the taxpayer concerned are treated as one qualifying activity, to which the above requirements are applied.

In the case of a company which is a member of a group of companies, the requirements apply to the group as a whole. The group which has to be considered in this context includes any international group of which the company is a member. If, at the time any expenditure is incurred, arrangements exist which, had they been put into effect immediately before that time, would have resulted in the company being a member of a group which did not meet the above requirements, the company is treated as being a member of that group at that time, so that first-year allowances are not available.

For the purpose of **5.16**(b) above, '*small enterprise*' is similarly defined, but by reference to the *Companies Act 1985* definition of 'small company', i.e. where two of the following three conditions are fulfilled: that the turnover does not exceed £5.6 million (£2.8 million for financial years ending before 30 January 2004); that the assets are not more than £2.8 million (£1.4 million for financial years ending before 30 January 2004); and that there be not more than 50 employees.

[*CAA 2001, ss 47–49, Sch 3 para 49; FA 2008, ss 75(3), 76(4); SI 2008 No 954, Arts 28–30*].

HMRC consider that neither a partnership which has one or more companies amongst its members nor a trust can be a small or medium-sized enterprise or a small enterprise. (HMRC Capital Allowances Manual, CA23170).

Entitlement to allowances

[5.25] A person carrying on a qualifying activity is entitled to a first-year allowance for the chargeable period in which the first-year qualifying expenditure was incurred if he owns the plant or machinery at some time during that period. For chargeable periods ending on or after 1 April 2012 the legislation is made explicit to confirm that first-year allowances cannot be claimed under more than one category in respect of the same expenditure. [*CAA 2001, ss 52(1)(2), 52A; FA 2012, Sch 11 paras 6, 8*].

A first-year allowance and an annual investment allowance cannot be claimed in respect of the same expenditure. [*CAA 2001, s 52A; FA 2012, Sch 11 paras 6, 8*]. Where expenditure would otherwise qualify for both types of allowance, taxpayers are free to decide which to claim. In general, where total qualifying expenditure exceeds the annual investment allowance limit, it will be beneficial to claim any 100% first-year allowances in priority to annual investment allowance, thereby leaving the limit intact for use for expenditure not qualifying for 100% first-year allowances.

Exclusions

[5.26] Subject to the exceptions noted, expenditure within any of the following categories is not first-year qualifying expenditure for the purposes of the allowances in **5.16**(1)–(8) and **5.16**(a) and (b) above.

(i) Expenditure incurred in the chargeable period in which the qualifying activity is permanently discontinued.

(ii) Expenditure incurred on the provision of a car, as defined at **5.51** below). This exclusion does not, of course, prevent expenditure on a car with low carbon dioxide emissions (as defined in **5.18** above) from qualifying for first-year allowances under **5.16**(2) above.

(iii) Expenditure incurred before 1 April 2013 on a ship (within *CAA 2001, s 94*) or railway asset (within *CAA 2001, s 95*) which is of a kind which was excluded from being a long-life asset where the expenditure was incurred before 1 January 2011 (see **5.66** below).

(iv) Expenditure where the plant or machinery would be long-life assets but for the provisions of *CAA 2001, Sch 3 para 20* (transitional provisions — see **5.66** below).

(v) Expenditure on the provision of plant or machinery for leasing (including the letting of a ship on charter or of any other asset on hire), whether in the course of a trade or otherwise. This exclusion does not apply for the purposes of the allowances in **5.16**(2) above to expenditure incurred before 1 April 2013. It does not apply, for expenditure incurred before 1 April 2006, to the allowances in **5.16**(3) above. It also does not apply for the purposes of the allowances in **5.16**(1) above, where the expenditure is incurred after 16 April 2002, and those in **5.16**(5) above, but only where, for expenditure incurred on or after 1 April 2006, the plant or machinery is provided for leasing under an excluded lease of background plant or machinery for a building within **6.29** below. The exclusion does not apply for the purposes of the allowances in **5.16**(a) above if the plant or machinery is provided for leasing under an excluded lease of background plant or machinery for a building.

(vi) Expenditure where the provision of the plant or machinery is connected with a change in the nature or conduct of a trade or business carried on by a person other than the person incurring the expenditure and the obtaining of a first-year allowance is the main benefit, or one of the main benefits, which could reasonably be expected to arise from the making of the change.

(vii) Expenditure where the provision of the plant or machinery is by way of gift (see **7.12** below).

(viii) Expenditure where the plant or machinery was previously used by the owner for purposes outside the qualifying activity (see **7.13** below) or for leasing under a long funding lease (see **6.39** below).

(ix) Expenditure where the plant or machinery is acquired in circumstances where the anti-avoidance provisions at **6.36**, **7.3**, **7.4** or **7.9** below apply.

[*CAA 2001, ss 46, 52(5); F(No 3)A 2010, Sch 7 paras 4, 5; FA 2012, Sch 11 paras 4, 5; FA 2013, ss 68(2)(5), 70; F(No 2)A 2017, s 38(4)*].

HMRC consider that where a business supplies plant or machinery with an operator, the business is supplying a service and is not merely letting the asset on hire, so that the exclusion at (v) above will not apply. The operator must remain with the equipment during its use and it must be operated by him alone save for exceptional circumstances. It is not sufficient for the plant or machinery to be delivered or installed by the hire firm. Where a particular piece of equipment is to be provided with an operator on some occasions, and without on others, provided that when the expenditure is incurred it is intended that the asset will predominantly be provided with an operator, HMRC will generally accept that the exclusion for letting on hire will not apply. HMRC also accept that provision of building access services by the scaffolding industry amounts to more than mere letting on hire. (HMRC Capital Allowances Manual, CA23115).

The exclusion at (v) above was considered In *MGF (Trench Construction Systems) Ltd v HMRC* FTT 2012, [2013] SFTD 281. A company claimed first-year allowances on excavation support equipment, which it hired out. HMRC rejected the claim on the basis that the exclusion at (v) above applied. None of the equipment required an operator or any labour to be supplied by the company to install it. The company contended that the equipment had not been acquired for leasing, since the company provided design services (through a subcontractor)to its customers as well as the equipment. The First-tier Tribunal accepted this contention and allowed the appeal. Judge Cannan held that 'there can be circumstances where plant is supplied without labour but with other services and benefits such that the expenditure on such plant falls outside' the exclusion. On the evidence, the company was 'providing an overall service beyond the leasing of assets referred to in [the exclusion]. It is analogous to a scaffolding firm hiring scaffolding but also providing something more, namely the labour to erect and dismantle the scaffolding'.

A claim for first-year allowances in respect of plant used by a subsidiary of the taxpayer for an annual charge based on the subsidiary's turnover failed, as the expenditure was held to be within (v) above, in *M F Freeman (Plant) Ltd v Jowett* Sp C, [2003] STC (SCD) 423.

Special rate expenditure within **5.49** below, and expenditure qualifying for first-year allowances under any of **5.16**(1)–(5) above, do not qualify for the 40% first-year allowance within **5.16**(a) above. [*FA 2009, s 24(2)*].

Expenditure on long-life assets within **5.66** below does not qualify for the 40% (or 50%) first-year allowance for expenditure incurred after 1 July 1998 within **5.16**(b) above. [*CAA 2001, s 44(2); FA 2008, s 75*].

See also **5.56** and **7.14** below for the reduction of first-year allowances where, respectively, plant or machinery is provided partly for purposes other than a qualifying activity or a partial depreciation subsidy is payable.

Miscellaneous

[5.27] A person is not obliged to claim a first-year allowance in respect of first-year qualifying expenditure. A claim for a first-year allowance may be made in respect of the whole or a part of the expenditure. [*CAA 2001, s 52(4)*]. Any part of the expenditure for which a first-year allowance is not claimed, may qualify for writing-down allowances for the same chargeable period.

In *Ensign Tankers (Leasing) Ltd v Stokes HL* , 1992, 64 TC 617, the taxpayer company entered two limited partnerships which were set up to produce films. The partnerships entered into agreements with third parties to distribute and exploit the films. The House of Lords rejected the Revenue's contention that the films did not 'belong' to the partnerships because the distribution agreements were entered into immediately after the films were acquired and were such that the partnerships sold the right to distribute the films and exploit them in perpetuity. It was held that the partnerships did not part with the right to exploit the films, but instead exploited them by entering into the agreements. (However, their Lordships found against the company on other grounds — see **1.9** above.) See **4.9** above regarding the change in the requirement as to 'belonging' under *CAA 2001*.

In *Jukes (HMIT) v SG Warburg & Co Ltd* [1996] STC 526 the High Court held that 100% first-year allowances were not available to Royal Ordnance Factories plc. The company which took over the privatised Royal Ordnance Factories in 1985 refinanced purchases of capital equipment made before the transfer by entering into new leasing contracts. The company maintained that it should be treated as the person who made the contracts for the purposes of claiming 100% first-year allowances which were withdrawn from 13 March 1984. The court held that although the company had assumed the assets and liabilities of the Crown service, sums paid after the transfer to the company were not to be regarded as having been paid by the original purchasers with the result that 100% capital allowances were not allowed.

For the treatment given to an additional VAT liability, see **17.53** below.

First-year tax credits

[5.28] *FA 2008* introduced new payable tax credits for companies making losses which are attributable to first-year allowances for expenditure on energy-saving or environmentally beneficial plant or machinery within **5.16**(1) or (5) above. The intention is to encourage investment in environmentally friendly technologies by companies who would not otherwise immediately benefit from the 100% first-year allowance as a result of making losses. (Treasury Explanatory Notes to the 2008 Finance Bill).

The credits are available only for expenditure incurred in the period beginning 1 April 2008 and ending on 31 March 2018, although the Treasury has the power to extend the qualifying period by order. In determining whether expenditure is incurred within the qualifying period, *CAA 2001, s 12* (pre-trading expenditure to be treated as incurred on the first day of trading — see **5.36** below) is ignored.

A company can claim a first-year tax credit for a chargeable period in which it has a 'surrenderable loss', unless it is an 'excluded company' for that period. A company has a '*surrenderable loss*' for a chargeable period for this purpose if a first-year allowance within **5.16**(1) or (5) above (other than one in respect of an additional VAT liability — see **17.53** below) is made in respect of expenditure incurred for the purposes of a qualifying activity the profits of which are chargeable to corporation tax and a loss (see below) is incurred in that activity. The amount of the surrenderable loss is so much of the loss as is 'unrelieved' or, if less, the amount of the first-year allowance.

A company is an '*excluded company*' for a chargeable period if at any time in that period it is entitled to make a claim under *CTA 2010, ss 642, 643* (rent etc. of co-operative housing associations disregarded for tax purposes) or *CTA 2010, ss 651, 652* (rent etc. of self-build societies disregarded for tax purposes) or is entitled to make one of certain claims under *CTA 2010, Pt 11* (tax exemptions for charitable companies and scientific research organisations).

Where the qualifying activity is a UK or overseas property business, a loss qualifies for a first-year tax credit only if the business is carried on on a commercial basis or in the exercise of statutory functions. If, however, the company is an insurance company, a loss from such a business qualifies so far as it is attributable to basic life assurance and general annuity business and is treated in accordance with *FA 2012, s 87(3)* (or, before the *FA 2012* insurance company regime took effect, in accordance with *ICTA 1988, s 432AB(3)*). If the insurance company is treated as carrying on more than one such business, the loss which qualifies is the aggregate net loss attributable to basic life assurance and general annuity business treated in accordance with *FA 2012, s 87(4)* (or *ICTA 1988, s 432AB(4)*). See **5.86** below for the taking effect of the *FA 2012* regime.

Where the qualifying activity is managing the investments of a company with investment business, the company incurs a loss for these purposes if the sum of the expenses and charges within *CTA 2009, s 1223(2)* for a chargeable period is greater than the profits from which they are deductible. The amount of the loss is the excess. If the qualifying activity is basic life assurance and general annuity business (before the *FA 2012* regime took effect, life assurance business) and the profits of the business are charged to tax under the I – E rules (previously the I minus E basis — see **5.86** below), the company incurs a loss in that activity if an amount falls to be carried forward under *FA 2012, s 73* (previously *ICTA 1988, s 76(12)* — carry forward of unrelieved expenses). The amount of the loss is the amount to be carried forward.

The amount of a loss which is 'unrelieved' is as follows.

(a) (Except where (d) or (f) below apply) where the qualifying activity is a trade or a UK or EEA furnished holiday lettings business, the amount of the loss less any relief that was or could have been obtained under *CTA 2010, s 37* (see **2.38** above) or *CTA 2010, s 42* (carry-back of loss of ring fence trade), any amount that was or could have been surrendered as group relief, any amount surrendered under another tax credit provision (see below) and any amount set off against the loss under *CTA 2010, ss 92–96* (write-off of government investment). No account is taken of any losses brought forward from an earlier period or carried back from a later period, or any loss incurred on a leasing contract in circumstances to which *CTA 2010, s 53* applies (see **17.7** below).

(b) (Except where (d) below applies) where the qualifying activity is a UK or overseas property business other than a furnished holiday lettings business, the amount of the loss less any relief that was or could have been claimed under *CTA 2010, s 62(1)–(3)* (loss relieved against profits of same accounting period — see **2.42** above), any amount that was or could have been surrendered as group relief, any amount surrendered under *CTA 2009, Pt 14 Ch 3* (tax credits for expenditure on remediation of contaminated land) and any amount set off against the loss under *CTA 2010, ss 92–96*. No account is taken of any losses brought forward from an earlier period.

(c) (Except where (d) below applies) where the qualifying activity is an overseas property business, the amount of the loss less any amount set off against the loss under *CTA 2010, ss 92–96* . No account is taken of any losses brought forward from an earlier period.

(d) Where the qualifying activity is a UK or overseas property business and the company is an insurance company, if no amount falls to be carried forward to a succeeding chargeable period under *FA 2012, s 73* (previously *ICTA 1988, s 76(12)*), no amount of the loss is unrelieved. If an amount does fall to be so carried forward, the unrelieved amount of the loss is the lesser of the amount carried forward and the amount of the loss (computed as above) less any amount surrendered under *CTA 2009, Pt 14 Ch 3* and any amount set off against the loss under *CTA 2010, ss 92–96*. In determining whether there is an amount falling to be carried forward, amounts brought forward from an earlier period by virtue of a previous application of *FA 2012, s 73, s 93* or *ICTA 1988, s 76(12)* or *(13)* or by virtue of *CTA 2009, s 391(3)* (loan relationship deficit carried forward) are disregarded.

(e) Where the qualifying activity is managing the investments of a company with investment business, the amount of the loss less any amount that was or could have been surrendered as group relief and any amount set off against the loss under *CTA 2010, ss 92–96*. No account is taken of any amount brought forward from an earlier period.

(f) Where the qualifying activity is basic life assurance and general annuity business (before the *FA 2012* regime took effect, life assurance business) and the profits of the business are charged to tax under the I – E rules (previously the I minus E basis), the amount of the loss less any amount surrendered under *CTA 2009, Pt 14 Ch 4* (tax credits for expenditure on remediation of contaminated land) and any amount set off against the loss under *CTA 2010, ss 92–96*. No account is taken of amounts brought forward from an earlier period by virtue of a previous application of *FA 2012, s 73, s 93* or *ICTA 1988, s 76(12)* or by virtue of *CTA 2009, s 391(3)* (loan relationship deficit carried forward).

For the purposes of (a) above, the other tax credit provisions to be taken into account are those under *CTA 2009, Pt 13, Chs 2 or 7* (research and development and vaccine research), *CTA 2009, Pt 14 Ch 3* (remediation of contaminated land), *CTA 2009, Pt 15 Ch 3* (films), *CTA 2009, Pt 15A Ch 3* (TV programmes), *CTA 2009, Pt 15B Ch 3* (video games), *CTA 2009, s 1217K* (theatre), *CTA 2009, Pt 15D Ch 3* (orchestral concerts) and *CTA 2009, Pt 15E Ch 3* (museum and gallery exhibitions).

[*CAA 2001, s 262A, Sch A1 paras 1, 3–16; FA 2011, Sch 14 para 12(16); FA 2012, Sch 16 para 106(2)–(5); FA 2013, Sch 18 para 6; FA 2014, Sch 4 para 7; FA 2016, Sch 8 para 7; F(No 2)A 2017, Sch 6 para 7; SI 2013 No 464*].

A transaction is disregarded in determining the amount of any tax credit for a chargeable period if it is attributable to arrangements (including any scheme, agreement or understanding, whether or not legally enforceable) one of whose main objects is to enable a company to obtain a tax credit to which it would not otherwise be entitled or a tax credit of a greater amount than that to which it would otherwise be entitled. [*CAA 2001, Sch A1 para 28*].

Claims to first-year tax credit must be separately identified as such in the return. [*CAA 2001, s 3(2B)*]. A fraudulent or negligent incorrect claim to a first-year tax credit attracts a penalty not exceeding the excess amount claimed. A similar penalty applies where a company discovers that a claim which was not made fraudulently or negligently is incorrect and does not remedy the error without unreasonable delay. [*FA 1998, Sch 18 para 83ZA(4)(5)*].

Amount of tax credit

[5.29] The amount of a first-year tax credit is 19% of the amount of the surrenderable loss, but this is subject to an upper limit of the greater of £250,000 or the company's total PAYE and NICs liabilities for 'payment periods' ending in the chargeable period. A company can claim the whole or only part of the amount.

For this purpose, a company's PAYE liability for a payment period is the amount of income tax for which it is required to account to HMRC under the PAYE regulations for that period, ignoring deductions for child tax credit and working tax credit. A company's NICs liability for a payment period is the Class 1 national insurance contributions for which it is required to account to HMRC for that period, ignoring deductions for statutory sick pay, statutory maternity pay, child tax credit and working tax credit. A '*payment period*' is a period ending on the fifth day of a month and for which the company is liable to account to HMRC for income tax and national insurance contributions.

The Treasury can alter the 19% rate by regulations. It may also provide for a different percentage to apply where the surrenderable loss relates to a qualifying activity that is a NI rate activity (see **17.46A** onwards below).

[*CAA 2001, Sch A1 paras 2, 17; CTNIA 2015, Sch 1 para 10; F(No 2)A 2017, Sch 7 para 28*].

Giving effect to tax credit

[5.30] Where a valid tax credit claim is made, the amount is normally paid to the company by HMRC. Alternatively, the amount, and any interest for late payment, can be applied to discharge the company's corporation tax liability. If HMRC open an enquiry into the company's tax return for the period concerned, they are not required to pay the tax credit until the enquiry is completed, but they may make a payment on a provisional basis as they think fit. HMRC are likewise not required to pay a tax credit for a chargeable period until the company has paid its PAYE and NICs liabilities for payment periods ending in the chargeable period. A payment of tax credit is not income of the company for tax purposes.

The company's loss from the qualifying activity for the chargeable period is reduced for the purposes of the following provisions by the amount of the surrenderable loss or that part of it in respect of which the tax credit was claimed.

(i) (Except where (v) or (vi) below apply) where the qualifying activity is a trade or a UK or EEA furnished holiday lettings business, *CTA 2010, ss 45, 45A, 45B* (see **2.38** above).

(ii) (Except where (v) below applies) where the qualifying activity is a UK property business other than a UK furnished holiday lettings business or, for chargeable periods beginning on or after 1 April 2011, an ordinary overseas property business, *CTA 2010, s 62(5)* (losses carried forward — see **2.42** above).

(iii) (Except where (v) below applies) where the qualifying activity is an overseas property business, *CTA 2010, s 66* (see **2.42** above).

(iv) Where the qualifying activity is managing the investments of a company with investment business, *CTA 2009, s 1223* (relief of expenses and charges against future profits).

(v) Where the qualifying activity is an ordinary UK property business or ordinary overseas property business (for chargeable periods beginning before 1 April 2011, a UK or overseas property business), and in a chargeable period the company's loss, as a result of *FA 2012, s 87(3)*, is treated for the purposes of *FA 2012, s 76* as a deemed BLAGAB management expense, and an amount falls to be carried forward under *FA 2012, s 73*, that amount is reduced by the loss surrendered. Before the *FA 2012* regime for insurance companies took effect (see **5.86** below), this provision applied where the company's loss was one treated under *ICTA 1988, s 432AB(3)*, for the purposes of *ICTA 1988, s 76(7)*, as expenses which fell to be brought into account at Step 3 in *s 76(7)*, and an amount fell to be carried forward under *s 76(12)*. The latter amount was reduced by the loss surrendered.

(vi) Where the qualifying activity is basic life assurance and general annuity business (before the *FA 2012* regime took effect, life assurance business) and the profits of the business are charged to tax under the I – E rules (previously the I minus E basis), the total amount which can be carried forward under *FA 2012, s 73* (previously *ICTA 1988, s 76(12)*) is reduced by the loss surrendered.

[*CAA 2001, Sch A1 paras 18–23; FA 2011, Sch 14 paras 12(16), 13; FA 2012, Sch 16 para 106(6)(7); F(No 2)A 2017, Sch 4 para 126*].

Clawback of tax credit

[5.31] First-year tax credit is clawed back where 'tax-relieved' plant or machinery is 'disposed' of within the period beginning with the date when the 'relevant first-year expenditure' is incurred and ending four years after the end of the chargeable period for which the tax credit was paid. The provisions apply equally to tax credit which was otherwise payable but not yet paid and to tax credit applied to meet a corporation tax liability. Any necessary adjustments to assessments can be made to effect the clawback. If a company which has made a tax return becomes aware that, as a result of these provisions, the return has become incorrect, it must notify HMRC within three months of so becoming aware, specifying how the return needs to be amended.

The appropriate part (the 'restored loss') of the loss surrendered in that chargeable period is treated as if it were not a surrenderable loss and the tax credit paid in respect of the restored loss is treated as if it should never have been paid. For this purpose, the tax credit paid in respect of the restored loss is 19% of the restored loss (or, where the Treasury have exercised their power to vary that percentage, the percentage applicable for the chargeable period for which the tax credit was paid).

An item of plant or machinery is '*tax-relieved*' if a first-year allowance meeting the requirements at **5.28** above was made in respect of any expenditure on it in the chargeable period for which the tax credit was paid. For the purpose only of the calculation of the amount of the restored loss below, the amount of that expenditure is the '*original expenditure*' on the item.

A company '*disposes*' of an item of tax-relieved plant or machinery if a disposal event within **5.41**(i)–(viii) below occurs or if there is a change in ownership of the item in circumstances such that a provision (a '*continuity or business provision*') applies under which, for the purposes of plant and machinery allowances, anything done to or by the company is treated as having been done to or by the person becoming the owner of the item. For the purpose only of the calculation of the amount of the restored loss below, the disposal value of the item is the normal disposal value except where either the company disposes of the item to a connected person for less than its market value or there is a change in ownership to which a continuity of business provision applies, in which case the disposal value is the market value of the item. For the same purpose, '*retained tax-relieved plant and machinery*' is tax-relieved plant or machinery of which the company has not disposed.

The amount of the '*restored loss*' is:

$$(LS - OERPM) - (OE - DV) - ARL$$

where:

LS is the amount of loss surrendered for the chargeable period for which the tax credit was paid;

OERPM is the amount (or aggregate of amounts) of the original expenditure on the retained tax-relieved plant and machinery after the item is disposed of;

OE is the aggregate of the original expenditure on the item disposed of and any other tax-relieved plant and machinery which the company has previously disposed of;

DV is the aggregate of the disposal values of the item disposed of and any other tax-relieved plant and machinery which the company has previously disposed of; and

ARL is the aggregate of any restored losses calculated on a previous application of this provision.

[*CAA 2001, Sch A1 paras 24–27*].

Writing-down allowances and balancing events

Pooling and availability of allowances

[5.32] For the purpose of calculating writing-down allowances, balancing allowances and balancing charges, qualifying expenditure (see **4.9** above) on plant and machinery is pooled. Expenditure relating to different qualifying activities carried on by the same person must not be allocated to the same pool. Expenditure is generally allocated to a single pool (the 'main pool') but there are specific requirements for certain types of expenditure to be allocated to a single asset pool or to a class pool instead (see **5.48** onwards below). Entitlement to allowances is determined separately for each pool. [*CAA 2001, ss 53, 54, 55(1)*].

A writing-down allowance is available for a chargeable period where the 'available qualifying expenditure' (see **5.36** below) in the particular pool for that period exceeds the total of any 'disposal values' (see **5.41** below) falling to be brought into account, unless the period is the 'final chargeable period' (in which case a balancing allowance will be available — see **5.46** below).

The allowance is currently given at the rate of 18% of the excess per annum, except in the case of special rate expenditure or an overseas leasing pool (8%; see **5.49** and **6.47** below). See **5.35** below for the 100% writing-down allowance for balances of £1,000 or less in the main or special rate pool.

For chargeable periods beginning before 6 April 2012 (1 April 2012 for corporation tax purposes), the allowance were given at the rate of 20% per annum, except in the case of special rate expenditure (10%) or an overseas leasing pool (10%). For chargeable periods beginning before and ending on or after 6 April 2012 (or 1 April 2012), the 20% rate is replaced by a hybrid rate calculated by reference to the proportion of the period falling before, and that falling on or after, that date. The rate is found using the formula:

$$x = \left(20 \times \frac{BRD}{CP}\right) + \left(18 \times \frac{ARD}{CP}\right)$$

where:

x = the rate (rounded up to two decimal places);

BRD = the number of days in the chargeable period before 6 April 2012 (or 1 April 2012 for corporation tax purposes);

ARD = the number of days in the chargeable period on and after 6 April 2012 (or 1 April 2012); and

CP = the total number of days in the chargeable period.

Similar transitional provisions apply in relation to special rate expenditure but by reference to 10% and 8% rates: see **5.49** below.

For chargeable periods beginning before 6 April 2008 (1 April 2008 for corporation tax purposes), the allowance was given at the rate of 25% per annum, except in the case of a long-life asset pool (6%; see **5.66** below) or an overseas leasing pool (10%). For chargeable periods beginning before, but ending on or after, 6 April 2008 (or 1 April 2008), the 25% rate is replaced by a hybrid rate calculated by reference to the proportion of the period falling before, and that falling on or after, that date. The rate is found using the formula:

$$x = \left(25 \times \frac{BRD}{CP}\right) + \left(20 \times \frac{ARD}{CP}\right)$$

where x, BRD, ARD and CP are defined as above, except by reference to 1/6 April 2008 rather than 1/6 April 2012.

HMRC have made available a ready reckoner for calculating the hybrid rate, which can be accessed at www.cahrcalculator.gov.uk/CAHR01.aspx.

Similar transitional provisions apply in relation to long-life asset pools, but by reference to 6% and 10% rates: see **5.69** below.

The reductions in the rate from 25% to 20% and from 20% to 18% do not apply to qualifying expenditure incurred wholly for the purposes of a ring fence trade (see **5.40** below) to which the supplementary charge in *CTA 2010, s 330(1)* applies. Writing-down allowances continue at a rate of 25% per annum for such expenditure.

If the chargeable period is longer than a year, the writing-down allowance is proportionately increased. Where the chargeable period is shorter than a year, or the qualifying activity is carried on only for part of the period, the allowance is proportionately reduced.

After deducting any writing-down allowance, any remaining balance left in the pool (the '*unrelieved qualifying expenditure*') is carried forward to the next chargeable period to form part of the available qualifying expenditure for that period. This amount is usually referred to as the 'written-down value'. No unrelieved qualifying expenditure can be carried forward from the final chargeable period. See **5.33** and **5.34** below for further circumstances in which unrelieved qualifying expenditure cannot be carried forward.

A writing-down allowance may be reduced to an amount specified in the claim.

For the purposes of the main pool, the '*final chargeable period*' is the chargeable period in which the qualifying activity is permanently discontinued. For the meaning of the term for class and single asset pools, see **5.48** onwards below.

[*CAA 2001, s 55(1), (2), (4), s 56(1)–(5), s 59(1)–(3), s 65(1); FA 2011, s 10(2)(4)(8)–(13)*].

For the treatment of an additional VAT liability, see **17.53** below.

Person entering the cash basis

[5.33] Plant and machinery allowances are not available to a person carrying on a trade, profession, vocation or property business to which the cash basis applies, except in relation to expenditure on the provision of a car (as defined at **5.51** below). See **17.1D** below.

Accordingly, where a person 'enters the cash basis' for a tax year, no 'cash basis deductible amount' may be carried forward as unrelieved qualifying expenditure from the chargeable period ending with the basis period for the previous tax year (or, where the qualifying activity is a property business, the chargeable period which is the previous tax year). This rule does not apply to expenditure on the provision of a car. A '*cash basis deductible amount*' is any amount that would have been deductible on the cash basis if it had been paid in the tax year for which the person enters the cash basis. For 2016/17 and earlier years, the rule was simply that no unrelieved qualifying expenditure could be carried forward unless it was on a car. Except where unrelieved qualifying expenditure is in a single asset pool, the amounts that can and cannot be carried forward must be determined on a just and reasonable basis.

For this purpose, a person carrying on a trade, profession or vocation '*enters the cash basis*' for a tax year if a cash basis election has effect for that year and such an election did not have effect immediately before the beginning of the basis period for that year. A person carrying on a property business '*enters the cash basis*' for a tax year if profits are calculated on the cash basis for that tax year but were not so calculated for the preceding tax year.

[*CAA 2001, s 59(4)–(7A); ITTOIA 2005, s 240B; FA 2013, Sch 4 paras 38, 47; F(No 2)A 2017, Sch 2 paras 52, 64*].

Although capital allowances are not available in respect of the unrelieved qualifying expenditure which is not carried forward, a deduction for that expenditure is allowable in the first cash basis year. This rule applies only to the extent that the amounts of expenditure in question are cash basis deductible amounts. Special rules apply if the plant or machinery in question has not been paid for in full. If the capital allowances given in respect of 'relevant expenditure' exceed the amount actually paid, the difference is treated as a receipt in calculating the profits for the first cash basis year. If the amount paid exceeds the allowances the excess is allowed as a deduction in that year. If the amount of the allowances was reduced because the asset was provided or used only partly for the purposes of the trade, profession or vocation or property business (see **5.56** below), the relevant expenditure is similarly proportionately reduced in making the comparison. '*Relevant expenditure*' is any amount of expenditure which is a cash basis deductible amount. For 2016/17 and earlier years, '*relevant expenditure*' was simply expenditure on plant or machinery (other than a car). The amount of capital allowances given and whether or to what extent expenditure is relevant expenditure are determined on a just and reasonable basis.

Where a person (the 'successor') enters the cash basis for a tax year and plant or machinery is treated as sold to him during the basis period for that tax year (or, in the case of a property business, during that tax year) as a result of an election under the provisions at **7.18** below (successions between connected persons), these rules apply as if everything done to or by the predecessor (i.e. the person previously carrying on the trade, profession or vocation) had been done to or by the successor and any expenditure actually incurred by the successor on acquiring the plant or machinery is not deductible under the cash basis.[

ITTOIA 2005, ss 240C, 240D, 240E, 334B–334E; FA 2013, Sch 4 para 38; F(No 2)A 2017, Sch 2 paras 7, 9, 29, 64].

See **17.1D** below for the requirement to bring into account a disposal value or balancing charge in certain cases where qualifying expenditure was incurred before entry into the cash basis which would not have been deductible under the cash basis if it had been incurred in the first cash basis year. See **5.47** below where a person leaves the cash basis.

For 2017/18 onwards, similar provisions apply where a person carrying on a trade enters the cash basis in respect of mineral extraction, patent and know-how allowances. See **10.2A** and **12.1A** below.

Vehicle for which fixed rate deduction made

[5.34] For income tax purposes for 2013/14 onwards, a person carrying on a trade, profession or vocation may choose to apply a fixed rate deduction under *TTOIA 2005, s 94D* for expenditure on a vehicle rather than claiming capital allowances for the cost of the vehicle and a deduction for other expenditure (such as repairs, fuel etc.). Where the fixed rate deduction option is chosen at the time the vehicle is acquired, expenditure on the vehicle is not qualifying expenditure — see **4.20**(g) above. Where the taxpayer initially claims capital allowances it is possible subsequently to switch to the fixed rate deduction. Where, therefore:

(a) at the end of the basis period for a tax year, the person has unrelieved qualifying expenditure incurred on a vehicle to carry forward from the period of account ending with that basis period;
(b) in calculating the profits of the trade, profession or vocation for the following tax year a fixed rate deduction is made in respect of the vehicle; and
(c) the person does not enter the cash basis for the following tax year;

none of the unrelieved qualifying expenditure can be carried forward from the period of account in (a) above. If the expenditure is not in a single asset pool, the amount of the unrelieved qualifying expenditure in respect of the vehicle is to be determined on a just and reasonable basis.

Note that any allowances already obtained in respect of the expenditure on the vehicle are not withdrawn. Once a fixed rate deduction for a particular vehicle has been obtained for a period, it is compulsory for all subsequent periods for that vehicle; it is not possible to switch back to capital allowances.

[*CAA 2001, s 59(8)–(10); FA 2013, Sch 5 paras 5(3), 6*].

Small balance on main pool or special rate pool

[5.35] For chargeable periods beginning on or after 6 April 2008 (1 April 2008 for corporation tax purposes), where the amount by which the available qualifying expenditure in either the main pool or the special rate pool for the period exceeds the total of any 'disposal values' (see **5.41** below) falling to be brought into account by £1,000 or less, a writing-down allowance of an amount up to 100% of that excess can be claimed in respect of that pool.

If the chargeable period is longer than a year, the £1,000 limit is proportionately increased. Where the chargeable period is shorter than a year, or the qualifying activity is carried on only for part of the period, the limit is proportionately reduced. The Treasury can alter the limit by order.

[*CAA 2001, s 56A*].

This provision is intended to reduce the compliance burden for small businesses where, following the introduction of the annual investment allowance, existing pools are unlikely to grow in future (Treasury Explanatory Notes to the 2008 Finance Bill).

Available qualifying expenditure

[5.36] The '*available qualifying expenditure*' in a particular pool for a chargeable period is made up of any qualifying expenditure allocated to the pool for the period (see below) plus any unrelieved qualifying expenditure (see **5.32** above) in the pool brought forward from the previous chargeable period. The available qualifying expenditure for a period may also include certain other amounts which are to be allocated to the pool for the period under the following provisions:

(a) *CAA 2001, s 26(3)* (demolition costs — see **5.37** below);
(b) *CAA 2001, ss 86(2)* or *87(2)* (available qualifying expenditure in a short-life asset pool to be allocated to the main pool in the circumstances mentioned at **5.61** and **5.63** below);
(c) *CAA 2001, s 111(3)* (overseas leasing — see **6.51** below);
(d) *CAA 2001, ss 129(1), 132(2), 133(3),* or *137* (special provisions relating to ships — see **5.72** onwards below);
(e) *CAA 2001, s 161C(2)* (North Sea oil industry decommissioning expenditure — see **5.39** below);
(f) *CAA 2001, s 165(3)* (North Sea oil industry general decommissioning expenditure — see **5.40** below);
(g) *CAA 2001, s 206(3)* (plant or machinery used partly for purposes other than those of a qualifying activity — see **5.55** below); and
(h) *CAA 2001, s 211(4)* (partial depreciation subsidy paid — see **7.14** below).

The available qualifying expenditure does not, however, include expenditure excluded under the provisions preventing double allowances (see **2.2** above) or expenditure excluded under specific anti-avoidance provisions.

See **5.38** below for special provisions relating to finance lessors.

In allocating qualifying expenditure to a particular pool, the following rules must be applied.

(1) An amount is not to be allocated to a pool if it has been taken into account in determining the available qualifying expenditure for an earlier chargeable period.
(2) Expenditure is not to be allocated to a pool for a chargeable period before that in which it is incurred.
(3) Expenditure is not to be allocated to a pool for a chargeable period unless the person owns the plant or machinery at some time in the period.

Nothing in these rules requires a person to allocate expenditure to a pool for the chargeable period in which it is incurred. Expenditure can be allocated instead for a later period (provided that the requirement in (3) above is still met). Of course, it would not normally be in a taxpayer's interest to delay allocation of expenditure to a pool, but this possibility would be useful where, for example, expenditure has not been allocated through an oversight.

For these purposes (and for the purposes of plant and machinery allowances generally), where a person incurs qualifying expenditure for the purposes of a qualifying activity which he is about to carry on, the expenditure is treated as being incurred on the first day on which the qualifying activity is carried on.

[*CAA 2001, ss 12, 57, 58(1)–(4); FA 2012, Sch 9 para 2, Sch 10 para 8; FA 2013, Sch 32 para 4*].

Where an annual investment allowance is claimed in respect of an amount of AIA qualifying expenditure (see **5.2** above), the amount must be allocated to the pool for the chargeable period in which it is incurred, but the available qualifying expenditure in the pool is then immediately reduced by the same amount. This provision enables a disposal value to be allocated to the pool on the disposal etc. of the assets concerned.

Where a first-year allowance is claimed in respect of an amount of first-year qualifying expenditure none of that amount can be allocated to the pool for the chargeable period in which it is incurred, unless a disposal event occurs in relation to the plant or machinery concerned in that period (see below). Only the balance remaining after deducting the allowance can be allocated to the pool for a subsequent chargeable period. Expenditure qualifying for first-year allowances can, however, be allocated to the pool for the chargeable period in which it is incurred where the taxpayer does not claim the allowance.

Equally, where the taxpayer has chosen to take a first-year allowance in respect of only part of any first-year qualifying expenditure incurred in a chargeable period, the remaining part of that expenditure can be allocated to the pool for that chargeable period. This enables a taxpayer to avoid a potential balancing charge (see **5.45** below) by increasing his available qualifying expenditure sufficiently to cover a disposal value (see **5.41** below).

Where a first-year allowance is made in respect of an amount of expenditure, the balance of the expenditure, or at least part of it, must be allocated to a pool for a chargeable period in which a disposal event occurs in relation to the plant or machinery concerned, if it has not been allocated for any previous period. Where a 100% first-year allowance is made, a nil balance is treated as so allocated. This provision enables a disposal value to be allocated to the pool in question, and may override the prohibition on allocating expenditure to a pool for the chargeable period in which it is incurred if a first-year allowance is claimed. It will normally be in the taxpayer's interest to allocate the entire balance.

[*CAA 2001, s 58(4A)–(7)*].

Demolition costs

[5.37] Where plant or machinery is demolished and its last use was for the purposes of a qualifying activity, then:

(a) if the person carrying on the qualifying activity replaces the plant or machinery, the net cost of demolition (i.e. the cost of demolition less any money received for the remains of the plant or machinery) is treated as expenditure incurred on the replacement plant or machinery; and
(b) if the plant or machinery is not replaced, the net cost of demolition is allocated to the appropriate pool for the chargeable period of demolition.

[*CAA 2001, s 26; FA 2013, Sch 32 para 3*].

Allocation of expenditure under leases

[5.38] There are provisions which allow only a proportion of capital expenditure incurred during a chargeable period on the provision of plant or machinery for leasing under certain types of lease to be taken into account in determining the available qualifying expenditure for that period.

For expenditure incurred on or after 1 April 2006, the provisions apply only to companies and only in limited circumstances involving groups. The company incurring the expenditure must be a member of a 'group' at the end of the 'period of account' (meaning, for this purpose, a period for which it draws up accounts) which is the 'basis period' for the chargeable period in which the expenditure is incurred, and the last day of the period of account must not be the last day of a period of account of the group's 'principal company'. A period of account is, for this purpose, the '*basis period*' for a chargeable period if the chargeable period coincides with, or falls within, the period of account. The terms '*group*' and '*principal company*' are defined as for capital gains purposes under *TCGA 1992, s 170(3)–(6)*. In applying the definitions, however, a subsidiary company that does not have ordinary share capital is treated as being a qualifying 75% subsidiary of another company if that other company has control of the subsidiary (within *CAA 2001, s 574*) and is beneficially entitled to at least 75% of any of the subsidiary's profits available for distribution to equity holders and would be beneficially entitled to at least 75% of the subsidiary's assets available to equity holders on a winding-up.

Previously, no such restrictions applied to the operation of the provisions.

The provisions apply to 'finance leases' (see **7.4** below) and, for expenditure incurred on or after 1 April 2006, 'qualifying operating leases', i.e. 'plant or machinery leases' (see **6.27** below) other than finance leases which are 'funding leases' (see **6.26** below) with a 'term' (see **6.22** below) of more than four years but not exceeding five years.

The proportion of the capital expenditure which can be taken into account in the chargeable period in which it is incurred is the same as the proportion of the chargeable period which falls after the time the expenditure was incurred, so that e.g. only one-quarter is brought in where expenditure is incurred ninety-one days before the end of a twelve-month period. HMRC consider that the apportionment is to be made using the number of whole days in each period for each item of expenditure.

These provisions do not apply where a disposal value is brought in in respect of the plant or machinery in the chargeable period in which the expenditure is incurred. They do not prevent the balance of the expenditure from being taken into account for any subsequent chargeable period.

[*CAA 2001, s 220*].

North Sea oil industry decommissioning expenditure

[5.39] Where a person carrying on a trade of oil extraction incurs 'decommissioning expenditure' in connection with plant or machinery which has been brought into use for the purposes of the trade and is 'offshore infrastructure' (or was when last in use for those purposes), the expenditure is allocated to the appropriate pool for the chargeable period in which it is incurred.

This provision does not apply in the case of plant or machinery which is 'UK infrastructure' unless the expenditure is incurred in connection with measures taken wholly or substantially to comply with an abandonment programme within the meaning of *Petroleum Act 1998, s 29* or any condition to which the approval of such a programme is subject. It also does not apply if an allowance or deduction could otherwise be made in respect of the expenditure in computing the person's income for tax purposes. See **5.40** below for the provision for an enhanced allowance in respect of 'general decommissioning expenditure' incurred by a person carrying on a 'ring fence trade' which may apply, by election, in place of this provision. See also **17.21** below for restrictions on allowances where either a connected person supplies decommissioning services or there is an avoidance purpose to a transaction.

Plant or machinery is '*offshore infrastructure*' for this purpose if it is:

(i) an offshore installation, or part of an offshore installation, within *Petroleum Act 1998, s 44*;
(ii) something that would be, or would be part of, such an installation if, in that *Act*, the meaning of 'offshore installation' included installations in waters in a foreign sector of the continental shelf and other foreign tidal waters;
(iii) a pipeline, or part of a pipeline, within *Petroleum Act 1998, s 26*, that is in, under or over, waters in the territorial sea adjacent to the UK or an area designated under *Continental Shelf Act 1964, s 1(7)*; or
(iv) a pipeline, or part of a pipeline, within *Petroleum Act 1998, s 26*, that is in, under or over, waters in a foreign sector of the continental shelf.

'*UK infrastructure*' is offshore infrastructure which is, or was when last in use for the purposes of the trade, within (i) or (iii) above.

'*Decommissioning expenditure*' is expenditure incurred in connection with

(a) preserving plant or machinery pending its reuse or demolition;
(b) preparing plant or machinery for reuse; or
(c) arranging for the reuse of plant or machinery.

Expenditure within (a)–(c) is decommissioning expenditure whether or not the plant or machinery is in fact reused, partly reused or demolished. Expenditure incurred on the demolition of offshore infrastructure is not decommissioning expenditure as it falls within the provisions at **5.37** above.

[*CAA 2001, ss 161A–161D; FA 2013, Sch 32 para 5*].

[5.40] A person carrying on a 'ring fence trade' can elect to have a special capital allowance for a chargeable period (the '*relevant chargeable period*') if he incurs 'general decommissioning expenditure' in the relevant chargeable period in respect of decommissioning carried out in that period or a previous period or if he incurred such expenditure in a previous period in respect of decommissioning that has not been carried out until the relevant chargeable period. The plant or machinery concerned must have been brought into use for the purposes of the ring fence trade. For expenditure incurred on decommissioning carried out on or after 17 July 2013, 'incidentally-acquired redundant plant or machinery' is deemed, for this purpose, to have been brought into use for such purposes.

'*Incidentally-acquired redundant plant or machinery*' is plant or machinery which has in fact not been brought into use for the purposes of the ring fence trade but which forms part of an offshore installation or submarine pipeline (within the meaning of *Petroleum Act 1998, Pt IV*) or an 'onshore installation' which has been brought into use for such purposes. The plant or machinery must not have been in use for any purpose when it was acquired and its acquisition must have been merely incidental to the acquisition of the interest in the installation or pipeline. An '*onshore installation*' is a building or structure within *Oil Taxation Act 1975, s 3(4)(c)(ii)–(iv)* which is not an offshore installation and which is or has been used for purposes connected with the winning of oil from an oil field any part of which lies within the territorial sea of the UK or an area designated under *Continental Shelf Act 1964, s 1(7)*.

For expenditure incurred before 22 April 2009 the election could be made by a person carrying on a ring fence trade who incurred general decommissioning expenditure (for expenditure incurred before 12 March 2008, 'abandonment expenditure') in relation to plant or machinery which had been brought into use for the purposes of the trade, for the chargeable period in which that expenditure was incurred (or, under the preceding year basis, for the chargeable period related to the incurring of the expenditure).

Where an election is made, the special allowance is, subject to the reductions below and the restrictions at **17.21** below (where either a connected person supplies decommissioning services or there is an avoidance purpose to a transaction), an amount equal to the amount of the expenditure to which the election relates. That amount does not then increase available qualifying expenditure as mentioned in **5.37**(b) or **5.39** above. The election is irrevocable, must specify the expenditure to which it relates and, in the case of demolition, any amounts received for the remains. For expenditure incurred after 21 April 2009, the election must also specify the chargeable period in which the expenditure was incurred, the decommissioning to which it relates and the chargeable period in which the decommissioning was carried out (the '*specified decommissioning period*'). The election must be made in writing within two years after the end of the chargeable period for which it is made.

For expenditure incurred after 21 April 2009, where the amount of expenditure to which an election relates is disproportionate to the decommissioning carried out in the specified decommissioning period, the election is treated as specifying only a proportionate amount of the expenditure. This does not prevent an election for a subsequent chargeable period being made in respect of the disallowed expenditure.

Where the plant or machinery concerned is demolished, the total of any special allowances is reduced by any amounts received for the remains, by setting the amount against the allowances for the chargeable period in which the amount is received. Any remaining part of the amount is then set off against special allowances for earlier periods (latest first) and if there is then any part of the amount remaining it is set off against special allowances for later periods (earliest first).

'*Ring fence trade*' means activities falling within *ITTOIA 2005, s 16* or *CTA 2010, s 274* (treatment of oil extraction activities etc. for tax purposes) and constituting a separate trade, whether or not under those provisions.

'*General decommissioning expenditure*' means expenditure incurred on 'decommissioning' plant or machinery which has been brought into use wholly or partly for the purposes of a ring fence trade, and which either:

(1) is, or forms part of, an offshore installation or submarine pipeline, or when last in use for the purposes of a ring fence trade was, or formed part of, such an installation or pipeline; or
(2) for expenditure incurred on decommissioning carried out on or after 17 July 2013, is, or forms part of, an onshore installation, or when last in use for the purposes of a ring fence trade was, or formed part of, such an installation.

Where (1) above applies, expenditure incurred after 21 April 2009 must be incurred wholly or substantially in complying with an approved abandonment programme, a condition to which the approval of an abandonment programme is subject or a condition imposed by (or an agreement made with) the Secretary of State, before the approval of an abandonment programme, in relation to the decommissioning of the plant or machinery. In either case, the plant or machinery decommissioned must not be replaced.

The amount of the expenditure qualifying as general decommissioning expenditure is reduced to an amount which is just and reasonable where it appears that the decommissioned plant and machinery was brought into use only partly for 'qualifying purposes' or has, at any time since it was brought into use, not been used wholly for qualifying purposes. Use for '*qualifying purposes*' is, for this purpose, use for the purposes of any ring fence trade of any person or other use (except use wholly or partly in connection with an oil field (within the meaning of *Oil Taxation Act 1975, s 12(2)*)) in the UK or its territorial sea or in an area designated under *Continental Shelf Act 1964, s 1(7)*. For expenditure incurred before 22 April 2009, use for '*qualifying purposes*' is use for the purposes of the ring fence trade.

'*Abandonment expenditure*' has the same meaning as general decommissioning expenditure, except that:

(a) the expenditure must be incurred for the purposes of, or in connection with, the closing down of, or of part of, an oil field;
(b) the decommissioning must be carried out, wholly or substantially, in compliance with an abandonment programme or with any condition to which the approval of such a programme is subject; and
(c) the 'just and reasonable' reduction for partial use other than for ring fence trade purposes does not apply.

For these purposes, '*decommissioning*', in relation to any plant or machinery, means:

- demolishing the plant or machinery,

- preserving the plant or machinery pending its reuse or demolition,
- preparing the plant or machinery for reuse, or
- arranging for the reuse of the plant or machinery.

It is immaterial whether the plant or machinery is in fact reused, demolished or partly reused and partly demolished.

A further relief applies where a person ('the former trader') ceases to carry on a ring fence trade (as defined above) and meets the 'decommissioning condition' in relation to a 'notional accounting period'. The general decommissioning expenditure concerned must not otherwise be tax-deductible.

For this purpose, the '*decommissioning condition*' is met in relation to a notional accounting period (the '*relevant period*') if the former trader incurs general decommissioning expenditure in that period in respect of decommissioning carried out in that period, in a previous notional accounting period or in a chargeable period before the first notional accounting period. The condition is also so met if the former trader incurred general decommissioning expenditure in a previous notional accounting period or a chargeable period before the first notional accounting period in respect of decommissioning which has not been carried out until the relevant period. Each of the following is a '*notional accounting period*': the period beginning with the day following the last day on which the former trader carried on the ring fence trade and ending with the day on which the first 'termination event' occurs; and each period beginning with the day following the last day of a notional accounting period and ending with the day of the first subsequent termination event. There can, however, be no notional accounting periods after the end of the 'post-cessation period'. '*Termination events*' are:

(A) the end of the period of twelve months beginning with the first day of the notional accounting period;

(B) the occurrence of the accounting date of the former trader or, if there is a period for which the former trader does not make up accounts, the end of that period; and

(C) the end of the post-cessation period.

If the former trader carries on more than one trade and makes up accounts of any of them to different dates, then if he does not make up general accounts for the whole of the company's activities, (B) above applies by reference to the accounting date of one of the trades, to be determined by the former trader, or by HMRC where they consider that the former trader's choice is inappropriate.

For expenditure incurred after 30 June 1991 and before 22 April 2009, the provisions applied where the former trader ceased to carry on a ring fence trade and within the post-cessation period, incurred general decommissioning expenditure (for expenditure incurred before 12 March 2008, abandonment expenditure) which is not otherwise tax-deductible.

Where the trade ceases on or after 12 March 2008, the '*post-cessation period*' is the period beginning with the day after that on which the trade ceased and ending with the day on which the following two conditions are both met (or, if they are met on different days, the later of those days). The conditions are that:

(i) each approved abandonment programme (within *Petroleum Act 1998, Pt 4*) that relates wholly or partly to 'relevant plant and machinery' has ceased to have effect; and

(ii) the Secretary of State is satisfied that no other abandonment programmes relating wholly or partly to such plant and machinery will be approved.

For the purpose of (i) above, '*relevant plant and machinery*' is plant and machinery which has been brought into use for the purposes of the trade which has ceased, and which, when last in use for the purposes of that trade was, or formed part of, an offshore installation or submarine pipeline (within *Petroleum Act 1998, Pt 4*). An approved abandonment programme ceases to have effect if and when it has been carried out to the satisfaction of the Secretary of State or approval has been withdrawn under *Petroleum Act 1998, Pt* 4.

Where the trade ceases before 12 March 2008, the post-cessation period is the three years after the date of cessation.

For expenditure incurred after 21 April 2009, where the relief applies to a notional accounting period, an amount equal to the 'relevant decommissioning cost' for that period, or the aggregate of all general decommissioning costs for that period, is allocated to the appropriate pool for the chargeable period in which the ring fence trade ceased. This rule is subject to the restrictions at **17.21** below (where either a connected person supplies decommissioning services or there is an avoidance purpose to a transaction). For expenditure incurred before 22 April 2009, the relief applied in simpler terms: an amount equal to the relevant decommissioning cost was allocated to the appropriate pool for the chargeable period in which the trade ceased.

For expenditure incurred after 21 April 2009, the '*relevant decommissioning cost*' for a notional accounting period is the general decommissioning expenditure by reference to which the decommissioning condition is met for that period less any amounts received before or during the period for the remains of any plant or machinery on whose demolition any of the expenditure was incurred. Previously, the '*relevant decommissioning cost*' meant the amount by which the general decommissioning expenditure (or abandonment expenditure) exceeded any amount received in the post-cessation period for the remains of any plant or machinery on whose demolition any of the expenditure was incurred.

Any amounts received for the remains of plant or machinery which are set against general decommissioning or abandonment expenditure are not then to be treated as taxable income.

Adjustments of assessments, whether by discharge or repayment of tax or otherwise, may be made to give effect to this relief.

For expenditure incurred after 21 April 2009, if an amount of expenditure is disproportionate to the decommissioning carried out, only a proportionate amount of the expenditure is treated as having been incurred in the notional accounting period concerned. This does not prevent the disallowed expenditure being taken into account in relation to a subsequent notional accounting period.

Where the trade ceases on or after 12 March 2008, expenditure is excluded from these provisions if it is incurred after an abandonment programme relating wholly or partly to relevant plant and machinery has had its approval withdrawn if no other abandonment programme relating wholly or partly to the plant and machinery is then approved. It is, however, immaterial for the purposes of these provisions whether approval of an abandonment programmed relating to relevant plant and machinery is given before or after the start of the post-cessation period.

[*CAA 2001, ss 162(2), 163–165, Sch 3 paras 26, 27; FA 2013, ss 90, 91, Sch 32 paras 6, 7*].

For the carrying back of losses referable to an allowance for general decommissioning or abandonment expenditure, see **2.38** above.

Disposal value

[5.41] Writing-down allowances are calculated for each pool in respect of any chargeable period (other than the final chargeable period) on the excess of available qualifying expenditure over any 'disposal value'. A person who has incurred qualifying expenditure on plant or machinery is required to bring a disposal value into account in a chargeable period on the happening of one of the following events.

(i) The person ceases to own the plant or machinery. Before *CAA 2001* had effect (see **1.2** above), this provision was expressed in terms of the plant or machinery ceasing to belong to the person.
(ii) The person loses possession of the plant or machinery in circumstances where it is reasonable to assume that the loss is permanent.
(iii) In the case of plant or machinery in use for mineral exploration and access, the person abandons it at the site where it was in use for that purpose.
(iv) The plant or machinery ceases to exist as such (whether through destruction, dismantling or otherwise).
(v) It begins to be used wholly or partly for purposes other than those of the qualifying activity.
(vi) The qualifying activity is permanently discontinued.
(vii) The vesting of the plant or machinery in the trustee for civil recovery or any other person by a recovery order made under *PCA 2002, Part 5* or in pursuance of an order made under *PCA 2002, s 276* (i.e. a '*Part 5* transfer' of the plant or machinery — see **2.29** above).
(viii) The plant or machinery begins to be leased under a long funding lease (see **6.21–6.40** below).

In addition to the above events, the following provisions may also require a disposal value to be brought into account:

(1) *CAA 2001, s 67* (hire purchase: cessation of notional ownership — see **7.9** below);
(2) *CAA 2001, ss 72, 73* (grant of new software right — see **4.19** above);
(3) *CAA 2001, ss 111, 114* (overseas leasing: recovery of allowances — see **6.51** below);

(4) *CAA 2001, s 132* (ships — see **5.75** below);
(5) *CAA 2001, ss 140, 143* (ships; attribution of deferred balancing charge — see **5.75** below);
(6) *CAA 2001, s 169* (oil production sharing contracts — see **7.20** below);
(7) *CAA 2001, s 208* (significant reduction in proportion of business use of plant or machinery — see **5.56** below);
(8) *CAA 2001, s 211* (partial depreciation subsidy paid — see **7.14** below);
(9) *CAA 2001, s 238* (additional VAT rebates — see **17.53** below);
(10) *ITA 2007, s 614BS; CTA 2010, s 918* (finance lease: receipt of major lump sum — see **17.8** below);
(11) *ITTOIA 2005, s 825* (special provisions for qualifying carers — see **17.44** below);
(12) *CAA 2001, s 70E* (disposal event in relation to long funding lease — see **6.37** below);
(13) *FA 2009, Sch 61 paras 15–17* (alternative finance investment bonds — see **17.46** below);
(14) *FA 2013, s 73(8)* (disposal value to be brought into account in a chargeable period including 29 May 2013 following changes to the rules for contribution allowances — see **2.8**(iv) above); and
(15) *CAA 2001, s 218ZB* (disposal of plant of machinery in avoidance cases — see **7.3B** below).

There are also special provisions relating to fixtures under leases — see **6.17** below.

An event requiring a disposal value to be brought into account is known as a '*disposal event*'.

A disposal value is only required to be brought into account in respect of a particular item of plant or machinery in connection with the first disposal event, except in the case of events within (2), (5) and (9) above. An event within (14) above is not a disposal event for this purpose.

[*CAA 2001, ss 60, 61(1), 66; PCA 2002, Sch 10 paras 2(1), 12; FA 2013, s 73(11); FA 2016, s 70(10)*].

The amount of disposal value depends on the nature of the disposal event, as follows.

(a) On a sale, except where (b) or (c) below applies, the disposal value equals the net sale proceeds (see **2.33** above) plus any insurance moneys received by reason of any event affecting the price obtainable and any other compensation consisting of capital sums.
(b) On a sale below market value, the disposal value is market value unless
    (i) the buyer's expenditure qualifies for either plant and machinery or research and development (formerly scientific research) allowances, and the buyer is not a dual resident investing company (within *CTA 2010, s 949*) connected (within **2.34** above) with the seller, or
    (ii) there is a charge to tax under *ITEPA 2003*.
(c) On a sale below market value, the disposal value is market value if:

- (i) the seller is a company or a partnership with one or more corporate partners and before the sale the plant or machinery is used wholly or partly for the purposes of a qualifying activity which is not an NI rate activity for the purposes of the Northern Ireland rate of corporation tax (see **17.46B** below); and
- (ii) the buyer is an SME (NI employer) company, NIRE company, NI Chapter 6 firm or NI Chapter 7 firm in the chargeable period in which it buys the plant or machinery, the expenditure is qualifying expenditure under the plant and machinery or research and development codes and the plant or machinery is used by the buyer wholly or partly for the purposes of a NI rate activity.

(d) On demolition or destruction, the disposal value is equal to the net amount received for the remains plus any insurance and other compensation consisting of capital sums received.

(e) On the abandonment of plant or machinery used for mineral exploration or access at the site at which it was used, the disposal value is any insurance money and other compensation consisting of capital sums received.

(f) On permanent loss otherwise than in consequence of demolition or destruction, the disposal value is any insurance and other compensation consisting of capital sums received.

(g) On plant or machinery beginning to be leased under a long funding lease, the disposal value depends on whether the lease is a long funding finance lease or a long funding operating lease (see **6.22** below). If the lease is a long funding finance lease whose inception is on or after 13 November 2008, the disposal value is the greater of the market value of the plant or machinery at the commencement of the term of the lease and the 'qualifying lease payments'. For such leases whose inception is before that date, the disposal value is the amount that would be recognised as the lessor's net investment in the lease if accounts were prepared in accordance with generally accepted accounting practice on the date (the '*relevant date*') on which the lessor's net investment in the lease is first recognised in his books or other financial records. If the lease is a long funding operating lease, the disposal value is the market value of the plant or machinery at the commencement of the term of the lease (see **6.22** below).

The '*qualifying lease payments*' are the minimum payments under the lease, including any initial payment, but excluding so much of any payment as falls, or would fall, under generally accepted accounting practice, to be treated as the gross return on investment and so much of any payment as represents charges for services or UK or foreign tax or duty payable by the lessor other than income tax, corporation tax or similar tax.

In determining the disposal value in respect of the commencement of a long funding finance lease whose inception is before 13 November 2008, the following applies. For such leases granted on or after 13 December 2007, rentals under the lease made or due on or before the relevant date are treated for this purpose as made and due after that date. For such leases granted on or after 12 March 2008, the lessor is treated as having no 'liabilities' of any kind at any time on the relevant date (but only if this would increase the disposal value). Where the lessor is a company, liabilities for this purpose include any share capital issued by the company which falls to be treated as a liability for accounting purposes.

(h) On the permanent discontinuance of the qualifying activity before the occurrence of any of the above mentioned events, the disposal value is the same as the value specified for that event. In practice, where there is likely to be a long delay between the date of cessation of trade and any of the above events, HMRC take market value at the date of cessation as being the disposal value (CCAB Memorandum, June 1971).

(i) On a *PCA 2002, Part 5* transfer, the disposal value is determined as follows.

  (i) If a compensating payment (as defined at **2.29** above) is made to the transferor, the disposal value is the amount of the payment.

  (ii) If no compensating payment is made and the plant or machinery was allocated to the main pool or a class pool, the disposal value is equal to the notional written-down value of the qualifying expenditure, calculated on the assumption that the plant or machinery in question was the only item provided for the qualifying activity (and therefore was the only item in its pool) and that all allowances had been made in full. Where, however, the transfer takes place in the same chargeable period as that in which the qualifying expenditure was incurred and a first-year allowance is made, the disposal value is equal to the balance left after deducting that allowance.

  (iii) If no compensating payment is made and the plant or machinery was allocated to a single asset pool, the disposal value is such amount as gives rise neither to a balancing allowance nor a balancing charge.

  (iv) If the qualifying activity is carried on in partnership, the plant or machinery is partnership property (see *Partnership Act 1890, ss 20, 21*), and compensating payments are made to one or more, but not all, of the partners, the disposal value is the aggregate of all the compensating payments and, for each partner not receiving a compensating payment, his share of the '*tax-neutral amount*' (being the amount that would have been the disposal value under (ii) or (iii) above had those provisions applied). For this purpose, a partner's share of the tax-neutral amount is determined according to the partnership's profit-sharing arrangements for the twelve months prior to the transfer.

  (v) If the qualifying activity is carried on in partnership, the plant or machinery is not partnership property but is owned by two or more of the partners and is used for the purposes of the qualifying activity, and compensating payments are made to one or more, but not all, of the owners, the disposal value is the aggregate of all the compensating payments and, for each owner not receiving a compensating payment, his share of the tax-neutral amount. For this purpose, an owner's share of the tax-neutral amount is determined in proportion to the value of his interest in the plant or machinery.

(j) On the plant or machinery beginning to be used for purposes other than those of a qualifying activity as a result of the coming into force of an election under *CTA 2009, s 18A* (exemption for profits of foreign permanent establishments of companies — see **17.36** below), the disposal value is the transition value (see **17.36** below).

(k) On any other event, the disposal value is the market value at the time of the event.

For the disposal value in the case of any of the disposal events within (1) to (13) above, see the appropriate paragraph referred to in the list. For further provisions determining the disposal value in certain cases, see also **5.49** (special rate expenditure: cushion gas and anti-avoidance provisions) **5.52** and **5.53** (cars: anti-avoidance), **5.64** (short-life assets: disposal at under-value or to connected person), **5.70** (long-life assets: anti-avoidance), **7.4** (anti-avoidance: sale and finance leaseback), **17.16** (disposal of plant or machinery subject to lease where income retained) and **17.20** (arrangements reducing disposal value of leased asset: anti-avoidance) below.

In no case can the disposal value exceed the qualifying expenditure incurred by the person required to bring it into account, except in certain circumstances where he has acquired the plant or machinery as a result of one or more transactions between connected persons (within **2.34** above), for which see **7.2** below.

A person is not required to bring into account a disposal value for a chargeable period in respect of qualifying expenditure which has not been taken into account in determining the available qualifying expenditure in the pool for that or any earlier chargeable period. See **5.36** above for the position where a first-year allowance has been made. See also **7.2** below for an exception to this rule in relation to transactions with connected persons.

[*CAA 2001, ss 61(2)–(4B)(5A), 62, 64(1), 66; PCA 2002, Sch 10 paras 13–17; FA 2011, s 48, Sch 13 para 16; CTNIA 2015, Sch 1 para 6; F(No 2)A 2017, Sch 7 para 24*].

Cases where disposal value is nil

[5.42] In the following circumstances, the disposal value to be brought into account is nil.

(a) Where plant or machinery is disposed of by way of gift in such circumstances that there is a charge to tax under *ITEPA 2003*, presumably on the recipient. [*CAA 2001, s 63(1); ITEPA 2003, Sch 6 para 250*].

(b) Where plant or machinery is disposed of by way of gift by a person carrying on a trade, profession or vocation or a property business within **4.4** above to a 'designated educational establishment'. [*CAA*

2001, s 63(2)(c)(3); FA 2011, Sch 14 para 12(10)]. For what constitutes a 'designated educational establishment', see *Taxes (Relief for Gifts) (Designated Educational Establishments) Regulations 1992 (SI 1992 No 42)*.

(c) Where plant or machinery is disposed of by way of gift by a person carrying on a trade, profession or vocation or a property business within **4.4** above to a 'charity' (see now *FA 2010, Sch 6 paras 1–7*) or to the Trustees of the National Heritage Memorial Fund; the Historic Buildings and Monuments Commission for England; the Trustees of the British Museum; or the Trustees of the Natural History Museum. The relief also applies to gifts made to registered community amateur sports clubs (within the meaning of *CTA 2010, Pt 13 Ch 9*). [*CAA 2001, s 63(2)(a)(b)(3); FA 2010, Sch 6 paras 16, 33, 34 FA 2011, Sch 14 para 12(10)*].

(d) Where expenditure is treated as having been incurred on plant or machinery under the provisions at **4.20** above. [*CAA 2001, s 63(5)*].

With regard to the reliefs at (b) and (c) above, if the donor or any connected person (within **2.34** above) receives any benefit in any way attributable to the gift, a charge to tax will arise under *ITTOIA 2005, s 109* or *CTA 2009, s 108*.

EXAMPLE 10

[5.43]

X, an individual trader, has for many years made up his accounts to 30 April each year and during the year ended 30 April 2015 incurs capital expenditure of £40,000 on plant and machinery. He also sells in that year plant and machinery costing £10,000 and receives net proceeds of £9,000 being equivalent to market value. Among the items sold is a machine which originally cost £1,000 and is sold for £1,200. He makes a gift during the year of a word processor (previously used in his trade) to his mother who uses it at home for personal correspondence; the word processor is valued at £100 (less than cost) at the date of the gift and his mother is not at that date his employee. In addition to the sales mentioned above, he sells an item of machinery to his brother for £500 (market value £1,000); his brother is also trading and will be entitled to capital allowances on his purchase of this item. X has unrelieved qualifying expenditure in the main pool of £60,000 brought forward at 30 April 2014.

X's plant and machinery allowances for the year ended 30 April 2014, assuming he claims all allowances to which he is entitled, will be calculated as follows.

	Main pool of expenditure	*Total allowances*
	£	£
WDV b/fwd	60,000	
Additions	40,000	
	100,000	
AIA	(40,000)	40,000
	60,000	
Disposal value (see **5.42** above)	(9,400)	
	51,600	
WDA 18%	(9,288)	9,288
WDV c/fwd	£42,312	

	Main pool of expenditure	*Total allowances*
	£	£
Total allowances claimed		£49,288

EXAMPLE 11

[5.44]

The trader in *Example 10* in **5.43** above makes no additions or disposals in the year ended 30 April 2016. Assuming that X makes a claim for the full amount of writing-down allowances, those allowances are calculated as follows.

	Main pool of expenditure	*Total allowances*
	£	£
Written-down value brought forward	42,312	
Writing-down allowances at 18%	7,616	7,616
Written-down value carried forward	£34,696	
Total allowances claimed		£7,616

If X again makes no additions or disposals in the year ended 30 April 2017, his capital allowances for that year will amount to £6,245, i.e. 18% of the written-down value brought forward of £34,696. If, however, X has a trading profit for that year, as adjusted for tax purposes but before capital allowances, of £14,000, has no other taxable income and wishes to utilise fully his personal allowance for 2017/18, which amounts to £11,500, he might wish to restrict his writing-down allowances to £2,500 so as to leave £11,500 within the charge to tax. If he restricts his claim accordingly as in **5.32** above, the computation proceeds as follows for the year ended 30 April 2017.

	Main pool of expenditure	*Total allowances*
	£	£
Written-down value brought forward	34,696	
Writing-down allowances restricted to	2,500	2,500
Written-down value carried forward	£32,196	
Total allowances claimed		£2,500

Balancing allowances and charges

[5.45] For any chargeable period (including the final chargeable period; see **5.32** above) any excess of disposal value over available qualifying expenditure in a pool will give rise to a balancing charge equal to the difference. [*CAA 2001, ss 55(3), 56(6)*].

[5.46] A balancing allowance can only arise in relation to a particular pool in the final chargeable period (see **5.32** above) and is equal to the excess, if any, of available qualifying expenditure over disposal value in that period. [*CAA 2001, s 55(2)(4), s 56(7)*]. See **17.25** below where a company transfers a trade for the purpose of obtaining a balancing allowance.

Person leaving the cash basis

[5.47] The following provisions apply where a person carrying on a trade, profession, vocation or property business leaves the cash basis (see **17.1A** below) in a chargeable period having incurred expenditure which would have been qualifying expenditure if it had not been incurred at a time when the cash basis applied. At least some of the expenditure must have been brought into account in calculating the profits of the business on the cash basis.

A person carrying on a trade, profession or vocation leaves the cash basis in a chargeable period for this purpose if immediately before the beginning of the period a cash basis election had effect but such an election does not have effect for the period itself. A person carrying on a property business leaves the cash basis in a chargeable period if profits are calculated in accordance with generally accepted accounting practice for the tax year which is the chargeable period but were calculated on the cash basis for the preceding tax year.

For the purpose of determining any entitlement to an annual investment allowance or first-year allowance, a person is treated as incurring the 'unrelieved portion' of the expenditure in the chargeable period in which he leaves the cash basis. For the purposes of determining the person's available qualifying expenditure (see **5.32** above) in a pool for the chargeable period in which he leaves the cash basis the whole of the expenditure must be allocated to the appropriate pool or pools and the available qualifying expenditure in each affected pool is then reduced by the 'relieved portion' of the expenditure allocated to it. These provisions provide for allowances where plant or machinery has not been fully paid for when the person leaves the cash basis, such as under a hire purchase agreement (see **7.7** below).

The '*relieved portion*' of expenditure is the higher of the amount for which a deduction has been allowed in computing the business profits and the amount for which such a deduction would have been allowed if the expenditure had been incurred wholly and exclusively for the purposes of the business. The '*unrelieved portion*' is any remaining amount of the expenditure.

For the purpose of determining any disposal values (see **5.41** above), the expenditure is treated as qualifying expenditure. As a result, where there is a disposal event in relation to the plant or machinery after the person leaves the cash basis, a disposal value must be brought into account in the pool to which the expenditure was allocated in the chargeable period in which the person left the cash basis.

[*CAA 2001, s 66A; FA 2013, Sch 4 para 48; F(No 2)A 2017, Sch 2 paras 53, 64*].

For similar provisions which apply in respect of mineral extraction, patent and know-how allowances. See **10.2A** and **12.1A** below.

Items excluded from the main pool of qualifying expenditure

[5.48] There are a number of items which do not form part of the main pool. Expenditure on such items is instead allocated either to a class pool or a single asset pool. A single asset pool cannot contain expenditure relating to more than one asset, whereas a class pool will include all expenditure on assets within the 'class' concerned. [*CAA 2001, s 54(2)(4)*]. These items are considered in **5.49–5.79** below.

Special rate expenditure

[5.49] 'Special rate expenditure' incurred wholly and exclusively for the purposes of a qualifying activity must, if allocated to a pool, be allocated to a class pool, known as the special rate pool. This does not apply to expenditure required to be allocated to a single asset pool. Where part only of expenditure on an asset is special rate expenditure, that part and the remainder are each treated as expenditure on a separate item of plant or machinery, any necessary apportionment being made on a just and reasonable basis. The final chargeable period (see **5.32** above) for the special rate pool is that in which the qualifying activity is permanently discontinued

Subject to the transitional rules below, '*special rate expenditure*' is:

(a) expenditure incurred on or after 6 April 2008 (1 April 2008 for corporation tax purposes) on thermal insulation of a building within **4.17**(b) above;
(b) expenditure incurred on or after that date on integral features of a building or structure within **4.23** above;
(c) long-life asset expenditure within **5.66** below incurred on or after that date;
(d) long-life asset expenditure incurred before that date but not allocated to a pool until a chargeable period beginning on or after that date;
(e) expenditure on or after 6 April 2009 (1 April 2009 for corporation tax purposes) on the provision of a car which is not a 'main rate car' (see **5.52** below);
(f) expenditure incurred on or after 1 April 2010 on the provision of cushion gas (i.e. gas which functions, or is intended to function, as plant in a particular gas storage facility); and
(g) expenditure on or after 6 April 2012 (1 April 2012 for corporation tax purposes) on the provision of solar panels.

See also **5.66** below for the transfer of the unrelieved balance of the long-life asset pool to the special rate pool at the end of the first chargeable period ending on or after 5 April 2008 (31 March 2008 for corporation tax purposes). Unrelieved long-life asset expenditure in a single asset pool at the end of the first such chargeable period is treated as special rate expenditure in subsequent chargeable periods.

Writing-down allowances in respect of special rate expenditure are given at the rate of 8% per annum. This applies both to expenditure within the special rate pool and expenditure in a single asset pool. If the chargeable period is longer than a year, the writing-down allowance is proportionately increased. Where the chargeable period is shorter than a year, or the qualifying activity is carried on only for part of the period, the allowance is proportionately reduced. See also **5.35** above for the rate of writing-down allowance where there is a balance of £1,000 or less in the special rate pool.

For chargeable periods ending before 6 April 2012 (1 April 2012 for corporation tax purposes), the special rate was 10% per annum. For chargeable periods beginning before and ending on or after 6 April 2012 (or 1 April 2012), a hybrid rate applies, calculated by reference to the proportion of the period falling before, and that falling on or after, that date. The rate is found using the formula:

$$x = \left(10 \times \frac{BRD}{CP}\right) + \left(8 \times \frac{ARD}{CP}\right)$$

where:

x = the rate (rounded up to two decimal places);

BRD = the number of days in the chargeable period before 6 April 2012 (or 1 April 2012 for corporation tax purposes);

ARD = the number of days in the chargeable period on and after 6 April 2012 (or 1 April 2012); and

CP = the total number of days in the chargeable period.

The reduction in the rate from 10% to 8% does not apply to qualifying expenditure incurred wholly for the purposes of a ring fence trade (see **5.40** above) to which the supplementary charge in *CTA 2010, s 330(1)* applies. Writing-down allowances continue at a rate of 10% per annum for such expenditure.

Where a disposal value less than the 'notional written-down value' would otherwise fall to be brought into account in respect of special rate expenditure on plant or machinery which has attracted restricted allowances as above (or, in the case of long-life asset expenditure not initially treated as special rate expenditure, 6% allowances as described at **5.69** below), an adjustment may be required. Where the event giving rise to the disposal value is part of a scheme or arrangement a main object of which is the obtaining of a tax advantage under *CAA 2001, Pt 2*, the 'notional written-down value' is treated as the disposal value. The '*notional written-down value*' is the qualifying expenditure on the item concerned less the total allowances which could have been made in respect of that expenditure (including allowances at the 6% rate), assuming that no other expenditure were taken into account in determining the available qualifying expenditure, that, where the asset is a long-life asset, the expenditure was not prevented from being long-life asset expenditure by reason of the application of the monetary limit referred to at **5.67** below, and that all allowances had been made in full.

Where, on or after 6 April 2008 (1 April 2008 for corporation tax purposes), there is a sale between connected persons (within **2.34** above) of an integral feature (see **4.23** above) on which expenditure was incurred by the seller before that date and the buyer's expenditure would otherwise be special rate expenditure, the buyer's expenditure is qualifying expenditure only if the seller's original expenditure was qualifying expenditure or if the buyer's expenditure would have been qualifying expenditure if incurred at the time the original expenditure was incurred. If expenditure is prevented by this rule from being qualifying expenditure, the rule is applied again if there is a further sale of the integral feature between connected persons, but reference to the original expenditure is always to the expenditure incurred before 6 April 2008 (or 1 April 2008). This rule is intended to prevent taxpayers using connected person sales to obtain allowances on integral features purchased before 6 April 2008 (or 1 April 2008) if allowances would not have been available for that feature on or before that date (Treasury Explanatory Notes to the 2008 Finance Bill).

A further transitional rule applies where, on or after 1 April 2008, there is a sale between members of a group of companies (as defined in *TCGA 1992, s 170(3)–(6)*) of an integral feature on which expenditure was incurred, and allocated to its main pool, by the seller before that date and the buyer's expenditure would otherwise be special rate expenditure. The buyer and seller can make a joint election for the following treatment to apply:

(i) the integral feature is treated as having been sold by the seller to the buyer at a price giving rise to neither a balancing allowance or charge;
(ii) the buyer's expenditure is treated as qualifying expenditure other than special rate expenditure (and, if allocated to a pool, must be allocated to the main pool); and
(iii) allowances and charges are made to or on the buyer as if everything done to or by the seller had been done to or by the buyer.

The election must be made by notice within two years after the date of the sale. If expenditure is allocated to a main pool as a result of an election under this provision, the provision is applied again if there is a further sale of the integral feature between group members.

A further transitional rule applies where cushion gas used in a particular gas storage facility includes gas the expenditure on which includes both special rate expenditure (i.e. expenditure incurred on or after 1 April 2010) and '*old expenditure*' (i.e. expenditure incurred before 1 April 2010). Where a disposal event occurs in relation to the expenditure on the gas the event is treated as relating to the special rate expenditure before the old expenditure. This rule has the effect of ensuring that, where only part of the gas is subject to the disposal event, any remaining old expenditure in the main pool will continue to attract writing-down allowances at 20%, so maximising the continuing allowances. If the disposal event is treated as relating to both special rate and old expenditure it is treated as two separate disposals, the first relating to the special rate expenditure and the second to the old expenditure.

[*CAA 2001, ss 65(1), 104A–104E, 104G; FA 2011, s 10(3)(4)(8)–(13); FA 2012, s 45(4)*].

The rate of writing-down allowances for special rate expenditure is to be reduced to 8% for chargeable periods ending on or after 6 April 2012 (1 April 2012 for corporation tax). Transitional rules will apply for chargeable periods straddling those dates, similar to those which applied to the change in the main rate of writing-down allowances in 2008 (see **5.32** above).

EXAMPLE 12

[5.50]

Lakeman Ltd begins trading on 1 April 2017 and makes up accounts to 31 March. In the year ending 31 March 2018 the company incurs capital expenditure on plant and machinery of £925,000, of which £600,000 is special rate expenditure and the remainder falls to be allocated to the main pool. Lakeman Ltd carries on no other qualifying activity and none of the restrictions at **5.11** above apply to restrict the maximum annual investment allowance. None of the capital expenditure qualifies for first-year allowances.

Lakeman Ltd's plant and machinery allowances for the year ended 31 March 2018, assuming it claims all allowances to which it is entitled, will be calculated as follows.

	Main pool of expenditure	*Special rate pool*	*Total allowances*
	£	£	£
Additions	325,000	600,000	
AIA (note (a))		(200,000)	200,000
		400,000	
WDA (18% p.a.)	58,500		58,500
WDA (8% p.a.)		32,000	32,000
WDV c/fwd	£266,500	£368,000	
Total allowances claimed			£290,500

Note

(a) The taxpayer is free to choose how to allocate the annual investment allowance to expenditure. In this example the allowance has been allocated to special rate expenditure as this maximises the writing-down allowances available.

Cars

[5.51] Certain expenditure incurred on cars (but not all such expenditure) is excluded from the main pool. The current rules which determine what expenditure is allocated to the main pool and what is excluded apply to expenditure incurred on or after 6 April 2009 (1 April 2009 for corporation tax purposes). For such expenditure, the allocation depends on the level of the car's carbon dioxide emissions, with expenditure on cars which are not 'main rate cars' treated as special rate expenditure qualifying for writing-down allowances only at the special rate (currently 8%). Previously, it was the amount of the expenditure that determined whether or not expenditure was excluded from the main pool, with a ceiling of £3,000 per year for writing-down allowances on cars costing more than £12,000.

The *FA 2009* legislation which made these changes divided expenditure into 'new expenditure' to which the new regime applies, and 'old expenditure', to which the old rules continued to apply for chargeable periods beginning before 6 April 2014 (1 April 2014 for corporation tax purposes). '*New expenditure*' is expenditure incurred on or after 6 April 2009 (1 April 2009 for corporation tax purposes) and also expenditure incurred under an agreement for the provision of a car entered into after 8 December 2008 under which the car is not required to be made available before 6 August 2009 (or 1 August 2009). For this purpose, an agreement is treated as entered into on the date on which there is a written contract for the provision of the car, the contract is unconditional or, if it is conditional, the conditions have been met, and no terms remain to be agreed. '*Old expenditure*' is expenditure which is not new expenditure. [*FA 2009, Sch 11 paras 26, 27*]. If both old and new expenditure was incurred on a single car or motor cycle, the old and new expenditure were treated as if they were incurred on separate but identical cars or motor cycles, and any disposal value was apportioned on a just and reasonable basis. [*FA 2009, Sch 11 para 30*].

In relation to new expenditure '*car*' means a mechanically propelled road vehicle other than:

(a) a motor cycle (within the meaning of *Road Traffic Act 1988* — see below);
(b) a vehicle of a construction primarily suited for the conveyance of goods or burden of any description (see **5.54** below); or
(c) a vehicle of a type not commonly used as private vehicles and unsuitable to be so used (see **5.54** below).

In relation to old expenditure, '*car*' means a mechanically propelled road vehicle other than one within (b) or (c) above (and therefore including motor cycles).

[*CAA 2001, ss 81, 268A; FA 2009, Sch 11 paras 5, 11*].

A motor cycle is defined as a mechanically propelled vehicle, other than an invalid carriage, with fewer than four wheels and an unladen weight of more than 410 kilograms. A quadricycle or quad bike is outside of this definition and is accordingly treated as a car for allowances purposes. (HMRC Capital Allowances Manual, CA23510).

See **5.52** below for the provisions applying to new expenditure. The previous regime for cars costing over £12,000 is covered at **5.53** below.

For the restriction on the deduction available to a trader for expenses incurred on the hiring of a car, see *ITTOIA 2005, ss 48–50B* and *CTA 2009, ss 56–58B* and Tolley's Income Tax and Corporation Tax.

Note that allowances are available for expenditure on the provision of a car to a person carrying on a trade, profession or vocation and using the cash basis (see **2.3** above), despite the general prohibition of allowances in such cases. See also **4.20** and **5.34** above for the capital allowances consequences of an income tax fixed rate deduction in respect of a vehicle under *ITTOIA 2005, s 94D*.

New expenditure

[5.52] New expenditure (see **5.51** above) incurred on or after 6 April 2009 (1 April 2009 for corporation tax purposes) on the provision of a car which is not a 'main rate car' is special rate expenditure, with the consequences described at **5.49** above (i.e. it must be allocated to the special rate pool (or a single asset pool) and writing-down allowances are at the special rate (currently 8% per year)). Otherwise, new expenditure is to be allocated to the main pool (unless it is to be allocated to a single asset pool) and therefore qualifies for writing-down allowances at the main rate (currently 18%).

A 'main rate car' is:

- a car that is registered before 1 March 2001;
- a car that has 'low carbon dioxide emissions'; or
- a car that is 'electrically propelled'.

For this purpose, a car has 'low carbon dioxide emissions' if:

(i) it is first registered on the basis of either an 'EC certificate of conformity' or a 'UK approval certificate' specifying carbon dioxide emissions figures in terms of grams per kilometre driven, and
(ii) it has an 'applicable carbon dioxide emissions figure' not exceeding 130 grams per kilometre driven (110 grams per kilometre for expenditure incurred on or after 1 April 2018; 160 grams for expenditure incurred before 6 April 2013 (1 April 2013 for corporation tax purposes)).

The expressions 'electrically propelled' 'EC certificate of conformity', 'UK approval certificate' and 'applicable carbon dioxide emissions figure' are all defined as at **5.18** above. (Note, however, that the definition of 'low carbon dioxide emissions' for the purposes of the first-year allowances described at **5.18** above applies by reference to emissions not exceeding 95 grams per kilometre (previously 110 grams per kilometre) rather than the more generous limit of 130 grams per kilometre applicable to the above provisions.)

The Treasury may by order amend the amount in (ii) above.

[*CAA 2001, ss 104AA, 268B, 268C; FA 2013, s 68(3)(6)(8); SI 2016 No 984, Arts 2, 5*].

Expenditure on a car may be allocated to a single asset pool where the car is only partly used for the purposes of the qualifying activity (see **5.55** below). In such circumstances, there is a special provision to prevent the creation of an excessive balancing allowance by reference to an artificially low disposal value where a person ceases to own such a car by reason of an event which is a sale or the performance of a contract, and allowances in respect of that person's expenditure under that transaction are restricted under the anti-avoidance provisions of *CAA 2001, s 217* or *218* (see **7.3** below).

Where the special provision applies, the disposal value on the event is the lower of the capital expenditure incurred by the person disposing of the car and its market value at the time of disposal, such disposal value being then deemed to be the amount of the capital expenditure incurred on the provision of the car by the acquirer of it. [*CAA 2001, s 208A; FA 2009, Sch 11 para 10*].

A further anti-avoidance provision applies where a qualifying activity carried on by a company is permanently discontinued. The provision applies if the company has incurred expenditure on a car which has been allocated to the special rate pool and:

(a) the qualifying activity consisted of or included (other than incidentally) making cars available to other persons;

(b) at any time in the six months after the discontinuance, the qualifying activity of a 'group relief company' consists of or includes (other than incidentally) making cars available to other persons; and

(c) the balancing allowance to which the company would otherwise be entitled in respect of the special rate pool (SBA) is greater than: BC – OBA.

In (b) above, a 'group relief company' means a company to which group relief (see **2.38** above) would be available in respect of balancing allowances surrendered by the taxpayer company in its final chargeable period or a company to which such relief would be available in respect of balancing allowances surrendered by such a company. In (c) above, BC is the total of any balancing charges (for any pool) to which the taxpayer company is liable for the chargeable period, and OBA is the total of balancing allowances for that period for any pool other than the special rate pool. If BC – OBA is a negative amount it is treated as nil.

The effect of the provisions is that the company's balancing allowance on the special rate pool is reduced to BC – OBA and the 'relevant company' is treated as having incurred qualifying special rate expenditure on cars equal to SBA – (BC – OBA). on the day after the end of the taxpayer company's final chargeable period. If part of the relevant company's chargeable period overlaps with the chargeable period of the taxpayer company that immediately precedes its final chargeable period, a proportional part of the expenditure which the relevant company is treated as incurring is not taken into account in determining its available qualifying expenditure for the acquisition period. This does not prevent that part of the expenditure from being so taken into account for any subsequent chargeable period. It is not necessary for the relevant company to own any cars previously owned by the taxpayer company.

The 'relevant company' is the group relief company in (b) above or, if there is more than one such company, the one nominated by the taxpayer company. The nomination must be made not more than six months after the end of the taxpayer company's final chargeable period and if no nomination is made, HMRC will nominate the relevant company.

[*CAA 2001, s 104F*].

Old expenditure — cars costing over £12,000

[5.53] The following provisions apply only to qualifying expenditure which is old expenditure (see **5.51** above). Where such expenditure exceeding £12,000 is incurred on the provision of a 'car' (see **5.51** above and see also below regarding qualifying hire cars), it must be allocated to a single asset pool, unless (for expenditure incurred after 16 April 2002) the expenditure is first-year qualifying expenditure for the purposes of **5.16**(2) above (first-year allowances for cars with low carbon dioxide emissions).

These provisions apply to cars (see **5.51** above) which are not 'qualifying hire cars'. For this purpose, a car is a '*qualifying hire car*' if it is provided wholly or mainly for hire to, or for the carriage of, members of the public in the ordinary course of a trade. A car is not, however, a qualifying hire car unless:

(i) it is not normally on hire to, or used for the carriage of, the same person for *either* as many as 30 consecutive days *or* as many as 90 days in any period of twelve months;
(ii) it is hired to a person who will himself use it wholly or mainly for hire to, or the carriage of, members of the public in a trade and within the limits in (i) above; or
(iii) it is provided wholly or mainly for the use of a person in receipt of certain disability living allowances, mobility allowances and supplements as described in the legislation.

For the purposes of both (i) and (ii) above, connected persons (within **2.34** above) are treated as the same person.

[*CAA 2001, ss 74, 81, 82, Sch 3 para 19; Disability Living Allowance and Disability Working Allowance Act 1991, Sch 2 para 21; FA 2009, Sch 11 paras 4, 5, 25, 28(1), 29(1)*].

Writing-down allowances in respect of each single car pool are limited to a maximum of £3,000 (or £2,000 for expenditure incurred before 11 March 1992). If the chargeable period is less than or more than a year the £3,000 and £2,000 limits are proportionately reduced or increased. The maximum allowance is also subject to reduction where, as a result of a contribution having been made to the cost of the car within **2.8** above, only part of the expenditure qualifies for an allowance. Similarly, a person making a contribution towards the cost, and entitled to an allowance by virtue of the provisions in **2.9** above has his maximum allowance proportionately reduced.

There is no disposal event where a car in a single asset pool begins to be used partly for purposes other than those of a qualifying activity. Subject to this, the normal rules limiting allowances and charges apply where an asset is used partly for such purposes or where a partial depreciation subsidy is received (see **5.55** and **7.14** below, respectively).

[*CAA 2001, ss 75–78, Sch 3 para 19; FA 2009, s 30, Sch 11 paras 4, 24, 28(1), 29(1)*].

The above provisions are repealed with effect for chargeable periods beginning on or after 6 April 2014 (1 April 2014 for corporation tax purposes). Any unrelieved expenditure which is in a single asset pool at the end of a chargeable period beginning before, and ending on or after that date, is then carried forward into the main pool, unless the expenditure would have to be allocated to a single asset pool for a different reason (such as where the car is used only partly for the purposes of the qualifying activity (see **5.55** below)), in which case the single asset pool treatment continues. [*FA 2009, Sch 11 paras 4, 26, 29(1), 31*].

As noted at **5.46** above, a balancing allowance in respect of a pool can only arise in the final chargeable period for that pool. In the case of a single car pool, the final chargeable period is the first chargeable period in which a disposal event within **5.41**(i)–(vi) occurs. There is a special provision to prevent the creation of an excessive balancing allowance by reference to an artificially low disposal value where a person ceases to own a car which is in a single car pool under the above provisions by reason of an event which is a sale or the performance of a contract within **7.3**(i)–(iii) below. The provisions of *CAA 2001, Pt 2 Ch 17* discussed at **7.3** and **7.4** below cover circumstances such as a seller and buyer being connected persons, the car continuing to be used in a seller's trade etc. or the sole or main benefit of a sale being the obtaining of an allowance, but it would appear that there is a drafting error in the *CAA 2001* provision in that a transaction within **7.3**(i)–(iii) below (see *CAA 2001, s 213*) is simply a sale, etc. without reference to any of the avoidance scenarios dealt with by CHAPTER **17**. On a strict interpretation of the wording used in *CAA 2001, s 79*, therefore, *all* sales etc. of a car in a single car pool would fall within this provision. It is not thought that this can have been intended, for a number of reasons: the previous legislation (*CAA 1990, s 34(4)*) applied the provision directly to a sale or performance of a contract to which the anti-avoidance provisions (then in *CAA 1990, s 75*) applied; no change in the law on this point was mentioned in Annex 1 to the Revenue's Explanatory Notes to the Capital Allowances Bill, which gives details of all the changes in the law made by *CAA 2001*; and, the strict interpretation of *CAA 2001, s 79* would make little sense in the overall context of the scheme of allowances.

Where the special provision applies, the disposal value on the event is the lower of the capital expenditure incurred by the person disposing of the car and its market value at the time of disposal, such disposal value being then deemed to be the amount of the capital expenditure incurred on the provision of the car by the acquirer of it. (The legislation does not make clear whether an election under *CAA 2001, s 266* (see **7.18** below) is available so as to override the above provisions. However, it would seem that the mandatory provisions of *CTA 2010, ss 940A–953* (see **17.22** below) do override them.)

[*CAA 2001, ss 65(2), 79; FA 2009, Sch 11 paras 4, 28(2), 29(2)*].

Case law on meaning of 'car'

[5.54] The meaning of provisions, in earlier legislation, similar to those described in **5.51**(a) and (b) above has been considered by the courts in a number of cases.

In *Tapper v Eyre* ChD 1967, 43 TC 720 the mini-van of a dealer in radios, etc. was held to be of a type commonly used as a private vehicle and suitable to be so used. A similar fate befell a 7-cwt van used by an electrical contractor, licensed as a goods vehicle but not adapted in any way for use in the business (*Laing v CIR* CS 1967, 44 TC 681). However, in *Roberts v Granada TV Rental Ltd* ChD 1970, 46 TC 295, mini-vans and light vans, all licensed as goods vehicles and used as such, were held to be of a type not commonly used as a private vehicle and unsuitable to be so used.

Three separate appeals relating to driving school cars were heard together in *Bourne v Auto School of Motoring (Norwich) Ltd*; *Coghlin v Tobin*; *Frazer v Trebilcock* ChD 1964, 42 TC 217. It was held that cars fitted with dual control were of a type not commonly used as private vehicles and unsuitable for such use, but that the same could not be said of a private car not specially adapted. A contention that this car was used for public hire was also rejected.

A saloon car fitted with a flashing light for use by a fire officer was held to be of a type not commonly used as a private vehicle and unsuitable to be so used, in view of the fact that use of such a vehicle on a public road in the UK would be an offence other than for fire brigade or police purposes (*Gurney v Richards* ChD 1989, 62 TC 287).

Plant or machinery used partly for purposes of a qualifying activity

[5.55] Where plant or machinery is acquired partly for the purposes of a qualifying activity and partly for other purposes (e.g. a motor car to be used to some extent for private motoring by a sole trader or a machine to be used partly for the purposes of the UK branch of a non-UK resident company — see **4.3** above), the qualifying expenditure can only be allocated to a single asset pool. The final chargeable period (see **5.32** and **5.46** above) for the pool is the first chargeable period in which a disposal event within **5.41**(i)–(vi) occurs or, in certain cases, where the proportion of use other than for the purposes of the qualifying activity increases (see **5.56** below).

Where an item has been used wholly for the purposes of a qualifying activity and a disposal value under **5.41**(v) is required to be brought into account in the pool to which the expenditure on the item was allocated because it begins to be used partly for other purposes, an amount equal to the disposal value is allocated to a single asset pool for that chargeable period (see **2.1** above). The disposal value is market value, or cost if lower (see **5.41** above).

[*CAA 2001, ss 65(2), 206*].

Reduction of available allowances

[5.56] Where it appears that a person carrying on a qualifying activity has incurred expenditure only partly for the purposes of that activity, any annual investment allowance or first-year allowance is reduced to such an amount as is 'just and reasonable' in the circumstances. A reduction in a first-year allowance is, however, ignored, in determining the balance of the expenditure left after deducting the allowance which can be allocated to the single asset pool.

Writing-down allowances, balancing allowances and balancing charges in respect of expenditure allocated to a single asset pool as in **5.55** above are likewise reduced to an amount which is 'just and reasonable' in the circumstances. Again, the reduction made to a writing-down allowance is ignored in determining the unrelieved qualifying expenditure to be carried forward in the pool.

In the case of annual investment allowance and first-year allowances the reduction is made having particular regard to the extent to which it appears that the plant or machinery is likely to be used for purposes other than those of the qualifying activity. In the case of writing-down allowances and balancing adjustments, the reduction is made having particular regard to the extent to which it appears that the plant or machinery was used for purposes other than those of the qualifying activity in the chargeable period concerned. If, for any chargeable period, a writing-down allowance is not claimed, or only claimed in part, then the unrelieved qualifying expenditure carried forward in the pool is treated as not reduced or only proportionately reduced accordingly.

[*CAA 2001, ss 205, 207*].

If, therefore, an item of machinery or plant is used as to three-fifths for 'business' purposes and two-fifths for non-business purposes, a taxpayer will be entitled to only three-fifths of the full writing-down allowances. It is, however, the full amount of the writing-down allowances, before any reduction, that is deducted in determining the amount of unrelieved qualifying expenditure carried forward.

If the proportion of business use remains the same until such time as a balancing allowance or charge arises, that allowance or charge will be reduced in the same proportion as the allowances previously given; but where the proportion of business use has varied, the balancing allowance or charge will usually be reduced in the same proportion that the total amount of allowances previously given bears to the amount that would have been available had there been no non-business use.

Where the proportion of use other than for the purposes of the qualifying activity increases and the market value of the plant or machinery at the end of the chargeable period of the increase exceeds the available qualifying expenditure for the period by more than £1 million, then, if not otherwise required, a disposal value must be brought into account for that period. The amount of the disposal value is then treated as if it were expenditure incurred at the beginning of the next chargeable period on the provision of the plant or machinery partly for the purposes of the qualifying activity and partly for other purposes. [*CAA 2001, s 208, Sch 3 para 42*].

The proportion of business use will be a matter for negotiation between taxpayer and HMRC; where a vehicle is concerned, a fraction based on business mileage over total mileage would be appropriate, although in practice a fixed and reasonable fraction or percentage is commonly adopted.

EXAMPLE 13

[5.57]

C, a sole trader of many years' standing, purchases a car for £6,000 shortly after the start of his accounting year ending 5 April 2016 and uses it privately as well as for his business. The car qualifies for allowances at the main rate. The private use is agreed at 30% for the year to 5 April 2016. Shortly after the start of the following accounting year, C buys another car for private use only, and the private usage of the first car falls so that the private use proportion is agreed at 10% for the year to 5 April 2017. On 14 April 2017 the first car is sold for £3,000 and is replaced by a leased one. There are no further changes in the year to 5 April 2018. The capital allowances for the three years affected are as follows.

	Car		*Allowances*
	£		£
Year ended 5 April 2016			
Acquisition	6,000		
Writing-down allowance (18% p.a.)	(1,080)	× 70% =	£756
Written-down value carried forward	4,920		
Year ended 5 April 2017			
Writing-down allowance (18% p.a.)	(886)	× 90% =	£797

	Car		Allowances
	£		£
Written-down value carried forward	4,034		
Year ended 5 April 2018			
Disposal value	3,000		
Balancing allowance	£1,034	$\times\frac{1,553}{1,966}=$	£817

Because the first car is used for most of the period of account in which it was acquired and was not used for most of the period of account in which it was disposed of, the limiting of the balancing allowance by the ratio of allowances actually given to the allowances potentially available produces a reasonable result.

Personal choice

[5.58] HMRC may contend that in addition to the reduction for non-business use in **5.56** above, a further reduction should be made to take into account any element of personal choice inherent in an item of plant or machinery acquired. This might be the case, for example, where a taxpayer chose to drive a particularly expensive and/or ostentatious car where the choice of such a car might have little relevance to the qualifying activity carried on and, objectively, could be seen as merely the result of a personal desire.

In *G H Chambers (Northiam Farms) Ltd v Watmough* ChD 1956, 36 TC 711, the Commissioners, in addition to disallowing one-twelfth of the capital allowances in respect of private use calculated on a mileage basis, also disallowed more than half the remaining allowances in order to reflect personal choice, the car in question being a Bentley. Their decision was upheld by the High Court. In *Kempster v McKenzie* ChD 1952, 33 TC 193, a contention by the Revenue that an abatement of allowances should be made on grounds of personal choice was rejected on the evidence. Every case must be considered on its merits, taking into account 'all the relevant circumstances' as expressly required by the legislation. See also HMRC Capital Allowances Manual, CA23530.

Restrictions on balancing allowances and charges where there has previously been a restriction of allowances because of an element of personal choice will be dealt with in the same way as for non-business use in **5.56** above.

Short-life assets

[5.59] A person can make a 'short-life asset' election for expenditure on an item of plant or machinery, with certain exceptions, not to be included in the main pool. Instead the expenditure is allocated to a single asset pool. The result is that a balancing adjustment can arise when the short-life asset is disposed of, whereas one could not normally arise if the item were included in the main pool unless the qualifying activity were to cease simultaneously. The election may apply to any item of plant or machinery except any of the following description.

(a) Ships.

(b) Cars, as defined at **5.51** above, except for those provided wholly or mainly for hire to a person in receipt of certain independence payments, disability living allowances, mobility allowances and supplements mentioned at *CAA 2001, s 268D* (previously *CAA 2001, s 82(4)*). See also (g) below.

(c) Plant or machinery which is the subject of special leasing (see **6.19** below).

(d) Plant or machinery acquired partly for purposes other than those of the qualifying activity (see **5.55** above).

(e) Plant or machinery which is the subject of a partial depreciation subsidy (see **7.14** below).

(f) Plant or machinery received by way of gift or whose previous use did not attract capital allowances (see **7.12** and **7.13** below).

(g) Plant or machinery provided for leasing, except:
  (i) plant or machinery which will be used in the 'designated period' for a 'qualifying purpose' (see **5.63** and **6.21** onwards below);
  (ii) cars provided wholly or mainly for hire to persons in receipt of certain independence payments, disability living allowances, mobility allowances and supplements (see (b) above).

(h) Plant or machinery which is leased to two or more persons jointly in such circumstances that *CAA 2001, s 116* (see **6.53** below) applies.

(i) Plant or machinery leased outside the UK which qualifies for only a 10% p.a. writing-down allowance (see **6.45** below).

(j) An asset expenditure on which is within the long-life asset provisions (see **5.66** below).

(k) Plant or machinery whose previous use was for leasing under a long funding lease (See **6.39** below).

(l) An asset expenditure on which is special rate expenditure (see **5.49** above) except cars provided wholly or mainly for hire to persons in receipt of certain independence payments, disability living allowances, mobility allowances and supplements (see (b) above).

[*CAA 2001, ss 83, 84*].

Requirements of election

[5.60] It should be noted that whilst the legislation is clear as to what is *not* a short-life asset, it does not state that an asset, to which an election refers, must have a short life. Nor does it formally define what is meant by a short life, although the advantages of the election are negated if the asset is held for more than eight years following the chargeable period of purchase (four years for expenditure incurred before 6 April 2011 (1 April 2011 for corporation tax purposes)). An election should, therefore, normally relate to assets which are expected to be sold (at less than original cost) or scrapped within that period.

Consequences of election

[5.61] The election is irrevocable and the time limit within which it must be made is, for income tax, twelve months after 31 January following the tax year in which ends the chargeable period in which the expenditure (or earliest expenditure) is incurred, and for corporation tax, two years after the end of the chargeable period. The election must be made by notice to HMRC and must specify the short-life asset, the amount of qualifying expenditure incurred and the date on which it was incurred.

On the making of an election, the qualifying expenditure on the short-life asset to which it relates can only be allocated to a single asset pool (known as a short-life asset pool). The 'final chargeable period' (see **5.32** above) for a short-life asset pool is the first chargeable period in which a disposal event within **5.41**(i)–(vi) above occurs.

If no such disposal event occurs in any of the chargeable periods ending on or before the cut-off date (see below), then the short-life asset pool comes to an end and the available qualifying expenditure is allocated to the main pool (or, in the case of new expenditure on a car which is not a main rate car, the special rate pool) for the first chargeable period ending after that date. For expenditure incurred on or after 6 April 2011 (1 April 2011 for corporation tax purposes), the cut-off date, for these purposes, is the eighth anniversary of the end of the chargeable period in which the expenditure (or the first part of the expenditure) was incurred. For expenditure incurred before 6 April 2011 (or 1 April 2011) the cut-off date is the fourth anniversary of the end of that chargeable period. No balancing allowance or charge arises on the ending of the short-life asset pool in these circumstances.

[*CAA 2001, ss 65(2)(3), 85, 86; FA 2011, s 12(2)(3)*].

For the further application of these rules to an additional VAT liability, see **17.53** below.

EXAMPLE 14

[5.62]

A company with a 31 October accounting date purchases in January 2011 two machines costing £10,000 and £20,000 respectively. Both are expected to become obsolescent within four years and an election is made to treat them as short-life assets. The first machine is scrapped during the year to 31 October 2015 and only proceeds of £200 are received. The second machine continues to be used for the purposes of the trade at 31 October 2015 but is sold for £2,000 in May 2016. The company has qualifying expenditure of £30,000, on 'main pool' plant and machinery only, brought forward at 1 November 2010 and incurs additional qualifying expenditure, allocated to the main pool, of £50,000 on 31 December 2010. Annual investment allowance is claimed in respect of that expenditure. There are no further additions or disposals during the following six years.

	Main pool	*Machine 1*	*Machine 2*	*Allow-ances*
	£	£	£	£
Year ended 31.10.11				
Written-down value brought forward	30,000			
Acquisitions	50,000	10,000	20,000	
Annual investment allowance (100%)	(50,000)			£50,000
	30,000			
Writing-down allowance (20%)	(6,000)	(2,000)	(4,000)	£12,000
Written-down values at 31.10.11	24,000	8,000	16,000	

	Main pool £	*Machine 1* £	*Machine 2* £	*Allow-ances* £
				£62,000
Year ended 31.10.12				
Writing-down allowances (18.83% (note (b))	(4,520)	(1,507)	(3,013)	£9,040
Written-down values at 31.10.12	19,480	6,493	12,987	
Year ended 31.10.13				
Writing-down allowances (18%)	(3,507)	(1,169)	(2,337)	£7,013
Written-down values at 31.10.13	15,973	5,324	10,650	
Year ended 31.10.14				
Writing-down allowances (18%)	(2,875)	(958)	(1,917)	£5,750
Written-down values at 31.10.14	13,098	4,366	8,733	
Year ended 31.10.15				
Disposal value		200		
Balancing allowance		£4,136		4,136
Writing-down allowances (18%)	(2,358)		(1,572)	3,930
Written-down values at 31.10.15	10,740		7,161	
Total allowances				£8,066
Year ended 31.10.16				
Transfer to pool	7,161		(7,161)	
	17,901		—	
Disposal value	(2,000)			
	15,901			
Writing-down allowance (18%)	(2,862)			£2,862
Written-down value carried forward	£13,039			

Note

(m) For chargeable periods straddling 1 April 2012 (6 April 2012 for income tax purposes) a hybrid rate is used to calculate writing-down allowances. Applying the formula in **5.32** above, for the year ended 31 October 2012 the rate is:

$$\left(20 \times \frac{152}{366}\right) + \left(18 \times \frac{214}{366}\right) = 18.83\%$$

Leasing

[5.63] If an item of machinery or plant is leased, it can still qualify as a short-life asset providing it is used for a 'qualifying purpose' within the 'designated period'. However, if, in a chargeable period ending on or before the cut-off date, and within the eight years of the designated period, the asset begins to be used otherwise than for a qualifying purpose, the short-life asset pool comes to an end, without a final chargeable period, and the available qualifying expenditure is allocated to the main pool for that chargeable period (with suitable modifications where the short-life asset is a car). For expenditure incurred before 6 April 2011 (1 April 2011 for corporation tax purposes), this rule applies by reference to the first four years of the designated period. (See **6.48** and **6.50** below for the meaning of 'designated period' and 'qualifying purposes' respectively and **6.18–6.55** below for leasing of plant and machinery in general.) [*CAA 2001, s 87; FA 2011, s 12(4)*].

Transfer to connected person

[5.64] If, at a time before the cut-off date, a person disposes of a short-life asset to a connected person (within **2.34** above), the short-life asset election continues in force as if the connected person had made that election in respect of expenditure incurred at the time when it was incurred by the transferor. Also, if the transferor and connected person jointly so elect within two years of the end of the chargeable period in which the disposal takes place, the disposal is deemed to be made for an amount equal to the available qualifying expenditure in the short-life asset pool for the period (i.e. at tax written-down value) so that no balancing allowance or charge arises. In the absence of such an election, the normal connected persons rules apply (see **7.2** below). Where an item of plant or machinery is sold at less than market value, it is normally obligatory to bring in the actual sale price rather than market value if the buyer will himself be entitled to capital allowances in respect of the item (see **5.41**(b)(i) above). This does not apply to a short-life asset; market value must be substituted for the sale price (unless there is a tax charge under *ITEPA 2003* or the transaction is between connected persons and they elect as above for tax written-down value to be substituted instead). [*CAA 2001, ss 88, 89; FA 2011, s 12(5)*].

HMRC practice

[5.65] In response to representations received, the Revenue issued a Statement of Practice (SP 1/86, 15 January 1986) dealing with some practical aspects of the legislation. The statement gives guidance on the making of elections, the preparation of computations and the submission of elections and computations. In particular, the statement recognises that there is a difficulty in preparing computations where there is a large number of short-life assets; whereas the legislation requires a separate computation for each such asset, HMRC are prepared to accept certain alternative treatments. The statement gives two specific examples, but goes on to say that other forms of computation may be equally acceptable.

The first example given is in respect of a particular class of assets, held in large numbers such that individual identification is impracticable and having similar average lives of less than five years. HMRC will allow such assets to be grouped together in a single pool of expenditure, but with a separate pool being opened for each year. In the last year of the agreed life of the assets, a balancing allowance will arise and the pool for that particular year will cease to exist. The second example deals with the situation where a large number of similar items are used in the trade etc. and whilst individual identification is possible, it is not practicable to keep track of them all on an individual basis. Again, a form of pooling is allowed with expenditure being apportioned by reference to the number of individual items within the pool.

It should be noted that any extra-statutory system of pooling will need to be capable of being adapted if it is likely that some assets, within the class of assets included in the pool, may be disqualified from being short-life assets. A company leasing gaming machines might lease them both to UK traders, e.g. pubs and casinos (a qualifying purpose within **6.50** below), and to non-trading concerns, e.g. private clubs and associations (a non-qualifying purpose).

Notwithstanding Statement of Practice SP 1/86, a trader, before making a short-life asset election, will need to consider carefully the extra costs involved in record-keeping and preparing of computations and to balance this against the potential benefits of an election. He should also bear in mind that if the main pool of qualifying expenditure has reached a relatively low level and there are likely to be future disposals which might give rise to a balancing charge, it might be worthwhile to inflate the pool by including all additions therein, even if such additions could be the subject of a short-life asset election. Similarly, a short-life asset election would not normally be advantageous in respect of an item which qualifies for a 100% first-year allowance (see **5.16** above) as this would invite a balancing charge on a disposal before the cut-off date.

Long-life assets

[5.66] There are special provisions for chargeable periods ending on or after 26 November 1996 relating to certain 'long-life asset expenditure'. These do not apply to expenditure incurred before 26 November 1996, or to expenditure incurred before 1 January 2001 under a contract entered into before 26 November 1996 (except that the later start date does not apply to any increased expenditure resulting from a variation of the contract on or after 26 November 1996). Subject to the exclusions noted at **5.67** below, 'long-life asset expenditure' is qualifying expenditure incurred on the provision of a 'long-life asset' for the purposes of a qualifying activity.

A '*long-life asset*' is plant or machinery which can reasonably be expected to have a useful economic life of at least 25 years (or where such could be reasonably expected when it was new). The useful economic life is taken as the period from first use until it ceases to be, or to be likely to be, used as a fixed asset of a business.

Where part only of expenditure on an asset falls within these provisions (see **5.67** below), that part and the remainder are each treated as expenditure on a separate item of plant or machinery, any necessary apportionment being made on a just and reasonable basis. For expenditure incurred, or allocated to a pool, on or after 6 April 2008 (1 April 2008 for corporation tax purposes) (i.e. expenditure which is special rate expenditure — see **5.69** below) this rule is replaced by an equivalent rule operating by reference to the part of the expenditure which is special rate expenditure. See **5.49** above.

[*CAA 2001, ss 90–92, Sch 3 para 20(1)*].

As an introduction to a detailed discussion of what constitutes a long-life asset (including twelve examples), the Revenue stated that they 'will generally accept the accounting treatment as determining whether an asset is long-life provided it is not clearly unreasonable'. (Revenue Tax Bulletin August 1997 pp 445–450). Where, however, there is an active second-hand market for a particular type of asset, the Revenue will take into account other factors, such as how long the business concerned typically keeps that type of asset before it is replaced, whether it has a history of selling assets into the second-hand market or scrapping them, and whether there are rapid technological or market changes in the sector (Revenue Tax Bulletin February 2002, p 916).

HMRC are willing to enter into industry-wide agreements about which types of assets used in the industry are, or are not, long-life assets. Agreements will be entered into with the representative body for the particular industrial sector, but only at the instigation of the body. If there is more than one representative body for the industry, the request for an agreement should be made jointly. Where the industry is dealt with by the Large Business Office or the Oil Taxation Office, applications should be made to the relevant office. In other cases, applications should be sent to HMRC CTISA (Technical), Third floor, 100 Parliament Street, London SW1A 2BQ (HMRC Capital Allowances Manual, CA23780).

The Revenue entered into an agreement with the British Air Transport Association (BATA) on the application of the long-life rules to jet aircraft with 60 or more seats. See Revenue Tax Bulletin, June 1999 and December 2003 and HMRC Capital Allowances Manual, CA23781. For HMRC's views on the application of the rules to aircraft outside the BATA agreement see Tax Bulletin, April 2000 and December 2003 and HMRC Capital Allowances Manual, CA23782. The agreement applies only to aircraft purchased before 1 July 2013.

An agreement was also made with the National Farmers Union that sophisticated greenhouses which qualify for machinery and plant allowances were not long-life assets (HMRC Capital Allowances Manual, CA23785). The agreement applied only to expenditure incurred before 1 January 2006.

For HMRC's views on modern printing equipment see Tax Bulletin February 2002 (at pages 916, 917) and HMRC Capital Allowances Manual, CA23790.

Expenditure excluded

[5.67] Expenditure on the following *cannot* be long-life asset expenditure.

(i) Fixtures (see **6.2** onwards below) in, or plant or machinery provided for use in, a building used wholly or mainly as a dwelling-house, showroom, hotel, office or retail shop or similar retail premises, or for purposes ancillary to such use.
(ii) Cars and motor cycles (see **5.51** above).
(iii) (In relation to expenditure incurred before 1 January 2011) ships of a seagoing kind, other than 'offshore installations' (as now defined in *CTA 2010, s 1132*) and ships of a kind used or chartered primarily for sport or recreation (which does not encompass passenger ships or cruise liners).
(iv) (In relation to expenditure incurred before 1 January 2011) 'railway assets' used only for a 'railway business' (as defined).

[*CAA 2001, ss 93–96*].

A *de minimis* monetary limit applies, in certain circumstances, to prevent expenditure from being treated as long-life asset expenditure. The limit applies to expenditure incurred, in the case of an individual, in a chargeable period in which the whole of his time is substantially devoted to carrying on the qualifying activity for the purposes of which the expenditure is incurred. In the case of a partnership of individuals, at least half of the partners must devote the whole or a substantial part of their time to carrying on the qualifying activity throughout the chargeable period concerned. The limit applies for corporation tax purposes without any such restriction. The following types of expenditure are not, however, prevented in any case from being long-life asset expenditure by the application of the monetary limit:

(a) expenditure on a share in plant or machinery; or
(b) a contribution treated as plant or machinery expenditure under *CAA 2001, s 538* (see **2.9** above); or
(c) expenditure on plant or machinery for leasing (whether or not in the course of a trade).

The monetary limit is, for a chargeable period of one year, £100,000 and is applied to the total expenditure which would, apart from the operation of the limit (and excluding expenditure within (a) to (c) above), be long-life asset expenditure. In applying the limit, all the expenditure incurred under a contract is treated as incurred in the first chargeable period in which any expenditure under the contract is incurred. Where the limit is exceeded, all the expenditure concerned is long-life asset expenditure, and not merely the excess.

Where the chargeable period is longer or shorter than one year the limit is increased or decreased proportionately. For companies, the limit is, where relevant, divided by one plus the number of related 51% group companies within *CTA 2010, s 279F* (for accounting periods beginning before 1 April 2015, one plus the number of associated companies).

[*CAA 2001, ss 97–100; FA 2014, Sch 1 paras 8, 21*].

Transitional provisions for second-hand assets

[5.68] A second-hand asset is excluded from the long-life asset provisions where the previous owner has properly claimed plant and machinery allowances for expenditure on its provision, and that expenditure did not fall to be treated as long-life asset expenditure, but would have done so if:

(1) expenditure incurred before the commencement dates referred to at **5.66** above was not prevented from being long-life asset expenditure; or
(2) the exclusion of second-hand assets did not apply; or
(3) the long-life asset provisions applied for chargeable periods ending before 26 November 1996.

[*CAA 2001, Sch 3 para 20(2)(3)(5)*].

A provisional claim to writing-down allowances at the higher rate may be made by a purchaser before the vendor has made the appropriate return, provided that reasonable steps have been taken to establish that entitlement will arise, and that the appropriate revisions will be made, and assessments accepted, if entitlement does not in the event arise. (Revenue Tax Bulletin August 1997 p 450).

Treatment of long-life asset expenditure

[5.69] Long-life asset expenditure incurred on or after 6 April 2008 (1 April 2008 for corporation tax purposes) is special rate expenditure and treated as described at **5.49** above. Expenditure incurred before that date but not allocated to a pool until a chargeable period beginning on or after that date is likewise treated as special rate expenditure.

Previously, long-life asset expenditure incurred wholly and exclusively for the purposes of a qualifying activity, and which was not required to be allocated to a single asset pool under other provisions, was allocated to a class pool (see **5.48** above), known as the long-life asset pool. The final chargeable period (see **5.32** above) for the long-life asset pool was that in which the qualifying activity is permanently discontinued.

Any unrelieved expenditure in a long-life asset pool at the end of the first chargeable period ending on or after 5 April 2008 (31 March 2008 for corporation tax purposes) is transferred to the special rate pool and treated in subsequent chargeable periods as special rate expenditure. Unrelieved long-life asset expenditure in a single asset pool at the end of the first such chargeable period is likewise treated as special rate expenditure in subsequent chargeable periods.

Writing-down allowances in respect of long-life expenditure which is (or is treated as) special rate expenditure are at a maximum of the special rate (whether allocated to the special rate pool or a single asset pool). See **5.49** above. Previously, allowances were given at a maximum annual rate of **6%**. A hybrid rate applies for a chargeable period which begins before, and ends on or after, 6 April 2008 (1 April 2008 for corporation tax purposes) in respect of long-life asset expenditure which is not special rate expenditure in that period. The rate is calculated by reference to the proportion of the period falling before, and that falling on or after, 6 April 2008 (1 April 2008 for corporation tax purposes) and is found using the formula:

$$x = \left(6 \times \frac{BRD}{CP}\right) + \left(10 \times \frac{ARD}{CP}\right)$$

where:

x = the rate (rounded up to two decimal places);

BRD = the number of days in the chargeable period before 6 April 2008 (or 1 April 2008 for corporation tax purposes);

ARD = the number of days in the chargeable period on and after 6 April 2008 (or 1 April 2008); and

CP = the total number of days in the chargeable period.

See **5.16**(4) above for the rate of first-year allowances available for long-life asset expenditure incurred after 16 April 2002 where the plant or machinery is for use wholly for the purposes of a ring fence trade.

[*CAA 2001, ss 65(1), 101, 102; FA 2008, s 83, Sch 26 paras 9, 10, 14*].

Anti-avoidance provisions

[5.70] Where plant and machinery allowances have been claimed for long-life asset expenditure, any earlier or later expenditure on the same asset for which allowances are subsequently claimed is also treated as being long-life asset expenditure if it would not otherwise be so, unless it is within the excluded categories described at **5.67**(i)–(iv) above. This over-rides the exclusion of expenditure within the monetary limit referred to at **5.67** above.

Where a disposal value less than the 'notional written-down value' would otherwise fall to be brought into account in respect of expenditure on plant or machinery which has attracted restricted allowances as described at **5.69** above, an adjustment may be required. Where the event giving rise to the disposal value is part of a scheme or arrangement a main object of which is the obtaining of a tax advantage under *CAA 2001, Pt 2*, the 'notional written-down value' is treated as the disposal value. The '*notional written-down value*' is the qualifying expenditure on the item concerned less the total allowances which could have been made in respect of that expenditure, assuming that no other expenditure were taken into account in determining the available qualifying expenditure, that the expenditure was not prevented from being long-life asset expenditure by reason of the application of the monetary limit referred to at **5.67** above, and that all allowances had been made in full. For long-life asset expenditure which is special rate expenditure, this provision is replaced by the equivalent provision described at **5.49** above.

[*CAA 2001, ss 103, 104; FA 2008, Sch 26 paras 11, 14*].

EXAMPLE 15

[5.71]

Bertie prepares trading accounts to 31 December. In the year to 31 December 2006, he has built new factory premises for use in his trade, which include a building mainly in use as offices (on which 20% of the cost of the premises is expended). Industrial buildings allowances are available on the construction expenditure. The plant and machinery main pool written-down value at 1 January 2006 is £800,000, and the disposal value brought in in respect of plant and machinery on his previous premises is £720,000. Machines installed in the new factory cost £920,000.

He also claims plant and machinery allowances for the expenditure of £520,000 incurred on fixtures integral to the new premises, which are agreed to have an expected life in excess of 25 years. Of this expenditure, it is agreed £120,000 should be apportioned to the offices.

On 1 May 2007 he incurs additional expenditure on upgrading the fixtures of £19,000, none of it relating to office fixtures.

On 1 October 2008 he moves to new premises, disposing of the old premises for a consideration including £425,000 relating to the integral fixtures (of which £95,000 relates to the office fixtures) and £510,000 relating to other plant and machinery.

Plant and machinery in the new premises costs £960,000, of which £300,000 relates to integral features (see **4.23** above).

None of Bertie's qualifying expenditure is eligible for first-year allowances. None of the restrictions at **5.11** above apply to reduce Bertie's maximum annual investment allowance.

The plant and machinery allowances computations for relevant periods are as follows.

	Main pool	Long-life asset pool	Special rate pool	Total allowances
	£	£	£	
Year ending 31.12.06				
WDV b/f	800,000	—		
Additions (note (a))	1,040,000	400,000		
Disposals	(720,000)	—		
	1,120,000	400,000		
WDA	280,000	24,000		£304,000
WDV c/f	840,000	376,000		
Year ending 31.12.07				
Additions (note (b))	—	19,000		
	840,000	395,000		
WDA	210,000	23,700		£233,700
WDV c/f	630,000	371,300		
Year ending 31.12.08				
Additions	660,000	—	300,000	
AIA (note (c))			36,885	£36,885
Disposals	(605,000)	(330,000)		
	685,000	41,300	263,115	
WDA (21.31%) (note (d))	145,974			£145,974
WDA (8.95%) (note (e))		3,697		£3,697
WDA			26,312	£26,312
	539,026	37,603	236,803	
Transfer to special rate pool (note (f))		(37,603)	37,603	
WDV c/f	£539,026	—	£274,406	
Total allowances y/e 31.12.08				£212,868

Notes

(a) Expenditure on fixtures provided for use in offices is excluded from being long-life asset expenditure (regardless of whether the office building itself attracts industrial buildings allowances because it represents not more than 25% of the overall cost of premises otherwise qualifying).

(b) Additional expenditure on long-life assets is within the provisions even if within the annual *de minimis* limit.

(c) Chargeable periods straddling 6 April 2008 (1 April 2008 for corporation tax purposes) are treated as beginning on that date for the purposes of determining the maximum annual investment allowance. In this case, therefore the maximum allowance is determined as if the chargeable period were 270 days long (6 April 2008 to 31 December 2008). The maximum allowance is therefore £50,000 × 270/366 = £36,885. See **5.4** above.

(d) For chargeable periods straddling 6 April 2008 (1 April 2008 for corporation tax purposes) a hybrid rate is used to calculate writing-down allowances. Applying the formula in **5.32** above, for the year ended 31 December 2008 the rate is:

$$\left(25\times\frac{96}{366}\right)+\left(20\times\frac{270}{366}\right)=21.31\%$$

(e) The final chargeable period for the long-life asset pool (in which period only a balancing allowance can arise) is that in which the qualifying activity is permanently discontinued. Allowances therefore continue to be given on the residue of expenditure on long-life assets despite their having been disposed of. For chargeable periods straddling 6 April 2008 (1 April 2008 for corporation tax purposes) a hybrid rate is used to calculate writing-down allowances. Applying the formula in **5.66** above, for the year ended 31 December 2008 the rate is:

$$\left(6 \times \frac{96}{366}\right) + \left(10 \times \frac{270}{366}\right) = 8.95\%$$

(f) Any unrelieved expenditure in a long-life asset pool at the end of the first chargeable period ending on or after 5 April 2008 (31 March 2008 for corporation tax purposes) is transferred to the special rate pool.

Ships

[5.72] The legislation described at **5.73** to **5.77** below relates to expenditure incurred after 31 March 1985 or, in the case of a new (which means unused and not second-hand) ship, after 13 March 1984. A ship which is not new can nevertheless be regarded as new if the previous owner was precluded from obtaining first-year allowances by virtue of his having disposed of the ship without having brought it into use for the purposes of his trade.

The legislation is silent as to what exactly is meant by a 'ship' but the term is defined by the *Merchant Shipping Act 1995* as including 'every description of vessel used in navigation'. The term is specifically extended for value added tax purposes to include a hovercraft, although it would seem doubtful if this would apply if an ordinary meaning is given. HMRC's practice is to accept that anything which is covered by the Merchant Shipping Act definition is a ship for capital allowance purposes. This means that HMRC will treat any vessel which is capable of being manoeuvred under direct or indirect power as a ship. HMRC also treat any vessel registered by the Maritime Coastguard Agency as a ship for capital allowance purposes (HMRC Capital Allowances Manual, CA25100).

See **17.58** onwards below for details of the tonnage tax regime and its associated capital allowances provisions.

Single ship pool

[5.73] Qualifying expenditure incurred on the provision of a ship for the purposes of a qualifying activity can only be allocated to a single asset pool (a 'single ship pool'). This does not, however, apply if:

(a) an election is made as described at **5.77** below;
(b) the qualifying activity is special leasing; or
(c) the ship is otherwise provided for leasing or letting on charter unless
  (i) the ship is not used for 'overseas leasing', or, if it is, is used only for 'protected leasing', and
  (ii) it appears the ship will be used for a 'qualifying purpose' in the 'designated period' and will not at any time in that period be used for any other purpose.

See **6.18–6.55** below as regards (b) and (c) above and for leasing of plant or machinery in general.

[*CAA 2001, ss 127, 128*].

Postponement of first-year and writing-down allowances

[5.74] A person entitled to a first-year or writing-down allowance for a chargeable period in respect of expenditure on a ship may elect to postpone the whole or part of the allowance. The time limit within which notice of the election must be given is, for income tax, ftwelve months after 31 January following the tax year in which ends the chargeable period concerned and, for corporation tax, two years after the end of the chargeable period. This does not prejudice his right to claim a first-year allowance in respect of only part of the expenditure or to claim a reduced writing-down allowance or to make no claim for an allowance. Where a first-year allowance is claimed in respect of part only of the expenditure, it is the allowance claimed that may be postponed (in whole or in part) Where a writing-down allowance is reduced, it is the reduced amount which may be postponed (in whole or in part).

Where an allowance, or part thereof, is postponed, it is nevertheless deemed to have been given for the purpose of arriving at the amount of available qualifying expenditure on which writing-down allowances fall to be calculated in later chargeable periods.

The taxpayer may claim to have all or part of a postponed allowance treated as a first-year or, as appropriate, writing-down allowance for one or more subsequent chargeable periods during which he is carrying on the qualifying activity. The total amount of allowances made in this way must not, of course, exceed the amount of the postponed allowance. A writing-down allowance made in this way is ignored in computing the unrelieved qualifying expenditure carried forward in any pool (see **5.32** above). The claiming of a postponed writing-down allowance does not affect entitlement to, or the amount of, any other writing-down allowance for the same chargeable period.

The fact that first-year or writing-down allowances have been postponed does not mean that they are regarded as allowances brought forward from an earlier year under the group relief provisions of *CTA 2010, s 101(3)*. A postponed allowance is treated as an allowance of the chargeable period *to* which it is postponed as opposed to the chargeable period *for* which it is postponed.

[*CAA 2001, ss 130, 131*].

Treatment of disposal value

[5.75] Where a disposal value falls to be brought into account in respect of a single ship pool, the available qualifying expenditure in the pool for the chargeable period concerned is allocated to the appropriate non-ship pool (the pool to which the expenditure would have been allocated but for the single ship pool provisions), and the disposal value is brought into account for that period in the non-ship pool. The single ship pool is treated as coming to an end without any final chargeable period (so that no balancing allowance arises in respect of it) and without any liability to a balancing charge. [*CAA 2001, ss 127(3), 132(2)*]. Obviously a balancing charge could arise as a result of the bringing into account of the disposal value in the appropriate non-ship pool.

In addition to the disposal events listed at **5.41** above, a disposal value must be brought into account in respect of the single ship pool where a ship is provided for leasing and begins to be used otherwise than for a 'qualifying purpose' within the first four years of the 'designated period' (see **6.48** and **6.50** below). [*CAA 2001, s 132(1)(4)*].

Balancing charges on 'qualifying ships' may be deferred and set against subsequent expenditure on ships for a maximum of six years from the date of disposal.

A '*qualifying ship*' is a ship of a sea-going kind of 100 gross registered tons or more, excluding ships of a kind used or chartered primarily for sport or recreation (but passenger ships and cruise liners are not so excluded) and 'offshore installations' (as now defined in *CTA 2010, s 1132*). The provisions also apply to registered ships of less than 100 tons in cases where the old ship is totally lost or is damaged beyond worthwhile repair. A ship brought into use in the qualifying activity on or after 20 July 1994 must within three months of first use (unless disposed of during those three months) be registered in the UK, the Channel Islands, Isle of Man, a colony (as defined by *Interpretation Act 1978, Sch 1*, including Anguilla, Bermuda, British Virgin Islands, Cayman Islands, Falkland Islands, Gibraltar, Montserrat, St. Helena, and Turks and Caicos Islands (Revenue Tax Bulletin April 1995, p 208)), or a European Economic Area State, and must continue to be so until at least three years from first use or, if earlier, until disposed of to an unconnected person.

No amount in respect of the old ship must have been allocated to an overseas leasing pool (see **6.45** below), a single asset pool within **5.56** above (partial use other than for the purpose of a qualifying activity) or **7.14** below (partial depreciation subsidy) or a pool for a qualifying activity consisting of special leasing (see **6.19**).

Deferment is achieved by allocating the amount deferred to the appropriate non-ship pool (see above) for the chargeable period for which the deferral claim is made. This effectively sets the amount deferred against the disposal value of the old ship which is brought into account in the non-ship pool for the same period, as described above. The *maximum deferment* is the lowest of the following amounts.

(1) The amount treated as brought into account in respect of the old ship under *CAA 2001, s 139*. If no election has been made under **5.77** below to allocate expenditure on the old ship to the appropriate non-ship pool, the amount is effectively the balancing charge on the old ship, i.e. the disposal value less the available qualifying expenditure transferred from the single ship pool to the appropriate non-ship pool as above. In all other cases the amount is a notionally computed balancing charge on the assumption that all the expenditure on the old ship was allocated to the appropriate non-ship pool and no other expenditure was allocated to that pool and that all first-year and writing-down allowances available to him had been made (including any first-year allowance postponed).
(2) The amount to be expended on new shipping (see below), so far as not already set against an earlier balancing charge, in the six years starting with the date of disposal of the old ship.

(3) The amount of any balancing charge which would, but for the deferment claim, have been made for the chargeable period in question in the appropriate non-ship pool. Before *CAA 2001* had effect (see **1.2** above), this amount could also include any balancing charges made for the chargeable period concerned in a short-life asset pool, an expensive car single asset pool, or a long-life asset pool.

(4) the amount needed to reduce the profit or income of the qualifying activity to nil (disregarding losses brought forward).

Where an amount is expended on new shipping within the six-year period allowed and is attributed by the shipowner, by notice to HMRC, to any part of an amount deferred, an amount equal to the amount so matched is brought into account as a disposal value in the single ship pool to which the expenditure is allocated for the chargeable period in which (or in the basis period for which) the expenditure is incurred, thus reducing the amount on which allowances may be claimed on the new ship. No amount of expenditure can be attributed to a deferment if there is earlier expenditure on new shipping within the said six-year period which has not been attributed to that or earlier deferments. An attribution may be varied by the shipowner by notice to HMRC within the time limit which would apply for making a claim for deferment of a balancing charge (see below) incurred in the earliest chargeable period in which matched expenditure is incurred.

An amount is expended on new shipping for the above purposes if it is qualifying expenditure incurred by the shipowner wholly and exclusively for the purposes of a qualifying activity carried on by him on the provision of a ship (the new ship) which will be a qualifying ship for at least three years after first use or, if earlier, until disposed of to an unconnected person. The expenditure must be allocated to a single ship pool. Expenditure will not qualify and will be deemed never to have qualified where:

(A) a notice under **5.77** below has the effect of requiring any of the expenditure to be allocated to the appropriate non-ship pool, or

(B) the ship is used for overseas leasing (see **6.44** below), or

(C) the shipowner (or a person connected with him) has already owned the ship at some time in the previous six years, or

(D) the main object, or one of the main objects, of the provision of the ship for the shipowner's qualifying activity (including a series of transactions of which that was one) is to secure the deferment of a balancing charge.

Expenditure will be treated as incurred by the shipowner if it is incurred by the persons for the time being carrying on the qualifying activity where the only changes in the persons carrying it on were changes which did not involve all of the persons carrying it on permanaently ceasing to do so or changes not treated as discontinuations by virtue of *CTA 2010, s 948*. In such circumstances, any notice stated to be given by the shipowner is to be given by the persons then carrying on the qualifying activity. A person is connected with the shipowner for the purposes of the above provisions if he is carrying on the qualifying activity previously carried on by the shipowner in the above circumstances or he is connected (within **2.34** above).

Specified time limits are laid down for the claiming of deferment of a balancing charge:

(a) for corporation tax purposes, *FA 1998, Sch 18 Pt IX* applies (see **2.21** above), i.e. broadly, the claim must be made within two years of the end of the accounting period in which the charge would have been made (or, if later, at any time before the assessment for the accounting period becomes final); and

(b) for income tax purposes, the claim must be made within twelve months from 31 January following the year of assessment in which the chargeable period of deferment ends.

Where a charge has been deferred and circumstances subsequently arise requiring that deferment to be treated as one to which the shipowner was not entitled, either in whole or in part, the shipowner must, within three months of the end of the chargeable period in which those changes first arise, give notice to HMRC specifying the circumstances. Failure to do so will result in a penalty under *TMA 1970, s 98*. Any assessments to tax chargeable as a result of the circumstances may be made at any time up to twelve months after the changed circumstances have been notified to HMRC.

There is provision for the balancing charge to be set against expenditure on new shipping by another member of the same group of companies as the shipowner (within *CTA 2010, Pt 5*). Such expenditure is, however, excluded where the ship ceases to belong to the fellow group member without being brought into use for the purposes of the member's qualifying activity, or where, within three years of being so brought into use, a disposal value falls to be brought in in respect of the ship (although these exclusions do not apply in the case of total loss of, or irreparable damage to, the ship). Expenditure is similarly excluded where the group relationship between the two companies ceases after the expenditure is incurred and within three years after the commencement of use for the purposes of a qualifying activity (again disregarding events after the total loss etc. of the ship).

[*CAA 2001, ss 134–158, Sch 3 para 24; F(No 2)A 2017, Sch 4 para 125; SI 1996 No 1323; SI 1997 No 133*].

Note that the above provisions do not apply to a balancing charge arising to a company whilst it is subject to tonnage tax (see **17.58** below). Where a company which has deferred a balancing charge under the above provisions subsequently enters tonnage tax, the operation of the provisions in relation to the balancing charge are not affected by the entry. However, expenditure on new shipping incurred by a company subject to tonnage tax is not taken into account unless the company which incurred the balancing charge was a qualifying company for tonnage tax purposes (see **17.58** below) at the time the charge arose (or would have been had the tonnage tax provisions then been in force). [*FA 2000, Sch 22 paras 72, 80(4)*].

Ship not brought into use

[5.76] If a ship ceases to be owned by a person carrying on a qualifying activity without its having been brought into use for the purposes of the qualifying activity, any writing-down allowances previously made in respect of expenditure in the single ship pool are withdrawn. The person loses his right to claim any allowances previously postponed. All writing-down allowances, including postponed allowances, thus withdrawn are added to the appropriate non-ship pool for the chargeable period in which the ship ceases to be owned by the person. These adjustments are in addition to those described in **5.75** above. [*CAA 2001, s 133*].

Single ship pool provisions not to apply

[5.77] A person who has incurred qualifying expenditure on a ship may elect, for any chargeable period, for the single ship pool provisions not to apply so that

- all or part of any qualifying expenditure that would otherwise be allocated to a single ship pool, or
- all or part of the available qualifying expenditure already in a single ship pool,

is allocated instead to the appropriate non-ship pool (see **5.75** above). The time limit within which the election must be made is, for income tax, twelve months after 31 January following the tax year in which the chargeable period concerned ends and, for corporation tax, two years after the end of the chargeable period. [*CAA 2001, s 129*].

EXAMPLE 16

[5.78]

A company carrying on a trade of merchant shipping purchases three ships during its 12-month accounting period ended 31 March 2018. The ships, 1, 2 and 3, cost £900,000, £1,000,000 and £1,200,000 respectively. There are no single ship pools brought forward at 1 April 2017, but there is unrelieved qualifying expenditure of £2,000,000 brought forward in the main pool. The company makes the following elections in respect of the chargeable period ended 31 March 2018.

(i) The writing-down allowance on Ship 1 be postponed in full.
(ii) The special provisions should not apply to Ship 2.
(iii) £1,000,000 of the expenditure on Ship 3 be taken outside the scope of the special provisions and included in the main pool.

The capital allowance computations for the accounting period to 31 March 2018 are as follows.

	Main pool	*Ship 1*	*Ship 3*	*Allowances*
	£'000	£'000	£'000	£'000
WDV b/fwd	2,000			
Additions:				
Ship 1		900		
Ship 2	1,000			
Ship 3	1,000		200	
	4,000	900	200	
AIA	200			200
	3,800			
WDA (18%)	(684)	(162)	(36)	882
WDV c/fwd	£3,116	£738	£164	
WDA postponed				(162)
Total allowances for the period				£920

EXAMPLE 16

[5.79]

A company with a single ship pool sells that ship for £800,000 during its 12-month accounting period ended 31 March 2018. Unrelieved qualifying expenditure brought forward at 1 April 2017 amounted to £1,000,000 in respect of the single ship pool and £3,000,000 in respect of the main pool. Assuming no other additions or disposals, the capital allowances computation for the accounting period in question is as follows.

	Pool	*Ship*	*Allowances*
	£'000	£'000	£'000
WDV b/fwd	3,000	1,000	
Transfer to main pool	1,000	(1,000)	
Disposal value	(800)		
	3,200	—	
WDA (18%)	(576)		£576
WDV c/fwd	£2,624		

General

[5.80] In addition to the items described in **5.53–5.79** above which are excluded from the main pool, certain plant and machinery which is leased overseas must be excluded as must plant and machinery for use in a qualifying activity consisting of special leasing (see **6.19** below). In addition, items in respect of which the person incurring the expenditure receives a partial depreciation subsidy (see **7.14** below) are similarly excluded. Where a person claims a contribution allowance in respect of plant or machinery, the expenditure is allocated to a single-asset pool (see **2.9** above).

Manner of making allowances and charges

[5.81] The manner of making allowances and charges in respect of plant and machinery is determined as below, with the general provisions of CHAPTER 2 also applying.

Trades, professions and vocations

[5.82] Plant and machinery allowances (or balancing charges) for a chargeable period in respect of a trade are treated as trading expenses (or receipts) of that period. The same rules apply to professions and vocations. See **17.46A** onwards below for the making of allowances to a company or partnership where the Northern Ireland rate of corporation tax applies (expected to be 2018 onwards). [*CAA 2001, ss 247(1), 251; CTNIA 2015, Sch 1 para 9*].

Property businesses

[5.83] Where the qualifying activity is an ordinary UK property business, a UK furnished holiday lettings business, an ordinary overseas property business or an EEA furnished holiday lettings business (or, previously, an overseas property business — see **4.4** above), allowances for a chargeable period are treated as expenses of the business for that period and charges are treated as receipts of the business. [*CAA 2001, ss 248–250A; FA 2011, Sch 14 para 12(11)–(14)*].

Where an individual carries on an ordinary overseas property business or an EEA furnished holiday lettings business in a tax year which is a 'split year' for the purposes of the statutory residence test for 2013/14 onwards, only the part of the profits arising in the UK part of the year are chargeable and allowances and charges are treated as expenses and receipts in calculating the profits arising in that part only. For this purpose, the profits for the tax year, before adjustment for the allowances and charges, must be apportioned between the UK and overseas parts of the year on a just and reasonable basis. [*ITTOIA 2005, s 270(3)–(5); FA 2013, Sch 45 paras 81, 153(2)*].

Concerns within CTA 2009, s 39(4) or ITTOIA 2005, s 12(4)

[5.84] Where the qualifying activity is a concern within *CTA 2009, s 39(4)* or *ITTOIA 2005, s 12(4)* (see **4.5** above), allowances for a chargeable period are treated as expenses of, and charges as receipts of, the concern for that period. [*CAA 2001, s 252*].

Companies with investment business

[5.85] Where the qualifying activity is managing the investment business of a company, allowances for a chargeable period are given effect by deduction from income of the business for that period, and any excess allowances become management expenses which can be offset against total profits for the same period or carried forward as excess management expenses to future periods. Balancing charges are given effect as income of the business. Allowances in respect of an item of plant or machinery cannot be given under both these provisions and in another way. Thus, expenditure qualifying for allowances by virtue of another qualifying activity carried on by the company (for example, an ordinary property business) cannot also qualify for allowances under these provisions.

[*CAA 2001, s 253; CTA 2009, s 1233; FA 2015, Sch 5 para 8*].

See also **17.42** below for further consideration of companies with investment business.

Life assurance companies

[5.86] The taxation of life insurance companies was fundamentally reformed by *FA 2012, Pt 2* with effect, subject to certain transitional provisions, from 1 January 2013. If an insurance company would otherwise have had an accounting period beginning before and ending on or after that date, the accounting period ends instead on 31 December 2012. [*FA 2012, ss 148, 149*].

Where the *FA 2012* regime applies to a company carrying on 'long-term business', a division is made between 'management assets' (those provided for use or used in the management of a long-term business) and 'investment assets' (assets held otherwise than for management purposes). Where the company is entitled or liable to any allowances or charges for a chargeable period in respect of any plant or machinery which is a management asset, the allowances or charges are apportioned between the company's 'basic life assurance and general annuity business' and any 'non-BLAGAB long-term business'. The apportionment must be made using the general provisions governing the calculation of the corporation tax profits of the two categories of business. Broadly, this requires an apportionment in accordance with an 'acceptable commercial method' (as defined). See *FA 2012, ss 114, 115*. '*Long-term business*' means life assurance business or other business consisting of the effecting or carrying out of contracts of long-term insurance.

Where a company carries on basic life assurance and general annuity business and is charged to tax in respect of that business under the I – E rules, allowances are given effect by treating them as deemed BLAGAB management expenses for the purposes of *FA 2012, s 76*. Charges are chargeable directly to corporation tax on income. It is not possible to claim allowances on management assets more than once, but they may be taken account of in computing the policy holder's share of I – E profit under *FA 2012, s 103* or in a computation under *FA 2012, s 93(5)* (minimum profits test).

The expressions 'basic life assurance and general assurance business', 'I – E rules', and 'non-BLAGAB long-term business' are all defined in *FA 2012* (see, respectively, *ss 57* and *67(5)*; *s 70(1)(2)*; and *ss 66* and *67*).

Before the introduction of the *FA 2012* regime, similar provisions applied to the management assets of companies carrying on life assurance business ('management assets' in this case being those provided for use or used in the management of a life assurance business). Where a company carrying on any such business was entitled or liable to any allowances or charges for a chargeable period in respect of any plant or machinery which was a management asset, the allowances or charges were apportioned between the different classes of business carried on by reference to mean liabilities. For periods of account (i.e. periods for which accounts are made up) beginning after 31 December 2006, the apportionment was between 'basic life assurance and general annuity business' (as defined), 'gross roll-up business' and 'PHI business'. '*Gross roll-up business*' for this purpose is any of the following: pension business, child trust fund business, ISA business, life reinsurance business and overseas life assurance business. '*PHI business*' is long-term business other than life assurance business. Apportionment did not apply to allowances and charges on management assets held for the purposes of a permanent establishment outside the UK through which the company carried on gross roll-up business. Such allowances were allocated to that business without apportionment. For periods of account (as above) beginning before 1 January 2007 this rule applied only to allowances and charges on management assets provided outside the UK falling to be made in respect of an overseas life assurance business.

Allowances and charges in respect of gross roll-up business were given effect as expenses and receipts of the business in computing the profits under *ICTA 1988, s 436A*. Where a company carried on basic life assurance and general annuity business and was charged to tax in respect of the life assurance business under the I minus E basis (or, for periods of account (as above) beginning before 1 January 2007, where the profits arising from the basic life assurance and general annuity business were not charged under Schedule D, Case I), allowances were treated as expenses falling to be brought into account in calculating the company's expenses deduction at step three in *ICTA 1988, s 76(7)*. Charges were chargeable directly to corporation tax on income. Allowances on management assets could be taken account of in computing the policy holder's proportion of the profits or in a computation:

(a) of the company's adjusted life assurance trade profits for the purposes of *FA 1989, s 85A*; or
(b) for the purposes of restricting the company's expenses deduction (see step nine in *ICTA 1988, s 76(7)*).

[*CAA 2001, ss 254–257, 544, 545(1)(2), ICTA 1988, ss 431(2), 431EA, 434D; FA 2012, ss 63(1), 146, Sch 16 paras 96–100, 103, 104(2), 107; SI 2004 No 2310, Sch paras 55, 56; SI 2004 No 2680, Regs 20, 21*].

In the case of plant or machinery which is an investment asset and is let, otherwise than in the course of a property business (see **5.83** above), allowances will be given under the special leasing provisions (see **5.87** below), the letting being regarded as otherwise than in the course of any other qualifying activity. Under the *FA 2012* regime, no allowance in respect of an investment asset can be taken into account in calculating the taxable profits of any non-BLAGAB long-term business carried on by a company. Previously, allowances on investment assets were apportioned between the different categories of business in the same way as income. Allowances were not available against profits from gross roll-up business. [*CAA 2001, ss 19(5), 545, Sch 2 para 39; ICTA 1988, s 434E; FA 2012, Sch 16 paras 95, 104(3)*].

See also **17.42** below for further consideration of life assurance companies.

Special leasing

[5.87] Where the qualifying activity is special leasing (see **4.7** above and **6.19** below), an allowance for a chargeable period is given effect by deducting it from (or setting it off against) income (including a balancing charge) from any special leasing for the tax year or accounting period (i.e. the chargeable period) concerned. Where the plant or machinery was not used for the whole or any part of that tax year or accounting period for the purposes of a qualifying activity carried on by the lessee, the allowance, or a proportionate part of it, is given effect by deducting it from income from that special leasing only. For income tax purposes, the deduction is given effect at Step 2 of the calculation in *ITA 2007, s 23*.

A balancing charge falling to be made in respect of special leasing is, for corporation tax purposes, treated as income from special leasing. For income tax purposes, charges are assessed directly to income tax. [*CAA 2001, ss 258, 259*].

No allowance in respect of special leasing may be given to any extent by deduction from a company's oil contractor profits subject to the ring fence in *CTA 2010, s 356M*. [*CTA 2010, s 356NG; FA 2014, Sch 16 para 4*].

For the restriction on the use of the above allowances, see **2.17** and **2.44** above. For the treatment of excess allowances, see **2.43** and **2.44** above.

Employments and offices

[5.88] Allowances available for a chargeable period to a person carrying on a qualifying activity which is an employment or office are given effect by treating them as a deduction from the taxable earnings of the employment or office. Charges are treated as earnings from the employment or office. [*CAA 2001, s 262*; *ITEPA 2003, Sch 6 para 253*].

A balancing charge is considered to be treated as earnings only for the limited purpose of giving effect to it, so that, for example, a charge is not taken into account in calculating earnings to determine whether the employment is lower-paid employment for the purposes of the benefits code for 2015/16 and earlier years (see *ITEPA 2003, ss 216–220*). (See the Revenue Explanatory Notes to the Capital Allowances Bill, Annex 2 Note 41.)

6

Plant and Machinery — Fixtures and Leasing

Introduction

[6.1] Special provisions apply to determine entitlement to capital allowances for expenditure on plant or machinery that is, or becomes, a 'fixture', i.e. plant or machinery 'that is so installed or otherwise fixed in or to a building or other description of land as to become, in law, part of that building or other land'. Also included in the definition are any boiler or water-filled radiator installed in a building as part of a space or water heating system. The provisions are complex and are described at **6.2–6.17** below.

Expenditure on plant or machinery used for leasing is subject to the general rules for capital allowances, as modified by the special provisions described in this chapter.

Special leasing (see **4.7** above) is treated as a separate qualifying activity as in **6.19** below. For plant or machinery provided by a lessee, see **6.20** below.

For restrictions on first-year allowances, see **5.26**(v) above.

Following *FA 2006* there is a special regime for certain 'long funding leases' under which it is the lessee who obtains capital allowances. See **6.21–6.40** below.

Writing-down allowances on plant or machinery used for certain overseas leasing were previously either restricted to 10% per annum or prohibited altogether. The restrictions are abolished for new leases on the introduction of the long funding lease regime. See **6.21–6.55** below.

Fixtures under leases

Background to the provisions

[6.2] The case of *Stokes v Costain Property Investments Ltd* CA 1984, 57 TC 688 focused attention on an anomaly whereby a person, incurring capital expenditure on fixtures which thereupon formed part of a building which he did not own, could not obtain capital allowances on such expenditure because the plant or machinery installed as fixtures were not 'owned' by him, even though he might have an interest in the building, for example as a lessee. Indeed the case highlighted a genuinely unsatisfactory area of revenue law which, when superimposed on already complex land law, gave rise to widespread concern. The concern was compounded because of the general feeling that the Revenue had hitherto in practice been prepared to ignore the 'owning' test. Ultimately the law was changed.

Scope of the provisions

[6.3] Legislation, originally contained in *FA 1985*, introduced rules determining entitlement to capital allowances for expenditure on plant or machinery that is, or becomes, a 'fixture'. The rules operate by deeming a particular person to be the owner of the fixture for the purpose of making allowances. For this purpose a '*fixture*' is plant or machinery 'that is so installed or otherwise fixed in or to a building or other description of land as to become, in law, part of that building or other land'. Also included in the definition are any boiler or water-filled radiator installed in a building as part of a space or water heating system.

Where there is any dispute over whether or not plant or machinery has become, in law, part of a building or land and it has a material effect on the tax liabilities of two or more persons, the question may be determined by the tribunal broadly as if it were an appeal with the persons affected entitled to be a party to the proceedings. The provisions do not preclude the granting of an allowance under *CAA 2001, s 538* to any person who has made a contribution towards the expenditure (see **2.9** above). Assessments and adjustments of assessments may be made to give effect to the provisions.

[*CAA 2001, ss 172, 173(1), 203(4), 204(1)–(3)*].

FA 2012 introduced provisions that require the buyer and seller of a building containing fixtures to meet certain requirements before the buyer can claim allowances in respect of the fixtures. Broadly, the seller must pool the expenditure on the fixtures before the sale and the buyer and seller must either formally agree a value for the fixtures within two years of the transfer or start formal proceedings to agree the value within that time.

Although the provisions strictly apply on an asset by asset basis, HMRC accept that in practice they may be applied to groups of assets provided that this does not distort the tax computation (Revenue Tax Bulletin June 1998, p 552).

Where fixtures are purchased under hire-purchase contracts etc., so that both these provisions and *CAA 2001, s 67* (see **7.7** onwards below) potentially apply, these provisions take priority and *CAA 2001, s 67* is disapplied. [*CAA 2001, s 69(1)*]. See **7.9** below for the position where plant or machinery purchased under a hire-purchase contract etc. subsequently becomes a fixture.

A person is not entitled to allowances under the fixtures provisions in respect of an asset if capital allowances other than plant and machinery allowances have previously been made to any person in respect of expenditure relating, in whole or in part, to that asset. This does not apply if the previous allowances were industrial buildings allowances (now abolished) research and development allowances or business premises renovation allowances and *CAA 2001, s 186(2)*, *186A(2)* or *187(2)* (see **6.15** and **6.16** below) apply. Similarly, where allowances have been made under the fixtures provisions for expenditure on an asset, no one is later entitled to a capital allowance other than a plant or machinery allowance in respect of any capital expenditure relating to the asset. [*CAA 2001, s 9, Sch 3 para 10; FA 2012, Sch 10 para 7*].

Exclusion for fixtures subject to long funding lease

[6.4] Where plant or machinery that is or becomes a fixture is the subject of a long funding lease (see **6.21–6.40** below), the fixtures provisions do not apply to determine the entitlement of the lessor or lessee to plant or machinery allowances, or to determine whether the lessor or the lessee is to be treated as the owner of the plant or machinery. This applies also where, in such a case, the lessee is or becomes the lessor of some or all of the plant or machinery under a further lease which is not a long funding lease. In the latter case, the fixtures provisions are disapplied in respect of the lessor and lessee under both leases. [*CAA 2001, s 172A*].

Relevant land

[6.5] For the purposes of the fixtures provisions, '*relevant land*' in relation to a fixture means the building or other description of land of which it becomes part or, in the case of boilers and radiators, in which it is installed. [*CAA 2001, s 173(2)*]. An '*interest in land*' is defined as:

(a) the fee simple estate in the land or an agreement to acquire that estate;
(b) in Scotland, the interest of the owner (or, before the appointed day for the coming into force of the *Abolition of Feudal Tenure etc. (Scotland) Act 2000*, the estate or interest of the proprietor of the *dominium utile* (or, in the case of property other than feudal property, of the owner)) and any agreement to acquire such an estate or interest;
(c) a lease (defined for the purpose of these provisions as any leasehold estate in, or in Scotland lease of, the land (whether a headlease, sublease or underlease) and any agreement to acquire such an estate, or in Scotland, lease);
(d) an easement or servitude or any agreement to acquire an easement or servitude; and
(e) a licence to occupy land.

Where an interest in land is conveyed or assigned by way of security and subject to a right of redemption, the person having that right is treated as having the interest in the land.

[*CAA 2001, ss 174(4), 175, Sch 3 para 29*].

HMRC consider that a licence to occupy land within (e) above will only arise where the claimant has an exclusive licence to occupy the land in question, since a licence to occupy is a permission to enter and remain on land for such a purpose as enables the licensee to exert control over the land (Revenue Tax Bulletin, June 2000).

Expenditure incurred by holder of interest in land

[6.6] Where a person incurs capital expenditure on plant or machinery which becomes a fixture at a time when he has an interest in the relevant land, then, providing the expenditure is incurred for the purposes of a qualifying activity carried on by him, he is treated as the owner of the fixture for capital allowance purposes. This is subject to the exceptions in **6.7** to **6.9** below.

If, in accordance with the above, two or more persons, each with a different interest in the land, would be treated as the owner of the fixture, only one interest is to be taken into account, determined in the following order of priority.

(i) The interest, if any, which is, or is an agreement to acquire, an easement or servitude.
(ii) The interest, if any, which is a licence to occupy land.
(iii) Except in Scotland, the interest which is not directly or indirectly in reversion on any of the interests held by any of the persons in question. In Scotland, the interest of whichever person has, or last had, the right of use of the land.

[*CAA 2001, s 176*].

In *JC Decaux (UK) Ltd v Francis (Inspector of Taxes)* SpC, [1996] SSCD 281 the taxpayer company leased various items of street furniture (including automatic public conveniences, electric information boards, bus shelters etc) to local authorities. The Special Commissioner dismissed the company's appeal for capital allowances on fixtures under what is now *CAA 2001, s 176* because the company would need to have an interest in the relevant land. The company did not have such an interest under English law, nor did its contractual rights to clean and maintain the equipment amount to a licence to occupy the land.

Expenditure incurred by equipment lessor

[6.7] For the purpose of the provisions below, an 'equipment lease' is an agreement, or a lease entered into under or as a result of an agreement, entered into in the following circumstances. The circumstances are that a person ('the equipment lessor') incurs capital expenditure on plant or machinery for leasing; an agreement is entered into for the lease, either directly or indirectly from the equipment lessor, of the plant or machinery to another person ('the equipment lessee'); and that plant or machinery becomes a fixture. The agreement must not be an agreement for the plant or machinery to be leased as part of the relevant land.

Provided that:

(i) the equipment lease is for the lease of the plant or machinery for the purposes of a qualifying activity carried on by (or to be carried on by) the equipment lessee;
(ii) the use of the plant or machinery under the equipment lease is not in a dwelling-house;
(iii) if the expenditure had been incurred by the lessee, he would, under **6.6** above, have been entitled to allowances in respect of that expenditure as being expenditure on the fixtures; and
(iv) the equipment lessor and equipment lessee are not connected persons (within **2.34** above).

the equipment lessee and equipment lessor may jointly elect for the equipment lessor, and not the equipment lessee, to be treated, from the time the expenditure is incurred, as the owner of the fixture. Where, however, the lessee's qualifying activity is not being carried on at the time the lessor incurs the expenditure, the election takes effect from the time the qualifying activity begins to be carried on.

Where the following conditions are met, conditions (i) and (iii) above do not have to be satisfied, and the potentially later start date for the election is not relevant:

(1) the plant or machinery becomes a fixture by being fixed to land which is neither a building nor part of a building;
(2) the lessee has an interest in that land when he takes possession of the plant or machinery under the equipment lease;
(3) under the terms of the equipment lease the lessor is entitled, at the end of the lease period, to sever the plant or machinery from the land to which it is then fixed, whereupon it will be owned by the lessor;
(4) the nature of the plant or machinery and the way it is fixed to the land are such that its use does not, to any material extent, prevent its being used, after severance, for the same purposes on different premises; and
(5) the equipment lease is such as falls under normal accountancy practice to be treated, in the accounts of UK incorporated equipment lessors, as an operating lease.

Where the expenditure is incurred on or after 28 July 2000 and before 1 January 2008, the plant or machinery consists of a boiler, heat exchanger, radiator or heating control installed in a building as part of a space or water heating system, and the equipment lease is approved under the Affordable Warmth Programme (a Government scheme intended to support the installation of efficient central heating systems in low income homes), these provisions have effect without conditions (i)–(iii) above having to be satisfied. Approval for this purpose is to be given, with the consent of the Treasury, by the Secretary of State, or where appropriate by the Scottish Ministers, the National Assembly for Wales or the Department for Social Development in Northern Ireland. Where such approval is withdrawn, it is treated as never having had effect, and all necessary consequential adjustments must be made. The taxpayer must notify HMRC, within three months of first becoming aware that a return of his has become incorrect by reason of the withdrawal of approval, of the amendments to the return required in consequence of the withdrawal, subject to penalties under *TMA 1970, s 98* for failure.

The election must be made by notice to HMRC:

(a) for income tax, within twelve months after 31 January following the tax year in which ends the equipment lessor's chargeable period in which the expenditure was incurred, and
(b) for corporation tax, within two years after the end of the equipment lessor's chargeable period in which the expenditure was incurred.

[*CAA 2001, ss 174(1)–(3), 177–180, 203*].

If no election is made or can be made (e.g. the parties are connected persons or the time limit for an election expires), no capital allowances are available as the equipment lessee has not incurred capital expenditure and the equipment lessor has no interest in the land of which the fixture forms a part. *CAA 2001, s 538* (see **2.9** above) does not seem to be of any help in such a situation as it could not be said that the equipment lessor has contributed 'a capital sum to expenditure . . . which . . . would have been regarded as wholly incurred by another person'. It seems this is a trap for the tardy in general or for unwary connected persons.

Expenditure incurred by energy services provider

[6.8] The provisions below apply in relation to expenditure incurred by an 'energy services provider' under an 'energy services agreement'.

For this purpose, an '*energy services provider*' is a person carrying on a qualifying activity consisting wholly or mainly in the provision of energy management services. An '*energy services agreement*' is an agreement between an energy services provider and another person ('*the client*') that provides, with a view to saving energy or using it more efficiently, for:

- the design of, or of systems incorporating, plant or machinery;
- obtaining and installing the plant or machinery;
- the operation and maintenance of the plant or machinery; and
- the amount of payments in respect of that operation to be linked, wholly or partly, to energy savings or increases in energy efficiency resulting from the provision or operation of the plant or machinery.

Where an energy services agreement is entered into under which the energy services provider incurs capital expenditure on the provision of plant or machinery which becomes a fixture, then provided that:

- at the time the plant or machinery becomes a fixture the client has an interest in the relevant land but the energy services provider does not;
- the plant or machinery is not leased or used in a dwelling-house;
- the operation of the plant or machinery is carried out wholly or substantially by the energy services provider (or a person connected with him); and
- the client and energy services provider are not connected persons (within **2.34** above);

the client and energy service provider may jointly elect that the energy services provider, and not the client, be treated as the owner of the fixture from the time the expenditure is incurred. Where the client would not have been entitled to an allowance by virtue of the provisions in **6.6** above (for example, as a local authority outside the charge to tax), the election can only be made if the plant or machinery is of a class designated by Treasury order. For this purpose, *SI 2001 No 2541, Art 6* designates the 'combined heat and power' technology class referred to at **5.17** above.

The election must be made by notice to HMRC no later than two years after the end of the chargeable period in which the expenditure is incurred for corporation tax purposes, or, for income tax purposes, within one year after 31 January following the tax year in which the chargeable period in which the expenditure is incurred ends.

[*CAA 2001, ss 175A, 180A*].

These provisions were introduced with the intention of enabling energy services providers to claim the 100% first-year allowances in 5.16 (1) above (where the conditions at 5.17 above are satisfied).

Expenditure included in consideration for acquisition of existing interest in land

[6.9] Where, after any item of plant or machinery has become a fixture, a person (the 'purchaser') acquires an existing interest in the relevant land and gives consideration for the interest which is or includes a capital sum that is, or is in part, treated for capital allowances purposes as expenditure on the provision of the fixture, then the purchaser is treated as the owner of the fixture in consequence of his expenditure on it.

The same applies:

(i) where, before the acquisition, the plant or machinery was let under an equipment lease (see 6.7 above) and the capital sum paid by the purchaser is to discharge the obligations of the equipment lessee; or
(ii) where, before the acquisition, the plant or machinery was provided under an energy services agreement (see 6.8 above) and the capital sum paid by the purchaser is to discharge the obligations of the client under that agreement.

See 6.15 below for circumstances in which the above provisions do not apply.

[*CAA 2001, ss 181(1)(4), 182(1), 182A(1)*].

CAA 2001, s 562 provides that, where more than one item of property is sold in one bargain, the purchase price is to be apportioned between the various items on a just and reasonable basis, notwithstanding that separate prices are agreed for the individual items of property. Any dispute as to the apportionment of the price may be determined by the Commissioners. See 4.21 above for HMRC's approach to apportionments. By virtue of *CAA 2001, s 185* (see 6.15 below), the purchaser of a building containing landlord's fixtures cannot claim capital allowances on a larger sum than the original cost of the fixtures.

Expenditure incurred by incoming lessee: election to transfer right to allowances

[6.10] An election can be made where, after any item of plant or machinery has become a fixture, a person (the 'lessor'), who has an interest in the relevant land, grants a lease and the consideration given by the lessee is, or includes, a capital sum that falls, in whole or part, to be treated for capital allowances purposes as expenditure on provision of the fixture, provided that the lessor was entitled to allowances on that fixture for the chargeable period in which the lease is granted (or, under the preceding year basis, the chargeable period related to the granting of the lease), or would have been so entitled if he were within the charge to tax. The lessor and lessee may jointly elect that the lessee be treated, as from the date of the lease, as the owner of the fixture. An election must be made by notice to HMRC within two years after the date on which the lease takes effect but no election can be made by connected persons (within **2.34** above). [*CAA 2001, s 183*].

Expenditure incurred by incoming lessee: lessor not entitled to allowances

[6.11] Where:

(i) after an item of plant or machinery has become a fixture, a person (the 'lessor') who has an interest in the relevant land grants a lease,
(ii) **6.10** above does not apply because the lessor is not entitled to capital allowances in respect of the fixtures (and would not be even if within the charge to tax),
(iii) before the lease is granted, the fixture has not been used for the purposes of a qualifying activity carried on by the lessor or a person connected with him (see **2.34** above), and
(iv) the consideration given by the lessee includes a capital sum falling to be treated for plant and machinery allowance purposes wholly or partly as expenditure on the provision of the fixture,

the lessee is treated as the owner of the fixture from the time the lease is granted. [*CAA 2001, s 184(1)*].

In *West Somerset Railway plc v Chivers*, Sp C [1995] SSCD 1, a railway line in Somerset was closed by British Rail in 1971. In 1975 Somerset County Council purchased the freehold of the railway and leased it to a company. In 1989 the company paid a premium of £210,000 for a new lease. The company claimed writing-down allowances on the basis that £107,000 of this related to plant and machinery on the railway line. The Revenue rejected the claim and the company appealed to the Special Commissioners. The Commissioner dismissed the appeal. Under the provisions applying at that time, the company could only claim allowances if 'no person has previously become entitled to an allowance in respect of any capital expenditure incurred on the provision of the fixture'. It appeared that most of the fixtures in question had been installed before the railway was nationalised in 1948, so that the Great Western Railway (which operated the line before nationalisation) would have been entitled to claim allowances thereon.

Cases where fixture is to be treated as ceasing to be owned by a particular person

[6.12] The rules requiring a disposal value to be brought into account on the happening of certain specified disposal events (see **5.41** above) apply equally to fixtures. One such event occurs when plant or machinery ceases to be owned by a person. Where a person is treated as the owner of a fixture under:

- *CAA 2001, s 176* (see **6.6** above);
- *CAA 2001, ss 181, 182, 182A* (see **6.9** above);
- *CAA 2001, s 183* (see **6.10** above); or
- *CAA 2001, s 184* (see **6.11** above),

he is treated as ceasing to own the fixture when he ceases to have the 'qualifying interest'. The qualifying interest is the interest in the relevant land referred to at **6.6** or **6.9** above, or in the case of **6.10** and **6.11** above, the lease there referred to. [*CAA 2001, s 188*].

If the qualifying interest is an agreement to acquire an interest in land, and the interest in land is granted or transferred to the person concerned, the interest so granted is regarded as being the qualifying interest.

There are certain circumstances in which an alteration in the interest held is disregarded in determining whether or not a person still has a qualifying interest, and these are as follows:

(i) where the qualifying interest is merged with another interest acquired by the same person;
(ii) where the qualifying interest is a lease, and on its termination a new lease of the same land, with or without other land, is granted to the lessee;
(iii) where the qualifying interest is a licence, and on its termination a new licence to occupy the land, with or without other land, is granted to the licensee; and
(iv) where the qualifying interest is a lease, and the lessee remains in possession of the land with the lessor's consent following termination of the lease with no new lease being granted to the lessee, the lessee's qualifying interest being deemed to continue for so long as he retains possession of the land.

[*CAA 2001, s 189*].

Where, in the circumstances described in **6.10** above (right to allowances transferred to incoming lessee), a fixture is treated as beginning to be owned by the lessee, it is treated as ceasing to be owned by the lessor. [*CAA 2001, s 190*].

Where a fixture is treated as ceasing to be owned by an outgoing lessee or licensee following the termination of the lease or licence, it is treated as beginning to be owned by the person who, immediately prior to termination, was the lessor or licensor. [*CAA 2001, s 193*].

Where, at any time, a fixture is permanently severed from the relevant land, thus ceasing to be a fixture, then it is treated as ceasing to be owned by the person treated as the owner under these provisions if, once severed, it is not in fact owned by him. [*CAA 2001, s 191*].

Special provisions as to equipment lessors

[6.13] Where an equipment lessor is treated as the owner of a fixture under *CAA 2001, s 177* (see **6.7** above), and either the lessor assigns his rights under the equipment lease or the financial obligations of the equipment lessee (or a person in whom those obligations have become vested (by assignment etc.)) are discharged by payment of a capital sum or otherwise, the equipment lessor is treated as ceasing to be the owner of the fixture at that time (or the earliest such time). [*CAA 2001, s 192*].

On an assignment, the assignee is treated as becoming the owner of the fixture and as having incurred expenditure on the provision of the fixture equal to the consideration given by him for the assignment. The assignee then takes over the role of equipment lessor. Where a capital sum is paid in order to discharge the financial obligations of the equipment lessee (or assignee etc.), the lessee (or assignee etc.) is treated as becoming the owner of the fixture and as having incurred expenditure on the provision of the fixture equal to the capital sum.

[*CAA 2001, ss 194, 195*].

Following publication of the 1985 Finance Bill, the Revenue confirmed, in discussions with the Law Society, that the phrase 'or otherwise' above embraced a capital sum of nil and that the use of the phrase was not intended to imply the need to bring into account market value as required by **5.41**(g) above.

Special provisions as to energy services providers

[6.14] Where an energy services provider is treated as the owner of a fixture under the provisions at **6.8** above and either he assigns his rights under the energy services agreement or the financial obligations of the client (or a person in whom those obligations have become vested (by assignment etc.)) in relation to the fixture under the agreement are discharged by payment of a capital sum or otherwise, the energy services provider is treated as ceasing to own the fixture at that time (or the earliest such time). [*CAA 2001, s 192A*].

On an assignment, the assignee is treated as being an energy services provider who owns the fixture by virtue of the provisions at **6.8** above and as having incurred expenditure on the provision of the fixture equal to the consideration given for the assignment. Where a capital sum is paid in order to discharge the financial obligations of the client (or assignee etc.), the client (or assignee etc.) is treated as becoming the owner of the fixture and as having incurred expenditure on the provision of the fixture equal to the capital sum. [*CAA 2001, ss 195A, 195B*].

Fixtures in respect of which more than one person would get an allowance

[6.15] Where **6.9** or **6.11** above would otherwise apply, they are treated as not applying (and as never having applied) where a person has a 'prior right' in relation to the fixture immediately after the relevant time (i.e. in relation to **6.9** above, the time when the purchaser acquires his interest in the relevant land, or, in relation to **6.11** above, the time of the grant of the lease). For this purpose, a person has a '*prior right*' if:

(i) that person is treated as the owner of the fixture (other than under *CAA 2001, s 538* (contributions to expenditure), see **2.9** above) immediately before the relevant time, as a result of his having incurred expenditure on its provision; and
(ii) that person is entitled to, and claims, an allowance in respect of that expenditure.

Where any person becomes aware that a return of his has become incorrect because of the operation of this provision, the necessary amendments to the return must be notified to HMRC within three months of his becoming so aware, subject to penalties for failure.

[*CAA 2001, ss 181(2)(3), 182(2)(3), 182A(2)(3), 184(2)(3), 203*].

Where:

(A) a person (the 'current owner') is treated as the owner of a fixture as a result of incurring capital expenditure ('new expenditure') on its provision;
(B) the fixture is treated (other than under *CAA 2001, s 538* (contributions to expenditure, see **2.9** above)) as having been owned at a 'relevant earlier time' by a person (the 'past owner', who may be the same as the current owner) as a result of incurring expenditure other than that within (A) above; and
(C) the past owner, having claimed an allowance for that expenditure, is or has been required to bring in a disposal value for the fixtures by reason of an event occurring after 23 July 1996,

so much (if any) of the new expenditure referred to in (A) above as exceeds the 'maximum allowable amount' is left out of account in determining the current owner's qualifying expenditure or, as the case may be, is taken to be expenditure which should never have been taken into account.

A '*relevant earlier time*' is any time before that taken under these provisions to be the earliest time when the current owner is treated as the owner of the fixture as a result of incurring the new expenditure. If, before that earliest time, the plant or machinery was sold other than as a fixture to an unconnected person (see **2.34** above), any time before the sale is not treated as a relevant earlier time.

The '*maximum allowable amount*' is the sum of the disposal value referred to in (C) above and so much (if any) of the expenditure referred to in (A) above as is deemed under *CAA 2001, s 25* (installation costs, see **4.16** above) to be on provision of the fixtures. Where (C) above is satisfied in relation to more than one event, only the most recent event is taken into account for this purpose.

Where any person becomes aware that a return of his has become incorrect because of the operation of this provision, the necessary amendments to the return must be notified to HMRC within three months of his becoming so aware, subject to penalties for failure.

[*CAA 2001, ss 185, 203*].

Change in ownership of a fixture

[6.15A] The following provisions require the buyer and seller of a building containing fixtures to meet certain requirements before the buyer can claim allowances in respect of the fixtures. Broadly, the seller must pool the expenditure on the fixtures before the sale and the buyer and seller must either formally agree a value for the fixtures within two years of the transfer or start formal proceedings to agree the value within that time.

The provisions apply where:

(a) a person (the 'current owner') is treated as the owner of a fixture as a result of incurring capital expenditure ('new expenditure') on or after 6 April 2012 (1 April 2012 for corporation tax purposes) on its provision for the purposes of a qualifying activity carried on by him;
(b) the fixture is treated (other than under *CAA 2001, s 538* (contributions to expenditure, see **2.9** above)) as having been owned at a relevant earlier time (see **6.15** above, and see further below) by a person as a result of incurring other capital expenditure ('historic expenditure') on its provision for the purposes of a qualifying activity carried on by him; and
(c) a person within (b) above was entitled to claim an allowance in respect of the historic expenditure.

Where the provisions apply, in determining the current owner's qualifying expenditure, the new expenditure is treated as nil if, in relation to the 'past owner' (i.e. the person in (b) or, if there is more than one such person, the person by whom expenditure was most recently incurred):

- the 'pooling requirement' is not satisfied;
- the 'fixed value requirement' applies but is not satisfied; or
- the 'disposal value statement requirement' applies but is not satisfied.

Note that the current owner and the past owner may be the same person. The treatment of new expenditure as nil does not affect any disposal value to be brought into account by the past owner. The provisions do not apply where the period of ownership in (b) above begins and ends before 6 April 2012 (1 April 2012 for corporation tax purposes).

The '*pooling requirement*' is that either the historic expenditure has been allocated to a pool in a chargeable period beginning on or before the day on which the past owner ceased to be treated as the owner of the fixture or a first-year allowance has been claimed in respect of that expenditure (or part of it). The pooling requirement does not apply if the period for which the fixture is treated as owned by the past owner ends before 6 April 2014 (1 April 2014 for corporation tax purposes).

The '*fixed value requirement*' applies if the past owner is or has been required to bring a disposal value of the fixture into account under **6.17**(1), (5) or (9) below. The requirement is that:

(1) either:
    (I) the tribunal has determined the part of the sale price or, where **6.17**(5) below applies, capital sum given by the lessee for the lease that constitutes the disposal value, on an application by one of the past owner and either the purchaser from the past owner or, where **6.17**(5) below applies, the lessee (the '*affected parties*') before the end of the two-year period (the '*relevant two-year period*') beginning with the date when the purchaser acquires the qualifying interest or the lessee is granted the lease; or

(II) an election under *CAA 2001, s 198* or *s 199* (see **6.17** below) is made jointly by the affected parties in respect of the sale price or capital sum before the end of the relevant two-year period or, if later, before any application within (I) above has been determined or withdrawn; or

(2) where the purchaser from the past owner or the lessee was not entitled to allowances on capital expenditure on the fixture, the current owner has obtained, directly or indirectly, a written statement made by that purchaser or lessee, that (I) above has not been met and can no longer be met, and a written statement made by the past owner of the amount of the disposal value in fact brought into account.

Note that copies of the written statements in (2) above are sufficient to meet the requirement.

The '*disposal value statement requirement*' applies if the past owner is or has been required to bring a disposal value of the fixture into account under **6.17**(2) or (3) below or **5.41**(j) above. The requirement is that the past owner must have made a written statement of the amount of the disposal value within two years of ceasing to own the fixture and the current owner must have obtained that statement or a copy of it.

The onus is on the current owner to show that the fixed value requirement or disposal value statement requirement apply and are satisfied and, for this purpose, to provide HMRC on request with a copy of any relevant tribunal decision, election or statement. Any apportionment made in a written statement of the amount of a disposal value applies for capital allowances purposes in place of any apportionment that would otherwise be made under the provisions at **2.25** and **2.30**(a) above. If subsequent circumstances reduce the disposal value shown in a written statement, the statement is treated as showing that reduced amount.

[*CAA 2001, ss 187A, 187B; FA 2012, s 43, Sch 10 paras 2, 11, 13*].

Fixtures on which an allowance has been made under another code

[6.16] Where, for chargeable periods ending after 23 July 1996:

(1) a person has claimed industrial buildings allowances for expenditure partly on the provision of plant or machinery, and transfers the relevant interest in the building concerned; and

(2) the transferee, or any other person who is subsequently treated as the owner of the plant or machinery under these provisions, claims allowances for expenditure ('new expenditure') incurred at a time after 23 July 1996 on the provision of that plant or machinery at a time when it is a fixture in the building,

the claim may not exceed the '*maximum allowable amount*', i.e. an amount equal to the proportion of the residue of qualifying expenditure (as defined for the purposes of industrial buildings allowances, now abolished) attributable to the relevant interest immediately after the transfer referred to in (1) above (calculated on the assumption that the transfer was a sale) that the part of the consideration for the transfer attributable to the fixture bears to the total consideration. Where the transfer takes place in a chargeable period beginning on or after 6 April 2011 for income tax purposes or 1 April 2011 for corporation tax purposes (i.e. following the abolition of industrial buildings allowances), in calculating the maximum allowable amount, a notional residue of qualifying expenditure is used, equal to the amount that would have been the residue had the transfer taken place immediately before the repeal of those allowances. If, however, the total consideration for the transfer does not exceed the notional residue, the maximum allowable amount is the part of that consideration which is attributable to the fixture.

A similar restriction applies where research and development allowances have previously been claimed. A similar restriction also applies where business premises renovation allowances have previously been claimed and a balancing event (see **8.10** below) occurs on or after 6 April 2012 (1 April 2012 for corporation tax purposes).

[*CAA 2001, ss 186–187; FA 2012, Sch 10 paras 6, 12*].

Disposal value of fixtures in certain cases

[6.17] Special provisions apply, in addition to the normal provisions (see **5.41** above), to determine the disposal value of fixtures, as follows.

(1) On the cessation of ownership of a fixture under *CAA 2001, s 188* (see **6.12** above) because of a sale of the qualifying interest, the disposal value is (unless (2) below applies) the part of the sale price that falls to be treated for plant and machinery allowance purposes as expenditure incurred by the purchaser on the provision of the fixture, or would so fall if the purchaser were entitled to allowances.

(2) On the cessation of ownership of a fixture under *CAA 2001, s 188* (see **6.12** above) because of a sale of the qualifying interest where the sale is at less than market value and the purchaser cannot claim plant and machinery or research and development (formerly scientific research) allowances in respect of his expenditure on the fixture or is a dual resident investing company connected with the seller, the disposal value is the part of the price that, if the qualifying interest were sold at market value (determined without regard to the actual sale), would be treated for plant and machinery allowance purposes as expenditure incurred by the purchaser on the provision of the fixture.

(3) On the cessation of ownership of a fixture under *CAA 2001, s 188* (see **6.12** above) where neither (1) nor (2) above applies but the qualifying interest continues in existence (or would do so but for its becoming merged in another interest), the disposal value is determined as in (2) above.

(4) On the cessation of ownership of a fixture under *CAA 2001, s 188* (see **6.12** above) because of the expiry of the qualifying interest, it is any capital sum received by reference to the fixture, or otherwise nil.

(5) On cessation of ownership under *CAA 2001, s 190* (see **6.12** above), the disposal value is the part of the capital sum given by the lessee for the lease that falls to be treated for plant and machinery allowance purposes as the lessee's expenditure on the provision of the fixture.

(6) On cessation of ownership under *CAA 2001, s 191* (see **6.12** above), the disposal value is the market value of the fixture at the time of severance.

(7) On cessation of ownership under *CAA 2001, s 192* (see **6.13** above), the disposal value is either the consideration given by the assignee for the assignment or the capital sum, if any, paid to discharge the equipment lessee's financial obligations, as appropriate.

(8) On cessation of ownership under *CAA 2001, s 192A* (see **6.13** above), the disposal value is either the consideration given by the assignee for the assignment or the capital sum, if any, paid to discharge the client's financial obligations, as appropriate.

(9) On the permanent discontinuance of the qualifying activity followed by sale of the qualifying interest, the disposal value is determined as in (1) above.

(10) On the permanent discontinuance of the qualifying activity followed by the demolition or destruction of the fixture, the disposal value is the net amount received for the remains of the fixture, plus any insurance or capital compensation received.

(11) On the permanent discontinuance of the qualifying activity followed by the permanent loss of the fixture (otherwise than as in (10) above), the disposal value is any insurance or capital compensation received.

(12) On the fixture's beginning to be used wholly or partly for purposes other than those of the qualifying activity, the disposal value is the part of the price that would be treated for plant and machinery allowance purposes as expenditure incurred by the purchaser on the provision of the fixture if the qualifying interest were sold at market value.

[*CAA 2001, s 196*].

Fixtures are treated as disposed of at their 'notional written-down value' (if greater than would otherwise be the case) where the event giving rise to the bringing in of a disposal value is part of a scheme or arrangement having the obtaining of a tax advantage under *CAA 2001, Pt 2* as a main object. The '*notional written-down value*' is qualifying expenditure on the fixture concerned less the maximum allowances that could have been made in respect of it, on the assumption that all allowances had been made in full. [*CAA 2001, s 197*].

A special election is available where the disposal value of fixtures falls to be determined under (1), (5) or, for 'new expenditure' (see **6.15** above) incurred on or after 6 April 2012 (1 April 2012 for corporation tax purposes), (9) above. Subject as below and to *CAA 2001, ss 186–187* (see **6.16** above) and *s 197* (above), the seller and the purchaser (or where (5) above applies, the persons who are the lessor and lessee for the purposes of *CAA 2001, s 183* (see **6.10** above)) may jointly elect to fix the amount so determined at a figure not exceeding either the capital expenditure treated as incurred on the fixtures by the seller (or lessor) or the actual sale price (or capital sum). The remainder (if any) of the sale price (or capital sum) is attributed to the other property included in the sale. The notice of election must be given to HMRC within two years after the qualifying interest is acquired or the lease granted, and is irrevocable. The time limit is extended where an application to the tribunal is made under **6.15**(1)(I) above; in such cases notice may be given at any time before the tribunal determines the application or the application is withdrawn. A copy of the notice must also accompany the returns of the persons making the election. The notice must contain prescribed information and must quantify the amount fixed by the election, although if subsequent circumstances reduce the maximum below that fixed, the election is treated as being for that reduced maximum amount. There are provisions for the determination of questions relating to such elections by the tribuna. Where any person becomes aware that a return of his has become incorrect because of such an election (or because of subsequent circumstances affecting the election), the necessary amendments to the return must be notified to HMRC within three months of his becoming aware, subject to penalties for failure. [*CAA 2001, ss 198–201, 203, 204(4)–(6); FA 2012, Sch 10 paras 3, 4, 9–11; F(No 2)A 2017, Sch 14 para 33*]. In practice, HMRC normally accept an election covering a group of fixtures, or all the fixtures in a single property, but not one covering fixtures in different properties (Revenue Tax Bulletin June 1998 p 552).

Leasing

Introduction

[6.18] Expenditure on plant or machinery used for leasing is subject to the general rules for capital allowances, as modified by the special provisions described below.

Special leasing (see **4.7** above) is treated as a separate qualifying activity as in **6.19** below. For plant or machinery provided by a lessee, see **6.20** below.

For restrictions on first-year allowances, see **5.26**(v) above.

Following *FA 2006* there is a special regime for certain 'long funding leases' under which it is the lessee who obtains capital allowances. See **6.21–6.40** below.

Writing-down allowances on plant or machinery used for certain overseas leasing were previously either restricted to 10% per annum or prohibited altogether. The restrictions are abolished for new leases on the introduction of the long funding lease regime. See **6.21–6.55** below.

There are special provisions applying to leases of ships which are qualifying ships for tonnage tax purposes (see **17.58** below) provided to companies within tonnage tax (see **17.60** below). Also, a claim for capital allowances by a lessor in respect of such a qualifying ship, whether or not the lessee is a tonnage tax company, must be accompanied by a certificate by the lessor and the lessee stating that:

- the ship is not leased (directly or indirectly) to a company subject to tonnage tax, or
- neither **17.60**(a) nor (b) below apply and, where the lease would otherwise be a long funding lease, **17.60**(d) below applies.

Where circumstances change so that any matter certificated ceases to be the case, the lessor must, subject to a penalty for failure, inform HMRC within three months after the end of the chargeable period of the change. [*FA 2000, Sch 22 para 93; FA 2003, Sch 32 para 4(1)(3); FA 2006, Sch 9 para 10*].

For provisions applying to companies carrying on a business of leasing plant or machinery, see **7.18** (election on succession between connected persons not to have effect in respect of qualifying leased plant or machinery), **15.11** (restrictions on use of losses and excess allowances in relation to leasing partnerships), **17.16** (disposal of plant or machinery subject to lease where income retained) and **17.30** (sale etc. of lessor company) below.

For anti-avoidance provisions applying to leased plant and machinery where there are arrangements to reduce the value of the leased asset or to reduce its disposal value see **17.20** below.

See also HMRC's Business Leasing Manual.

Special leasing

[6.19] As noted at **4.7** above, the hiring out of plant or machinery otherwise than in the course of any other qualifying activity is in itself a qualifying activity, known as 'special leasing'. Expenditure on plant or machinery for special leasing is allocated to a main pool, although the pool can only include one asset because each item of plant or machinery that is subject to special leasing is treated as leased in the course of a separate qualifying activity. The 'final chargeable period' in respect of the pool (see **5.32** and **5.46** above) is the chargeable period in which the special leasing is permanently discontinued. This is deemed to occur when the lessor permanently ceases to hire out the item in question. [*CAA 2001, ss 19(1)–(4), 65(1)*]. See also **5.87** above.

Plant or machinery provided by lessee

[6.20] If:

(a) a lessee incurs capital expenditure on the provision, for the purposes of a qualifying activity carried on by him, of plant or machinery which the lease requires him to provide,
(b) the plant or machinery is not so installed or fixed in or to a building or any other land so as to become part of the building or land, and
(c) he does not own the plant or machinery,

then, for capital allowances purposes:

(i) the lessee is treated as owning the plant or machinery for so long as it is used for the purposes of the qualifying activity, but
(ii) he is not required to bring a disposal value into account because the lease ends.

If the plant or machinery continues to be so used until the lease ends and the lessor holds the lease in the course of his own qualifying activity, the lessor is required to bring a disposal value into account in the appropriate pool where a disposal event occurs on or after the ending of the lease and at a time when the lessor owns the plant or machinery. For this purpose the appropriate pool is the pool which would be applicable if the expenditure incurred by the lessee had been incurred by the lessor.

For the purposes of the above, a 'lease' includes an agreement for a lease where the term to be covered by the lease has begun, and also includes any tenancy, but does not include a mortgage, and that 'lessee' and 'lessor' should be construed accordingly.

[*CAA 2001, s 70*].

Long funding leases

Introduction

[6.21] As discussed at **6.18** above, *FA 2006, s 81, Sch 8* introduced a new regime for the tax treatment of 'long funding leases'. The intention of the regime is to ensure that lease finance and loan finance are taxed in much the same way, removing any distortionary effect on taxpayer behaviour resulting from the previous differences in tax treatment. The regime is therefore restricted to leases which are essentially financing transactions, comprising mainly finance leases but also some operating leases. The tax treatment of other leases is unaffected.

Under the regime, capital allowances in respect of the leased plant or machinery are given to the lessee rather than, as would be the case on normal principles, the lessor. As a consequence, the lessee's allowable deductions in computing profits are restricted to exclude any expenditure to the extent that it qualifies for allowances.

Whether a lease is a long funding lease is determined independently for the lessor and the lessee. There are, however, provisions to ensure that only one person is able to claim capital allowances in respect of the leased plant or machinery (see **6.25** below).

There are also detailed rules to determine the amounts which lessors are required to bring into account in calculating their profits in respect of a long funding lease which ensure that the capital element of rentals is excluded. For capital gains purposes, a lessor is treated as disposing of and immediately reacquiring plant or machinery for specified amounts both at the commencement of the term of a long funding lease and at the time of its termination (see *TCGA 1992, s 25A*) and capital losses on disposals of fixtures that have been leased under a long funding lease are restricted under *TCGA 1992, s 41A*.

The regime applies from 1 April 2006 subject to the detailed commencement and transitional provisions at **6.23** below. Short leases (as defined) and (broadly) leases finalised before 1 April 2006 are excluded.

The regime is described in detail at **6.21–6.40** below. Basic definitions are given at **6.22** below and the commencement provisions are at **6.23** below. The definition of 'long funding lease' is covered at **6.24–6.35** below. The tax treatment of lessees, including their capital allowances, is at **6.36–6.38** below and that of lessors is at **6.39**, **6.40** below. (The detailed capital gains provisions are outside the scope of this book — see Tolley's Capital Gains Tax for full coverage.)

See **6.4** above for the exclusion from the fixtures provisions of fixtures subject to a long funding lease.

HMRC published a technical note on long funding leases on their website (www.hmrc.gov.uk) on 1 August 2006. Their Business Leasing Manual, available on their website, also includes guidance on long funding leases at BLM 20000–25200, 40000–42400.

Basic definitions

[6.22] The following basic definitions apply for the purposes of the long funding lease regime.

A '*lease*' includes any agreement or arrangement which is or includes a 'plant or machinery lease' (see **6.27** below). A lease, in relation to land, includes an underlease, sublease or any tenancy, an agreement for a lease, underlease, sublease or tenancy (or in Scotland an agreement (including missives of let not constituting a lease) under which a lease, underlease, sublease or tenancy is to be executed) and, in the case of land outside the UK, any interest corresponding to a lease as so defined. A lease, in relation to plant or machinery, includes a sublease.

'*Lessor*' and '*lessee*' and other related expressions are to be construed accordingly. '*Lessee*' includes any person entitled to the lessee's interest under a lease, and '*lessor*' includes any person entitled to the lessor's interest under a lease.

The date of the commencement of the term of a lease is the date on and after which the lessee is entitled to exercise his right to use the complete leased asset under the lease, and for this purpose an asset is regarded as complete if its construction is substantially complete.

The date of the inception of a plant or machinery lease is the earliest date on which there is a contract in writing for the lease between the lessor and the lessee, no terms remain to be agreed and either the contract is unconditional or, if conditional, the conditions have been met.

The term of a lease is the period comprising so much of the period of the lease beginning with the commencement of the term as is a 'non-cancellable period' and any subsequent periods for which the lessee has an option to continue to lease the asset (with or without further payment) which it is reasonably certain, at the inception of the lease, he will exercise. A '*non-cancellable period*' is any period during which the lessee may terminate the lease only upon the occurrence of some remote contingency or upon payment of such an additional amount that, at the inception of the lease, the continuation of the lease is reasonably certain. Special rules apply where the market value (see below) of the leased asset exceeds £1 million at the commencement of the lease's term and at that time the estimated market value five years later is more than half of the market value at that time. Where the term of the lease would otherwise be five years or less (so that the lease would be a short lease — see **6.24** below) but:

(i) the lessee has one or more options to continue to lease the asset;
(ii) the term of the lease would exceed seven years on the assumption that it is reasonably certain, at the inception of the lease, that the lessee will exercise those options; and
(iii) on failing to exercise those options the lessee may be required to make a payment to the lessor,

it is to be assumed that those options will be exercised (so that the lease will not be a short lease), unless it is reasonably certain, at the inception of the lease, that the options will not be exercised. This does not apply if, leaving out of account any options that would result in the term of the lease exceeding seven years, conditions (a)–(c) at **6.24** below are met.

The '*termination*' of a lease means the coming to an end of the lease, whether by the passing of time or in any other way and includes in particular the bringing to an end of the lease by any person or by operation of law. Related expressions are to be construed accordingly.

A '*long funding finance lease*' is a long funding lease which meets the finance lease test at **6.26**(i) below in the case of a particular person by virtue of falling to be treated under generally accepted accounting practice as a finance lease or loan in the accounts of that person. A '*long funding operating lease*' is a long funding lease which is not a long funding finance lease.

'*Arrangement*' includes any transaction or series of transactions.

References to a '*building*' include a structure or part of a building or structure. '*Fixture*' is defined as at **6.3** above, and references to plant or machinery in relation to a lease include references to fixtures.

The market value of plant or machinery is to be determined on the assumption of a disposal by an absolute owner (or, in Scotland, an owner) free from all leases and encumbrances.

Apportionments are to be made on a just and reasonable basis.

Generally accepted accounting practice is defined at *CTA 2010, s 1127*. See also *FA 2011, s 53* which, in effect, preserves the distinction between finance leases and operating leases for tax purposes where accounting standards have been revised to remove it.

[*CAA 2001, ss 70YF, 70YI*].

Commencement

[6.23] The long funding lease regime applies to a lease (which is within the definition of a long funding lease at **6.24** onwards below) if either of the following conditions are met.

(i) The first condition is that the lease is not an 'excepted lease' and either it was 'finalised' on or after 1 April 2006 or the commencement of its term (see **6.22** above) was on or after that date.

(ii) The second condition is that the commencement of the term of the lease was before 1 April 2006 but the plant or machinery is brought into use on or after that date for the purposes of a qualifying activity carried on by the person concerned (i.e. the lessor or lessee). This could apply, for example, where plant or machinery is leased before 1 April 2006 to or by a non-resident trading outside the UK who becomes UK-resident on or after that date (so that the trade becomes a qualifying activity — see **4.3** above).

A lease finalised before 21 July 2005 cannot be a long funding lease. This let-out is itself disapplied as respects any time after 17 May 2006 if the lessor does not come within the charge to UK tax until after 17 May 2006.

A lease is '*finalised*' for the above purposes on the earliest day on which there is a contract in writing for the lease between the lessor and the lessee, no terms remain to be agreed and either the contract is unconditional or, if conditional, the conditions have been met.

Where a lease is excluded from the regime by the commencement rules above, there are provisions to ensure that a transfer (within **6.31** below) of the leased plant or machinery from one lessor to another or from one lessee to another does not of itself bring the lease within the regime. The provisions apply where, on the assumption that before the transfer the lease was not a long funding lease, the transfer is in circumstances such that, were the provisions at **6.31**(a) or (b) below to apply, they would treat the 'new lease' (i.e. the lease deemed to be created on the transfer under those provisions) as not being a long funding lease. The provisions do not apply unless the person making the transfer is within the charge to UK tax immediately before the transfer.

For the purposes of (i) above, a lease is an '*excepted lease*' if the following conditions are met.

(a) Before 21 July 2005 there was evidence in writing that there was agreement or a common understanding between the 'lessor's side' and the 'lessee's side' as to the 'principal terms' of the lease (the '*pre-existing heads of agreement*'). For this purpose, the '*lessor's side*' means any of the lessor, a person who controls (within *CAA 2001, s 574*), or is to control, the lessor and any two or more persons who together control, or are to control the lessor. The '*lessee's side*' means any of the lessee, a person who controls or is to control the lessee and any two or more persons who together control or are to control the lessee. The '*principal terms*' of a lease are the identity of the lessee, the identity or description of the asset to be leased and particulars or a description of the rentals payable and the term.
(b) The leased plant or machinery was 'under construction' before 1 April 2006. For this purpose, an asset is 'under construction' during the period beginning when construction begins and ending when construction is completed. An asset consisting of more than one component part is treated as under construction at any time after the start of construction of any component part identified as a component part before its construction begins. A leased asset is not, however, under construction at any time after the commencement of the term of the lease.

(c) The lease has been finalised before 1 April 2007 (but see below).
(d) The commencement of the term of the lease is before 1 April 2007 (but see below).
(e) The lessee is the particular person or persons identified as such in the pre-existing heads of agreement.
(f) The principal terms of the lease are not materially different from those in the pre-existing heads of agreement (or would not be but for the provisions at **6.28** below dividing mixed leases into derived leases).

The date in (c) and (d) above is deferred to 1 April 2009 if, at the latest, the commencement of the term of the lease is as soon as is reasonably practicable after construction of the asset is substantially complete and the construction proceeded continuously after 31 March 2006. The construction must have proceeded at the normal pace for an asset of its type, i.e. at the pace required to construct the asset in a reasonable time without delays or interruptions and consistent with normal business practice. These conditions are not failed if any breaches are due only to abnormal or unusual events beyond the control of each of the 'principal parties' where:

- the events are unforeseen, and could not reasonably have been foreseen, when the main contract for construction of the asset was entered into, and
- the consequences of the event as respects the condition breached could not have been avoided by the exercise of all due care, or the taking of all reasonable steps, by any of the principal parties.

The '*principal parties*' are the lessor's side, the lessee's side and the main constructor (i.e. the contractor under the main contract for construction of the asset).

Where the pre-existing heads of agreement (see (a) above) relate to more than one asset, the above provisions (and those below) apply as follows. Where any of the assets are for use individually, the provisions apply to that asset separately as if it were the subject of its own pre-existing heads of agreement and, where there is a finalised lease, its own separate finalised lease. In determining the terms of the deemed lease, the same principles are used as are used in determining the terms of a derived lease at **6.28** below. Where any of the assets are constituent assets of a combined asset, the combined asset is treated as a single asset and the provisions apply to that asset separately as if it were an asset for use individually. For this purpose there is a combined asset only if each of the constituent items of plant or machinery was constructed with a view to its use in conjunction with the others as a single combined asset to be used individually. Plant or machinery that can be used individually is not treated as part of a combined asset just because it is one of a number of assets of a similar description each of which is intended for use individually and that use is to be co-ordinated to any extent.

Special transitional provisions apply where a person incurs expenditure on the provision of plant or machinery for leasing under a long funding lease and some or all of that expenditure was incurred before 19 July 2006. If the long funding lease is not an excepted lease and there were pre-existing heads of agreement before 21 July 2005, then, for the purpose of determining the liability to income tax or corporation tax of any person who is or has been the lessor or lessee, the lease is treated as two separate leases. So much of the expenditure as was incurred before 19 July 2006 is treated as if it had been incurred on a separate asset for leasing under a separate long funding lease. The lease is then treated as an excepted lease. Any remaining expenditure is treated as incurred on a second separate asset for leasing under a second separate long funding lease to which the long funding lease regime applies. (These provisions do not prevent this second deemed lease from being further divided under any of the other commencement provisions.) Rentals under the actual lease are to be apportioned between the two deemed leases on a just and reasonable basis.

In determining whether expenditure is incurred before 19 July 2006 for this purpose, the general rule at **2.5** above applies subject to the following exceptions. If under an agreement an unconditional obligation to pay an amount of expenditure comes into being as a result of the giving of a certificate, or any other event occurring, before 19 August 2006, the expenditure is treated as incurred on 18 July 2006. If under an agreement there is an unconditional obligation to pay an amount of expenditure on a date earlier than accords with normal commercial practice and the sole or main benefit expected to result is that the amount is treated as incurred under the general rule at an earlier time, the expenditure is treated as incurred on the date by which payment is due. If the payment terms of an agreement are varied on or after 22 March 2006 so that an unconditional obligation to pay an amount which would otherwise have come into being on or after 19 July 2006 in fact comes into being before that date, then, unless the lease was finalised before 22 March 2006, the amount is treated as incurred on the date that it would have been treated as incurred but for the variation.

For the purposes of the above commencement provisions, a 'lease' includes a plant or machinery lease (see **6.27** below) and a mixed lease (see **6.28** below). 'Lessor', 'lessee' and related expressions are to be construed accordingly.

The provisions apply to mixed leases in accordance with the following. If the mixed lease is an excepted lease it is not within the long funding lease regime. If the mixed lease is not an excepted lease then the principles at **6.28** below are applied to divide the lease into derived leases. The commencement provisions are then applied separately to each of those leases.

[*FA 2006, Sch 8 paras 15, 17–27*].

Meaning of long funding lease

[6.24] A '*long funding lease*' is a 'funding lease' (see **6.26** below) which:

- (i) is not a 'short lease';
- (ii) is not an excluded lease of background plant or machinery for a building (see **6.29** below); and
- (iii) is not excluded by the *de minimis* provision for plant or machinery leased with land at **6.30** below.

A lease is not a long funding lease in the case of the lessee unless the lease is treated in his tax return for the 'initial period' as a long funding lease in respect of which he is taxable under *CTA 2010, ss 360–376* or *ITTOIA 2005, ss 148G–148I* (see **6.38** below). This does not apply in circumstances where a person transfers plant or machinery to another person and, subsequently, the plant or machinery is available to be used by the transferor or a connected person under a plant or machinery lease the commencement of the term of which is after 12 November 2008. Where a return for the initial period has been made, a claim under the recovery of overpaid tax etc. provisions of *TMA 1970, Sch 1AB* or *FA 1998, Sch 18 para 51* (previously an error or mistake relief claim under *TMA 1970, s 33* or *FA 1998, Sch 18 para 51*) cannot be made to amend the way that the lease is treated. There is, however, nothing to prevent an amendment to a return being made within the appropriate time limit. The '*initial period*' is the first accounting period or tax year for which there is a difference in the amount of profits or losses to be included in the return according to whether or not the lease is a long funding lease. The effect of this provision is that the lessee can choose whether to apply the long funding lease lessee provisions (see **6.36–6.38** below) to a particular lease. If the lessee does not choose to apply the long funding lease provisions but the lease is a long funding lease in the case of the lessor, neither will be able to claim capital allowances. For leases entered into on or after 13 December 2007, the lessee cannot choose whether to apply the provisions in this way if, at any time in the period beginning with the inception of the lease and ending with the making of, or of the last amendment to, the return for the initial period, he is the lessor of a long funding lease of any of the same plant or machinery. In such cases, it is immaterial whether or not the lease is treated as a long funding lease in the return.

A further exclusion applies in relation to lessees where the lessor etc. can claim capital allowances in respect of the leased plant or machinery; see **6.25** below.

Where, at the commencement of the term of a lease (see **6.22** above), the plant or machinery is not used for the purposes of a qualifying activity but is subsequently so used, the lease is a long funding lease if it would have been such a lease at its inception (see **6.22** above) if the plant or machinery had then been used for the purposes of a qualifying activity carried on by the person who carries on the subsequent qualifying activity. This could apply, for example, where plant or machinery is leased to or by a non-resident trading outside the UK who subsequently becomes UK-resident (so that the trade becomes a qualifying activity — see **4.3** above).

See also **17.60**(d) below for the exclusion applying in the case of certain leases of ships to companies within the tonnage tax regime.

In certain circumstances, a lessor can make an election for all its 'eligible leases' and 'qualifying incidental leases' to be treated as long funding leases in its case (but not as regards the lessee). The election must specify the date from which it is to take effect (the '*effective date*'), which date may not be earlier than the later of 1 April 2006 and the beginning of the 'relevant accounting period' (i.e. the accounting period in which the effective date falls) or the 'tax year to which the election relates' (i.e. the tax year in which the basis period in which the effective date falls ends). For income tax purposes, the election must be made within the period beginning with the end of the tax year to which it relates and ending twelve months after the 31 January next following that tax year. For corporation tax purposes, the election must be made within two years of the end of the relevant accounting period. The election must be included in the tax return, or amended tax return, for the tax year to which it relates or for the relevant accounting period. It may be withdrawn by amending the return before the time limit for making the election expires, but is otherwise irrevocable.

The effect of the election is to treat the electing lessor as if all its eligible leases and qualifying incidental leases finalised on or after the effective date had been long funding leases since they were finalised.

An '*eligible lease*' is a plant or machinery lease finalised on or after 1 April 2006 which would not otherwise be a long funding lease and which has a term of twelve months or more. The leased asset must:

(I) have been unused and not second-hand at the commencement of the term of the lease;
(II) if leased previously, have been last leased under a long funding lease (including a lease treated as a long funding lease under an election) before the commencement of the term of the lease;
(III) have been the subject of a valid election under *CAA 2001, s 227* (see **7.5** below) before the electing lessor made a return for the period in which the commencement of the term of the lease occurred; or
(IV) replace plant or machinery of the same type and quantity previously leased by the electing lessor to the lessee under a lease which was an eligible lease under (I), (II) or (III) above.

Leases of assets valued (at commencement) at more than £10 million or cars, leases of background plant or machinery for a building (see **6.29** below) and leases of plant or machinery leased with land (see **6.30** below) are not eligible leases.

Where the original lessor's interest under a lease has been assigned, then, for the lease to be an eligible lease, the assignment or assignments must all have occurred within four months of the commencement of the term of the lease and the original lessor and any person later owning the leased assets and through whom the lessor making the election derives title to them, must not claim, or have claimed, capital allowances at any time in respect of those assets.

A '*qualifying incidental lease*' is a lease of plant or machinery which is wholly incidental to an eligible lease and which, if the requirement for an eligible lease to have a term of twelve months or more were disregarded, would have been an eligible lease.

A '*short lease*' for the purpose of (i) above is one whose term is five years or less. A lease with a term of more than five years but not more than seven years is also a short lease if

(a) under generally accepted accounting practice it would be treated as a finance lease;
(b) the residual value of the plant or machinery which is implied in the lease is not more than 5% of its market value (see **6.22** above) at the commencement of the term of the lease, as estimated at the inception of the lease; and

(c) under the lease's terms the total rentals due in the first reference year are no more than 10% less than the total rentals due in the second reference year and the total rentals due in the final year or in any reference year after the second are no more than 10% greater than those due in the second reference year. In determining whether this condition is met, variations in rentals resulting from changes in a standard published interest base rate are excluded.
The first reference year is the period of twelve months beginning the day next after the commencement of the lease's term. The other reference years are then successive twelve month periods beginning on an anniversary of that day and ending before the last day of the lease's term. The final year is the twelve months ending with the last day of the term of the lease (and may therefore overlap with a reference year).

A lease, the inception of which is on or after 7 April 2006, is not a short lease if, at or about the time of inception, arrangements are entered into for the asset to be leased to one or more other persons under one or more other leases and in the aggregate the term of the lease and the terms of the leases to such of those other persons as are connected (within **2.34** above) with the original lessee exceed five years.

Where plant or machinery is the subject of a sale and finance leaseback (as defined at **7.4** below) and the date of the transaction within **7.3**(i)–(iii) below is on or after 9 October 2007, any finance lease (where the date of the transaction is before 12 March 2008, the finance lease) in consequence of which the plant or machinery is available to be used by the seller after the date of the transaction within **7.3**(i)–(iii) below is not a short lease if it would otherwise be. Where, however, the conditions for an election under *CAA 2001, s 227* are met (see **7.5** below), the buyer and seller can make a joint election, the effects of which are to disapply this provision and to apply the effects at **7.5**(a) and (b) below. *CAA 2001, s 225* (see **7.4** below) is not prevented from applying. The election is irrevocable and must be made by notice to HMRC not more than two years after the date of the transaction within **7.3**(i)–(iii) below.

Where plant or machinery is the subject of a lease and finance leaseback (as defined at **17.13** below) and the head lease (i.e. the lease of the plant and machinery by S to B) is entered into on or after 12 March 2008), the finance lease in consequence of which the plant or machinery is used as in **17.13** (a)–(c) below, and any other finance lease (other than the head lease) which forms part of the arrangements for the lease and finance leaseback is a short lease if it would otherwise be.

[*CAA 2001, ss 70G–70I, 70YI(4); SI 2007 No 304*].

For the purposes of determining whether (c) above applies, HMRC consider that variations in rentals that cannot reasonably be predicted (such as result from tax variation clauses) need not be taken into account. (HMRC Technical Note 'Leased Plant or Machinery', 1 August 2006).

For the treatment of mixed leases of plant or machinery and other assets, see **6.28** below.

For provisions which determine whether or not a plant or machinery lease is a long funding lease following a transfer of the leased plant or machinery by the lessor or lessee or following a sale and leaseback, etc. see **6.31** below. For the treatment of a lease following a change in accountancy classification, an extension in the term or an increase in the proportion of the residual amount guaranteed by the lessee etc., see **6.32–6.34** below.

For anti-avoidance provisions applying to situations involving international leasing, see **6.35** below.

Lessor entitled to claim capital allowances

[6.25] A lease is not a long funding lease if the lessor or any 'superior lessor':

(i) is entitled at the commencement of the lease's term to claim a capital allowance in respect of the leased plant or machinery;
(ii) would have been so entitled but for the international leasing anti-avoidance provision at **6.35** below;
(iii) has at any earlier time been entitled to claim such an allowance and has not been required to bring a disposal value into account under **5.41**(viii) above (plant or machinery beginning to be leased under long finance lease); or
(iv) would fall within any of (i)–(iii) above if he had been within the charge to income tax or corporation tax at the inception of the lease and any earlier times.

In determining whether (iv) above applies where the lessor (or superior lessor) is not within the charge to income tax or corporation tax by reason of not being UK-resident for any period, if the lessor etc. does not prepare accounts for that period in accordance with international accounting standards or UK generally accepted accounting practice, then any question relating to generally accepted accounting practice in relation to the lessor etc. and that period is determined by reference to international accounting standards.

This exclusion does not apply if the inception of the lease is before 28 June 2006 and the lease is not a funding lease in the case of the lessor by virtue only of the exclusion for plant or machinery leased for at least ten years before 1 April 2006 (see **6.26** below).

There is a superior lessor for the above purposes only where there is a chain of superior leases, i.e. where the immediate lessor has his interest in the leased plant or machinery under a lease from a third person (who may himself have his interest under a lease from a fourth person and so on). Lessors under the chain other than the immediate lessor are '*superior lessors*'.

[*CAA 2001, s 70Q*].

Under self assessment it is for the lessee to take appropriate steps to ensure that (i)–(iv) above do not apply to the lessor or any superior lessor. HMRC consider that this will be particularly important where the lease is close to the boundary between a long funding lease and a non-long funding lease. Lessees may need to obtain assurances from the lessor. (HMRC Technical Note 'Leased Plant or Machinery', 1 August 2006).

Meaning of funding lease

[6.26] A '*funding lease*' is a 'plant or machinery lease' (see **6.27** below) which at its inception meets one or more of the tests at (i)–(iii) below. A plant or machinery lease whose inception is on or after 1 April 2010 is also a funding lease if the plant or machinery is 'cushion gas' (and such a lease does not need to meet any of the tests below). '*Cushion gas*' is gas which functions, or is intended to function, as plant in a particular gas storage facility.

(i) *The finance lease test.* A lease meets this test in the case of any person if it is one which would be treated under generally accepted accounting practice as a finance lease or a loan in the accounts of that person or, where that person is the lessor, in the accounts of any connected person (within **2.34** above).
For this purpose, the accounts of a company include any consolidated accounts drawn up under generally accepted accounting practice which relate to two or more companies of which that company is one. In determining whether the test is met, where a person is not within the charge to income tax or corporation tax by reason of not being UK-resident for any period, if accounts are not prepared for that period in accordance with international accounting standards or UK generally accepted accounting practice, then any question relating to generally accepted accounting practice is determined by reference to international accounting standards.
The Treasury has the power to vary the finance lease test by regulations. See also *FA 2011, s 53* which, in effect, preserves the distinction between finance leases and operating leases for tax purposes where accounting standards have been revised to remove it.

(ii) *The lease payments test.* A lease meets this test if the present value of the 'minimum lease payments', calculated using the interest rate implicit in the lease, is 80% or more of the 'fair value' of the leased plant or machinery.
The interest rate implicit in a lease is for this purpose the interest rate that would apply using normal commercial criteria including, where applicable, generally accepted accounting practice. If the rate cannot be determined on that basis (which may be the case for some operating leases) then the temporal discount rate under *FA 2005, s 70* is used, i.e. 3.5% (subject to amendment by Treasury regulations). The '*fair value*' of leased plant or machinery is its market value (see **6.22** above) less any grants receivable towards its purchase or use.
The '*minimum lease payments*' under a lease are the minimum payments under the lease over the term of the lease (including any 'initial payment') together with, in the case of the lessee, so much of any 'residual amount' as is guaranteed by him or a person connected with him, and in the case of the lessor, so much of any residual amount as is guaranteed by any person who is not connected with him or by the lessee. Any amounts which represent charges for services or any UK or foreign tax or duty payable by the lessor other than income tax, corporation tax or similar foreign tax are excluded. An '*initial payment*' under a lease is a payment by the lessee at or before the time the lease is entered into in respect of the plant or machinery which is the subject

of the lease. The '*residual amount*' is so much of the fair value of the plant or machinery as cannot be reasonably expected to be recovered by the lessor from the payments under the lease.

(iii) *The useful economic life test.* A lease meets this test if its term is more than 65% of the 'remaining useful economic life' of the leased plant or machinery. The '*remaining useful economic life*' of leased plant or machinery is, for this purpose, the period beginning with the commencement of the lease's term and ending when the asset is no longer used and no longer likely to be used by any person for any purpose as a fixed asset of a business.

A lease is not a funding lease if:

(a) the lease is a contract to which *CAA 2001, s 67* (hire-purchase etc. — see **7.9** below) applies; or

(b) before the commencement of the term of the lease, the lessor has leased the plant or machinery under one or more other plant or machinery leases none of which were funding leases and the aggregate terms of which exceed 65% of the remaining useful economic life of the plant or machinery at the commencement of the earliest such lease. For this purpose, all pre-1 April 2006 lessors are treated as if they were the same person as the first lessor on or after that date.

A lease is not a funding lease in the case of the lessor if before 1 April 2006 the plant or machinery had been the subject of one or more leases for at least ten years and the lessor under the lease in question was also lessor of the plant or machinery on the last day before that date on which the plant or machinery was the subject of a lease. HMRC consider that in applying this provision the item of plant or machinery in question should be looked at as a whole rather than as a set of component parts. Therefore, where capital expenditure is incurred on updating or improving an asset, then, provided that the expenditure is not on, or does not create, a separate asset, the provision will apply if the plant or machinery as a whole has been leased out for 10 years before 1 April 2006. (HMRC Technical Note 'Leased Plant or Machinery', 1 August 2006).

[*CAA 2001, ss 70J, 70N–70P, 70YE, 70YI(1)(4), 70YJ; FA 2010, s 28(2)–(5)(8)*].

Meaning of plant or machinery lease

[6.27] A '*plant or machinery lease*' is any of the following:

(i) any agreement or arrangement under which a person grants to another person the right to use plant or machinery for a period and which would be treated as a lease under generally accepted accounting practice;

(ii) any other agreement or arrangement to the extent that:
- under generally accepted accounting practice, it would be treated as a lease, and
- for the purposes of generally accepted accounting practice the agreement or arrangement conveys or would be regarded as conveying the right to use an asset which is plant or machinery; or

(iii) where plant or machinery is the subject of a 'sale and finance leaseback' within **7.4** above, the finance lease involved.

For the purposes of (i) and (ii) above, where an agreement or arrangement would be treated as a lease under generally accepted accounting practice immediately after the commencement of the term of the lease, it is deemed to be so treated during the period beginning with the inception of the lease and ending with the commencement of the lease's term.

The Treasury has the power to vary the meaning of plant or machinery lease by regulations.

[*CAA 2001, ss 70K, 70YJ*].

In practice, an agreement or arrangement would be treated as a lease under generally accepted accounting practice if it would be so treated under Statement of Standard Accounting Practice 21, International Accounting Standard (IAS) 17 or International Financial Reporting Interpretations Committee (IFRIC) 4. An agreement or arrangement would not be treated as a lease if it would be accounted for as a financial transaction under IAS 39 or as a service concession (under Financial Reporting Standard 5, Application Note B or IFRIC draft interpretation 12). (HMRC Technical Note 'Leased Plant or Machinery', 1 August 2006).

Mixed leases

[6.28] An agreement or arrangement which at any time relates to, or is to relate to, or has come to relate to, both plant or machinery of a particular description and other assets (whether or not also plant or machinery) is a '*mixed lease*'.

For the purposes of the long funding lease provisions, the mixed lease, so far as relating to the particular plant or machinery, and the mixed lease, so far as relating to other assets, are treated as separate agreements or arrangements (each referred to as a '*derived lease*'). The normal rules are then applied to each derived lease to determine whether it is a plant or machinery lease and, if so, whether it is a funding lease.

The term of a derived lease is limited to the remaining useful economic life (see **6.26**(iii) above) of the plant or machinery at the commencement of the derived lease's term, but subject to this is determined under the normal rules (see **6.22** above). The rentals deemed to be payable under the derived lease are such rentals as are just and reasonable in all the circumstances of the case, and for this purpose regard must be had to:

- all the provisions of the mixed lease;
- the nature of the plant or machinery;
- the value of the plant or machinery at the commencement of the term of the derived lease;
- the amount which is expected, at the commencement of that term, to be the market value (see **6.22** above) of the plant or machinery at the end of the term;
- the remaining useful economic life (see **6.26**(iii) above) of the plant or machinery at the commencement of the term of the derived lease; and

- the term of the derived lease.

It is to be assumed that rentals under the derived lease are payable in equal instalments throughout the term of the lease, unless it is reasonable to draw a different conclusion from all the circumstances of the case.

The above applies only if the mixed lease would be treated as a lease under generally accepted accounting practice or if the plant or machinery concerned is the subject of a sale and finance leaseback within **7.4** above and the mixed lease is or includes the finance lease involved. For this purpose, where an agreement or arrangement would be treated as a lease under generally accepted accounting practice immediately after the commencement of the term of the lease, it is deemed to be so treated during the period beginning with the inception of the lease and ending with the commencement of the lease's term.

[*CAA 2001, ss 70L, 70M*].

Excluded leases of background plant or machinery for a building

[6.29] As indicated at **6.24** above, a lease is not a long funding lease if it is an excluded lease of background plant or machinery for a building. The exclusion applies to a derived lease (see **6.28** above) of plant or machinery where:

(i) the plant or machinery is affixed to, or otherwise installed in or on, any land which consists of or includes a building;
(ii) the plant or machinery is 'background plant or machinery for the building'; and
(iii) the plant or machinery is leased with the land under a mixed lease.

The exclusion does not apply where:

(a) the amounts payable under the mixed lease or any other arrangement vary, or may be varied, by reference to the value to the lessor of any capital allowances in respect of expenditure incurred by him on the plant or machinery; or
(b) the main purpose, or one of the main purposes, of entering into the mixed lease, a series of transactions of which the mixed lease is one, or any of the transactions in such a series is to secure that capital allowances are available to the lessor for expenditure incurred in the provision of background plant or machinery for a building.

Plant or machinery is '*background plant or machinery for a building*' if it is of a type which might reasonably be expected to be installed in, or in or on the sites of, a variety of different buildings and whose sole purpose is to contribute to the functionality of the building or its site as an environment within which activities can be carried on. The Treasury have the power by order to specify types of plant or machinery which will be deemed to fall within (or not to fall within) the definition and have exercised that power with effect from 1 April 2006 as follows.

In determining whether any particular plant or machinery does or does not fall within the definition, the following descriptions of plant or machinery are prescribed as examples that may be regarded as falling within the definition (unless they fall within the list of exclusions below):

- heating and air conditioning installations;
- ceilings which are part of an air conditioning system;
- hot water installations;
- electrical installations that provide power to a building, such as high and low voltage switchgear, all sub-mains distribution systems and standby generators;
- mechanisms, including automatic control systems, for opening and closing doors, windows and vents;
- escalators and passenger lifts;
- window cleaning installations;
- fittings such as fitted cupboards, blinds, curtains and associated mechanical equipment;
- demountable partitions;
- protective installations such as lightning protection, sprinkler and other equipment for containing or fighting fires, fire alarm systems and fire escapes; and
- building management systems.

The following descriptions of plant or machinery are deemed to be background plant or machinery:

- lighting installations including all fixed light fittings and emergency lighting systems;
- telephone, audio-visual and data installations incidental to the occupation of the building;
- computer networking facilities incidental to the occupation of the building;
- sanitary appliances and other bathroom fittings including hand driers, counters, partitions, mirrors, shower and locker facilities;
- kitchen and catering facilities for producing and storing food and drink for the occupants of the building;
- fixed seating;
- signs;
- public address systems; and
- intruder alarm systems and other security equipment including surveillance equipment.

Plant or machinery use for any of the following purposes is deemed not to be background plant or machinery (unless it falls within the above list of items deemed to be background plant or machinery). The purposes are:

- storing, moving or displaying goods to be sold in the course of a trade, whether wholesale or retail;
- manufacturing goods or materials;
- subjecting goods or materials to a process; and
- storing goods or materials:
  - which are to be used in the manufacture of other goods or materials;
  - which are to be subjected, in the course of a trade, to a process;
  - which, having been manufactured or produced or subjected in the course of a trade to a process, have not yet been delivered to any purchaser; or

- on their arrival in the UK from a place outside the UK.

[*CAA 2001, ss 70R–70T; SI 2007 No 303*].

HMRC consider that leases of residential property will not include derived long funding leases unless the lease includes plant or machinery that is not normally found in residential property and which is not there to contribute to the functionality of the building as residential property (and so does not fall within the definition of background plant or machinery for the building). (HMRC Technical Note 'Leased Plant or Machinery', 1 August 2006).

Exclusion for plant or machinery with low percentage value leased with land

[6.30] As indicated at **6.24** above, there is an exclusion from the long funding lease regime for certain leases where plant or machinery is leased with land and the plant or machinery has a low percentage value. The exclusion applies where the following conditions are satisfied:

(i) any plant or machinery (the '*relevant plant or machinery*') is affixed to, or otherwise installed in or on, any land;
(ii) the plant or machinery is not background plant or machinery for any building on the land;
(iii) the plant or machinery is leased with the land under a mixed lease; and
(iv) at the commencement of the term of the derived lease (see **6.28** above) of the relevant plant or machinery, the aggregate market value (see **6.22** above) of the relevant plant or machinery and any other plant or machinery within (i)–(iii) above does not exceed both 10% of the 'BMV' and 5% of the 'LMV'. For this purpose, '*BMV*' is the aggregate market value of all the background plant or machinery leased with the land, and '*LMV*' is the market value of the land, including buildings and fixtures. The market value of the land is to be determined on the assumption of a sale of the land by an absolute owner (or, in Scotland, an owner) free from all leases and other encumbrances.

Where the above conditions are satisfied, the derived lease of the relevant plant or machinery is not a long funding lease.

The exclusion does not apply where:

(a) the amounts payable under the mixed lease or any other arrangement vary, or may be varied, by reference to the value to the lessor of any capital allowances in respect of expenditure incurred by him on the relevant plant or machinery; or
(b) the main purpose, or one of the main purposes, of entering into the mixed lease, a series of transactions of which the mixed lease is one, or any of the transactions in such a series is to secure that capital allowances are available to the lessor for expenditure incurred in the provision of relevant plant or machinery.

[*CAA 2001, ss 70U, 70YI(1)*].

Transfers, assignments, leasebacks etc.

[6.31] There are provisions to determine whether or not a plant or machinery lease is a long funding lease following a transfer of the leased plant or machinery by the lessor or lessee or following a sale and leaseback, etc. For the purposes of the provisions, a transfer of plant or machinery by a person includes:

(i) any kind of disposal of, or of the person's interest in, the plant or machinery (including, in the case of a sale and leaseback etc., the grant of a lease);
(ii) any arrangements under which the person's interest in the plant or machinery is terminated and another person becomes lessor or lessee of the plant or machinery, or becomes entitled to, or to an interest in, the plant or machinery; or
(iii) in a case where the plant or machinery is a fixture and the person is treated as the owner under **6.6** above, any cessation of ownership within **6.12–6.14** above.

[*CAA 2001, ss 70W(7), 70X(7), 70Y(3)*].

The provisions are as follows.

(a) *Transfer by lessor.* The provisions apply where, during the term of a plant or machinery lease (the '*old lease*'), the lessor (the '*old lessor*') transfers the plant or machinery to another person (the '*new lessor*') in circumstances such that the transfer is not the grant of a plant or machinery lease by the old lessor and, immediately after the transfer, the new lessor is the lessor of the plant or machinery under a lease (the '*new lease*'), whether or not the new lease is the same lease as the old lease. If it is not otherwise the case, the old lessor is treated as if the old lease terminated immediately before the transfer and the new lessor is treated as if the new lease had been entered into immediately after the transfer. The date of transfer is treated as the date of the inception of, and the commencement of the term of, the new lease.
The new lease is treated as a long funding lease in the case of the new lessor only if the old lease was a long funding lease in the case of the old lessor immediately before the transfer and if:
    (I) the term of the new lease is the unexpired portion of the term of the old lease, and
    (II) the amounts receivable under the new lease are the same as would have been receivable under the old lease had it continued in effect.
Where (I) and (II) above apply, the lessee is treated as if the old lease and the new lease were the same continuing lease.
[*CAA 2001, s 70W*].
(b) *Transfer by lessee.* The provisions apply where, during the term of a plant or machinery lease (the '*old lease*'), the lessee (the '*old lessee*') transfers the plant or machinery to another person (the '*new lessee*') in circumstances such that the transfer is not the grant of a plant or machinery lease by the old lessee and, immediately after the transfer, the new lessee is the lessee of the plant or machinery under a lease (the '*new lease*'), whether or not the new lease is the same lease as the old lease.

If it is not otherwise the case, the old lessee is treated as if the old lease terminated immediately before the transfer and the new lessee is treated as if the new lease had been entered into immediately after the transfer. The date of transfer is treated as the date of the inception of, and the commencement of the term of, the new lease.

The new lease is treated as a long funding lease in the case of the new lessee only if the old lease was a long funding lease in the case of the old lessee immediately before the transfer and if:

(A) the term of the new lease is the unexpired portion of the term of the old lease, and

(B) the amounts payable under the new lease are the same as would have been payable under the old lease had it continued in effect.

Where (A) and (B) above apply, the lessor is treated as if the old lease and the new lease were the same continuing lease.

[*CAA 2001, s 70X*].

(c) *Sale and leasebacks etc.* Where:

- a person ('X') transfers plant or machinery to another person ('Y'), and
- the plant or machinery is directly or indirectly leased back to X, and
- immediately before the commencement of the term of the lease back to X, X is the lessor of the plant or machinery to another person under a lease which is a long funding lease in X's case,

the lease back to X is a long funding lease in the case of both X and Y. If the plant or machinery is leased back to X indirectly via a chain of leases, each lease in the chain is also a long funding lease in the case of both of the parties to it. [*CAA 2001, s 70Y*].

Change in accounting classification

[6.32] Special provisions apply where, after the inception of a long funding lease, there is a change in its accountancy classification as a 'finance lease' or an operating lease in the 'relevant accounts'. The change must be in accordance with generally accepted accounting practice.

For the purposes of the provisions, the '*relevant accounts*' are, broadly, the accounts of the lessee, the lessor or a person connected (within **2.34** above) with the lessor. In the case of a company, any consolidated accounts drawn up under generally accepted accounting practice which relate to two or more companies of which that company is one are also included. Where a person is not within the charge to income tax or corporation tax by reason of not being UK-resident for any period, if accounts are not prepared for that period in accordance with international accounting standards or UK generally accepted accounting practice, then any question relating to generally accepted accounting practice is determined by reference to international accounting standards. A '*finance lease*' includes a loan.

Where the change is in the accounts of the lessee, the lessee is treated as if the lease had terminated immediately before the change and a new lease which was a long funding lease in the case of the lessor had been entered into immediately afterwards. The date of the change is treated as the date of the inception of, and the commencement of the term of, the new lease. Where the change is in the accounts of the lessor or connected person, the same consequences apply to the lessor.

The Treasury has the power to restrict the application or operation of these provisions by regulations.

[*CAA 2001, ss 70N(2)(3), 70YA, 70YI(4)*].

Extension of term of lease

[6.33] The following provisions apply to determine whether a plant or machinery lease is a long funding lease following an event which extends the lease's term (whether by variation of the provisions of the lease, the grant or exercise of an option or in any other way). The events concerned are as follows:

(i) an event which has the effect of making a further period, falling wholly or partly after the end of the pre-existing term of the lease, a non-cancellable period (see **6.22** above);
(ii) the grant of an option to the lessee to continue to lease the plant or machinery for such a further period, where it is reasonably certain at the time of grant that the lessee will exercise the option;
(iii) the exercise by the lessee of an option to continue to lease the plant or machinery for a further period; and
(iv) an event not within (i)–(iii) above which has the effect that the lessee will continue, or is reasonably certain to continue, to lease the plant or machinery for a further period.

Where the existing lease was a long funding operating lease (see **6.22** above) before the event, the lessor and the lessee are treated as if the existing lease terminated at the end of the day before the 'effective date' and a new lease was entered into on that date. That date is treated as the date of both the inception of the new lease and the commencement of its term. The new lease is taken to be a long funding operating lease whose term is the unexpired portion of the existing lease, as extended. This does not apply if the event is one by reason of which the accountancy classification of the lease as an operating lease changes in the relevant accounts within **6.32** above. The '*effective date*' is the earlier of the day after the end of the pre-existing term of the existing lease and the date on which any variation of the rentals payable resulting from or otherwise in connection with the event takes effect.

Where the existing lease is not a long funding lease, if, on the following assumptions, the 'new lease' would be a long funding lease, the lessor is to be treated on those assumptions. The assumptions are that:

- the existing lease terminates immediately before the effective date (as above);
- a '*new lease*' is entered into on the effective date;
- the term of the new lease is the portion of the term of the existing lease, as extended, that remains unexpired at the effective date; and
- the effective date is the date of both the inception of the new lease and the commencement of its term.

If, on those assumptions, the new lease would not be a long funding lease, then the term of the existing lease is treated as extended for the purpose of any subsequent application of this provision or that at 6.34 below.

[*CAA 2001, ss 70YB, 70YC*].

Increase in proportion of residual amount guaranteed

[6.34] Where a lessor under a lease which is not a long funding lease enters into an arrangement which meets the conditions listed below, or enters into arrangements which taken together meet the conditions, he is treated as if the lease terminated immediately before the time of the 'relevant transaction' and a new lease was entered into immediately afterwards. The date of the relevant transaction is treated as the date of both the inception of the new lease and the commencement of its term. The term of the new lease is taken to be the unexpired portion of the existing lease.

The conditions are that:

- as a result of the arrangement or arrangements, there is an increase, after the inception of the lease, in the proportion of the residual amount that is guaranteed by the lessee or a person not connected (within 2.34 above) with the lessor; and
- had the arrangement or arrangements been entered into before the inception of the lease, the lease would have been a long funding lease.

The '*relevant transaction*' is the arrangement or, where two or more arrangements have been entered into, the latest of them.

The Treasury has the power to restrict the application or operation of these provisions by regulations.

[*CAA 2001, ss 70YD, 70YI(4)*].

Avoidance involving international leasing

[6.35] Anti-avoidance provisions apply where there are plant or machinery leases such that:

(i) under a lease by a non-resident, an asset is provided directly or indirectly to a resident;
(ii) the direct provision of the asset to the resident is under a lease which, in the case of the resident, is a long funding lease or a lease to which *CAA 2001, s 67* (hire-purchase etc. — see 7.9 below) applies;
(iii) the asset is used by the resident for the purpose of leasing it under a lease (the '*relevant lease*') that would not otherwise be a long funding lease in the case of the resident; and
(iv) under the relevant lease, the asset is provided directly or indirectly (but by a lease) to a non-resident.

If the sole or main purpose of arranging matters as in (i)–(iv) above is to obtain a 'tax advantage' by securing that capital allowances are available to a resident under either *CAA 2001, s 67* or *s 70A* (see 6.36 below), the relevant lease is treated as a long funding lease in the case of the resident lessor.

A person is non-resident for this purpose if he is not resident in the UK and does not use the plant or machinery exclusively for earning profits chargeable to tax and, conversely, a person is resident if either he is resident in the UK or uses the plant or machinery exclusively for earning profits chargeable to tax. The definition of '*tax advantage*' at **2.32** above is extended to include a relief or increased relief from, or repayment or increased repayment of, tax, or the avoidance or reduction of a charge to tax or an assessment to tax or the avoidance of a possible assessment thereto.

[*CAA 2001, ss 70V, 577(4); CTA 2010, s 1139*].

HMRC have indicated that these provisions will not apply to normal commercial arrangements where the leasing into and the leasing out of the UK are incidents of an activity that has a real commercial presence in the UK. They give the example of an aircraft leasing company entering into a long funding lease as part of its arrangements to acquire an aircraft from an overseas manufacturer. If the company subsequently, and in the course of its trade, entered into a short term operating lease to provide the aircraft to a non-UK airline, the provisions would not apply to treat that lease as a long funding lease. (Treasury Notes to the Finance (No 2) Bill 2006).

Tax treatment of lessee

Capital allowances

[6.36] Where a person carrying on a qualifying activity incurs expenditure (whether or not of a capital nature) on the provision of plant or machinery for the purposes of the activity under a long funding lease, the plant or machinery is treated as owned by him at any time when he is the lessee under the lease. This applies whether or not the lease is a long funding lease in the case of the lessor.

The lessee is then treated for capital allowances purposes as having incurred capital expenditure on the provision of the plant or machinery at the commencement of the term of the lease.

The effect of these provisions is that the lessee under a long funding lease is treated as incurring qualifying expenditure of an amount equal to the amount of the deemed capital expenditure calculated as below. Subject to the anti-avoidance provision for long funding leasebacks below, the qualifying expenditure may qualify for first-year allowances (see **5.26**(v) above).

If the lease is a long funding finance lease (see **6.22** above), the amount of the capital expenditure so treated as incurred is, subject to the following, the amount that would be recognised, if the lessee prepared 'appropriate accounts', as the present value of the minimum lease payments (see **6.26**(ii) above) at the later of the commencement of the lease's term and the date on which the plant or machinery is first brought into use for the purposes of the qualifying activity. For this purpose, '*appropriate accounts*' are accounts prepared according to generally accepted accounting practice on the date on which the amount is first recognised in the books or other financial records of the lessee. Where the minimum lease payments include a 'relievable amount', the present value of that amount is excluded in determining the present value of the minimum lease payments for this purpose. An amount is a '*relievable amount*' if:

- an arrangement entered into on or after 9 March 2011 is in place under which all or part of any residual amount (see **6.26**(ii) above) is guaranteed by the lessee or a person connected with him;
- the amount is within the minimum lease payments because of that arrangement; and
- it is reasonable to assume that, were the amount to be incurred under the arrangement, relief (by way of a capital allowance or income tax or corporation tax deduction) would be available as a result (beyond relief resulting from the inclusion of the amount within the minimum lease payments under the above provisions or *CAA 2001, s 70E* (see **6.37** below)). In deciding for this purpose if relief would be available no account is taken of any part of the arrangement other than that under which all or part of the residual amount is guaranteed or of any other arrangement connected with, or forming part of a set of arrangements which includes, the arrangement.

If the lessee has paid rentals under the lease before the commencement of its term, any such rentals which are otherwise unrelievable are also included in the amount of the deemed capital expenditure incurred. Pre-commencement rentals are unrelievable for this purpose if they do not, apart from this provision, qualify for any capital allowance or any income tax or corporation tax deduction or, where the plant or machinery was not used for the purposes of a qualifying activity pre-commencement, if they would not have qualified for such an allowance or deduction even if the plant or machinery had been so used.

The amount of the deemed capital expenditure is restricted to an amount equal to the market value of the asset at the commencement of the term of the lease if the main purpose, or one of the main purposes, of entering into the lease, a series of transactions of which the lease is one, or any of the transactions in such a series is to obtain capital allowances under these provisions in respect of an amount of expenditure materially exceeding the asset's market value.

If the lease is a long funding operating lease (see **6.22** above), the amount of the capital expenditure so treated as incurred is the market value of the plant or machinery at the later of the commencement of the lease's term and the date on which the plant or machinery is first brought into use for the purposes of the qualifying activity.

In the case of a long funding finance lease, where the lessor incurs expenditure in relation to the plant or machinery as a result of which there is an increase in the present value of the minimum lease payments, the lessee is treated as having incurred further capital expenditure on the plant or machinery on the date on which the increase is first recognised in his books or other financial records. Any increase attributable to a relievable amount (as above) is, however, ignored. The amount of the deemed expenditure is the amount that would fall to be recognised as the amount of the increase in accounts prepared by the lessee on that date in accordance with generally accepted accounting practice.

If a long funding finance lease would fall, under generally accepted accounting practice, to be treated as a loan, the above provisions apply as if the lease fell to be treated as a finance lease.

[*CAA 2001, ss 70A–70D; FA 2011, s 33(2)(3)(6)*].

Anti-avoidance provisions apply where a person (S) 'transfers' (as defined to include any kind of disposal and the grant of a lease) plant or machinery to another person (B) and, at any subsequent time, the plant or machinery is available to be used by S or a connected person under a plant or machinery lease which is a long funding lease (i.e. there is a long funding leaseback). The commencement of the term of the lease must be after 12 November 2008. In such circumstances, no annual investment allowance or first-year allowance is available to S or the connected person. The qualifying expenditure of S or the connected person is limited to the amount of any disposal value that S has to bring into account because of the transfer. If no such disposal value has to be brought into account, then (subject to the further provision below) the qualifying expenditure is limited to the lowest of the market value of the plant or machinery and any capital expenditure incurred by S or a connected person on the original provision of the plant or machinery before the transfer to B.

Where the lease is entered into on or after 26 February 2015, the qualifying expenditure of S or the connected person is nil if S is not required to bring a disposal value into account on the transfer and at any time before the transfer S or a 'linked person' became the owner of the plant or machinery without incurring capital expenditure or 'qualifying revenue expenditure' on its provision. For this purpose, '*qualifying revenue expenditure*' is revenue expenditure of an amount at least equal to that which would reasonably have been expected to have been incurred on the provision of the plant or machinery by a transaction at arm's length in the open market or revenue expenditure which is incurred by the manufacturer of the plant or machinery and which is of an amount at least equal to what would reasonably be expected to be the normal manufacturing cost. A '*linked person*' is a person who owned the plant or machinery at any time before the transfer and who was connected with S at any time in the period beginning with that person's acquisition of the plant or machinery and ending with the transfer.

[*CAA 2001, s 70DA; FA 2015, Sch 10 para 2*].

Disposal events and disposal values

[6.37] Where the provisions at **6.36** above apply to a lessee, certain 'relevant events' are disposal events (see **5.41** above) and the lessee must bring a disposal value into account for the chargeable period in which the event occurs. The following are 'relevant events':

- the termination of the lease;
- the plant or machinery beginning, on or after 13 November 2008, to be used wholly or partly for purposes other than those of a qualifying activity; and
- the permanent discontinuance of the qualifying activity on or after that date.

Where the relevant event occurs on or after 13 November 2008, the disposal value is:

(QE – QA) + R

where QE is the qualifying expenditure on the provision of the plant or machinery, QA is the 'qualifying amount' and R is the sum of any 'relevant rebate' and other 'relevant lease-related payment'. For relevant events occurring before 21 March 2012, R is simply any relevant rebate. The disposal value cannot be less than nil.

Where the lease is a long funding operating lease, the '*qualifying amount*' is the aggregate of the reductions made under *ICTA 1988, s 502K* or *ITTOIA 2005, s 148I* (see **6.38** below) for periods of account in which the lessee in question was the lessee.

In the case of a long funding finance lease, the 'qualifying amount' is the aggregate of the payments made to the lessor by the lessee under the lease (including any initial payment) and the payments made under a guarantee of any residual amounts (see **6.26** above) other than any 'relievable payment' made on or after 9 March 2011. If the lease is not a transaction at arm's length, only so much of the payments as would reasonably be expected to have been paid if the lease had been such a transaction are included. Any part of a payment which would be shown in the lessee's accounts, in accordance with generally accepted accounting practice, as finance charges or which represents charges for services or UK or foreign tax or duty (other than income tax, corporation tax or a similar foreign tax) payable by the lessor is excluded. A payment is a '*relievable payment*' for this purpose if:

- an arrangement is in place under which all or part of any residual amount is guaranteed by the lessee or a person connected with him;
- the payment is within the minimum lease payments because of that arrangement; and
- it is reasonable to assume that relief (by way of a capital allowance or income tax or corporation tax deduction) would be available as a result of making the payment (beyond relief resulting from the inclusion of the amount within the minimum lease payments under the above provisions or *CAA 2001, ss 70C, 70D* (see **6.36** above)). In deciding for this purpose if relief would be available no account is taken of any part of the arrangement other than that under which all or part of the residual amount is guaranteed or of any other arrangement connected with, or forming part of a set of arrangements which includes, the arrangement.

Where the relevant event is the termination of the lease, the '*relevant rebate*' is any amount calculated by reference to the 'termination value' that is payable directly or indirectly for the benefit of the lessee or a connected person. In any other case, the '*relevant rebate*' is any such amount that would have been so payable had the lease terminated when the relevant event occurred and the plant or machinery had been sold for its market value. If the lease is not a transaction at arm's length, the relevant rebate includes any amount that would reasonably be expected to be included if the lease had been such a transaction.

A '*relevant lease-related payment*' is any payment which:

- is payable at any time for the benefit (directly or indirectly) of the lessee or a connected person;

- is connected with the long funding lease or an arrangement connected with it;
- is not an initial payment or other payment made by the lessee to the lessor, a payment under the lease or under a guarantee of any residual amount (see **6.26**(ii) above);
- is not an initial payment or any other payment made under a superior lease (i.e. a lease of the plant or machinery to which the long funding lease is inferior) to the lessor under that lease by the lessee under that lease; and
- is not a payment to the seller of the proceeds of a sale of the plant or machinery to which **7.3**(c) or (d) below (sale and leaseback) applies and in respect of which the conditions mentioned in **7.5** below are met,

if, and to the extent that, the payment is not otherwise brought into account for tax purposes as income or a disposal receipt by the person for whom the benefit is payable (or would not be if that person were within the charge to tax). For this purpose, 'payment' includes the provision of any benefit, the assumption of any liability and any other transfer of money's worth. If the lease is not a transaction at arm's length, 'relevant lease-related payment' includes any amount that would reasonably be expected to be included if the lease had been such a transaction.

Where the relevant event occurs before 13 November 2008 and the lease is a long funding operating lease, the disposal value is the aggregate of:

(i) the sum of any amounts payable to the lessee which are calculated by reference to the 'termination value' (for example, a refund of rentals); and

(ii) the amount (if any) by which the market value of the plant or machinery at the later of the commencement of the lease's term and the date on which it was first brought into use for the purposes of the qualifying activity exceeds the aggregate of the amounts by which the tax deductions of the lessee fell to be reduced under *CTA 2010, s 379* or *ITTOIA 2005, s 148I* (see **6.38** below) for the periods of account in which he was the lessee.

Where the relevant event occurs before 13 November 2008 and the lease is a long funding finance lease, the disposal value is the sum of:

(a) any amounts payable to the lessee which are calculated by reference to the termination value; and

(b) where the lease terminates before the end of its term, the amount that would be recognised as the present value immediately before termination of the 'balance of the minimum lease payments', if accounts were prepared by the lessee in accordance with generally accepted accounting practice at that time,

reduced (but not below nil) by any amount payable by the lessee to the lessor for or in consequence of the termination. The '*balance of the minimum lease payments*' is, for this purpose, the amount by which the actual minimum lease payments exceed the amount that would have been the minimum lease payments had the term of the lease expired on the day of the termination.

These provisions take priority over any other provision under which a relevant event gives rise to a disposal event: any such disposal event is ignored.

[*CAA 2001, s 70E; FA 2011, s 33(4)(5)(7); FA 2012, s 46*].

The '*termination value*' of any plant or machinery is its value at or about the time when the lease terminates. References above to calculation by reference to the termination value should be read as including:

- where the plant or machinery is sold after the lease comes to an end, calculation by reference to the proceeds of sale;
- calculation by reference to any insurance proceeds, compensation or similar sums;
- calculation by reference to an estimate of the plant or machinery's market value;
- determination in a way which, or by reference to factors or criteria which, might reasonably be expected to produce a broadly similar result to calculation by reference to the termination value; and
- any other form of calculation indirectly by reference to the termination value.

[*CAA 2001, s 70YH*].

Lessee's taxable profits

[6.38] The following provisions apply to ensure that, broadly, the lessee under a long funding lease does not obtain a tax deduction in computing his profits for expenditure under the lease to the extent that it qualifies for capital allowances as in **6.37** above.

Where the lease is a long funding finance lease, only those amounts in respect of the lease which, in accordance with generally accepted accounting practice, would be treated as finance charges can be deducted in calculating the lessee's taxable profits. (A lease which falls to be treated under generally accepted accounting practice as a loan is treated for this purpose as if it fell to be treated as a finance lease.)

A payment made to the lessee on termination of a long funding finance lease which is calculated by reference to the termination value (see **6.37** above) is not taxable (but will be taken into account in calculating any capital allowances disposal value — see **6.37** above).

[*CTA 2010, ss 377, 378; ITTOIA 2005, ss 148G, 148H*].

Where the lease is a long funding operating lease, in computing the taxable profits of the lessee, the allowable deductions for each period for which he draws up accounts and in which he is the lessee are reduced by the proportion of the 'expected gross reduction' in the value of the plant or machinery that the period (to the extent that it falls within the term of the lease) bears to the term of the lease.

The '*expected gross reduction*' for the above purposes is the 'starting value' less the amount which, at the commencement of the term of the lease, is expected to be the market value of the plant or machinery at the end of the term. The '*starting value*' is the market value of the plant or machinery at the commencement of the term of the lease. Where, however, the lessee initially incurred the expenditure on the provision of the plant or machinery for purposes other than those of a qualifying activity but subsequently, and after 31 March 2006, brings the plant or machinery into use for the purposes of such an activity, the starting value is the lower of:

- the market value of the plant or machinery at the time it is first so brought into use, and
- the value of the plant or machinery at that time on the assumption that the market value at the commencement of the term of the lease has been written off on a straight line basis (as defined) over the plant or machinery's remaining useful economic life (see **6.26**(iii) above).

[*CTA 2010, ss 379, 380; ITTOIA 2005, ss 148I, 148J(3)*].

Tax treatment of lessor

Capital allowances

[6.39] Expenditure incurred on the provision of plant or machinery for leasing under a long funding lease is not qualifying expenditure. [*CAA 2001, s 34A*]. As a result, a lessor under such a lease cannot claim capital allowances in respect of the leased plant or machinery. Where expenditure on plant or machinery is incurred for other purposes such that it is qualifying expenditure, if the plant or machinery is subsequently leased under a long funding lease, the commencement of the term of the lease is a disposal event requiring a disposal value to be brought into account (see **5.41** above).

Where a lessor ceases to use plant or machinery for the purpose of leasing it under a long funding lease without ceasing to use it for the purposes of a qualifying activity, he is treated as having incurred qualifying expenditure on the plant or machinery on the day after the cessation of an amount equal to the 'termination amount' in the case of the last long funding lease. This applies only if, on the day of cessation, the lessor owns the plant or machinery as a result of having incurred capital expenditure on its provision for the purpose of the qualifying activity. The plant or machinery after the day of cessation is treated as different plant or machinery from the plant or machinery on or before that day, so that, where a disposal event subsequently occurs, a disposal value is not prevented from being brought into account because of the provisions at **5.41** above requiring a disposal value to be brought into account for a particular item of plant or machinery only in respect of the first disposal event. First-year allowances are not, however, available and a short-life asset election (see **5.59** above) cannot be made.

The '*termination amount*' in the case of a long funding lease is:

(i) if the lease terminates as a result of an event that would have been a disposal event had *CAA 2001, s 34A* above not applied to prevent the lessor claiming allowances or if such an event occurs as a result of, or in connection with, the termination, the disposal value that would have been brought into account by reason of the event had the lessor qualified for allowances and claimed all the allowances to which he would have been entitled;

(ii) if (i) above does not apply and the lease is a long funding finance lease (see **6.22** above), the value at which, immediately after the termination of the lease, the plant or machinery is recognised in the books or other financial records of the lessor; or

(iii) if (i) above does not apply and the lease is a long funding operating lease (see **6.22** above), the market value of the plant or machinery immediately after the termination of the lease.

[*CAA 2001, ss 13A, 46(2), 70YG*].

Lessor's taxable profits

[6.40] In calculating the taxable profits of a person for any period of account (meaning, in this case, a period for which he draws up accounts) in which he is the lessor of any plant or machinery under a long funding finance lease, the following provisions apply, subject to the anti-avoidance provisions below.

The amount to be brought into account as taxable income from the lease is the amount of the 'rental earnings' in respect of the lease for the period. The '*rental earnings*' for a period is the amount which, in accordance with generally accepted accounting practice, would be treated as the gross return on investment for the period in respect of the lease. If the lease would be treated in the accounts as a loan under generally accepted accounting practice, so much of the rentals under the lease which fall to be treated as interest are treated as rental earnings. [*CTA 2010, s 360; ITTOIA 2005, s 148A*].

A profit (whether capital or otherwise) arising to the lessor in connection with the lease which:

- would not otherwise be brought into account for tax purposes, and
- falls to be recognised under generally accepted accounting practice in the lessor's profit and loss account, income statement, statement of recognised gains and losses, statement of changes in equity or any other statement of items brought into account in computing the lessor's profits or losses for a period,

is treated as income attributable to the lease for the period. A loss meeting these conditions is treated as a revenue expense incurred in connection with the lease in the period. [*CTA 2010, s 361; ITTOIA 2005, s 148B*].

Where a long funding finance lease terminates and a sum calculated by reference to the termination value (see **6.37** above) is paid to the lessee (for example, as a rebate of rentals), no deduction is allowed in respect of the sum, except to any extent that it is brought into account in determining the lessor's rental earnings. [*CTA 2010, s 362; ITTOIA 2005, s 148C*].

In calculating the profits of a person for any period of account (as above) in any part of which he is the lessor of any plant or machinery under a long funding operating lease, the following provisions apply.

A deduction is allowable for each period of an amount equal to so much of the 'expected gross reduction' in the value of the plant or machinery over the term of the lease as is attributable to the period (apportioning the reduction on a time basis).

The '*expected gross reduction*' for the above purposes is the 'starting value' less the amount which, at the commencement of the term of the lease, is expected to be the 'residual value' of the plant or machinery. The '*starting value*' is:

(i) if the only use of the plant or machinery by the lessor has been the leasing of it under the long funding operating lease as a qualifying activity, the cost (i.e. the expenditure incurred by the lessor on provision of the plant or machinery);

(ii) if the last previous use of the plant or machinery by the lessor was the leasing of it under another long funding operating lease as a qualifying activity, the market value of the plant or machinery at the commencement of the term of the lease under consideration;

(iii) if the last previous use of the plant or machinery by the lessor was the leasing of it under a long funding finance lease as a qualifying activity, the value at which the plant or machinery is recognised in the books or other financial records of the lessor at the commencement of the lease under consideration;

(iv) if the last previous use of the plant or machinery by the lessor was for the purposes of a qualifying activity other than leasing under a long funding lease, the lower of the amounts in (i) and (ii) above; or

(v) if the lessor initially incurred the expenditure on the provision of the plant or machinery for purposes other than those of a qualifying activity but subsequently, and after 31 March 2006, brings the plant or machinery into use for the purposes of a qualifying activity consisting of the leasing of the plant or machinery under the lease, the lower of:
    - the market value of the plant or machinery at the time it is first so brought into use, and
    - the value of the plant or machinery at that time on the assumption that the initial cost of the plant or machinery has been written off on a straight line basis (as defined) over its remaining useful economic life (see **6.26**(iii) above) and any further capital expenditure incurred has been written off on the same basis over so much of the remaining useful economic life as remains at the time it is incurred.

The '*residual value*' of plant or machinery is its estimated market value on a disposal at the end of the term of the lease less the estimated costs of disposal.

A further deduction is allowable where the lessor incurs additional capital expenditure in relation to the plant or machinery which is not reflected in the market value of the plant or machinery at the commencement of the term of the lease (or, where the circumstances are as in (v) above, at the time the plant or machinery is first brought into use for the purposes of the qualifying activity). The deduction is for each period ending after the incurring of the additional expenditure and is an amount equal to the proportion of the 'expected reduction' in the value of the additional expenditure that the period (to the extent that it falls within the remaining term of the lease) bears to the remaining term of the lease.

The '*expected reduction*' for this purpose is the amount of the additional capital expenditure less 'RRV'. '*RRV*' is, where 'ARV' exceeds the aggregate of

'CRV' and 'PRV', the portion of the excess that is a result of the additional capital expenditure. If ARV does not exceed that aggregate, RRV is nil. '*ARV*' is the amount which, when the additional expenditure is incurred, is expected to be the residual value (as above) of the plant or machinery. '*CRV*' is the amount which is expected at the commencement of the term of the lease to be the residual value. '*PRV*' is the sum of any previous RRVs in respect of previous additional expenditure in relation to the leased plant or machinery.

On termination of a long funding operating lease, no deduction is allowed to the lessor for any sums paid to the lessee which are calculated by reference to the termination value (see **6.37** above). Any profits or losses arising at the termination are, however, taxed or relieved as follows.

The profit or loss is equal to:

$$TA - (ERV + EAE + LP)$$

where:

- TA is the termination amount (see **6.39** above);
- ERV is the amount, if any, by which the starting value (as above) exceeds the lessor's total deductions in respect of the expected gross reduction (as above);
- EAE is the amount, if any, by which the lessor's total additional capital expenditure (within the above provisions) exceeds his total deductions in respect of the expected partial reduction (as above); and
- LP is the total of any sums paid to the lessee that are calculated by reference to the termination value.

If the formula produces a positive result, there will be a profit; and if it produces a negative result there will be a loss. A profit is treated as income of the lessor attributable to the lease for the period in which the lease terminates. A loss is treated as a revenue expense incurred in connection with the lease in that period.

[*CTA 2010, ss 363–369, 381(4); ITTOIA 2005, ss 148D–148F, 148J*].

The above provisions are disapplied in relation to a lessor if any of the following four situations applies.

The first situation is where any part of the expenditure incurred on acquiring the plant or machinery for leasing under the lease is (apart from those provisions) allowable as a deduction in computing his profits or losses as a result of forming part of his trading stock. This rule applies also if the lessor becomes entitled to such a deduction at any time after the expenditure is incurred as a result of the plant or machinery forming part of the trading stock at that later time (i.e. where the plant or machinery is appropriated to trading stock having originally been acquired as, for example, a fixed asset). If the above provisions have been given effect before the appropriation, the amounts to be taken into account in computing the profits or losses are adjusted on a just and reasonable basis. This provision applies where the expenditure is incurred on or after 9 October 2007 or where a person becomes entitled to a deduction as a result of any plant or machinery forming part of the trading stock on or after that date. [*CTA 2010, ss 370, 371; ITTOIA 2005, s 148FA*].

The second situation in which the provisions are disapplied is where a person is the lessee of any plant or machinery under a lease (lease A) which is not a long funding lease and, on or after 13 December 2007, he enters, as lessor, into a long funding lease (lease B) of any of the same plant or machinery. If lease A subsequently becomes a long funding lease as a result of *CAA 2001, s 70H* (tax return by lessee treating lease as long funding lease — see **6.24** above) and does not cease to be such a lease, this provision is treated as never having applied to lease B. [*CTA 2010, s 372; ITTOIA 2005, s 148FB*].

The third situation in which there is a disapplication of the provisions is where:

(a) the long funding lease forms part of any arrangement entered into (whether before or after the inception of the lease) by the lessor on or after 9 October 2007 which includes one or more other transactions;
(b) the main purpose, or one of the main purposes, of the arrangement is to secure that, over the period of the lease, there would be a substantial difference between the total amounts taken into account under the arrangement under generally accepted accounting practice and those taken into account for tax purposes; and
(c) the difference would be wholly or partly attributable to the application of any of the above provisions.

For this purpose it does not matter if the parties to one transaction forming part of the arrangement differ from the parties to any other such transaction. The circumstances in which two or more transactions are treated as forming an arrangement include any case where it would be reasonable to assume that one or more of them would not have been entered into independently, or if entered into independently, would not have taken the same form of been on the same terms. If the above provisions have been given effect before (a)–(c) above are met, the amounts to be taken into account in computing the profits or losses of the lessor are adjusted on a just and reasonable basis.

[*CTA 2010, ss 373–375; ITTOIA 2005, s 148FC*].

Where, at the beginning of 13 December 2007, a lessor under a long funding lease ('lease B') is also the lessee of the same plant or machinery under a lease ('lease A') that is not a long funding lease, the following apply.

(A) *CTA 2010, s 360* or *ITTOIA 2005, s 148A* above does not apply to any period of account beginning on or after 13 December 2007 if no rentals due under lease B before that date are in respect of any part of that period.
(B) In calculating his profits under lease B for a period of account ending on or after 13 December 2007 which is not within (A) above, the lessor is treated as receiving for that period (in addition to any amount brought into account under *CTA 2010, s 360* or *ITTOIA 2005, s 148A*) income attributable to the lease equal to so much of the rentals which become due on or after 13 December 2007 and which are wholly or partly in respect of the period as would not reasonably be regarded as reflected in the rental earnings for the period. Any rental paid for a rental period beginning before 13 December 2007 or which is not wholly within the period of account is apportioned on a time basis for this purpose.

(C) *CTA 2010, s 361* or *ITTOIA 2005, s 148B* does not apply to any profit or loss arising on or after 13 December 2007.

(D) If *CTA 2010, s 362* or *ITTOIA 2005, s 148C* applies to the termination of lease B on or after 13 December 2007, a deduction is allowed in calculating the lessor's profits in respect of the sum paid to the lessee, but restricted to the total amount brought into account under (A) or (B) above.

If lease A subsequently becomes a long funding lease as a result of *CAA 2001, s 70H* (tax return by lessee treating lease as long funding lease — see **6.24** above) and does not cease to be such a lease, (A)–(D) above are treated as never having applied to lease B.

[*FA 2008, Sch 20 para 11*].

The fourth situation in which the provisions are disapplied is where a person is or has been a lessor under a long funding lease of a film, the inception of which is on or after 13 November 2008. For this purpose, a '*film*' includes any record, however made, of a sequence of visual images that is capable of being used as a means of showing that sequence as a moving picture, and also includes the film soundtrack. [*CTA 2010, s 376; ITTOIA 2005, s 148FD; CTA 2009, s 1181*].

Similar provisions to those at (A)–(D) above apply in respect of a long funding finance lease of a film whose inception is before 13 November 2008 and which has not terminated before that date. The provisions apply by reference to 13 November 2008 and as if references to lease B were to the lease. [*FA 2009, Sch 33 paras 4–9; CTA 2010, Sch 1 para 718, Sch 2 para 64*].

Provisions in *ICTA 1988, s 502H* deal with the taxable profits of a lessor which is a company carrying on life assurance business.

Overseas leasing

Repeal of provisions

[6.41] The overseas leasing provisions at **6.43–6.55** below are, in effect, repealed on the introduction of the long funding lease provisions at **6.10** above. The repeal operates by disregarding leases 'finalised' on or after 1 April 2006 in determining whether plant or machinery is used for overseas leasing. For this purpose, a lease is '*finalised*' on the earliest day on which there is a contract in writing for the lease between the lessor and the lessee, no terms remain to be agreed and either the contract is unconditional or, if conditional, the conditions have been met. [*CAA 2001, s 105(2A); FA 2006, Sch 8 para 23, Sch 9 para 13*].

Lessee resident in EEA country

[6.42] HMRC announced on 24 May 2007 that they now accept that in some circumstances the overseas leasing provisions at **6.43–6.55** below are contrary to EU law. Accordingly (and subject to the repeal provisions at **6.41** above), where plant or machinery is used for overseas leasing and the lessee is resident in a European Economic Area ('EEA') country, HMRC will now adopt the following approach.

Where the EEA country concerned gives the lessee a relief that is broadly equivalent to capital allowances, HMRC will apply *CAA 2001, s 109* (see **6.45** below) to restrict writing-down allowances to 10% but will not seek to apply *CAA 2001, s 110* (see **6.46** below) to deny allowances altogether.

Where the EEA country concerned does not give the lessee a relief broadly equivalent to capital allowances, HMRC will accept that the lessor is entitled to normal writing-down allowances at 25% per annum.

(HMRC Brief 40/07).

Lease

[6.43] References to a lease include references to a sublease; and references to lessors and lessees are construed accordingly. Letting a ship or aircraft on charter, or any other asset on hire, is treated as leasing even if it would not otherwise be regarded as such. [*CAA 2001, s 105(1)*].

Overseas leasing and other definitions

[6.44] For the purposes of the following provisions, plant or machinery is, subject to the repeal provisions at **6.41** above, used for overseas leasing if it is used for the purpose of being leased to a person who:

- (a) is not resident in the UK, and
- (b) does not use the plant or machinery exclusively for earning profits chargeable to UK tax (including profits chargeable under *ICTA 1988, s 830(4)* (profits from the exploration and exploitation of the seabed etc.), but excluding profits in respect of which relief from UK tax under a double taxation agreement pursuant to *TIOPA 2010, s 2(1)* (previously *ICTA 1988, s 788*) is available).

The Inland Revenue's view was previously that where there was a chain of leases, the tests in (a) and (b) above applied to the end lessee only. However, in their Tax Bulletin, April 1999, they stated a change of view with effect from 19 April 1999 that the above tests should apply to any lessee in the chain.

[*CAA 2001, s 105(2)–(4), Sch 3 para 21; TIOPA 2010, Sch 8 para 58*].

The provisions at **6.45** and **6.46** below apply to qualifying expenditure incurred on the provision of plant or machinery for leasing which is at any time in the 'designated period' (see **6.48** below) used for overseas leasing which is not 'protected leasing'. For this purpose, 'protected leasing' is 'short-term leasing' (see **6.49** below) or the use of a ship, aircraft or transport container for a 'qualifying purpose' under *CAA 2001, ss 123 or 124* (see **6.50**(e)–(g) below). [*CAA 2001, ss 105(5), 107(2), 109(2), 110(2)*].

HMRC consider that where there is a chain of leases, each of the leases must be examined to determine if the leasing under it is protected leasing. If the leasing under any of the leases is not protected leasing then the provisions at **6.45** and **6.46** below are not prevented from applying. This position represents a change of view: previously it was considered that the protected leasing tests applied to the end lessee only. HMRC will accept the application of the old interpretation to leasing arrangements entered into before 3 February 2005 and to arrangements entered into before 3 May 2005 where the principal terms of the arrangement were agreed in writing before 3 February 2005 and have not materially altered since that date. (Revenue Statement, 3 February 2005).

Note that the restriction in the meaning of the term 'qualifying activity' referred to at **4.3** above does not apply for the purpose of these provisions, so that 'qualifying activity' includes any activity listed at **4.2** above, even if any profits or gains from it are not chargeable to UK tax. [*CAA 2001, s 105(6)*].

References in any of the following paragraphs (up to and including **6.55** below) to expenditure having qualified for a first-year allowance is a reference to such an allowance having fallen to be made in respect of the whole or any part of that expenditure. [*CAA 2001, s 126(3)*].

Pooling and restriction of allowances

[6.45] Where the lessee is resident in an EEA country, the provisions below apply subject to **6.42** above.

Expenditure meeting the conditions in **6.41** and **6.44** above can only be allocated to a class pool (see **5.48** above), known as the overseas leasing pool. This does not apply where such expenditure is long-life asset expenditure (see **5.66** above) or expenditure required to be allocated to a single asset pool (see **5.48** onwards above). The final chargeable period (see **5.32** and **5.46** above) for the overseas leasing pool is the chargeable period at the end of which the circumstances are such that no more disposal values could fall to be brought into account.

Writing-down allowances in respect of expenditure meeting the conditions at **6.44** above are restricted to 10% per annum (where such allowances are not prohibited altogether as described at **6.46** below). This applies both to expenditure within the overseas leasing pool and expenditure in a single asset pool, including, for chargeable periods for which *CAA 2001* has effect (see **1.2** above), expenditure on plant or machinery used partly for purposes other than those of a qualifying activity (see **5.55** above). The restriction does not, however, apply to long-life assets (see **5.66** above), as writing-down allowances are restricted in any event to 6% per annum for such assets. The 10% allowance is proportionately increased if the chargeable period is longer than one year and proportionately reduced if the chargeable period is shorter than one year or the qualifying activity is carried on only for part of the chargeable period. A claim for a writing-down allowance may require it to be reduced to a specified amount.

[*CAA 2001, ss 56(5), 65(4), 107, 109*].

If plant or machinery allocated to the overseas leasing pool is disposed of to a connected person within **2.34** above (otherwise than where there is a change in the persons carrying on the qualifying activity which does not involve all the persons carrying on that activity before the change permanently ceasing to carry it on or where the qualifying activity is treated as continuing under *CTA 2010, ss 940A–953* (previously *ICTA 1988, s 343*), the disposal value to be brought into account is the lesser of market value and cost, and the transferee is treated as acquiring the plant at the same figure. [*CAA 2001, s 108*].

Prohibition of allowances

[6.46] Where the lessee is resident in an EEA country, the provisions below apply subject to **6.42** above.

No balancing allowances or writing-down allowances are available in respect of expenditure meeting the conditions noted above if the plant or machinery is used otherwise than for a 'qualifying purpose' (see **6.50** below) and the lease is within one of the following items:

(A) there is more than a year between the dates when two consecutive payments become due under the lease;
(B) any payments other than periodical ones are due under the lease, or under any agreement which might reasonably be construed as being collateral to it;
(C) any payment under the lease or under such a collateral agreement, expressed as a monthly amount over the period for which it is due, differs from any other such payment expressed in the same way, unless this is attributable to a change in:
  (i) the rate of corporation tax or income tax, or
  (ii) the rate of capital allowances, or
  (iii) any rate of interest linked to a change in the rate of interest applicable to inter-bank loans, or
  (iv) any change in insurance premiums charged by a person not connected with the lessor or lessee;
(D) the lease is for more than 13 years; or the lease or a separate agreement provides for extension or renewal of the lease, or for the grant of a new lease, with the result that the plant or machinery could be leased for a period exceeding 13 years;
(E) at any time the lessor or a person connected with him (within **2.34** above) will or may become entitled to receive from the lessee or any other person a payment, other than insurance money, of an amount determined before the expiry of the lease and referable to a value of the plant or machinery on or after expiry, but not necessarily relating to a disposal of the plant or machinery.

[*CAA 2001, s 110*].

In *BMBF (No 24) Ltd v CIR* CA, [2004] STC 97 it was held that the lease referred to in (A) to (E) above is the lease by the owner of the machinery or plant, i.e. in the case of a chain of leases, the headlease.

If a balancing, first-year or writing-down allowance has been made, and an event during the designated period results in the expenditure falling within the above provisions, the amount of the allowances already made, less any amount recovered as excess relief (see **6.51** below), is treated as a balancing charge, on the person who owns the plant or machinery immediately before the event, for the chargeable period (see **2.1** above) in which the event occurs. The allowances already made are determined as if the plant or machinery in question was the only item provided for the qualifying activity (and therefore was the only item in its pool). A disposal value is also to be brought into account in the actual pool concerned (thereby removing the item from the pool) equal to the amount of the expenditure on the item on which allowances have been given less the balancing charge. [*CAA 2001, s 114*].

If a person liable to such a balancing charge acquired the plant or machinery through one or more transactions between connected persons (within **2.34** above) and a first-year, balancing or writing-down allowance was made to any of those persons, the following provisions apply for the computation of the balancing charge, except where the transaction or transactions involved a change in the persons carrying on the qualifying activity which did not involve all the persons carrying on that activity before the change permanently ceasing to carry it on or where the continuation or succession provisions in *CTA 2010, ss 940A–953* (previously *ICTA 1988, s 343(1)*) applied:

(1) all capital allowances made to the connected persons are taken into account;
(2) consideration passing between the connected persons is disregarded;
(3) if a balancing adjustment is made, the total allowances taken into account under (1) above are adjusted in a just and reasonable manner.

[*CAA 2001, s 115*].

EXAMPLE 1

[6.47]

K Ltd, which carries on a leasing trade and makes up its annual accounts to 30 June, has qualifying expenditure of £28,000 on plant within the main pool at 1 July 2004. During the year ended 30 June 2005 it incurs the following expenditure.

(1)	various items of plant for leasing to UK traders	£80,000
(2)	various items of plant for overseas leasing such that *CAA 2001, s 109* applies to restrict writing-down allowances to 10% p.a.	£40,000
(3)	items of plant for overseas leasing such that *CAA 2001, s 110* precludes writing-down allowances	£10,000

No other additions or disposals take place within the year. The company's capital allowances computation for the year to 30 June 2005 is as follows.

	Expenditure qualifying for FYAs	*Main pool*	*Overseas leasing pool*	*Total Allowances*
	£	£	£	£
WDV b/fwd		28,000		
Additions	—	80,000	40,000	
		108,000		

	Expenditure qualifying for FYAs	*Main pool*	*Overseas leasing pool*	*Total Allowances*
	£	£	£	£
WDA		(27,000)	(4,000)	31,000
WDV c/fwd		£81,000	£36,000	
Total allowances				£31,000

Note

(a) Where allowances are excluded altogether by virtue of *CAA 2001, s 110* expenditure on the plant in question must in practice be omitted from the overseas leasing pool for the purposes of calculating writing-down allowances, although strictly the legislation does not prevent the expenditure being allocated to the pool.

Designated period

[6.48] The '*designated period*' is the period beginning when the plant or machinery is first brought into use by the person who incurred the new expenditure, and ending at the earlier of:

(a) ten years later; and
(b) the plant ceasing to be owned by that person.

For the purposes of (a) above, however, if the lease was entered into before 16 March 1993, the designated period was reduced to four years if the plant or machinery was used throughout that time for a 'qualifying purpose' within **6.50** below. For the purposes of (b) above, the plant or machinery is treated as continuing to be owned by that person whilst it is owned by a connected person (within **2.34** above) or a person who acquired it from him through one or more disposals on the occasion of which either there was a change in the persons carrying on the qualifying activity which did not involve all the persons carrying on that activity before the change permanently ceasing to carry it on. [*CAA 2001, s 106*].

Short-term leasing

[6.49] '*Short-term leasing*' is the leasing of plant or machinery in such a manner:

(a) that:
    (i) the number of consecutive days of leasing to the same person will normally be below 30, and
    (ii) the total number of days of leasing to the same person in any period of 12 months will normally be below 90; or
(b) that:
    (i) the number of consecutive days of leasing to the same person will not normally exceed 365, and

(ii) the aggregate of the periods of leasing in any period of four consecutive years within the designated period to lessees in circumstances not falling within **6.50**(a) below will not exceed two years.

For these purposes:

(A) persons connected with each other (within **2.34** above) are treated as the same person, and
(B) where plant or machinery is leased as one of a number of items which form part of a group of similar items and are not separately identifiable, all the items in the group may be treated as used for short-term leasing if substantially all are so used.

[*CAA 2001, s 121*].

Qualifying purpose

[6.50] Plant or machinery is used for a '*qualifying purpose*' at any time when one of the following situations exists:

(a) the plant or machinery is leased to a lessee who uses it for the qualifying activity without leasing it and it would have been included, wholly or partly, in his available qualifying expenditure for any period under the general writing-down allowances provisions if he had bought it at that time;
(b) the person who incurred the expenditure, or a person connected with him (within **2.34** above), or a person who acquired the asset from him through one or more disposals on the occasion of which there was a change in the persons carrying on the qualifying activity which did not involve all the persons carrying on that activity before the change permanently ceasing to carry it on, uses the plant or machinery for short-term leasing (within **6.49** above);
(c) the plant or machinery is leased to a lessee who uses it for short-term leasing and *either* is resident in the UK *or* uses it in a qualifying activity carried on in the UK;
(d) the person who incurred the expenditure, or a person connected with him, or a person who acquired the asset from him through one or more disposals on the occasion of which there was a change in the persons carrying on the qualifying activity which did not involve all the persons carrying on that activity before the change permanently ceasing to carry it on, uses the plant or machinery for a qualifying activity without leasing it;
(e) the plant or machinery is a ship which is let on a charter in a trade involving the operation of ships, and
    (i) the trader is resident in the UK or carries on the trade there,
    (ii) he is responsible as principal (or appoints another person to be responsible in his place) for navigating and managing the ship throughout the charter period and for defraying all expenses in connection with the ship throughout the period, or substantially all expenses other than those directly incidental to a particular voyage or to the employment of the ship during that period, and

(iii) the main object, or one of the main objects, of the chartering, or a series of transactions including the chartering, or any transaction in such a series, was not for any person to obtain a first-year allowance or a writing-down allowance of an amount determined without regard to the restriction of the rate to 10% per annum by *CAA 2001, s 109* for certain overseas leasing (see **6.45** above);

(f) the plant or machinery is an aircraft within the scope, with suitable modifications, of (e) above;

(g) the plant or machinery is a transport container which leased in a trade carried on by a person who is resident in the UK or who carries on the trade there, and either:
   (i) the trade involves the operation of ships or aircraft, and the container is at other times used by him in connection with the operation of them, or
   (ii) the container is leased under a succession of leases to different persons most or all of whom are not connected with each other.

[*CAA 2001, ss 122–125*].

As regards (a) above, the meaning of the word 'leasing' was examined in *Barclays Mercantile Industrial Finance Ltd v Melluish* ChD 1990, 63 TC 95. The lessee of the master print of a film, capital expenditure on the provision of which by the lessor qualified for capital allowances under the legislation then in force, was held not to have used the print for leasing when it entered into exclusive distribution agreements whereby the print would be exploited by third parties in return for licence fees. As regards (e) above see *Lloyds TSB Equipment Leasing (No 1) Ltd v HMRC* CA, [2014] STC 2770; [2014] EWCA Civ 1062 and *Lloyds Bank Leasing (No 1) Ltd v HMRC* FTT, [2015] SFTD 1012.

Recovery of excess relief

[6.51] If new expenditure has qualified for a first-year allowance or a 'normal writing-down allowance' and at any time in the designated period the plant or machinery is used for overseas leasing which is not protected leasing (see **6.44** above), the following provisions apply to the person who owns the plant or machinery when it is first so used.

(a) A balancing charge for the chargeable period in which the plant is first so used is made equal to the amount by which the first-year and normal writing-down allowances made in respect of the qualifying expenditure for chargeable periods up to and including that period exceed the total allowances that could have been made for those periods if no first-year or normal writing-down allowances could have been made (i.e. if the provisions at **6.45** or **6.46** above had applied from the outset). The allowances already made are determined as if the plant or machinery in question was the only item provided for the qualifying activity (and therefore was the only item in its pool).

(b) A disposal value must be brought into account in the appropriate pool equal to the qualifying expenditure on the plant or machinery concerned less the actual allowances made as calculated in (a) above.

(c) The aggregate of the balancing charge and the disposal value is then allocated to whichever pool is appropriate for plant or machinery used for overseas leasing (usually the overseas leasing pool — see **6.45** above) for the next chargeable period.

For the above purposes, a '*normal writing-down allowance*' is a writing-down allowance not subject to the 10% per annum rate restriction in **6.45** above or the 6% restriction for long-life asset expenditure (see **5.66** above).

[*CAA 2001, ss 111, 126(1)(2)*].

If the person who owns the plant or machinery at the time when overseas leasing other than protected leasing begins acquired it through one or more transactions between connected persons (within **2.34** above), and a first-year or normal writing-down allowance was made to any of those persons or, where no first-year allowance or normal writing-down allowance was claimed but a balancing allowance was made to any of those persons, the following provisions apply for the computation of the amounts in (a)–(c) above.

(A) Only the expenditure by the first connected person is taken into account, and any consideration passing between the connected persons is disregarded.
(B) All the allowances made to the connected persons are taken into account.
(C) If a balancing adjustment has been made on any of the transfers between the connected persons, the total relief taken into account under (a) above is adjusted as is just and reasonable.

This does not apply where the transaction or transactions involved a change in the persons carrying on the qualifying activity which did not involve all the persons carrying on that activity before the change permanently ceasing to carry it on or where the continuation or succession provisions now in *CTA 2010, ss 940A–953* applied. [*CAA 2001, s 112*].

If the plant or machinery is a ship, the following further provisions apply. No first-year or writing-down allowance postponed under *CAA 2001, s 130* (see **5.74** above), and not subsequently made, can be made for the first chargeable period of use for overseas leasing which is not protected leasing or for any subsequent chargeable period. Instead the outstanding amount is allocated to the long-life asset or overseas leasing pool of the following chargeable period. The provisions described in (a)–(c) above take precedence over those in *CAA 2001, s 132(2)* concerning potential balancing adjustments (see **5.75** above). [*CAA 2001, s 113*].

EXAMPLE 2

[6.52]

In 2003 X Ltd, which makes up accounts to 31 December annually, buys two items of plant, machines A and B, for use in its manufacturing trade, for £1,500 each. In 2004 it leases them overseas in circumstances such that capital allowances are obtainable at 10% per annum for machine A in accordance with *CAA 2001, s 109*, but are prohibited by *CAA 2001, s 110* for machine B. X Ltd has unrelieved qualifying expenditure of £16,000 in its main pool at 1 January 2003 and makes no transactions on plant, etc. other than those mentioned above. Machines A and B qualified for a 40% first-year allowance. The capital allowances are computed as follows for the years ended 31 December 2003, 2004 and 2005.

	Expenditure qualifying for FYAs	*Main pool*	*Overseas leasing pool (Machine A)*	*Total Allowances*
	£	£	£	£
Year to 31.12.03				
WDV b/fwd		16,000		
Additions	3,000			
FYA (40%)	(1,200)			1,200
	1,800	16,000		
WDA (25%)		(4,000)		4,000
Transfer to main pool	(1,800)	1,800		
WDV c/fwd		13,800		
Total allowances				£5,200
Year to 31.12.04				
Disposal value**		(1,350)		
WDA (25%)		(3,113)		3,113
WDV c/fwd		9,337		
Balancing charge*				(1,365)
Total allowances				£1,748
Year to 31.12.05				
Qualifying expenditure on Machine A***			1,215	
WDA (25%)/(10%)		(2,334)	(122)	£2,456
WDV c/fwd		£7,003	£1,093	

The balancing charge is computed as follows (see* **6.51*(a) above):*

Machine A

Actual allowances

	Machine A	*Total Allowances*
	£	£
Expenditure incurred	1,500	
FYA at 40%, year to 31.12.03	(600)	600
WSDV c/fwd	900	
WDA at 25%,		
year to 31.12.04	(225)	225
WDV c/fwd	£675	
Total actual allowances		£825

Notional allowances (on the basis that *CAA 2001, s 109* applied from the outset)

	Machine A	*Total Allowances*
	£	£
Expenditure incurred	1,500	
WDA at 10%, year to 31.12.03	(150)	150
WDV c/fwd	1,350	
WDA at 10%,		
year to 31.12.04	(135)	135
WDV c/fwd	£1,215	
Total notional allowances		£285

	£
Total actual allowances	825
Total notional allowances	285
Balancing charge on machine A	£540

Machine B

	£
Total actual allowances (as for machine A)	825
Total notional allowances	Nil
Balancing charge on machine B	£825

The total balancing charge is therefore £540 + £825 = £1,365.

The disposal value is equal to the qualifying expenditure less the total actual allowances computed as above (see* **6.51(b) above).*

	Machine A	*Machine B*
	£	£
Qualifying expenditure	1,500	1,500
Actual allowances (see above)	825	825

	Machine A	*Machine B*
	£	£
Disposal values	£675	£675

Total disposal value is therefore £675 + £675 = £1,350.

****Qualifying expenditure is allocated to the overseas leasing pool in respect of machine A as follows (see* **6.51***(c) above)*

	£
Balancing charge (machine A)	540
Disposal value	675
	£1,215

The figure of £1,215 is equivalent to notionally writing down the original cost of £1,500 at 10% p.a. for two years as above.

Joint lessees

[6.53] The following provisions apply, in respect of new expenditure, if plant or machinery is leased to two or more persons jointly and at least one of them is not resident in the UK and does not use the plant or machinery exclusively for earning profits chargeable to UK tax, and the leasing is not 'protected leasing' (as in **6.44** above).

If, at any time when the plant or machinery is so leased, the lessees use it for the purposes of a qualifying activity or activities but not for leasing, the expenditure is treated as not subject to *CAA 2001, ss 107* and *109* (overseas leasing pool and restriction of allowances — see **6.45** above) or *s 110* (prohibition of allowances — see **6.46** above) if, and to the extent that, it appears that the profits arising throughout the designated period (or the period of the lease, if shorter) will be chargeable to UK tax. If this provision applies to only part of the expenditure, that part is treated as relating to an item of plant or machinery separate from the remainder and apportionments are made as necessary.

[*CAA 2001, s 116*].

[6.54] If, in consequence of the provisions described in **6.53** above, the whole or part of any expenditure has qualified for a normal writing-down allowance (as defined in **6.51** above), and at any time in the designated period while the plant or machinery is leased as specified in **6.53** above:

(a) no lessee uses the plant or machinery for any qualifying activity of which the profits or gains are chargeable to UK tax, and
(b) the provisions in *CAA 2001, s 114* for recovery of prohibited allowances (see **6.46** above) do not otherwise apply and have not applied earlier,

the provisions in *CAA 2001, ss 111, 112* for the recovery of excess allowances (see **6.51** above) apply as if the plant or machinery (or the notional separate item of plant or machinery specified in **6.53** above) had at that time begun to be used for overseas leasing which is not protected leasing. [*CAA 2001, s 117(1), Sch 3 para 22*].

If:

(A) any expenditure has qualified for a normal writing-down allowance otherwise than as a result of the provisions in **6.53** above,
(B) the plant or machinery is subsequently leased in the designated period as described in **6.53** above, and
(C) at any time in the designated period while the plant or machinery is so leased, (a) and (b) above apply,

the provisions in *CAA 2001, ss 111, 112* for the recovery of excess allowances (see **6.51** above) apply as if the plant or machinery (and not any notional separate item of plant or machinery specified in **6.53** above) had at that time begun to be used for overseas leasing which is not protected leasing. [*CAA 2001, s 117(2)*].

If:

(i) under the provisions in **6.53** above, any new expenditure has qualified for a normal writing-down allowance,
(ii) at the end of the designated period the plant or machinery is leased as specified in **6.53** above,
(iii) *CAA 2001, s 117(1)* above has not applied, and
(iv) it appears that the extent to which the plant or machinery has been used for any qualifying activity or activities the profits of which are chargeable to UK tax is less than that which was taken into account in determining the amount of expenditure which qualified for a normal writing-down allowance,

the following provisions apply:

- the provisions in *CAA 2001, ss 111, 112* concerning recovery of excess relief (see **6.51** above) apply as if a part of the expenditure corresponding to the reduction in the extent of the use specified were expenditure on a separate item of plant, used, on the last day of the designated period, for overseas leasing which is not protected leasing;
- any disposal value subsequently brought into account in respect of the plant or machinery is apportioned by reference to the extent its use, determined at the end of the designated period, for the purposes of a qualifying activity or activities the profits of which are chargeable to UK tax instead of in accordance with the provisions of **6.53** above.

[*CAA 2001, s 117(3)–(6)*].

Information

[6.55] If plant or machinery which has not yet qualified for a first-year allowance or a normal writing-down allowance (or has qualified for one but not the other) is used for overseas leasing which is protected leasing, a claim for a first-year allowance/writing-down allowance must be accompanied by a certificate to that effect, specifying the description of the protected leasing, the lessee and the item or items of plant or machinery. If plant or machinery which has qualified for a first-year allowance or a normal writing-down allowance is used at any time in the designated period for overseas leasing other than protected leasing, the person who then owns it must give written notice to HMRC, specifying the lessee and the item or items of plant or machinery. The notice must be given within three months of the end of the chargeable period (see **2.1** above) in which the plant or machinery is first so used; but if after the three months the person concerned does not know, and cannot reasonably be expected to know, that the plant or machinery has been so leased, he must give notice within 30 days of coming to know of it.

If expenditure is incurred on plant or machinery which is leased to joint lessees within *CAA 2001, s 116(1)* (see **6.53** above), the lessor must, within the time limits set out above, give written notice to HMRC specifying:

(a) the names and addresses of the joint lessees,
(b) the portion of the expenditure properly attributable to each of them, and
(c) so far as it is within his knowledge, which of them is resident in the UK.

If circumstances occur such that *CAA 2001, s 117(1)* or *(2)* (recovery of allowances — see **6.54** above) applies, the then lessor must give written notice to HMRC specifying any of the joint lessees who is not resident in the UK and the item or items of plant or machinery. The notice must be given within three months of the end of the chargeable period (see **2.1** above) in which the circumstances occur; but if after the three months the person concerned does not know, and cannot reasonably be expected to know of the circumstances, he must give notice within 30 days of coming to know of it.

[*CAA 2001, ss 118–120*].

The usual penalties apply for failure to comply with the foregoing provisions. [*TMA 1970, s 98*].

7

Plant and Machinery — General Matters

Introduction

[7.1] This chapter deals with the miscellaneous remaining aspects of the plant and machinery code not covered in CHAPTERS **4–6**. Those aspects are as follows.

(1) **Anti-avoidance.** See **7.2** below for the effect of disposals to connected persons and **7.3–7.6** below for the restriction of allowances on certain sales, hire-purchase etc. arrangements. See also **17.2** onwards below for further anti-avoidance provisions.
(2) **Hire-purchase and leasing agreements.** Special provisions apply to expenditure incurred under a contract providing that the person incurring it may become the owner of the plant or machinery on the performance of the contract — see **7.7–7.10** below.
(3) **Abortive expenditure.** See **7.11** below.
(4) **Gifts.** Where plant or machinery is received by a person carrying on a qualifying activity as a gift for use in that activity it is treated as acquired at its market value. See **7.12** below.
(5) **Previous use outside qualifying activity.** Where plant or machinery previously used for other purposes begins to be used for the purposes of a qualifying activity, it is treated as acquired at that time, usually at its market value or actual cost if lower. See **7.13** below.
(6) **Partial depreciation subsidies.** Where such a subsidy is received in respect of plant or machinery allowances and charges are restricted. See **7.14** below.
(7) **Renewals basis.** Before 6 April 2016 (1 April 2016 for corporation tax purposes), the renewals basis could be used as an alternative to capital allowances, particularly for small items. No allowance or deduction was given on the cost of an original item but the cost of replacement is allowed as a revenue deduction. See **7.15** below.
(8) **Replacement domestic items relief.** A limited renewals basis for landlords of residential property continues to be available in the form of replacement domestic items relief. See **7.16A** below.
(9) **Successions to trades etc.** Special provisions apply to successions to qualifying activities. See **7.17–7.19** below.
(10) **Oil production sharing contracts.** See **7.20** below.
(11) **Co-ownership authorised contractual schemes.** See 7.21 below.

Anti-avoidance

Connected persons

[7.2] There are certain provisions which are designed to prevent a tax advantage being obtained as a result of transactions in plant or machinery between connected persons (within **2.34** above).

Where a disposal value falls to be brought into account in accordance with **5.41** above, the normal rule, that the disposal value cannot exceed the cost of acquisition to the person in question, is amended for disposals in cases where the person acquired the plant or machinery as a result of a transaction or series of transactions between connected persons. In such cases, the disposal value is limited to the greatest amount of expenditure incurred on the plant or machinery by any party to any of the transactions involved. [*CAA 2001, s 62(2)–(4)*]. For modifications of this provision where an additional VAT rebate is made, see **17.53** below.

The normal rule that no disposal value need be brought into account if none of the qualifying expenditure in question has been taken into account in determining available qualifying expenditure of the person (C) concerned (see **5.41** above), does not apply where C acquired the plant or machinery as a result of a transaction or series of transactions between connected persons and any of those connected persons were required to bring a disposal value into account. Instead, C's qualifying expenditure is treated as allocated to the appropriate pool for the chargeable period in which the disposal event occurs. [*CAA 2001, s 64(2)–(4)*]. As a result C is required to bring a disposal value into account in that pool for that chargeable period. The amount of the disposal value is then subject to the above limit.

Restriction of allowances on sale, hire-purchase etc.

[7.3] Anti-avoidance provisions operate to restrict the availability and amount of allowances or to impose or increase a balancing charge in certain cases where:

(i) a person (the '*buyer*') purchases plant or machinery from another (the '*seller*'); or
(ii) a person (the '*buyer*') enters into a contract such that on the performance thereof he will or may become the owner of plant or machinery belonging to another person (the '*seller*') (e.g. hire-purchase), or
(iii) a person (the '*buyer*') is assigned the benefit of a contract by another person (the '*seller*'), where the contract is one that on the performance thereof the seller will or may become the owner of plant or machinery.

Where a person is treated as having incurred capital expenditure on the provision of plant or machinery under **7.12** below (receipt of plant or machinery by way of gift), he is treated for this purpose as having done so by way of purchase from the donor.

The provisions apply only if any of the following conditions are met:

(a) the parties to the transaction are connected persons (within **2.34** above); or

(b) (for expenditure incurred before 6 April 2012 (1 April 2012 for corporation tax purposes)) it appears that the sole or main benefit which might be expected to accrue is the obtaining of a plant or machinery allowance; or

(c) the plant or machinery continues to be used for the purposes of a qualifying activity carried on by the seller or, where the transaction within (i)–(iii) above takes place after 21 April 2009, by a person (other than the buyer) who is connected with the seller; or

(d) the plant or machinery is used at any time after the date of the transaction for the purposes of a qualifying activity carried on by either the seller or any person, other than the buyer, who is connected with the seller, and has not in the meantime been used for the purposes of any other qualifying activity except that of leasing the plant or machinery; or

(e) (for expenditure incurred on or after 6 April 2012 (1 April 2012 for corporation tax purposes)) the transaction either has an 'avoidance purpose' or is part, or occurs as a result of, a scheme or arrangement that has such a purpose.

For these purposes a qualifying activity includes any activity within **4.2** above, regardless of whether or not any profits would be chargeable to UK tax (i.e. the restriction at **4.3** above does not apply).

In (e) above, a transaction, scheme or arrangement has an '*avoidance purpose*' if a main purpose of a party entering into it is to enable a person to obtain a tax advantage under the plant and machinery allowances code that would not otherwise be obtained (and this includes obtaining an allowance that is more favourable than the one that would otherwise be obtained and, for transactions within (i) (ii) or (iii) above occurring on or after 25 November 2015, avoiding liability for the whole of part of a balancing charge to which a person would otherwise be liable). It is immaterial whether a scheme or arrangement was made before or after the transaction in (i), (ii) or (iii) above was entered into and whether or not a scheme or arrangement is legally enforceable.

For the effect of the provisions where any of the conditions in (a)–(d) above are met, see **7.3A** below. For their effect where (e) above applies see **7.3B** below.

In relation to transactions within (i), (ii) or (iii) above occurring on or after 25 November 2015 it is explicitly provided that references in **7.3A** onwards below to the disposal value of the plant or machinery under such a transaction are references to the disposal value to be brought into account by the seller as a result of the sale, contract or assignment.

Any assessments or adjustments of assessments can be made to give effect to the provisions.

[*CAA 2001, ss 213–216, 231, 232, 268E; FA 2012, s 42, Sch 9 paras 1, 3, 4, 8, 9; FA 2016, s 70(2)–(7)(11)*].

The provisions were examined in *Barclays Mercantile Industrial Finance Ltd v Melluish* ChD 1990, 63 TC 95. They are modified to some extent where an additional VAT liability or rebate is incurred (see **17.53** below).

Transactions other than to obtain tax advantage

[7.3A] Where the anti-avoidance provisions in 7.3 above apply because any of the conditions in 7.3(a)–(d) are met, the buyer's allowances are restricted as follows.

(A) No annual investment allowance or first-year allowance is available to the buyer (where one would otherwise be due).

(B) In determining the buyer's qualifying expenditure, there is left out of account the excess of his actual capital expenditure over the disposal value brought into account by the seller.

Where the transaction in 7.3(i), (ii) or (iii) above is entered into on or after 26 February 2015, the qualifying expenditure of the buyer is nil if the seller is not required to bring a disposal value into account and at any time before the transaction the seller or a 'linked person' became the owner of the plant or machinery without incurring capital expenditure or 'qualifying revenue expenditure' on its provision. For this purpose, '*qualifying revenue expenditure*' is revenue expenditure of an amount at least equal to that which would reasonably have been expected to have been incurred on the provision of the plant or machinery by a transaction at arm's length in the open market or revenue expenditure which is incurred by the manufacturer of the plant or machinery and which is of an amount at least equal to what would reasonably be expected to be the normal manufacturing cost. A '*linked person*' is a person who owned the plant or machinery at any time before the transaction in (i), (ii) or (iii) above and who was connected with the seller at any time in the period beginning with that person's acquisition of the plant or machinery and ending with the transaction.

In any other case in which no disposal value falls to be brought into account by the seller (for example, if he is not within the charge to tax in the UK), the qualifying expenditure of the buyer (if otherwise greater) is limited to the lowest of:

(1) market value;

(2) where capital expenditure was incurred by the seller on the provision of the plant or machinery, the amount of that expenditure; and

(3) where capital expenditure was incurred by any person connected with the seller on the provision of the plant or machinery, the amount of the expenditure incurred by that person.

Except where the transaction is within 7.3(iii) above, the restrictions in (A) and (B) above are not applied if:

- before the sale or making of the contract, the plant or machinery has never been used; and
- the business of the seller is, or includes, the manufacture of plant or machinery of the same class; and
- the sale is effected, or the contract made, in the ordinary course of that business.

For expenditure incurred on or after 12 August 2011 and before 6 April 2012 (1 April 2012 for corporation tax purposes), (A) above is not so disapplied unless the buyer can show that, had 7.3(e) above then been in effect, (A) above would have been disapplied.

The restrictions at (A) and (B) above also do not apply if the plant or machinery is the subject of a sale and finance leaseback (see **7.4** below).

[*CAA 2001, ss 214–218, 230; FA 2012, ss 41, 42, Sch 9 paras 1, 3–5, 7, 9(1)(3); FA 2015, Sch 10 para 3*].

Transactions to obtain tax advantage

[7.3B] Where the anti-avoidance provisions in 7.3 above apply because the condition in 7.3(e) above is met, they have effect as follows.

(1) If the tax advantage is that an allowance to which the buyer is entitled for a chargeable period is calculated at a rate higher than would otherwise be used:
- no annual investment allowance or first-year allowance is available to the buyer (where one would otherwise be due); and
- the allowance in question is to be calculated at that lower rate.

(2) If the tax advantage is that the buyer is entitled to an allowance sooner than would otherwise be the case:
- no annual investment allowance or first-year allowance is available to the buyer (where one would otherwise be due); and
- the allowance is to be available as and when it would have been but for the tax advantage.

(3) In any case not within (1) or (2) above or (4) below, no annual investment allowance or first-year allowance is available to the buyer (where one would otherwise be due) and in determining the buyer's qualifying expenditure there is left out of account such amount as would, or would in effect, cancel out the tax advantage (whether that advantage is obtained by the buyer or another person and whether it relates to the transaction within 7.3(i)–(iii) above or something else).

(4) (In relation to transactions occurring on or after 25 November 2015) if the tax advantage relates to the disposal value of the plant or machinery to be brought into account by the seller as a result of the sale, contract or assignment in 7.3(i), (ii) or (iii) above (whether the advantage is the obtaining of a more favourable allowance or the avoidance of all or part of a balancing charge), then if:
- a 'payment' is payable to any person under the transaction, scheme or arrangement in 7.3(e) above, some or all of which would not be taken into account in determining the disposal value of the plant or machinery, and
- as a result, the seller would otherwise obtain a tax advantage under the plant and machinery allowances code;

the disposal value is to be adjusted in a just and reasonable manner so as to include an amount representing so much of the payment as would cancel out the tax advantage.
'*Payment*' for this purpose includes providing any benefit, assuming any liability and any other transfer of money or money's worth.

Where (3) above applies, the amount left out of account cannot be more than the buyer's expenditure under the transaction in **7.3**(i)–(iii) above. If a transaction, scheme or arrangement involves a tax advantage within (1) or (2) above and one of another kind (other than one within (4) above), then the restrictions in (1)–(3) above apply separately to each tax advantage.

Where an amount is to be left out of account under (3) above and an amount is also to be left out of account under either **7.3A**(B) above or *CAA 2001, s 228* (see **7.5** below), the amount to be left out of account is the greater of the two amounts. (1) and (2) above apply whether or not **7.3A**(B) above also applies or *CAA 2001, s 228* also applies.

The denial of annual investment allowance and first-year allowances to the buyer does not apply if the plant or machinery is the subject of a sale and finance leaseback (see **7.4** below).

[*CAA 2001, ss 215, 217, 218ZA, 218ZB; FA 2012, s 42, Sch 9 paras 1, 6, 9(1)(3); FA 2016, s 70(4)–(9)(11)*].

Sale and finance leasebacks

[7.4] Plant or machinery is subject to a '*sale and finance leaseback*' if a transaction within **7.3**(i)–(iii) above occurs and, after the date of the transaction, the plant or machinery

(a) continues to be used for the purposes of an activity carried on by the seller or a person (other than the buyer) connected with the seller (where the date of the transaction within **7.3**(i)–(iii) above is before 22 April 2009, continues to be used for the purposes of a qualifying activity carried on by the seller); or
(b) is used for the purposes of a qualifying activity carried on by either the seller or any person, other than the buyer, who is connected with the seller, and has not in the meantime been used for the purposes of any other qualifying activity except that of leasing the plant or machinery, or
(c) is used for the purposes of a non-qualifying activity carried on by the seller or any person (other than the buyer) who is connected with the seller, without having been used in the meantime for the purposes of any qualifying activity other than leasing of the plant or machinery,

and the plant or machinery is available to be so used directly or indirectly as a consequence of having been leased under a 'finance lease'.

A '*finance lease*' is any arrangements for plant or machinery to be leased or made available which, under generally accepted accounting practice, either would fall to be treated in the accounts (including any consolidated group accounts) of the lessor or person connected (within **2.34** above) with the lessor as a finance lease or a loan, or are comprised in arrangements which would fall to be so treated. A lease which is a long funding lease within the regime at **6.21** above is not a finance lease for this purpose where the transaction within **7.3**(i)–(iii) above takes place before 9 October 2007. See also *FA 2011, s 53* which, in effect, preserves the distinction between finance leases and operating leases for tax purposes where accounting standards have been revised to remove it.

[*CAA 2001, ss 219, 221*].

If plant or machinery is the subject of a sale and finance leaseback and the finance lease, or any transaction or series of transactions of which it forms part, makes provision, other than by guarantee from a person connected with the lessee, removing from the lessor (or a connected person) the whole or greater part of any risk which would fall on him of any person sustaining a loss if payments are not made in accordance with the lease's terms, the buyer's (and, if the buyer is not the lessor, the lessor's) capital expenditure under the transaction within **7.3**(i)–(iii) above is not qualifying expenditure for the purposes of plant and machinery allowances. This provision applies regardless of any election within **6.24** above or **7.5** below. [*CAA 2001, s 225*]. See Revenue Tax Bulletin, June 1998 for examples of circumstances in which this provision will apply.

For expenditure incurred before 6 April 2012 (1 April 2012 for corporation tax purposes) the above provision does not apply if

- before the sale or making of the contract, the plant or machinery has never been used; and
- the business of the seller is, or includes, the manufacture of plant or machinery of the same class; and
- the sale is effected, or the contract made, in the ordinary course of that business.

This exclusion does not apply where the transaction is within **7.3**(iii) above.

[*CAA 2001, s 230(2)(3); FA 2012, Sch 9 paras 7(3), 9*].

The provisions are modified to some extent where an additional VAT liability or rebate is incurred (see **17.53** below).

See also **17.10** to **17.15** below for the calculation of the income or profits of lessors and lessees under a sale and finance leaseback.

Election for special treatment

[7.5] Where a transaction within 7.3(i)–(iii) above occurs and the provisions at 7.3 above apply by virtue of (c) or (d) (i.e. a sale and lease-back), then if the conditions listed below are met, the seller and the buyer may make a joint election, the effect of which is that:

(a) no allowance is made to the seller in respect of the expenditure (with the result that no disposal value will fall to be brought into account); and
(b) in determining the allowances due to the lessor (i.e. the buyer), his qualifying expenditure is limited to the lesser of his capital expenditure or the capital expenditure incurred by the seller, or a person connected to the seller, on the provision of the plant or machinery (i.e. disregarding the market value and, where the lease-back is a finance lease, the seller's notional written-down value).

The conditions are that:

- the seller incurred capital expenditure on the provision of the plant or machinery which was unused and not second-hand at or (e.g. where the acquisition is by hire-purchase) after the time when he acquired it and was not acquired by him as a result of a transaction within the provisions at **7.3** above;
- the transaction within **7.3**(i)–(iii) above takes place not more than four months after the first occasion on which the plant or machinery is brought into use by any person for any purpose; and
- the seller has not made a claim for allowances in respect of the expenditure or included it in a pool of expenditure in any return or amended return.

The election is irrevocable and must be made by notice to HMRC not more than two years after the date of the transaction within **7.3**(i)–(iii) above.

[*CAA 2001, ss 227, 228(1)–(3)(5)*].

Oil fields

[7.6] Without affecting the operation of **7.3** to **7.5** above, additional provisions apply where

(a) there is, for the purposes of *FA 1980, Sch 17*, a transfer by a participator (the '*old participator*') in an oil field of the whole or part of his interest in the field; and

(b) as part of that transfer, the old participator disposes of, and the '*new participator*' (i.e. the person to whom the interest in the field is transferred) acquires plant or machinery used, or expected to be used, in connection with the field, or a share in such plant or machinery (see **4.18** above).

For plant and machinery allowance purposes, the qualifying expenditure incurred by the new participator in the acquisition in (b) above is, if it would otherwise be greater, restricted to the disposal value brought into account on the disposal.

'*Oil field*' and '*participator*' have the same meanings as they have in *Oil Taxation Act 1975, Pt I*.

[*CAA 2001, s 166*].

See also **7.18** below as regards successions to trades between connected persons.

Hire-purchase and leasing agreements

[7.7] Subject to the exclusions noted at **7.9** below, special provisions apply where capital expenditure on the provision of plant or machinery is incurred under 'a contract providing that [the person incurring the expenditure] shall or may become the owner of the plant or machinery on the performance of the contract'. The words are taken from the relevant legislation (*CAA 2001, s 67*), which is headed 'Hire-purchase and similar contracts'.

They would equally apply to a so-called lease-purchase contract which is similar to a hire-purchase contract in all but name, but which must be distinguished from leasing agreements under which the lessee is neither to become nor given the right to become the owner of the plant or machinery in question. (For leasing generally, see CHAPTER 6 above.) In order to avoid confusion and to emphasise the distinction and different tax treatment between the two types of arrangement, the Inland Revenue confirmed that, regardless of accounting treatment, lessees, as opposed to buyers under hire-purchase or lease-purchase agreements, are not entitled to capital allowances, the entitlement to such allowances normally resting with the lessor (Inland Revenue Press Release 27 October 1986). See now, however, **6.21** onwards above for capital allowances available to lessees under long funding leases.

A properly computed commercial rate of depreciation which is charged to the profit and loss account in respect of the asset acquired under the lease will normally be tax deductible (SP 3/91). Note, however, that this is subject to the rules introduced by *FA 2004* restricting the tax deductions available in the case of a sale and finance leaseback or lease and finance leaseback (see **17.10** to **17.15** below) and those introduced by *FA 2006* for long funding leases (see the computational provisions at **6.38** above).

Where a business is seeking to finance an acquisition of plant or machinery, therefore, it will need to take into account the differing tax treatment of the various options: hire-purchase, loan or lease. If the lease option is taken, the tax treatment will depend on whether or not the lease falls within the long funding lease regime.

EXAMPLE 1

[7.8]

A decision has to be made by a business on whether to enter into a hire-purchase agreement or a finance lease to acquire some computer equipment for £1,000. The business has a policy of writing-off the cost of computer equipment over a period of three years. Interest is assumed to be £300 in both cases and is computed under the sum-of-digits method. If the equipment purchase is financed by hire-purchase the tax deductions will be:

	Year 1	*Year 2*	*Year 3*
	£	£	£
Capital allowances (18% WDA)	180	148	121
H.P. interest	171	99	30
	£351	£247	£151

Alternatively, if the equipment is hired under a finance lease (which is not a long funding lease) the tax deductions will be:

	Year 1	*Year 2*	*Year 3*
	£	£	£
Depreciation over three years	334	333	333
Finance interest	171	99	30
	£505	£432	£363

In this example the total tax deductions over the three year period under hire-purchase are £749, whereas the finance lease alternative generates total tax deductions over the same period of £1,300, which is an additional £551. If annual investment allowance or a 100% first-year allowance could be claimed, the hire-purchase alternative would become more attractive, with deductions in the first year totalling £1,171, and the total over the three years equal to that for the finance lease option.

[7.9] Where a person carrying on a qualifying activity or, for contracts 'finalised' on or after 1 April 2006, a 'corresponding overseas activity' incurs capital expenditure on plant or machinery for the purposes of that activity under a hire-purchase etc. contract (as defined at **7.7** above), the plant or machinery is (subject to the exclusions below) treated as owned by that person (and not by any other person) at any time when he is entitled to the benefit of the contract.

All capital expenditure incurred by the buyer under the contract after the plant or machinery is brought into use for the purposes of the qualifying activity is treated as having been incurred at the time when it was first so brought into use. In other words, the full cost of an item of plant or machinery bought on hire-purchase and immediately used in the qualifying activity is eligible for writing-down allowances (or, where available, first-year allowances) for the chargeable period (see **2.1** above) in which the transaction takes place, notwithstanding the fact that such cost is to be paid in instalments extending beyond the end of that chargeable period. If the item is not immediately brought into use, capital expenditure incurred under the contract will qualify for allowances as it is incurred (i.e. subject to **2.4** above), until the item is brought into use, at which point all the remaining such expenditure qualifies for allowances. The cost for capital allowances purposes does not of course include hire-purchase interest charges or equivalent charges.

For these purposes, a '*corresponding overseas activity*' is an activity that would be a qualifying activity if the person carrying it on were resident in the UK (see **4.3** above). The inclusion of such activities within the provisions ensures that sellers under hire-purchase contracts are treated the in the same way whether or not the buyer is UK-resident. A contract is '*finalised*' on the earliest day on which there is a contract in writing between the parties, no terms remain to be agreed and either the contract is unconditional or, if conditional, the conditions have been met.

[*CAA 2001, s 67(1)(2)(3)(8), Sch 3 para 15*].

For contracts finalised on or after 1 April 2006, where a person enters into two or more agreements (or undertakings, whether or not legally enforceable) and those agreements are such that, if considered together as a single contract, that person would or could become the owner of the plant or machinery on their performance, the agreements are treated for the purposes of these provisions as parts of a single contract. [*CAA 2001, s 67(6)*]. This provision is intended to apply the hire-purchase provisions to arrangements such as those developed to be Shari'a compliant.

When a person is entitled to the benefit of a contract within the above provisions and ceases to be so entitled without becoming the owner of the plant or machinery in question, the person is treated as ceasing to own the plant or machinery at that time. The amount of any disposal value required to be brought into account as a result (see **5.41** above) depends on whether or not the item has been brought into use for the purposes of the qualifying activity. If it has been brought into use, the disposal value is the sum of:

(a) any capital sums received, or receivable, by way of compensation, consideration, damages or insurance moneys in respect of either the person's rights under the contract or the plant or machinery in question, and

(b) any capital expenditure payable under the contract, treated as paid under the above provisions and not in fact yet paid. The disposal value may not, however, exceed the total capital expenditure that would have been payable under the contract had it continued until completion. This follows the general rule that a disposal value cannot exceed the amount of the original qualifying expenditure in respect of a particular item of plant or machinery.

If the plant or machinery has not been brought into use, the amount of the disposal value is any capital sums received or receivable within (a) above.

[*CAA 2001, ss 67(4), 68)*].

For any contract finalised on or after 1 April 2006 which would fall under generally accepted accounting practice (within *FA 2004, s 50*) to be treated as a lease, the buyer is treated as owning the plant or machinery under the above provisions only if the lease would so fall to be treated by him as a finance lease. Where this exclusion applies, the plant or machinery is nevertheless treated as not owned by any other person. [*CAA 2001, s 67(2)–(2C)*].

The provisions do not apply to expenditure on plant or machinery that is a fixture (as defined at **6.3** above) and they do not prevent *CAA 2001, Pt 2 Ch 14* (the special provisions relating to fixtures — see **6.2** onwards above) applying to such expenditure incurred under a hire-purchase contract, etc. [*CAA 2001, s 69(1)(3)*]. Where a person is treated as owning plant or machinery under these provisions and the plant or machinery becomes a fixture, then, unless it is also treated as owned by that person under *CAA 2001, Pt 2 Ch 14*, it is treated as ceasing to be owned by him at the time it becomes a fixture. [*CAA 2001, s 69(2), Sch 3 para 16*].

The provisions also do not apply (except in relation to deemed ownership of the asset concerned) to expenditure incurred on the provision of plant or machinery for leasing under a 'finance lease' (see **7.4** above). [*CAA 2001, s 229(1)(3), Sch 3 para 44*].

Where the person entitled to the benefit of a hire-purchase etc. contract assigns the benefit of the contract before the plant or machinery is brought into use in such circumstances that the allowances due to the assignee fall to be restricted under the anti-avoidance provisions of *CAA 2001, Pt 2 Ch 17* (see **7.3** above), the disposal value provisions above do not apply. Instead, the disposal value is equal to the total of any capital sums within (a) above and any capital expenditure which the person would have incurred if he had wholly performed the contract. The latter amount is, however, added to the assignor's available qualifying expenditure for the chargeable period of the assignment, leaving him effectively in the same position as under *CAA 2001, s 68* above. The purpose of the provision is to protect the assignee from an undue depression of his qualifying expenditure by reference to the disposal value under the provisions at **7.3** above. The provision also applies to cases involving the provision of plant or machinery for leasing under a finance lease. [*CAA 2001, s 229(1)(2)(4)–(7); Sch 3 para 44*].

Anti-avoidance provisions apply where a person (S) 'transfers' (as defined to include any kind of disposal and the grant of a lease) plant or machinery to another person (B), at any subsequent time, the plant or machinery is available to be used by S or a connected person under a hire purchase etc. contract and S or the connected person incurs capital expenditure on the provision of the plant or machinery under that contract. The contract must be entered into after 12 November 2008.

In such circumstances, no annual investment allowance or first-year allowance is available to S or the connected person. The qualifying expenditure of S or the connected person is limited to the disposal value brought into account by S on the transfer of the plant or machinery to B. If S is not required to bring such a disposal value into account, then (subject to the further provision below), the qualifying expenditure is limited to the lowest of the market value of the plant or machinery and any capital expenditure incurred by S or a connected person on the original provision of the plant or machinery before the transfer to B.[

Where the hire purchase etc. contract is entered into on or after 26 February 2015, the qualifying expenditure of S or the connected person is nil if S is not required to bring a disposal value into account on the transfer to B and at any time before the transfer S or a 'linked person' became the owner of the plant or machinery without incurring capital expenditure or 'qualifying revenue expenditure' on its provision. For this purpose, '*qualifying revenue expenditure*' is revenue expenditure of an amount at least equal to that which would reasonably have been expected to have been incurred on the provision of the plant or machinery by a transaction at arm's length in the open market or revenue expenditure which is incurred by the manufacturer of the plant or machinery and which is of an amount at least equal to what would reasonably be expected to be the normal manufacturing cost. A '*linked person*' is a person who owned the plant or machinery at any time before the transfer and who was connected with S at any time in the period beginning with that person's acquisition of the plant or machinery and ending with the transfer.

CAA 2001, s 229A; FA 2009, s 64, Sch 32 paras 21, 22; FA 2015, Sch 10 para 4].

EXAMPLE 2

[7.10]

K Ltd, a trading company with a 30 June accounting date, buys a forklift truck on 1 July 2014 and immediately brings it into use in its trade. The price of the truck, if purchased with an immediate cash settlement, would have been £14,000 but K Ltd buys it on hire-purchase, involving the payment of 24 monthly instalments, beginning on 20 July 2014, of £500 each, following an initial deposit of £5,000 made on 1 July 2014, a total of £17,000 of which £3,000 represents hire-purchase charges. The company has qualifying expenditure of £9,000 on plant and machinery at 30 June 2014. On 31 October 5, the forklift truck is irreparably damaged by fire. K Ltd's insurers offer a payment of £2,000 on the basis that they will settle the outstanding instalments directly with the finance company handling the hire-purchase. Assuming that K Ltd accepts this offer and that there are no other additions or disposals of plant or machinery, K Ltd's capital allowances computations for the years ended 30 June 2015 and 2016 will be as follows.

	Main pool £	*Allowances* £
Year ended 30 June 2015		
Written-down value brought forward	9,000	
Addition	14,000	
	23,000	
Annual investment allowance	14,000	£14,000
	9,000	
WDA (18% p.a.)	1,620	£1,620
Written-down value carried forward	7,380	
Year ended 30 June 2016		
Disposal value (note (a))	5,000	
	2,380	
WDA (18% p.a.)	428	£428
Written-down value carried forward	£1,952	

Note

(a) 8 instalments unpaid at 31 October 2015. It is assumed that each instalment comprises capital of £375 (£(14,000 – 5,000) ÷ 24) and interest of £125 (£3,000 ÷ 24). 8 × £375 = £3,000 (capital expenditure unpaid). This amount together with the £2,000 received direct from the insurers gives a disposal value of £5,000.

Abortive expenditure

[7.11] Although *CAA 2001, s 67* (see **7.9** above) applies principally to hire-purchase contracts, it can also apply in respect of other contracts which provide that a person shall or may become the owner of plant or machinery on the performance of the contract, where that person incurs expenditure but then ceases to be entitled to the benefit of the contract without becoming the owner of the plant or machinery. Thus, where such a contract exists, a person can obtain allowances in respect of, for example, a deposit paid on plant or machinery which is never actually supplied, either because the buyer withdraws from the contract and the deposit is non-refundable or because the supplier defaults or for some other reason. Without the operation of *CAA 2001, s 67*, the 'buyer' would be denied allowances on the basis that he never actually owns the plant or machinery.

As in **7.9** above, a disposal value will need to be brought into account, by virtue of *CAA 2001, s 68*, at the time that the 'buyer' ceases to be entitled to the benefit of the contract without becoming the owner of the plant or machinery. (Revenue Tax Bulletin February 1992 p 13).

Gifts

[7.12] Where a person receives as a gift plant or machinery which he brings into use for the purposes of his qualifying trade, he is regarded, for the purposes of plant and machinery allowances, as having incurred capital expenditure of an amount equal to the market value of the plant or machinery on the date when it was so brought into use in the qualifying activity.

First-year allowances are not available for plant or machinery received by way of gift.

The plant or machinery is treated as owned by the person in consequence of his having incurred the expenditure. The expenditure is treated as incurred on the date on which the plant or machinery is brought into use in the qualifying activity.

[*CAA 2001, s 14, Sch 3 para 12*].

See also **7.3** above for certain gifts within these provisions to be treated as purchases. For plant used in mineral extraction these provisions are subject to those in **10.12** below.

Previous use outside qualifying activity

[7.13] Similar provisions as in 7.12 above apply where a person brings into use, for the purposes of a qualifying activity, plant or machinery which he then owns as a result of having incurred capital expenditure on its provision for purposes other than those of the qualifying activity. Thus he is entitled to writing-down allowances on an amount of expenditure deemed to be incurred on the date on which the plant or machinery is first brought into use in the qualifying activity.

The amount of expenditure on which allowances are given is restricted to the lowest of:

- open market value at the time of first such use;
- the expenditure actually incurred on the plant or machinery; and

- the amount of expenditure on which allowances could have been claimed had the plant or machinery qualified for allowances at the time of acquisition, if that amount would have been restricted to less than cost under the anti-avoidance provisions of *CAA 2001, ss 218* or *224* (see **7.3**, **7.4** above).

First-year allowances are not available.

[*CAA 2001, s 13; FA 2008, Sch 20 para 6(2)*].

See also **4.4** above for the special rule applying where a person carrying on one of the above four types of property business uses an item of plant or machinery in rotation between the different types whilst retaining ownership throughout.

Partial depreciation subsidies

[7.14] Special rules apply to plant and machinery in respect of which a 'partial depreciation subsidy' is received. A 'partial depreciation subsidy' is a sum which

(a) is payable directly or indirectly to a person who has incurred qualifying expenditure for the purposes of a qualifying activity;
(b) is in respect of, or takes account of, part of the depreciation of the plant or machinery resulting from its use for the purposes of that activity; and
(c) does not fall to be taxed as income of that person, or in computing the profits of a qualifying activity carried on by him.

Where it appears that a partial depreciation subsidy is or will be payable, any annual investment allowance or first-year allowance available must be reduced to an amount which is 'just and reasonable having regard to the relevant circumstances'. A reduction in a first-year allowance is, however, disregarded for the purpose of allocating the balance of the expenditure to a pool.

If a partial depreciation subsidy has been paid, the qualifying expenditure can only be allocated to a single asset pool (see **5.48** above). If expenditure has otherwise been allocated to a pool and a partial depreciation subsidy is paid for the first time, it is transferred to a single asset pool, by bringing a disposal value into account in the original pool and allocating the amount of that disposal value to the single asset pool for the chargeable period in which the subsidy is first paid. The 'final chargeable period' (see **5.32** and **5.46** above) for the single asset pool is the first chargeable period in which a disposal event within **5.41**(i)–(vi) occurs.

Writing-down allowances, balancing allowances and balancing charges for the pool are reduced to a 'just and reasonable' amount. In calculating the unrelieved qualifying expenditure to be carried forward in the pool, however, the reduction in the writing-down allowance is disregarded. If a writing-down allowance is not claimed or claimed only in part, the unrelieved qualifying expenditure carried forward is treated as not reduced, or only proportionately reduced.

The legislation is not explicit as regards the meaning of 'just and reasonable' and this must be a matter for negotiation with HMRC in much the same way as for plant and machinery used partly for non-qualifying activity purposes (see **5.56** above). If, for example, a contribution was regarded as being in respect of 25% of the 'cost' of depreciation for a specific chargeable period, the writing-down allowance should be reduced by that percentage. This example is perhaps an over-simplification and the facts and circumstances may well differ from one chargeable period to another even if, or perhaps especially if, a fixed annual sum is received towards depreciation. (It may well be that the item of plant or machinery concerned is not one for which a uniform rate of depreciation would normally be suitable.) Balancing allowances and charges are likely to be restricted in the same proportion that the total allowances previously given bears to the total allowances that could have been given had no reduction applied (see **5.56** above for the similar treatment as regards assets used partly for non-qualifying activity purposes).

[*CAA 2001, ss 65(2), 209–212*].

See **4.20**(c) above for the position where a subsidy is received in respect of the whole of the depreciation of plant or machinery.

Renewals basis

[7.15] As an alternative to the claiming of capital allowances on plant and machinery, it was possible, for expenditure incurred before 6 April 2013 (1 April 2013 for corporation tax purposes) to use a non-statutory renewals basis, whereby no capital allowances were claimed on the cost of an original item, or all the original items within one class, but the cost of replacement of that item, or those items, was a revenue expense to be deducted in arriving at the profit. This effectively meant a 100% allowance for replacements, although any proceeds received in respect of assets being replaced were deducted from the cost of the replacements in arriving at the amount allowable against profits. The non-statutory renewals basis is abolished in relation to expenditure on replacing plant and machinery which is incurred on or after 6 April 2013 for income tax purposes or 1 April 2013 for corporation tax purposes (http://webarchive.nationalarchives.gov.uk/20140109143644/http://www.hmrc.gov.uk/budget-updates/06dec11/withdraw-tech-note.pdf).

There was also a statutory renewals basis in *ITTOIA 2005, s 68* and *CTA 2009, s 68* which allowed a deduction in calculating trading profits for expenditure on replacing or altering any implement, utensil or article used for the purposes of the trade. The statutory renewals basis is, however, abolished for expenditure incurred on or after 6 April 2016 (1 April 2016 for corporation tax purposes).

In general, the renewals basis (both statutory and non-statutory) was used for small items such as loose tools in a factory or crockery, etc. in a restaurant. It was possible for other classes of plant or machinery to attract capital allowances so that the two bases ran side by side. For example, a factory or workshop operation may employ both heavy machinery and loose tools. The disadvantages of the renewals basis were that relief was only available to the extent that like was replaced with like, any improvement element being disregarded, and that no relief was available for additions to the class of plant or machinery concerned, as opposed to replacements.

Change from renewals to capital allowance basis and vice versa

[7.16] The renewals basis was more popular, especially as regards larger items, under the pre-*FA 1971* regime than subsequently. Once first-year allowances were increased to 100% in March 1972, there seemed to be little to commend the renewals basis and the Inland Revenue introduced Extra-Statutory Concession B1. Under this concession, a change from the renewals basis to a normal capital allowances basis could be made at any time, but if more than one item of a class of plant or machinery was used, the change had to apply to all items in that class. Allowances for the same class of plant or machinery could not be given on both bases for the same chargeable period (see **2.1** above); thus, in the chargeable period for which the change was to apply, no renewals allowances were given. Acquisitions during that period, whether they were replacements or additions, qualified for capital allowances. The treatment of an item to be replaced following the change, being an item to which the renewals basis previously applied, was as follows. Its 'commercial written-down value' was added to the available qualifying expenditure for the pool for the period for which the change applied, unless it was replaced during that period. In this case no adjustment was made if the proceeds, if any, exceeded the commercial written-down value; but if that value exceeded the proceeds, the excess was added to the qualifying expenditure.

'*Commercial written-down value*' means the value arrived at by writing down the item from cost at a commercial rate of depreciation having regard to its age and expected life.

There was no statutory procedure for transferring from a capital allowances basis to a renewals basis for one or more classes of plant or machinery, nor was there any extra-statutory concession equivalent to the one outlined above for transferring from a renewals basis to a capital allowances basis.

See generally HMRC Business Income Manual, BIM46960, BIM46985.

Replacement domestic items relief

[7.16A] A limited form of the renewals basis is available for certain expenditure incurred on or after 6 April 2016 (1 April 2016 for corporation tax purposes) on replacement 'domestic items' by landlords of residential property. The relief is available where all the following conditions are met:

- a person (P) carries on a property business in relation to land which consists of or includes a dwelling-house;
- P incurs expenditure on replacing a domestic item; the new item must be provided solely for the use of the 'lessee' in the dwelling-house, and the old item must no longer be available for such use following its replacement;

- the expenditure is incurred wholly and exclusively for the purposes of the business and no deduction is otherwise allowable because it is of a capital nature; and
- no capital allowances are available on the expenditure.

'*Domestic items*' are items for domestic use, such as furniture, furnishings, appliances (including white goods) and kitchenware. A 'fixture' is not, however, a domestic item for this purpose, and '*fixture*' is defined as plant or machinery that is so installed, or otherwise fixed in or to, a dwelling-house as to become, in law, part of that dwelling-house and includes any boiler or water-filled radiator installed in a dwelling-house as part of a space or water heating system. A '*lessee*' is a person who is entitled to the use of the dwelling-house under a lease or other arrangement under which payment for such use is required

Where the conditions are satisfied, a deduction is allowed for the expenditure in calculating the taxable profits of the business. A claim is not required. The amount of the deduction is the cost of the replacement item, unless the new item is not the same or substantially the same as the old. In the latter case, the deduction is limited to the cost of an item which is the same or substantially the same as the old item. The amount of the deduction is increased by any incidental capital expenditure incurred by P in connection with the disposal of the old item or the acquisition of the new item. The deduction is reduced by the amount or value (in money or money's worth) of any consideration which P, or a connected person, receives, or is entitled to receive, for the disposal. If the disposal is in part-exchange for the new item, the part-exchange value is treated as expenditure incurred on the new item but the deduction is then reduced by the same amount.

No deduction is allowed if the business consists of or includes the commercial letting of furnished holiday accommodation and the dwelling-house constitutes some or all of that accommodation for the tax year or accounting period in which the expenditure is incurred. Similarly, no deduction is allowed if rent-a-room relief (under *ITTOIA 2005, ss 784–802*) applies in respect of the dwelling-house for the tax year.

[*ITTOIA 2005, s 311A; CTA 2009, s 250A; FA 2016, s 73(1)(2)(8)(9); F(No 2)A 2017, Sch 2 para 24*].

Successions to trades, etc.

[7.17] These provisions deal with successions to qualifying activities only insofar as they affect plant and machinery allowances. For transfers of a company's trade within *CTA 2010, ss 938–953*, see the comment made in the following paragraph and **17.22** below, and for the effect of partnership changes on capital allowances, see **7.18** and Chapter **15** below.

For the purpose of these provisions, 'qualifying activity' does not include an employment or office, but includes any other activity listed in **4.2** above even if any profits are not chargeable to UK tax (i.e. the restriction at **4.3** does not apply).

When such a qualifying activity changes hands and, where the activity is a trade or property business, all of the persons carrying it on before the succession permanently cease to carry it on or, for corporation tax purposes, no company carrying on the activity in partnership immediately before the change continues to carry it on in partnership after the change, any plant or machinery which immediately beforehand was owned by the person then carrying on the discontinued activity and was either in use or provided and available for use for that activity and immediately afterwards, without being sold, is in use or provided and available for use for the new qualifying activity, is treated as if it had been sold to the successor at the time when the succession took place. The sale is treated as being at market value. The former owner must therefore bring disposal values into account, and the successor is entitled to writing-down allowances (but not to annual investment allowance or first-year allowances, even where such allowances would otherwise be available). These provisions do not apply to a succession where an election is made under the provisions in **7.18** below. Where no such election is made it would appear that these provisions are overridden by those in *CTA 2010, ss 938–953*. [*CAA 2001, ss 265, 266(7), Sch 3 para 52*]. See also **17.31** below for the application of these provisions with modifications where the predecessor is a company to which ring fence treatment under *CTA 2010, ss 398A–398G* applies.

Where a person succeeds to a deceased person's qualifying activity under the terms of a will or on intestacy, he may elect, in respect of any plant or machinery previously owned by the deceased which passes to him with the activity, that such plant or machinery be treated as sold to him when the succession takes place. The net proceeds of the sale are treated as the lower of market value and the unrelieved qualifying expenditure which would have been taken into account in calculating a balancing allowance for the chargeable period in which the deceased's qualifying activity was permanently discontinued, on the assumption that the disposal value of the plant or machinery had been nil. Any subsequent disposal value of plant or machinery covered by the election which has to be ascertained in relation to the beneficiary cannot exceed the cost incurred by the deceased on its provision. If the plant or machinery is software or a right to software, in determining whether the limit on the disposal value is exceeded under *CAA 2001, s 73* (see **4.19** above) the previous disposal values to be taken into account are those of the deceased. [*CAA 2001, s 268*].

Successions between connected persons

[7.18] Where a person ('the successor') succeeds to a qualifying activity previously carried on by another person ('the predecessor') they may jointly elect, within two years after the succession, that the provisions below apply provided that

(a) the two persons are 'connected' with each other;
(b) each of them is within the charge to tax in the UK on the profits of the qualifying activity; and
(c) the successor is not a dual resident investing company within *CTA 2010, s 949*.

An election results in plant or machinery, which immediately before the succession was owned by the predecessor and was in use or provided and available for use for the purposes of the qualifying activity and which immediately after the succession is owned by the successor and is in use or provided and available for use for that purpose, being treated as sold to the successor at a price which produces neither balancing allowance nor balancing charge. Subsequent plant and machinery allowances are made to or on the successor as if everything done to or by the predecessor had been done to or by the successor. The deemed sale is treated as taking place at the time of the succession.

Predecessor and successor are 'connected' with each other for the purposes of (a) above if

- (i) they are connected with each other within **2.34** above;
- (ii) one of them is a partnership and the other has the right to a share of the assets or income of that partnership;
- (iii) one of them is a corporate body and the other has control (within *CAA 2001, s 574*) of that body;
- (iv) both of them are partnerships and some other person has the right to a share of the assets or income of both of them; or
- (v) both of them are corporate bodies, or one of them is a corporate body and the other is a partnership, and (in either case) some other person has control (as in (iii) above) over both of them.

An election will preclude the application of *CAA 2001, s 104* (disposal of long-life assets in avoidance cases; see **5.70** above), *CAA 2001, s 104E* (disposal of special rate expenditure assets in avoidance cases: see **5.49** above), *CAA 2001, s 108* (effect of disposal to connected person on overseas leasing pool; see **6.55** above), *CAA 2001, s 265* (see **7.17** above).

Assessments and adjustments of assessments may be made to give effect to the above.

For corporation tax purposes, where a succession occurs on or after 5 December 2005 and the predecessor was carrying on a 'business of leasing plant or machinery' (whether alone or in partnership), an election under the above provisions has no effect in relation to any plant or machinery meeting conditions (A)–(C) at **17.32** below or, for successions before 23 March 2011, in relation to any 'qualifying leased plant or machinery'. For the meaning of the expressions 'business of leasing plant or machinery' and 'qualifying leased plant or machinery', see **17.32** below.

[*CAA 2001, ss 266–267A, Sch 3 para 52; FA 2011, Sch 6 paras 23, 27(3)*].

It would appear that first-year allowances are not available to the successor on a succession between connected persons where an election under the above provisions has been made. In correspondence with the Revenue concerning the *CAA 1990* legislation, they have said that there is nothing in *CAA 1990, s 77* (now *CAA 2001, s 267*) which confers title to a first-year allowance and have pointed out that when the legislation introduces a fiction, one has to consider how far the deeming goes. *Section 77(4)(a)* (now *CAA 2001, s 267(2)*) treats the plant or machinery as being sold for a price which does not give rise to a balancing charge or allowance, but it does not go so far as to treat the successor as incurring expenditure equal to that amount. The successor is effectively treated as stepping into the shoes of his predecessor and takes over his pool value and capital allowances history (so that, for example, on any subsequent disposal by the successor the disposal value for capital allowance purposes is limited to the predecessor's original expenditure on the asset in question and not the value of the asset at the date of the succession).

The Revenue concede that the successor may actually incur capital expenditure in acquiring assets from his predecessor, but note that *s 77(4)(b)* necessarily requires such expenditure to be disregarded (this requirement is only implicit in *CAA 2001, s 267*). However, if the Revenue's view is incorrect and the *s 77* successor does incur expenditure, the Revenue state that *CAA 1990, s 75(1)* (now *CAA 2001, s 217*; see **7.3** above) means that the successor cannot claim first-year allowances because the deemed sale is between connected persons.

Before *CTA 2010* took effect there was no formal disapplication of the above provisions where the mandatory provisions of *ICTA 1988, s 343* (now *CTA 2010, ss 940A–953* — transfer of company trade without change of ownership as in **17.22** below) apply, but in practice it would seem unnecessary to consider an election under the above provisions where such mandatory provisions applied.

EXAMPLE 3

[7.19]

P, a sole trader for many years with a 30 June accounting date, transfers the whole of her trade, including all plant and machinery used therein, to Q, the wife of her husband's brother, on 1 November 2016. P had unrelieved qualifying expenditure carried forward in the main pool of £10,000 at 30 June 2015. P then incurred capital expenditure on plant and machinery of £3,600 during the final period of account 1 July 2016 to 31 October 2016. No disposals were made during that final period. Q makes up her first accounts for the year ending 31 October 2017 and incurred capital expenditure on plant and machinery of £5,600 in her first year. The capital allowances computations for P for the period of account ended 31 October 2016 and for Q for the year ended 31 October 2017, assuming that an election under **7.18** above is made, are as follows.

	Qualifying for AIA	*Main pool*	*Allowances*
P	£	£	
Written-down value brought forward by P		10,000	
Additions 1.7.16 to 31.10.16		3,600	
		13,600	
Deemed sale price		(13,600)	
Balancing allowance or charge to or on P		Nil	
Q	£	£	
Qualifying expenditure incurred 1.11.16 by Q		13,600	
Additions 1.11.16 to 31.10.17	5,600		
Annual investment allowance (100%)	(5,600)		5,600

	Qualifying for AIA	*Main pool*	*Allowances*
Writing-down allowance (18% p.a.)		(2,448)	2,448
Written-down value carried forward		£11,152	
Total allowances			£8,048

Oil production sharing contracts

[7.20] The governments of many oil-producing countries enter into contracts with foreign oil companies to exploit their oil and gas reserves. Under a typical such contract, known as a production sharing contract, the state continues to own all the oil rights, while the contractor carries out all exploration, production and marketing. Under the terms of most such contracts, ownership of plant and machinery used by the oil company for the purposes of the contract will pass at some time to the host government, whilst still continuing to be used by the company to fulfil its contractual obligations. *Finance Act 2000* introduced provisions to treat such plant and machinery as continuing to be owned by the company after the transfer of ownership. The provisions apply where:

(a) a person ('*the contractor*') is entitled to an interest in a contract made with the government (or its authorised representative) of a country or territory in which oil (as defined in *CAA 2001, s 556(3)*) is or may be produced;

(b) the contract provides (among other things) that any plant or machinery of a description specified in the contract which is provided by the contractor and has an 'oil-related use' under the contract will (whether immediately or at some later time) be transferred to the government or representative;

(c) the contractor incurs capital expenditure after 20 March 2000 on the provision of plant or machinery of a description so specified which, for the purposes of a trade of oil extraction carried on by him, is to be have an oil-related use under the contract; and

(d) the amount of that expenditure is commensurate with the value of the contractor's interest under the contract.

Plant or machinery has an '*oil-related use*' if it is used to explore for, win access to, or extract oil, for the initial storage or treatment of oil, or for other purposes ancillary to the extraction of oil.

Where, in accordance with (b) above, the plant or machinery is transferred to the government or representative, it is deemed (subject to the deemed disposal below on transfer of an interest in the contract) to continue to be owned by the contractor (and not by any other person) until such time as it ceases to be owned by the government or representative or ceases to be used, or held for use, by any person under the contract.

Where a person ('*the participator*') acquires an interest in the contract, whether from the contractor or from another person who has acquired it (directly or indirectly) from the contractor, the provisions also apply to capital expenditure incurred after 20 March 2000 by the participator on the provision of plant or machinery which, for the purposes of a trade of oil extraction carried on by him, is to have an oil-related use under the contract. Provided that the amount of that expenditure is commensurate with the value of the participator's interest under the contract; such plant or machinery transferred in accordance with (b) above is deemed (subject to the deemed disposal below on transfer of an interest in the contract) to be owned by the participator (and not by any other person) until such time as it ceases to be owned by the government or representative or ceases to be used, or held for use, by any person under the contract.

Where some of the expenditure incurred by a participator to acquire his interest in the contract is attributable to plant or machinery which is deemed under these provisions to be owned by the contractor or to another participator; that plant or machinery is, subject to any subsequent application of this provision, deemed instead to be owned by that participator (and not by any other person) until such time as it ceases to be owned by the government or representative or ceases to be used, or held for use, by any person under the contract. The contractor, or the other participator, is deemed to have disposed of the plant or machinery for a consideration equal to the expenditure of the participator so attributable to it, on a just and reasonable basis. The participator is deemed to have incurred capital expenditure on the provision of the plant or machinery, of the same amount except that so much of it as exceeds any disposal value to be brought into account by the contractor or the other participator by reason of his deemed disposal is disregarded.

[*CAA 2001, ss 167–170, Sch 3 para 28*].

Where the above provisions apply and the plant or machinery ceases to belong to the government or representative or ceases to be used, or held for use, by any person under the contract, and is therefore deemed to cease to be owned by the contractor or participator, the disposal value (see **5.41** above) is determined as follows.

- Where capital compensation is received by the contractor or participator, the disposal value is the amount of that compensation.
- Where no such compensation is so received, the disposal value is nil.

[*CAA 2001, s 171*].

Co-ownership authorised contractual schemes

[7.21] Co-ownership authorised contractual schemes (CoACS) are a type of collective investment scheme which are authorised under *Financial Services and Markets Act 2000, s 261D*. Such schemes are transparent for tax purposes so that they are not subject to tax on their income. Instead, participants (i.e. investors) in the scheme are treated as if the assets of the scheme were held by them directly. Income of the scheme is then taxed as income of the participants.

Where the participants in a CoACS together carry on a qualifying activity, then, with effect from the date of Royal Assent to *F(No 2)A 2017*, each participant is treated as carrying on the activity to the extent that the profits or gains arising to him from the activity are chargeable to tax (or would be chargeable if there were any profits). In determining whether or to what extent the participants are together carrying on a qualifying activity, it must be assumed that profits or gains arising to *all* the participants from the activity are chargeable to tax (or would be if there were any). The rule in **4.3** above is therefore treated as satisfied by all of the participants.

The operator of a CoACS may, however, make an election under which it will calculate allowances on the basis that it carries on the qualifying activity itself and then allocate a proportion of the allowances to each participant. The election must be made by notice to HMRC and must specify the first accounting period for which it will take effect; that accounting period must begin on or after 1 April 2017 and must not be longer than twelve months. The election has effect for that first period and all subsequent accounting periods of the scheme and is irrevocable.

For each accounting period for which the election has effect, the operator must calculate the allowances on the basis of the following assumptions:

- the scheme itself is a person;
- the period is a chargeable period for capital allowances purposes;
- any qualifying activity carried on by the scheme participants together is carried on by the scheme;
- property which was subject to the scheme at the beginning of the first period to which the election applies ceased to be owned by the participants, and was acquired by the scheme, at that time
- the disposal value for that disposal and acquisition is the tax written-down value (i.e. the amount which, on the assumption that the expenditure in question is in its own pool, results in there being neither a balancing allowance nor a balancing charge);
- any property which subsequently becomes subject to the scheme is acquired by the scheme when it becomes so subject;
- any property which ceases to be subject to the scheme ceases to be owned by the scheme when it so ceases;
- the disposal value for that disposal is the tax written-down value; and
- the scheme is not entitled to any annual investment allowance or first-year allowances.

For each period the operator must allocate a proportion of the allowances (which may be zero) to each participant on a just and reasonable basis, by reference in particular to the relative size of each participant's holding of units in the scheme. The extent to which a participant is liable to income tax or corporation tax and any other circumstances relating to a participant's liability to tax must be disregarded. If more than one qualifying activity is carried on by the participants together, a calculation and allocation must be made separately for each activity.

Where allowances in respect of a qualifying activity are allocated by an operator in this way, participants can claim no other allowances for that activity. Participants are treated as ceasing to own their interests in the property subject to the scheme at the beginning of the first period for which the election has effect and must bring into account a disposal value of an amount equal to the tax written-down value (as above).

Where property consisting of a fixture (see **6.3** above) has ceased to be subject to the scheme at a time when an election is in effect and a person is subsequently treated as the owner of the fixture as a result of incurring capital expenditure on its provision (the '*new expenditure*'):

- the new expenditure is treated as nil if the 'disposal value statement requirement' is not met; and
- in any other case the new expenditure is left out of account in determining the new owner's qualifying expenditure to the extent that it exceeds the disposal value brought into account by the operator when the fixture ceased to be subject to the scheme.

The '*disposal value statement requirement*' is that the operator has, within two years after the fixture's ceasing to be property subject to the scheme, made a written statement of the disposal value, and that the new owner has obtained the statement or a copy of it. *CAA 2001, s 185* (see **6.15** above) and *s 187A* (see **6.15A** above) which restrict allowances and impose certain requirements following the transfer of fixtures generally are disapplied in relation to the new expenditure.

[*CAA 2001, ss 262AA–262AF; F(No 2)A 2017, s 40*].

Note that, at the time of writing, *F(No 2)A 2017* had not completed its passage through Parliament. These provisions are therefore subject to any changes made during the Parliamentary process.

8

Business Premises Renovation

Introduction

[8.1] *FA 2005, s 92, Sch 6 Pt 1* introduced a temporary new code of capital allowances ('business premises renovation allowances') for certain expenditure incurred on or after 11 April 2007 on converting or renovating qualifying buildings in designated disadvantaged areas of the UK into business premises (*CAA 2001, Pt 3A*). Allowances under the code are available only for expenditure incurred before 6 April 2017 (1 April 2017 for corporation tax purposes).

There are stringent conditions which must be met for expenditure to qualify and further restrictions were introduced for expenditure incurred on or after 6 April 2014 (1 April 2014 for corporation tax purposes) as a result of what the Government considered to be use of the allowances for avoidance purposes. See **8.2** onwards below.

Allowances are available to a person who incurs qualifying expenditure in respect of a 'qualifying building' and who holds the 'relevant interest' in it. Allowances cannot be transferred to a purchaser on sale of the relevant interest. An initial allowance of 100% of qualifying expenditure can be claimed, and where this is not claimed, or claimed only in part, writing-down allowances of 25% a year on the straight-line basis are available. If the relevant interest is sold, or certain other balancing events occur, within five years of the time the premises are first brought back into use or are first suitable for letting, a balancing adjustment is made. For expenditure incurred before 6 April 2014 (1 April 2014 for corporation tax purposes), this rule applies by reference to a period of seven years. For expenditure incurred on or after 11 April 2012, allowances are restricted to a maximum of 20 million euros for any single project.

[*CAA 2001, ss 360A, 360B(1)(2); FA 2014, s 66(2)(10)(12); SI 2007 No 945, reg 2A; SI 2007 No 949; SI 2012 No 868, reg 3*].

A claim to business premises renovation allowances must be separately identified as such in the return in which it is made (see **2.20** and **2.21** above). [*CAA 2001, s 3(2A)*]. A claim made on or after 1 July 2016 must include any information required by HMRC for the purpose of complying with certain EU State aid obligations. See **2.21A** above.

Business premises renovation allowances are not available for qualifying expenditure if certain grants or payments are made towards that expenditure or any other expenditure incurred by any person in respect of the same building and on the same 'single investment project'. The grants or payments are either a grant or payment which is a State Aid (other than a business premises renovation allowance) or any other grant or subsidy designated by the Treasury by Order. An investment project is a '*single investment project*' when investments are undertaken during a period of three years by the same undertaking or undertakings and consists of fixed assets combined in an economically indivisible way (see EU Commission Regulation 651/2014). Allowances already given are withdrawn if such a grant or payment is subsequently made towards the expenditure or is made within three years of the incurring of the expenditure towards any other expenditure incurred by any person in respect of the same building and on the same single investment project. Assessments and adjustments of assessments can be made as necessary to give effect to these provisions. If a person's return becomes incorrect as a result of the provisions, he must give notice to HMRC specifying how the return needs to be amended within three months of becoming aware that the return has become incorrect. These provisions, as described above, apply where a relevant grant or payment is made on or after 6 April 2014 (1 April 2014 for corporation tax purposes), whether the expenditure is incurred before or after those dates. They also apply where the relevant grant or payment is made before those dates but the expenditure is incurred on or after those dates.

Previously, business premises renovation allowances were not available for expenditure taken into account for the purposes of a 'relevant grant or payment' made towards it. A '*relevant grant or payment*' is defined for this purpose as above except that the reference to a State Aid is restricted to a notified State Aid. Allowances given before such a grant or payment was received are withdrawn. A relevant grant or payment is treated as never having been made to the extent that it is repaid by the grantee to the grantor. Assessments and adjustments of assessments can be made as necessary to give effect to these provisions, and such assessments or adjustments are not out of time if made within three years of the end of the chargeable period in which the grant, payment or adjustment was made.

[*CAA 2001, s 360L; FA 2014, s 66(8)(11)(12)*].

For the purposes of the allowances, '*lease*' includes an agreement for a lease where the term to be covered by the lease has begun, and also includes any tenancy, but does not include a mortgage. The terms 'lessor', 'lessee' and 'leasehold interest' are to be construed accordingly. In relation to Scotland, '*leasehold interest*' (or '*leasehold estate*') means the interest of a tenant in property subject to a lease, and a reference to an interest reversionary on a leasehold interest or lease is a reference to the interest of the landlord in the property subject to the leasehold interest or lease. [*CAA 2001, s 360Z4*].

See **17.1D** below for the prohibition on allowances where profits of a trade, profession, vocation are calculated on the cash basis.

Qualifying expenditure

[8.2] Capital expenditure incurred on or after 6 April 2014 (1 April 2014 for corporation tax purposes) is '*qualifying expenditure*' for the purposes of business premises renovation allowances if it is incurred before 6 April 2017 (1 April 2017 for corporation tax purposes), is not excluded (as below) and meets the following two conditions.

The first condition is that the expenditure must be incurred on:

(i) the conversion of a 'qualifying building' (see **8.4** below) into 'qualifying business premises' (see **8.5** below);
(ii) the renovation of a qualifying building if it is, or will be, qualifying business premises; or
(iii) repairs to a qualifying building (or a building of which the qualifying building forms part) which are incidental to expenditure within (i) or (ii) above.

For the purposes of (iii) above, expenditure on repairs to a building is treated as capital if it is not allowable in calculating the taxable profits of a property business or a trade, profession or vocation.

The second condition is that the expenditure must be incurred on:

(1) building works;
(2) architectural or design services;
(3) surveying or engineering services;
(4) planning applications; or
(5) statutory fees or statutory permissions.

The condition is treated as met by expenditure not within (1)–(5) above to the extent that it does not (in total) exceed 5% of the qualifying expenditure on items within (1)–(3) above.

Capital expenditure incurred before 6 April 2014 (1 April 2014 for corporation tax purposes) is qualifying expenditure if it is incurred on, or in connection with (i)–(iii) above.

Expenditure incurred on or in connection with:

(a) the acquisition of, or of rights in or over, land;
(b) the extension of a qualifying building (except to the extent required to provide a means of getting to or from qualifying business premises);
(c) the development of land adjoining or adjacent to a qualifying building; or
(d) the provision of plant and machinery (other than plant or machinery which is, or becomes, a 'fixture' and, for expenditure incurred on or after 6 April 2014 (1 April 2014 for corporation tax purposes) falls within one of the categories listed below),

is excluded if incurred on or after 6 April 2014 (1 April 2014 for corporation tax purposes). Such expenditure incurred before those dates is not qualifying expenditure.

A '*fixture*' is defined for the purposes of (d) above as at **6.3** above. The categories of fixture mentioned in (d) above are:

- integral features (see **4.23** above) or parts of such a feature;
- automatic control systems for opening and closing doors, windows and vents;

- window cleaning installations;
- fitted cupboards and blinds;
- protective installations such as lightning protection, sprinkler and other equipment for containing or fighting fires, fire alarm systems and fire escapes;
- building management systems;
- cabling in connection with telephone, audio-visual data installations and computer networking facilities, which are incidental to the occupation of the building;
- sanitary appliances and bathroom fittings which are hand driers, counters, partitions, mirrors or shower facilities;
- kitchen and catering facilities for producing and storing food and drink for the occupants of the building;
- signs;
- public address systems; and
- intruder alarm systems.

Expenditure incurred on or after 6 April 2014 (1 April 2014 for corporation tax) is also excluded:

- if, and to the extent that, it exceeds the amount of expenditure which it would have been normal and reasonable to incur on the works, services or other matters concerned on a transaction between parties acting at arm's length in the open market in the market conditions prevailing at the time of the expenditure; or
- if the qualifying building was used at any time in the twelve months ending with the day on which the expenditure is incurred.

Expenditure incurred on or after 11 April 2012 on or in connection with a building which is not in a disadvantaged area (see **8.4** below) on the date the expenditure is incurred is not qualifying expenditure. Expenditure incurred on or after that date is also not qualifying expenditure to the extent that it exceeds 20 million euros or to the extent that it, together with the aggregate amount of the 'single project investment expenditure' on which business premises renovation allowances have previously been made, exceeds 20 million euros. Expenditure not in euros is to be converted for this purpose using the spot rate of exchange for the day on which the expenditure is incurred. 'Single project investment expenditure' is expenditure incurred by any person within three years before the date on which the expenditure in question is incurred and which, together with the expenditure in question, would be treated as incurred as part of a single investment project for the purposes of *Article 14 para 13* of the *EU General Block Exemption Regulation (651/2014)* (or, for expenditure incurred before 22 July 2014, would be treated as incurred in an economically indivisible way for the purposes of *Commission Regulation (EC) 800/2008, Art 13(10)* (relating to State Aid)).

The Treasury has the power to make regulations further defining qualifying expenditure. See now *SI 2007 No 945, reg 5*.

[*CAA 2001, s 360B; FA 2014, s 66(1)–(6)(10)(12); SI 2007 No 945, reg 5; SI 2012 No 868, regs 1, 5; SI 2014 No 1687, regs 1, 6*].

Time when qualifying expenditure is incurred

[8.3] The normal rules for determining when qualifying expenditure is incurred (see **2.4–2.6** above) apply subject to an exception where expenditure is incurred on or after 6 April 2014 (1 April 2014 for corporation tax purposes) on works, services or other matters in a chargeable period and those works etc. are not completed or provided within the 36 months beginning with the date the expenditure is incurred. Such expenditure, to the extent that it relates to so much of the works etc. as is so uncompleted or unprovided, is treated for the purposes of business premises renovation allowances as incurred at the time that the works etc. are completed or provided. If a person's tax return becomes incorrect as a result of this provision, he must give notice to HMRC specifying how the return needs to be amended within three months of first becoming aware that the return has become incorrect. Assessments can be made or adjusted as necessary to give effect to these provisions. [*CAA 2001, s 360BA; FA 2014, s 66(7)(10)(12)*].

Qualifying building

[8.4] A '*qualifying building*' is a building or structure, or part of a building or structure, which meets the following requirements.

(i) It must be situated in an area which was a 'disadvantaged area' on the date the renovation or conversion work began. (See below where only part of the building or structure is in a disadvantaged area.)

(ii) It must have been unused throughout the year ending immediately before that date.

(iii) On that date, it must have last been used either for the purposes of a trade, profession or vocation, or as an office or offices.

(iv) On that date, it must not have last been used as, or as part of, a dwelling.

(v) In the case of a part of a building or structure, on that date it must not have last been occupied and used in common with any other part of the building or structure other than a part which met requirement (ii) above or which had last been used as a dwelling.

For the purposes of (i) above, a '*disadvantaged area*' is an area designated as such by regulations made by the Treasury for the purposes of these provisions (or, where no such regulations are made, regulations made for the purposes of *FA 2003, Sch 6* (stamp duty land tax disadvantaged areas relief)). The *Business Premises Renovation Allowances Regulations 2007 (SI 2007 No 945), reg 3* designates Northern Ireland and areas specified as development areas by the *Assisted Areas Order 2014 (SI 2014 No 1508)* (previously the *Assisted Areas Order 2007 (SI 2007 No 107)*) as disadvantaged areas.

Where a qualifying building is only partly in a disadvantaged area, only so much of the expenditure as is attributable, on a just and reasonable apportionment, to the part of the building or structure which is in the area is treated as qualifying expenditure.

In *Senex Investments Ltd v HMRC* FTT, [2015] SFTD 501; [2015] UKFTT 107 (TC), the previous use of a building as a Wesleyan Reform Union church satisfied the requirement in (iii) above.

The Treasury has the power to make regulations further defining qualifying buildings.

[*CAA 2001, s 360C; SI 2007 No 945, reg 3; SI 2014 No 1687, reg 4*].

Qualifying business premises

[8.5] Any 'premises' in respect of which the following requirements are met are '*qualifying business premises*'.

(i) The premises must be a qualifying building within 8.4 above.
(ii) The premises must be used, or available and suitable for letting for use, for the purposes of a trade, profession or vocation or as an office or offices.
(iii) The premises must not be used, or available for use as, or as part of, a dwelling.

Premises are not, however, qualifying business premises where the person entitled to the relevant interest (see 8.6 below) is carrying on an excluded trade or where the premises are used, or used in part, for the purposes of such a trade.

For these purposes, '*premises*' means any building or structure or part of a building or structure. For expenditure incurred on or after 22 July 2014, the trades excluded from obtaining allowances are any trade (or part of a trade):

(a) in the fishery and aquaculture sector;
(b) in the coal, steel, shipbuilding or synthetic fibres sectors;
(c) in the transport sector or in related infrastructure;
(d) relating to the development of broadband networks;
(e) relating to energy generation, distribution and infrastructure;
(f) in the primary agricultural production sector; or
(g) carried on by any undertaking (as defined) which is either subject to an outstanding recovery order made under Treaty on the Functioning of the European Union, Article 108(2) or which it is reasonable to assume would be regarded as a firm in difficulty for the purposes of the *EU General Block Exemption Regulation (651/2014)*.

For expenditure incurred on or after 11 April 2012 and before 22 July 2014, the trades excluded are any trade (or part of a trade) in any sector to which *Commission Regulation (EC) No 800/2008* (on State Aid) does not apply by virtue of *Article 1 para 3*. For expenditure incurred before 11 April 2012, the trades excluded were any trade (or part of a trade) in any sector to which *Commission Regulation (EC) No 1628/2006* (on State Aid) did not apply by virtue of *Article 1 para 2*. Broadly, these are trades within (a), (b) or (f) above, (for expenditure incurred on or after 11 April 2012) trades consisting of the processing and marketing of certain agricultural products and (for expenditure incurred before 11 April 2012) the manufacture and marketing of products which imitate or substitute for milk and milk products. Trades within (g) above are also excluded, but by reference to the Community Guidelines on State Aid for Rescuing and Restructuring Firms in Difficulty rather than the General Block Exemption Regulation.

Where, immediately before a period of temporary unsuitability for use as in (ii) above, premises are qualifying business premises, they are deemed to continue to be qualifying business premises during that period. 'Temporary' unsuitability is not defined but should, presumably, be distinguished from 'permanent' unsuitability, which would cause premises to cease to be qualifying business premises and thereby trigger a balancing adjustment (see **8.10** below).

The Treasury has the power to make regulations amending the definition of qualifying business premises; this power has already been used to exclude the trades listed above.

[*CAA 2001, s 360D; SI 2007 No 945, reg 4; SI 2012 No 868, regs 1, 4; SI 2014 No 1687, regs 1, 5*].

Relevant interest

[8.6] As indicated at **8.1** above, business premises renovation allowances are available to a person incurring qualifying expenditure in respect of a qualifying building if he holds the relevant interest in it. The '*relevant interest*' in relation to any qualifying expenditure is the interest in the qualifying building held by the person incurring the expenditure at the time it is incurred. If that person is then entitled to more than one such interest, then if one of those interests is reversionary on the others, only that interest is the relevant interest.

The creation of a lease (see **8.1** above) or other interest to which the relevant interest is subject does not cause that interest to cease to be the relevant interest (but the grant of a long lease for consideration is a balancing event; see **8.10** below). Where the relevant interest is a leasehold interest and is extinguished on the person entitled to it acquiring the interest which is reversionary on it, the interest into which the leasehold interest merges then becomes the relevant interest.

[*CAA 2001, s 360E*].

In determining the relevant interest in a qualifying building, a person who incurs expenditure on the conversion of a qualifying building into qualifying business premises is treated as having an interest in the flat at the time it is incurred if he is entitled to that interest on, or as a result of, the completion of the conversion. [*CAA 2001, s 360F*].

If, on the termination of a lease, the lessee remains in possession of the qualifying building with the consent of the lessor but without entering into a new lease, his old lease is treated as continuing whilst he remains in possession (so that if that lease is the relevant interest he will preserve his right to writing-down allowances and there will be no balancing event as in **8.10**(iii) below). If a lease contains an option to renew which is exercised, the new lease is similarly treated as if it were a continuation of the old. [*CAA 2001, s 360Z3(1)–(3)*]. Conversely, the entering into of a new lease by a lessee remaining in possession, other than under option arrangements contained in a lease which has expired, will bring about a balancing event (if occurring within the five or seven-year time limit in **8.10** below). In the absence of capital sums being received from the lessor (see below), a balancing allowance will be generated should there be any residue of qualifying expenditure (see **8.9** below).

If, on the termination of a lease, the lessor makes a payment to the lessee in respect of business premises comprised in the lease, the lease is treated as if it had come to an end by surrender in consideration of that payment. [*CAA 2001, s 360Z3(4)*]. This brings into play *CAA 2001, s 572*, which treats the deemed surrender as a sale of property (see **2.26** above). If the lease is the relevant interest, therefore, this will be a balancing event (if occurring within the five or seven-year time limit). The net proceeds of the deemed sale for the purpose of calculating any balancing adjustment (see **8.11** below) include the payment made by the lessor.

If on the termination of the lease another lease is granted to a different lessee, and, in connection with the transaction, the incoming lessee makes a payment to the former lessee, the new lease is treated for business premises renovation allowance purposes as if it were a continuation of the old and as if it had been assigned in consideration of that payment. [*CAA 2001, s 360Z3(5)*]. This will trigger a balancing adjustment, again subject to the five or seven-year limit.

Allowances available

Initial allowances

[8.7] An initial allowance of 100% is available to a person who has incurred qualifying expenditure in respect of a qualifying building, for the chargeable period (see **2.1** above) in which the expenditure is incurred. A claim for an initial allowance may require it to be reduced to a specified amount.

No initial allowance can be made if, at the time when the premises are first used by the person with the relevant interest or, if they are not so used, at the time when they are first suitable for letting for purposes within **8.5**(ii) above, they are not qualifying business premises (see **8.5** above), and, if an initial allowance has previously been made it is withdrawn. Likewise, if the relevant interest is sold before the premises are first used by the person with the relevant interest or before they are first suitable for letting for purposes within **8.5**(ii) above any initial allowance already made is withdrawn. Assessments and adjustments of assessments can be made as necessary to give effect to these provisions.

[*CAA 2001, ss 360G, 360H*].

See **17.52** below for the treatment of additional VAT liabilities in respect of qualifying expenditure.

Writing-down allowances

[8.8] Where the initial allowance is not claimed, or not claimed in full, a writing-down allowance can be claimed by the person who incurred the qualifying expenditure for a chargeable period at the end of which he is entitled to the relevant interest in the qualifying building, provided that the building is then qualifying business premises and that a 'long lease' (see below) of the qualifying building has not been granted in consideration of a capital sum.

Writing-down allowances are given at the rate of 25% of the qualifying expenditure (i.e. on the straight-line basis), the amount being proportionately increased or reduced if the chargeable period is more or less than one year. A writing-down allowance cannot, however, exceed the 'residue of qualifying expenditure' (see **8.9** below) immediately before it is made. A person can require the allowance to be reduced to an amount specified in the claim.

For the above purposes, a '*long lease*' is one of a duration exceeding 50 years. The property business rules of *ITTOIA 2005, s 303* apply to determine whether the lease exceeds 50 years, but without regard to *CAA 2001, s 360Z3(3)* (option for renewal; see **8.6** above).

[*CAA 2001, ss 360I, 360J*].

See **17.52** below for the treatment of additional VAT liabilities in respect of qualifying expenditure.

Residue of qualifying expenditure

[8.9] Qualifying expenditure is treated as written off to the extent and at the times given below. What remains at any time is termed the '*residue of qualifying expenditure*'. [*CAA 2001, ss 360K, 360Q*].

Any initial allowance made in respect of the expenditure is treated as written off as at the time the qualifying business premises are first used, or suitable for letting for use, for purposes within **8.5**(ii) above. A writing-down allowance made for a chargeable period (see **2.1** above) is treated as written off as at the end of that period. For the purposes of calculating what balancing adjustment arises out of a balancing event (see **8.10** below) which occurs at the same time as a writing-down allowance is required to be written off, the write-off is taken into account in computing the residue of qualifying expenditure immediately before the event. [*CAA 2001, s 360R*].

Where a qualifying building is demolished and the cost of demolition is borne by the person who incurred the qualifying expenditure, that cost less any money received for the remains of the building is added to the residue of qualifying expenditure immediately before the demolition. Where this applies, neither the cost of demolition nor the amount added to the residue can be treated for any capital allowance purpose as expenditure on property replacing the demolished qualifying building. [*CAA 2001, s 360S*].

See **17.52** below for the treatment of additional VAT liabilities and rebates in respect of qualifying expenditure.

Balancing adjustments

Balancing events

[8.10] A balancing adjustment is made on or to the person who incurred the qualifying expenditure if a 'balancing event' occurs within the five years (seven years for expenditure incurred before 6 April 2014 (1 April 2014 for corporation tax purposes)) after the time when the premises were first used, or suitable for letting, for purposes within **8.5**(ii) above. If more than one balancing event occurs within those years, however, only the first such event gives rise to a balancing adjustment. The following are '*balancing events*':

(i) the sale of the relevant interest (see **8.6** above);
(ii) the grant of a long lease (see **8.8** above) out of the relevant interest in consideration of a capital sum;
(iii) where the relevant interest is a lease, the coming to an end of the lease otherwise than on the person entitled to it acquiring the interest reversionary on it;
(iv) the death of the person who incurred the qualifying expenditure;
(v) the demolition or destruction of the qualifying building; and
(vi) the qualifying building ceasing to be qualifying business premises without being demolished or destroyed.

[*CAA 2001, ss 360M, 360N; FA 2014, s 66(9)(10)(12)*].

It should be noted that the transfer of the relevant interest otherwise than by way of sale is treated as a sale of the relevant interest at market value. [*CAA 2001, s 573*]. See also **8.6** above, for the termination of a lease which is the relevant interest.

Balancing adjustments will continue to be made under these provisions, where applicable, following the abolition of allowances from April 2017 (see **8.2** above).

See **17.52** below for the treatment of additional VAT rebates in respect of qualifying expenditure.

Proceeds of balancing events

[8.11] To calculate a balancing adjustment, the proceeds from the balancing event must be ascertained. The following amounts received or receivable in connection with the event by the person who incurred the qualifying expenditure are treated as the proceeds from the event.

- If the event is the sale of the relevant interest: the net proceeds of sale (see **2.33** above).
- If the event is the grant of a long lease out of the relevant interest: the sum paid in consideration of the grant, or the commercial premium (i.e. premium that would have been given if the transaction had been at arm's length) if higher.
- If the event is the coming to an end of a lease and the lessee and a holder of any superior interest are connected (within **2.34** above): the market value of the relevant interest in the qualifying building.

- If the event is the death of the person who incurred the qualifying expenditure: the residue of qualifying expenditure (see **8.9** above) immediately before the death.
- If the event is the demolition or destruction of the qualifying building: the net amount received for the remains plus any insurance moneys or other compensation consisting of capital sums.
- If the event is the qualifying building ceasing to be qualifying business premises: the market value of the relevant interest in the qualifying building.

If the proceeds from a balancing event are only partly attributable to assets representing expenditure for which a business premises renovation allowance can be made, only that part of the proceeds as is so attributable, on a just and reasonable apportionment, is taken into account.

[*CAA 2001, ss 360O, 360Z2*].

See **8.6** above for further provisions applying on the termination of a lease. See also **17.2** onwards below for the anti-avoidance provision applying to controlled and main benefit sales, and note that an election under *CAA 2001, s 569* cannot be made in relation to business premises renovation allowances.

Calculation of balancing adjustments

[8.12] Where there is a residue of qualifying expenditure at the time of the balancing event and the proceeds of the balancing event are less than that residue or there are no such proceeds, a balancing allowance is given for the chargeable period in which the balancing event occurs. The allowance is equal to the amount by which the residue of qualifying expenditure exceeds the proceeds.

If the proceeds exceed the residue of qualifying expenditure (including a nil residue), a balancing charge is made for the chargeable period in which the balancing event occurs, equal to that excess. The charge cannot, however, exceed the total of any initial allowance made in respect of the expenditure and any writing-down allowances made for chargeable periods ending on or before the date of the balancing event.

[*CAA 2001, ss 360M(2), 360P*].

For the denial of a balancing allowance where the proceeds of a balancing event are reduced as a result of a tax avoidance scheme, see **17.6** below.

EXAMPLE 1

[8.13]

Lyra is a travel agent who has been in business for many years and makes up accounts to 30 April each year. On 1 May 2013, she buys the freehold of a building in the Charles Dickens ward in Portsmouth. The building has been empty since April 2009, having been used before that time as a restaurant. In the year ended 30 April 2014, Lyra incurs qualifying expenditure of £30,000 in renovating the building for use as her business premises. Lyra claims a reduced business premises renovation initial allowance of 50% of the expenditure for the year ended 30 April 2014.

The renovation is completed on 1 June 2014 and Lyra starts to use the building for the purposes of her trade on that date. In July 2015 Lyra sells the freehold of the building for £250,000. Of the net sale proceeds, £36,000 is attributable to assets representing the renovation expenditure.

Lyra's allowances are as follows:

Year ended		£	Residue of expenditure £
30 April 2014	Qualifying expenditure		30,000
	Initial allowance (maximum 100%)	15,000	(15,000)
30 April 2015	Writing-down allowance (25% of £30,000)	7,500	(7,500)
			7,500
30 April 2016	Writing-down allowance	—	—
	Sale proceeds		(36,000)
	Excess of sale proceeds over residue of expenditure		£28,500
	Balancing charge (restricted to allowances made, £15,000 + £7,500)		£22,500

Note

(a) No writing-down allowance is available for the year ended 30 April 2014 as the building is not in use for the purposes of the trade (and hence is not qualifying business premises) on 30 April 2014. It becomes qualifying business premises on 1 June 2014, so that a writing-down allowance is available for the year ended 30 April 2015. Lyra does not hold the relevant interest in the flat on 30 April 2016, having sold the building in July 2015, so no writing-down allowance is available for the year ended 30 April 2016.

Method of making allowances and charges

[8.14] Business premises renovation allowances and charges are made in calculating the profits of a trade, profession or vocation by treating an allowance as an expense, and a charge as a receipt, of the trade etc. See **17.46A** onwards below for the making of allowances to a company or partnership where the Northern Ireland rate of corporation tax applies (2017 onwards).

Where the interest in the building or structure concerned is subject to a lease or licence at any time in a chargeable period, then allowances and charges are treated as expenses and receipts of a property business, or where the taxpayer is not, in fact, carrying on such a business, of a deemed property business.

[*CAA 2001, ss 360Z(1)–(3), 360Z1; CTNIA 2015, Sch 1 para 11(1)*].

9

Flat Conversion

Introduction

[9.1] *FA 2001, s 67, Sch 19 Pt I* introduced a new code of capital allowances ('flat conversion allowances') for certain expenditure incurred on or after 11 May 2001 on converting or renovating parts of qualifying buildings in the UK into flats for short-term letting (*CAA 2001, Pt 4A*). The code was expected to provide allowances on the conversion of around 1,300 flats a year and was introduced as part of the then Government's strategy to regenerate rundown areas of the UK (Hansard Standing Committee A, 1 May 2001, cols 122–124). The allowances are abolished by *FA 2012* for expenditure incurred after 5 April 2013 (31 March 2013 for corporation tax purposes), and writing-down allowances cannot be obtained in chargeable periods beginning after those dates. The detailed provisions are at **9.2** below.

Subject to the above, allowances are available to a person who incurs qualifying expenditure in respect of a flat and who holds the 'relevant interest' in it. Allowances cannot be transferred to a purchaser on sale of the relevant interest. An initial allowance of 100% of qualifying expenditure can be claimed, and where this is not claimed, or claimed only in part, writing-down allowances of 25% a year on the straight-line basis are available. If the relevant interest is sold, or certain other balancing events occur, within seven years of the time the flat is first suitable for letting, a balancing adjustment is made.

For the purpose of the allowances, a '*flat*' is a 'dwelling' which forms part of a building and which is a separate set of premises (whether or not all on the same floor) divided horizontally from another part of the building. A '*dwelling*' is a building or part of a building occupied or intended to be occupied as a separate dwelling.

'*Lease*' includes an agreement for a lease where the term to be covered by the lease has begun, and also includes any tenancy, but does not include a mortgage. The terms 'lessor', 'lessee' and 'leasehold interest' are to be construed accordingly.

In relation to Scotland, '*leasehold interest*' (or '*leasehold estate*') means the interest of a tenant in property subject to a lease, and a reference to an interest reversionary on a leasehold interest or lease is a reference to the interest of the landlord in the property subject to the leasehold interest or lease.

[*CAA 2001, ss 393A, 393W*].

Abolition of allowances

[9.2] No flat conversion allowances can be obtained for expenditure incurred on or after 6 April 2013 (1 April 2013 for corporation tax purposes).

For expenditure incurred before the above dates, no writing-down allowances are available for chargeable periods beginning on or after those dates (i.e. where the initial allowance was not claimed, or only claimed in part). For chargeable periods of companies which straddle 1 April 2013, writing-down allowances are restricted by time apportionment of the allowance otherwise due. The allowance is the amount of the allowance otherwise due multiplied by the number of days in the part of the chargeable period falling before 1 April 2013 and divided by the number of days in the whole period. Time apportionment does not apply to any initial allowance due for a straddling period and does not apply for income tax purposes.

The provisions for withdrawal of an initial allowance (see **9.7** below) and for balancing adjustments (see **9.10–9.12** below) continue to apply despite the abolition of the allowances.

[*FA 2012, s 227, Sch 39 paras 36, 37, 40–42*].

Qualifying expenditure

[9.3] Capital expenditure is '*qualifying expenditure*' for the purposes of flat conversion allowances if it is incurred before 6 April 2013 (1 April 2013 for corporation tax purposes) on, or in connection with:

(i) the conversion of part of a 'qualifying building' (see **9.4** below) into a 'qualifying flat' (see **9.5** below); or
(ii) the renovation of a flat in a qualifying building if the flat is, or will be, a qualifying flat,

provided that the part of the building or flat concerned has been unused or used only for storage for at least one year immediately before the time at which the conversion or renovation work begins. Expenditure incurred on repairs to a qualifying building which are incidental to expenditure within (i) or (ii) above is also qualifying expenditure if it is not allowable in calculating the taxable profits of a UK property business.

Expenditure incurred on or in connection with:

- the acquisition of, or of rights in or over, land;
- the extension of a qualifying building (except to the extent required to provide a means of getting to or from a qualifying flat);
- the development of land adjoining or adjacent to a qualifying building; or
- the provision of chattels or furnishings

is not, however, qualifying expenditure.

[*CAA 2001, s 393B(1)–(4); FA 2012, Sch 39 para 36*].

Expenditure incurred in connection with the conversion or renovation of a flat may include costs outside the direct boundary of the new or renovated flat; for example, the creation of stairwells within the building or, as noted above, the creation of an extension, solely to provide access to the new flats. It may also include architect's and surveyor's fees. Examples of associated costs that may qualify include inserting and removing walls, windows, or doors, installing and upgrading plumbing, central heating, etc., re-roofing, providing access to the flat separate from the part of the building which is authorised for business use (see 9.4 and 9.5(c) below), and providing external fire escapes where regulations require (HMRC Capital Allowances Manual, CA43150).

The Treasury has the power to make regulations further defining qualifying expenditure. [*CAA 2001, s 393B(5)*].

Qualifying building

[9.4] A building which is situated in the UK and meets all of the following requirements is a '*qualifying building*'.

(i) All or most of the ground floor (see below) must be 'authorised for business use'.
(ii) It must appear that, at the time the building was constructed, the storeys above the ground floor were for use primarily as one or more dwellings.
(iii) There must be not more than four storeys above the ground floor, not counting the attic storey (unless that storey is or has been in use as a dwelling or as part of a dwelling).
(iv) Construction of the building must have been completed before 1 January 1980. Where the building has been extended on or after 1 January 1980 it is not thereby prevented from being a qualifying building provided that the extension was completed before 1 January 2001.

For the purposes of (i) above, a building is '*authorised for business use*' if it is authorised for a specified category of use. The categories specified are:

(a) shops, i.e. use for all or any of the following purposes:
- for the retail sale of goods other than hot food (but see (c) below),
- as a post office,
- for the sale of tickets or as a travel agency,
- for the sale of sandwiches or other cold food for consumption off the premises,
- for hairdressing,
- for the direction of funerals,
- for the display of goods for sale,
- for the hiring out of domestic or personal goods or articles,
- for the washing or cleaning of clothes or fabrics on the premises, or
- for the reception of goods to be washed, cleaned or repaired;

(b) financial and professional services, i.e. use for the provision of
- financial services,
- professional services (other than health or medical services), or
- any other services (including use as a betting office) which it is appropriate to provide in a shopping area,

where the services are provided principally to visiting members of the public;

(c) food and drink, i.e. use for the sale of food and drink for consumption on the premises or of hot food for consumption off the premises;
(d) business, i.e. use for all or any of the following purposes:
- as an office other than within (b) above,
- for research and development of products or processes, or
- for any industrial process,

being a use which can be carried out in any residential area without detriment to the amenity of that area by reason of noise, vibration, smell, fumes, smoke, soot, ash, dust or grit; and
(e) use (not including residential use) for the provision of any medical or health services except the use of premises attached to the residence of the consultant or practitioner.

[*CAA 2001, s 393C(1)–(4); Town and Country Planning (Use Classes) Order 1987, SI 1987 No 764; Planning (Use Classes) Order (Northern Ireland) 1989, SR 1989 No 290; Town and Country Planning (Use Classes) (Scotland) Order 1997, SI 1997 No 3061*].

In most cases, which is the ground floor of a building for the purposes of (i) above will be obvious. However, if the building is on a considerable slope it may not be so clear. HMRC consider that the ground floor in such a case will normally be the floor which contains the main entrance to the shop etc., unless there are clear reasons to take a different view.

Some business use of the storeys above the ground floor will not prevent condition (ii) above being met provided that the greater part of the upper storeys was originally for use primarily as dwellings. Thus a four-storey building could qualify even where there was originally an office, showroom etc. on the first floor, provided that the second and third floors were residential.

(Revenue Guidance Note: Flat Conversion Allowances, October 2001).

The Treasury has the power to make regulations further defining qualifying buildings. [*CAA 2001, s 393C(5)*].

Qualifying flat

[9.5] For a flat (see **9.1** above) to be a '*qualifying flat*' it must meet the following conditions.

(a) It must be in a qualifying building (see **9.4** above).
(b) It must be suitable for letting as a dwelling and held for the purpose of short-term letting (i.e. letting as a dwelling on a lease (see **9.1** above) for a term or period of not more than five years).
(c) Access to the flat must be possible without using the part of the ground floor which is authorised for business use (see **9.4** above).
(d) The flat must not have more than four rooms, excluding any bathroom or kitchen and any closet, cloakroom or hallway of an area not exceeding five square metres.
(e) It must not be a 'high value flat' (see below) or created or renovated as part of a scheme involving the creation or renovation of one or more high value flats.
(f) It must not be let to a connected person (within **2.34** above).

[*CAA 2001, s 393D*].

A qualifying flat can be situated in the basement of a qualifying building and may occupy more than one storey (HMRC Capital Allowances Manual, CA43200, CA43250).

In considering whether a flat is held for the purpose of short-term letting within (b) above, HMRC look at the end-use of the flat. Thus the grant of a longer lease to an intermediate lessor does not disqualify the flat provided that the letting to the occupying tenant will be short-term (HMRC Capital Allowances Manual, CA43250).

Whether a space in a flat amounts to a 'room' for the purposes of (d) above is a matter of fact and appearance. Generally, HMRC will accept that a lounge diner, a through living room, a kitchen/diner or a kitchen/living room will comprise one room. (Revenue Guidance Note: Flat Conversion Allowances, October 2001).

A flat is a '*high value flat*' within (e) above if the rent that could reasonably be expected for it on the date on which expenditure on the conversion or renovation is first incurred exceeds certain limits. This '*notional rent*' is calculated on the assumption that on that date:

- the renovation or conversion has been completed;
- the flat is let furnished to a tenant who is not connected with the person incurring the conversion or renovation expenditure;
- the tenant is not required under the lease (see **9.1** above) to pay a premium or make any other payment to the landlord (or a person connected with him); and
- the flat is let on an assured shorthold tenancy (where it is situated in England or Wales) or a short assured tenancy (if situated in Scotland).

For a flat in Greater London the limits are £350 per week for a one or two room flat, £425 per week for a three room flat, and £480 per week for a four room flat. For a flat elsewhere in the UK the limits are £150 per week for a one or two room flat, £225 per week for a three room flat, and £300 per week for a four room flat. In determining the number of rooms for this purpose, the same exclusions are made as in (d) above.

Where, immediately before a period of temporary unsuitability for letting, a flat is a qualifying flat, it is deemed to continue to be a qualifying flat during that period. 'Temporary' unsuitability is not defined but should, presumably, be distinguished from 'permanent' unsuitability, which would cause a flat to cease to be a qualifying flat and thereby trigger a balancing adjustment (see **9.10** below).

The Treasury has the power to make regulations amending the definition of a qualifying flat and varying the notional rent limits for high value flats.

[*CAA 2001, s 393E*].

Relevant interest

[9.6] As indicated at **9.1** above, flat conversion allowances are available to a person incurring qualifying expenditure in respect of a qualifying flat if he holds the relevant interest in the flat. The '*relevant interest*' in relation to any qualifying expenditure is the interest in the flat held by the person incurring the expenditure at the time it is incurred. If that person is then entitled to more than one such interest, then if one of those interests is reversionary on the others, only that interest is the relevant interest.

The creation of a lease (see **9.1** above) or other interest to which the relevant interest is subject does not cause that interest to cease to be the relevant interest (but the grant of a long lease for consideration is a balancing event; see **9.10** below). Where the relevant interest is a leasehold interest and is extinguished on the person entitled to it acquiring the interest which is reversionary on it, the interest into which the leasehold interest merges then becomes the relevant interest.

[*CAA 2001, s 393F*].

In determining the relevant interest in a flat, a person who incurs expenditure on the conversion of part of a building into the flat is treated as having an interest in the flat at the time it is incurred if he is entitled to that interest on, or as a result of, the completion of the conversion. [*CAA 2001, s 393G*].

If, on the termination of a lease, the lessee remains in possession of the flat with the consent of the lessor but without entering into a new lease, his old lease is treated as continuing whilst he remains in possession (so that if that lease is the relevant interest he will preserve his right to writing-down allowances and there will be no balancing event as in **9.10**(iii) below). If a lease contains an option to renew which is exercised, the new lease is similarly treated as if it were a continuation of the old. [*CAA 2001, s 393V(1)–(3)*]. Conversely, the entering into of a new lease by a lessee remaining in possession, other than under option arrangements contained in a lease which has expired, will bring about a balancing event (if occurring within the seven-year time limit in **9.10** below). In the absence of capital sums being received from the lessor (see below), a balancing allowance will be generated should there be any residue of qualifying expenditure (see **9.9** below).

If, on the termination of a lease, the lessor makes a payment to the lessee in respect of a flat comprised in the lease, the lease is treated as if it had come to an end by surrender in consideration of that payment. [*CAA 2001, s 393V(4)*]. This brings into play *CAA 2001, s 572*, which treats the deemed surrender as a sale of property (see **2.26** above). If the lease is the relevant interest, therefore, this will be a balancing event (if occurring within the seven-year time limit). The net proceeds of the deemed sale for the purpose of calculating any balancing adjustment (see **9.11** below) include the payment made by the lessor.

If on the termination of the lease another lease is granted to a different lessee, and, in connection with the transaction, the incoming lessee makes a payment to the former lessee, the new lease is treated for flat conversion allowance purposes as if it were a continuation of the old and as if it had been assigned in consideration of that payment. [*CAA 2001, s 393V(5)*]. This will trigger a balancing adjustment, again subject to the seven-year limit.

Allowances available

Initial allowances

[9.7] An initial allowance of 100% is available to a person who has incurred qualifying expenditure in respect of a flat, for the chargeable period (see **2.1** above) in which the expenditure is incurred. A claim for an initial allowance may require it to be reduced to a specified amount.

No initial allowance can be made if, at the time the flat is first suitable for letting as a dwelling, it is not a qualifying flat (see **9.5** above), and, if an initial allowance has previously been made it is withdrawn. Likewise, if the relevant interest is sold before the flat is suitable for letting as a dwelling any initial allowance already made is withdrawn. Assessments and adjustments of assessments can be made as necessary to give effect to these provisions. The provisions continue to apply to expenditure in respect of which an initial allowance has been given despite the abolition of allowances from April 2013 (see **9.2** above).

[*CAA 2001, ss 393H, 393I; FA 2012, Sch 39 para 42*].

Writing-down allowances

[9.8] Where the initial allowance is not claimed, or not claimed in full, a writing-down allowance can be claimed by the person who incurred the qualifying expenditure for a chargeable period at the end of which he is entitled to the relevant interest in the flat, provided that the flat is then a qualifying flat and that a 'long lease' (see below) of the flat has not been granted in consideration of a capital sum.

Writing-down allowances are given at the rate of 25% of the qualifying expenditure (i.e. on the straight-line basis), the amount being proportionately increased or reduced if the chargeable period is more or less than one year. A writing-down allowance cannot, however, exceed the 'residue of qualifying expenditure' (see **9.9** below) immediately before it is made. A person can require the allowance to be reduced to an amount specified in the claim. See also **9.2** above for the restriction of writing-down allowances for companies for chargeable periods straddling 1 April 2013.

For the above purposes, a '*long lease*' is one of a duration exceeding 50 years. The property business rules of *CTA 2009, ss 243, 244* apply to determine whether the lease exceeds 50 years, but without regard to *CAA 2001, s 393V(3)* (option for renewal; see **9.6** above).

[*CAA 2001, ss 393J, 393K*].

Residue of qualifying expenditure

[9.9] Qualifying expenditure is treated as written off to the extent and at the times given below. What remains at any time is termed the '*residue of qualifying expenditure*'. [*CAA 2001, ss 393L, 393Q*].

Any initial allowance made in respect of the expenditure is treated as written off as at the time the flat concerned is first suitable for letting as a dwelling. A writing-down allowance made for a chargeable period (see **2.1** above) is treated as written off as at the end of that period. For the purposes of calculating what balancing adjustment arises out of a balancing event (see **9.10** below) which occurs at the same time as a writing-down allowance is required to be written off, the write-off is taken into account in computing the residue of qualifying expenditure immediately before the event. [*CAA 2001, s 393R*].

Where a qualifying flat is demolished and the cost of demolition is borne by the person who incurred the qualifying expenditure, that cost less any money received for the remains of the flat is added to the residue of qualifying expenditure immediately before the demolition. Where this applies, neither the cost of demolition nor the amount added to the residue can be treated for any capital allowance purpose as expenditure on property replacing the demolished flat. [*CAA 2001, s 393S*].

Balancing adjustments

Balancing events

[9.10] A balancing adjustment is made on or to the person who incurred the qualifying expenditure if a 'balancing event' occurs within the seven years after the time when the flat is first suitable for letting as a dwelling. If more than one balancing event occurs within those years, however, only the first such event gives rise to a balancing adjustment. The following are '*balancing events*':

(i) the sale of the relevant interest (see **9.6** above);
(ii) the grant of a long lease (see **9.8** above) out of the relevant interest in consideration of a capital sum;
(iii) where the relevant interest is a lease, the coming to an end of the lease otherwise than on the person entitled to it acquiring the interest reversionary on it;
(iv) the death of the person who incurred the qualifying expenditure;
(v) the demolition or destruction of the flat;
(vi) the flat ceasing to be a qualifying flat without being demolished or destroyed; and
(vii) the relevant interest in the flat vests in the trustee for civil recovery or any other person by a recovery order made under *PCA 2002, Part 5* or in pursuance of an order made under *PCA 2002, s 276* (i.e. there is a '*Part 5* transfer' of the relevant interest — see **2.29** above).

Balancing adjustments will continue to be made under these provisions, where applicable, following the abolition of allowances from April 2013 (see **9.2** above).

[*CAA 2001, ss 393M, 393N; PCA 2002, Sch 10 paras 2(1), 22; FA 2012, Sch 39 para 42*].

It should be noted that the transfer of the relevant interest otherwise than by way of sale is treated as a sale of the relevant interest at market value. [*CAA*

2001, s 573; FA 2012, Sch 39 para 38(7)]. See also **9.6** above, for the termination of a lease which is the relevant interest.

Proceeds of balancing events

[9.11] To calculate a balancing adjustment, the proceeds from the balancing event must be ascertained. The following amounts received or receivable in connection with the event by the person who incurred the qualifying expenditure are treated as the proceeds from the event.

- If the event is the sale of the relevant interest: the net proceeds of sale (see **2.33** above).
- If the event is the grant of a long lease out of the relevant interest: the sum paid in consideration of the grant, or the commercial premium (i.e. premium that would have been given if the transaction had been at arm's length) if higher.
- If the event is the coming to an end of a lease and the lessee and a holder of any superior interest are connected (within **2.34** above): the market value of the relevant interest in the flat.
- If the event is the death of the person who incurred the qualifying expenditure: the residue of qualifying expenditure (see **9.9** above) immediately before the death.
- If the event is the demolition or destruction of the flat: the net amount received for the remains plus any insurance moneys or other compensation consisting of capital sums.
- If the event is the flat ceasing to be a qualifying flat: the market value of the relevant interest in the flat.
- If the event is a *Part 5* transfer of the relevant interest as in **9.10**(vii) above and a compensating payment (defined as at **2.29** above) is made to the transferor: the amount of that payment. If no such payment is made, the proceeds are treated as being equal to the residue of qualifying expenditure immediately before the transfer. Where, however, the relevant interest is partnership property (see *Partnership Act 1890, ss 20, 21*) and one or more, but not all, of the partners receive compensating payments, the proceeds are taken to be the aggregate of the compensating payments and, for each partner not receiving a compensating payment, his share of the residue of qualifying expenditure immediately before the transfer. For this purpose, a partner's share of the residue of qualifying expenditure is determined according to the partnership's profit-sharing arrangements for the twelve months prior to the transfer.

If the proceeds from a balancing event are only partly attributable to assets representing expenditure for which a flat conversion allowance can be made, only that part of the proceeds as is so attributable, on a just and reasonable apportionment, is taken into account.

[*CAA 2001, ss 393O, 393U; PCA 2002, Sch 10 paras 23, 24*].

See **9.6** above for further provisions applying on the termination of a lease. See also **17.2** and onwards below for the anti-avoidance provision applying to controlled and main benefit sales, and note that an election under *CAA 2001, s 569* cannot be made in relation to flat conversion allowances.

Calculation of balancing adjustments

[9.12] Where there is a residue of qualifying expenditure at the time of the balancing event and the proceeds of the balancing event are less than that residue or there are no such proceeds, a balancing allowance is given for the chargeable period in which the balancing event occurs. The allowance is equal to the amount by which the residue of qualifying expenditure exceeds the proceeds.

If the proceeds exceed the residue of qualifying expenditure (including a nil residue), a balancing charge is made for the chargeable period in which the balancing event occurs, equal to that excess. The charge cannot, however, exceed the total of any initial allowance made in respect of the expenditure and any writing-down allowances made for chargeable periods ending on or before the date of the balancing event.

[*CAA 2001, ss 393M(2), 393P*].

For the denial of a balancing allowance where the proceeds of a balancing event are reduced as a result of a tax avoidance scheme, see **17.6** below.

EXAMPLE 1

[9.13]

Frances is a travel agent in Brighton operating from the ground floor of a building of which she is the freeholder. The building was constructed in 1960 and has two storeys above the ground floor which were originally used as a dwelling but which have been empty since 1997. In the year ended 5 April 2011, Frances incurs capital expenditure of £15,000 in converting the second storey into a flat for the purpose of short-term letting as a dwelling. The flat has three rooms plus kitchen and bathroom. Included in the expenditure is £5,000 for an extension to the building which is required to provide access to the flat. Frances claims a reduced flat conversion initial allowance of 50% of the expenditure for 2010/11.

The flat is completed and suitable for letting on 1 May 2011. It is let to a person who is not connected with Frances on 1 June 2011 under a three-year lease for £200 a week. In March 2013 Frances sells the freehold of the building for £250,000. Of the net sale proceeds, £18,000 is attributable to assets representing the conversion expenditure.

Frances' allowances are as follows:

			Residue of expenditure
		£	£
2010/11	Qualifying expenditure		15,000
	Initial allowance (maximum 100%)	7,500	(7,500)
2011/12	Writing-down allowance (25% of £15,000)	3,750	(3,750)
			3,750
2012/13	Writing-down allowance	—	—
	Sale proceeds		(18,000)

	£	Residue of expenditure £
Excess of sale proceeds over residue of expenditure		£14,250
Balancing charge (restricted to allowances made, £7,500 + £3,750)		£11,250

Notes

(a) No writing-down allowance is available for 2010/11 as the flat is not suitable for letting as a dwelling on 5 April 2010 and is not therefore a qualifying flat at that time. It becomes a qualifying flat on 1 May 2011, so that a writing-down allowance is available for 2011/12. Frances does not hold the relevant interest in the flat on 5 April 2013, having sold the building in March 2013, so no writing-down allowance is available for 2012/13.

(b) Had the sale of the freehold taken place one year later, a writing-down allowance of £3,750 would have been available for 2012/13, reducing the residue of expenditure to nil. Notwithstanding the abolition of flat conversion allowances (see **9.2** above), a balancing charge would have arisen for 2013/14; this would have been restricted to the total allowances made and would thus have amounted to £15,000.

(c) Expenditure on the extension of a building is not qualifying expenditure except to the extent that it is required for the purpose of providing a means of entry to the flat (see **9.3** above).

(d) Assuming that Frances is not otherwise carrying on a property business, the initial allowance of £7,500 will create a loss for 2010/11 in the UK property business which she is deemed to carry on in accordance with **9.14** below, as no income from the flats arises until 2011/12. Frances may claim to set off that loss (which consists entirely of capital allowances) against other income of 2010/11 or 2011/12 or may carry it forward against future rental income (see **9.14** below).

Method of making allowances and charges

[9.14] Where the interest in the flat is an asset of a UK property business, initial, writing-down and balancing allowances are given effect by treating them as expenses of that business. Balancing charges are treated as receipts of the business. If the interest in the flat is not an asset of such a business, the person concerned is treated as if he were carrying on such a business and allowances and charges are made accordingly. [*CAA 2001, s 393T*].

Where the full 100% initial allowance is claimed, in many instances a UK property business loss will arise for the chargeable period in which the expenditure is incurred. See **2.40** and **2.42** above for the carry forward of such losses and for relief against general income. See also *Example 1* at **9.13** above.

10

Mineral Extraction

Introduction

[10.1] A significant amount of capital expenditure is likely to be incurred before and after the commencement of a trade of mineral extraction, or even if no such trade is ultimately commenced. For example, initial pre-trading expenditure may be on the acquisition of prospecting and exploration rights, geological and geophysical surveys, exploratory drilling and evaluation of a site's commercial prospects. It may be that circumstances are such that the intending trader abandons his plans for the intended mineral extraction activities. In so doing he may endeavour to sell the fruits of the knowledge he has gained to somebody else. However, once a viable site has been found and any necessary production rights acquired, the development of the source can begin (such development being the stage at which HMRC usually acknowledge that a trade has begun). This will involve capital expenditure on works such as the sinking of oil wells and mine shafts and the setting up of facilities for production, transport, storage, staff, etc., before finally the stage is reached at which the raw material begins to be produced from the source. Similar observations can be made in the case of an existing trade and an additional source of mineral deposits. Although some of the capital expenditure may qualify under other capital allowances provisions, a large amount will not.

The current code of mineral extraction allowances, which provides tax relief for some of the above mentioned expenditure, was introduced by *FA 1986* and is now consolidated as *CAA 2001, Pt 5*. This code relates to expenditure incurred after 31 March 1986 (subject to certain exceptions) and replaces a previous code. There are transitional provisions for unrelieved balances of expenditure qualifying under the old code of allowances and for balancing adjustments relating to such balances. See the 2010/11 or earlier edition of this work for details.

Allowances are available for qualifying expenditure incurred in a '*mineral extraction trade*', i.e. a trade consisting of, or including, the working of a 'source of mineral deposits' but, for claims to allowances made on or after 6 April 2014 (1 April 2014 for corporation tax purposes), only to the extent that the profits or gains from that trade are, or (if there were any) would be, chargeable to UK tax. The term '*mineral deposits*' is limited to deposits of a wasting nature, and includes any natural deposits capable of being lifted or extracted from the earth. For this purpose, geothermal energy is treated as a natural deposit. A '*source of mineral deposits*' includes a mine, an oil well and a source of geothermal energy. The code applies to shares in assets as *CAA 2001, s 571* (see **2.32** above) applies to parts of assets. A share in an asset is treated as used for trade purposes only if the underlying asset is so used. [*CAA 2001, ss 394, 435; FA 2014, s 67(2)(8)*].

It must always be acknowledged that some capital expenditure will not qualify for allowances under any of the capital allowance provisions. Pre-trading expenditure that is not capital expenditure may be the subject of relief as a trading deduction under *ITTOIA 2005, s 57* or *CTA 2009, s 61* when incurred in the seven years prior to the commencement of trading.

See **17.36** below for the effect on mineral extraction allowances of an election for exemption of profits of foreign permanent establishments of a UK resident company.

Research and development allowances

[10.2] There is a great deal of capital expenditure that has to be incurred before the decision can be made to develop a source of mineral deposits with a view to producing raw material from it. Much of this capital expenditure will be incurred on the accumulation of knowledge in the fields of natural and applied science so that research and development allowances will be available (see **Chapter 11** below for additional conditions).

For income tax purposes for 2000/01 and subsequent tax years, and for corporation tax purposes for accounting periods ending after 31 March 2000, research and development allowances are specifically made available for expenditure on 'oil and gas exploration and appraisal' (as defined in **11.3** below).

For earlier periods, such expenditure was not included in the statutory definition of expenditure qualifying for scientific research allowances (as research and development allowances were then known). However, in 1967, the Revenue and the UK Oil Industry Taxation Committee published a memorandum which set out an agreed approach to the making of scientific research allowances in relation to the stages of development of an oil well. The memorandum can also be useful in categorising expenditure on mineral extraction activities other than those involving oil, etc.

It was agreed that there were five stages in the development of an oil well. The first stage involved studies of the available geological information on the areas which had been selected; the acquisition of a prospecting concession in respect of all or part of an area; and initial, and then detailed, geological and geophysical surveys of likely fields. The second stage entailed the drilling of exploration wells in order to obtain physical samples of the geology below the surface of the land or sea-bed. If sufficient promise was shown by the second stage, the third stage would consist of the drilling of appraisal wells which would determine whether there was oil in commercial quantities. If there was, the fourth stage would be the drilling of development wells and the provision of facilities for production, transport, storage and staff. The fifth stage would be that of production operations.

The Revenue agreed that, *provided* that the capital expenditure in question would otherwise qualify for scientific research allowances, they were prepared to treat expenditure within the first three phases above as so qualifying rather than under the mineral extraction old code. However, once it was generally known that a particular field did have commercial quantities of oil, no further expenditure within the first three stages and relating to that field, even if incurred by another trader, would be treated as qualifying for scientific research allowances.

It will usually be to a trader's or prospective trader's advantage (unless mineral extraction first-year allowances are available) to claim a research and development allowance in preference to a mineral extraction allowance, because the former provides a 100% allowance immediately. Where a research and development allowance is made in respect of any expenditure, no mineral extraction allowance is to be made. See **2.2** above.

Effect of the cash basis

[10.2A] Although mineral extraction trades are currently excluded trades for cash basis purposes (see *ITTOIA 2005, s 31C(8)* and **17.1A** below), provisions have been introduced for 2017/18 onwards dealing with the effect of the cash basis on mineral extraction allowances. Such allowances are not generally available to a person carrying on a trade to which the cash basis applies. See **17.1D** below.

Where a person carrying on a mineral extraction trade 'enters the cash basis' for a tax year, only the 'non-cash basis deductible portion' of qualifying expenditure incurred before entering the cash basis is taken into account in determining the unrelieved qualifying expenditure (see **10.23** below) for tax years for which the cash basis applies. The '*non-cash basis deductible portion*' of qualifying expenditure is any amount that would not have been deductible on the cash basis if it had been paid in the tax year for which the person enters the cash basis.

For this purpose, a person '*enters the cash basis*' for a tax year if a cash basis election has effect for that year and such an election did not have effect immediately before the beginning of the basis period for that year.

[*CAA 2001, s 419A; F(No 2)A 2017, Sch 2 paras 54, 64*].

A deduction is allowable in the first cash basis year for any amount which would have been unrelieved qualifying expenditure but for the above provision and which would have been deductible on the cash basis if it had been paid in that year. Special rules apply if the expenditure in question has not been paid in full. If the capital allowances given in respect of 'relevant expenditure' exceed the amount actually paid, the difference is treated as a receipt in calculating the profits for the first cash basis year. If the amount paid exceeds the allowances the excess is allowed as a deduction in that year. '*Relevant expenditure*' is any amount of expenditure which would have been deductible on the cash basis if it had been paid in the tax year for which the person enters the cash basis. The amount of capital allowances given and whether or to what extent expenditure is relevant expenditure are determined on a just and reasonable basis.

ITTOIA 2005, ss 240CA, 240D; FA 2013, Sch 4 para 38; F(No 2)A 2017, Sch 2 paras 8, 9, 64].

See **17.1D** below for the requirement to bring into account a disposal value or balancing charge in certain cases where qualifying expenditure was incurred before entry into the cash basis which would not have been deductible under the cash basis if it had been incurred in the first cash basis year.

The following provisions apply where a person carrying on a mineral extraction trade leaves the cash basis in a chargeable period having incurred expenditure which would have been qualifying expenditure if it had not been incurred at a time when the cash basis applied. At least some of the expenditure must have been brought into account in calculating the profits of the trade on the cash basis. A person leaves the cash basis in a chargeable period for this purpose if immediately before the beginning of the period a cash basis election had effect but such an election does not have effect for the period itself.

An amount equal to the excess of the 'unrelieved portion' of the expenditure over the 'relieved portion' is treated as qualifying expenditure incurred in the chargeable period in which the person leaves the cash basis.

The '*relieved portion*' of expenditure is the higher of the amount for which a deduction has been allowed in computing the trade profits and the amount for which such a deduction would have been allowed if the expenditure had been incurred wholly and exclusively for the purposes of the trade. The '*unrelieved portion*' is any remaining amount of the expenditure.

[*CAA 2001, s 431D; F(No 2)A 2017, Sch 2 paras 55, 64*].

For similar provisions which apply in respect of plant and machinery, patent and know-how allowances. See **5.33** and **5.47** above and **12.1A** below.

Note that, at the time of writing, *F(No 2)A 2017* had not completed its passage through Parliament. These provisions are therefore subject to any changes made during the Parliamentary process.

Qualifying expenditure

Introduction

[10.3] Subject to the matters set out further in **10.13–10.20** below and the anti-avoidance provisions at **17.21** below, '*qualifying expenditure*' is capital expenditure of any of the following kinds.

(i) Expenditure on 'mineral exploration and access'; see **10.5** below.
(ii) Expenditure on acquiring a 'mineral asset'; see **10.6** below.
(iii) Expenditure on constructing certain works; see **10.7** below.
(iv) Pre-trading expenditure on plant or machinery which is sold, etc.; see **10.8** below.
(v) Pre-trading exploration expenditure; see **10.9** below.
(vi) Contributions to buildings or works, etc. overseas; see **10.10** below.
(vii) Restoration expenditure; see **10.11** below.

[*CAA 2001, s 395; FA 2013, s 92(2), Sch 32 para 10*].

Expenditure on the following is excluded from the above categories.

(a) Plant or machinery other than within (iv) above.
(b) Works for processing the raw product, except to prepare it for use as such.
(c) Buildings for occupation by or for the welfare of workers (but see also **10.10** below).
(d) A building the whole of which was constructed for use as an office.
(e) So much of a building or structure which was constructed for use as an office, unless the capital cost of construction of that part did not exceed one-tenth of the capital cost of construction of the whole building.

For claims to allowances made on or after 6 April 2014 (1 April 2014 for corporation tax purposes), expenditure incurred for the purposes of a mineral extraction trade is not qualifying expenditure if:

(1) when the expenditure is incurred the trade is being carried on but is not then a mineral extraction trade (because, for example, the trade is not within the charge to UK tax; see **10.1** above); or
(2) the trade has not begun to be carried on when the expenditure is incurred and when it begins to be carried on it is not a mineral extraction trade.

An event treated by the Taxes Acts as a deemed commencement of a trade is not a commencement of a trade for the purposes of (2) above.

[*CAA 2001, s 399; FA 2014, s 67(3)(8)*].

What constitutes an 'office' and a whole building has been considered by the courts in the context of allowances for industrial buildings (which have now been repealed).

In *CIR v Lambhill Ironworks Ltd* CS 1950, 31 TC 393, it was held that the drawing office of a business of structural engineers was an industrial building and not an office or ancillary to an office: a distinction was made between the 'managerial' and 'industrial' sides of the business.

Buildings which are offices include buildings which house wages offices and purchasing and sales departments, and buildings providing accommodation for the board and senior executives, planning and administration, personnel, works planning and control, and the works manager and staff dealing with costing and despatch (HMRC Capital Allowances Manual, CA32312).

There is no real definition of what constitutes a whole or separate building. In *Abbott Laboratories Ltd v Carmody* ChD 1968, 44 TC 569, it was held that an administrative block was a separate building and the company then had no opportunity to claim allowances using the industrial buildings de minimis rule (similar to the rule in (e) above). However, there was little consideration of whether a complex of buildings could be the 'whole of a building'. In *O'Conaill v Waterford Glass Ltd* HC/I 1982, TL 122, a separate building was regarded as part of a whole industrial complex and could be included for the de minimis calculation under similar Irish legislation.

In two other cases (but under different legislation) 'separated' parts of buildings were held to be part of the whole of a building. In *Sinclair v Cadbury*

Bros Ltd CA 1933, 18 TC 157 it was held that a dining block connected by bridges and walkways to the factory building was part of the premises used as a mill or factory. In *Bedford College v Guest* CA 1920, 7 TC 480 a school designed in separate blocks but connected by a covered corridor which enabled access to be obtained without going out into the open air was held to be one unit.

An important point to note is that the 10% rule in (e) above is applied by reference to expenditure rather than to area.

Capital or revenue?

[10.4] The question of whether expenditure is on capital or revenue account will occur in connection with mineral extraction activities as it will with any other activities. In the case of *RTZ Oil & Gas Ltd v Elliss* ChD 1987, 61 TC 132, provisions for expenditure to be made in the future on the restoration of North Sea oil well sites were disallowed as trading deductions because the expenditure, when incurred, would be on capital account. That case, although probably of general application to all mineral extraction, is of special interest to the UK oil and gas sector involved in the North Sea since the restoration costs to be incurred there will probably involve the incurring of some thousands of millions of pounds. Some of the concerns raised by the case have been met by the relieving provisions at **5.39** and **5.40** above in connection with qualifying expenditure for plant and machinery allowances. Although the *RTZ* case involved expenditure to be incurred after extraction ceased, it will often be the particular pre-production stages involved in researching and developing a mineral extraction activity so that production can actually take place, as exemplified in the 1967 memorandum mentioned in **10.2** above, that will allow ample scope for argument as to the treatment of a particular amount of expenditure, particularly as the fruits of the capital expenditure, as with revenue expenditure, will often be intangible.

In this connection, it is perhaps ironic that the first report in the Official Reports of Tax Cases concerned a claim by a coal and iron master to deduct a percentage for the cost of sinking pits. The claim was refused because the payments made were chargeable to capital (*In re Robert Addie & Sons CE(S)* 1875, 1 TC 1). A similar decision was reached a few years later in *Coltness Iron Co. v Black* HL 1881, 1 TC 287.

Although these cases were decided over a century ago, it would appear that the principles enunciated in them still hold good.

Some further guidance was given as regards intangible drilling costs by a decision of the Special Commissioners, published by the Revenue in 1967 with the latter's approval, which indicates that the cost of drilling oil wells before there is final proof of commercial quantities of oil is on capital account but that similar costs thereafter in the same 'area or group of sands', e.g. for the purpose of producing oil, will be on revenue account. The decision also indicated that if a well was producing commercial quantities of oil from one group of sands, the cost of deepening the well to further an investigation of whether there were such quantities in a lower group of sands would also be on capital account until it was shown that the lower level was productive.

It may be possible to apply the above reasoning to other mineral extraction activities, both in the oil sector and elsewhere. The accounting treatment of any expenditure may, or may not, be called upon by the taxpayer to assist his case depending on the circumstances. Such evidence will not be conclusive (*Heather v P-E Consulting Group Ltd* CA 1972, 48 TC 293). Ultimately it will be for the courts to decide the status of any disputed expenditure.

Mineral exploration and access

[10.5] Capital expenditure incurred for the purposes of a mineral extraction trade on mineral exploration and access is qualifying expenditure. For this purpose, '*mineral exploration and access*' means searching for, or discovering and testing, the mineral deposits of any source, or winning access to any such deposits.

Expenditure incurred on seeking, or appealing against a refusal of, planning permission for mineral exploration and access to be undertaken, or for mineral deposits to be worked, is included in this category (and is not expenditure on acquiring a mineral asset within **10.6** below). Such expenditure incurred before 17 July 2014 is within this category only if the planning application is unsuccessful (and expenditure incurred before that date on a successful application is treated as expenditure on acquiring a mineral asset).

Expenditure on mineral exploration and access incurred by a person in connection with a mineral extraction trade (whether before or after the trade began to be carried on) is treated as incurred for the purposes of the trade.

[*CAA 2001, ss 396, 400(1)(2), 436; FA 2014, s 68(2)(4)*].

Acquisition of a mineral asset

[10.6] Capital expenditure incurred for the purposes of a mineral extraction trade on acquiring a mineral asset is qualifying expenditure. It does not, however, qualify for first-year allowances (see **10.22** below). '*Mineral asset*' means any mineral deposits or land comprising such deposits, or any interest in or right over such deposits or land. The 'undeveloped market value' of land is excluded from the qualifying expenditure (see **10.13** below) as is a proportion of any premium relief previously allowed (see **10.14** below). A mineral asset which consists of or includes an interest in or right over mineral deposits or land is not regarded as situated in the UK unless the deposits or land are situated there. (It should be noted that *ITA 2007, s 1013* and *CTA 2010, s 1170* deem the territorial sea to be in the UK for all income and corporation tax purposes but that *CTA 2009, s 1313* and *ITTOIA 2005, s 874* only treat profits arising from exploration or exploitation activities in a 'designated area' of the continental shelf as arising from a UK source. Hence a designated area will be treated as outside the UK for mineral extraction purposes.)

Expenditure incurred on restoration of the site of a source (which includes land used in connection with the working of the source) to the working of which a ring fence trade relates (or related) carried out on or after 17 July 2013 is not expenditure on acquiring a mineral asset.

Insofar as it is necessary to determine whether expenditure should fall within **10.5** above or this paragraph, expenditure on the acquisition of, or of rights over, the site of a source, and expenditure on the acquisition of, or of rights over, mineral deposits, is treated as falling within this paragraph and not within **10.5** above. See **10.5** above for the treatment of expenditure on planning applications.

[*CAA 2001, ss 397, 398, 403, Sch 3 para 87(4); FA 2013, s 92(3)(10); FA 2014, s 68(3)*].

Construction of works

[10.7] Capital expenditure incurred for the purposes of a mineral extraction trade on the construction of works in connection with the working of a source of mineral deposits is qualifying expenditure provided that the works are likely to have little or no value to the person last working the source when it is no longer worked or, if the source is worked under a foreign concession, are likely to become valueless to the person then working it when the concession ends. A foreign concession is a right or privilege granted by the government of a territory outside the UK or any municipality or other authority in such a territory.

Not included in the above qualifying expenditure is any expenditure incurred on acquiring the site of the works, or acquiring any right in or over the site.

[*CAA 2001, s 414*].

Pre-trading expenditure on plant and machinery which is sold, etc.

[10.8] Plant and machinery provided specifically for mineral exploration and access within **10.5** above is frequently not of use for mineral extraction. If any plant or machinery has been so provided before the commencement of a mineral extraction trade, and is still owned when the trade commences, capital allowances will be available under the normal code of allowances for plant and machinery (see Chapter 3 onwards above), which was extended for this purpose by the provisions in **10.12** below. If, however, the plant has been sold, demolished, destroyed or abandoned before the commencement of the trade, the trader is treated as incurring qualifying expenditure, called '*pre-trading expenditure on plant or machinery*', on the first day of trading.

The amount of this deemed expenditure is the excess of the actual capital expenditure incurred over any 'relevant receipts' received. Expenditure incurred more than six years before the first day of trading is left out of account if the mineral exploration and access at the source at which the plant or machinery was used ceased before that day. If the plant or machinery is sold, the '*relevant receipts*' are the net sale proceeds. If the plant or machinery is demolished or destroyed, they are the net amount received for the remains plus any insurance money or other capital compensation received. Where the plant or machinery is abandoned, the relevant receipts are any insurance money or other capital compensation received.

The legislation does not require the mineral extraction trade to be commenced at the source at which the plant was used. Relief is therefore available for abortive expenditure.

[*CAA 2001, s 400(2)–(5), s 402*].

Pre-trading exploration expenditure

[10.9] Other pre-trading capital expenditure of any kind incurred for mineral exploration or access within 10.5 at a source is qualifying expenditure, called '*pre-trading exploration expenditure*'. It is treated as incurred on the first day of trading.

The amount of this is the excess of the expenditure incurred over any '*relevant capital sums*', i.e. capital sums which the person incurring the expenditure received before commencing the trade, to the extent that they are reasonably attributable to the incurring of the expenditure at the source. Expenditure incurred more than six years before the first day of trading is left out of account if the mineral exploration and access at the source ceased before that day.

The legislation refers to 'a source', and does not require the trade of mineral extraction to be commenced at the source which was explored. Relief is therefore available for abortive expenditure.

[*CAA 2001, ss 400(2)–(5), 401*].

Contributions to buildings or works overseas

[10.10] Where a mineral extraction trade is carried on outside the UK, it is frequently necessary for accommodation to be made available for persons employed in the trade and their families. Accordingly, capital contributions to the cost of buildings for occupation by employees employed at or in connection with the working of a source outside the UK, or works for the supply of water, gas or electricity to such buildings, or works for the welfare of such employees or their dependants, are qualifying expenditure if:

(a) the buildings or works are likely to be of little or no value, when the source is no longer worked, to the last person working it;
(b) the expenditure does not result in his acquiring an asset;
(c) the expenditure is incurred for the purposes of the mineral extraction trade; and
(d) no allowance is available under any other provision of the *Taxes Acts*.

[*CAA 2001, s 415*].

Legislation relating to industrial buildings allowances (now repealed) which was phrased similarly to that in (a) above, was tested in *CIR v National Coal Board* HL 1957, 37 TC 264. It was held that colliery dwelling-houses remaining after mining had finished at a site in Nottinghamshire were capable of alternative use by persons other than colliery employees and were therefore of some residual value. If the mining site had been more remote, the decision might have been different.

Restoration expenditure

[10.11] Certain expenditure is qualifying expenditure if it is incurred on the 'restoration' of the site of a source (which includes land used in connection with the working of the source). For expenditure on such restoration carried out on or after 17 July 2013, there are separate rules for ring fence trades.

The following rules apply to expenditure on site restoration incurred after the trade of mineral extraction has ceased. Expenditure on restoration carried out on or after 17 July 2013 is excluded if the trade was a ring fence trade.

'*Restoration*' includes landscaping. It also includes the carrying out of any works required by a condition subject to which planning permission for working the source was granted in respect of land in the UK, or required by an equivalent condition imposed under local law in respect of land overseas. In relation to expenditure on restoration carried out on or after 17 July 2013, it does not include decommissioning any plant or machinery (for which see **5.40** above).

The expenditure must have been incurred within the period of three years from the last day of trading, and must not have been deducted for income tax or corporation tax purposes in relation to the trade of mineral extraction or any other trade carried on by the trader. It must also be expenditure which, if it had been incurred while the trade of mineral extraction was being carried on, would either have been qualifying expenditure within **10.5–10.10** above or would have been deductible as a trading expense.

The amount of the above expenditure treated as qualifying expenditure is limited to the '*net cost*' of restoration, i.e. the amount (if any) by which the actual expenditure incurred exceeds any sums which are received within the three-year period mentioned above and which are attributable to the restoration (e.g. for spoil or other assets removed from the site or for tipping rights). None of the expenditure (not just that part of it which is treated as qualifying expenditure) is deductible in any computation of income, and to the extent that receipts are taken into account they do not constitute income for any other purpose.

The expenditure treated as qualifying expenditure is treated as incurred on the last day of trading. Adjustments, whether by way of discharge or repayment of tax or otherwise, may be made as required by the above provisions.

[*CAA 2001, s 416; FA 2013, s 92(4)(10)*].

Where expenditure is incurred by a person who is carrying on, or has carried on, a ring fence trade on restoration carried out on or after 17 July 2013, the 'net cost' of restoration is qualifying expenditure for the chargeable period (or, where the work is carried out after the trade has ceased, for the 'notional accounting period') in which that part of the work to which the expenditure relates is carried out. Qualifying expenditure for a notional accounting period is treated as incurred on the last day of trading. Expenditure which has been deducted in calculating the taxable profits of any trade carried on by the person is not qualifying expenditure.

If the expenditure incurred on any part of the restoration work in a chargeable period or notional accounting period is disproportionate to that part of the work, only a proportionate amount of the net cost of the restoration is qualifying expenditure for that period. This does not prevent expenditure excluded by this rule from being qualifying expenditure of a later period.

'*Restoration*' includes landscaping and, in relation to UK land, the carrying out of any works required as a condition of granting planning permission for development relating to the winning of oil from an oil field. It also includes, in relation to land in the UK marine area (within the meaning of *Marine and Coastal Access Act 2009, s 42*), the carrying out of works required to comply with an approved abandonment programme (within *Petroleum Act 1998, Pt IV*), a condition to which the approval of an abandonment programme is subject or a requirement imposed by, or an agreement made with, the Secretary of State in relation to the site. In relation to land in a foreign sector of the continental shelf, 'restoration' also includes works required in order to comply any corresponding programme, condition, requirement or agreement under local law. It does not include decommissioning any plant or machinery (for which see **5.40** above).

The '*net cost*' of restoration is the amount (if any) by which the actual expenditure incurred exceeds any sums which are received or are to be received by the person which are attributable to the restoration of the site. None of the restoration expenditure (not just that part of it which is treated as qualifying expenditure) is deductible in any computation of income, and to the extent that receipts are taken into account in the net cost they do not constitute income for any other purpose.

The first '*notional accounting period*' begins on the day after the ring fence trade ceases and ends on the day on which the first subsequent 'termination event' occurs. The next notional accounting period begins on the following day and ends on the day of the next subsequent termination event, and so on. There are, however, no notional accounting periods after the end of the post-cessation period (i.e. the period from cessation of the trade to the day on which the 'appropriate authority' is satisfied that the restoration has been completed). For land in the UK marine area the '*appropriate authority*' is the Secretary of State; in any other case the appropriate authority is a person or body specified by HMRC. The following are termination events:

(a) the end of the twelve-month period starting with the first day of the notional accounting period;
(b) the occurrence of an accounting date of the former trader or, if there is a period for which accounts are not made up, the end of that period; and
(c) the end of the post-cessation period.

If the former trader carries on more than one trade and makes up accounts for any of them to different dates (without making up general accounts for the whole of its activities), the former trader can choose which of the accounting dates to use for the purposes of (b) above. If, however, HMRC are of the opinion, on reasonable grounds, that a chosen date is inappropriate, they may by notice direct that another of the dates should be used.

[*CAA 2001, ss 416ZA, 416ZB; FA 2013, s 92(5)(10)*].

CTA 2009, ss 142, 145 and *ITTOIA 2005, ss 165, 168* allow trading deductions for certain 'site preparation expenditure' and 'site restoration payments' made in connection with waste disposal activities carried on or to be carried on. As the site of such activities may well have been previously a source for mineral extraction, it is provided that relief is not available for any part of the expenditure or payment for which a capital allowance (although not necessarily one under the mineral extraction code) has been, or may be, made. [*ITTOIA 2005, ss 166, 168; CTA 2009, ss 143, 145; FA 2012, s 53*].

Expenditure which is not qualifying expenditure

[10.12] The following points relate to expenditure which is not qualifying expenditure.

(a) The cost of a site, or of any rights in or over a site, does not constitute qualifying expenditure (see **10.6** above and **10.13** below). Representations were made, in the consultation process prior to the introduction of the current code of allowances, for relief to be given because the value of some land (such as that used for tipping mineral waste) may depreciate but it was thought not to be right to make an exception in favour of mineral extraction activities.

(b) In general, expenditure on plant and machinery is not qualifying expenditure for the purposes of mineral extraction allowances (see **10.3** above), but may well qualify for plant and machinery allowances generally (for which see CHAPTER 3 onwards above). Plant and machinery acquired for mineral exploration and access within **10.5** above, which on the first day of a mineral extraction trade (see **10.1** above) is still owned and has not been demolished, destroyed or abandoned, is treated for the purposes of plant and machinery allowances as having been sold immediately before that day and reacquired on that day at its original cost (or at its last cost if there has previously been an actual sale and reacquisition). For claims to allowances made on or after 6 April 2014 (1 April 2014 for corporation tax purposes), this rule does not apply if there is a prior time when the taxpayer carried on the trade and the trade was not a mineral extraction trade (and a deemed commencement of a trade does not count as a commencement of the trade for these purposes). [*CAA 2001, s 161; FA 2014, s 67(5)(6)(8)*].

Limitations on qualifying expenditure

Expenditure on acquisition of land

[10.13] Certain expenditure within 10.6 above incurred in acquiring an interest in land which includes a source of mineral deposits is not qualifying expenditure. The reasoning given by the Revenue in their consultative document of 16 July 1985 is that if the relief were based on the value of the source including the land, the result could be that a deduction would be given in respect of something not generally considered to be a wasting asset. Conversely, a balancing charge could ultimately arise because of an inflationary increase in the value of the land, thus diminishing the relief given for the mineral extraction.

The amount to be excluded is the '*undeveloped market value*' of the interest acquired in the land. This is the amount which the interest in the land would be expected to fetch on a sale in the open market if:

(a) there were no source of mineral deposits, and
(b) development of the land, apart from any already lawfully carried out or begun, or for which planning permission has been granted by a general development order in force at the time, were, and would continue to be, unlawful.

Where the land is outside the UK, whether development has been lawfully carried out or begun is determined for the purposes of (b) above by reference to local law, and whether development could be lawfully carried out under planning permission granted by a general development order is determined as if the land were in England.

Where the undeveloped market value of an interest in land includes the value of buildings or other structures on the land which, at the time of acquisition or subsequently, cease permanently to be used for any purpose, 'the unrelieved value' of them is treated as qualifying expenditure incurred at that time on the acquisition of a mineral asset.

'*The unrelieved value*' is the value of the buildings, etc., at the time of acquisition (disregarding the value of the land on which they stand) less the excess of any allowances over balancing charges received on them by the trader under *CAA 2001* (or former equivalent provisions) but excluding any allowances or charges under the provisions for dwelling-houses let on assured tenancies and, in cases where the buildings, etc. ceased permanently to be used for any purpose before 27 July 1989, agricultural buildings.

In these provisions the special rules in *CAA 2001, s 434* (see **10.21** below) about the timing of expenditure do not apply.

[*CAA 2001, ss 404, 405*].

Premiums

[10.14] If a person:

(a) incurs capital expenditure on acquiring a mineral asset (see **10.6** above) which is or includes an interest in land, and
(b) in any chargeable period before he became entitled to a capital allowance on it as qualifying expenditure, he has obtained any deduction under *CTA 2009, ss 62–67* or *ITTOIA 2005, ss 60–67* in respect of a taxable premium paid on a lease of it,

the expenditure is treated as reduced by an amount equal to the proportion of the total deductions that the part of the expenditure on the interest in land which would have been qualifying expenditure had the person been entitled to mineral extraction allowances for those earlier chargeable periods bears to the total expenditure on the interest.

[*CAA 2001, s 406*].

Assets formerly owned by traders

[10.15] If:

(a) a person carrying on a mineral extraction trade ('*the buyer*') incurs capital expenditure for the purposes of the trade on acquiring an asset ('*the purchased asset*') from another person, and
(b) either:
  (i) the other person incurred expenditure on the acquisition or creation of the purchased asset in connection with a mineral extraction trade carried on by him, or
  (ii) the other person did not so incur such expenditure but an earlier owner did (after 31 March 1986 in the case of an asset situated in the UK),

the provisions described in **10.16** and **10.17** below apply.

The last person to incur expenditure within (b)(i) or (b)(ii) above is called '*the previous trader*'.

A purchased asset includes two or more assets which together make it up, and one or more assets from which it is derived.

[*CAA 2001, s 407(1)(3)(a)(6)(7), s 411(1)(5)(6)*].

For the purposes of these provisions, '*the buyer's expenditure*' means the expenditure incurred by the buyer as described above, less any amount of undeveloped market value (see **10.13** above). [*CAA 2001, ss 407(2), 411(2)*].

Limitation of qualifying expenditure

[10.16] In the circumstances described in **10.15** above, the amount of the buyer's expenditure which constitutes qualifying expenditure in respect of the acquisition of the purchased asset is limited to the '*residue of the previous trader's qualifying expenditure*', i.e. that part of the previous trader's expenditure on acquiring or creating the purchased asset which constitutes qualifying expenditure for the purposes of the new code of allowances less any new code mineral extraction allowances received, plus any new code mineral extraction balancing charge made. If the purchased asset is derived from one or more assets created or acquired by the previous trader, the residue of his qualifying expenditure is computed by reference to so much of those amounts as are attributable to the purchased asset on a just and reasonable basis. [*CAA 2001, s 411(3)(4)(7)*].

The limitation applies subject to **10.17** and **10.18** below. [*CAA 2001, s 411(8)*].

Previous expenditure on mineral exploration and access

[10.17] If:

(i) the circumstances are as described in **10.15** above,
(ii) the purchased asset is a mineral asset,

(iii) part of the value of the asset is properly attributable to expenditure by the previous trader on mineral exploration and access, and
(iv) part of the buyer's expenditure is, on a just and reasonable basis, attributable to that part of the value of the asset,

the following provisions apply:

(a) the lesser of the part of the buyer's expenditure so attributable and the previous trader's expenditure on mineral exploration and access is treated as qualifying expenditure on mineral exploration and access; and
(b) the remainder of the buyer's expenditure is treated as expenditure on the acquisition of a mineral asset.

In determining the amount of the previous trader's expenditure on mineral exploration and access, any amount deducted in calculating the profits of a trade carried on by him is excluded.

[*CAA 2001, s 407(3)–(5)*].

Oil licences, etc.

[10.18] The amount of any expenditure eligible to be qualifying expenditure may also be restricted where the capital expenditure is on the acquisition of a mineral asset which is, or is an interest in, a '*UK oil licence*', i.e. a licence under the *Petroleum Act 1998, Part I* or the *Petroleum (Production) Act (Northern Ireland) 1964* authorising the winning of oil.

The amount of the purchaser's expenditure treated as qualifying expenditure is restricted to the payment made for obtaining the licence by the person to whom the licence was granted, to the Secretary of State (or, in Northern Ireland, the Department of Enterprise, Trade and Investment), or, if only an interest in a licence is acquired, a just and reasonable portion of that payment.

The provisions do not affect any expenditure treated as qualifying expenditure on mineral exploration and access under *CAA 2001, s 407(5)* (see **10.17** above) or *s 408(2)* (see **10.20** below).

[*CAA 2001, ss 410, 552(2), 556(2)*].

See also **10.20** below.

Transfer of mineral assets within a company group

[10.19] Rules similar to those applying where an asset is acquired from a previous trader apply in the case of transfers of mineral assets to a group company (i.e. a company which controls or is controlled by, or is controlled by the same person as, the transferee). These rules are important in preventing groups from gaining an advantage over single companies by using several companies to deal with different aspects of a project. The rules do not apply where

(a) an election is made under *CAA 2001, s 569* (but, subject to that, do apply notwithstanding anything in *CAA 2001, s 568*) (see **17.2** below in both cases), or

(b) the provisions at **10.18** above apply.

The rules do not affect any expenditure treated as qualifying expenditure on mineral exploration and access under *CAA 2001, s 407(5)* (see **10.17** above) or *s 408(2)* (see **10.20** below).

Any excess of capital expenditure incurred by the transferee on the acquisition of the asset over the expenditure incurred on it by the transferor is disregarded. Where only an interest or right in an asset is granted by the transferor, the transferor's expenditure is apportioned accordingly on a just and reasonable basis.

If the transferee is carrying on a trade of mineral extraction, and the asset acquired is an interest in land, the following provisions apply.

(A) References in *CAA 2001, ss 404* and *405* (see **10.13** above) to the time of acquisition are to the time of acquisition by the transferor, or, if there was a series of transfers within these provisions, to the time of acquisition by the first transferor.

(B) If there was a series of transfers, the allowances and charges to be taken into account in calculating the 'unrelieved value' (see **10.13** above) include all allowances and charges made to or on any transferor in the series.

[*CAA 2001, ss 412, 413*].

Assets formerly owned by non-traders

[10.20] If:

(a) a person carrying on a mineral extraction trade ('*the buyer*') incurs capital expenditure for the purposes of the trade on acquiring an asset ('*the purchased asset*') from another person, and

(b) the person from whom the purchased asset was acquired ('*the seller*') disposed of it without having carried on a mineral extraction trade,

the following provisions apply:

if the purchased asset is an interest in an oil licence and:

(i) part of the value of the interest is attributable to expenditure by the seller on mineral exploration and access, and

(ii) part of the buyer's expenditure is, on a just and reasonable basis, attributable to that part of the value of the interest,

the lesser of that part of the buyer's expenditure and the seller's expenditure on mineral exploration and access is treated as qualifying expenditure on mineral exploration and access. The buyer's expenditure on acquiring the interest is treated as reduced by the amount in (ii) above. For this purpose, an oil licence is a UK oil licence (see **10.18** above) or a 'foreign oil concession' (as defined in *CAA 2001, s 552(3)*) and an interest in an oil licence includes an entitlement to a share of, or the proceeds of the sale of, oil under an agreement relating to oil from the whole or part of the licensed area made before the extraction of the oil to which it relates.

In all other cases, where the purchased asset represents expenditure by the seller on mineral exploration and access, the buyer's qualifying expenditure is limited to so much of the price paid as does not exceed the seller's expenditure which is represented by the asset.

References above to assets representing mineral exploration and access expenditure include results obtained from any search, exploration or inquiry on which the expenditure was incurred.

[*CAA 2001, ss 408, 409, 552*].

Allowances and charges

[10.21] Writing-down allowances and balancing allowances are available to a person who carries on a mineral extraction trade, in respect of qualifying expenditure. [*CAA 2001, s 394(1)*]. First-year allowances are available only to companies for expenditure incurred after 16 April 2002 solely for the purposes of a 'ring fence trade' (see **10.22** below). [*CAA 2001, ss 416A, 416B(1)*].

Expenditure incurred for the purposes of a trade about to be carried on is treated as incurred on the first day of trading. Pre-trading expenditure on plant or machinery and pre-trading exploration expenditure (see **10.8** and **10.9** above) are also treated as incurred on that day. [*CAA 2001, ss 400(4), 434*]. These provisions are, however, ignored when determining whether expenditure qualifies for first-year allowances. [*CAA 2001, s 416C*]. In other words, expenditure actually incurred before 17 April 2002 cannot qualify for first-year allowances even if treated for allowances purposes as incurred when a trade commences on or after that day.

A separate computation is strictly made for each item of qualifying expenditure, and therefore there is no pooling. In practice, however, HMRC make no objection to the grouping together of assets for computational convenience, provided that each source is dealt with separately and expenditure to be written down at 10% a year is distinguished from other expenditure. Where a disposal value falls to be brought into account, or a balancing allowance is due, it may in certain circumstances be necessary to reconstruct separate computations for individual items of expenditure previously grouped (HMRC Capital Allowances Manual, CA50410).

First-year allowances

[10.22] Expenditure qualifies for a first-year allowance of 100% (and is referred to below as '*first-year qualifying expenditure*') if:

(a) it is incurred by a company after 16 April 2002;
(b) it is incurred solely for the purposes of a 'ring fence trade' in respect of which tax is chargeable under *CTA 2010, s 330(1)* (supplementary charge on ring fence trades);
(c) it is not expenditure on acquiring a mineral asset (within **10.6** above); and

(d) it is not incurred by a company on the acquisition of an asset representing expenditure incurred by a company connected with that company (see **2.34** above).

To the extent that the reference in (d) above to an asset representing expenditure incurred by a company includes a reference to expenditure on mineral exploration and access (see **10.5** above), it also includes a reference to any results obtained from any exploration, search or inquiry on which any such expenditure was incurred.

A 'ring fence trade' means activities falling within *CTA 2010, s 274* (treatment of oil extraction activities etc. for tax purposes) and constituting a separate trade, whether or not under that provision.

The first-year allowance is given for the chargeable period in which the first-year qualifying expenditure is incurred. The allowance may be claimed in respect of the whole or part of the expenditure.

[*CAA 2001, ss 416B, 416D; CTA 2010, s 277; FA 2013, s 92(6)*].

An anti-avoidance provision applies under which a transaction is disregarded in determining the amount of any first-year allowance to the extent that it is attributable to 'arrangements' where the object, or one of the main objects, is to enable a person to obtain a first-year allowance or a greater first-year allowance than that to which he would otherwise be entitled. For this purpose, '*arrangements*' include any scheme, agreement or understanding, whether or not legally enforceable. [*CAA 2001, s 416E*].

Writing-down allowances

[10.23] Writing-down allowances are given for a chargeable period (unless a balancing allowance is provided for — see **10.25** below), on the excess of the 'unrelieved qualifying expenditure' for that period over the total of any 'disposal values' (see **10.27** below) required to be brought into account, at a rate which depends on the type of expenditure.

The rate is 10% for expenditure on the acquisition of a mineral asset (see **10.6** above), and for all other expenditure, it is 25%.

If a chargeable period (see **2.1** above), or, under the preceding year basis, its basis period, is a period of less or more than a year or if the trade has been carried on for only part of it, the amount of the allowance is correspondingly reduced or, as the case may require, increased. A writing-down allowance may be reduced to a specified amount. No writing-down allowance is due for a period for which a balancing charge or allowance is made (see **10.24** and **10.25** below).

'*Unrelieved qualifying expenditure*' means, for the chargeable period in which it is incurred, the whole of the qualifying expenditure itself or, if the expenditure is first-year qualifying expenditure (see **10.22** above), none of it. This means that a writing-down allowance is not available for the chargeable period in which a first-year allowance can be claimed. For later periods, the unrelieved qualifying expenditure is the qualifying expenditure less the total of any allowances made and disposal values brought into account for earlier periods (i.e. the tax written-down value). Where a first-year allowance is claimed in respect of only part of any first-year qualifying expenditure (or not claimed at all) and a disposal value is to be brought into account for the same chargeable period, then, for the purpose only of determining whether, and in what amount, a balancing allowance or charge arises for that period, the unrelieved qualifying expenditure is taken to be so much of the expenditure as remains after deducting the allowance claimed.

[*CAA 2001, ss 417(1)(2)(4), 418(1)–(3)(6), 419*].

Balancing charges

[10.24] If the disposal values to be brought into account for a chargeable period exceed the unrelieved qualifying expenditure, a balancing charge is made. The charge is equal to the excess or, if less, to the excess of any new code allowances received over any such balancing charges made for earlier periods. For this purpose, a first-year allowance made for the period in which the balancing charge arises is treated as made in an earlier period. [*CAA 2001, ss 417(3), 418(4)*].

Balancing allowances

[10.25] A balancing allowance equal to the unrelieved qualifying expenditure less the sum of any disposal values to be brought into account is made for any of the following periods. No writing-down allowance is made for that period.

(a) The chargeable period in which the first day of trading occurs, where the qualifying expenditure concerned is:
 (i) pre-trading expenditure on plant or machinery (see **10.8** above), or
 (ii) pre-trading exploration expenditure (see **10.9** above) if the mineral exploration and access has ceased before that day.

(b) The chargeable period in which a person who has incurred qualifying expenditure on mineral exploration and access gives up the search, exploration or inquiry without then or later carrying on a mineral extraction trade involving any mineral deposits to which the expenditure related.

(c) The chargeable period in which the trader permanently ceases the working of particular mineral deposits. In this case a balancing allowance is due only in respect of qualifying expenditure on:
 (i) mineral exploration and access relating solely to that source, or
 (ii) the acquisition of a mineral asset consisting of the whole or part of those deposits.

 In a case where two or more assets were once comprised in, or have otherwise derived from, a single mineral asset, a balancing allowance is not available until the trader permanently ceases to work the deposits comprised in all the said assets. For this purpose if a mineral asset relates to, but does not consist of, mineral deposits, the related deposits are treated as comprised in the asset.

(d) Where the qualifying expenditure is a contribution within *CAA 2001, s 415* (see **10.10** above) to the cost of buildings or works overseas, the chargeable period in which they permanently cease to be used for or in connection with the trade.
(e) The chargeable period in which an asset is disposed of or otherwise permanently ceases to be used for the trade.
(f) The chargeable period in which the trader loses possession of assets, and it is reasonable to assume that the loss is permanent.
(g) The chargeable period in which assets cease to exist as such, through destruction, dismantlement or otherwise.
(h) The chargeable period in which assets begin to be used wholly or partly for purposes other than the mineral extraction trade carried on by the person concerned.
(i) The chargeable period in which the mineral extraction trade is permanently discontinued.

[*CAA 2001, ss 417(1)(2)(4), 418(5), 426–431*].

A trader claiming a balancing allowance may require it to be reduced to a specified amount (although this is unlikely to be of advantage, as the balance would be lost). [*CAA 2001, s 418(6)*].

For the denial of a balancing allowance where a disposal value is reduced as a result of a tax avoidance scheme, see **17.6** below.

Manner of making allowances and charges

[10.26] Allowances and charges made to or on any person under the new code are made by treating an allowance as an expense of, and a charge as a receipt of, the mineral extraction trade. See **17.46A** onwards below for the making of allowances to a company or partnership where the Northern Ireland rate of corporation tax applies (2017 onwards). [*CAA 2001, s 432; CTNIA 2015, Sch 1 para 13*].

Disposal values

[10.27] A disposal value is required to be brought into account in accordance with the following provisions, and may also be required to be brought into account under the provisions at **17.9** below).

If:

- qualifying expenditure has been incurred on the provision of any assets (including the construction of any works), and
- in any chargeable period any of those assets is disposed of, or for any reason otherwise permanently ceases (whether on the cessation of the trade or otherwise) to be used by the trader for a mineral extraction trade,

the 'disposal value' of the asset must be brought into account (see **10.23** above) for that chargeable period.

If a person has acquired a mineral asset and it begins to be used in a chargeable period by anyone in a way which constitutes development but is neither 'existing permitted development' nor development for the purposes of a mineral extraction trade carried on by that person, the disposal value of the asset must be brought into account for that chargeable period.

'*Existing permitted development*' is development which, at the time of the acquisition:

(i) had been, or had begun to be, lawfully carried out, or
(ii) could be lawfully carried out under planning permission granted by a general development order.

If the land is situated outside the UK, whether development is lawful is determined by reference to local law, and whether development could be lawfully carried out under planning permission granted by a general development order is determined as if the land were in England. [*CAA 2001, ss 420–422, 436*].

The amount of the disposal value depends on the nature of the event by reason of which it falls to be taken into account, as follows.

(a) On a sale, except where (b) below applies, the disposal value equals the net sale proceeds (see **2.33** above) plus any insurance moneys received by reason of any event affecting the price obtainable and any other compensation consisting of capital sums.
(b) On a sale below market value, the disposal value is market value unless:
    (i) the buyer's expenditure qualifies for either plant and machinery or research and development allowances, and the buyer is not a dual resident investing company (within *CTA 2010, s 949*) connected (within **2.34** above) with the seller, or
    (ii) there is a charge under *ITEPA 2003*.
(c) On demolition or destruction, the disposal value is equal to the net amount received for the remains plus any insurance and other compensation consisting of capital sums received.
(d) On permanent loss otherwise than in consequence of demolition or destruction, the disposal value is any insurance and other compensation consisting of capital sums received.
(e) On the permanent discontinuance of the trade before the occurrence of any of the above mentioned events, the disposal value is the same as the value specified for that event. In practice, where there is likely to be a long delay between the date of cessation of trade and any of the above events, HMRC take market value at the date of cessation as being the disposal value (CCAB Memorandum, June 1971).
(f) On any other event, the disposal value is the market value at the time of the event.

If, however, the asset is an interest in land, the disposal value is restricted by excluding the undeveloped market value (determined as in **10.13** above) at the time of the disposal etc.

[*CAA 2001, ss 423, 424*].

Where a disposal occurs, in whole or in part, of an oil licence (see **10.20** above) relating to an 'undeveloped area', and the consideration for the disposal includes either another oil licence relating to an undeveloped area or an obligation to undertake 'exploration or appraisal work' on the 'licensed areas' being disposed of, the value of the consideration is treated as nil. [*CAA 2001, ss 552–554, 556*].

Other cases

[10.28] If:

(a) a person has incurred qualifying expenditure,
(b) in any chargeable period (see **2.1** above) he receives a capital sum which it is reasonable to attribute, wholly or partly, to that expenditure, and
(c) the sum is not brought into account as a disposal value by the provisions described at **10.27** above,

so much of the sum as is reasonably attributable to the expenditure must be brought into account as a disposal value. [*CAA 2001, s 425*].

Demolition costs

[10.29] The 'net cost' of demolition of an asset representing qualifying expenditure is added to the qualifying expenditure when any balancing adjustment is calculated. The '*net cost*' is the excess (if any) of the cost of demolition over any moneys received for the remains of the asset. Where this provision applies, the net cost of demolition is not treated as expenditure on any asset replacing that demolished. [*CAA 2001, s 433*].

EXAMPLE 1

[10.30]

Arthur has carried on a mining trade at two UK sources, X and Y, for many years having first incurred qualifying expenditure relating to the sources in 1998. Arthur makes up accounts to 30 September each year. On 1 January 2017, the mineral deposits and mine works at X were sold at market value (which was below original cost) to Digger Ltd, an unconnected company, for £100,000 and £205,000 respectively (excluding undeveloped market values). Digger Ltd had not previously traded but commenced to carry on a mining trade at source X on the date of purchase (1 January 2017). Digger Ltd decided to make up its annual accounts to 30 June and in its six-month accounting period to 30 June 2017 incurs no capital expenditure relating to source X other than that previously mentioned. A new UK source, Z, was purchased by Arthur on 30 April 2017 and the following capital expenditure is incurred by him in respect of it during the year ended 30 September 2017.

	£
Purchase of UK mineral deposits (excluding undeveloped market value of land)	125,000
Construction of administration office (not part of a larger building)	30,000
Construction of mining works likely to have little value when working of source ceases	60,000
Staff hostel	40,000
Winning access to the deposits	180,000

The unrelieved qualifying expenditure brought forward at 1 October 2016 (the first day of the period of account ending on 30 September 2017) was:

	£
Source X: mineral asset	117,500
mining works and winning access	187,000
Source Y: mineral asset	95,000
mining works and winning access	200,000

Allowances due to Arthur for year ending 30 September 2017

	£	*Allow-ances* £
Source X: mineral asset		
Written-down value at 1.10.16	117,500	
Deduct: Sale proceeds	100,000	
Balancing allowance	£17,500	17,500
Source X: works and access		
Written-down value at 1.10.16	187,000	
Deduct: Sale proceeds	205,000	
Balancing charge	£18,000	(18,000)
Source Y: mineral asset		
Written-down value at 1.10.16	95,000	
Deduct: Writing-down allowance at 10% p.a.	9,500	9,500
Written-down value at 30.9.17	£85,500	
Source Y: works and access		
Written-down value at 1.10.16	200,000	
Deduct: Writing-down allowance at 25% p.a.	50,000	50,000
Written-down value at 30.9.17	£150,000	
Source Z: mineral asset		
Qualifying expenditure for period	125,000	
Deduct: Writing-down allowance at 10% p.a.	12,500	12,500
Written-down value at 30.9.17	£112,500	
Source Z: works		
Qualifying expenditure for period	60,000	
Deduct: Writing-down allowance at 25% p.a.	15,000	15,000
Written-down value at 30.9.17	£45,000	
Source Z: winning access		
Qualifying expenditure for period	180,000	
Deduct: Writing-down allowance at 25% p.a.	45,000	45,000
Written-down value at 30.9.17	£135,000	
Net mineral extraction allowances for year ended 30.9.17		£131,500

Allowances due to Digger Ltd for six-month accounting period ended 30 June 2017

		Allow-ances
	£	£
Source X: mineral asset		
Residue (£117,500 – £17,500)	100,000	
Deduct: Writing-down allowance at 10% p.a. × 6/12	5,000	5,000
Written-down value at 30.6.17	£95,000	
Source X: works and access		
Residue (£187,000 + £18,000)	205,000	
Deduct: Writing-down allowance at 25% p.a. × 6/12	25,625	25,625
Written-down value at 30.6.17	£179,375	
Mineral extraction allowances due for period		£30,625

The net allowances due to Arthur consist of writing-down and balancing allowances of £149,500 as reduced by a balancing charge of £18,000. In strictness the two amounts should be allowed and charged separately, the allowances as a trading expense and the charge as a trading receipt.

No mineral extraction allowance is due to Arthur in respect of the administration office or the hostel.

11

Research and Development

Introduction

[11.1] Capital allowances are available to a trader who incurs capital expenditure on research and development undertaken directly by him or on his behalf which is related to the trade. Allowances are also available for capital expenditure on research and development undertaken by a person directly or on his behalf if he subsequently begins a trade which is connected with the research and development. The allowance is equal to the whole of the expenditure and is given for the chargeable period in which it is incurred or, if later, the chargeable period in which the trade commences. A balancing adjustment is made if the trader ceases to own an asset representing qualifying expenditure or such an asset is demolished or destroyed. In most cases, the adjustment will be a balancing charge equal to the lesser of the disposal value and the allowance made.

It should be noted that the allowances are available to companies despite the introduction of the corporation tax intangible assets regime (see *CTA 2009, Pt 8*). The legislation governing the interaction of the regime with the capital allowances rules is not entirely clear, but it would appear that the intention is that those provisions of the regime which would otherwise override the capital allowances rules are to be disapplied. The provisions of the regime dealing with the realisation of intangible assets apply as if the cost of the asset did not include any expenditure on research and development. [*CTA 2009, s 814*]. See also **11.12** below.

See **17.1D** below for the prohibition on allowances where profits of a trade are calculated on the cash basis.

Qualifying expenditure

Definition

[11.2] Capital allowances are available in respect of 'qualifying expenditure' on 'research and development' (see **11.3** below).

'*Qualifying expenditure*' is capital expenditure incurred by a person on research and development directly undertaken by him or on his behalf if:

(a) he is a trader, and the research and development is related to his trade, or
(b) he subsequently sets up and commences a trade connected with the research and development.

The reference above to research and development related to a trade includes

- research and development which may lead to or facilitate an extension of the trade, and
- research and development of a medical nature which has a special relation to the welfare of workers employed in the trade.

All capital expenditure incurred for the carrying out of, or the provision of facilities for the carrying out of, research and development is treated as expenditure on research and development, except any incurred in the acquisition of rights in, or arising out of, research and development and any which is met by another person (see **2.8** above). Further exclusions relating to land are discussed at **11.4** below.

Where a person incurs capital expenditure which is only partly within the above definition, the expenditure may be apportioned as is just and reasonable for the purpose of granting allowances.

[*CAA 2001, s 437(1), s 438(1)(2), s 439*].

Research and development

[11.3] '*Research and development*' for these purposes means activities that are treated as research and development in accordance with 'generally accepted accounting practice' (see now *CTA 2010, s 1127*).

The statutory definition of research and development is supplemented by *The Research and Development (Prescribed Activities) Regulations 2004 (SI 2004 No 712)*. The Regulations operate by reference to the '*Guidelines on the Meaning of Research and Development for Tax Purposes*' issued by the Secretary of State for the Department of Trade and Industry on 5 March 2004 and updated by the Department for Business, Innovation and Skills on 6 December 2010. Activities treated as research and development in accordance with the Guidelines are to be treated as research and development for tax purposes. Likewise, activities excluded by the Guidelines are also excluded for tax purposes. The Guidelines consider the boundary of research and development and other related supporting activities that may be part of the wider innovation process. There is also detailed consideration of the treatment of computer software.

'*Oil and gas exploration and appraisal*' means activities carried out for the purpose of searching for 'petroleum' (as defined in *Petroleum Act 1998, s 1*) or for the purpose of ascertaining the extent, characteristics or reserves of a petroleum-bearing area in order to determine whether the petroleum is suitable for commercial exploitation.

[*CAA 2001, s 437(2)(3); ITA 2007, s 1003; CTA 2010, s 1134*].

Exclusion of land and dwellings in some cases

[11.4] The following two further restrictions apply for the purposes of research and development allowances.

(a) Expenditure on the acquisition of, or of rights in or over, land is not qualifying expenditure, except to the extent that the expenditure is referable, on a just and reasonable basis, to the acquisition of, or of rights in or over, or of plant or machinery which forms part of, a building or structure already constructed on the land.
(b) Expenditure on the provision of a dwelling is not expenditure on research and development, except that if:
   (i) the dwelling is part of a building the rest of which is used for research and development, and
   (ii) the expenditure apportionable, on a just and reasonable basis, to the dwelling is not more than one-quarter of the capital expenditure which is referable to the construction or acquisition of the whole building,

   the whole building is treated as used for research and development.

[*CAA 2001, ss 438(3)–(6), 440*].

An additional VAT liability or rebate is disregarded in applying (b)(ii) above (see **17.48** onwards below).

Exclusion of patents and know-how

[11.5] The exclusion of rights in, or arising out of research and development in **11.2** above presumably refers to patents and know-how. Although capital allowances may be available for capital expenditure on such assets when acquired for the purposes of a trade or otherwise (see CHAPTER **12** below), the rate of them is less generous than the immediate 100% rate under the research and development head. The distinction no doubt recognises that the acquisition of a patent, etc. implies that the initial research, which may have had a slim chance of success in producing any fruitful results, has resulted in a marketable product which may be exploited personally by the trader or assigned or licensed. The legislation gives a higher rate of allowance to the initial research and development expenditure than it does to any subsequent expenditure on the acquisition of 'safer' assets arising out of successful research.

'Asset'

[11.6] For the purpose of these provisions, 'asset' includes any part of an asset and the same expenditure is not to be taken into account for more than one trade. [*CAA 2001, ss 439(2), 571*].

Making of allowances

[11.7] Subject to **11.12** below, the allowance is equal to the whole of the expenditure and is given for the 'relevant chargeable period' (see **11.8** below). The allowance is given effect by treating it as an expense of the trade. Specific provision is made for a person to claim for the allowance to be reduced to a specific amount, although if this is done, no relief at all can be obtained for the balance of the expenditure. See **17.46A** onwards below for the making of allowances to a company or partnership where the Northern Ireland rate of corporation tax applies (2017 onwards).

[*CAA 2001, ss 441(1)(3), 450; CTNIA 2015, Sch 1 para 15*].

For the broadly similar treatment applying to an additional VAT liability, see **17.48** and onwards below.

Relevant chargeable period

[11.8] For corporation tax purposes the '*relevant chargeable period*' is the accounting period in which the expenditure was incurred or, if it was incurred before the accounting period in which the trade is set up and commenced, that accounting period.

For income tax purposes the '*relevant chargeable period*' is the period of account in which the expenditure was incurred or, if it is pre-trading expenditure, the period of account in which the trade commenced.

[*CAA 2001, s 441(2)*].

Separate company carrying out research and development

[11.9] A group of companies may form a separate company purely for the purpose of carrying out research and development for associated trading companies. Capital expenditure incurred for the purpose of carrying on its trade of research and development qualifies for research and development allowances unless specifically excluded (HMRC Capital Allowances Manual, CA60400). Associated companies making payments for carrying out the research receive research and development allowances (for capital payments), or the deduction available under **11.17** below for non-capital payments, or a deduction under general principles.

Case law

[11.10] The issue in *Gaspet Ltd v Elliss* CA 1987, 60 TC 91 turned on the words 'directly undertaken by him or on his behalf' (see **11.2** above). A fellow subsidiary of the taxpayer company was a member of two syndicates which held oil exploration licences granted by the Irish government. The actual exploration was done by other members of the syndicates ('the operators'), with operating costs being borne in proportion to the members' respective interests. The taxpayer company entered into an agreement with its fellow subsidiary under which it agreed to pay the latter company's share of the operating costs of the two syndicates' operations in return for all of the latter company's share of the oil won and saved. Although it was agreed that the taxpayer's contribution in its accounting period ended 14 September 1978 was on capital account, that oil exploration constituted scientific research (as the capital allowances legislation then required), that the taxpayer company did not directly undertake the research and that the operators did directly undertake the research, it was held that a claimant had to prove a close and direct link between himself and the work undertaken. This link could be forged by a wider form of relationship than agency under a contractual relationship but it could not merely be formed by the claimant contributing finance without himself procuring the research and taking direct responsibility for it. The taxpayer company's claim accordingly failed. (The judgment stated that if a person had stepped into the shoes of a member of a syndicate with the agreement of all concerned, but had not been a party to the original grant of the licence or to the arrangements commissioning the research, such a novation would have fallen within the ambit of the words at issue. Although the operating agreements allowed a member's involvement to be assigned, it was common ground that there had been no such assignment.) See also HMRC Capital Allowances Manual, CA60400.

In *Salt v Golding*, SpC [1996] SSCD 269, a writer (S) had published a book about film technology, which he had written himself, and a booklet about the construction of plays, which had been written in 1911. He claimed scientific research allowances in respect of a television, a video cassette recorder, a scanner and a tape streamer. The Revenue accepted that they qualified for allowances as plant or machinery but rejected the claim to scientific research allowances. The Special Commissioner dismissed S's appeal, holding that even if S were to be treated as carrying on a trade of publishing, he had not conducted any scientific research relating to that trade as required.

In *Brain Disorders Research Ltd Partnership v HMRC* FTT, [2015] UKFTT 325 (TC) allowances were denied to a partnership on the grounds that certain elements of the documentation under which research and development was sub-contracted were a sham and that the partnership was not trading.

Exclusion of double allowances

[11.11] See 2.2 above for the provisions preventing double allowances.

Balancing adjustments

Disposal event

[11.12] There is a '*disposal event*' where the person carrying on the trade ceases to own an asset representing qualifying expenditure or such an asset is demolished or destroyed.

For this purpose, a person ceases to own an asset in the case of a sale at the earlier of the time of completion or the time when possession is given.

On the happening of a disposal event, the trader must, unless a balancing charge arises under the industrial buildings (now repealed) or plant and machinery capital allowance provisions, bring a 'disposal value' (see **11.13** below) into account in respect of the expenditure concerned as follows.

(a) If the disposal event occurs in or after the chargeable period (see **2.1** above) for which an allowance under **11.7** above is made for the expenditure represented by the asset, the disposal value is brought into account for that period, unless it occurs after the trade has been permanently discontinued, in which case it is brought into account for the chargeable period of the discontinuance.

(b) If the disposal event occurs before the chargeable period for which an allowance under **11.7** above would fall to be made, the disposal value is brought into account for that later period.

The effect of bringing a disposal value into account is as follows.

(i) If the disposal value is required to be brought into account for the chargeable period for which an allowance under **11.7** above is made for the qualifying expenditure concerned, then the allowance is restricted to the excess (if any) of the expenditure over the disposal value.

(ii) If the disposal value is to be brought into account in a chargeable period later than that in which the allowance is made, the trader is liable to a balancing charge for that later period equal to the disposal value less any unclaimed allowance, except that the charge cannot exceed the allowance made. The balancing charge is given effect by treating it as a receipt of the trade.

[*CAA 2001, ss 441(1)(b), 442, 443(1)–(3)(7), 444, 450, 451*].

For the purposes of the above provisions, the disposal of an interest in an 'oil licence' (see **10.20** above) where part of the value is attributable to 'allowable exploration expenditure' incurred by the transferor is deemed to be a disposal by which the transferor ceases to own an asset representing the expenditure to which that part of the value is attributable. For this purpose, '*allowable exploration expenditure*' means qualifying expenditure on 'mineral exploration and access' (see **10.5** above). [*CAA 2001, ss 552, 555(1)(2)(4)*].

See **17.4** below for *CAA 2001, s 569*, which provides for a transferee to take on, in certain circumstances, the capital allowances position of the transferor.

The above provisions are adapted where an additional VAT rebate is incurred (see **17.48** and onwards below).

Where the asset representing qualifying expenditure is within the corporation tax intangible assets regime (see *CTA 2009, Pt 8*), a credit is to be brought into account under the provisions of that regime broadly equal to the excess of the realisation proceeds over the tax cost of the asset. [*CTA 2009, s 736*]. As noted at **11.1** above, the cost for this purpose excludes any expenditure on research and development, so that, on the face of it, a double charge could arise if a disposal value is also to be brought into account under the capital allowances provisions. It would appear that this result is avoided by virtue of *CTA 2009, s 906(1)* which provides that amounts brought into account in respect of any matter under the intangible assets regime are the only amounts to be brought into account for corporation tax purposes in respect of that matter. This implies that the realisation proceeds are not to be brought into account as a disposal value for capital allowances purposes and there is therefore no balancing adjustment. This interpretation of the legislation does, however, appear anomalous (see, for example, the position regarding computer software at **4.19** above), and it is not clear whether it is the intended result.

Disposal value

[11.13] Subject to the modifications below, '*disposal value*' in **11.12** above is determined as follows.

(a) If the disposal event is a sale at a price not below market value: the *net* proceeds (see **2.33** above).
(b) If the disposal event is the destruction of the asset: any proceeds from the remains together with any insurance or other compensation consisting of capital sums received.
(c) If the disposal event is the vesting of the asset in the trustee for civil recovery or any other person by a recovery order made under *PCA 2002, Part 5* or in pursuance of an order made under *PCA 2002, s 276* (i.e. a '*Part 5* transfer' of the asset — see **2.29** above): any compensating payment (see **2.29** above) made to the transferor. If no such payment is made, the disposal value is nil. If the asset is partnership property and compensating payments are made to one or more, but not all, of the partners, the disposal value is the sum of the payments.
(d) In any other case: market value.

[*CAA 2001, s 443(4)(5); PCA 2002, Sch 10 paras 26–29*].

If the disposal event is brought about by the demolition of the asset, the disposal value is reduced (or extinguished) by any costs of demolition. If the demolition costs exceed the disposal value, the excess is treated as qualifying expenditure on research and development incurred at the time of the demolition (or, if earlier, immediately before the trade is permanently discontinued), provided that, prior to its demolition, the asset had not begun to be used for purposes other than research and development related to the trade. Where these provisions apply, the demolition costs are not to be treated for any capital allowance purposes as expenditure on any property replacing the demolished asset. [*CAA 2001, s 445*].

If an asset representing qualifying research and development expenditure is likely to have to be demolished at appreciable cost when no longer required, it may be expedient to use it for research and development purposes only until the time of demolition. Presumably disuse (rather than use for another purpose) before demolition and after research and development use had ceased would not disallow relief for demolition costs.

Subject to the exception below for oil licences relating to undeveloped areas, where the disposal event is the disposal of an interest in an oil licence where part of the value of the interest is attributable to allowable exploration expenditure incurred by the transferor (see **11.12** above), the disposal value is so much of the transferee's expenditure as is, on a just and reasonable basis, attributable to that part of the value. The normal procedure for dealing with apportionments applies (see **2.30** above). [*CAA 2001, s 555(3)*].

Where a disposal occurs, in whole or in part, of an oil licence (see **10.20** above) relating to an 'undeveloped area', and the consideration for the disposal includes either another oil licence relating to an undeveloped area or an obligation to undertake 'exploration or appraisal work' on the 'licensed areas' being disposed of, the value of the consideration is treated as nil. [*CAA 2001, ss 552–554, 556*].

See also **17.2** onwards below (controlled and main benefit sales, etc.).

EXAMPLE 1

[11.14]

Adventure Ltd, which makes up its annual accounts to 31 December, has the following transactions in respect of capital expenditure incurred on research and development.

	Asset A	*Asset B*
	£	£
Cost on 20.5.17	10,000	10,000
Disposal value on 2.1.18	6,000	11,000

The following allowances and deemed trading receipts arise.

	Asset A	*Asset B*
	£	£
Accounting period to 31.12.17		
Allowance	£10,000	£10,000
Accounting period to 31.12.18		
Disposal value	6,000	11,000
Balancing charge (restricted to allowance received)	£6,000	£10,000

EXAMPLE 2

[11.15]

Adventure Ltd, as in Example 1 at **11.14** above, has the following further transactions in respect of capital expenditure incurred on research and development.

	Asset C	*Asset D*
	£	£
Cost on 1.9.12	10,000	10,000
Both assets destroyed on 1.12.17 after being used throughout for research and development		
Insurance proceeds	700	700
Scrap proceeds	500	500
Cost of demolition, etc.	300	2,000

The following allowances and deemed trading receipts or deductions arise.

	Asset C	*Asset D*
Accounting period to 31.12.12		
Allowance	£10,000	£10,000

Accounting period to 31.12.17	*Asset C* £	*Asset D* £
Insurance proceeds	700	700
Scrap proceeds	500	500
Disposal value before demolition costs	1,200	1,200
Demolition costs	(300)	(2,000)
Disposal value	900	(800)
Balancing charge	£900	
Allowance		£800

Allowances for certain expenditure given as trading deductions

[11.17] Where a person carrying on a trade:

(a) incurs expenditure not of a capital nature on research and development related to that trade and directly undertaken by him or on his behalf, or

(b) pays any sum to any scientific research association for the time being approved for these purposes by the appropriate Secretary of State, being an association which has as its object the undertaking of scientific research related to the class of trade to which the trade he is carrying on belongs, or

(c) pays any sum to be used for such scientific research as is mentioned in (b) above to any such university, college, research institute or other similar institution as is for the time being approved for these purposes by the appropriate Secretary of State,

the expenditure incurred or sum paid, as the case may be, may be deducted as an expense in computing the profits of the trade for tax purposes. The same expenditure may not be taken into account in relation to more than one trade.

Note that any question as to whether any activities constitute scientific research for the purposes of (b) and (c) above is to be referred by the Board to the appropriate Secretary of State, whose decision is final.

The definition in **11.3** above applies for the purposes of these provisions.

[*ITTOIA 2005, ss 87, 88; CTA 2009, ss 87, 88*].

The wording of the above provisions should be noted carefully. For both (b) and (c) above it does not matter whether the research is directly related to the trade concerned or whether the sum paid is on revenue or capital account provided the research is related to the class of trade concerned. In such circumstances, and where a payment on capital account is concerned, a deduction under this head may be an alternative to 'true' capital allowances. To qualify under (a) above, the expenditure must be on revenue account; be directly undertaken by the trader or on his behalf; and be related to the trade carried on. It does not matter whether the expenditure is deductible or not under the general trading deductions rules (but obviously a double deduction is not allowed).

It should be noted that additional reliefs are available for certain revenue expenditure of companies on research and development. See *CTA 2009, Pt 3 Ch 6A, Pt 13*.

12

Patents and Know-how

Introduction

[12.1] Separate, but similar, capital allowance codes are available for expenditure on the purchase of patent rights and the acquisitions of industrial know-how. Patent allowances are available whether or not the rights are to be used for trade purposes, provided that any income in respect of the rights is liable to UK tax. Know-how allowances are only available where the know-how is acquired for use in a trade. Both codes operate under a pooling system similar to that for plant and machinery allowances. Writing-down allowances are given at 25% of the unrelieved balance on each pool and there is provision for balancing adjustments. See **12.2–12.13** below for the patents code and **12.14–12.22** below for the know-how code.

Capital allowances are not available under either code for corporation tax purposes where the intangible assets regime applies to the patent rights or know-how. See **12.2** below.

Effect of the cash basis

[12.1A] Patent and know-how allowances are not available to a person carrying on a trade to which the cash basis applies. See **17.1D** below.

Accordingly, for 2017/18 onwards, where a person 'enters the cash basis' for a tax year, no 'cash basis deductible amount' may be carried forward as unrelieved qualifying expenditure under either code (see **12.5** and **12.18** below) from the chargeable period ending with the basis period for the previous tax year. A '*cash basis deductible amount*' is any amount that would have been deductible on the cash basis if it had been paid in the tax year for which the person enters the cash basis. The amounts that can and cannot be carried forward must be determined on a just and reasonable basis. For this purpose, a person '*enters the cash basis*' for a tax year if a cash basis election has effect for that year and such an election did not have effect immediately before the beginning of the basis period for that year. [*CAA 2001, ss 461A, 475A; F(No 2)A 2017, Sch 2 paras 56, 58, 64*].

Although capital allowances are not available in respect of the unrelieved qualifying expenditure which is not carried forward, for 2017/18 onwards, a deduction for that expenditure is allowable in the first cash basis year. This rule applies only to the extent that the amounts of expenditure in question are cash basis deductible amounts. Special rules apply if the expenditure in question has not been paid in full. If the capital allowances given in respect of 'relevant expenditure' exceed the amount actually paid, the difference is treated as a receipt in calculating the profits for the first cash basis year. If the amount paid exceeds the allowances the excess is allowed as a deduction in that year. '*Relevant expenditure*' is any amount of expenditure which is a cash basis deductible amount. The amount of capital allowances given and whether or to what extent expenditure is relevant expenditure are determined on a just and reasonable basis.

ITTOIA 2005, ss 240C, 240D; FA 2013, Sch 4 para 38; F(No 2)A 2017, Sch 2 paras 7, 9, 64].

See **17.1D** below for the requirement to bring into account a disposal value or balancing charge in certain cases where qualifying expenditure was incurred before entry into the cash basis which would not have been deductible under the cash basis if it had been incurred in the first cash basis year.

The following provisions apply for 2017/18 onwards where a person carrying on a trade leaves the cash basis in a chargeable period having incurred expenditure which would have been qualifying expenditure under the know-how code or qualifying trade expenditure under the patents code if it had not been incurred at a time when the cash basis applied. At least some of the expenditure must have been brought into account in calculating the profits of the trade on the cash basis. A person leaves the cash basis in a chargeable period for this purpose if immediately before the beginning of the period a cash basis election had effect but such an election does not have effect for the period itself.

For the purpose of determining the person's available qualifying expenditure (see **12.5** and **12.18** below) for the chargeable period in which he leaves the cash basis the whole of the expenditure must be allocated to the pool and the available qualifying expenditure in the pool is then reduced by the 'relieved portion' of the expenditure allocated to it.

The '*relieved portion*' of expenditure is the higher of the amount for which a deduction has been allowed in computing the trade profits and, for the purposes of know-how allowances, the amount for which such a deduction would have been allowed if the expenditure had been incurred wholly and exclusively for the purposes of the trade.

For the purpose of determining any disposal values (see **12.7** and **12.20** below), the expenditure is treated as qualifying expenditure or, for patent allowances, qualifying trade expenditure. As a result, where there is a sale of the patent rights or know-how after the person leaves the cash basis, a disposal value must be brought into account.

[*CAA 2001, ss 462A, 477A; F(No 2)A 2017, Sch 2 paras 57, 59, 64*].

For the similar provisions dealing with the effect of entering the cash basis on allowances for plant and machinery and mineral extraction see **5.33**, **5.47** and **10.2A** above.

Note that, at the time of writing, *F(No 2)A 2017* had not completed its passage through Parliament. These provisions are therefore subject to any changes made during the Parliamentary process.

Patents

Qualifying expenditure

[12.2] Capital allowances are available on 'qualifying expenditure' incurred on the purchase of 'patent rights'. '*Patent rights*' means the right to do, or authorise the doing of, anything which would otherwise be an infringement of a patent. See also **12.4** below.

'*Qualifying expenditure*' is either:

(a) '*qualifying trade expenditure*', meaning capital expenditure incurred by a person on the purchase of patent rights for the purposes of a trade within the charge to UK tax carried on by him; or
(b) '*qualifying non-trade expenditure*', meaning capital expenditure incurred by a person on the purchase of patent rights if any income receivable by him in respect of the rights would be liable to UK tax and the expenditure is not qualifying trade expenditure.

Expenditure incurred for the purposes of a trade about to be carried on is treated as incurred on the first day of trading, unless all the rights have been sold before that day. The same expenditure cannot be qualifying trade expenditure in relation to more than one trade.

[*CAA 2001, ss 464, 467–469*].

Note that capital allowances are not available for corporation tax purposes where the intangible assets regime applies to the patent rights. The regime applies to 'intangible fixed assets' (as defined, which definition will normally include patent rights) which are:

(A) created by the company on or after 1 April 2002;
(B) acquired by the company on or after 1 April 2002 from a person who is not a 'related party' (as defined); or
(C) acquired by the company on or after 1 April 2002 from a related party in the following cases:
    (i) where the asset is acquired from a company in whose hands the asset fell within the intangible fixed asset regime;
    (ii) where the asset is acquired from an intermediary who acquired the asset on or after 1 April 2002 from a third party which was not a related party of the intermediary (at the time of the intermediary's acquisition of the asset) or of the company (at the time of the company's acquisition); or
    (iii) where the asset was created by any person on or after 1 April 2002.

Where an asset excluded from the regime by these provisions is transferred after 27 June 2002 to another company in circumstances where *TCGA 1992, s 139* (reconstruction or amalgamation involving transfer of business) or *s 140A* (transfer of UK trade to company resident in another EU member State) apply to treat the transfer as giving rise to neither gain nor loss, the asset is likewise excluded in the hands of the transferee company.

Anti-avoidance provisions apply, broadly, to treat an asset created on or after 1 April 2002 and acquired by a company from a related party as excluded from the regime by the above provisions where either the asset is derived from assets themselves so excluded or the acquisition is directly or indirectly in consequence of, or in connection with, the disposal of an excluded asset. The provisions apply in relation to the debits and credits to be brought into account under the regime for accounting periods ending on or after 5 December 2005 (treating, for this purpose only, accounting periods straddling that date as two separate periods, the first ending on 4 December 2005 and the second beginning on 5 December 2005).

For the purposes of the above provisions (and subject to certain exceptions), an intangible asset is regarded as created or acquired after 31 March 2002 to the extent that expenditure on its creation or acquisition is incurred after that date. Where the expenditure would, but for the intangible assets regime, be qualifying expenditure for capital allowances purposes, expenditure is for this purpose treated as incurred when an unconditional obligation to pay it comes into being (even if payment is not required until a later date).

[*CTA 2009, ss 880–895, 906(1)*].

Patent law

[12.3] Patent law is obviously outside the scope of this book but a patent can be defined as a monopoly granted, usually by the government of the country in which it is sought to have such a monopoly, to an inventor or his assignee in connection with the exploitation of an invention or technical innovation. The patent will probably have a limited life but during that time it may be retained by the patentee for his own use, or it may be sold or otherwise transferred, or a licence may be granted in respect of it whilst still being retained (whether or not it is exploited by the patentee himself).

Transfer of rights

[12.4] The grant of a licence in respect of a patent is treated as a sale of part of patent rights; and if it gives exclusive rights for the remainder of the term, it is treated as a sale of the whole of the rights. The acquisition of a licence in respect of a patent is treated as a purchase of patent rights. Expenditure on a right to acquire in the future rights in respect of a patent which has not yet been granted is treated as expenditure on the purchase of patent rights; and if the patent rights are subsequently acquired, the expenditure is treated as expenditure on the purchase of those rights. The recipient of such expenditure is treated as having received the proceeds of a sale of patent rights. Use of a patent by the Crown or the government of the country concerned is treated as taking place in pursuance of a licence, and any sums paid in respect of the use are treated accordingly. [*CAA 2001, ss 465, 466, 482*].

Allowances and charges

Writing-down and balancing allowances

[12.5] Qualifying expenditure is pooled, with a separate pool for each trade in respect of which a person has qualifying trade expenditure and one pool for all of the person's qualifying non-trade expenditure.

For each pool, a writing-down allowance is available for a chargeable period where the 'available qualifying expenditure' for that period exceeds the total of any 'disposal values' (see **12.7** below) falling to be brought into account, unless the period is the 'final chargeable period' (in which case a balancing allowance will be available, see below). The allowance is given at the rate of 25% of the excess per annum. If the chargeable period is longer than a year, the writing-down allowance is proportionately increased. Where the chargeable period is shorter than a year, or (where relevant) the trade is carried on only for part of the period, the allowance is proportionately reduced. After deducting any writing-down allowance, any remaining balance left in the pool (the '*unrelieved qualifying expenditure*') is carried forward to the next chargeable period to form part of the available qualifying expenditure for that period. This amount is usually referred to as the 'written-down value'. No unrelieved qualifying expenditure can be carried forward from the final chargeable period. A writing-down allowance may be reduced to an amount specified in the claim.

The '*final chargeable period*', in relation to a pool of qualifying trade expenditure is the chargeable period in which the trade is permanently discontinued. In relation to a pool of qualifying non-trade expenditure, it is the chargeable period in which the last of the patent rights concerned either comes to an end without being revived or is wholly disposed of. Where the available qualifying expenditure exceeds the disposal values to be brought into account for the final chargeable period, a balancing allowance equal to the excess is made.

The '*available qualifying expenditure*' in a pool for a chargeable period is made up of any qualifying expenditure allocated to the pool for the period plus any unrelieved qualifying expenditure (see above) in the pool brought forward from the previous chargeable period. In allocating qualifying expenditure to a pool, the following rules must be applied.

(1) An amount is not to be allocated to a pool if it has been taken into account in determining the available qualifying expenditure for an earlier chargeable period.
(2) Expenditure is not to be allocated to a pool for a chargeable period before that in which it is incurred.
(3) Expenditure is not to be allocated to a pool for a chargeable period if in any earlier chargeable period the patent rights concerned have come to an end without being revived or have been wholly disposed of.

Nothing in these rules requires a person to allocate expenditure to a pool for the chargeable period in which it is incurred. Expenditure can be allocated instead for a later period (provided that the requirement in (3) above is still met). Of course, it would not normally be in a taxpayer's interest to delay allocation of expenditure to a pool, but this possibility would be useful where, for example, expenditure has not been allocated through an oversight.

[*CAA 2001, ss 470, 471(1)(2)(4)–(6), s 472(1)–(4)(6), ss 473–475*].

Balancing charges

[12.6] If in any chargeable period, the disposal values to be brought into account in a pool exceed the available qualifying expenditure in the pool, a balancing charge equal to the excess arises for that period. [*CAA 2001, ss 471(1)(3), 472(5)*].

Disposal value

[12.7] A 'disposal value' must be brought into account in the chargeable period in which the whole or any part of patent rights on which qualifying expenditure has been incurred are sold, which includes the granting of a licence. A disposal value may also be required to be brought into account under the provisions for finance lessors at **17.9** below.

The '*disposal value*' is normally the lower of the net sale proceeds (see **2.33** above) and the cost of the patent rights sold (but see **12.8** below where connected persons are involved). The net proceeds are limited to capital sums.

[*CAA 2001, ss 476, 477(1)*].

Connected persons, etc.

[12.8] If patent rights were previously acquired through transactions involving connected persons (within **2.34** above), the disposal value on a sale is restricted by reference to the highest price paid for those rights by any of the connected persons.

If capital expenditure is incurred on the purchase of patent rights, and either:

(a) the parties are connected (within **2.34** above), or
(b) it appears the sole or main benefit which might otherwise have been expected to accrue to the parties from the sale, or the sale and other transactions, would have been the obtaining of an allowance under **12.5** above,

the expenditure is treated for the purpose of making allowances and charges under **12.5** and **12.6** above as not exceeding the 'relevant limit'. The '*relevant limit*' is:

(i) where a disposal value falls to be brought into account by the seller, an amount equal to that disposal value;
(ii) where no disposal value falls to be brought into account by the seller but the seller receives on the sale a capital sum in respect of which he is chargeable to tax under *CTA 2009, s 912* or *ITTOIA 2005, s 587*, an amount equal to that sum;
(iii) in any other case, an amount which is the smallest of: the market value of the rights; the amount of expenditure incurred as capital expenditure by the seller on acquiring the rights; and the amount of expenditure incurred as capital expenditure by any person connected with the seller on acquiring the rights.

[*CAA 2001, ss 477(2)(3), 481*].

[12.9] Because of the effect of the provisions in **12.8** above, *CAA 2001, ss 567–570* (controlled and main benefit sales, etc. as discussed in **17.2** below) do not apply. [*CAA 2001, s 567(1)*].

EXAMPLE 1

[12.10]

X has the following transactions in respect of patents used for the purposes of his trade. He makes up accounts to 31 March each year.

	Patent A	*Patent B*
	£	£
Year ended 31.3.16		
Cost	10,000	
Year ended 31.3.17		
Cost		6,500
Proceeds	8,000	
Year ended 31.3.18		
Proceeds		7,000

The capital allowance computations are as follows.

	£	£
Year ended 31.3.16		
Expenditure		10,000
WDA (25% p.a.)	2,500	2,500
		7,500
Year ended 31.3.17		
Expenditure		6,500
		14,000
Deduct: Disposal value		
		6,000
WDA (25% p.a.)	1,500	1,500
		4,500
Year ended 31.3.18		
Deduct: Disposal value (lower of cost and proceeds)		6,500
Balancing charge		£2,000

Note

(a) The excess of proceeds over cost, (£7,000–£6,500) = £500 is chargeable to income tax over six years, commencing with the year in which the proceeds are received, by reason of *ITTOIA 2005, ss 587–591*. An election can be made for the excess of £500 to be taxed in one sum in the year in which it is received. Such an election must be made within one year from 31 January following the tax year in which the proceeds are received. [*ITTOIA 2005, s 590(6)*].

Making of allowances and charges

[12.11] Allowances and charges in respect of qualifying trade expenditure (see **12.2** above) are given effect by treating allowances as expenses of the trade and charges as trade receipts.

An allowance to which a person is entitled in respect of qualifying non-trade expenditure (see **12.2** above) is given effect by deducting it or setting it off against the person's 'income from patents' for the current tax year or accounting period. For income tax purposes, the deduction is given effect at Step 2 of the calculation in *ITA 2007, s 23*. For income tax purposes, a charge is assessable directly to income tax. For corporation tax purposes, a charge is treated as income from patents. Where an allowance exceeds the income from patents for a tax year or accounting period, the excess is carried forward and set, at the first opportunity, against subsequent income from patents.

'*Income from patents*' means any royalty or other sum paid in respect of the use of a patent, any balancing charge or any amount taxed as income under *CTA 2009, ss 912* or *918* or *ITTOIA 2005, ss 587, 593* or *594*.

[*CAA 2001, ss 478–480, 483*].

Other expenditure

[12.12] Fees or expenses incurred by a trader to obtain a grant or extension of a patent, or in connection with a rejected or abandoned application for one, are deductible as trading expenses. [*ITTOIA 2005, s 89; CTA 2009, s 89*]. Fees or expenses incurred by a non-trader in connection with the grant, maintenance or extension of a patent, or a rejected or abandoned patent application, are deductible from patent income if in a trade they would have been allowable as trading expenses. For income tax purposes, the deduction is given effect at Step 2 of the calculation in *ITA 2007, s 23*. [*ITTOIA 2005, ss 600, 601; CTA 2009, ss 924, 925*].

Whether expenditure capital or revenue

[12.13] As might be expected there have been a number of cases in which the issue hinged on whether a payment made for the benefit of acquiring or using a patent has been on account of capital or revenue (e.g. a royalty which might also be an annual payment and therefore subject to the deduction of income tax by the payer).

A fixed amount (payable in instalments) for a licence to use a patent for five years was held to be capital expenditure by the payer (*Desoutter Brothers Ltd v J E Hanger & Co. Ltd and Artificial Limb Makers Ltd KB*, [1936] 1 All E R 535). See also **12.4** above for the treatment of licences. A UK resident company acquired a licence to use a French patent for ten years on payment of £25,000, of which £15,000 was payable immediately with £5,000 after six months and another £5,000 after twelve months, and ten annual payments of £2,500 each as royalty. It was held that the £25,000 was the payment of a capital sum but the other payments of £2,500 were in respect of the user of a patent (*CIR v British Salmson Aero Engines* CA 1938, 22 TC 29).

Know-how

Introduction

Qualifying expenditure

[12.14] Capital allowances are available for 'qualifying expenditure' incurred on the acquisition of 'know-how' (see **12.16** below). For this purpose, '*qualifying expenditure*' is capital expenditure, not otherwise deducted for tax purposes, incurred by a person where:

(a) the know-how is acquired for use in a trade then carried on by him; or
(b) he subsequently sets up and commences a trade in which the know-how is used.

Where the know-how is acquired together with a trade, or part of a trade, in which it is used, the consideration for it is treated (if the buyer provided the consideration) as a payment for goodwill by virtue of *CTA 2009, s 178(3)* or *ITTOIA 2005, s 194(3)* and is not qualifying expenditure, except that this does not apply if:

(i) the parties jointly so elect under *CTA 2009, s 178* or *ITTOIA 2005, s 194(5)* within two years of the disposal, or
(ii) the trade was previously carried on wholly outside the UK,

in which case the expenditure is qualifying expenditure.

Expenditure is not, however, qualifying expenditure where the buyer is a body of persons (which includes a partnership) over whom the seller has control (within **2.31** above), or vice versa, or both buyer and seller are bodies of persons over whom some other person has control.

Qualifying expenditure within (b) above is treated as incurred on the first day of trading. The same expenditure cannot be qualifying expenditure in relation to more than one trade.

[*CAA 2001, ss 452(1), 454, 455*].

Note that capital allowances are not available for corporation tax purposes where the intangible assets regime applies to the know-how. [*CTA 2009, s 906(1); FA 2002, Sch 29 para 1(3)*]. See **12.2** above for the commencement provisions for the regime.

Sale with a trade, etc.

[12.15] Where know-how is sold with a trade or part of a trade and the circumstances are that a joint election could be made, it may well be in the purchaser's interest to persuade the seller to enter into the joint election so that the purchaser can claim allowances. This will be no problem provided that the seller is prepared to accept the receipt (to the extent it is not taken into account as a disposal value — see **12.20** below) being taxable as income and not as disposal proceeds for goodwill under the capital gains tax regime. The situation will obviously depend upon the tax situation of the seller generally, e.g. availability of trading or other losses.

Meaning of know-how

[12.16] '*Know-how*' means any industrial information and techniques likely to assist in the manufacture or processing of goods or materials, or in the working of a mine, oil well or other source of mineral deposits (including the searching for, discovery or testing of, or obtaining access to deposits), or in the carrying out of any agricultural, forestry or fishing operations. [*CAA 2001, s 452(2)(3)*].

Being essentially information, e.g. secret processes, know-how cannot be protected under patent law (although it may be protected under other statute law, such as copyright, and under other legal process, such as breach of confidence). Although the legislation is in terms of the 'disposal' of know-how, a better term might be 'disclosure' since know-how is incapable, in English law at least, of being assigned or licensed since it is not, in its true sense, 'property' (although undoubtedly it is an 'asset' for such purposes as capital gains tax). Know-how is, however, to be treated as property for capital allowances purposes, and references in the capital allowances provisions to the purchase or sale of property include the acquisition or disposal of know-how. [*CAA 2001, s 453*].

[12.17] The definition of 'know-how' is obviously restricted in its scope covering, broadly, only information and techniques of an 'industrial' nature for use in the manufacture and processing of goods etc., mining, and agriculture, forestry and fishing. It must probably be assumed that the word 'industrial' in the definition given in **12.16** above qualifies both the words 'information' and 'techniques'. If the ordinary meaning of 'industrial', taken as 'relating to or consisting in any branch of manufacture or trade', is used, it may be possible, for example, to obtain allowances on an appropriate part of a capital payment made for the grant of a right to operate a high street printing and duplicating business under the terms of a franchise. As no special meaning is given to the meaning of 'industrial' by the legislation, it could be argued that the fact that stationery is being manufactured and processed at the rear of a retail shop may not prevent allowances being claimed. If so, it may be possible to demonstrate that any capital franchise fee is at least partly for the provision of information and techniques, the remainder of the payment being referable to any goodwill element. Whether HMRC will agree to this broad definition of what is 'industrial' must, however, be open to question.

HMRC do not regard expenditure on 'commercial know-how' as qualifying for allowances, commercial know-how being 'know-how' which does not directly assist in manufacturing and processing operations. Examples of commercial know-how given by HMRC include information about marketing, packaging or distributing a manufactured product. Such information, they argue, does not assist in the manufacture of that product, but is concerned with selling the product once it has been manufactured (Revenue Tax Bulletin August 1993, p 86).

Where non-qualifying information and techniques are in point, and the payment made for them is definitely not allowable as a revenue expense under general principles, it might be possible to apply existing case law as regards the meaning of 'plant' (for a general discussion of which, see **4.9** onwards above). In the case of *Munby v Furlong* CA 1977, 50 TC 491 (which allowed the costs of law books and reports of a barrister who had just started practice to rank as plant and thus overruled *Daphne v Shaw* KB 1926, 11 TC 256) it was said that '"plant" ... extends to the intellectual storehouse which ... any ... professional man has in the course of carrying on his profession'. If it is remembered that capital allowances were first introduced for know-how acquisitions in 1968, i.e. well before the overruling of *Daphne* by *Munby*, there seems to be a sensible case for arguing that certain capital expenditure on the provision of information which is to be a permanent 'data bank' for the purposes of a *trade* (as well as a profession) may constitute expenditure on 'plant'. However, even if the hurdle of demonstrating that a payment is for plant can actually be overcome, there will sometimes be a problem with the requirement of such legislation as *CAA 2001, s 11(4)(b)* that the plant be 'owned' by the person carrying on the trade. The ICAEW in their memorandum TR 637 of October 1986 pointed out that lump sum payments for licences to use computer software for a five-year term were probably on capital account, but since the asset remained the property of the licensor, capital allowances for plant were unavailable to the licensee. They pointed out that this situation applied generally to computer software where the payment made was not on revenue account and did not qualify under the plant and machinery code of allowances because of this problem (but see **4.19** above). Unless the information, etc. included in the software was likely to be of assistance in a manufacturing process, for example, no allowances would be due under the statutory 'know-how' heading.

However, *F(No 2)A 1992* removed this discrimination against software by introducing provisions to allow computer software acquired after 9 March 1992 for the purposes of a trade etc. to be treated as plant for the purposes of claiming capital allowances (see **4.19** above).

Writing-down and balancing allowances

[12.18] Qualifying expenditure is pooled, with a separate pool for each trade in respect of which a person has qualifying expenditure.

For each such pool, a writing-down allowance is available for a chargeable period where the 'available qualifying expenditure' for that period exceeds the total of any 'disposal values' (see **12.20** below) falling to be brought into account, unless the period is the 'final chargeable period' (in which case a balancing allowance will be available, see below). The allowance is given at the rate of 25% of the excess per annum. If the chargeable period is longer than a year, the writing-down allowance is proportionately increased. Where the chargeable period is shorter than a year, or the trade is carried on only for part of the period, the allowance is proportionately reduced. After deducting any writing-down allowance, any remaining balance left in the pool (the '*unrelieved qualifying expenditure*') is carried forward to the next chargeable period to form part of the available qualifying expenditure for that period. This amount is usually referred to as the 'written-down value'. No unrelieved qualifying expenditure can be carried forward from the final chargeable period. A writing-down allowance may be reduced to an amount specified in the claim.

The '*final chargeable period*' is the chargeable period in which the trade is permanently discontinued. Where the available qualifying expenditure exceeds the disposal values to be brought into account for that period, a balancing allowance equal to the excess is made.

The '*available qualifying expenditure*' in the pool for a chargeable period is made up of any qualifying expenditure allocated to the pool for the period plus any unrelieved qualifying expenditure (see above) in the pool brought forward from the previous chargeable period. In allocating qualifying expenditure to the pool, the following rules must be applied.

(1) An amount is not to be allocated to the pool if it has been taken into account in determining the available qualifying expenditure for an earlier chargeable period.
(2) Expenditure is not to be allocated to a pool for a chargeable period before that in which (or, under the preceding year basis, before that in the basis period for which) it is incurred.

Nothing in these rules requires a person to allocate expenditure to a pool for the chargeable period in which it is incurred. Expenditure can be allocated instead for a later period. Of course, it would not normally be in a taxpayer's interest to delay allocation of expenditure to a pool, but this possibility would be useful where, for example, expenditure has not been allocated through an oversight.

[*CAA 2001, ss 457(1)(2)(4)(5), 458(1)–(4)(6), 459–461*].

Balancing charges

[12.19] If in any chargeable period the disposal values to be brought into account in the pool exceed the available qualifying expenditure, a balancing charge equal to the excess arises for that period. [*CAA 2001, ss 457(1)(3), 458(5)*].

Disposal value

[12.20] A 'disposal value' must be brought into account in the chargeable period in which the trader sells know-how on which he has incurred qualifying expenditure. No disposal value need be brought into account if the consideration for the sale is treated as a payment for goodwill under *CTA 2009, s 178(2)* (previously *ICTA 1988, s 531(2)*) or *ITTOIA 2005, s 194(2)*.

The '*disposal value*' is the net sale proceeds (see **2.33** above) so far as they consist of capital sums.

[*CAA 2001, s 462; CTA 2009, Sch 1 para 511*].

It should be noted that the disposal value is not limited to allowances previously given.

EXAMPLE 2

[12.21]

P has the following transactions in respect of know-how used for the purposes of his trade. He makes up accounts to 31 March each year.

	Know-how A	*Know-how B*
Year ended 31.3.16	£	£
Cost	10,000	
Year ended 31.3.17		
Cost		6,500
Proceeds	8,000	
Year ended 31.3.18		
Proceeds		7,000

The capital allowance computations are as follows.

Year ended 31.3.16	£
Expenditure	10,000
WDA (25% p.a.)	2,500
	7,500
Year ended 31.3.17	
Expenditure	6,500
	14,000
Deduct: Disposal proceeds	8,000
	6,000
WDA (25% p.a.)	1,500
	4,500
Year ended 31.3.18	
Deduct: Disposal value (proceeds)	7,000
Balancing charge	£2,500

Making of allowances and charges

[12.22] Allowances and charges are given effect by treating allowances as expenses of the trade and charges as trade receipts. [*CAA 2001, s 463*].

13

Dredging

Introduction

[13.1] Capital allowances for expenditure on dredging undertaken in the interests of navigation are available only to traders within limited specified categories. Writing-down allowances are given on a straight-line basis at 4% per annum over a 25-year writing-down period. Initial allowances were historically available but were discontinued in 1986. If the trade is permanently discontinued a balancing allowance is given for any remaining unrelieved expenditure. There is no provision for a balancing charge to arise.

See **17.1D** below for the prohibition on allowances where profits of a trade are calculated on the cash basis.

Entitlement to allowances

[13.2] Capital allowances are available to a person carrying on a 'qualifying trade' (see **13.3** below) where 'qualifying expenditure' is incurred on 'dredging'. '*Dredging*' is not fully defined, but:

(a) does not include things done otherwise than in the interests of navigation, and
(b) subject to (a) above, does include the removal, by any means, of anything forming part of or projecting from the bed of the sea or of any inland water, even if it is wholly or partly above water.

The provisions apply equally to the widening of an inland waterway in the interests of navigation.

Expenditure is 'qualifying expenditure' if it is capital expenditure and:

- it is incurred for the purposes of the qualifying trade by the person carrying it on, and
- if the qualifying trade is within **13.3**(ii) below, the dredging is for the benefit of vessels coming to, leaving or using any dock or other premises occupied by him for the purposes of the trade.

If expenditure is incurred only partly for a qualifying trade, the qualifying expenditure is limited to only so much of it as can justly and reasonably be treated as incurred for the qualifying trade. For this purpose a trade of which only part is a qualifying trade is treated as two trades.

[*CAA 2001, ss 484(1)(3)(4), 485*].

See HMRC Capital Allowances Manual, CA80400 for the treatment of claims for dredging allowances by the operator of a marina.

For the purpose of the allowances, a person who contributes a capital sum to dredging expenditure incurred by another person is treated as incurring capital expenditure on that dredging; but capital expenditure incurred by a person is not treated as incurred for a trade of his if it is met, directly or indirectly, by the Crown or any UK or overseas government or public or local authority, or by capital sums contributed by another person for purposes other than those of that trade. [*CAA 2001, ss 533, 543*].

The provisions of **2.2** above apply to prevent double allowances.

Qualifying trade

[13.3] A '*qualifying trade*' is a trade or undertaking which, or part of which, either:

(i) consists of the maintenance or improvement of the navigation of a harbour, estuary or waterway, or

(ii) is of a kind listed in *CAA 2001, s 274* (which related to industrial buildings allowances before their repeal).

The following trades fall within (ii) above:

- (a) a trade consisting of manufacturing goods or materials;
- (b) a trade consisting of subjecting goods or materials to a process (including maintaining or repairing goods or materials;
- (c) a trade consisting of storing goods or materials:
  - to be used in the manufacture of other goods or materials; or
  - to be subjected, in the course of a trade, to any process; or
  - which, having been manufactured or produced, or subjected, in the course of a trade, to a process, have not yet been delivered to any purchaser; or
  - on their arrival in any part of the UK from a place outside the UK;
- (d) a trade consisting of ploughing or cultivating land occupied by another, carrying out any other agricultural operation on such land or threshing another's crops (including vegetable produce);
- (e) a trade consisting of working land outside the UK used for growing and harvesting crops (including vegetable produce), husbandry or forestry;
- (f) a trade consisting of catching or taking fish or shellfish;
- (g) a trade consisting of working a source (including a mine, oil well or source of geothermal energy) of mineral deposits (including any natural deposits or geothermal energy capable of being lifted or extracted from the earth);
- (h) an undertaking for the generation, transformation, conversion, transmission or distribution of electrical energy which is carried on by way of trade;
- (i) an undertaking for the supply of water for public consumption carried on by way of trade;
- (j) an undertaking for the supply of hydraulic power carried on by way of trade;

(k) an undertaking for the supply of sewerage services (within Water Industry Act 1991) carried on by way of trade;

(l) a highway undertaking (i.e. so much of any undertaking relating to the design, building, financing and operation of roads as is carried on for the purposes of, or in connection with, the exploitation of highway concessions) carried on by way of trade;

(m) a tunnel, bridge or inland navigation undertaking carried on by way of trade; and

(n) a dock (including any harbour, wharf, pier, jetty or other works in or at which vessels can ship or unship merchandise or passengers, other than a pier or jetty primarily used for recreation) undertaking carried on by way of trade

For the purposes of (2) above, maintaining or repairing goods or materials is not a qualifying trade if the goods or materials are employed in a trade or undertaking, the maintenance or repair is carried out by the person employing the goods or materials and the trade or undertaking is not itself a qualifying trade.

As noted above, trades within (a) to (n) above were also qualifying trades for the purposes of the now repealed industrial buildings allowances. In the context of those allowances there is a considerable body of case law concerned, in particular, with processing and storage (see (b) and (c) above) and with whether a part of a trade is a qualifying trade. Leading cases include *Crusabridge Investments Ltd v Casings International Ltd* ChD 1979, 54 TC 246; *Bestway (Holdings) Ltd v Luff* ChD [1998] STC 357 and *Maco Door & Window Hardware (UK) Ltd v HMRC* HL [2008] STC 2594. For detailed discussion of the case law see the 2010/11 and earlier editions of this work.

[*CAA 2001, ss 274, 276(3), 484(2)*].

Initial allowance

[13.4] An initial allowance of 15% was available on qualifying expenditure incurred before 1 April 1986, or incurred before 1 April 1987 under a contract entered into before 14 March 1984 by the person incurring the expenditure. The allowance was made for the chargeable period in which the expenditure was incurred or, for income tax purposes, the chargeable period related to the incurring of the expenditure. [*CAA 1968, s 67(1)(a); FA 1985, s 61(1)*].

Writing-down allowance

[13.5] A writing-down allowance is available to a person for a chargeable period if he is at any time in that period carrying on a qualifying trade for the purposes of which qualifying expenditure on dredging has been incurred and that time falls within the 'writing-down period'. The allowance is at a rate of 4% per annum on a straight-line basis on expenditure incurred after 5 November 1962. The rate was 2% per annum on expenditure incurred before 6 November 1962. If the chargeable period is longer than a year, the writing-down allowance is proportionately increased. Where the chargeable period is shorter than a year the allowance is proportionately reduced. The total allowances made in respect of an item of expenditure must not exceed the amount of the expenditure. Where an initial allowance was also available, the first annual writing-down allowance was available in the same year as the initial allowance.

A writing-down allowance is not available for a chargeable period in which a balancing allowance is made, and the legislation specifically provides that a writing-down allowance may be reduced to a specified amount.

The 'writing-down period' is the period of 25 years (50 years for expenditure incurred before 6 November 1962) beginning with the first day of the chargeable period in which the qualifying expenditure was incurred (or, under the preceding year basis, the first day of the chargeable period in the basis period for which the expenditure is incurred). If:

(i) any allowance was made under *FA 1965, Sch 14 para 27(2)* for a company's accounting period falling wholly or partly within 1964/65 or 1965/66, and
(ii) any allowance was made for income tax purposes for either year,

all the periods for which allowances were made are added together in calculating the writing-down period, even though (according to the calendar) the same time is counted twice. For the meaning of 'basis period' in relation to the preceding year basis see the 2010/11 or earlier edition of this work.

[*CAA 2001, s 487, Sch 3 paras 103, 105*].

Balancing allowance

[13.6] If the qualifying trade is permanently discontinued or sold, a balancing allowance is made equal to the excess of the qualifying expenditure over the allowances previously made, whether to the same or different persons. A trade is not treated as permanently discontinued by virtue of provisions deeming such a discontinuance to occur where a person ceases to carry on a trade (see now *CAA 2001, s 577(2A)* and *ITTOIA 2005, s 18*). No balancing allowance is made in the case of a sale if:

(i) the buyer is a body of persons (including a partnership) over whom the seller has control (within **2.31** above), or vice versa, or both are connected persons (see **2.34** above) or are bodies of persons under common control; or
(ii) the sole or main benefit to be expected from the sale, or transactions of which the sale is one, is the obtaining of a tax advantage (see **2.32** above) other than under the plant and machinery code.

The balancing allowance is made for the chargeable period in which the trade is permanently discontinued or sold.

[*CAA 2001, s 488, Sch 3 para 104*].

Whether expenditure capital or revenue

[13.7] Whether expenditure on dredging is on capital or revenue account will often be a point of contention. In *Ounsworth v Vickers Ltd* KB 1915, 6 TC 671 the yards of the taxpayer company were approached by a channel. Since the company's initial occupation of the yards some 15 years before, the harbour authorities had neglected their duty to dredge the channel and it had silted up. The authorities were unable to meet the cost of restoring the channel to its condition of 15 years before and so, after negotiations with the company, a cheaper scheme was devised. The company and the authorities contributed to the cost, the company's contribution being the greater. Certain work was carried out; all but a small part of it related to a partial restoration of the channel to its original condition. An essential feature of the scheme was that, because the channel was only partly to be restored, provision had to be made for a deep-water berth so that vessels could rest there to await high water before crossing a bar which crossed the channel on its entry to the sea. If the work had not been carried out, the company would not have been able to deliver a vessel it was building at that time, but there was also evidence that the general business of the company could no longer be safely carried on because of the inability of vessels to enter or leave the company's yards readily.

It was accepted by Rowlatt J that, compared with revenue expenditure being made every year on dredging, expenditure would still be on revenue account if 'the dredging was not done for a year or two because it was not worthwhile to do so and was only done when matters became serious enough, say in three years'. However, he observed that the company did not 'simply put right the default of the harbour authority, they enter into an agreement by which in conjunction a new thing is done. They do not dredge enough to enable their ships to get out merely by virtue of dredging, but they adopt a different plan'. It was held that the expenditure was incurred in making what was in effect a new means of access to the yards, and was therefore not deductible as a revenue expense in computing the taxpayer's trading profits.

Harbour authorities have been accepted as making revenue expenditure where such expenditure related to dredging necessary to remove the accumulation of silt over a number of years (*Dumbarton Harbour Board v Cox* CS 1918, 7 TC 147). Although the removal of a wreck, as capital expenditure, would now qualify for allowances under **13.2**(b) above, it was held in the special circumstances pertaining in *Whelan v Dover Harbour Board* CA 1934, 18 TC 555 that expenditure relating to the removal of wrecks by the Board was on revenue account.

EXAMPLE 1

[13.8]

X Ltd, which makes up its accounts to 31 December annually, incurs qualifying capital expenditure on dredging two estuaries, under a contract made by it in 2013. £1,000,000 is incurred in February 2015 in dredging Estuary A and £500,000 is incurred in May 2015 in dredging Estuary B. On 31 December 2017 the trade is sold to an unconnected third party.

	Estuary A	*Estuary B*
	£'000	£'000
Accounting period to 31.12.15		
Expenditure	1,000	500
Writing-down allowance (4% p.a.)	40	20
	960	480
Accounting period to 31.12.16		
Writing-down allowance (4% p.a.)	40	20
	920	460
Accounting period to 31.12.17		
Balancing allowance	920	460

Advance expenditure

[13.9] If a person incurs capital expenditure:

(a) with a view to carrying on a trade (or part); or
(b) in connection with a dock or other premises and with a view to occupying the dock or premises for the purposes of a qualifying trade within **13.2**(ii),

the expenditure is treated as being incurred on the first day of trading or occupation as appropriate. [*CAA 2001, s 486*].

Making of allowances

[13.10] A writing-down or balancing allowance is given effect by treating it as an expense of the trade. See **17.46A** onwards below for the making of allowances to a company or partnership where the Northern Ireland rate of corporation tax applies (2017 onwards). [*CAA 2001, s 489; CTNIA 2001, Sch 1 para 17*].

14

Other Reliefs for Capital Expenditure

Introduction

[14.1] As noted in Chapter 1 above, capital allowances constitute the main exception to the rule that capital expenditure is not allowable in computing taxable income. This chapter describes three further exceptions to that rule, which provide reliefs similar to capital allowances without being part of the capital allowances code. The three reliefs are:

- landlord's energy-saving allowance (now abolished; see **14.2** below);
- contaminated or derelict land remediation relief (see **14.3** below); and
- relief for capital expenditure on cemeteries and crematoria (see **14.4** below).

Landlord's energy-saving allowance

[14.2] A taxpayer who carries on a property business where the land involved includes or consists of a dwelling-house can obtain a deduction in computing the profits of the business for capital expenditure incurred on installing certain energy-saving items in or for the benefit of the dwelling-house. For income tax purposes the relief is available for expenditure incurred within any of the tax years 2004/05 to 2014/15 inclusive. For corporation tax purposes the relief is available for expenditure incurred on or after 8 July 2008 and before 1 April 2015. A deduction is given for expenditure which:

- is capital expenditure incurred in the acquisition, and installation in the dwelling-house or alternatively, (for income tax purposes, in relation only to expenditure incurred on or after 6 April 2007) and insofar as the expenditure is for the benefit of the dwelling-house, in a building containing the dwelling-house, of a 'qualifying energy-saving item'; and
- is incurred wholly and exclusively for the purposes of the property business, is not otherwise deductible in computing the profits of that business and does not qualify for any capital allowance.

'*Qualifying energy-saving items*' are cavity wall insulation; loft insulation; (from 7 April 2005) solid wall insulation; (from 6 April 2006) hot water system insulation and draught proofing; and (from 6 April 2007) floor insulation.

The deduction is limited to a maximum of £1,500 per dwelling-house, irrespective of the number of persons incurring expenditure or entitled to make a deduction in respect of that dwelling-house. Before 6 April 2007, the deduction was limited to a maximum of £1,500 per *building*, irrespective of the number of dwelling-houses contained in the building and the number of persons eligible to make a deduction in respect of it. Any contribution received from another person towards the expenditure must be excluded in arriving at the deductible amount.

Where expenditure is incurred in acquiring and installing an energy-saving item in more than one dwelling-house, in a building containing more than one dwelling-house or in a building containing one or more dwelling-house and one or more properties which are not dwelling-houses, the expenditure must be apportioned between all of the properties which benefit from it on a just and reasonable basis, The deduction in respect of each dwelling-house is then restricted to the amount apportioned to it (subject to the £1,500 maximum). A similar apportionment must be made where a dwelling-house or the building containing it is owned jointly or in common by the taxpayer and other persons or is subject to differing estates or interests.

For 2004/05 only for income tax purposes, it was necessary to make a claim for the deduction to be given.

The deduction is not available if, at the time the item is installed, the dwelling-house is under construction or is comprised in land in which the taxpayer does not have an interest or is in the course of acquiring an interest or a further interest. The property business must not consist in the commercial letting of furnished holiday accommodation (within *ITTOIA 2005, ss 322–328B; CTA 2009, ss 264–269A*) or, if it does so consist to any extent, the dwelling-house must not itself constitute any of that accommodation for the tax year or accounting period in question. The taxpayer must not also be taking rent-a-room relief (within *ITTOIA 2005, s 793* or *s 797*) in respect of any qualifying residence which consists of or includes the dwelling-house.

Where the qualifying conditions are satisfied in relation to part only of any expenditure, a deduction is allowed on the basis of a just and reasonable apportionment of the expenditure. Relief under *ITTOIA 2005, s 57* or *CTA 2009, s 61* for *pre-trading expenditure* (as applied to property businesses by *ITTOIA 2005, s 272* and *CTA 2009, s 210*) is allowed only for expenditure incurred within the *six months* before the claimant commences the property business.

The Treasury are given wide powers to vary these provisions by regulation; this includes the power to vary the definition of a 'qualifying energy-saving item' and to impose conditions by reference to which a specified item will qualify. The current regulations include an appeals procedure where their application raises any question as to the amount of deduction to which a person is entitled.

[*ITTOIA 2005, ss 312–314, Sch 2 para 73; CTA 2009, ss 251–253, Sch 2 para 50; SI 2007 No 3278; SI 2008 No 1520*].

Contaminated or derelict land remediation expenditure

[14.3] Relief is available for expenditure on land in the UK incurred by a company carrying on a trade or UK property business for the purpose of remedying contamination or, for expenditure incurred on or after 1 April 2009, dereliction of the land. The relief consists of three elements:

- a deduction in computing the profits of the trade or business for capital expenditure which is 'qualifying land remediation expenditure';
- an additional deduction of 50% for qualifying land remediation expenditure (whether capital or revenue expenditure); and
- where the trade or business makes a loss, the option to convert that part of the loss which is attributable to land remediation relief into a payable tax credit.

Relief is available for expenditure incurred on or after 11 May 2001 which is 'qualifying land remediation expenditure' incurred by a company in respect of 'land' in the UK acquired by the company for the purposes of a trade or UK property business carried on by it (pre-trading expenses being ignored). '*Land*' is defined as 'any estate, interest or rights in or over land' and, for these purposes, includes buildings (see HMRC Corporate Intangibles, Research & Development Manual, CIRD60130 and *Interpretation Act 1978, Sch 1*). To qualify for the relief, the taxpayer must acquire a major interest in the land. A major interest is a freehold interest in the land or a leasehold interest which is either a grant or an assignment of a lease for a term of at least seven years. Relief is not available if all or part of the land was in a contaminated or derelict state wholly or partly as a result of the company's own actions or inaction (or the actions or inaction of a person with a 'relevant connection' to the company (see below)).

Capital expenditure is, if the company so elects by written notice, allowed as a deduction in computing the profits of the trade or business for the accounting period in which the expenditure was incurred (and may also attract the enhanced deduction described below). The election must specify the accounting period in respect of which it is made and must be made within two years after the end of that period. The relief does not apply to so much of the 'qualifying land remediation expenditure' as represents expenditure which has been allowed as a deduction for an earlier accounting period or in respect of which any capital allowances have been, or may be, given.

'*Qualifying land remediation expenditure*' is expenditure meeting the following five conditions.

(a) It must be on land all or part of which is in a '*contaminated state*'. For expenditure incurred before 1 April 2009, this means that the land is in such a condition, by reason of substances in, on or under it, that 'harm' is being caused (or there is a possibility of harm being caused) or '*pollution of controlled waters*' (i.e. the entry into 'controlled waters' of any poisonous, noxious or polluting matter or any solid waste matter) is being, or is likely to be, caused. For expenditure on or after 1 April 2009, land is in a '*contaminated state*' if something in, on or under the land is in such a condition that 'relevant harm' is likely to be caused. However land is not contaminated by reason only of the presence in, on or under it of living organisms or decaying matter deriving from living organisms, air or water or anything other than the result of industrial activity, although this may be disapplied by statutory instrument.
'*Harm*' in this context means:
    (i) harm to the health of living organisms (an example of harm would be illness caused by asbestos);

- (ii) interference with the ecological systems of which any living organisms form part;
- (iii) offence to the senses of human beings; or
- (iv) damage to property.

'*Relevant harm*' is defined as death, significant injury or damage to living organisms, significant pollution of controlled water, material adverse impact on the ecosystem or structural or other significant damage to buildings or other structures or interference with buildings or other structures that significantly compromises their use.

For expenditure incurred on or after 1 April 2009, the relief is extended to remedial expenditure to clear land of arsenic, arsenical compounds, radon or Japanese Knotweed. Only such part of a site as is contaminated by these items qualifies for relief.

Also for expenditure incurred on or after 1 April 2009, the relief is also available for expenditure on land which is in a '*derelict state*' (i.e. it is not in productive use and cannot be put into such use without the removal of buildings etc.).

A nuclear site is not contaminated or derelict land for the purpose of this relief.

'*Controlled waters*' are as under *Water Resources Act 1991, Pt III* or comparable Scottish or Northern Irish legislation. For expenditure incurred on or after 1 April 2009, HMRC accept that a 'substance' includes plants, e.g. Japanese Knotweed. Any cases open at 24 November 2008 were settled on the basis of the revised guidance in HMRC Brief 62/2008.

The land must be in a contaminated state when acquired, or in the case of derelict land, be in such a state throughout the period beginning on the earlier of 1 April 1998 and the date the major interest was acquired. These requirements may be varied by statutory instrument.

(b) It must be on 'relevant contaminated land remediation' or, for expenditure incurred on or after 1 April 2009, 'relevant derelict land remediation' undertaken directly by the company or on its behalf. '*Relevant contaminated land remediation*' is the doing of any works, the carrying out of any operations or the taking of any steps in relation to the land (or adjoining or adjacent land), or any controlled waters affected by the state of that land, for the purpose of preventing or minimising, or remedying or mitigating the effects of, any harm, or any pollution of controlled waters, by reason of which the land is in a contaminated state, or restoring the land or waters to their former state. Preparatory activities are included provided that they are for the purpose of assessing the condition of the land or waters concerned and are connected to the remediation activities undertaken by the company or on its behalf. The removal of Japanese Knotweed to a landfill site is not relevant contaminated land remediation. '*Relevant derelict land remediation*' is the doing of any works, the carrying out of any operations or the taking of any steps for the removal of post-tensioned concrete heavyweight construction, building foundations and machinery bases, reinforced concrete pilecaps, reinforced concrete basements, or redundant services which are located below the ground. Again, preparatory activities are included provided that they are for the purpose of assessing the condition of the land concerned and are connected to the remediation activities undertaken by the company or on its behalf.

(c) It must be incurred on employee costs (see below) or on materials employed directly in the remediation or be 'qualifying expenditure on sub-contracted land remediation'.

(d) It must be expenditure which would not have been incurred had the land not been in a contaminated or derelict state. Any increase in expenditure by reason only of the land being in a contaminated or derelict state is treated as satisfying this condition, as is expenditure on works done, operations carried out or steps taken mainly for the purposes described in (b) above.

(e) No grant or subsidy may be received in respect of the expenditure, nor may it be met directly or indirectly by any person other than the company (any unallocated payment being allocated for this purpose in a just and reasonable manner).

As regards (c) above, employee costs include all employment income (other than benefits in kind), employer NICs and pension contributions paid to, or in respect of, directors or employees directly and actively engaged in the relevant land remediation in (b) above. If between 20% and 80% of a director's or employee's time is spent directly and actively so engaged, an appropriate proportion of costs related to him or her qualify. If less than 20% is so spent, none of the costs qualify, and if more than 80%, all of the costs qualify. (For expenditure incurred before 1 April 2004, employment costs include benefits in kind.) Staff providing support services (e.g. secretarial or administrative services) are not thereby treated as engaged in the activities they support.

'*Qualifying expenditure on sub-contracted land remediation*' is expenditure consisting of payments made for sub-contracted land remediation work. Except where the company and the sub-contractor are connected persons (within *CTA 2010, s 1122*), such payments qualify in full. Where the company and the sub-contractor are connected persons, then provided that, in accordance with generally accepted accounting practice, the whole of the sub-contractor payment and all of the sub-contractor's 'relevant expenditure' has been brought into account in determining the sub-contractor's profit or loss for a 'relevant period', the whole of the sub-contractor payment (up to the amount of the sub-contractor's 'relevant expenditure') qualifies. '*Relevant expenditure*' is expenditure on employee costs or materials (as under (c) above), not of a capital nature, which is incurred by the sub-contractor in carrying on, on behalf of the company, the activities to which the sub-contractor payment relates, and which satisfies (e) above. A '*relevant period*' is a period for which the sub-contractor draws up accounts and which ends not more than twelve months after the end of the period of account of the company in which, in accordance with generally accepted accounting practice, the sub-contractor payment is brought into account in determining the company's profit or loss. Any necessary apportionment of expenditure for these purposes is made on a just and reasonable basis.

A person has a '*relevant connection*' to a company if he is or was a 'connected person' within *CTA 2010, s 1122* either when the action (or inaction) in question occurred, or when the land in question was acquired by the company, or at any time when the remediation work was undertaken.

[*CTA 2009, ss 1144–1148, 1170–1179; SI 2009 No 2037*].

For any accounting period in which the company is carrying on a trade or UK property business in computing profits from which qualifying land remediation expenditure is deductible (including capital expenditure allowed as a trade deduction), the company may claim relief for an additional 50% of that expenditure, i.e. for 150% of that expenditure in total. For contaminated land the land must be in a contaminated state at the time of acquisition and for derelict land the land must be have been derelict throughout the period beginning with the earlier of 1 April 1998 and the date of acquisition. Any capital expenditure allowed as a deduction in computing profits is not an allowable deduction for capital gains purposes under *TCGA 1992, s 39*. [*CTA 2009, s 1149*].

For any accounting period in which the company has a 'qualifying land remediation loss', it may claim a 'land remediation tax credit' equal to 16% of the amount of that loss. The 16% figure is subject to revision by the Treasury by order. A '*qualifying land remediation loss*' arises for an accounting period in which the company is entitled to an enhanced deduction as above and incurs a loss in the trade or UK property business concerned. The amount of the qualifying land remediation loss is so much of the trading or UK property business loss as is 'unrelieved' or, if less, 150% of the related qualifying land remediation expenditure. A trading or UK property business loss is '*unrelieved*' for this purpose to the extent that the loss has not been relieved under *CTA 2010, s 62(1)–(3)* or has not and could not have been relieved by a claim under *CTA 2010, s 37* for relief against profits of the same period, and has not otherwise been relieved (including under *CTA 2010, s 37* against profits of earlier periods, and has not been surrendered as group relief or group relief for carried-forward losses. Losses carried back or brought forward to the accounting period in question are disregarded for this purpose. The amount of the tax credit may be applied in discharging any liability of the company to corporation tax, or if PAYE and NIC payments are in arrears for the period to which the payment relates. Where the company's return is under enquiry, HMRC may make a provisional payment of such amount as they think fit.

On receiving a claim for land remediation tax credit, HMRC will pay to the company the amount of the tax credit, and the amount of the company's trading or UK property business losses available to be carried forward from the period will accordingly be reduced by the amount of the qualifying land remediation loss for the period (or by a corresponding proportion thereof where the amount of the tax credit claimed was less than 16% of the qualifying land remediation loss). Where a tax credit has been claimed in respect of a qualifying land remediation loss, the related qualifying land remediation expenditure is treated as non-allowable expenditure for capital gains tax purposes under *TCGA 1992, s 39*.

A claim for payment of a land remediation tax credit must be made in a company tax return (or amended return) for the accounting period for which the credit is claimed, within one year of the filing date for that return or by such later time as HMRC may allow. It can similarly only be amended or withdrawn by amendment of the company tax return within the same time limit. It must specify the quantum of the amount claimed.

[*CTA 2009, ss 1151–1158; FA 1998, Sch 18 paras 10(2A), 83G–83L; FA 2012, Sch 16 paras 193, 194; F(No 2)A 2017, Sch 4 paras 137, 138*].

Any transaction attributable to arrangements (including any scheme, agreement or understanding, whether or not legally enforceable) whose sole or main object is to enable a company to obtain a relief or payment under any of the above provisions to which it would not otherwise be entitled, or a greater relief or payment than that to which it would otherwise be entitled, is disregarded in determining the amount of any such relief or payment. [*CTA 2009, s 1169; FA 2012, Sch 16 para 206*].

Cemeteries and crematoria

[14.4] In computing profits of a trade consisting of, or including, the carrying on of a cemetery or the carrying on of a crematorium (and, in connection with it, the maintenance of memorial garden plots), a deduction as a trading expense for any period of account (i.e. any period for which accounts are drawn up) is allowed for:

- the capital cost of purchasing and preparing land (including cost of levelling, draining or otherwise making suitable) sold for interments or memorial garden plots *in that period*; and
- a *proportion* (based on the ratio of number of grave-spaces/garden plots sold in the period to that number plus those still available — see Example 1 at **14.5** below) of 'residual capital expenditure'.

'*Residual capital expenditure*' is the total 'ancillary capital expenditure' incurred before the end of the period of account in question after subtracting:

(i) amounts previously deducted under these provisions;
(ii) any sale, insurance or compensation receipts for assets representing ancillary capital expenditure and sold or destroyed; and
(iii) certain expenditure before the basis period for 1954/55.

'*Ancillary capital expenditure*' is capital expenditure incurred on any building or structure (other than a dwelling-house), or on the purchase or preparation of other land not suitable or adaptable for interments or garden plots, which is in the cemetery or memorial garden and is likely to have little or no value when the cemetery or garden is full; it also includes capital expenditure on the purchase or preparation of land taken up by said buildings and structures.

For these purposes, sales of land in a cemetery include sales of interment rights, and sales of land in a memorial garden include appropriations of part of the garden in return for dedication fees etc. Expenditure met by subsidies cannot be deducted as above (the detailed rules being similar to those for capital allowances at **2.8** above).

Any change in the persons carrying on the trade is ignored; allowances continue as they would to the original trader, disregarding any purchase price paid in connection with the change itself.

[*ITTOIA 2005, ss 169–172; CTA 2009, ss 146–149*].

As regards crematoria, see also *Bourne v Norwich Crematorium* Ch D 1967, 44 TC 164.

EXAMPLE 1

[14.5]

GE, who operates a funeral service, owns a cemetery for which accounts to 31 December are prepared. The accounts to 31.12.17 reveal the following:

(i)	Cost of land representing 110 grave spaces sold in period	£3,400
(ii)	Number of grave spaces remaining	275
(iii)	Residual capital expenditure on buildings and other land unsuitable for interments	£18,250

The allowances available are:		£
(a)	Item (i)	3,400
(b)	$\frac{110}{110 + 275} \times £18,250$	5,214
		£8,614

Note

(a) £8,614 will be allowed as a deduction in computing GE's trading profits for the period of account ending on 31 December 2017.

15

Partnerships

Introduction

[15.1] This chapter concentrates on those provisions of the capital allowances legislation which are peculiar to partnerships. Many other provisions do, of course, apply equally to partnerships as they do to individuals and companies. The coverage below concerns itself with exceptions to the norm and assumes the reader to be familiar with the basic rules relating to the taxation of partnerships.

Assets used by the partnership

Assets owned by the partnership

[15.2] This section deals with assets to which all the partners can be considered to be entitled and which are partnership property (see *Partnership Act 1890, ss 20, 21*).

Assets owned by a partnership qualify for capital allowances if they would have so qualified if owned by an individual. As to whether an asset is owned by the partnership, as opposed to being owned by an individual partner, each of the points listed below may be relevant.

(i) Is the asset held in the partnership name or on trust for the continuing partners? This would be of particular relevance as regards land, but will not always be applicable to machinery and plant.
(ii) Where the capital expenditure was pursuant to a written contract, is the contract in the partnership name?
(iii) Was the expenditure invoiced to the partnership?
(iv) Was payment made through the partnership bank account or otherwise with moneys belonging to the firm?
(v) Does the asset appear in the partnership accounts?

If the answer to any one or more of the above questions is 'no', it does not necessarily mean that the asset is not partnership property. For example, an asset may be acquired by a partner personally on behalf of the firm. Similarly, a positive answer to one of the above questions will not always be conclusive. An asset may be paid for by the firm but charged to an individual partner as part of his drawings. It is necessary to consider all the facts.

Treatment of allowances

[15.3] Individual partners are assessed to tax separately on their respective shares of the profits of a partnership for the period of account. Partners are assessed on the basis of each having a separate notional sole trade or profession taxed in accordance with the normal basis period rules and which begins on entry to the partnership or when the partnership itself commences and finishes upon exit from the partnership or when the partnership itself ceases. Thus, each partner will have his or her own overlap, overlap relief and, if applicable, terminal loss relief. Untaxed income received by the partnership is treated similarly. [*ITTOIA 2005, ss 849–856*]. As capital allowances are given as trading expenses of periods of account of the partnership business (see **2.11** above) they are not dealt with as a separate matter.

Assets owned by individual partners

[15.4] Capital allowances may also be due in respect of property owned by an individual partner but used in a trade carried on by the partnership. Under self-assessment it is not, however, possible for partners to make individual claims for capital allowances with regard to expenditure they have incurred personally. To obtain allowances for such personal expenditure, claims have to be included in the partnership return. [*TMA 1970, s 42(6)(7); CTA 2009, Sch 1 para 302*]. The Revenue have stated that they will accept adjustments for such expenditure in the tax computations included in the partnership return providing the adjustments are made before apportionment of the net profit between the partners (SAT 1 (1995), para 5.17).

There is specific legislation concerning a partnership using, for the purposes of its qualifying activity, plant or machinery belonging to one or more partners but not being partnership property. The same allowances, deductions and charges are given or made as if such plant or machinery had at all material times belonged to all the partners and had been partnership property, and as if everything done by or to any of the partners in relation to the plant or machinery had been done by or to all of them. No balancing adjustment will arise, or disposal value fall to be brought into account, on a sale or gift of the plant or machinery by one or more partners to another partner or other partners, if it continues to be used for the qualifying activity after the sale or gift. These provisions do not apply if the plant or machinery is let by the individual partner or partners to the partnership or is used in consideration of any payment which would be an allowable deduction in computing the partnership profits. [*CAA 2001, s 264*].

EXAMPLE 1

[15.5]

A and B have been in partnership trading as interior decorators and sharing profits in the ratio 2:1 for many years. The firm's accounting date is 31 March, and after the calculation of the allowances for the year ended 31 March 2017, unrelieved qualifying expenditure in the partnership plant and machinery main pool amounts to £10,000. A owns a van which is used, by both A and B, entirely for partnership business; its tax written-down value at 31 March 2017 is £1,000. B buys a car for £5,000 on 4 April 2017 and uses it partly for partnership business; the proportion of business use to total use, based on mileage, for the period from date of purchase to 31 March 2018 is 40%. There are no other additions or disposals, either by the partnership or by either of the partners. The adjusted profit for tax purposes before capital allowances for the year to 31 March 2018 amounts to £40,000.

Capital allowances and the partnership trade profit for the year ended 31 March 2018 are as follows.

	Main pool	*Property owned by A*	*Property owned by B*
	£	£	£
Written-down values brought forward	10,000	1,000	—
Additions			5,000
Writing-down allowances (18%)	(1,800)	(180)	(900)
Written-down values carried forward	£8,200	£820	£4,100
Total allowances due	£1,800	£180	£360[1]

1 (This footnote refers to the figure above, £360, which is on the 'Total allowances due' line) Restricted to 40% of £900.

The trade profit for the year ended 31 March 2018 and its division between the partners is as follows.

	Total profit	*A's share*	*B's share*
	£	£	£
Profit before capital allowances	40,000		
Capital allowances (£1,800 + £180 + £360)	(2,340)		
	37,660		
Add back: capital allowances —			
property owned by A	(180)		
property owned by B	(360)		
Adjusted profit (shared 2:1)	38,200	25,467	12,733
Less: capital allowances —			
property owned by A	(180)	(120)	(60)
property owned by B	(360)		(360)
Taxable profit	£37,660	£25,347	£12,313

Partnership changes

[15.6] As a consequence of the rules at **15.3** above, where a partner leaves or joins a partnership, the partnership trade etc. is not treated as discontinued and recommenced provided that there is at least one continuing partner (which also applies to a sole trader beginning to carry on the trade etc. in partnership or a former partner beginning to carry on the trade etc. as a sole trader). The opening year and cessation basis period provisions only apply to the individuals who joining or leaving the partnership.

On a change of partners in a partnership which carries on a 'relevant activity' capital allowances (except those for research and development) therefore continue to be calculated as if there had been no change (unless there is a cessation). Allowances and charges are made to the present partners as if they had carried on the relevant activity at all times and everything done by or to their predecessors had been done by or to them. For this purpose, a '*relevant activity*' is a trade, profession, vocation or property business.

Slightly different rules apply in the case of plant and machinery allowances, in that the partnership must be carrying on a qualifying activity (within **4.2** above, but excluding an office or employment, and without the restriction mentioned in **4.3** above) rather than a relevant activity, and annual investment, first-year and writing-down allowances are made to the present partners as if the plant or machinery had been owned at all times by all the partners as partnership property, and everything done by or to their predecessors had been done by or to them. A balancing charge or allowance is made on or to the partners at the time of the event giving rise to the adjustment and is calculated as if those partners had carried on the qualifying activity at all times and everything done by or to their predecessors had been done by or to them.

[*CAA 2001, ss 263, 557, 558*].

It follows that when there are unused allowances brought forward, an outgoing partner will not obtain any benefit therefrom, but nor will he have any liability for balancing charges arising from assets in use at the time he was a partner. If, of course, an outgoing partner has, say, plant or machinery which he personally owns and which is withdrawn from the business, a balancing adjustment will arise due to the items in question ceasing to be used for the purposes of the business.

If all of the partners are replaced simultaneously so that the change is treated as the permanent cessation of one 'relevant activity' (as above), or in the case of plant and machinery, 'qualifying activity' (modified as above), and the commencement of another (i.e. the new partnership succeeds to the activity), any property which was in use, immediately before the change, for the purposes of the discontinued activity and, without being sold, is in use, immediately after the change, for the purposes of the new activity, is treated for capital allowance purposes (save those for research and development) as if it had been sold by the old partnership to the new partnership at its open market value. However, no annual investment allowance or initial or first-year allowances (where such would otherwise have been available) are available to the new partnership. [*CAA 2001, ss 265, 557, 559*].

As regards plant and machinery only, an election may in certain circumstances be made as under **7.18** above for capital allowances to continue to be made as if the trade had not been discontinued.

Claim for reduced allowances

[15.7] Capital allowances are made to the partnership, being the person or persons from time to time carrying on the trade or other activity. A claim for a reduced capital allowance (including a claim for a nil allowance) (see **2.46** above) must be made by the partnership as a whole. It is not open to an individual partner to claim that his share of capital allowances be reduced. This is the case even if the allowance is in respect of plant or machinery provided by the individual partner for use in the trade. The plant or machinery is regarded as partnership property for capital allowances purposes by virtue of *CAA 2001, s 264* (see **15.4** above).

Partnerships involving companies

Anti-avoidance: restriction of loss reliefs

[15.8] There are anti-avoidance provisions in *CTA 2010, ss 958–962* which can prevent a company, which is a member of a partnership carrying on a trade, from setting off its share of partnership losses and gift aid donations against income not derived from the partnership and denies the company the right to offset its own losses against its share of partnership profits. These provisions operate where certain arrangements are in existence, whereby a partner other than the company (or a person connected with that partner) receives any payment, or enjoys any benefit in money's worth, in respect of the company's share of partnership profits or losses, or the company itself (or a person connected with it) receives any payment, or enjoys any benefit in money's worth, in respect of its share of partnership losses. A payment between companies in consideration of losses surrendered in respect of group relief does not, however, bring these provisions into operation. [*CTA 2010, ss 958–962*].

These provisions apply to a company's share of partnership profits or losses falling within any of the provisions listed in *CTA 2010, s 1173* as if they were trading profits or losses. Any plant or machinery allowances due in respect of special leasing (see **6.19** above) are treated as allowances given effect in calculating the profits of that trade. [*CTA 2010, s 961(3)*].

[15.9] See **2.36** above for provisions preventing an individual member of a partnership involving a company from setting off a loss against general income to the extent that the loss is attributable to first-year allowances on plant or machinery provided for leasing in the course of the partnership qualifying activity. This restriction can also apply in certain circumstances where no company is involved.

Leasing partnerships

[15.10] Further restrictions apply to the use of certain losses and excess allowances incurred by a company where it carries on a 'business of leasing plant or machinery' (see **17.32** below) in partnership. See below for the commencement provisions.

The loss restrictions apply to a loss incurred by a company in its 'notional business' for any accounting period comprised wholly or partly in an accounting period of the partnership during any day of which the business carried on in partnership (the '*leasing business*') is a business of leasing plant or machinery if the interest of the company in the leasing business during the accounting period of the partnership is not determined on an 'allowable basis'. The restrictions apply only where the company is within the charge to corporation tax in respect of the business.

For this purpose, a company's interest in a leasing business is determined on an '*allowable basis*' for an accounting period if, for the purposes of *CTA 2009, ss 1262–1264* (see **15.8** above), the company's share in the profits (other than chargeable gains) or loss of the leasing business and in any 'relevant capital allowances' (i.e. capital allowances in respect of expenditure incurred on plant or machinery wholly or partly for the purposes of the leasing business) are determined for the period wholly by reference to the same, single percentage. A company's '*notional business*' is the business the profits or loss are determined under *CTA 2009, s 1259*.

Where the above conditions are met, the restrictions apply in respect of so much of the loss incurred by the company in its notional business as derives from the relevant capital allowances (treating those allowances as the final amounts to be deducted).

Relief for the restricted part of the loss cannot be given under any of the following provisions:

(i) *CTA 2010, s 62* (UK property business losses);
(ii) *CTA 2010, s 66* (overseas property business losses — see **2.42** above);
(iii) *CTA 2010, s 45* (carry forward of trading losses — see **2.38** above); or
(iv) *CTA 2010, s 91* (losses from miscellaneous transactions),

except by way of set off against any income of the notional business deriving from any lease (including an underlease, sublease, tenancy or licence or any agreement for any of those things) of plant or machinery entered into before the end of the accounting period in which the loss is incurred.

Where the notional business is a trade, the restricted part of the loss cannot be set off against other profits of the company under *CTA 2010, s 37* (see **2.38** above). The restricted part of the loss cannot be surrendered as group relief.

[*CTA 2010, ss 887–889*].

The excess allowance restriction applies where a company carries on a business in partnership, the business (the '*leasing business*') is a business of leasing plant or machinery and the company's qualifying activity for the purposes of plant and machinery allowances is special leasing (see **4.7** above). If, for any chargeable period comprised wholly or partly in a chargeable period of the partnership, the company has excess allowances, no claim can be made under *CAA 2001, s 260(3)–(6)* to set off the excess against other profits (see **2.44** above) unless the interest of the company in the leasing business during the chargeable period of the partnership is determined on an allowable basis (as above). [*CAA 2001, s 261A*].

The above provisions apply for accounting periods of a partnership ending on or after 5 December 2005. For accounting periods beginning before and ending on or after that date, the provisions apply only if the company starts to carry on the business in partnership after 4 December 2005 or if its interest in the business ceases to be determined on an allowable basis after that date. [*FA 2006, s 83(4)–(6)*].

Limited liability partnerships

[15.11] A trade, profession or business carried on by a limited liability partnership is treated for tax purposes as carried on in partnership by its members (and not by the limited liability partnership as such); and the property of the limited liability partnership is treated as partnership property. [*ITTOIA 2005, s 863; CTA 2009, s 1273; Limited Liability Partnership Act 2000, s 10(1)*]. The provisions described in this chapter apply accordingly.

16

Interaction with Capital Gains Tax

Introduction

[16.1] This chapter deals with specific areas of capital gains tax which affect, or are affected by, capital allowances. A detailed consideration of the capital gains tax provisions in general is outside the scope of this book, so the coverage in it has been based on the assumption that the reader will already have a basic working knowledge of the tax. Reference can, of course, be made to Tolley's Capital Gains Tax.

Time of disposal

[16.2] The time of disposal of an asset for capital gains tax purposes can sometimes differ from that for capital allowances purposes. As regards an asset disposed of under a contract, the time of disposal for capital gains tax purposes is the time the contract is made and not, if different, the time at which the asset is conveyed or transferred. [*TCGA 1992, s 28(1)*]. The rule is modified for conditional contracts, and in particular where the contract is conditional on the exercise of an option, the time of disposal then being the time when the condition is satisfied. [*TCGA 1992, s 28(2)*]. However, any reference for capital allowance purposes to the time of any sale is broadly construed as a reference to the time of completion or the time when possession is given, whichever is the earlier. [*CAA 2001, ss 451, 572(4)*]. Where this last provision applies, it effectively means that a person can, in respect of the same disposal, incur a capital gain in one chargeable period and have a balancing adjustment in another.

Destruction, etc. giving rise to receipt of capital sums

[16.3] The application of *TCGA 1992, s 28(1)* is subject to *TCGA 1992, s 22(2)*. The latter deals with the time of disposal in respect of certain capital sums derived from an asset which are deemed to give rise to a disposal notwithstanding that no asset is acquired by the person paying the capital sum. *Section 22(2)* provides that the time of disposal is to be the time when the capital sum is received.

The capital sums included cover, *inter alia*, capital compensation received for the loss of an asset, an event giving rise to a balancing adjustment under most of the capital allowances provisions. For most capital allowances purposes, the balancing event occurs in the chargeable period (see **2.1** above) in which an asset is demolished or destroyed, the charge or allowance for the chargeable period being the difference between the asset's tax written-down value and, *inter alia*, any capital compensation moneys received. It may well be that the payment of compensation moneys is delayed and that such payment is not received until a later chargeable period than that related to the event for capital allowance purposes; so, again, there could be different disposal dates for capital allowance and capital gains tax purposes. In this case, the capital gains tax disposal date would be on the receipt of the compensation moneys; e.g. an asset belonging to a company is destroyed in one chargeable period, giving rise to a balancing adjustment for that chargeable period, but the related compensation moneys are received in a subsequent chargeable period, at which time a disposal takes place for capital gains tax purposes. It will be noted that for a non-corporate taxpayer, the relevant year of assessment for capital gains tax is the year of assessment in which the related disposal falls, whilst for capital allowances (income tax) it will be the year of assessment in which the end of the period of account containing the related disposal falls.

Destruction, etc. of whole asset without receipt of capital sums

[16.4] Although *TCGA 1992, s 24(1)* provides that the entire loss, destruction, dissipation or extinction of an asset is to constitute a disposal of the asset whether or not any capital sum is received by way of compensation or otherwise, it is not thought that this provision, as regards the date of disposal, overrides *TCGA 1992, s 22(2)* where an actual capital sum is received (see, for example, the words of Hoffman J in the High Court in *Powlson v Welbeck Securities Ltd* CA 1987, 60 TC 269). However, where no capital sums are eventually received, *s 24(1)* will have the effect of making the time of disposal the time when the entire loss, etc. occurs. A negligible value claim under *s 24* can be related back up to two years from the beginning of the year in which the claim is made. The asset must have negligible value both at the time of the claim and at the earlier date specified in the claim.

Allowable expenditure

[16.5] *TCGA 1992, s 38* sets out the sums allowable as a deduction from consideration in the computation of a chargeable gain accruing to a person on the disposal of an asset and is thus used to determine the acquisition cost of an asset for capital gains tax purposes. Generally, such acquisition cost is limited to:

(a) the amount or value of the consideration, in money or money's worth, given wholly and exclusively for the acquisition of the asset,
(b) the incidental costs of acquisition, as limited by *TCGA 1992, s 38(2)* (see **16.7** below),
(c) the amount of any expenditure wholly and exclusively incurred for the purpose of enhancing the value of the asset, being expenditure reflected in the state or nature of the asset at the time of disposal, and
(d) the amount of any expenditure wholly and exclusively incurred in establishing, preserving or defending title to, or to a right over, the asset.

Comparison of two bases

[16.6] It should be borne in mind that the acquisition cost of an asset for capital gains tax purposes, computed under the above rules, may differ from its cost for the purposes of capital allowances. For example, an entitlement to capital allowances on enhancement expenditure will not depend on the state or nature of the asset at the time of disposal. Furthermore, there are cases where special provisions apply for capital allowances. One of general application is that expenditure for rights over land can only rarely be the subject of a capital allowance claim. Furthermore, there seems to be little or no scope for taking incidental costs into account for allowance purposes.

Incidental costs

[16.7] As regards incidental costs, *TCGA 1992, s 38(2)* defines them, so far as they relate to acquisition, as:

(a) fees, commission or remuneration paid for the professional services of any surveyor or valuer, or auctioneer, or accountant, or agent or legal adviser;
(b) costs of transfer or conveyance, including stamp duty; and
(c) costs of advertising to find a seller.

Capital allowances legislation, on the other hand, generally tends to be silent as to the possibility of including such costs as part of the capital expenditure incurred on an asset and thus qualifying for allowances. As regards plant and machinery, for example, writing-down allowances are given in respect of capital expenditure incurred *on the provision of* plant or machinery for the purposes of a qualifying activity. [*CAA 2001, s 11*]. Whilst it is generally accepted that the cost of providing plant must include incidental costs of acquiring title, bringing the plant to the location where it will be used in the trade, and setting it up in working order, the legislation is by no means specific. Whilst *TCGA 1992, s 38(2)* may be useful as a guideline in determining what incidental costs may be taken into account in a capital allowances claim, it has no authority other than for capital gains tax purposes. (See also **4.16** above with regard to ancillary expenditure.)

[16.8] The other side of the coin is the extent to which incidental costs of disposal may be taken into account in computing a balancing charge or allowance on the sale or other disposal of an asset which has qualified for capital allowances. For the purposes of flat conversion allowances, plant and machinery allowances, mineral extraction allowances, and research and development allowances, the legislation requires the 'net proceeds of sale' to be brought into account. The expression 'net proceeds' is not further defined, but is generally taken to mean that costs of disposal, to the extent that they are not allowed as a revenue expense in computing profits, may be deducted in arriving at the amount of sale proceeds to be taken into account in the calculation of a balancing adjustment.

Exclusion of allowable expenditure for capital gains tax purposes by reference to tax on income

[16.9] Allowable expenditure for capital gains tax purposes is restricted so as to exclude any expenditure allowable against income, including any amount deductible in computing the profits of a trade, profession or vocation, or which would be allowable were it not for an insufficiency of income or trading profits. In addition, if the assets, to which the capital gains tax computation relates, were and had always been held or used as part of the fixed capital of a trade, the profits of which were chargeable to income tax, any expenditure in respect of those assets which would be allowable as a deduction in computing the profits or gains or losses of the trade is excluded from being an allowable deduction in the capital gains tax computation. [*TCGA 1992, s 39(1)–(3)*].

This could be interpreted as meaning that any expenditure which has been the subject of a capital allowance is not therefore an allowable deduction for capital gains tax purposes. This is not, however, the case as *TCGA 1992, s 41(1)* specifically provides, *inter alia*, that *s 39* is not to require the exclusion, from the sums allowable as a deduction for capital gains tax purposes, of any expenditure in respect of which a capital allowance (or renewals allowance) is made. However, this only applies if the capital gains tax computation results in a gain (after deducting indexation allowance where applicable) according to HMRC (see HMRC Capital Gains Tax Manual, CG17450). See **16.11** below for the restriction of losses on the disposal of an asset which has qualified for capital allowances. See also Example 3 at **16.13** below for the application of the above principles.

Exclusion of consideration chargeable to tax on income

[16.10] Whereas *TCGA 1992, s 39* excludes, from the capital gains tax computation, expenditure allowable for income tax purposes (see **16.9** above), *TCGA 1992, s 37* similarly excludes, from consideration to be brought into account for capital gains tax purposes, any money or money's worth charged to income tax or taken into account as a receipt in computing income, profits or losses. [*TCGA 1992, s 37(1)*]. This precludes a double charge to both income tax (or corporation tax on income) and capital gains tax (or corporation tax on chargeable gains). Again there is an exception for assets which have been the subject of capital allowances, in that any amount brought into account in the making of a balancing charge or which is brought into account as the disposal value of plant or machinery or an asset representing research and development expenditure is not excluded from consideration for capital gains tax purposes. [*TCGA 1992, s 37(2)*]. For 2017/18 onwards, any amount taken into account as a receipt of a trade, profession, vocation or property business as a result of the operation of the cash basis deemed disposal provisions of *ITTOIA 2005, ss 96A(4)(5), 307F* (see **17.1C** below) is also excluded from consideration to be brought into account for capital gains tax purposes (but only to the extent that it has not been so excluded in respect of an earlier disposal of the asset). [*TCGA 1992, s 37(1A)–(1C); F(No 2)A 2017, Sch 2 paras 44, 64*].

The combined effect of *sections 37* and *39* is to disregard, for the purpose of computing an unindexed gain (see **16.11** below as regards losses), the fact that capital allowances have been given and/or balancing charges made in respect of the asset under consideration, the capital gains tax computation proceeding in the same way as if the asset were one on which capital allowances were never available.

Restriction of losses by reference to capital allowances, etc.

[16.11] Where a person incurs a capital loss on an asset which has been the subject of capital allowances, the amount of expenditure allowable as a deduction in computing the loss is restricted so as to exclude any expenditure to the extent to which any 'capital allowance' or 'renewals allowance' has been made or may be made in respect of it. [*TCGA 1992, s 41(2)*]. For this purpose, the meaning of '*capital allowance*' is extended to mean any allowance under *CAA 2001*, (for 2017/18 onwards) any deduction under *ITTOIA 2005, ss 33A* or *307B* (deduction for capital expenditure in calculating profits on the cash basis — see **17.1B** below), any deduction under *ITTOIA 2005, s 311A* or *CTA 2009, s 250A* (replacement domestic items relief — see **7.16A** above), any deduction under *ITTOIA 2005, s 315* or *CTA 2009, s 254* (sea walls) or any deduction under *ITTOIA 2005, s 170* or *CTA 2009, s 147* (cemeteries — see **14.4** above). [*TCGA 1992, s 41(4); FA 2016, s 73(3); F(No 2)A 2017, Sch 2 paras 45(2), 64*]. A '*renewals allowance*' is defined as a deduction allowable, in computing the profits or gains of a trade, profession or vocation for income tax purposes, in respect of the replacement of one asset by another, and the deduction is treated as allowable in respect of the asset which is being replaced. [*TCGA 1992, s 41(5)*]. See also **7.15** above for renewals allowances for expenditure incurred before 6 April 2016 (1 April 2016 for corporation tax purposes).

The amount of capital allowances to be taken into account under *TCGA 1992, s 41* includes any balancing allowance in respect of the disposal in question and is after deducting the amount of any balancing charge, in respect of either that disposal or any earlier event. If the capital allowances include a deduction for capital expenditure on the cash basis, the capital allowances to be taken into account are the total expenditure which has qualified for capital allowances less any balancing charge. Where this provision does not apply and the disposal is of plant or machinery, the amount of capital allowances to be taken into account is the difference between the capital expenditure incurred, or treated as incurred, and the disposal value to be brought into account under **5.41** above. This provision is necessary as the pooling provisions of the plant and machinery code of allowances would make it difficult, if not impossible, to identify the capital allowances given in respect of a single item of plant or machinery. The provision does not apply either to assets used partly for non-trading purposes and falling within *CAA 2001, Pt 2 Ch 15* (see **5.55** above) or to assets which are the subject of a partial depreciation subsidy and fall within *CAA 2001, Pt 2 Ch 16* (see **7.14** above); so it is necessary to identify separately the capital allowances given on assets within these classes. [*TCGA 1992, s 41(6)–(7); F(No 2)A 2017, Sch 2 para 45(3)(4)*].

See **16.12–16.15** below for provisions supplementary to *TCGA 1992, s 41*.

Note that, at the time of writing, *F(No 2)A 2017* had not completed its passage through Parliament. The changes made to these provisions for 2017/18 onwards are therefore subject to any changes made during the Parliamentary process.

Purpose of TCGA 1992, s 41

[16.12] The purpose of *TCGA 1992, s 41* is to prevent double relief for expenditure. For example, in *Example 1* at **16.13** below, B Ltd has made a commercial loss of £10,000 in respect of the item of plant. Relief for this loss is obtained via the capital allowances which will ultimately be received of £10,000 (£20,000 having been added to the main pool on acquisition and a disposal value of £10,000 deducted on disposal). But for *s 41*, B Ltd would additionally have an allowable capital loss of £10,000, giving overall tax relief for the loss of £20,000.

Section 41 only applies if a capital loss has been incurred; in general there is no need for a similar provision if a capital gain is made, as for most types of expenditure any capital allowances given would be recovered by a balancing charge or through the deduction of disposal proceeds from a pool of existing expenditure.

EXAMPLE 1

[16.13]

B Ltd, a trading company with a 31 October accounting date, buys an item of plant in May 2015 for £20,000 and sells it for £10,000 in May 2017. At 1 November 2016, the company had unrelieved qualifying expenditure of £50,000 on plant and machinery in its main pool and apart from the above, makes no additions or disposals during the year commencing on that date.

Capital allowances computation — year ending 31 October 2017

	Main pool	*Total allowances*
	£	£
Qualifying expenditure brought forward	50,000	
Disposal value	(10,000)	
	40,000	
Writing-down allowance (18%)	(7,200)	£7,200
Written-down value carried forward	£32,800	

Capital gains tax computation on disposal

	£	£	£
Proceeds			10,000
Cost		20,000	
Reduction under *TCGA 1992, s 41*:			
Original cost	20,000		
Disposal value	10,000		
		10,000	
			10,000
Unindexed gain/loss			Nil
Indexation allowance restricted to			Nil
Allowable loss			Nil

Transfers of assets at written-down value

[16.14] There are certain provisions embodied in the capital allowances legislation which, on the making of the appropriate election, enable a person to be deemed to acquire an asset at its tax written-down or residual value for capital allowances purposes where, in the absence of an election, the transfer would be deemed to be at market value. *TCGA 1992, s 41* specifies the following such cases:

(a) a sale, between controlled bodies or connected persons, in respect of which an election is made under *CAA 2001, s 569* (or equivalent previous legislation) (see **17.4** below); and
(b) a transfer of plant or machinery, passing to a person as part of a trade transferred by will or intestacy, in respect of which an election is made under *CAA 2001, s 268* (or equivalent previous enactment) (see **7.17** above).

For the purpose of applying the loss restricting provisions of *TCGA 1992, s 41* to a subsequent disposal, the transferee is deemed to have received the benefit of any capital allowances made to the transferor. Where there is a series of transactions covered by one or more of the above-mentioned provisions, the allowances made to every transferor are deemed to have been made to the transferee. This effectively means that the amount of capital allowances which can restrict the capital loss on a disposal (by the transferee) is not limited to allowances made to him but extends to allowances made to all of the transferors. However, where capital allowances are used to restrict a capital loss arising on a disposal, those allowances cannot again be used to restrict a capital loss on a subsequent disposal. [*TCGA 1992, s 41(3)*].

EXAMPLE 2

[16.15]

B succeeds to a trade under the will of her late husband, A, who died on 28 August 2016. She inherits various items of plant and machinery used in the trade and elects under *CAA 2001, s 268* to take these over at their written-down values for capital allowances purposes and which total £24,000 (such total being less than that of the market values). One particular item of plant cost £20,000 in 2015 and had a market value of £16,000 at 28 August 2016. In December 2017, B sells that item for £11,000 and thus brings that amount into her capital allowances computation as a disposal value.

B is treated for capital gains tax purposes as acquiring the asset at its value at the date of A's death (£16,000), and will have, subject to *TCGA 1992, s 41*, a capital loss of £5,000 (£16,000 – £11,000). However, her acquisition cost will be limited by £9,000 (this being the difference between the expenditure incurred by A and the disposal value) which is deemed to be the total of the allowances made to A and B in respect of the asset. Her acquisition cost is thus reduced to £7,000, and her loss is reduced to nil. Note that she does not make a chargeable gain by reference to the difference between her proceeds of £11,000 and her reduced cost of £7,000 as *s 41* operates only to restrict losses and cannot create gains where none would otherwise exist.

Transfers within groups of companies

[16.16] Where there is a disposal of an asset acquired in 'relevant circumstances', the provisions of *TCGA 1992, s 41* in **16.14** above are applied in relation to capital allowances made to the person from whom it was acquired (so far as not taken into account in relation to a disposal of the asset by that person), and so on as respects previous transfers of the asset in relevant circumstances. '*Relevant circumstances*' means circumstances in which *TCGA 1992, s 171* (transfers within a group) or *TCGA 1992, s 172* (transfer of UK branch or agency before 1 April 2000) applied or in which *TCGA 1992, s 171* would have applied but for the provisions of *TCGA 1992, s 171(2)* (certain intra-group disposals not treated as at a no gain/no loss consideration). The application of *TCGA 1992, s 41* is not to be taken as affecting the consideration for which an asset is deemed under *TCGA 1992, s 171* (or *172*) to be acquired. [*TCGA 1992, ss 41(8), 174(1)(2)(3)*].

Part disposals

[16.17] *TCGA 1992, s 42* deals with part disposals of assets and sets out a formula for apportioning the acquisition cost of an asset between the part disposed of and the part retained. Such apportionment is to be made before the application of *TCGA 1992, s 41* where the last-named provision would restrict the acquisition cost by reference to capital allowances.

If, following a part disposal, there is a disposal of an asset and *s 41* applies to the disposal, the amount of capital allowances or renewals allowances to be taken into account in restricting the loss on the subsequent disposal are those arising by virtue of expenditure falling within *TCGA 1992, s 38(1)(a)(b)* (see **16.5** above) and attributable to the asset whether before or after the part disposal. However, where a loss on the part disposal was restricted by capital allowances, those allowances cannot again restrict a loss on the subsequent disposal. [*TCGA 1992, s 42(3)*].

The above is subject to a general rule concerning part disposals which is that there should be no apportionment of any expenditure which, on the facts, is wholly attributable either to the part disposed of or to the part retained. [*TCGA 1992, s 42(4)*].

Assets held on 6 April 1965 and 31 March 1982

[16.18] Under various provisions of *CGTA 1979, Sch 5*, an asset held on 6 April 1965 can, in certain circumstances, be regarded for capital gains tax purposes as having been sold by the owner on 6 April 1965 and immediately reacquired by him at its market value at that date. Following the rebasing provisions introduced by *FA 1988, s 96*, a deemed sale and reacquisition is now generally treated as taking place on 31 March 1982 where the disposal takes place after 5 April 1988 and relates to an asset held on 31 March 1982. The relevant provisions are now contained in *TCGA 1992, Sch 2*. For capital gains tax purposes, re-basing to 31 March 1982 applies automatically and with no exceptions for disposals on or after 6 April 2008. Exceptions continue to apply for the purposes of corporation tax on chargeable gains.

The gain or loss on a subsequent disposal is computed by reference to the value of the asset at 6 April 1965, or 31 March 1982 as appropriate, rather than its original cost. Where the gain or loss is computed by reference to 6 April 1965 value, the provisions of *TCGA 1992, s 41* apply in relation to any capital allowances and/or renewals allowances made in respect of the actual expenditure incurred by the owner in providing the asset and so made for the year 1965/66 and subsequent years of assessment, as if those allowances had been made in respect of the notional expenditure deemed to have been incurred on reacquiring the asset on 6 April 1965 (the legislation states the relevant date to be 7 April 1965, but this appears to be a drafting error as such a date is inconsistent with the general tenor of *TCGA 1992, Sch* 2). [*TCGA 1992, Sch 2 para 20*]. Where the gain or loss is computed by reference to 31 March 1982 value, the provisions of *TCGA 1992, s 41* apply *mutatis mutandis* in relation to the deemed reacquisition at 31 March 1982. [*TCGA 1992, s 55(3)(5), Sch 3 para 3*].

TCGA 1992, s 35(5) allows a person to make an irrevocable election so that, in relation to assets disposed of after 5 April 1988, all assets held by him on 31 March 1982 are deemed to have been sold on 31 March 1982 and immediately reacquired at market value. The election is no longer relevant for capital gains tax purposes because, as indicated above, re-basing applies automatically and without exceptions. Elections continue to be relevant for the purposes of corporation tax on chargeable gains. An election does not, *inter alia*, cover a disposal of, or of an interest in, plant or machinery eligible for a capital allowance, any asset eligible for a capital allowance which has been held etc. at some time for the purposes of the working of a source of mineral deposits or a 'UK oil licence' (see **10.18** above) whether or not eligible for a capital allowance. Eligibility for an allowance in this context includes eligibility in the hands of certain former holders of the asset. [*TCGA 1992, ss 35(5), 55(2); FA 2008, Sch 2 paras 58(6), 71*]. In practice, this provision will mean that a capital loss arising on such an asset is calculated by reference to the smaller of the losses arising from comparing proceeds on disposal with the original cost of the asset concerned and its market value at 31 March 1982. As explained above, *TCGA 1992, s 41* will also apply to reduce the loss arising in each of these circumstances.

Assets exempt from capital gains tax

[16.19] It is beyond the scope of this book to consider all the types of asset which are exempt from capital gains tax. The coverage below only mentions those which are commonly the subject of a capital allowances claim.

Cars

[16.20] Cars are not chargeable assets for capital gains tax purposes regardless of whether or not they have qualified for capital allowances. This applies only to 'passenger vehicles', i.e. mechanically propelled road vehicles constructed or adapted for the carriage of passengers, except vehicles of a type not commonly used as private vehicles and unsuitable to be so used. [*TCGA 1992, s 263*]. It should be noted that whilst the above definition of a 'passenger vehicle' is similar to that of a 'car' which applies for the purposes of plant and machinery allowances (see **5.53** above), it is not as extensive. Occasionally therefore, a mechanically propelled road vehicle may be within one definition and not the other.

Tangible movable assets (chattels)

[16.21] A gain on the disposal of a tangible movable asset is, with some minor exceptions, exempt from capital gains tax if the disposal consideration does not exceed £6,000. As the criterion is consideration, rather than proceeds, it is applied without deduction of any costs of sale. Assets which have qualified for capital allowances can nevertheless qualify for this exemption; the obvious example is plant and machinery, although not all items of plant and machinery are tangible movable assets. Marginal relief is available in that where consideration exceeds £6,000, the chargeable gain is limited to five-thirds of the excess. Where a loss is incurred and the consideration is less than £6,000, the consideration is deemed to be £6,000 with the result that the loss is restricted. [*TCGA 1992, s 262*].

There are special rules for dealing with disposals of rights or interests in or over tangible movable property. [*TCGA 1992, s 262(5)*].

Where two or more articles form part of a set of articles of any description all owned at one time by one person, and those articles are sold by that person either to one other person or to two or more persons acting in concert or who are connected persons, then, regardless of whether the sale is by a single transaction or two or more transactions, the articles are treated as a single asset. Thus if each article is sold for £6,000 or less but the combined proceeds exceed that figure, full exemption will not be available, although marginal relief may still apply by reference to the excess of total combined proceeds over £6,000. [*TCGA 1992, s 262(4)*].

As to whether or not different items of plant and machinery might be regarded as forming part of a set, it is likely that this would not be the case where two or more items can be put to practical or commercial use independently. However, if, for example, the use of one item was entirely dependent on the use of another so that each item was of no use on its own, or the items were part of a range of different size, shape, etc. in circumstances where the only commercial use that could be made of an item was in conjunction with the use made of the rest of the range, the two items might well be regarded as forming a set or part of a set.

The relevance of the above provisions, insofar as they might be applied to plant and machinery, is perhaps limited by the fact that the very nature of plant and machinery (being depreciating assets) would suggest that such items are more likely to be disposed of at less than original cost than at a profit, with the result that no chargeable gain would arise but losses could be restricted, both as above and under *TCGA 1992, s 41* (see **16.12** above).

EXAMPLE 3

[16.22]

C, a trader, has an item of plant which is tangible movable property, which he uses in his trade and on which he has obtained capital allowances. He sells it in 2017 for £10,000. His acquisition cost was £8,000 in April 2015.

Computation

	£
Consideration	10,000
Cost	8,000
Chargeable gain	£2,000

The chargeable gain is limited to $\frac{5}{3}$ × (£10,000 – £6,000) = £6,667, but as this is more than the actual gain of £2,000, the actual gain stands.

Tangible movable assets (chattels) which are wasting assets

[16.23] Tangible movable assets which are also wasting assets (see **16.25** below) are exempt from capital gains tax whatever the amount of consideration received. However, this exemption does not apply to the disposal of an asset or of an interest in an asset, if the asset in question has been used, throughout the entire period of ownership of the person making the disposal, solely for the purposes of a trade, profession or vocation and if that person either has claimed or could have claimed capital allowances in respect of any expenditure that would be allowable as a deduction, under *TCGA 1992, s 38(1)(a)(b)*, in a capital gains tax computation on the disposal of the asset. If this restriction does not apply, but the person making the disposal has incurred any expenditure on the asset, or interest therein, which has otherwise qualified in full for any capital allowance (e.g. special leasing of plant or machinery), then, again, the exemption does not apply.

A process of apportionment applies where a tangible movable asset, which is also a wasting asset, has either:

(a) been used only partly for the purposes of a trade, profession or vocation and partly for other purposes; or
(b) been used for the purposes of a trade, etc. for only part of the period of ownership of the person making the disposal; or
(c) otherwise qualified in part only for capital allowances.

The consideration and the allowable expenditure are both apportioned by reference to the extent to which the said expenditure qualified for capital allowances and separate capital gains tax computations are prepared in respect of each of the two apportioned parts of consideration and expenditure. The exemption then applies only to that part of the total gain which is not attributable to that part of the expenditure which has qualified for capital allowances.

For disposals on or after 6 April 2015 (1 April 2015 for corporation tax purposes), the exemption also does not apply (and no apportionment can be made) where the asset has become plant as a result of its use for the purposes of a trade, profession or vocation carried on by a person other than the owner and it would not otherwise have been a wasting asset. This exclusion does not, however, apply if the asset is plant under a long funding lease and the disposal takes place during the term of the lease or it is a deemed disposal on termination of the lease under *TCGA 1992, s 25A(3)(a)* (see **6.21** above). This rule effectively reverses the effect of the decision in *Executors of Lord Howard of Henderskelfe v HMRC* CA, [2014] STC 1100 in which a painting which was informally loaned to a company for display to the paying public as part of its trade was held to be plant and therefore a wasting asset.

[*TCGA 1992, s 45; FA 2015, s 40*].

For the purposes of the above provisions, the term 'capital allowance' is as defined in **16.11** above. [*TCGA 1992, ss 41(4), 52(5)*].

An asset is not to be regarded as having qualified for capital allowances if such allowances have been given and then fully withdrawn otherwise than by way of a balancing adjustment (*Burman v Westminster Press Ltd* ChD 1987, 60 TC 418). This case concerned the sale of a printing press on which first-year plant and machinery allowances had been given and later withdrawn due to the fact that the asset before being sold had never been used for the purposes of the trade; the withdrawal of allowances was made under *FA 1971, s 41(2)* which was repealed as regards chargeable periods or basis periods ending after 31 March 1985, and thus the case is now of limited interest.

EXAMPLE 4

[16.24]

D, a greengrocer, purchases a lorry for £12,000 for use in his trade. It is not a passenger vehicle within *TCGA 1992, s 263* (see **16.20** above) and is thus a chargeable asset, albeit a tangible movable and wasting asset. Nevertheless, D does use it to some extent for private purposes and capital allowances are restricted by 10% to reflect the private usage, the expenditure incurred on the lorry being excluded from the main pool of qualifying expenditure by virtue of *CAA 2001, s 206(1)*. After a few months of ownership, D receives and accepts an offer of £16,000 for the van from a trader who is anxious to acquire the van because of a scarcity of such vehicles caused by a strike at the manufacturers.

	Total	*Part qualifying for capital allowances*	*Remainder*
	£	£	£
Sale proceeds	16,000	14,400	1,600
Cost	12,000	10,800	1,200
Gain	£4,000	3,600	400
Chargeable gain		£3,600	
Exempt gain			£400

Notes

(a) The gain of £400 attributable to non-trade use is exempt under *TCGA 1992, s 45*.

(b) Strictly, the cost of £1,200 attributed to the part not qualifying for capital allowances should be reduced in accordance with the wasting asset provisions of *TCGA 1992, s 46* (see **16.25** below), but there is no point in making the necessary calculation as the gain is exempt in any case. The £10,800 cost is not reduced because the wasting asset provisions do not apply to expenditure on which capital allowances are available (see **16.26** below).

Wasting assets

Definition

[16.25] A wasting asset is one that has a predictable life of fifty years or less. The following further qualifications are relevant.

(a) Freehold land can never be a wasting asset, whatever its nature and whatever the nature of any buildings or works upon it.

(b) A lease of land is not a wasting asset until such time as its remaining duration does not exceed fifty years.

(c) Plant and machinery are always regarded as having a predictable life of less than fifty years and are thus always wasting assets.

(d) As regards tangible movable property, 'life' means useful life having regard to the purpose for which the tangible assets were acquired or provided by the person making the disposal.

[*TCGA 1992, s 44(1), Sch 8 para 1(1)*].

It should be noted that although freehold land is excluded from being a wasting asset, the legislation does not explicitly exclude buildings and structures on freehold land, in the rare cases where their predictable life does not exceed fifty years. (It is accepted that other legal provisions may treat the building as part of the freehold land.)

Allowable expenditure, within *TCGA 1992, s 38(1)(a)(b)*, on a wasting asset is written off at a uniform rate over the predictable life of the asset, after first deducting any predictable residual or scrap value. The writing-off of expenditure is calculated in accordance with a formula laid down by *TCGA 1992, s 46(2)* or, in the case of leases, in accordance with a table contained in *TCGA 1992, Sch 8 para 1*.

Assets qualifying for capital allowances

[16.26] The wasting asset provisions of *TCGA 1992, s 46, Sch 8 para 1*, i.e. the writing-off of allowable expenditure, do not apply to wasting assets qualifying for capital allowances. More specifically, the provisions do not apply to a disposal of an asset which satisfies the conditions set out in the first paragraph of **16.23** above, i.e. used in a trade and qualifying in full for capital allowances or otherwise so qualifying.

Similar rules for apportionment as set out in the second paragraph of **16.23** above apply in the case of an asset which meets one or more of the criteria in **16.25**(a)–(c) above. The part of the total gain which is attributable to the part of the expenditure qualifying for capital allowances is calculated without taking into account the writing-off provisions of *TCGA 1992, s 46*. The remaining part of the gain is computed in accordance with those provisions. The consideration for the disposal is apportioned in the same way as any apportionment of consideration made for the purpose of making any capital allowance or balancing charge to or on the person making the disposal. Where no such apportionment for capital allowances purposes has been made, the consideration is apportioned for capital gains tax purposes in the same proportions as the allowable expenditure, i.e. by reference to the extent to which the expenditure qualified for capital allowances. [*TCGA 1992, s 47*].

For the purposes of these provisions, the term 'capital allowance' has the same meaning as in **16.11** above. [*TCGA 1992, ss 41(4), 52(5)*].

If, under any of the provisions of *TCGA 1992, Sch 2*, an asset is deemed to have been sold and immediately reacquired at its market value on 6 April 1965, the provisions of *TCGA 1992, s 47* apply in relation to any capital allowances made in respect of the actual expenditure incurred by the owner in providing the asset and so made for the year 1965/66 and subsequent years of assessment, as if those allowances had been made in respect of the notional expenditure deemed to have been incurred in reacquiring the asset on 6 April 1965. [*TCGA 1992, Sch 2 para 20*]. Where a gain or loss is computed by reference to market value at 31 March 1982, the provisions of *TCGA 1992, s 47* apply *mutatis mutandis* in relation to the deemed reacquisition at 31 March 1982. [*TCGA 1992, s 55(3), Sch 3 para 3*]. See also **16.18** above.

Effect of the cash basis

[16.27] For income tax purposes for 2013/14 onwards, an election can be made for the profits of certain small trades, professions or vocations to be calculated using the cash basis. For 2017/18 onwards, the cash basis also applies (without election) for income tax purposes to certain small property businesses. See **17.1A** below. Capital allowance are not available (except in respect of expenditure on the provision of a car) where the cash basis is used.

For 2017/18 onwards, no chargeable gain arises on the disposal of an asset other than land (or an interest in such an asset) if at any time during the period of ownership of the person making the disposal the asset was used for the purposes of a trade, profession, vocation or property business carried on by him and 'disposal proceeds' arising from the disposal are brought into account as a receipt of the trade etc. under *ITTOIA 2005, s 96A* or *s 307E* (capital receipts under, or after leaving, the cash basis — see **17.1C** below). 'Disposal proceeds' has the same meaning here as at **17.1C** below.

For 2016/17 and earlier years, this provision applied only to tangible moveable property which was a wasting asset (because the only capital expenditure which could be deducted under the cash basis was expenditure on acquiring plant and machinery (other than a car)) and only where the disposal took place whilst the cash basis was in effect (see below for disposals after leaving the cash basis). No chargeable gain arose if expenditure on acquiring or enhancing the value of the asset was deducted in calculating profits on the cash basis or would have been if the cash basis had applied when the expenditure was paid.

[*TCGA 1992, s 47A(1)–(5A); FA 2013, Sch 4 para 45*].

For 2016/17 and earlier years where a person disposed of, or an interest in, an asset used for the purposes of a trade, profession or vocation after leaving the cash basis and any acquisition or enhancement expenditure on the asset was brought into account in calculating the profits under the cash basis, the following modifications applied to the chargeable gains rules in this chapter:

- *TCGA 1992, s 39* (exclusion of expenditure by reference to tax on income — see **16.9** above) did not apply to the acquisition and enhancement expenditure;
- *TCGA 1992, s 41* (restriction of losses by reference to capital allowances — see **16.11** above) applied as if the cash basis had not been in effect when the expenditure was incurred and as if expenditure which would have been qualifying expenditure but for the cash basis applying, were qualifying expenditure; and
- *TCGA 1992, s 45* (exemption for wasting assets — see **16.23** above) and *s 47* (wasting assets qualifying for capital allowances — see **16.26** above) applied as if the cash basis had not been in effect when the expenditure was incurred, and references to qualifying expenditure in those sections were to be read as references to expenditure which would have been qualifying expenditure but for the cash basis applying.

[*TCGA 1992, s 47B; FA 2013, Sch 4 paras 45, 56; F(No 2)A 2017, Sch 2 paras 47, 64*].

Note that, at the time of writing, *F(No 2)A 2017* had not completed its passage through Parliament. The changes made to these provisions for 2017/18 onwards are therefore subject to any changes made during the Parliamentary process.

17

Problem Areas

Introduction

[17.1] This chapter considers a number of complex capital allowances rules which are not covered in the main chapters either because they affect more than one type of allowance or because they apply only in limited circumstances. The rules are covered under the following headings.

- **Cash basis for small businesses.** See **17.1A–17.1D** below.
- **Anti-avoidance provisions.**
  - Controlled and main benefit sales, etc. See **17.2–17.5** below.
  - Avoidance affecting the proceeds of a balancing event. See **17.6** below.
  - Annual investment allowance and first-year allowances. See **17.7** below.
  - Finance lessors: receipt of major lump sum. See **17.8, 17.9** below.
  - Income and profits of parties to finance leasebacks of plant or machinery. See **17.10–17.15** below.
  - Disposal of plant or machinery subject to lease where income retained. See **17.16** below
  - Avoidance involving allowance buying. See **17.17–17.19** below.
  - Leased plant and machinery. See **17.20** below.
  - Ring fence trades — decommissioning and site restoration. See **17.21** below.
- **Company reconstructions without change in ownership.** See **17.22–17.26** below.
- **Transfer or division of a UK business.** See **17.27** below.
- **Transfers of assets during cross-border merger.** See **17.28** below.
- **Change in ownership of a company: disallowance of trading losses.** See **17.29** below.
- **Sale of lessor companies.** See **17.30–17.33** below.
- **Plant and machinery used for business entertaining.** See **17.34** below.
- **Overseas matters.**
  - Assets purchased in foreign currency. See **17.35** below.
  - Exemption for profits of foreign permanent establishments of a UK resident company. See **17.36** below.
  - Non-UK residents. See **17.37, 17.38** below.
  - Controlled foreign companies. See **17.39** below.
  - Dual resident investing companies. See **17.40** below.
- **Special cases.**
  - Post-cessation, etc. receipts. See **17.41** below.
  - Companies with investment business and life assurance companies. See **17.42, 17.43** below.
  - Foster carers and shared lives carers. See **17.44** below.

- – Alternative finance investment bond arrangements where the underlying asset is land. See **17.46** below.
- – Workers' services provided to public sector through intermediaries. See **17.46ZA** below.
- **The Northern Ireland rate of corporation tax.** See **17.46A** below.
  - – Capital allowance provisions. See **17.46B** below.
- **Self-built, etc. assets.** See **17.47** below.
- **Value added tax.**
  - – General principles. See **17.48** below.
  - – VAT capital goods scheme. See **17.49–17.56** below.
- **Trusts.** See **17.57** below.
- **Tonnage tax.** See **17.58–17.60** below.
- **Real estate investment trusts.** See **17.61** below.

Cash basis for small businesses

[17.1A] *FA 2013* introduced a cash basis for 2013/14 onwards under which the profits of certain trades, professions or vocations can be calculated for income tax purposes. It is optional, and is available to unincorporated trades, professions and vocations (including those carried on in a partnership of individuals) with an annual turnover not exceeding £150,000. For 2016/17 and earlier years, the turnover threshold was the VAT registration threshold for the year. For recipients of universal credit, the turnover threshold is twice the normal amount. Businesses must leave the cash basis the year after their receipts exceed £300,000 (for 2016/17 and earlier years, twice the VAT registration threshold). Elections to adopt the cash basis are made via the tax return. If more than one business is carried on by the same person, the combined receipts must be taken into account when applying the turnover test.

F(No 2)A 2017 extended the cash basis so that it applies for income tax purposes to certain property businesses. For 2017/18 and subsequent tax years, the profits of a property business must be calculated for income tax purposes on the cash basis unless any of the following applies:

(a) the person carrying on the business makes an election to disapply the cash basis for the tax year;

(b) the business is carried on at any time in the year by a company, a limited liability partnership, a partnership in which any of the partners are not individuals, or the trustees of a trust;

(c) the receipts for the year (calculated as if the cash basis applied) exceed £150,000 (proportionately reduced if the property business is carried on only for part of the year);

- the business is carried on by an individual and its profits include a share of 'joint property income'; and
- a share of that joint property income is brought into account in calculating the profits for the year of a property business carried on by the individual's spouse or civil partner and those profits are not calculated on the cash basis; or

(e) business premises renovation allowances (see CHAPTER 8) have been made to the business at any time and, if profits were not calculated on the cash basis, a balancing event (see **8.10** below) would give rise to a balancing adjustment for the year.

'*Joint property income*' in (d) above is income to which the spouses or civil partners are treated for income tax purposes as beneficially entitled in equal shares under *ITA 2007, s 836*.

Businesses using the cash basis calculate their taxable income by deducting business expenses paid in a year from business receipts for the year. They do not have to compute figures of debtors, creditors and, where relevant, stock. Allowable expenses are those paid wholly and exclusively for the purposes of the trade or business. For full details of the cash basis see Tolley's Income Tax.

[*ITTOIA 2005, ss 271A–271D; F(No 2)A 2017, Sch 2 paras 13, 64*].

Note that, at the time of writing, *F(No 2)A 2017* had not completed its passage through Parliament. The changes made to these provisions for 2017/18 onwards are therefore subject to any changes made during the Parliamentary process.

Capital expenditure

[17.1B] For 2017/18 onwards, no deduction is allowed for expenditure of a capital nature incurred on, or in connection with:

(1) the acquisition or disposal of a business (or part of a business);
(2) education or training;
(3) the provision, alteration or disposal of:
  (a) an asset that is not a 'depreciating asset';
  (b) an asset that was not acquired or created for use on a continuing basis in the trade or business;
  (c) a car (as defined at **5.51** below);
  (d) land;
  (e) a 'non-qualifying' 'intangible asset'; or
  (f) a 'financial asset'; or
(4) for 'ordinary property businesses' only, the provision, alteration or disposal of an asset for use in a dwelling-house or part of a dwelling-house. This rule does not, however, deny relief for replacement domestic items (see **7.16A** above).

The references in (3) and (4) above to provision, alteration or disposal include *potential* provision, alteration or disposal. Reference to the provision of an asset includes its creation or construction as well as its acquisition.

In (3)(a) above, an asset is a '*depreciating asset*' if, based on a reasonable expectation at the time the capital expenditure is incurred, the asset either has a useful life of less than 20 years or will decline in value by at least 90% in that time. For this purpose, the useful life of an asset ends when it is no longer of use to any person as an asset of a business.

The exclusion in (3)(d) above does not prohibit a deduction for expenditure incurred on the provision of a depreciating asset installed or otherwise fixed to land so as to become, in law, part of it. In the case of an ordinary property business, the land must not be a dwelling-house or part of a dwelling-house. No deduction can be made for expenditure incurred on, or in connection with, the provision of a building or other fixed structure; a wall, floor, ceiling, door, gate, shutter or window or stairs; a waste disposal system; a sewerage or drainage system; or a lift or escalator shaft or similar.

In (3)(e) above, '*intangible asset*' is defined by reference to Financial Reporting Standard (FRS) 105. In particular, it includes an internally-generated intangible asset and intellectual property (as defined). An intangible asset is '*non-qualifying*' unless it has a fixed maximum duration and must thereby cease to exist within 20 years from the time the capital expenditure is incurred. A right to obtain an intangible asset is itself non-qualifying if this would otherwise circumvent the 20-year rule. An intangible asset (asset A) is also non-qualifying if it consists of a licence or other right granted to the taxpayer in respect of another intangible asset (asset B) in respect of which the taxpayer grants a licence etc. to someone else.

In 3(f) above, a '*financial asset*' means any right under, or in connection with, either a 'financial instrument' or an arrangement capable of producing an economically equivalent return to that produced under any financial instrument. '*Financial instrument*' is defined by reference to FRS 105.

In (4) above, an '*ordinary property business*' is so much of a UK or overseas property business as does not consist of commercial letting of furnished holiday accommodation in the UK or other EEA states. Apportionments of expenditure must be made where an asset is provided partly for use in a dwelling-house or part of a dwelling-house and partly for other purposes or where there is a letting of accommodation only part of which is furnished holiday accommodation. Such apportionments must be made on a just and reasonable basis.

For 2016/17 and earlier years, a deduction was allowed for expenditure (other than on the provision of a car) that would otherwise be qualifying expenditure for the purposes of capital allowances on plant and machinery. No deduction was allowed for other items of a capital nature.

For 2017/18 only (but not for property businesses), if a deduction would have been allowed under the old rule above but is not allowed under the new rule, the old rule applies so that the deduction is allowed.

[*ITTOIA 2005, ss 33A, 307B; FA 2013, Sch 4 paras 8, 56; F(No 2)A 2017, Sch 2 paras 2, 23, 64*].

Note that, at the time of writing, *F(No 2)A 2017* had not completed its passage through Parliament. The changes made to these provisions for 2017/18 onwards are therefore subject to any changes made during the Parliamentary process.

Capital receipts

[17.1C] For 2017/18 onwards, 'disposal proceeds' of an asset received by a person at a time when the cash basis applies must be brought into account as a receipt in calculating the profits of the business on the cash basis if an amount of 'capital expenditure' relating to the asset:

(a) has been brought into account in calculating profits on the cash basis; or

(b) in the case of a trade, profession or vocation:
- was incurred (or treated as incurred) by the person before he last entered the cash basis;
- would have been deductible on the cash basis if incurred in the first tax year after he last entered the cash basis; and
- was brought into account in calculating profits for a tax year for which no cash basis election had effect. This includes its being brought into account for capital allowances purposes; or

(c) in the case of a property business:
  (i) was incurred (or treated as incurred) by the person before he last entered the cash basis;
  (ii) would have been deductible on the cash basis if incurred in the first tax year after he last entered the cash basis; and
  (iii) was brought into account in calculating profits in accordance with generally accepted accounting practice (GAAP), either:
  - by means of a deduction allowed under *ITTOIA 2005, ss 58, 59* (incidental costs of obtaining finance); or
  - by means of a deduction allowed under *ITTOIA 2005, s 311A* (replacement domestic items relief) (see **7.16** above); or
  - for the purposes of plant and machinery capital allowances.

For this purpose, a person carrying on a trade, profession or vocation enters the cash basis for a tax year if a cash basis election is in force for that tax year but no such election was in force for the preceding tax year. A person carrying on a property business enters the cash basis for a tax year if profits are calculated on the cash basis for that tax year but were calculated in accordance with GAAP for the preceding tax year.

'*Capital expenditure*' means expenditure of a capital nature incurred (or treated as incurred) on, or in connection with, the provision, alteration or disposal of an asset or the potential provision, alteration or disposal of an asset. Reference to the provision of an asset includes its creation or construction as well as its acquisition. If only part of the capital expenditure relating to an asset is brought into account in calculating profits (whether or not on the cash basis), the disposal proceeds to be brought into account are proportionately reduced. '*Disposal proceeds*' means:

- any proceeds on the disposal (or part disposal) of the asset;
- any proceeds arising from the grant of any right in respect of, or any interest in, the asset;
- any damages, insurance proceeds or other compensation received in respect of the asset; and
- any amount that is (in substance) a refund of capital expenditure relating to the asset.

In (c)(iii) above, expenditure is brought into account for plant and machinery allowances purposes if and to the extent that an allowance in respect of it has been treated as an expense in calculating the profits or if it has been allocated to a pool but has not been carried forward because a disposal value in respect of expenditure on a different asset (or more than one) has been allocated to the pool.

If the whole (or any part) of the proceeds that would fall to be brought into account is otherwise brought into account as a receipt of the trade or business, or as a disposal value for capital allowances, the proceeds (or that part) do not fall to be brought into account again under these rules. For property businesses, the reference to a disposal value is restricted to a disposal value under the plant and machinery code (see **5.41** above) and the proceeds of a balancing event under the business premises renovation code (see **8.11** above).

Also for 2017/18 onwards, proceeds of an asset arising to a person after leaving the cash basis must be brought into account as a receipt of the trade or business in calculating profits if an amount of capital expenditure relating to the asset meets condition A or B below (in the case of a trade etc.) or condition C or D below (in the case of a property business).

Condition A is that an amount of capital expenditure relating to the asset:

- was paid at a time when a cash basis election had effect;
- was brought into account in calculating profits on the cash basis; and
- would not have been qualifying expenditure for capital allowances purposes if no cash basis election had been in force.

Condition B is that is that an amount of capital expenditure relating to the asset was brought into account in calculating profits for a tax year for which no cash basis election had effect and which preceded the person's last entry into the cash basis. This does not include its being brought into account for capital allowances purposes.

Condition C is that an amount of capital expenditure relating to the asset:

- was paid in a tax year for which profits were calculated on the cash basis;
- was brought into account in calculating profits on the cash basis; and
- would not have been qualifying expenditure for the purposes of plant and machinery capital allowances if profits had not been calculated on the cash basis at the time the expenditure was paid.

Condition D is that is that an amount of capital expenditure relating to the asset was brought into account in calculating profits for a tax year in accordance with GAAP and that tax year preceded the person's last entry into the cash basis. The reference here to expenditure being brought into account is to its being brought into account as in (c)(iii) above, except that it does not include its being brought into account for capital allowances purposes.

If at any time the person ceases to use the asset (or any part of it) for the purposes of the trade, profession, vocation or property business, but does not dispose of the asset (or that part of it) at that time, he is treated for the purposes of the above provisions as disposing of the asset (or that part) at that time for its 'market value amount'. '*Market value amount*' is the amount that would be regarded as normal and reasonable in the market conditions then prevailing, and between persons dealing with each other on an arm's length basis in the open market.

If at any time there is a material increase in the person's non-business use of the asset (or any part of it), he is treated for the above purposes as disposing of the asset (or that part) at that time for an amount equal to the 'relevant proportion' of its market value amount. There is an increase in a person's non-business use of an asset (or part of an asset) only if the proportion of business use decreases *and* the proportion of use for other purposes increases. 'Material increase' is not defined. The '*relevant proportion*' is the difference between the proportion of non-business use before the increase and the proportion of non-business use after it.

If the business in question is an overseas property business, there is a deemed disposal at market value amount (as above) if the person ceases to be UK resident. The deemed disposal occurs on the last day of the tax year for which he is UK resident. If, however, a tax year is a split year as regards the person for the purposes of the statutory residence test, and the overseas part of the split year is the later part, the deemed disposal occurs on the last day of the UK part of the split year.

For 2016/17 and earlier years, if the whole or part of any expenditure incurred in acquiring, creating or improving an asset was brought into account in calculating profits on the cash basis (or would have been so brought into account if a cash basis election had been in force at the time the expenditure was paid), any 'disposal proceeds' relating to the asset had to be brought into account as a receipt in calculating profits on the cash basis. '*Disposal proceeds*' were defined as above, except that they did not include refunds of capital expenditure. If only part of the expenditure incurred in acquiring, creating or improving the asset was (or would have been) so brought into account, the capital receipt to be brought into account was proportionately reduced. There were rules identical to those described above for deemed disposals. There were no rules covering proceeds (or deemed disposal proceeds) arising after a person leaves the cash basis.

[*ITTOIA 2005, ss 96A, 96B, 307E, 307F; FA 2013, Sch 4 paras 20, 56; F(No 2)A 2017, Sch 2 paras 4, 5, 23, 64*].

Note that, at the time of writing, *F(No 2)A 2017* had not completed its passage through Parliament. The changes made to these provisions for 2017/18 onwards are therefore subject to any changes made during the Parliamentary process.

Effect of cash basis on capital allowances

[17.1D] With two exceptions, a person is not entitled to any capital allowance and is not liable to any balancing charge in calculating the profits of a trade, profession or vocation in relation to which an election for the cash basis is in effect. The first exception is that allowances under the plant and machinery code continue to be available (and balancing charges remain chargeable) for expenditure on the provision of a car (as defined at **5.51** above).

The second exception applies for 2017/18 onwards where

- qualifying expenditure under any of the capital allowances codes was incurred on an asset at a time when profits were not calculated on the cash basis;
- the person carrying on the business entered the cash basis for a tax year; and
- the expenditure would not have been deductible on the cash basis if it had been paid in that tax year.

In such circumstances, if any balancing charge or 'disposal value' would, but for the effect of the cash basis, arise in respect of the expenditure, the person carrying on the business is liable to the charge or must bring the value or proceeds into account. A '*disposal value*' for this purpose includes disposal values under the plant and machinery, flat conversion, mineral extraction, research and development, patents, know-how and assured tenancy codes and proceeds from balancing events under the industrial buildings and business premises renovations codes.

For this purpose, a person carrying on a trade, profession or vocation enters the cash basis for a tax year if a cash basis election is in force for that tax year but no such election was in force for the preceding tax year. A person carrying on a property business enters the cash basis for a tax year if profits are calculated on the cash basis for that tax year but were calculated in accordance with GAAP for the preceding tax year.

[*CAA 2001, ss 1(4)(5), 1A; FA 2013, Sch 4 paras 46, 56; F(No 2)A 2017, Sch 2 paras 49, 50, 64*].

There are provisions to deal with the consequences for capital allowances where a person enters or leaves the cash basis. For plant and machinery allowances see **5.33** and **5.47** above respectively. For mineral extraction allowances see **10.2A** above. For patent and know-how allowances see **12.1A** above. Note that the provisions for mineral extraction, patents, and know-how apply only to trades and for 2017/18 onwards. Provisions have been introduced for mineral extraction allowances even though mineral extraction trades are currently excluded trades for cash basis purposes (see *ITTOIA 2005, s 31C(8)*).

Note that, at the time of writing, *F(No 2)A 2017* had not completed its passage through Parliament. The changes made to these provisions for 2017/18 onwards are therefore subject to any changes made during the Parliamentary process.

Anti-avoidance provisions

Controlled and main benefit sales, etc.

[17.2] An anti-avoidance provision, as described in **17.3** below, applies in relation to sales of any property in any of the following circumstances.

(a) Where the buyer is a body of persons over whom the seller has 'control', or vice versa, or both buyer and seller are bodies of persons and some other person has control over both of them.
(b) Where the buyer and seller are connected persons within **2.34** above.
(c) Where it appears, with respect to the sale or with respect to transactions of which the sale is one, that the sole or main benefit which otherwise might be expected to accrue to the parties or any of them was:
  (i) the obtaining of an allowance,
  (ii) the obtaining of a greater allowance than would have otherwise been the case, or
  (iii) the avoidance or reduction of a charge,

  other than a plant or machinery allowance/charge.

References to a body of persons include references to a partnership.

'*Control*' is as defined in **2.31** above.

[*CAA 2001, s 567*].

See **17.5** below as regards the types of capital allowance to which these provisions relate.

[17.3] The anti-avoidance provision referred to in **17.2** above is that where property is sold at other than market value, and the sale is within **17.2** above, it is treated, subject to the making of an election as described in **17.4** below and the application of the anti-avoidance provision in **17.27** below, as if it had been sold at its market value. This affects both the buyer (as regards any allowances to which he will be entitled) and the seller (as regards balancing adjustments). [*CAA 2001, s 568*].

[17.4] Where a sale would be treated as being made at market value because the circumstances are as in **17.2**(a) (control) or (b) (connected persons) above, but **17.2**(c) above does not apply, the parties to the sale may elect for an amount to be substituted for market value. The amount substituted is the lower of the actual market value and a sum which is:

(a) for assets representing qualifying expenditure for the purposes of mineral extraction allowances, the unrelieved qualifying expenditure immediately before the sale;
(b) for assets representing allowable research and development expenditure, nil, if an allowance is made for that expenditure, and in any other case, the full amount of the qualifying expenditure (see **11.2** above).

Where the election is made, such balancing charge may be made on the buyer on any event occurring after the date of sale as would have fallen by reason of that event to be made on the seller if he had continued to own the property and had done all such things and been allowed all such allowances as were done by or allowed to the buyer.

[*CAA 2001, s 569*].

The election cannot be made if:

(i) the circumstances of the sale (including those of the parties to it) are such that no capital allowance or charge can be made on both parties, or

(ii) the buyer is a dual resident investing company within the meaning of *CTA 2010, s 949*.

An election has to be made within two years of the sale. It is therefore important for taxpayers affected not to let the two-year period elapse without action being taken. It should be noted that the time limit is not by reference to chargeable periods and can therefore be easily overlooked. Assessments and adjustments of assessments may be made as is necessary to give effect to an election.

[*CAA 2001, ss 569(7), 570*].

For the availability of an election on a partnership change, see **15.6** above.

[17.5] The provisions in **17.2** to **17.4** above apply in relation to all allowances subject to the following exceptions.

(a) Plant and machinery. There are separate provisions applicable to such plant or machinery as in **5.41**, **7.2**, **7.3–7.6**, **7.17** and **7.18** above.
(b) Dealings in know-how (see **12.14** above for alternative provisions).
(c) Expenditure on patent rights (see **12.8** above for alternative provisions).

[*CAA 2001, s 567(1); FA 2012, Sch 39 para 38(4)*].

In their relation to business premises renovation allowances and flat conversion allowances the provisions apply with the omission of the right to make the election described in **17.4** above. [*CAA 2001, s 570(1); FA 2012, Sch 39 para 38(5)*].

See **16.14** above for the capital gains tax provisions applying to a disposal at a loss of an asset in respect of which the election described in **17.4** above has been made.

Avoidance affecting the proceeds of a balancing event

[17.6] *FA 2003* introduced provisions to counter a particular avoidance scheme which sought to accelerate capital allowances artificially. Under the scheme, the market value of an asset would be artificially depressed, so that on disposal of the asset to a connected person, a greater balancing allowance would be obtained than would have otherwise been available. The provisions apply to the capital allowances codes for business premises renovation, flat conversion and mineral extraction.

Where an event occurs (a '*balancing event*') as a result of which a balancing allowance would otherwise arise, that allowance is denied if the amount to be brought into account as the proceeds or disposal value from the event is less than it would have otherwise been as a result of a tax avoidance scheme (i.e. a scheme or arrangement the main purpose, or one of the main purposes, of which is the obtaining of a tax advantage (see **2.32** above) by the person who would otherwise be entitled to the allowance).

Where a balancing allowance is denied under these provisions, the residue of qualifying expenditure (or, in the case of mineral extraction allowances, the unrelieved qualifying expenditure) immediately after the balancing event is calculated as if the balancing allowance had been made. This means that the allowances available to any purchaser of the asset will be reduced to the level that would have been available had the balancing allowance been made, so that, effectively, no allowances will ever be obtained for the amount of the balancing allowance forgone, even though the avoidance scheme at which the provisions are aimed merely achieved a timing advantage.

[*CAA 2001, s 570A; FA 2012, Sch 39 para 38(6)*].

Annual investment allowance and first-year allowances

[17.7] A number of anti-avoidance provisions are specifically concerned with annual investment allowance and first-year allowances on plant or machinery.

Where a company incurs expenditure on plant or machinery which it leases to another person and arrangements are made for another company (which may be either a successor company within *CTA 2010, ss 940A–953* as in **17.22** below or a connected person within **2.34** above) to take over such part of the first company's trade as includes its obligations under the leasing contract, the first company is not entitled to loss relief under *CTA 2010, ss 37, 45, 45A* or *45B* (see **2.38** above) in respect of losses incurred under the leasing contract either in the accounting period for which an annual investment allowance or first-year allowance is made in respect of that expenditure or in any subsequent accounting period, except against profits arising under that contract. The performance of the leasing contract is treated as a separate trade. [*CTA 2010, s 53; F(No 2)A 2017, Sch 4 para 150*].

On transfers between connected persons, sale and lease-back transactions and transfers the main benefit of which appears to be the obtaining of allowances, the buyer is not entitled to an annual investment allowance or first-year allowance. See **7.3–7.6** above.

See **2.36** above for denial of loss relief against general income in respect of annual investment allowance or first-year allowances in certain circumstances.

Finance lessors: receipt of major lump sum

[17.8] *FA 1997, Sch 12 Pt I* introduced anti-avoidance provisions, now contained in *ITA 2007, ss 614A–614DG* and *CTA 2010, ss 895–937*, with effect from 26 November 1996 in order to counter leasing schemes whereby finance lessors turned income into capital receipts, and to prevent tax deferral where rentals are concentrated towards the end of a lease term.

The provisions do not apply to the extent that, in the case of the current lessor, the lease is a long funding lease within the provisions at **6.21** onwards above.

The provisions apply to arrangements involving the lease of an asset which are dealt with by generally accepted accountancy practice as finance leases or loans where the effect of the arrangements is that some or all of the investment return is or may be in non-rental form and would not otherwise be wholly taxed as lease rentals. The principal purposes of the provisions are to charge any person entitled to the lessor's interest to tax by reference to the income return for accounting purposes (taking into account the substance of the matter as a whole, e.g. as regards connected persons or groups of companies); and to recover reliefs etc. for capital and other expenditure, including capital allowances (see **17.9** below), by reference to sums received which fall within the provisions.

The provisions apply where a lease of an asset (as widely defined) is or has at any time been granted in the case of which the following conditions are or have been satisfied at some time (the '*relevant time*') in an accounts period (i.e. a period for which accounts are drawn up) of the current lessor. Where the conditions have been satisfied at a relevant time, they are treated as continuing to be satisfied unless and until the asset ceases to be leased under the lease or the lessor's interest is assigned to a person not connected (see **2.34** above) with the assignor or certain other prior or subsequent lessors. Persons who are connected persons at any time in the period from the earliest time at which any of the leasing arrangements were made to the time when the current lessor finally ceases to have an interest in the asset or any arrangements relating to it are for these purposes treated as so connected throughout that period.

[*ITA 2007, ss 614B–614BB, 614DC; CTA 2010, ss 899–901, 933*].

The conditions referred to above are as follows.

(a) At the relevant time the leasing arrangements fall for accounting purposes to be treated as a finance lease or loan in relation to which either:
  (i) the lessor (or a connected person) is the finance lessor; or
  (ii) the lessor is a member of a group of companies for the purposes of whose consolidated accounts the finance lease or loan is treated as subsisting.

(b) A sum (a '*major lump sum*') is or may be payable to the lessor (or a connected person) under the leasing arrangements which is not rent but which falls to be treated for accounting purposes partly as repayment of some or all of the investment in respect of the finance lease or loan and partly as a return on that investment.

(c) Not all of the part of the major lump sum which is treated as a return on the investment (as in (b) above) would, apart from these provisions, be brought into account for tax purposes, as 'normal rent' from the lease for accounts periods of the lessor, in chargeable periods of the lessor ending with the 'relevant chargeable period'. For income tax purposes, the '*relevant chargeable period*' is the tax year (or latest year) whose trading basis period consists of or includes all or part of the accounts period in which the sum is or may be payable under the arrangements. For corporation tax purposes, the relevant chargeable period is the accounting period (or latest such period) which consists of or includes all or part of the accounts period in which the sum is or may be payable. A '*normal rent*' for an accounts period is the amount which (apart from the current provisions) the lessor would bring in for tax purposes in the period as rent arising from the lease.

(d) The accounts period of the lessor in which the relevant time falls (or an earlier period during which he was the lessor) is one for which the 'accountancy rental earnings' in respect of the lease exceed the normal rent. The '*accountancy rental earnings*' for a period are the greatest of the '*rental earnings*' for the period in respect of the lease (i.e. the amount treated under generally accepted accountancy practice as the gross return on investment for the period):
  (i) of the lessor;
  (ii) of any person connected with the lessor; and
  (iii) for the purposes of consolidated group accounts of a group of which the lessor is a member.

  Where (ii) or (iii) applies and the lessor's accounts period does not coincide with that of the connected person or the consolidated group accounts, amounts in the accounts periods of the latter are apportioned as necessary by reference to the number of days in the common periods. The normal rent for an accounts period for these purposes is determined by treating rent as accruing and falling due evenly over the period to which it relates (unless a payment falls due more than twelve months after any of the rent to which it relates is so treated as accruing).

(e) At the relevant time, either:
  (i) arrangements exist under which the lessee (or a connected person) may directly or indirectly acquire the leased asset (or an asset representing it — see *ITA 2007, s 614DD; CTA 2010, s 934*) from the lessor (or a connected person), and in connection with that acquisition the lessor (or a connected person) may directly or indirectly receive a '*qualifying lump sum*' from the lessee (or a connected person) (i.e. a non-rental sum part at least of which would, if the recipient were a UK-incorporated company, be treated under normal accountancy practice as a return on investment in respect of a finance lease or loan); or
  (ii) in the absence of such arrangements, it is in any event more likely that the acquisition and receipt described in (i) above will take place than that, before any such acquisition, the leased asset (or the asset representing it) will have been acquired in an open market sale other than by the lessor or lessee (or persons connected with either of them).

[*ITA 2007, ss 614BC–614BE, 614DA; CTA 2010, ss 902–904, 931*].

Where the above conditions are met, the consequences are broadly that the taxable rentals of the current lessor are increased or reduced as necessary to reflect the accountancy rental earnings over the life of the lease. In determining the chargeable gain on a disposal by the current lessor (or a connected person) of his interest under the lease (or of the leased asset or an asset representing it), the disposal consideration may also be reduced under the provisions to reflect the increased amount chargeable to tax as income.

[*ITA 2007, ss 614BF–614BO, 614D; CTA 2010, ss 905–914, 924; TCGA 1992, s 37A*].

Effect on capital allowances of receipt of major lump sum

[17.9] Where, in a case in which the provisions at **17.8** above apply, an occasion occurs on or after 26 November 1996 on which a major lump sum (as in **17.8**(b) above) falls to be paid, and capital expenditure incurred by the current lessor in respect of the leased asset has been taken into account for the purposes of any capital allowance or balancing charge, a countervailing receipt must be brought into account.

In the case of plant and machinery, mineral extraction, and patents, a disposal value is brought into account of an amount equal to the amount or value of the major lump sum, subject to the normal limiting provisions (see **5.41**, **10.27** and **12.7** above). Where, however, in addition to the disposal value arising under these provisions, a disposal value is to be brought into account in respect of the leased asset by reason of any other event occurring at the same time or subsequently, it is the aggregate amount of the disposal values which is not to exceed the limit concerned rather than any individual disposal value.

In the case of any of the other allowance codes in *CAA 2001*, a balancing charge is made on the current lessor of an amount equal to the lesser of:

- the aggregate of the allowances given (so far as not previously withdrawn); and
- the amount or value of the major lump sum.

These provisions apply equally to capital allowances for contributors to capital expenditure under *CAA 2001, ss 537–542*.

If a deduction under *ITTOIA 2005, ss 135, 138, 139* or *140* (films etc.) has been allowed to the current lessor in respect of expenditure incurred in connection with the leased asset, where a major lump sum falls to be paid on or after 26 November 1996, he must bring into account a revenue receipt equal to the excess of the amount of the major lump sum over that part of it which is treated as a revenue receipt under *ITTOIA 2005, s 134(2)*. Similar provisions apply to deductions made under *CTA 2009, s 147* or *ITTOIA 2005, s 170* (cemeteries and crematoria) and deductions under *CTA 2009, ss 142, 145* or *ITTOIA 2005, ss 165, 168* (restoration and preparation expenditure in relation to a waste disposal site).

[*ITA 2007, ss 614BR–614BW; CTA 2010, ss 917–922*].

For HMRC's views on various points of interpretation regarding these provisions and those in **17.8** above, see Revenue Tax Bulletin April 1997 pp 414–417.

Income and profits of parties to finance leasebacks of plant or machinery

[17.10] *Finance Act 2004* introduced anti-avoidance legislation to prevent the use by businesses of finance leasebacks of plant or machinery to obtain a double tax benefit by retaining the right to capital allowances whilst also obtaining a deduction for the leaseback rentals. The provisions were partly repealed by *Finance Act 2008* following which they apply only to lease and finance leasebacks (see **17.13** below). Although the provisions are enacted in *CAA 2001*, they do not in fact alter the capital allowances consequences of such leasebacks, but operate by restricting the deductions (or increasing profits).

Subject to the transitional provisions at **17.15** below, the provisions apply in relation to periods ending after 16 March 2004 where plant or machinery is the subject of a sale and finance leaseback (within **7.4** above) and the seller's disposal value (the '*restricted disposal value*') is restricted as in **7.4**(i) above. The provisions are repealed for sale and leasebacks where the sale takes place on or after 9 October 2007, but continue to apply in the case of a lease and finance leaseback — see **17.13** below. [*CAA 2001, s 228A; FA 2007, Sch 5 para 17(2); FA 2008, Sch 20 para 12(2)(12)*]. See **7.4** above for the meaning of 'finance lease' for the purposes of the provisions.

The provisions operate on the basis that 'correct accounts' are drawn up (i.e. accounts drawn up in accordance with generally accepted accounting practice (see *FA 2004, s 50*)). Where correct accounts are not drawn up, or no accounts at all are drawn up, the provisions apply as if correct accounts had been drawn up, and amounts referred to in the provisions as shown in accounts are those that would be shown in correct accounts. Where accounts have been drawn up in reliance on amounts derived from the accounts of an earlier period which were not correct accounts, amounts referred to in the provisions as shown in accounts for the later period are the amounts that would have been shown had the earlier accounts been correct accounts. [*CAA 2001, s 228H(2)–(4)*].

There is an oddity in the legislation in that the provisions operate by reference to 'periods of account'. For the purposes of *CAA 2001*, this term carries a specialised meaning relating to income tax only (see **2.1** and **2.22** above). It is difficult to reconcile the use of the term in these provisions with its stated meaning in the *Act*.

For HMRC guidance on the provisions, see HMRC Capital Allowances Manual, CA28900–CA28980.

The lessee

[17.11] Subject to the repeal of the provisions noted at **17.10** above, in calculating the lessee's income or profits for tax purposes, the amount deducted for a period of account in respect of amounts payable under the leaseback is restricted to the '*permitted maximum*', i.e. the aggregate of the finance charges shown in the accounts and the amount which would have been charged as depreciation had the value of the leased plant or machinery at the beginning of the leaseback been equal to the restricted disposal value. For the period of account in which the leaseback terminates (see below), the permitted maximum is increased by a proportion of the 'net book value' of the leased plant or machinery immediately before the termination (the '*current book value*') calculated according to the following formula:

$$\text{current book value} \times \frac{\text{original consideration}}{\text{original book value}}$$

where the '*original consideration*' is the consideration payable to the seller for entering into the transaction within **7.3**(i)–(iii) above and the '*original book* *value*' is the net book value of the plant or machinery at the beginning of the leaseback. These provisions do not affect the tax treatment of any amounts received by way of refund of amounts payable under a leaseback on its termination, including any amount which would be so received in respect of the lessee's interest under the leaseback if any amounts due to the lessor were disregarded.

For the period in which the leaseback terminates, the lessee's income or profits from the qualifying activity for the purposes of which the leased plant or machinery was used immediately before the termination are increased by a proportion of the 'net consideration' calculated according to the following formula:

$$\text{net consideration} \times \frac{\text{current book value}}{\text{original book value}}$$

where the '*net consideration*' is the original consideration as above less the restricted disposal value. This does not apply to the termination before 17 March 2004 of a leaseback which commenced before that date.

For these purposes, a '*termination*' of a leaseback includes the assignment of the lessee's interest, the making of any other arrangements under which a person other than the lessee becomes liable to make payments under the leaseback and any variation resulting in the leaseback ceasing to be a finance lease. The 'net book value' of an item of leased plant or machinery is its book value having regard to any relevant entry in the lessee's accounts and to depreciation up to the time in question, but disregarding any revaluation gains or losses and any impairment.

The above provisions do not apply where the lessee becomes the lessee by way of an assignment.

[*CAA 2001, ss 228B, 228C, 228H(1) as originally enacted*].

The above rules are adapted where the leaseback does not (or other arrangements in which the leaseback is comprised do not) fall under generally accepted accounting practice to be accounted for as a finance lease or loan in the accounts of the lessee and as a result an amount required for any of the above calculations cannot be ascertained. If the leaseback or arrangements fall under generally accepted accounting practice to be accounted for as a finance lease or loan in the accounts of a person connected (within **2.34** above) with the lessee, then, where the amount concerned can be ascertained in the accounts of the connected person, that amount is taken for the purpose of making the calculation.

If the leaseback or arrangements do not fall under generally accepted accounting practice to be accounted for as a finance lease or loan in the accounts of the lessee or any connected person, none of the above provisions apply. Instead, if the leaseback begins after 17 May 2004, the lessee's income or profits from the relevant qualifying activity for the period of account in which the leaseback begins are increased for tax purposes by the net consideration.

[*CAA 2001, s 228G; FA 2004, s 134(1); FA 2008, Sch 20 para 12(6)*].

The lessor

[17.12] Subject to the repeal of the provisions noted at **17.10** above, in calculating the lessor's income or profits for a period of account for tax purposes, the following adjustments are made unless the lessee became the lessee by means of an assignment of the lease before 17 March 2004. Amounts receivable in respect of the lessor's interest in the leaseback which fall to be included in such income or profits are so included without any reduction for amounts due to the lessee under the leaseback. However, the amounts receivable are themselves not included as income or profits to the extent that they exceed the '*permitted threshold*', i.e. the total of the 'gross earnings' under the leaseback and a proportion of the restricted disposal value calculated according to the following formula:

$$\text{restricted disposal value} \times \frac{\text{investment reduction for the period}}{\text{net investment}}$$

where the '*net investment*' is the amount shown in the lessor's accounts as the net investment in the leaseback at the beginning of its term, and the '*investment reduction for the period*' is the amount shown in those accounts in respect of the reduction in the net investment. The '*gross earnings*' under a leaseback are the amount shown in the lessor's accounts in respect of the lessor's gross earnings under the leaseback.

Where the leaseback terminates and the lessor disposes of the plant or machinery in circumstances such that the disposal value is limited by *CAA 2001, s 62* (disposal value limited, broadly, to the qualifying expenditure incurred on its acquisition — see **5.41** and **7.2** above), then in calculating for tax purposes the lessor's income or profits for the period in which the termination occurs, any amount refunded to the lessee may be deducted only to the extent that it does not exceed the limited disposal value. This does not apply in the case of a leaseback which commenced and terminated before 17 March 2004.

[*CAA 2001, ss 228D, 228E; FA 2008, Sch 20 para 12(5)*].

Lease and finance leaseback

[17.13] The provisions at **17.10**, **17.11** and (prior to the changes noted below) **17.12** above apply where plant or machinery is the subject of a 'lease and finance leaseback' with certain modifications. The modified provisions continue to apply following the repeal of the provisions applying to sale and finance leasebacks (see **17.10** above).

For this purpose, plant or machinery is subject to a '*lease and finance leaseback*' where a person ('S') leases plant or machinery to another ('B') and, after the date of the transaction, the plant or machinery:

(a) continues to be used by S for the purposes of a qualifying activity carried on by him; or
(b) is used for the purposes of a qualifying activity carried on by either S or any person, other than B, who is connected with S, and has not in the meantime been used for the purposes of any other qualifying activity except that of leasing the plant or machinery; or

(c) is used for the purposes of a non-qualifying activity carried on by S or any person (other than B) who is connected with S, without having been used in the meantime for the purposes of any qualifying activity other than leasing of the plant or machinery,

and the plant or machinery is available to be so used directly as a consequence of having been leased under a finance lease.

For this purpose S is regarded as leasing an item of plant or machinery to B only if he grants rights over the item for consideration and is not required to bring all of that consideration into account under the plant and machinery allowances code; but if this last condition is met only because of a joint election under *CAA 2001, s 199* (election to fix disposal value of fixtures — see **6.17** above) made before 18 May 2004 the item of plant or machinery in question is not regarded as leased by S to B. Where the lease granted by S is entered into on or after 9 October 2007, the consideration given for the grant of rights over the item to B excludes rentals payable under the grant and any 'relevant capital payments' (within *CTA 2010, s 890* or *ITA 2007, s 809ZA*; capital receipts from plant and machinery leases treated as income) to the extent that either of those sections applies to them.

In applying the provisions at **17.10–17.12** above to a lease and finance leaseback, S is the lessee and B (or an assignee of B) is the lessor, and the following modifications are made.

- The permitted maximum for the purposes of **17.11** above is restricted to the finance charges shown in the accounts, plus, on termination, a proportion of the current book value as calculated at **17.11** above (i.e. depreciation is excluded).
- Where the lease granted by S is entered into on or after 12 March 2008, if the use of the plant or machinery within (a)–(c) above includes use by a person other than B who is connected with S, the restriction of deductions to the permitted maximum at **17.11** above applies to that person as it applies to S.
- In calculating the amount to be added to the income or profits of the lessee on termination of the leaseback, or when the leaseback begins, as at **17.11** above, the net consideration is taken to be the consideration given by B for the grant by S of the rights over the plant or machinery.
- Amounts receivable by the lessor under the leaseback are disregarded in calculating his income or profits as at **17.12** above to the extent that they exceed the gross earnings.
- The restriction at **17.12** above on the deduction by the lessor of any amount refunded to the lessee does not apply.

The provisions at **17.12** above do not apply to a lease and finance leaseback in relation to 'post-commencement rentals' that fall to be taken into account in calculating for tax purposes the income or profits for any period of account ending on or after 6 December 2006. For this purpose, a '*post-commencement rental*' is an amount receivable on or after 6 December 2006 in respect of any period beginning on or after that date. A fraction of any amount receivable on or after 6 December 2006 in respect of any period straddling that date is also a post-commencement rental, the amount being apportioned on a time basis.

Amounts received before 6 December 2006 are excluded. Where, for any period of account ending on or after 6 December 2006, the amounts to be taken into account in calculating the income or profits for tax purposes under the provisions at **17.12** above, as applied by the above provisions, include both post-commencement rentals and other amounts, the gross earnings are taken to be so much of the gross earnings as relate, on a just and reasonable basis, to those other amounts.

[*CAA 2001, ss 228A–228C, 228F, 228G(6)(b), 228H(1A)(1B); FA 2007, Sch 5 para 17(3)(5)–(9); FA 2008, Sch 20 paras 12(2)–(5)(9)(12), 13; CTA 2010, Sch 1 para 345*].

Plant or machinery subject to further operating lease

[17.14] The following provisions apply where plant or machinery, whilst continuing to be the subject of a lease and finance leaseback or, before the partial repeal of the provisions at **17.10–17.12** above (see **17.10** above), a sale and finance leaseback, is leased to the original owner or a person connected (within **2.34** above) with him under an 'operating lease' commencing after 17 May 2004. For this purpose an '*operating lease*' is a lease not falling under generally accepted accounting practice to be treated as a finance lease or loan in the accounts of the lessee or a lease which is comprised in other arrangements, which arrangements do not fall to be so treated.

In calculating the income or profits of the lessee (i.e. the lessee under the operating lease) for tax purposes, the amount deducted for a period of account in respect of amounts payable under the operating lease is restricted to the permitted maximum under the leaseback (see **17.11** above).

In calculating the income or profits of the lessor (i.e. the lessor under the operating lease) for a period of account for tax purposes, the following adjustments are made. Amounts receivable in respect of the lessor's interest in the operating lease which fall to be included in such income or profits are so included without any reduction for amounts due to the lessee under the lease. However, the amounts receivable are themselves not included as income or profits to the extent that they exceed the amount which the lessee under the leaseback may deduct in respect of amounts payable under the leaseback (see **17.11** above).

Where only some of the plant or machinery which is the subject of the leaseback is also the subject of the operating lease these provisions apply subject to such apportionments as are just and reasonable.

[*CAA 2001, s 228J; FA 2008, Sch 20 para 12(10)*].

Transitional provisions

[17.15] Where a leaseback (an '*existing leaseback*') commenced before 17 March 2004, the provisions at **17.10–17.14** above operate subject to transitional rules. The complex rules seek to preserve the previous tax treatment for leaseback rentals payable or receivable in, or relating to, periods before that date.

For the purposes of the rules, a '*transitional period of account*' is a period of account that includes 17 March 2004. '*Pre-commencement rentals*' are any amounts payable by the lessee to the lessor before 17 March 2004 and any amounts so payable on or after that date in respect of a period ending before that date. Also included are the 'appropriate fraction' of any amounts payable on or after 17 March 2004 in respect of a period which includes that date. The '*appropriate fraction*' of any amount that relates to a particular period is the number of days in the part of the period falling before 17 March 2004 divided by the total number of days in the period.

[*FA 2004, s 134(4), Sch 23 paras 1, 11*].

Where the pre-commencement rentals are greater than the total 'actual rental deductions' for periods of account up to but not including the transitional period of account (i.e. there are '*excess rentals*'), the provisions at **17.11** restricting the amount which the lessee may deduct for tax purposes in respect of amounts payable under the leaseback to the permitted maximum are amended as follows.

No restriction applies to the transitional period of account if the lessee's excess rentals are greater than the 'notional rental deduction' for that period or to a subsequent period of account if the 'unrelieved portion' of the lessee's excess rentals is greater than the notional rental deduction for that period. In the first such period of account for which neither of these circumstances apply, the permitted maximum is the total of:

(i) the '*deductible excess*', i.e. the lessee's excess rentals (for the transitional period of account) or the unrelieved portion thereof (for a subsequent period of account); and
(ii) the amount given for the period by the calculation:

$$\text{basic amount} \times \frac{(\text{notional rental deduction} - \text{deductible excess})}{\text{notional rental deduction}}$$

where the '*basic amount*' is the normal permitted maximum given by the provisions at **17.11** above.

Where the period of account in question is the transitional period of account, however, where the total of (i) and (ii) above is less than the appropriate fraction of the notional rental deduction for that period, the latter amount is the permitted maximum.

The above rules do not prevent the inclusion on termination of the leaseback of a proportion of the current book value of the plant or machinery in the permitted maximum by the lessee. The rules do not apply to any period of account after the period of account for which the permitted maximum has been calculated as above (so that the provisions at **17.11** will apply in the normal way).

For the purposes of the above rules, the '*actual rental deduction*' for a period of account is the amount deductible in respect of amounts payable under the leaseback in calculating the lessee's income or profits for tax purposes for that period. The '*notional rental deduction*' for a period of account is the amount that would be so deductible if the provisions at **17.11** above did not apply. The '*unrelieved portion*' of the lessee's excess rentals for a period of account are the excess rentals less the total actual rental deductions for all previous periods of account from the transitional period of account onwards.

[*FA 2004, Sch 23 para 2*].

The permitted maximum is also increased for the period of account in which an existing leaseback terminates where, but for the termination, there would have been an unrelieved portion of the lessee's excess rentals (as above) for the following period of account. The increase is of an amount equal to that notional unrelieved portion. [*FA 2004, Sch 23 para 3*].

Where an existing leaseback terminates otherwise than by expiry of its term, the amount by which the lessee's income or profits are increased as at **17.11** above is restricted, if it would otherwise be greater, to the amount given by the calculation:

$$(\text{original consideration} - \text{relevant rentals}) \times \frac{\text{net consideration}}{\text{original consideration}}$$

where the '*relevant rentals*' are the pre-commencement rentals less the total of the finance charges shown in the accounts for periods ending before 17 March 2004 and the appropriate fraction of the finance charges shown in the accounts for the transitional period of account, and the original consideration and net consideration are defined as at **17.11** above). [*FA 2004, Sch 23 para 5*].

Special rules apply where the existing leaseback terminates other than by expiry and

(i) within one month beginning with the termination, the lessee becomes the owner of the plant or machinery by acquiring it either from the lessor or, where no person other than the lessor or a person connected (within **2.34** above) with the lessee has owned the plant or machinery at any time after the termination, from a person connected with the lessee;
(ii) the person who first acquires the plant or machinery from the lessor does so by incurring capital expenditure at least equal to its market value at the time of the termination; and
(iii) the amount of the '*lessee's acquisition expenditure*' (i.e. the capital expenditure incurred by him in acquiring the plant or machinery) that is qualifying expenditure for plant or machinery allowances purposes is restricted under *CAA 2001, s 226* (see **7.4** (iii) above).

If the 'section 226 restriction' exceeds the amount by which the lessee's income or profits would otherwise be increased, no such increase is made on termination but an increase, calculated as below, is subsequently made where there is a 'taxable disposal'. If the *section 226* restriction does not exceed the amount by which the lessee's income or profits would otherwise be increased, that amount is reduced by the *section 226* restriction and a further increase is made where there is a taxable disposal. For this purpose, the '*section 226 restriction*' is the lessee's acquisition expenditure less the '*restricted qualifying expenditure*' (i.e. the qualifying expenditure as restricted by *CAA 2001, s 226*). A '*taxable disposal*' occurs when, within six years beginning with the termination of the leaseback, there is an event requiring a disposal value to be brought into account for plant and machinery allowances purposes (see **5.41** above) in respect of the whole or part of the plant or machinery.

The increase to the lessee's income or profits required where there is a taxable disposal is made for the period in which the disposal occurs and is equal to the 'relevant fraction' of:

- where no increase was made to the lessee's income or profits on termination as a result of the above provisions, the amount given by the calculation:

$$\text{net consideration} \times \frac{\text{current book value}}{\text{original book value}}$$

  where net consideration and original book value are as defined at **17.11** above and the '*current book value*' is the net book value of the plant or machinery immediately before the cessation of ownership; or
- where the increase to the lessee's income or profits on termination was reduced by the amount of the *section 226* restriction, that amount.

The '*relevant fraction*' for this purpose is the 'disposal proceeds' less the restricted qualifying expenditure divided by the *section 226* restriction. The '*disposal proceeds*' are the higher of the consideration due to the lessee under the taxable disposal and the market value of the plant or machinery at the time of the disposal, but if either of those amounts is greater than the lessee's acquisition expenditure, that expenditure is the disposal proceeds, and if both of those amounts are less than the restricted qualifying expenditure, that expenditure is the disposal proceeds.

Where only part of the plant or machinery is the subject of a taxable disposal, the lessee's income or profits are increased only by the 'partial disposal fraction' of the amount given by the above rules. In calculating the disposal proceeds, the consideration due to the lessee is compared with the market value of the relevant part of the plant or machinery and the partial disposal fraction of the lessee's acquisition expenditure and restricted qualifying expenditure. For this purpose, the '*partial disposal fraction*' is so much of the lessee's acquisition expenditure as was attributable to the part of the plant or machinery subject to the taxable disposal divided by the total lessee's acquisition expenditure.

[*FA 2004, Sch 23 para 6*].

Where the pre-commencement rentals are greater than the total 'actual taxed rentals' for periods of account up to but not including the transitional period of account (i.e. there are '*lessor's excess rentals*'), the provisions at **17.12** determining the extent to which amounts receivable under the leaseback are included in the lessor's income or profits are amended as follows.

The provisions do not apply at all to the transitional period of account if the lessor's excess rentals are greater than the 'notional taxed rental' for that period or to a subsequent period of account if the 'untaxed portion' of the lessor's excess rentals is greater than the notional taxed rental for that period.

In the first such period of account for which neither of these circumstances apply, the permitted threshold for the purposes of the provisions is the total of:

(i) the '*deductible excess*', i.e. the lessor's excess rentals (for the transitional period of account) or the untaxed portion thereof (for a subsequent period of account); and

(ii) the amount given for the period by the calculation:

$$\text{basic amount} \times \frac{(\text{notional taxed rental} - \text{deductible excess})}{\text{notional taxed rental}}$$

where the '*basic amount*' is the normal permitted threshold given by the provisions at **17.12** above.

Where the period of account in question is the transitional period of account, however, where the total of (i) and (ii) above is less than the appropriate fraction of the notional taxed rental for that period, the latter amount is the permitted threshold. These rules do not prevent the inclusion of an amount in the permitted threshold for the period in question through the operation of the disregard of amounts due to the lessee in taking amounts receivable into account (see **17.12** above).

The rules do not apply to any period of account after the period of account for which the permitted threshold has been calculated as above (so that the provisions at **17.12** will apply in the normal way).

For the purposes of the above rules, the '*actual taxed rental*' for a period of account is the amount that should be taken into account in respect of amounts receivable under the leaseback in calculating the lessor's income or profits for tax purposes for that period. The '*notional taxed rental*' for a period of account is the amount that would be so taken into account if the provisions at **17.12** above did not apply. The '*untaxed portion*' of the lessor's excess rentals for a period of account are the excess rentals less the total actual taxed rentals for all previous periods of account from the transitional period of account onwards.

[*FA 2004, Sch 23 para 7*].

The permitted threshold is also increased for the period of account in which an existing leaseback terminates where, but for the termination, there would have been an untaxed portion of the lessor's excess rentals (as above) for the following period of account. The increase is of an amount equal to that notional untaxed portion. [*FA 2004, Sch 23 para 8*].

For 2003/04 onwards, or any accounting period ending after 16 March 2004, where a chargeable gain arises on a disposal by the lessee, on or after termination of an existing leaseback, of the whole or part of the plant or machinery subject to the leaseback, only a proportion of the gain is taken into account for tax purposes. The fraction to be applied to the gain to determine the part to be so taken into account is the 'net rentals' less the 'termination charge' divided by the 'lease premium'. This applies only in the case of a lease and finance leaseback. The '*net rentals*' for this purpose are the total amounts deducted in respect of amounts payable under the leaseback in calculating for tax purposes the lessee's income or profits less the total of the amounts shown in the lessee's accounts in respect of finance charges relating to the leaseback.

The '*termination charge*' is the amount by which the lessee's income or profits are increased in respect of the termination of the leaseback as at **17.11** above (subject to the modification at **17.13** above), and the '*lease premium*' is the consideration given for the grant of rights over the plant or machinery that constitutes the original lease (see **17.13** above). [*FA 2004, Sch 23 para 10*].

Disposal of plant or machinery subject to lease where income retained

[17.16] The following provisions apply where a lessor company carrying on a business of leasing plant or machinery (see **17.32** below), whether alone or in partnership, sells or otherwise disposes of any plant or machinery, on or after 5 December 2005, which it acquired wholly or partly for the purposes of the business and which is at the time of disposal subject to a 'lease' to another person. For this purpose, a '*lease*' includes an underlease, sublease, tenancy or licence or any agreement for any of those things.

If the lessor remains entitled immediately after the disposal to some or all of the rentals under the lease which are payable on or after the day of the disposal then the amount of any disposal value (see **5.41** above) which the company is required to bring into account is determined as follows.

Where the amount or value of the consideration for the disposal exceeds the limit that would otherwise be imposed by *CAA 2001, s 62* (disposal value not to exceed qualifying expenditure incurred by the company (see **5.41** above) or that incurred by a connected person (see **7.2** above)) or *CAA 2001, s 239* (limit on disposal value where additional VAT rebate received — see **17.53** below) that limit does not apply. Instead, the disposal value is the amount or value of the consideration.

In any other case the disposal value is the sum of the amount or value of the consideration and the total of the net present values (see below) of the rentals under the lease in respect of the plant or machinery which are payable during the 'term' of the lease (see **6.22** above) and on or after the day of the disposal and to which the lessor remains entitled immediately after the disposal. In this case the disposal value remains subject to the limit imposed by *CAA 2001, s 62* or *s 239*. Where the lease includes any land or other asset which is not plant or machinery, the net present value of rentals in respect of the plant or machinery is taken to be so much of the amount of the net present value of the rentals as, on a just and reasonable basis, relates to the plant or machinery.

To the extent that rentals are taken into account in the disposal value as above they are left out of account in calculating the income of the lessor's business for corporation tax purposes. Any apportionment required for this purpose is to be made on a just and reasonable basis.

The net present value of a rental is calculated by applying the formula:

$$\frac{\mathrm{RI}}{(1+\mathrm{T})^{i}}$$

where:

RI is the amount of the rental payment,

T is the temporal discount rate (i.e. 3.5% or such other rate as may be specified in regulations made by the Treasury), and

i is the number of days in the period beginning with the day of the disposal and ending with the day on which the payment is due, divided by 365.

Where the above provisions apply, any rentals receivable by the lessor before 22 March 2006 are left out of account in calculating the income of its business for corporation tax purposes.

[*CAA 2001, ss 228K–228M*].

Avoidance involving allowance buying

[17.17] *Finance Act 2010* introduced provisions to prevent the use by companies of schemes to, in effect, transfer an entitlement to capital allowances on plant or machinery where the written-down value is greater than the balance sheet value. Originally the provisions applied only to trades, but *FA 2013* extended their application to all qualifying activities (see below). The provisions apply where the relevant day (see below) is on or after 21 July 2009, although certain relaxations apply where the relevant day is before 9 December 2009.

The provisions apply where the following four conditions are met:

(a) a company carries on a trade or, where the relevant day is on or after 20 March 2013 (but see the transitional rule below), other qualifying activity either alone or in partnership;
(b) there is a 'qualifying change' in relation to the company on any day (the '*relevant day*') on or after 21 July 2009;
(c) the company or, where the trade or qualifying activity is carried on in partnership, the partnership had an 'excess of allowances' in relation to the trade or activity; and
(d) the qualifying change meets one of the limiting conditions.

Where the relevant day is before 20 March 2013, the condition in (d) above is that the qualifying change has to have an 'unallowable purpose'. This version of condition (d) also applies where the relevant day is on or after 20 March 2013 but the arrangements for the qualifying change were entered into before that date or there was an agreement or common understanding between the parties on the principal terms on which the qualifying change would happen. The extension of the provisions to all qualifying activities also does not apply in such circumstances.

[*CAA 2001, s 212B; FA 2010, Sch 4 paras 2, 5; FA 2013, Sch 26 paras 2, 5, 13*].

Definitions of the terms used in the above list are given at **17.18** below and the effect of the provisions is described at **17.19** below.

Definitions

[17.18] For the purposes of **17.17**(b) above, there is a '*qualifying change*' in relation to the company on the relevant day if any one or more of the following conditions is satisfied.

(A) Either the 'principal company' or principal companies of the taxpayer company at the start of the day is not, or are not, the same as at the end of the day, or, where the relevant day is on or after 9 December 2009, there is no such principal company at the start of the day but there is one or more at the end of the day.

(B) Any principal company of the taxpayer company is a 'consortium principal company' and its 'ownership proportion' at the end of the day is more than at the start of the day.

(C) The qualifying activity is a trade and the company ceases to carry on the whole or part of the trade on the relevant day and it begins to be carried on in partnership by two or more companies in circumstances to which *CTA 2010, ss 938–953* (company reconstructions without change in ownership — see **17.22** below) apply.

(D) The trade or other qualifying activity is carried on by the company in partnership at the start of the relevant day and its percentage share in the profits or losses of the trade or activity at the end of the day is less than at the start of the day (or is nil). A company's percentage share is determined on a just and reasonable basis, but regard must be had to anything which would be taken into account in allocating profits between partners under *CTA 2009, s 1262*.

A company (U) is a '*principal company*' of another company (C) if C is a qualifying 75% subsidiary of U and U is not a qualifying 75% subsidiary of another company. If U is a qualifying 75% subsidiary of another company (V) then V, but not U, is a principal company of C if V is not a qualifying 75% subsidiary of another company, and so on.

A company (X) is a principal company of C and also a '*consortium principal company*' of C if C is 'owned' by a consortium of which X is a member or C is a qualifying 75% subsidiary of a company owned by the consortium and, in either case, X is not a qualifying 75% subsidiary of another company. If X is a qualifying 75% subsidiary of another company (Y), then Y, but not X, is a principal company (and consortium principal company) of C if Y is not a qualifying 75% subsidiary of another company, and so on. For this purpose, a company is '*owned*' by a consortium if it is not a qualifying 75% subsidiary of another company but at least 75% of its ordinary share capital is beneficially owned between them by other companies, each of which owns no less that 5% of the capital. Those other companies are the members of the consortium.

A consortium principal company's '*ownership proportion*' is the lowest of:

- the percentage of the subsidiary company's ordinary share capital that it beneficially owns;
- the percentage to which it is beneficially entitled of any profits available for distribution to equity holders of the subsidiary company; and

- the percentage to which it would be beneficially entitled of any assets of the subsidiary company available to equity holders on a winding-up.

The expression 'equity holder' is interpreted, and the amounts available for distribution are determined, under the rules for group relief (see *CTA 2010, ss 157–182*) and where the subsidiary has no ordinary share capital those rules are applied as if its members were equity holders.

A company is a '*qualifying 75% subsidiary*' of another company if either of the first two of the following conditions is satisfied and the third condition is also satisfied. The first condition is that the subsidiary has ordinary share capital and at least 75% of that capital is beneficially owned directly or indirectly by the parent. The second condition is that the subsidiary does not have ordinary share capital and the parent has control of it. The third condition is that the parent is beneficially entitled to at least 75% of any profits available for distribution to equity holders of the subsidiary and of any assets of the subsidiary available for distribution to equity holders on a winding-up.

For the purposes of **17.17**(c) above, a company or partnership has an '*excess of allowances*' if the 'tax written-down value' is greater than the 'balance sheet value'. In computing each of these amounts, plant or machinery is excluded if it is provided for leasing under a long funding lease or if it is treated as owned by someone other than the company or partnership under *CAA 2001, s 67* (hire purchase etc. — see **7.8** above).

The '*tax written-down value*' is the total of amount 1 and, where the relevant day is on or after 9 December 2009, amount 2. Amount 1 is the total of any unrelieved qualifying expenditure in respect of plant and machinery in the main pool and any class or single asset pools which is available to be carried forward from the 'old period' (i.e. the accounting period which ends on the relevant day — see **17.19** below). The unrelieved expenditure in each pool at the end of the old period is calculated for this purpose on the assumption that all qualifying expenditure that could have been allocated to the pool has been so allocated, including any balance of first-year qualifying expenditure remaining after the giving of first-year allowances for the period. Where the relevant day is on or after 9 December 2009, the assumption is also made that any transaction on the relevant day which would reduce the unrelieved expenditure has not taken place.

Amount 2 is the total of any qualifying expenditure on the provision of a ship for the purposes of the trade or other qualifying activity which is in any pool and is unrelieved at the end of the old period as a result of a notice under *CAA 2001, s 130* (postponement of allowances — see **5.74** above).

Where the qualifying change is within (C) above, amounts 1 and 2 are taken to be what they would have been but for the change. Plant and machinery expenditure on which is included in amounts 1 and 2 is referred to below as '*relevant plant and machinery*'.

The '*balance sheet value*' is that of the relevant plant and machinery and is found by adding together any amounts shown in respect of it in a balance sheet of the company or partnership drawn up in accordance with generally accepted accounting practice at the beginning of the relevant day, but adjusted to reflect the disposal of any of the relevant plant and machinery on that day. The amounts to be added together are the amounts shown as the net book value or carrying amount of the relevant plant and machinery plus any amounts shown as the net investment in finance leases of it. Just and reasonable apportionments are to be made where any of the plant or machinery is a fixture in land (defined as at **6.3** above) and the amount to be shown in the balance sheet in respect of the land would include an amount in respect of the fixture and where any of the plant or machinery is subject to a finance lease and any land or other asset is also subject to the lease.

For the purpose of **17.17**(d) above, the limiting conditions are:

(1) the amount of the excess of allowances is £50 million or more;
(2) the amount of the excess allowances is £2 million or more but less than £50 million and is not insignificant as a proportion of the total amount or value of the benefits derived by any 'relevant person' as a result of the qualifying change or any 'arrangements' made to bring about the change or otherwise connected with the change;
(3) the amount of the excess of allowances is less than £2 million and the qualifying change has an unallowable purpose;
(4) the main purpose, or one of the main purposes, of any arrangements is to procure that the conditions in (1)–(3) above are not met.

A '*relevant person*' for the purpose of (2) above means a principal company of the taxpayer company, a person carrying on the qualifying activity in partnership or a person connected with such a company or partner.

For the purposes of (3) above and the pre-20 March 2013 condition (d) at **17.17** above, a qualifying change has an '*unallowable purpose*' if the main purpose, or one of the main purposes, of any arrangements made to bring about the change or any arrangements otherwise connected with the change is for any person to become entitled to a reduction in corporation tax profits or an increase in losses resulting from a claim to allowances for qualifying expenditure on the relevant plant or machinery or qualifying expenditure which would fall within amount 2 above.

'*Arrangements*' include any agreement, understanding, scheme, transaction or series of transactions, whether or not legally enforceable.

[*CAA 2001, ss 212C–212M; FA 2010, Sch 4 paras 2, 5, 6; FA 2013, Sch 26 paras 3, 6–9*].

Effect of provisions

[17.19] Where the provisions at **17.17** above apply, the accounting period of the taxpayer company which is current on the relevant day ends with that day and a new accounting period starts the next day. Where **17.18**(A), (B) or (D) apply and the trade or qualifying activity is carried on in partnership at the start of the relevant day it is the accounting period of the partnership which comes to an end with that day, and an accounting period of either the partnership or company which is carrying on the trade or activity after the qualifying change which starts the next day. The accounting period which ends on the relevant day is the '*old period*' below, and the accounting period starting on the next day is the '*new period*'.

Where the taxpayer company or the partnership carrying on the trade or activity at the beginning of the relevant day has an 'excess of allowances' (see below) at the end of the old period in any single asset, class or main pool the following apply in relation to each pool.

(1) The unrelieved qualifying expenditure in the pool is reduced at the start of the new period by the amount of the excess allowances (see below). Where **17.18**(C) applies, this rule applies from the time of the qualifying change rather than the start of the new period.

(2) The amount of the excess allowances is treated from the beginning of the new period as qualifying expenditure in a new pool of the same type. Where **17.18**(C) applies, this rule applies from the time of the qualifying change rather than the start of the new period.

(3) Where, following the qualifying change, a person ceases to carry on a trade or qualifying activity and the taxpayer company begins to carry it on as part of its trade or business, in claiming allowances on expenditure in the new pool the transferred trade or activity is treated as a separate trade or business. This rule applies equally where only part of a trade or activity is transferred or where the taxpayer company starts to carry on the trade or activity in partnership.

(4) A loss attributable to an allowance claimed on expenditure in the new pool cannot be set off under *CTA 2010, ss 37, 45A, 62 or 66* (relief for trade and property business losses — see **2.38** and **2.42** above) or *CAA 2001, ss 259, 260(3)* (excess allowances in respect of special leasing — see **2.44** above) except against profits of a qualifying activity carried on by the company, or a company which is a member of the partnership, at the start of the relevant day. For this purpose, any activity not carried on by the company or member at the start of the relevant day is not treated as forming part of a qualifying activity carried on by them at that time even if it would otherwise be so treated for corporation tax purposes.

(5) The amount of such a loss that can be so used by any person cannot exceed the amount which would have been available for use by that person but for the qualifying change.

(6) Similarly, a loss attributable to an allowance claimed on expenditure in the new pool cannot be claimed as group relief or group relief for carried-forward losses (see **2.38** above) unless it could have been claimed but for the qualifying change, and the amount of any such loss that can be claimed cannot exceed the amount which could have been claimed but for the qualifying change.

A company or partnership has an '*excess of allowances*' in a pool if 'PA' is greater than 'BSVP' and the amount of the excess is the difference between the two. For this purpose, 'PA' is the amount in relation to the pool used in calculating amount 1 at **17.18** above, and 'BSVP' is so much of the balance sheet value (see **17.18** above) as it is appropriate to attribute to the pool on a just and reasonable apportionment. If, however, PA is less than BSVP for any other pool, the amount of the excess of allowances for the pool in question is reduced by the difference between the two amounts for the other pool (or where a reduction under this rule has already been made in respect of any other pools or a reduction under the equivalent rule for postponed allowances below has already been made, by so much of the difference as is left).

Where there is a disposal event in respect of any of the relevant plant and machinery, the disposal proceeds must be apportioned between the new pool and the original pool on a just and reasonable basis.

Where amount 2 at **17.18** above is an amount other than nil (i.e. where the company or partnership has postponed allowances) and the relevant day is on or after 9 December 2009, provisions similar to those at (3) to (6) above apply by reference to the postponed allowances. If PA is less than BSVP for any pool, the amount of the postponed allowances is reduced by the difference between the two amounts for the pool (or where a reduction under the equivalent rule for pools above has already been made, by so much of the difference as is left).

If the relevant day is on or after 9 December 2009 and any plant or machinery is transferred on the relevant day and would, but for the requirement to ignore such transfers, reduce the tax written-down value as defined at **17.18** above, no person other then the company or partnership can claim an allowance in respect of that plant or machinery after the transfer.

[*CAA 2001, ss 212N–212S; FA 2010, Sch 4 paras 2, 5, 6; FA 2013, Sch 26 paras 10–12; F(No 2)A 2017, Sch 4 para 124*].

Leased plant and machinery

[17.20] *FA 2010* introduced provisions designed to reverse the effects of two avoidance schemes involving the leasing of plant and machinery which were disclosed to HMRC under the disclosure of tax avoidance schemes provisions. Under the first scheme arrangements are made to create a company that is taxed on very little income from the leasing but which can claim capital allowances on the full cost of the leased asset, so creating a tax loss from a commercial profit. The second scheme involves arrangements where a lessor has claimed capital allowances in the initial loss-making phase of the lease but avoids tax on the income arising once the loss is in its tax-profitable phase. (A variation on the first scheme relies on obtaining a deduction for a rebate of rentals to generate the tax loss; the provisions dealing with this variation are outside the scope of this work — see *ITTOIA 2005, s 55B; CTA 2009, s 60A*.)

The provisions aimed at the first scheme apply where capital expenditure is incurred on or after 9 December 2009 on provision of plant or machinery if at the time it is incurred the asset is leased, or arrangements exist under which it is to be leased, and arrangements have been entered into in relation to payments under the lease with the effect of reducing the value of the asset. For this purpose, a lease includes any arrangements under which plant or machinery is to be leased or otherwise made available by one person to another.

The lessor's qualifying expenditure is reduced to the amount VI + VR, where VI is the 'present value' of the lessor's 'income from the asset', and VR is the present value of the 'residual value' of the asset reduced by any 'rental rebate'.

Where expenditure on provision of the asset by the lessor has also been incurred previously, it is the total qualifying expenditure that is reduced in this way.

For this purpose, the lessor's '*income from the asset*' is the total of all amounts which have been received, or which it is reasonable to expect will be received, by the lessor in connection with the lease and which have been, or it is reasonable to expect will be, brought into account as income in computing taxable profits. Amounts to be brought into account as disposal values (see **5.41** above) are, however, excluded, as are amounts representing charges for services or any UK or foreign tax or duty other than income tax, corporation tax or similar foreign tax, to be paid by the lessor. The '*residual value*' of the asset is what it is reasonable to expect will be the market value of the lessor's interest in the asset immediately after the termination of the lease.

The '*present value*' of an amount is calculated using the interest rate implicit in the lease. In most cases, this will be the interest rate that would apply using normal commercial criteria, including generally accepted accounting practice. Where, however, the implicit interest rate cannot be determined in this way, it is taken to be 1% above LIBOR (i.e. the London interbank offered rate on the day on which the lease was entered into (or, if that was not a business day, the next business day) for deposits for a term of twelve months in the currency in which the lease rentals are payable).

A '*rental rebate*' is any sum payable to the lessee which is calculated by reference to the asset's termination value, i.e. in most cases its value at or about the time the lease terminates. Calculation by reference to the termination value also includes, however, calculation by reference to the proceeds of sale where the asset is sold, any insurance proceeds, compensation or similar sums arising from the asset and an estimate of the market value. It also includes any determination which might reasonably be expected to produce a broadly similar result to calculation by reference to the termination value and any other form of calculation indirectly by reference to the termination value.

[*CAA 2001, ss 228MA–228MC; FA 2010, Sch 5 para 1*].

The provision aimed at the second scheme applies where plant or machinery is subject to a lease and a disposal event occurs on or after 9 December 2009 which results in a disposal value within **5.41**(a), (b) or (i) being brought into account (i.e. the disposal event is a sale of the plant or machinery or any other event other than those specified at **5.41**(c)–(h)). If arrangements have been entered into which reduce the disposal value to the extent that it is attributable to rentals payable under the lease then the disposal value must be determined as if the arrangements had not been entered into.

This provision does not apply where arrangements take the form of a transfer of an income stream the value of which is taxed as income under *ITA 2007, s 809AZA* or *CTA 2010, s 752*. [*CAA 2001, s 64A; FA 2010, Sch 5 para 3*].

FA 2016 introduced a further provision to reverse the effects of an avoidance scheme involving arrangements under which non-taxable consideration is received when taking over tax deductible lease obligations. The provision applies where, under any 'arrangements', a person chargeable to income tax or a company chargeable to corporation tax (P) agrees on or after 25 November 2015 to take over the obligations of another person (Q) as lessee under a 'lease of plant or machinery' and as a result, P or a person connected with P, becomes entitled to 'income deductions'. If a 'payment' is payable to P or a connected person by way of consideration for the agreement, that payment is treated for tax purposes as income received by P or the connected person in the period of account or tax year in which P takes over the obligations. This does not apply to the extent that the payment is otherwise charged to tax as income of P or the connected person, brought into account in calculating taxable income of P or the connected person or brought into account by P or the connected person for capital allowances purposes as a disposal receipt or proceeds from a balancing or disposal event.

The provision applies however P takes over the obligations of Q, whether by assignment, novation, variation or replacement of the contract, by operation of law or otherwise. It applies in priority to any other tax provision other than the general anti-abuse rule.

A '*lease of plant or machinery*' is widely defined to include any agreement or arrangement under which sums are paid for the use of, or otherwise in respect of, plant or machinery. '*Income deductions*' are deductions in calculating income or from total profits. '*Arrangements*' include any scheme, arrangement, understanding, transaction or series of transactions, whether or not legally enforceable. '*Payment*' includes provision of any benefit, assumption of any liability or transfer of money or money's worth. A payment is by way of consideration if it is made, directly or indirectly, in consequence of or otherwise in connection with, the agreement to take over the obligations as lessee where it is reasonable to assume that the agreement would not have been made unless the arrangements included provision for the payment.

[*ITA 2007, s 809ZFA; CTA 2010, s 894A; FA 2016, s 68*].

Ring fence trades — decommissioning and site restoration expenditure

[17.21] *FA 2013* introduced anti-avoidance provisions under the plant and machinery and mineral extraction allowances codes which are specific to the oil industry. Under the provisions, plant or machinery allowances on 'decommissioning expenditure' and mineral extraction allowances on site restoration are restricted where either a connected person supplies services or there is an avoidance purpose to a transaction. The provisions apply to expenditure incurred on decommissioning and site restoration carried out on or after 17 July 2013.

Plant and machinery allowances are restricted where a person ('R') who is carrying on, or has ceased to carry on, a ring fence trade (see **5.40** above) enters into an arrangement under which a person ('S') who is connected with R provides a service to R and all or part of the consideration for the service is decommissioning expenditure. The service may be provided indirectly and it does not matter whether R and S are parties to the same contract or whether payments are made by R directly to S. Providing a service includes letting a ship on charter or any other asset on hire and providing goods which are to be used up in the course of providing a service.

'*Decommissioning expenditure*' means expenditure in connection with 'decommissioning'. '*Decommissioning*' means demolishing plant or machinery, preserving plant or machinery pending its reuse or demolition, preparing plant or machinery for reuse or arranging for plant or machinery to be reused. It does not matter whether, in fact, the plant or machinery is reused, demolished or partly reused and partly demolished.

The restriction is that the amount by which R's 'expenditure under the arrangement' exceeds 'amount D' is excluded from R's available qualifying expenditure (see **5.36** above). R's '*expenditure under the arrangement*' is so much of the consideration for the service as is decommissioning expenditure incurred by R. '*Amount D*' is:

(1) where neither of (2) or (3) below apply; the cost to S of providing the service (or the part of the service which relates to R's expenditure under the arrangement);
(2) where the service is a planning or project management service and the cost plus method is an appropriate method, under the OECD transfer pricing guidelines, to apply the transfer pricing rules; the cost to S of providing the service (or part) plus the appropriate mark up on that cost using the cost plus method (or 10% of the cost if less);
(3) where S decommissions the plant or machinery, R is not the only participator in the oil field in question and the expenditure on decommissioning is apportioned between the participators according to their share in the oil or the equity in the field; the part of the expenditure on decommissioning which is incurred by R.

Where plant or machinery has been used in more than one field and the expenditure on decommissioning is apportioned between those fields in accordance with the contribution from each field to the total oil won using the plant or machinery, (3) above applies separately to the expenditure apportioned to each field. The rule in (1) above applies instead of that in (3) above if the consideration received by S (or the method of determining it) or the apportionment of the expenditure between participators or fields has been agreed as, or as part of, an avoidance scheme (i.e. a scheme a main purpose of which is to enable a person to obtain a tax advantage under the plant and machinery allowances code that would not otherwise be obtained).

If the service, or part of it, is provided by more than one person, so that there would otherwise be more than one amount D, the lowest of those amounts is taken to be amount D.

Plant and machinery allowances are also restricted where:

(a) a person ('A') who is carrying on, or has ceased to carry on, a ring fence trade enters into a transaction with another person ('B');
(b) B receives consideration from A , all or part of which is decommissioning expenditure, for services provided under the transaction; and
(c) the transaction has an avoidance purpose or is part of or occurs as a result of a scheme or arrangement (whether or not legally enforceable) which has an avoidance purpose.

In (c) above, the scheme or arrangement may have been made before or after the transaction was entered into. A scheme, arrangement or transaction has an avoidance purpose if a main purpose of a party in entering into it or in agreeing an amount of consideration or a method of determining an amount of consideration to be paid under it is to enable a person to obtain a tax advantage under the plant and machinery allowances code that would not otherwise be obtained.

The restriction is that all or part of A's expenditure under the transaction is excluded from A's available qualifying expenditure (see **5.36** above). The amount to be excluded is the amount which would cancel out the tax advantage (but cannot exceed A's expenditure). This rule applies even if the tax advantage would be obtained by a person other than A.

[*CAA 2001, ss 165A–165E; FA 2013, Sch 32 paras 2, 8*].

Mineral extraction allowances are restricted where a person ('X') who is carrying on, or has ceased to carry on, a ring fence trade enters into an arrangement under which a person ('Y') who is connected with X provides a service to X in connection with work on the 'restoration' (see **10.11** above) of the site of a source (which includes land used in connection with the working of the source) and all or part of the consideration for the service would otherwise be qualifying expenditure of X under *CAA 2001, s 416ZA* (see **10.11** above).The service may be provided indirectly and it does not matter whether X and Y are parties to the same contract or whether payments are made by X directly to Y. Providing a service includes letting a ship on charter or any other asset on hire and providing goods which are to be used up in the course of providing a service.

The restriction is that the amount of the consideration for the service which exceeds 'amount D' is excluded from X's qualifying expenditure. '*Amount D*' is:

(i) where neither of (ii) or (iii) below apply; the cost to Y of providing the service (or, if the qualifying expenditure relates only to part of the service, that part);
(ii) where the service is a planning or project management service and the cost plus method is an appropriate method, under the OECD transfer pricing guidelines, to apply the transfer pricing rules; the cost to Y of providing the service (or part) plus the appropriate mark up on that cost using the cost plus method (or 10% of the cost if less);
(iii) where Y carries out the restoration, X is not the only participator in the oil field in question and the expenditure on restoration is apportioned between the participators according to their share in the oil or the equity in the field; the part of the expenditure on restoration which is incurred by X.

Where a site has been used in connection with winning oil from more than one field and the expenditure on restoration is apportioned between those fields in accordance with the contribution from each field to the total oil won using that site, (iii) above applies separately to the expenditure apportioned to each field. The rule in (i) above applies instead of that in (iii) above if the consideration received by Y (or the method of determining it) or the apportionment of the expenditure between participators or fields has been agreed as, or as part of, an avoidance scheme (i.e. a scheme a main purpose of which is to enable a person to obtain a tax advantage under the mineral extraction allowances code that would not otherwise be obtained).

If the service, or part of it, is provided by more than one person, so that there would otherwise be more than one amount D, the lowest of those amounts is taken to be amount D.

The plant and machinery restriction for transactions with an avoidance purpose described above applies, with the necessary modifications, to restrict site restoration expenditure as it applies to restrict decommissioning expenditure.

[*CAA 2001, ss 416ZC–416ZE; FA 2013, Sch 32 paras 9, 11*].

Company reconstructions without change of ownership

[17.22] Where one company succeeds to a trade formerly carried on by another and the two companies are under common ownership, there are special rules regarding the treatment of capital allowances in respect of that trade, these being contained in *CTA 2010, s 948*. The rules take priority over the normal capital allowances rules. [*CAA 2001, s 560A; CTA 2010, Sch 1 para 359*].

Subject to the exclusions at **17.24** below, the provisions apply where:

(a) on the transfer of the trade or at any time within two years after that event, the trade or an interest amounting to not less than a three-quarters share in it belongs to the same persons as the trade, or such an interest in it, belonged to at some time within a year before that event, and

(b) within the period taken as the period of comparison under (a) above, the trade is at no time carried on other than by a company which is within the charge to corporation tax or income tax in respect of it.

References to a trade include references to any other trade, the activities of which comprise the activities of that first-mentioned trade.

The provisions described below do not apply if the successor company is a dual resident investing company within *CTA 2010, s 949*.

[*CTA 2010, ss 940A–943, 949(1); F(No 2)A 2017, Sch 4 para 62*].

Where the above conditions are satisfied, all allowances and charges that would have fallen to be made to or on the predecessor, if it had continued to carry on the trade, are made instead to the successor. Such allowances or charges are to be calculated as if the successor had been carrying on the trade since the time when the predecessor began to carry it on and as if everything done to or by the predecessor had been done to or by the successor. No balancing allowances or charges arise by virtue of assets being sold or transferred by the predecessor to the successor on the transfer of the trade if they are in use for the purposes of the trade, such assets being treated as transferred at their tax written-down value. [*CTA 2010, s 948; FA 2011, Sch 6 para 24*].

These provisions apply also where only part of a trade is transferred and/or where the successor company carries on the transferred trade as part of its trade. [*CTA 2010, s 951; F(No 2)A 2017, Sch 4 para 67*].

See **5.53**, **7.17** and **7.18** above for comments on the interaction of these provisions with those contained therein (which deal with plant and machinery allowances on a transfer of an expensive car or a succession to a trade).

Where the above provisions apply, HMRC consider that the predecessor should be treated as having a chargeable period which ends on the transfer date and the successor as having a chargeable period which begins on that date. In the case of a transfer of part of a trade, that part should be treated as a separate notional trade of the predecessor from the beginning of the accounting period in which the transfer takes place. Capital allowance assets are to be apportioned for this purpose between that part and the balance of the trade on a just and reasonable basis. If the trade (or part) transferred from the predecessor to the successor expands a pre-existing trade, or if the successor has no pre-existing trade but acquires a trade (or part) from another person at the same time, each transferred trade (or part) should be treated as a separate notional trade of the successor for the successor's notional chargeable period commencing on the transfer date (HMRC Capital Allowances Manual, CA15400).

EXAMPLE 1

[17.23]

A Ltd, which makes up its accounts to 30 June, transfers the whole of its trade to B Ltd on 30 September 2017 in circumstances such that *CTA 2010, s 948* applies. B Ltd, which makes up its accounts to 31 December, then carries on the trade as part of its own trade. At 1 July 2017, A Ltd had unrelieved qualifying expenditure of £16,000 on plant and machinery in the main pool as well as a short-life asset (purchased in 2015) in a single asset pool, the written-down value of which was £3,000. B Ltd had unrelieved qualifying expenditure of £8,000 on plant and machinery in the main pool as at 1 January 2017. The following transactions took place in the six months to 31 December 2017.

(a) A Ltd sold the short-life asset mentioned above on 31 August 2017 for £2,000.
(b) B Ltd purchased plant on 1 October 2017 for £12,000.

The capital allowances for the period to 31 December 2017 are calculated as follows.

Plant and machinery allowances

A Ltd

	Main pool	*Short-life asset*	*Total allowances*
	£	£	£
WDV at 1.7.17	16,000	3,000	
Disposal		(2,000)	
Balancing allowance		£1,000	1,000
WDA (Three-month period —18% × $^{3}/_{12}$)	(720)		720
WDV at 30.9.17	15,280		

A Ltd

	Main pool	*Short-life asset*	*Total allowances*
	£	£	£
Transfer to B Ltd	(15,280)		
Total allowances (period 1.7.17 to 30.9.17)			£1,720

B Ltd

	Main pool	*Total allowances*
	£	£
WDV b/fwd at 1.1.17	8,000	
Purchase 1.10.17	12,000	
Transfer from A Ltd	15,280	
	35,280	
AIA	(12,000)	12,000
	23,280	
WDA on £8,000 (at 18%)	(1,440)	1,440
WDA on £15,280 (at 18% p.a.) × $^{3}/_{12}$	(688)	688
WDV at 31.12.17	£21,152	
Total allowances (year ended 31.12.17)		£14,128

Note

(a) This example applies the current HMRC guidance referred to at **17.22** above. It should be noted that previous Revenue guidance adopted a different approach which gave differing results. See CCAB statement TR 500, issued in March 1983, and the Revenue Capital Allowances Manual, CA2158 (as at December 2001).

Reconstructions involving business of leasing plant or machinery

[17.24] Following disclosures made to HMRC of schemes using *ICTA 1988, s 343(2)* (now *CTA 2010, s 948*) to avoid the application of *FA 2006, Sch 10* (now *CTA 2010, ss 382–437* — see **17.30** below), *FA 2007* introduced restrictions on the circumstances in which *s 948* (or *s 343(2)*) applies where the trade is or forms part of a 'business of leasing plant or machinery' (see **17.32** below).

For cessations occurring on or after 22 November 2006 and before 21 March 2007 where, on the day of cessation, neither the predecessor nor the successor carry on the trade in partnership, *s 343(2)* did not apply unless, on that day, each company which is a 'principal company' of the predecessor is also a 'principal company' of the successor.

For cessations occurring on or after 21 March 2007 where, on the day of cessation, neither the predecessor nor the successor carry on the trade in partnership, *s 948* does not apply unless:

(a) the principal company or companies of the predecessor immediately before the cessation are the same as the principal company or companies of the successor immediately afterwards, and
(b) if any of those principal companies is a 'consortium principal company', the 'ownership proportion' in relation to the predecessor immediately before the cessation is the same as the relevant fraction in relation to the successor immediately afterwards (regardless of whether the members of each consortium are the same).

For cessations occurring on or after 21 March 2012, for the purposes of (a) above, the principal company or companies of the predecessor immediately before the cessation are not regarded as the same as the principal company or companies of the successor immediately afterwards if there is a qualifying change of ownership of the successor within *CTA 2010, s 394ZA* (company joining tonnage tax group — see **17.30** below) before the day of cessation. This applies even if the qualifying change of ownership occurs before 21 March 2012, but where the change occurs as a result of a company becoming a member of a tonnage tax group without itself entering tonnage tax at the same time, the rule applies only where the day of cessation is on or after 23 April 2012.

For cessations occurring on or after 21 March 2007 where, on the day of cessation, the predecessor or the successor carries on the trade in partnership, *s 948* does not apply unless the predecessor ceases to carry on the whole of its trade and that trade is a business of leasing plant or machinery carried on in partnership on the day of cessation.

Where *s 948* does not apply because of the above provisions, the plant or machinery belonging to the trade is treated as sold by the predecessor to the successor at the higher of its 'ascribed value' immediately before the cessation and the disposal value that the predecessor would otherwise have been required to bring into account as a result of the cessation. For transfers before 23 March 2011, the plant or machinery was treated as sold by the predecessor to the successor at market value (determined on the assumption of a disposal by an absolute owner free from all leases and other encumbrances) on the day of cessation. 'Ascribed value' for this purpose is as defined at **17.33** below but treating references there to the company as references to the predecessor.

For the above purposes, a company is a '*principal company*' of another company if that other company is its 'qualifying 75% subsidiary' and it is not itself a qualifying 75% subsidiary of a third company. In the case of consortium relationships, a company (company B) is the principal company of another company if it is itself not a qualifying 75% subsidiary of any company and if that other company is owned by a consortium, or is a 'qualifying 90% subsidiary' of a company owned by a consortium, of which company B is a member. If company B is a qualifying 75% subsidiary of another company, company A, company A is the principal company provided it is not itself a qualifying 75% subsidiary of another company (and so on). A company is a '*qualifying 75% subsidiary*' of another if it is a 75% subsidiary within *CTA 2010, s 398* (or, if it has no ordinary share capital, it is controlled (within *CTA 2010, s 1124*) by the parent company) and the parent company is beneficially entitled to at least 75% of profits available for distribution by the subsidiary and would be so entitled to at least 75% of assets available for distribution to equity holders on a winding-up of the subsidiary. '*Qualifying 90% subsidiary*' is defined in the same way, but with references to 75% replaced by 90%.

A company is a '*consortium principal company*' if it is a principal company by virtue of a consortium relationship. The '*ownership proportion*' in the case of a consortium relationship is the lowest of the percentage of the ordinary share capital held by the principal company, its percentage entitlement to distributable profits and theist percentage entitlement to assets on a winding up.

[*CTA 2010, s 950; FA 2011, Sch 6 paras 25, 27(3); FA 2012, s 24(7)(11)*].

See also **17.31** for the disapplication of *CTA 2010, s 948* following the sale of a lessor company and an election for ring fence treatment.

Transfer of trade to obtain balancing allowances

[17.25] *FA 2008* extended the application of *ICTA 1988, s 343(2)* to certain transfers of a trade between companies which would not otherwise be within *ICTA 1988, s 343*, where the transfer is intended to obtain for the predecessor a balancing allowance under the plant and machinery code. Following the enactment of *CTA 2010*, this rule applies by way of stand alone provisions rather than by extending the application of *CTA 2010, s 948*, but the effect remains the same as previously (so that identical provisions to those in *s 948* apply). Where these provisions apply they are not, however, subject to the anti-avoidance rule at **17.24** above.

The provisions apply where the predecessor company ceases to carry on a trade on or after 12 March 2008 and another company begins to carry on the activities of the trade either as its trade or as part of its trade, if:

- the predecessor would otherwise be entitled to a balancing allowance in respect of the trade for the accounting period of cessation; and
- its ceasing to carry on the trade is part of a scheme or arrangement whose main purpose, or one of whose main purposes, is to obtain that allowance.

The provisions also apply where the predecessor company ceases to carry on part of a trade on or after 12 March 2008 and another company begins to carry on the activities of that part either as its trade or as part of its trade, if the predecessor's ceasing to carry on the part of the trade is part of a scheme or arrangement whose main purpose, or one of whose main purposes, is to obtain a balancing allowance on cessation of the trade.

In applying these provisions where the predecessor transfers a trade and the successor carries on the activities as part of its trade, that part is treated as a separate trade. Where the predecessor transfers only part of a trade, that part is treated for these purposes as a separate trade carried on by the predecessor and, where the successor carries on the activities as part of its trade, that part is likewise treated as a separate trade. For these purposes, receipts, expenses, assets and liabilities are apportioned on a just and reasonable basis.

[*CTA 2010, ss 954–957*].

Carry forward of losses

[17.26] *CTA 2010, ss 938–954* also allow for the carry forward of the predecessor company's trading losses against the successor company's trading profits under *CTA 2010, s 45*. [*CTA 2010, s 944*]. As capital allowances are treated as trading expenses of a company, they are deducted in arriving at the amount of a loss.

The amount of any loss to be carried forward may be restricted if the amount of any liabilities of the predecessor which are not taken over by the successor exceeds the value of any assets not so taken over plus the consideration for the transfer of the trade. [*CTA 2010, s 945*]. Where losses are restricted in this way, capital allowances which have enhanced the amount of a loss will effectively have been wasted.

It should be noted that as regards subsequent balancing charges, there is no equivalent provision to that described in **17.29** below where carry forward of losses is restricted on a change of ownership of a company. The provisions of *CAA 2001, s 577(3)*, whereby an allowance or deduction is deemed to have been made if it would have been made but for an insufficiency of profits against which to make it, will apply. Thus, in computing a balancing charge accruing to the successor, any allowance made to the predecessor would be taken into account even if the benefit of the allowance had been forgone due to its forming part of a loss carried forward which fell to be restricted on the succession.

Transfer or division of a UK business

[17.27] Where:

(a) a '*qualifying company*' (i.e. a body incorporated under the law of an EU member state) transfers the whole or part of a business carried on by it in the UK to one or more qualifying companies resident in one or more other member states;
(b) *TCGA 1992, s 140A* (transfer of assets treated as no-gain, no-loss disposal) applies to the transfer; and
(c) immediately after the transfer, the transferee (or one or more of the transferees) is either resident in the UK or carries on in the UK through a permanent establishment a business which consists of, or includes, the business or part transferred,

the transfer does not give rise to any capital allowances or balancing charges, and the transferee (or each transferee) inherits the capital allowances position of the transferor in relation to the assets transferred to it. Where it is not possible to distinguish expenditure on the assets transferred from expenditure on other assets, a just and reasonable apportionment is to be made.

For transfers before 1 January 2007, these provisions applied only to the transfer of a trade to a single transferee.

Where the provisions apply, the provisions of *CTA 2010, s 948* (company reconstructions without change of ownership — see **17.22** above), *CAA 2001,* *s 266* (successions between connected persons — see **7.18** above), *CAA 2001, s 560* (transfer of insurance company business — see **17.43** below), *CAA 2001, ss 568–570* (controlled and main benefit sales, etc. — see **17.2** above) and *CAA 2001, s 573* (transfers treated as sales — see **8.10**, and **9.10** above) do not apply.

[*CAA 2001, ss 266(8), 560(3), 561, 567(5), 573(4)*].

Note that it is a condition for the application of *TCGA 1992, s 140A* that the transfer must take place for *bona fide* commercial reasons, and that the avoidance of UK tax must not be the main reason, or one of the main reasons, for the transfer. [*TCGA 1992, s 140B*].

The intention of the above provisions is to ensure that no capital allowance adjustments take place when a trade is transferred as part of a transaction within the *EEC Mergers and Divisions Directive (90/434/EEC)*.

Transfers of assets during cross-border merger

[17.28] The following provisions apply to a transfer of 'qualifying assets' as part of the process of a merger to which *TCGA 1992, s 140E* applies (or would apply but for *TCGA 1992, s 139* applying). Broadly, *TCGA 1992, s 140E* applies to:

- the formation of a European Company (*Societas Europaea* ('SE')) on or after 1 April 2005 by the merger of two or more companies in accordance with *Council Regulation (EC) No 2157/2001, Arts 2(1), 17(2)*;
- the formation of a European Co-operative (*Societas Co-operative Europaea* ('SCE')) on or after 18 August 2006 by the merger of two or more co-operative societies (as defined), at least one of which is a society registered under *Industrial and Provident Societies Act 1965*, in accordance with *Council Regulation (EC) No 1435/2003*;
- a merger on or after 1 January 2007 effected by the transfer by one or more companies or co-operative societies of all their assets and liabilities to a single existing company or co-operative society; and
- a merger on or after 1 January 2007 effected by the transfer by two or more companies of all their assets to a single new company (which is not an SE or SCE) in exchange for the issue by the transferee company of shares or debentures to each person holding shares in or debentures of a transferee company.

Each of the merging companies or co-operative societies must be resident in a member state but they must not all be resident in the same state. *TCGA 1992, s 140E* does not apply if the merger is not effected for *bona fide* commercial reasons or if it forms part of a scheme or arrangements of which the main purpose, or one of the main purposes, is avoiding liability to UK tax.

Such a transfer does not give rise to any capital allowances or balancing charges, and the transferee inherits the capital allowances position of the transferor. Where it is not possible to distinguish expenditure on the assets transferred from expenditure on other assets, a just and reasonable apportionment is to be made.

Where these provisions apply, the provisions of *CTA 2010, s 948* (see **17.22** above) do not apply.

An asset is a '*qualifying asset*' if it is transferred to the transferee as part of the merger, either the transferor is resident in the UK at the time of transfer or the asset is an asset of the transferor's UK permanent establishment, and either the transferee is resident in the UK at the time of the transfer or the asset is an asset of the transferee's UK permanent establishment immmediately after the transfer.

[*CAA 2001, s 561A*].

Change in ownership of a company: disallowance of trading losses

[17.29] The following applies if there is a change in ownership of a company and either:

(a) within any five-year period beginning on more than three years before the change there is a major change in the nature or conduct of its trade; or

(b) there is a change of ownership of a company at any time after the scale of its trading activities has become small or negligible and before any considerable revival,

Where either the change in ownership or the major change in the nature or conduct of the trade took place before 1 April 2017, the condition in (a) above was that within any three-year period in which the change in ownership occurred, there was a major change in the nature or conduct of its trade.

No relief is given under *CTA 2010, s 45* or *s 45B* for a loss incurred before the change of ownership against income or profits arising after the change. Where a change of ownership takes place during an accounting period, that period is, for tax purposes, regarded as two separate periods, the first ending with the change of ownership and the second beginning at that time. [*CTA 2010, ss 673, 674; F(No 2)A 2017, Sch 4 paras 72, 73*].

The term 'major change in the nature or conduct of a trade' is not defined; but *CTA 2010, s 673(4)* specifies certain matters which it includes.

HMRC's interpretation of the term is set out in Statement of Practice SP 10/91 (revised in 1996). HMRC will consider factors such as the location of the company's business premises; the identity of its suppliers, management or staff; its methods of manufacture; its pricing and purchasing policies and whether it switches from investing in shares and securities to investing in real property, to the extent that these factors indicate that a major change has occurred. HMRC will not regard a major change as having occurred when a company simply makes changes to improve its efficiency or to make use of technological advantages, or when it rationalises its product range by withdrawing unprofitable items or when it makes changes to its portfolio of investments.

In *Willis v Peeters Picture Frames Ltd* CA(NI) 1982, 56 TC 436, the Court of Appeal held that whether there had been a major change was a question of fact and degree for the Commissioners to decide. Gibson LJ observed that 'major' meant more than 'significant'. This decision was considered by the High Court in the stock relief case of *Purchase v Tesco Stores Ltd* ChD 1984, 58 TC 46, where Warner J held that a 'major' change could take place even if the change was only quantitative rather than qualitative, and that a change could be 'major' without being 'fundamental'.

CTA 2010, ss 719–726 sets out rules for ascertaining whether or not there has been a change of ownership.

Normally, the effect of *CAA 2001, s 577(3)* is that where a capital allowance has been made but no benefit has thereby been obtained due to an insufficiency of profits or gains, the allowance is nevertheless deemed to have been given for the purpose of computing subsequent balancing charges, such charges being restricted to the total allowances given on the asset in question. However, there is an exception where the carry forward of a loss has been prohibited by *CTA 2010, s 674*. Any allowance or deduction falling to be made in taxing a company's trade before the change of ownership, to the extent that profits or gains arising in the same or subsequent chargeable periods before the change of ownership were insufficient to give effect thereto, is disregarded when computing the amount of any balancing charge arising from an event taking place after the change of ownership. In deciding the extent to which effect can be given to allowances or deductions against profits or gains arising before the change of ownership, such allowances, etc. are deemed to be set off against such profits in priority to any loss which is not attributable to such an allowance or deduction. [*CTA 2010, s 675*].

The provisions of *CTA 2010, s 674* apply also to prevent relief being given under *CTA 2010, s 37* or *s 42* (see **2.38** above) by setting a trading loss incurred by the company in an accounting period ending after the change in ownership against any profits of an accounting period beginning before the change in ownership or under *CTA 2010, s 45A* for a loss incurred in an accounting period beginning before the change by carry-forward to an accounting period ending after the change. [*CTA 2010, s 674(1); F(No 2)A 2017, Sch 4 para 73*]. No additional capital allowance provisions arise out of this denial of relief.

There are a number of similar provisions which apply to ensure that it is not possible to carry forward losses, excess management expenses or other reliefs of a company in particular circumstances where there is a change in its ownership. [*CTA 2010, ss 676A–705; F(No 2)A 2017, Sch 4 paras 80–88*].

Sale of lessor companies

[17.30] *FA 2006* introduced anti-avoidance provisions, for corporation tax purposes only, which apply where a company carrying on a 'business of leasing plant or machinery' on its own or in partnership, undergoes a change in ownership or changes its interest in a business carried on in partnership after 4 December 2005. Strictly, the provisions do not affect the capital allowances position of the company, and are to that extent outside the scope of this book. They are covered in summary here, however, as the charge arising under the provisions is calculated by reference to capital allowances and the intention of the provisions is to counter perceived avoidance using capital allowances. The charge under the provisions arises in respect of long leases where in the early years of a lease the capital allowances available to the lessor are greater than the rental income from the lease, giving rise to losses; the charge broadly equates to the tax benefit of such losses. This prevents the lessor making use of such losses, for example, by way of group relief, where the profits arising in the later years of the lease (when the rental income is greater than the capital allowances) are sheltered on the sale of the lessor company to a group with tax losses. The charge thus counteracts the losses available to the original owner and the corresponding relief treated as arising immediately after the change in ownership etc. counteracts the profits passed on to the new owner. The provisions were amended by *FA 2009* so that they apply equally to the sale of an intermediate lessor company. Further amendments were made by *FA 2010* to allow for a company otherwise falling within (i) below to elect instead for an alternative ring fence treatment: see **17.31** below. However, the option to make an election has been withdrawn by *FA 2011* where the relevant day (see below) is on or after 23 March 2011.

The provisions are summarised below. The meaning of the expression 'business of leasing plant or machinery', which is used for the purposes of a number of capital allowances provisions is covered in detail at **17.32** below.

For full coverage of the provisions, see Tolley's Corporation Tax. See also the HMRC Technical Note published on 31 March 2006.

(i) *Leasing business carried on by a company alone.* Where there is a 'qualifying change of ownership' on or after 5 December 2005 of a company within the charge to corporation tax which carries on a 'business of leasing plant or machinery' (see **17.32** below) otherwise than in partnership, the accounting period of the company ends on the day of the change (the '*relevant day*') and a new accounting period begins on the following day. The company is treated as receiving a taxable business receipt in the accounting period ending on the relevant day and as incurring a deductible business expense equal to that amount in the new accounting period. Where the relevant day is on or after 21 March 2012 or where the receipt arises as a result of a company becoming a member of a tonnage tax group (see below), losses cannot be carried back under *CTA 2010, s 37(3)(b)* or s *45F* to the extent that they are to be set against so much of the company's profits as derive from the deemed receipt (the profits being calculated for this purpose on the basis that the receipt is the final amount to be added). Previously, the rule was that any loss derived from the expense (calculated on the basis that the expense was the final amount to be deducted) could not be carried back under *CTA 2010, s 37(3)(b)* as a trading loss for offset against profits of earlier accounting periods.

Subject to exceptions for certain intra-group and consortium reorganisations or where an election for alternative treatment is made (see **17.31** below), there is a '*qualifying change of ownership*' of a company for this purpose if the company ceases to be a 'qualifying 75% subsidiary' of its 'principal company' (both terms as defined). In the case of a chain of companies where the principal company is at the top of the chain, a qualifying change in ownership occurs whenever any of the links in the 75% chain are broken. See *CTA 2010, s 394* for the circumstances in which there is a qualifying change in ownership in consortium cases. There is also a qualifying change of ownership where a subsidiary or consortium-owned company becomes a member of a tonnage tax group (see **17.58** below) on or after 21 March 2012 and enters tonnage tax itself at the same time or where a company becomes a member of a tonnage tax group on or after 23 April 2012 without entering tonnage tax at the same time. If there is a qualifying change of ownership on the same day both as a result of the company concerned becoming a member of a tonnage tax group and under another category, the sale of lessor provisions apply only to the former.

The basic amount of the taxable receipt (which is not to be less than nil and is subject to adjustment as below) is calculated by the formula PM – TWDV. For this purpose,

- Where the relevant day is on or after 13 November 2008, PM is the aggregate of any amounts which would be shown in respect of plant or machinery in the 'appropriate balance sheet' of the company drawn up as at the start of the relevant day, and any amounts which would be shown in the appropriate balance sheet of the company drawn up at the end of the relevant day in respect of 'relevant transferred plant or machinery'. For the meaning of amounts shown in an 'appropriate balance sheet' and 'relevant transferred plant or machinery' see **17.32** below. In certain circumstances, the 'ascribed value' (see **17.33** below) or, where the relevant day is before 23 March 2011, the market value, as at the relevant day of an item of plant or machinery is included in PM instead of the amount found as above. This applies where the company is the lessee of the plant or machinery under a long funding finance or operating lease (see **6.22** above) or is treated as the owner of the plant or machinery under *CAA 2001, s 67* (hire purchase etc. — see **7.7** above) either at the start of the relevant day or, the plant or machinery having been acquired from an associated company on that day, at the end of the relevant day.

  Plant or machinery on which the company has not incurred qualifying expenditure is excluded in calculating PM, as is plant or machinery of which the company is lessor under a long funding lease or which is treated as owned by another person under *CAA 2001, s 67* and plant or machinery ignored under *CTA 2010, s 407(2)* (migration).

  Where the relevant day is before 13 November 2008, PM is the aggregate of any amounts shown in the appropriate balance sheet of the company in respect of plant or machinery which it owns at the start of the relevant day and any amounts shown in the appropriate balance sheet of each associated company (see **17.32** below) in respect of plant or machinery which is transferred to the company on the relevant day. Plant or machinery treated as owned by other persons under *CAA 2001, s 67* (hire-purchase and similar contracts — see **7.9** above) or on which capital allowances are not available by virtue of *CAA 2001, s 34A* (long funding leasing — see **4.20** above) is excluded.

- TWDV is the total amount of unrelieved qualifying expenditure on plant or machinery in all single asset, class pools and main pool brought forward under the capital allowances provisions at the start of the new accounting period following the relevant day.

  The amount excludes any expenditure on the acquisition of plant or machinery on the relevant day, other than acquisitions from associated companies, and, where the relevant day is on or after 23 March 2011, also excludes any expenditure incurred (or treated as incurred) on the relevant day which is attributable to plant or machinery acquired by the company before that day. Also where the relevant day is on or after that date, the legislation specifies that the references to the acquisition of plant or machinery include deemed acquisition and also the plant or machinery being brought into use or made available for use for the first time for the purposes of the business.

An adjustment is made to the basic amount as calculated above where a company ceases to be a 75% subsidiary of another company and becomes instead owned by a consortium (or a 75% subsidiary (where the relevant day is before 9 December 2009, a 90% subsidiary) of a company owned by a consortium) of which that other company is a member.

[*CTA 2010, ss 383–386, 392–398, 399–406; FA 2010, s 29, Sch 18 paras 3–5; FA 2011, Sch 6 paras 7–9, 27(1); FA 2012, s 24(2)–(5)(9)(10); F(No 2)A 2017, Sch 4 para 164*].

(ii) *Change in interest of company in leasing business carried on in partnership*. Where on any day (the '*relevant day*') there is a 'qualifying change' in the interest of a company (the '*partner company*') in a business of leasing plant or machinery carried on in partnership with other persons, the partner company is treated as receiving a taxable receipt in relation to its 'notional business' and any other corporate partner is treated as incurring a deductible expense in relation to its notional business (or, where it is the only company carrying on the leasing business at the end of the relevant day, in relation to the actual business). The companies in question must be within the charge to corporation tax and the respective amounts are brought into account in the accounting periods in which they are treated as received or incurred. There is an exception in certain circumstances where all of the companies that carried on the business in partnership cease to have a share in the business. A company's '*notional business*' is the business profits or losses of which are determined under *CTA 2009, s 1259*.

There is a '*qualifying change*' in a company's interest in a business if there is a fall on any day of its percentage share in the profits or loss (excluding chargeable gains or allowable losses) of the business (which may include a nil share whether or not as a result of the dissolution of the partnership).

The basic amount of the taxable receipt (which is not to be less than nil and is subject to adjustment as below) is calculated using the formula PM – TWDV, as above, but suitably modified to take account of the plant or machinery owned by the partnership as a whole. The taxable receipt is then limited to the 'appropriate percentage' of the basic amount, i.e. the decrease in the company's percentage share at the end of the relevant day from that at the start of the day. A similar adjustment is also made to the basic amount to ascertain the expense treated as incurred by the other companies where the percentage of the company's share in the profits or loss of the business has increased as a result of a change in the partner company's interest.

[*CTA 2010, ss 415–424; FA 2011, Sch 6 paras 15, 27(1)*].

(iii) *Change in ownership of a corporate partner.* Where there is a qualifying change of ownership of a company within the charge to corporation tax, which carries on a business of leasing plant or machinery in partnership with other persons, the accounting period of the company ends on the day of the change (the '*relevant day*') and a new accounting period begins on the following day. The company is treated as receiving a taxable receipt of its notional business in the accounting period ending on the relevant day and as incurring a deductible business expense equal to that amount in the new accounting period. Where the relevant day is on or after 21 March 2012 or where the receipt arises as a result of a company becoming a member of a tonnage tax group (see (i) above), losses cannot be carried back under *CTA 2010, s 37(3)(b)* or *s 45F* to the extent that they are to be set against so much of the company's profits as derive from the deemed receipt (the profits being calculated for this purpose on the basis that the receipt is the final amount to be added). Previously, the rule was that any loss derived from such expense (calculated on the basis that the expense was the final amount to be deducted) could not be carried back under *CTA 2010, s 37(3)(b)* as a trading loss for offset against profits of earlier accounting periods. The amount of the income is calculated by first applying the PM – TWDV formula and then restricting the taxable income to the 'appropriate percentage', i.e. the company's percentage share in the profits or loss of the business on the relevant day or, if there is a qualifying change in the company's interest in the business on that day, its percentage share in the profits or loss of the business at the end of that day. [*CTA 2010, ss 425–429; FA 2012, s 24(6)(9); F(No 2)A 2017, Sch 4 para 166*].

(iv) *Disposal of leased asset.* The following provision applies only where the relevant day (within (i), (ii) or (iii) above) is before 13 November 2008. If, on such a relevant day, the company or the partnership of which the company is a member disposes of any 'relevant plant or machinery subject to a lease' in circumstances to which *CAA 2001, s 228K* (disposal of plant or machinery subject to lease where income retained

— see **17.16** above) applies, the above provisions do not apply to treat any person as receiving an amount of income or as incurring an expense to the extent that the income or expense arises by reference to that disposal. If, as a result, no income is treated as received by a company, its accounting period is not treated as coming to an end under (i) or (iii) above. In relation to disposals made before 2 June 2006, the above provisions are disapplied in their entirety in relation to the change in ownership or interest. [*FA 2006, s 82, Sch 10 para 40; FA 2009, s 63, Sch 31 paras 8, 12*].

Election for alternative treatment

[17.31] As noted at 17.30 above, a company otherwise falling within the provisions at **17.30**(i) above can instead make an irrevocable election for an alternative ring fence treatment where the relevant day (see **17.30**(i) above) is on or after 9 December 2009 and before 23 March 2011. Such an election must be made by notice to HMRC within the two years beginning with the relevant day.

The effect of the election is broadly to ring fence the company's leasing business by restricting the set off of losses and preventing the fragmentation of the business without tax effect, the reduction of the profits of the business through additional claims to capital allowances and the creation of artificial deductions. The company's accounting period ends on the relevant day and the ring fence operates from the first day of the new accounting period (i.e. the day after the relevant day). The ring fence comes to an end only if there is a further change in the ownership of the company which, where the relevant day is on or after 24 March 2010, results in a charge under **17.30**(i) above (or would do so but for the making of a further election).

For detailed coverage of the ring fence provisions see *Tolley's Corporation Tax*. The capital allowances implications are as follows.

Expenditure incurred by the company during the period in which the ring fence applies is not qualifying expenditure for plant and machinery allowances purposes if it is incurred on the acquisition or creation of an 'independent asset'. For this purpose an '*independent asset*' is one which in the normal course of business could be used individually (whether or not it could also be used as a constituent part of a 'combined asset') or could be used at different times as a constituent part of different combined assets. A '*combined asset*' is a single asset consisting of more than one asset. This rule does not apply to expenditure incurred under a written contract finalised before 9 December 2009 (and for this purpose a contract is finalised on the earliest date on which it is unconditional (or, if conditional, the conditions are met) and no terms remain to be agreed).

The capital allowances provisions which normally apply to company reconstructions without change of ownership (see **17.22** above) do not apply where a company to which the ring fence applies is either the predecessor or the successor. Instead, where the reconstruction takes place before 23 March 2011, the plant or machinery belonging to the transferred trade is treated as sold by the predecessor to the successor on the day of cessation at its market value (as defined at *CTA 2010, s 437(9)*).

Where an event occurs on or after 23 March 2011 which requires a company within the ring fence to bring a disposal value into account, the disposal value is the 'ascribed value' (see **17.33** below) of the plant or machinery if this is higher than what the disposal value would have been under the normal rules. This provision overrides *CAA 2001, s 265(2)(b)* (net proceeds of deemed sale to be taken as market value) which previously applied on a succession to a trade etc. (see **7.17** above) where a company within the ring fence was the predecessor, even if the plant or machinery concerned was actually sold to the successor (and it applied by reference to market value as determined under *CTA 2010, s 437(9)*).

[*CTA 2010, ss 398A–398G; FA 2011, s 54, Sch 6 paras 6, 27(2)(3); FA 2012, Sch 20 para 38; F(No 2)A 2017, Sch 4 para 165*].

Business of leasing plant or machinery

[17.32] For the purposes of 17.30(i) above, a company carries on a '*business of leasing plant or machinery*' on a particular day (the '*relevant day*') if either of the following conditions is met.

(i) At least half of the 'relevant plant or machinery value' relates to plant or machinery meeting conditions (A)–(C) below (or where the relevant day is before 23 March 2011, relates to 'qualifying leased plant or machinery' (see below)). Where the relevant day is before 13 November 2008, the condition is that at least half of the 'accounting value' of the plant or machinery owned by the company on the relevant day relates to qualifying leased plant or machinery.
For this purpose, the '*relevant plant or machinery value*' is the sum of:

- any amounts which would be shown in respect of plant or machinery in the appropriate balance sheet (as below) of the company drawn up as at the start of the relevant day; and
- any amounts which would be shown in the appropriate balance sheet of the company drawn up as at the end of the relevant day in respect of 'relevant transferred plant or machinery' (i.e. plant or machinery an amount in respect of which would be shown in the appropriate balance sheet of an 'associated' company drawn up as at the start of the relevant day).

In certain circumstances, the 'ascribed value' (where the relevant day is before 23 March 2011, the market value) as at the relevant day of an item of plant or machinery is included in the relevant plant or machinery value instead of the amount found as above. This applies where the company is the lessee of the plant or machinery under a long funding finance or operating lease (see **6.22** above) or is treated as the owner of the plant or machinery under *CAA 2001, s 67* (hire purchase etc. — see **7.7** above) either at the start of the relevant day or, the plant

or machinery having been acquired from an associated company on that day, at the end of the relevant day. For the meaning of the 'ascribed value' of plant or machinery see **17.33** below.
The '*accounting value*' of the plant or machinery is the sum of:

- any amounts shown in the appropriate balance sheet (as below) of the company in respect of plant or machinery which it owns at the start of the relevant day; and
- any amounts shown in the appropriate balance sheet of any 'associated' companies in respect of plant or machinery which they transfer to the company on the relevant day.

The amounts shown in the appropriate balance sheet of a company for these purposes are the amounts that would be shown as:

- the net book value or carrying amount of any plant or machinery, and
- the net investment in finance leases of any plant or machinery,

in a balance sheet drawn up (where the relevant day is before 13 November 2008, drawn up as at the start of the relevant day) in accordance with generally accepted accounting practice. The assumption is made, where the relevant day is after 21 March 2006, that any plant or machinery acquired directly or indirectly from a person connected (within **2.34** above) with the company had been acquired at its ascribed value (where the relevant day is before 23 March 2011, at its market value) as at the relevant day. Where the relevant day is after 21 April 2009, the assumption is to be made only if either the acquisition took place on or after 5 December 2005 or the person from whom the plant or machinery was acquired was also connected with the company on that date. Apportionments on a just and reasonable basis are to be made where the net book value or carrying amount of land includes any plant or machinery which is a fixture (within **6.3** above) or where a finance lease includes assets other than plant or machinery.
A company is '*associated*' with another company on any day if, at the start of the day, one of the two has control (within *CTA 2010, ss 450, 451*) of the other or both are under the control of the same person or persons. A company which is owned by a consortium or which is a qualifying 75% subsidiary (where the relevant day is before 9 December 2009, a qualifying 90% subsidiary — both terms as defined) of a company owned by a consortium is also associated with certain members of the consortium and their associated companies.

(ii) At least half of the company's income as calculated for corporation tax purposes over the twelve-month period ending on the relevant day derives from plant or machinery meeting conditions (A)–(C) below (or where the relevant day is before 23 March 2011, derives from qualifying leased plant or machinery). Any apportionment necessary to determine the amount of the company's income is to be made for this purposes on a time basis unless that basis would work in an unjust or unreasonable manner, in which case, the apportionment is on a just and reasonable basis. Any apportionment necessary to determine the proportion of the income that derives from plant or machinery meeting the conditions (or from qualifying leased plant or machinery) is to be made on a just and reasonable basis.

Plant or machinery meets the conditions referred to in (i) and (ii) above if:

(A) it is, or at any time in the twelve months ending on the relevant day has been, leased out by the company or a 'qualifying associate';
(B) the lease under which it is or has been leased out is a plant or machinery lease (see **6.27** above) but not an 'excluded lease of background plant or machinery for a building' (see **6.29** above); and
(C) if it satisfies (A) above only because it is or has been leased out by a qualifying associate, the lessee under the lease is or was someone other than the company.

For this purpose, plant or machinery is 'leased out' by a person if it is subject to a plant or machinery lease under which that person is a lessor. A '*qualifying associate*' is a person who is connected with the company at the start of the relevant day or at any time in the twelve months ending on that day. The circumstances in which a person is connected with a company (see **2.34** above) include, where the company is owned by a consortium or is a qualifying 75% subsidiary of such a company, any consortium member or person connected with a member.

Plant or machinery is '*qualifying leased plant or machinery*' if the company's expenditure on it was incurred (or treated as incurred) for the purposes of the business, the company is, or has been, entitled to claim capital allowances in respect of the expenditure (or would have been so entitled but for *CAA 2001, ss 34A, 70A* (lessees, and not lessors, under long funding leases entitled to allowances — see **6.21** onwards above)) and at any time in the twelve months ending on the relevant day it has been subject to a plant or machinery lease which is not an excluded lease of background plant or machinery for a building.

[*CTA 2010, ss 387–391, 408; FA 2010, s 29(6); FA 2011, Sch 6 paras 2–5, 27(1)*].

Similar provisions apply for the purposes of **17.30**(ii)(iii) above to determine whether, on any day, a company (the '*partner company*') carries on a business of leasing plant or machinery in partnership with other persons. The provisions differ from those above in the following ways.

(a) References above to the company carrying on the business are to be read as references to the partnership.
(b) The reference in (i) above to associated companies is to be read as a reference to the partner company, any other partner company in relation to whose interest in the business there is a qualifying change on the relevant day, any other partner company in relation to which there is a qualifying change in ownership on the relevant day, and any company associated on the relevant day with any of those partner companies.

[*CTA 2010, ss 410–414; FA 2011, Sch 6 paras 11–14, 27(1)*].

[17.33] For the purposes of **17.30–17.32** above, the '*ascribed value*' of plant or machinery at a particular time is determined as follows.

(I) If the plant or machinery is subject to a 'plant or machinery lease' (see **6.27** above) at the time in question, the company is a lessor under the lease and (II) below does not apply, the ascribed value at that time is the higher of the market value of the plant or machinery and the present value of the lease at that time.

(II) If the plant or machinery is subject to a plant or machinery lease at the time in question, the lease is an 'equipment lease' (see **6.7** above) and the company is the 'equipment lessor' and is treated at that time as the owner of the plant or machinery because of an election under the provisions at **6.7** above, the ascribed value is the present value of the lease at that time.

(III) If neither (I) nor (II) above apply, the ascribed value is the market value of the plant or machinery at the time in question.

Market value for the purposes of (I)–(III) above is determined on the assumption of a disposal by an absolute owner free from all leases and other encumbrances (including any agreement etc. which includes a plant or machinery lease). If the plant or machinery is a fixture, its market value is a proportion of the market value of the relevant land (see **6.5** above) and the fixture together, determined on a just and reasonable basis. The present value of a lease at a particular time is the present value of the amounts payable under the lease after that time together with any residual amount (see **6.26** above). Present value is calculated using the interest rate implicit in the lease, i.e. the rate that would apply based on normal commercial criteria (including generally accepted accounting practice). If there is no such rate, 1% above LIBOR (as defined) is used. Charges for services and any UK or foreign tax or duty payable by the lessor other than income tax, corporation tax or similar foreign tax are excluded from the amounts payable under a lease for this purpose. If the lessee has an option to extend the lease and it is reasonably certain at the time in question that he will do so, then any amounts payable under the lease as extended are included. If the lease also relates to anything which is not plant or machinery, only the proportion (determined on a just and reasonable apportionment) of the amounts payable under the lease and the residual amount which is attributable to the plant or machinery is taken into account.

[*CTA 2010, ss 437A–437C; FA 2011, Sch 6 paras 22, 27(1)(4)*].

Plant and machinery used for business entertaining

[17.34] Where plant or machinery is used by a person carrying on a qualifying activity, or an employee of that person (including a director of a company or other person engaged in management of the company) for providing 'business entertainment', this use is treated as use otherwise than for the purposes of the qualifying activity. [*CAA 2001, s 269(1)(5)*]. As capital allowances are given only on plant and machinery provided for the purposes of the qualifying activity (see **4.9** above), no allowances would be due in respect of an item used wholly for such business entertaining. As regards an item of plant or machinery which is used partly for qualifying activity purposes and partly for business entertaining, the provisions of *CAA 2001, Pt 2 Ch 15* (see **5.55** above) would restrict the allowances according to the proportion of qualifying activity use.

'*Business entertainment*' includes hospitality of any kind, and the use of an asset for entertainment includes its use for providing anything incidental to the entertainment. Business entertainment does not include anything provided for employees, except where this is incidental to the providing of entertainment for others. Also not included is the use of plant or machinery for the provision of anything if it is the function of the qualifying activity to provide it, and it is provided in the ordinary course of that activity for payment or free for the purpose of advertising to the general public. [*CAA 2001, s 269(2)–(4)*]. Thus, a billiard table provided for staff recreation would qualify for allowances, whilst an identical table provided for the enjoyment of visiting clients and suppliers would not, even though members of staff, e.g. directors, might well use it whilst performing their role as hosts.

Overseas matters

Assets purchased in foreign currency

[17.35] Where assets are purchased in foreign currency and qualify for capital allowances, it will usually be necessary to translate the cost into sterling. Using the provisions in **2.5** above to determine the date on which capital expenditure is to be treated as having been incurred, the translation will normally be at the exchange rate prevailing on that date. Due to exchange rate fluctuations, the sterling equivalent at the time of payment or entry into the company's books (on the invoice or delivery date) may be higher or lower than at the aforementioned date. HMRC consider that where a taxpayer enters a resulting exchange loss should be deducted from the expenditure on which capital allowances are to be given. (HMRC Capital Allowance Manual, CA 11750). Once the sterling cost has been determined, it cannot be altered in subsequent years, regardless of exchange rate movements and of the fact that the asset continues to attract writing down allowances. Where a disposal value falls to be brought into account by reference to sale proceeds received in foreign currency, the conversion to sterling will generally be at the rate prevailing at the date of sale with no account being taken of exchange rate fluctuations between that date and the date of the conversion of the proceeds into sterling. These provisions are subject to those of *CTA 2010, ss 8, 9* which permit companies which prepare their accounts, or those of a UK permanent establishment (previously branch or agency), in a foreign currency to use that currency to calculate their corporation tax profits or losses, converting only the final figure into sterling.

Exemption for profits of foreign permanent establishments of a UK resident company

[17.36] With effect from 19 July 2011, a UK resident company can make an election for profits arising from its foreign permanent establishments to be exempt from corporation tax (and for losses from those permanent establishments to be excluded). Such an election will apply to all accounting periods of the company beginning on or after the 'relevant day'. For this purpose, the 'relevant day' is the day on which, at the time of the election, the next or (for elections made on or after 1 January 2013) the first accounting period is expected to begin. If, in the event, an accounting period begins before and ends on or after the relevant day, then for corporation tax purposes that period is treated as two accounting periods, the first ending immediately before the relevant day and the second starting on that day. Profits and losses are to be apportioned to the two periods on a just and reasonable basis. An election can only be revoked by the company which made it before the relevant day, but it is revoked automatically where the company ceases to be UK resident on or after 1 January 2013. Otherwise the election is irrevocable.

With effect from 1 January 2013, an election can also be made by a non-UK resident company which expects to become UK resident. In such cases, the relevant day is the day on which the company becomes UK resident.

The exemption operates by making appropriate adjustments to the company's total taxable profits for each accounting period to which an election applies in order to secure that the profits and losses from each foreign permanent establishment of the company are excluded. This is done by excluding those profits and losses which make up the 'foreign permanent establishments amount' for the period in question. The '*foreign permanent establishments amount*' is the aggregate of the 'profits amount' for each territory outside the UK in which the company carries on, or has carried on, business through a permanent establishment, less the aggregate of the 'losses amount' for each such territory. The calculation of the profits amount and losses amount differs depending on whether or not there is a double tax treaty between the territory and the UK which includes a provision (a '*non-discrimination provision*') that a permanent establishment of an enterprise of a contracting state is not to be taxed less favourably in the other state than an enterprise of that other state carrying on the same activities. Where there is such a treaty, the '*profits amount*' is the profits which would be taken to be attributable to the permanent establishment in ascertaining the amount of any credit relief for foreign tax. The '*losses amount*' is calculated on the same basis. If an amount of credit relief does not depend on the profits taken to be attributable to the permanent establishment because, under the treaty, the foreign tax is not charged by reference to such profits, then only profits which would be taken to be attributable to the permanent establishment if the foreign tax were charged by reference to such profits are included in the profits amount (and only such losses are included in the losses amount). Where there is no such treaty, the profits amount and losses amount are the amounts which would be taken to be so attributable to the permanent establishment if there were such a treaty and it was in the terms of the OECD model tax convention. If a treaty does not include provisions for a credit to be allowed against tax computed by reference to the same profits as those by reference to which the tax was computed in the foreign territory concerned, it is assumed, for the above purposes, to do so

[*CTA 2009, ss 18A, 18F, 18R, 18S; FA 2011, s 48, Sch 13 paras 4, 31; FA 2012, Sch 20 paras 3, 5, 55*].

Special rules apply to the calculation of the adjustments in relation to chargeable gains and gains taken into account in computing income, capital allowances, payments subject to deduction of tax, certain employee share acquisitions and pre-entry losses. The capital allowances rules are described below.

For the purposes of plant and machinery allowances, a business carried on through one or more permanent establishments outside the UK by a company which has made an election which has taken effect is treated as an activity separate from any other activity of the company and as an activity from which any profits and gains are not chargeable to tax. The deemed activity is not, therefore, a qualifying activity (see **4.3** above). With effect from 1 January 2013, however, this rule does not apply to the business so far as it consists of a plant or machinery lease under which the company is a lessor if any profits or losses arising from the lease are to be left out of account under *CTA 2009, s 18C(3)* below. [*CAA 2001, s 15(2A)(2B); FA 2011, Sch 13 para 15; FA 2012, Sch 20 paras 9, 55*].

Despite the above rule, notional allowances and balancing charges are to be taken into account automatically in any calculation of profits and losses attributable to the permanent establishment for any accounting period for which the election is in effect, as if the deemed separate activity were a qualifying activity. This does not apply, however, if that activity would not have been a qualifying activity even if the above deeming provisions did not apply. [*CTA 2009, s 18C(1); FA 2011, Sch 13 para 4*].

When the election takes effect and as a result of *CAA 2001, s 15(2A)* above there is a disposal event because the plant or machinery in question begins to be used for purposes other than those of a qualifying activity (see **5.41** above), the disposal value is the 'transition value', i.e. the amount which gives rise to neither a balancing allowance nor a balancing charge. This rule does not apply, however, if the qualifying expenditure in respect of the asset, or of the asset together with any other assets with which it is used during any accounting period for which the election has effect, exceeds £5 million, and the asset has been used by the company otherwise than for the purposes of a non-UK permanent establishment at any time during the accounting period in which the election is made or any earlier accounting period ending less than six years before the end of that accounting period. [*CAA 2001, s 62A; FA 2011, Sch 13 para 17*].

In determining any profits amount or losses amount (as above) any profits or losses arising from a plant or machinery lease (see **6.27** above) under which the company is a lessor are to be left out of account if a capital allowance (other than a notional allowance under the above provisions) has been made to the company or a connected company in respect of the leased plant or machinery. [*CTA 2009, s 18C(3)(4); FA 2011, Sch 13 para 4*].

Similar rules apply to mineral extraction allowances, but only where the election takes effect on or after 1 April 2014. A trade which consists of, or includes, the working of a source of mineral deposits is treated, so far as it is carried on through one or more permanent establishments outside the UK by a company which has made an election which has taken effect, as a trade separate from any other trade of the company and as a trade from which any profits and gains are not chargeable to tax. The deemed trade is not, therefore, a mineral extraction trade (see **10.1** above). Notional allowances and balancing charges are, however, to be taken into account automatically in any calculation of profits and losses attributable to the permanent establishment for any accounting period for which the election has effect if those allowances and charges could have been claimed but for the election. If, when the election takes effect, the company has to bring into account at that time the disposal value of an asset which is treated as ceasing to be used for the purposes of a mineral extraction trade, the company is treated for the purpose of calculating the notional allowances as having incurred qualifying expenditure for the purpose of the deemed trade of an amount equal to the disposal value. [*CAA 2001, ss 431A, 431C; FA 2014, s 67(7)(9)*].

Where, whilst an election has effect, the company has to bring into account the disposal value of an asset which is treated as ceasing to be used for the purposes of a mineral extraction trade as a result of the above provisions, the disposal value is the amount which gives rise to neither a balancing allowance nor a balancing charge. This rule does not apply, however, if the qualifying expenditure in respect of the asset exceeds £5 million, the company has claimed any allowances for that expenditure and the asset has been used by the company otherwise than for the purposes of a non-UK permanent establishment at any time during an accounting period ending before, but not more than six years before, the relevant day. [*CAA 2001, s 431B; FA 2014, s 67(7)*].

Non-UK residents

[17.37] A non-UK resident company carrying on a trade in the UK through a permanent establishment is within the charge to UK corporation tax in respect of all profits, wherever arising, that are attributable to the permanent establishment. Its chargeable profits for the purposes of UK corporation tax comprise:

(i) any trading income arising directly or indirectly through or from the establishment and any income from property or rights used by, or held by or for, the establishment, and
(ii) chargeable gains falling within *TCGA 1992, s 10B* by virtue of assets either being used in or for the purposes of the trade carried on by the company through the establishment or being used or held for the purposes of the establishment or being acquired for use by or for the purposes of the establishment.

In computing the chargeable profits it is assumed that the permanent establishment is a distinct and separate enterprise, engaged in the same or similar activities under the same or similar conditions, dealing wholly independently with the non-resident company. Deductions are allowed for allowable expenses incurred for the purposes of the establishment, whether in the UK or elsewhere.

Subject to the above rules, non-resident companies are therefore entitled to capital allowances in respect of a UK permanent establishment in the normal way (but see the special provisions relating to plant and machinery below).

[*CTA 2009, ss 5(2)(3), 19, 21*].

Other UK income arising to a non-UK resident company is within the charge to income tax by virtue of *CTA 2009, s 3*. This would, for example, include rental income received from the letting of UK properties not within (i) above. Where a non-resident company is within the charge to corporation tax in respect of one source of UK income and to income tax in respect of another, capital allowances relating to any source of income are to be given effect against income chargeable to the same tax as is chargeable on income from that source. [*CAA 2001, s 566*].

Non-resident individuals, partnerships, etc. are within the charge to income tax in respect of a trade, profession or vocation carried on in the UK. [*ITTOIA 2005, s 6(2)(3)*]. They are therefore entitled to capital allowances in respect of the trade.

There are provisions to ensure that plant and machinery allowances are given (and balancing charges made) in respect of a qualifying activity as if activities are comprised in the qualifying activity only to the extent that any profits or gains are (or would be, if there were any) chargeable to income tax or corporation tax (see **4.3** above). The effect of these provisions is that, for example, allowances are due to a non-resident carrying on part of its trade through a UK branch or permanent establishment as if the branch or establishment were carrying on a separate qualifying activity. The part of the non-resident's trade that is outside the scope of UK tax is treated as if it were not a qualifying activity, and plant and machinery used for that part is treated as used for non-qualifying activity purposes.

Persons becoming resident or non-resident in the UK

[17.38] A company becoming UK resident and commencing to carry on a trade, or coming within the charge to corporation tax by virtue of its beginning to carry on a trade through a UK permanent establishment (see **17.37** above) is regarded, for corporation tax purposes, as commencing a trade notwithstanding that it may previously have carried on the trade abroad. [*CTA 2009, s 41*]. As regards plant and machinery previously owned and introduced into the UK trade, the provisions in **7.13** above apply so that the plant and machinery is deemed to be acquired at market value on the day on which it was brought into use in the UK trade.

Where a company ceases to be within the charge to corporation tax in respect of a trade, that trade is treated as having been discontinued. [*CTA 2009, s 41*]. Thus, a company which is resident in the UK and becomes non-resident (transferring any UK trade abroad), or which has traded through a UK permanent establishment (and has therefore been within the charge to UK corporation tax) and then transfers the trade abroad, will be treated as having ceased to carry on the trade regardless of whether or not it has actually done so. Any capital allowance provision which requires a disposal value, etc. to be brought into account and/or a balancing adjustment to be computed therefore comes into play on the deemed discontinuance.

A similar rule applies for income tax purposes. Where an individual ceases to be (or becomes) UK resident, the individual is treated as ceasing to carry on any trade etc. carried on wholly or partly outside the UK at the time of the change of residence and, where appropriate, as starting to carry on a new trade etc. immediately afterwards. [*ITTOIA 2005, s 17; FA 2013, Sch 45 para 76*].

Controlled foreign companies

[17.39] Provisions designed to prevent UK residents accumulating profits in non-resident companies subject to low rates of taxation were originally introduced by *FA 1984* but a new regime has been introduced by *FA 2012*. The new regime is contained in *TIOPA 2010, ss 371AA–371VJ* and applies, broadly, for accounting periods of controlled foreign companies beginning on or after 1 January 2013. Under the new regime, a controlled foreign company is simply a company which is not resident in the UK and is controlled by UK resident persons. [*TIOPA 2010, s 371AA(3); FA 2012, Sch 20 para 1*]. However, many such companies are excluded from the regime under one of five main exemptions.

Before the *FA 2012* regime was introduced, the controlled foreign companies rules were contained in *ICTA 1988, ss 747–756, Schs 24–26*. Under the old regime, a controlled foreign company was defined as one which, in any accounting period,

(a) is resident outside the UK,
(b) is 'controlled' (as defined) by persons resident in the UK, and
(c) is 'subject to a lower level of taxation' (as defined) in the territory in which it is resident.

[*ICTA 1988, s 747(1)(2)*].

Again, there are a number of exemptions.

Under both regimes, the profits of a controlled foreign company are apportioned among the shareholders and thus brought within the charge to UK tax where appropriate. Under the *FA 2012* regime, however, profits are so apportioned only to the extent that they pass through one of five 'charge gateways'.

For the purpose of computing the profits of a controlled foreign company for the purposes of apportionment, that company is assumed to be resident in the UK and profits are therefore calculated as they would be for a UK resident company, although this does not mean that the company is assumed to carry on its activities other than in the place or places where it does in fact carry them on. [*ICTA 1988, Sch 24 para 1(1)(2); TIOPA 2010, s 371SD(1)(2); FA 2012, Sch 20 para 1*]. The calculation of profits should therefore take into account deductions for capital allowances, where these would be due to a UK resident company. It should be noted that, if the company carries on its activities overseas, allowances will be precluded in some cases. If the company is carrying on a trade in the UK through a permanent establishment, it will of course be within the charge to UK tax in respect of that trade and be entitled to capital allowances accordingly, quite apart from the controlled foreign companies legislation.

Specific provisions concerning capital allowances apply in calculating the profits for the purposes of apportionment and are summarised briefly below. The following provisions apply under the *FA 2012* regime.

(1) If, before the accounting period which begins when the controlled foreign company becomes a controlled foreign company, that company incurred any capital expenditure on the provision of plant or machinery for the purposes of its trade, that plant or machinery is assumed to have been provided for purposes wholly other than those of the trade and to have been brought into use for the purposes of the trade at the beginning of that accounting period. The provisions in **7.13** above then come into play, the effect being that the plant or machinery is deemed to have been acquired at its market value at the beginning of that accounting period, allowances then being calculated accordingly. [*TIOPA 2010, s 371SM; FA 2012, Sch 20 para 1*].

(2) A company or companies which would have more than half of the profits of a controlled foreign company apportioned to them were the controlled foreign companies charge applied may by notice to HMRC request that the controlled foreign company be assumed to have made a long funding lease election (see **6.24** above) in the form specified in the notice. Such a notice must be given within the time period in which (applying the assumptions required to calculate its profits) the controlled foreign company itself could have made the election. Similarly, a notice can be withdrawn during the period in which the controlled foreign company could have withdrawn an actual election. [*TIOPA 2010, s 371SJ; FA 2012, Sch 20 para 1*].

The following provisions apply under the pre-*FA 2012* regime.

(i) If, prior to the first accounting period for which the company falls to have amounts apportioned to it in respect of the controlled foreign company, the controlled foreign company has incurred capital expenditure on plant or machinery for the purposes of its trade, that plant or machinery is assumed to have been provided for purposes wholly other than those of the trade and to have been brought into use for the purposes of the trade at the beginning of that first accounting period. The effect is then as in (1) above. For accounting periods of a controlled foreign company beginning on or after 28 November 1995 and before 1 July 2009, this rule also applies to any such capital expenditure incurred prior to the beginning of the first accounting period which is an ADP exempt period. An ADP exempt period is a reference to an accounting period of the company beginning on or after 28 November 1995 and in respect of which the company pursued an 'acceptable distribution policy' as defined by *ICTA 1988, Sch 25*. [*ICTA 1988, Sch 24 para 10; FA 2009, Sch 16 paras 2(6), 6*].

(ii) From the controlled foreign company's first accounting period beginning after 22 March 1995 it may compute its profits in the currency in which its accounts are prepared. The profits are then translated into sterling at the rate prevailing on the last day of the accounting period. [*ICTA 1988, ss 747(4A), (4B), 748(4)(5)*]. However, capital expenditure qualifying for allowances is translated into sterling at the London closing rate on the date on which the expenditure was incurred. [*ICTA 1988, Sch 24 para 11A*].

Where a company within the above provisions ceases to be controlled by UK residents and thus ceases to be a controlled foreign company, its deemed UK residence comes to an end. [*ICTA 1988, Sch 24 para 2*]. By virtue of *CTA 2009, s 41*, the trade is then regarded as being permanently discontinued, so that at the end of the last accounting period for which profits fall to be apportioned, any balancing adjustments that, under general principles, are brought about by a discontinuance must be taken into account in computing chargeable profits. This would include, for example, adjustments in respect of plant and machinery but not industrial buildings.

Dual resident investing companies

[17.40] Legislation was introduced in 1987 limiting the application of certain tax reliefs and provisions in dealings involving 'dual resident investing companies'. A '*dual resident investing company*' is defined by *CTA 2010, s 949* and means, broadly speaking, a company which:

(a) is not a trading company,
(b) is resident in the UK, and
(c) is also within a charge to tax under the laws of a foreign territory.

A trading company can in certain circumstances, mainly where it is used principally to borrow or to purchase or hold shares in another member of the group, be deemed to be an investing company for the purposes of this legislation. [*CTA 2010, s 949*].

Some of the provisions concern capital allowances and these can be summarised as follows.

(i) An election for the transfer of property between connected persons, etc. at tax written-down value as at **17.4** above cannot be made if the buyer is a dual resident investing company.
(ii) The legislation in **5.41**(b)(i) above provides an exclusion to the general rule that plant or machinery sold at less than market value is to be treated as transferred at market value. The exclusion applies where the buyer can claim allowances on the plant or machinery; and in such a case, the item is treated as transferred at its actual sale price. This exclusion does not apply to sales after 31 March 1987 if the buyer is a dual resident investing company and is connected with the seller within **2.34** above.
(iii) The continuity of capital allowances on company reconstructions without change of ownership as in **17.22** above does not apply if the successor is a dual resident investing company.

(iv) An election for continuity of capital allowances on successions to qualifying activities between connected persons as in **7.18** above cannot be made if the successor is a dual resident investing company.

The intention of the provisions was to prevent dual resident investing companies from obtaining tax reliefs twice, i.e. in both the UK and another country, by virtue of their dual residence. It was considered that such companies often generate very little income and usually make losses which, if there were no restrictions, could then be used in group relief claims (or their equivalent) in the UK and in the other country. However, the legislation is, unfortunately, not restricted to situations where such a company is used by a multinational group as a tax-avoidance vehicle, and company groups should therefore beware of being caught by the provisions unwittingly. The above provisions relating specifically to capital allowances appear to be aimed at preventing companies from avoiding balancing charges on transfers of assets and/or trades to dual resident investing companies bearing in mind that subsequent balancing charges accruing to such companies may escape a charge to tax because there are losses available.

Special cases

Post-cessation, etc. receipts

[17.41] When a trade, profession or vocation carried on wholly or partly in the UK has been permanently discontinued, certain sums received after cessation, to the extent that they have not already been taken into account either in the final year's accounts and tax computations or previously, are assessed to income tax or to corporation tax. [*ITTOIA 2005, ss 241–251; CTA 2009, ss 188–195*]. In calculating the amount chargeable, deductions are allowed for any loss, expense or debit (including capital allowances) which, but for the cessation, would have been deducted in calculating, or deducted from or set off against, the profits of the trade etc. for tax purposes. [*ITTOIA 2005, ss 254, 255; CTA 2009, ss 196, 197; FA 2013, Sch 4 para 39(3)*].

Companies with investment business and life assurance companies

[17.42] A company with investment business is defined by *CTA 2009, s 1218(1)* as 'any company whose business consists wholly or partly in the making of investments'.

A deduction is allowed in computing the total profits of a company with investment business for any management expenses which are referable to the accounting period in question. An excess of management expenses in any period is carried forward and treated as management expenses of the following period; there is effectively an indefinite carry forward. To the extent that expenses are deductible, under any other provision, in computing profits, they cannot be treated as management expenses. The obvious example is expenditure deductible in computing property income. Capital expenditure is specifically excluded (except to the extent that capital allowances are included under the provisions at 5.85 above). [*CTA 2009, ss 1218, 1219, 1223*].

A company with investment business may claim plant and machinery allowances as in 5.85 above.

A company carrying on long-term insurance business will be subject to *CAA 2001, ss 254–257* in claiming plant and machinery allowances, as in 5.85 above.

These provisions do not affect a company's entitlement to capital allowances under the general provisions.

[17.43] Where assets are transferred as part of, or in connection with, a transfer of the whole or part of the long term business of an insurance company to another company in accordance with an 'insurance business transfer scheme' (as defined), the transferor and transferee company are treated as the same company for capital allowance purposes and the actual transfer is ignored. This applies for transfers after 31 December 1989; and (subject to that) applies in relation to accounting periods ending before 6 April 1990 as well as in relation to later accounting periods. Any transfers of life business sanctioned or authorised after 30 June 1994 which result in assets being taken out of UK tax jurisdiction will cause an appropriate balancing adjustment to be made. [*CAA 2001, s 560, Sch 3 para 111; ICTA 1988, s 431(2); FA 2012, Sch 16 para 105; SI 2001 No 3629, Art 108*].

Foster carers and shared lives carers

[17.44] For 2003/04 and subsequent years special provisions apply to income from the provision by an individual of foster care. For 2010/11 and subsequent years the provisions apply also to the provision by an individual of 'shared lives care'. Broadly, '*shared lives care*' involves the provision of accommodation and care of an adult or child in an individual's home on the basis that the adult or child shares the individual's home and daily family life. The placement must be under a social care scheme and no more than three adults and/or children can usually be placed in a single residence. For 2010/11 only, shared lives carers can elect to continue to operate the existing concessional simplified income tax arrangements if this gives a better result than the new statutory provisions.

Broadly, where the total 'qualifying care receipts' (i.e. receipts in respect of the provision of foster and/or shared lives care which would otherwise be brought into account in calculating the profits of a trade or otherwise chargeable to income tax) for an 'income period' do not exceed the individual's limit (see below), his profits for the tax year related to that period are treated as nil for tax purposes. If the receipts would have been brought into account in calculating the profits of a trade, the '*income period*' is the basis period for the tax year. Otherwise, the tax year itself is the income period.

If the total such receipts for an income period exceed the limit, an election can be made for an alternative method to be used in calculating the taxable profits; the excess of the receipts over the limit are taken to be the profits for the period, with no deductions allowed for expenses. In the absence of an election, the normal income tax rules apply in calculating the profits. For the purposes of these provisions, an individual's limit is made up of two elements. The first is a fixed amount, limited to £10,000 per annum per residence. The second element is a weekly amount for each fostered child: £200 for a child aged under eleven and £250 for a child aged eleven or more or an adult.

[*ITTOIA 2005, ss 803–823; F(No 3)A 2010, s 1, Sch 1 paras 1–24, 36; FA 2013, Sch 4 paras 42, 43; F(No 2)A 2017, Sch 2 para 11*].

Capital allowances

[17.45] Carers may well be entitled to plant and machinery allowances, and therefore provisions are required for 'relevant chargeable periods' to ensure that the effect of the above provisions is broadly neutral for capital allowances purposes. The provisions have been amended for chargeable periods ending on or after 16 December 2010 to correct technical anomalies in the previous provisions.

For the purposes of the provisions, a '*relevant chargeable period*' is a chargeable period of an individual which corresponds to an income period for the individual's qualifying care receipts in a tax year where the qualifying care receipts would be chargeable to income tax but either the exemption or the alternative calculation method apply for that year. '*Care business expenditure*' is qualifying expenditure incurred wholly or partly for the purposes of the care business. A '*care business pool*' is a pool of care business expenditure.

The following applies for chargeable periods ending on or after 16 December 2010. Immediately after the beginning of any relevant chargeable period that was not immediately preceded by a relevant chargeable period and for which there is a care business pool, a disposal event is deemed to occur. The disposal value to be brought into account is equal to the unrelieved qualifying expenditure brought forward in the pool from the preceding chargeable period. For this purpose, any previous qualifying expenditure not yet allocated to the pool is treated as if it were now allocated and is thus added to the expenditure brought forward. The disposal value ensures that there is no remaining unrelieved qualifying expenditure in the pool.

Capital expenditure ('*excluded capital expenditure*') incurred in a relevant chargeable period on plant or machinery wholly or partly for the purposes of qualifying care is not qualifying expenditure for capital allowances purposes.

If on the first day of the first subsequent chargeable period which is not a relevant chargeable period, the carer still owns any of the plant or machinery which had been in a care business pool and is still using any of it for the purposes of the care business, the carer is deemed to have incurred notional capital expenditure on the provision of that plant or machinery (the '*retained plant or machinery*') at that time. He is then entitled to claim capital allowances on that expenditure. The notional expenditure is equal to the smaller of the market value of the retained plant or machinery on the first day of the chargeable period and the disposal value last brought into account as above.

If, following a disposal event as above, the carer begins to use some of the plant or machinery in question for the purposes of a qualifying activity other than the care business. The provisions at **7.13** above (previous use outside qualifying activity) have effect as if the notional qualifying expenditure incurred on that plant or machinery were equal to the smaller of its market value at the time it is so brought into use and the disposal value last brought into account as above.

In calculating the notional expenditure under either of the above rules, the disposal value is reduced in certain circumstances so as to prevent double allowances. In the case of the retained plant and machinery rule, the reduction applies where the change of use rule has previously applied to any plant or machinery in the pool. It does not apply, however, where the plant or machinery which began to be used for another qualifying activity is nevertheless retained plant or machinery (where, for example, it is used only partly in the other activity). In the case of the change of use rule, the reduction applies where either the change of use rule or the retained plant and machinery rule has previously applied to other plant or machinery in the pool. The amount of the reduction is equal to the notional expenditure previously treated as incurred.

If there is an actual disposal of plant and machinery on or after the date on which the carer is treated as having brought it into use under either the retained plant or machinery rule or the change of use rule above, a disposal value must be brought into account under the normal rules notwithstanding the deemed disposal under the above rules. The disposal value is not limited by the amount of any notional expenditure on that plant and machinery but only by the amount of qualifying expenditure originally incurred by the carer on the plant and machinery.

Also for the first subsequent chargeable period that is not a relevant chargeable period, the carer can claim allowances on any excluded capital expenditure which he still owns. He is treated as if he brought the plant or machinery into use on the first day of that chargeable period and the provisions at **7.13** above (previous use outside qualifying activity) apply accordingly. The plant or machinery will normally fall to be brought into account at its then market value.

The following applies for chargeable periods ended before 16 December 2010. Immediately after the beginning of any relevant chargeable period that was not immediately preceded by a such a period and for which there was a care business pool, a disposal event was deemed to have occurred as above. The disposal value to be brought into account was equal to the unrelieved qualifying expenditure brought forward from the preceding chargeable period. For the first subsequent chargeable period that was not a relevant chargeable period, but for which care receipts still arose, *CAA 2001, s 13* was brought into effect as if, on the first day of that chargeable period, the individual had brought into use for the purposes of the care business any such plant or machinery that he still owned and any plant or machinery acquired for those purposes during the time that allowances were not available.

If the last chargeable period ended before 16 December 2010 was a relevant chargeable period, the last deemed disposal event to have occurred (if any) under the rules for chargeable periods ended before 16 December 2010 is taken into account for the purposes of the rules for subsequent chargeable periods just as if it had occurred under those new rules.

If:

- for 2009/10 (or for a continuous series of tax years up to and including 2009/10), an individual had qualifying care receipts in respect of the provision of shared lives care;
- the receipts were receipts of a trade;
- the individual was taxed on those receipts in accordance with the previous non-statutory arrangements; and
- the individual did not derive any taxable income, other than qualifying care receipts, from the trade,

he is treated for capital allowances purposes as if the qualifying care relief rules had applied to him in 2009/10 (or, where applicable, in each of the continuous series of years) and as if that year (or each of those years) were a year for which either the full exemption applied or an election had been made to apply the alternative method of calculating profits. The effect is that if capital expenditure was incurred on qualifying plant and machinery whilst the non-statutory arrangements applied, an amount equal to the market value of any plant and machinery continuing to be used in the care business can be subsequently brought into account for capital allowances purposes under the main capital allowances rules above. If the individual already has unrelieved qualifying expenditure in a shared lives trade capital allowances pool, and the plant and machinery in question is retained for use in the qualifying care business, then the amount to brought in as qualifying expenditure in the qualifying care business is the smaller of the market value of the plant and machinery and the unrelieved qualifying expenditure from the shared lives trade (Treasury Explanatory Notes to the 2010 Finance (No 2) Bill).

If the shared lives carer makes the election to remain within the non-statutory arrangements for 2010/11 (see **17.44** above), the above transitional rule applies as if all references to 2009/10 were to 2010/11.

[*ITTOIA 2005, ss 824–827; F(No 3)A 2010, s 3, Sch 1 paras 25–28, 37*].

Alternative finance investment bond arrangements where the underlying asset is land

[17.46] The following provisions apply where the 'effective date' of the 'first transaction' (see below) under an alternative finance investment bond arrangement is on or after 21 July 2009. [*FA 2009, Sch 61 para 29*]. The provisions (together with equivalent provisions relating to stamp duty land tax and capital gains tax) are intended to ensure that the tax consequences of an alternative finance investment bond are the same as those for a conventional securitisation of land. The '*effective date*' of a land transaction is that date for the purposes of stamp duty land tax. Where a transaction is to be completed by conveyance, the effective date will in most cases be the date of completion. Where, however, 'substantial performance' of the contract takes place at an earlier date, that earlier date is the effective date. '*Substantial performance*' of a contract occurs when either the purchaser (or connected person) takes possession of substantially the whole of the interest or a substantial amount of the consideration is paid or provided. [*FA 2003, s 44; FA 2009, Sch 61 para 1(2)*]. See Tolley's Stamp Taxes for further details.

The provisions apply where:

(a) two persons ('P' and 'Q') enter into arrangements under which P transfers to Q a 'qualifying interest' in land (the '*first transaction*') and P and Q agree that when Q ceases to hold the interest as a 'bond asset' (see (b) below), Q will transfer the interest to P;
(b) Q, as 'bond issuer', enters into an 'alternative finance investment bond', either before or after making the arrangements in (a) above, and holds the interest in land as a bond asset; and
(c) to generate income or gains for the bond, Q and P enter into a leaseback agreement (i.e. Q grants a lease or sub-lease to P out of the interest transferred to Q by the first transaction).

The Treasury can make regulations specifying an alternative to condition (c) above. A '*qualifying interest*' in land is a major interest in land (within *FA 2003, s 117*), but leases with a term or period of less than 21 years are excluded. An 'alternative finance investment bond' is, broadly, arrangements which:

- provide for one person (the '*bond holder*') to pay a sum of money (the '*capital*') to another (the '*bond issuer*');
- identify assets or a class of assets which the bond issuer will acquire for the purpose of generating income or gains (the '*bond assets*');
- specify a term at the end of which they cease to apply;
- include an undertaking by the bond issuer to dispose of any bond assets still in his possession at the end of the bond term;
- include an undertaking by the bond issuer to make a repayment of the capital to the bond holder during or at the end of the bond term (whether or not in instalments);
- include an undertaking by the bond issuer to make additional payments not exceeding a reasonable commercial return on a loan of the capital during or at the end of the bond term;
- include an undertaking by the bond issuer to arrange for the management of the bond assets with a view to generating sufficient income to pay the redemption payment and the additional payments;
- allow the bond holder to transfer the rights under the arrangements;
- are a listed security on a recognised stock exchange; and
- are wholly or partly treated in accordance with international accounting standards as a financial liability of the bond issuer (or would be if he applied them).

[*FA 2005, s 48A; ITA 2007, s 564G; FA 2009, Sch 61 paras 1(1), 5(1)–(5); TIOPA 2010, Sch 2 para 8; Sch 8 para 229*].

If all of the above conditions are met within 30 days beginning with the effective date of the first transaction and an asset which is part of the subject matter of the first transaction constitutes plant or machinery, Q's expenditure under the first transaction in acquiring the asset is treated for capital allowances purposes as not being capital expenditure and Q is not treated as becoming, and P is not treated as ceasing to be, the owner of the asset as a result of that transaction. This rule applies also to the leaseback in (c) above and to any transaction by which, after the interest in the land ceases to be a bond asset, it is transferred by Q to P (but the rule applies as if the references to Q and P were reversed).

If the asset which is part of the subject matter of the first transaction is plant or machinery and, at any time when it is held as a bond asset, either the person with possession of it loses possession in circumstances in which it is reasonable to assume that the loss is permanent, or the asset ceases to exist as such (through destruction, dismantling or otherwise), that event is a disposal event (see **5.41** above) in relation to P. The disposal event is treated as occurring in the chargeable period in which the event occurs and the disposal value which P must bring into account is the market value of the asset at the time of the event. If, however, the event is the demolition or destruction or permanent loss of the plant or machinery, the disposal value is the amount within **5.41**(c) or (d) above unless that amount is zero, in which case the disposal value is market value.

If Q ceases to hold the asset as a bond asset at any time but does not transfer it to P or any other person, Q is treated as becoming, and P is treated as ceasing to be, the owner at that time. Q's ceasing to hold the asset as a bond asset is therefore treated as a disposal event (see **5.41** above) in relation to P occurring in the chargeable period in which the cessation takes place. If the asset is plant or machinery, the disposal value is its market value. Similar provisions apply where Q transfers the asset to a person other than P (i.e. the transfer is a disposal event or balancing event in relation to P).

[*FA 2009, Sch 61 paras 13–17*].

Workers' services provided to public sector through intermediaries

[17.46ZA] For 2017/18 onwards, special provisions apply where an individual worker provides services through an intermediary to a public sector body such as a Government department, NHS trust or local authority in circumstances such that, if the worker had been directly engaged by the body, he would have been an employee. Subject to detailed computational rules, the public sector body (or the recruiting agency through which the body engages) must make deductions for income tax and NICs from a deemed direct payment to the worker and account for them to HMRC as if the worker were in fact its employee.

A deemed direct payment arises where a 'chain payment' is made to the intermediary, whether directly from the public sector body or indirectly via a chain of other persons (such as a recruitment agency). A '*chain payment*' is a payment of money, a transfer of money's worth, or the providing of a benefit, that can reasonably be taken to be for the worker's services to the client. The chain payment is not required to be brought into account as income by the intermediary.

Although the deemed direct payment is treated as made to, and received by, the worker, the chain payment giving rise to it will actually have been received by the intermediary. There is potential double taxation where:

- the worker receives any payment or benefit (the '*end-of-line remuneration*') from the intermediary which can reasonably be taken to represent remuneration for his services to a public sector body;
- a deemed direct payment has been treated as made to the worker in respect of those same services; and
- the cost of the PAYE deductions on the deemed direct payment has been borne (by deduction at source or otherwise) by the recipient of the chain payment in question,

as the payment made by the intermediary to the worker is from income already subjected to PAYE. In such a case, the intermediary and the worker may treat the end-of-line remuneration as reduced (but not below nil) by the amount of the deemed direct payment. In addition, they may treat the end-of-line remuneration as reduced by any plant or machinery capital allowances on expenditure incurred by the intermediary that would have been deductible from employment income if the worker had been employed by the public authority and had incurred the expenditure himself. (A further reduction is allowed for certain excess pension contributions made by the intermediary.) All of the reductions can be made regardless of whether the end-of-line remuneration is earnings of the worker or is a dividend or other distribution of the intermediary or takes some other form.

For the detailed provisions see Tolley's Income Tax.

[*ITEPA 2003, ss 61K-61X; ITTOIA 2005, s 164B; CTA 2009, s 141A; FA 2017, Sch 1 paras 9, 13-17*].

The Northern Ireland rate of corporation tax

[17.46A] The *Corporation Tax (Northern Ireland) Act 2015* introduced provisions to enable the Northern Ireland Assembly to set a rate of corporation tax which will apply to trade profits of small and medium-sized companies whose workforce is largely in Northern Ireland and to trade profits of certain other companies and corporate partners to the extent that the profits are attributable to a Northern Ireland trading presence. The power of the Assembly to set the rate will apply from a financial year appointed by the Treasury, the first day of which is the '*commencement day*'. It is intended that the rate will commence when the Northern Ireland Executive can demonstrate that its finances are on a sustainable long term footing. Accounting periods which straddle the commencement day are treated for the purposes of the rate as two separate accounting periods, the first ending on the day before the commencement day.

The '*Northern Ireland profits*' that will be chargeable at the Northern Ireland rate instead of the UK rate are broadly:

(i) all of the trading profits of a company (an '*SME (NI employer) company*') that is a micro, small or medium-sized enterprise ('SME') if the company's workforce time and costs fall largely in Northern Ireland;

(ii) a corporate partner's share of the trade profits of a partnership (a '*NI Chapter 6 firm*'), if that company and partnership are both SMEs and the partnership's workforce time and costs fall largely in Northern Ireland;

(iii) the profits of a large company or an SME company which has made the necessary election (a '*NIRE company*') that are attributable to a 'Northern Ireland regional establishment'; and

(iv) a corporate partner's share of the profits of a partnership (a '*NI Chapter 7 firm*') that are attributable to a Northern Ireland regional establishment where either:
   - the partnership is either a large partnership or an SME which has made the necessary election; or
   - the partnership is an SME whose workforce time and costs fall largely in Northern Ireland and the corporate partner is not an SME.

A company may make the election mentioned in (iii) above for an accounting period if it is an SME which does not fall within (i) above but has a Northern Ireland regional establishment for the period. A partnership may make the election mentioned in (iv) above if it is an SME which does not fall within (ii) above but has a Northern Ireland regional establishment. A close company or a partnership may not make an election if it has its Northern Ireland regional establishment as a result of tax avoidance arrangements and certain additional workforce requirements are not met.

A company or partnership has a '*Northern Ireland regional establishment*' if it has a fixed place of business (as defined) in Northern Ireland through which it wholly or partly carries on its business or if a dependent agent acting on its behalf has and habitually exercises in Northern Ireland authority to do business on its behalf.

The rate applies only to profits of a '*qualifying trade*', i.e. a trade in relation to which the company is within the charge to corporation tax and which is not an 'excluded trade', or a '*qualifying partnership trade*', i.e. a trade carried on by a partnership which is not an excluded trade. '*Excluded trades*' are broadly oil industry ring-fence trades, certain lending activities and investment activities regulated under *FISMA 2000*, investment management, long-term insurance business and reinsurance. A company or partnership carrying on an excluded trade within the lending and investment, investment management or reinsurance categories can elect for the trade to be treated as a qualifying trade or qualifying partnership trade. By election, the Northern Ireland rate may apply to the proportion of the trade profits which relate to back-office activities (as defined).

[*CAA 2001, ss 6A, 6B; CTA 2010, ss 357H–357XI; CTNIA 2015, ss 1, 2, 5, Sch 1 para 2; F(No 2)A 2017, Sch 4 paras 94–105, Sch 7*].

Capital allowances provisions

[17.46B] The introduction of the Northern Ireland rate of corporation tax (see **17.46A** above) will require a number of special capital allowances provisions. The provisions are as follows and are subject to the transitional provisions at **17.46H** below.

For the purposes of determining entitlement to, and the amount of, capital allowances, the 'NI rate activity' carried on by a SME (NI employer) company, a NIRE company, a NI Chapter 6 firm or a NI Chapter 7 firm (see **17.46A** above) is treated as a separate trade, distinct from any other activities carried on by the company or partnership as part of the trade. In partnership cases this rule applies only for the purposes of determining the allowances and charges to which effect is given in determining the profits of the trade chargeable to corporation tax (i.e. for the purposes of the '*corporate partner calculation*').

Once calculated, all allowances and charges (whether or not relating to the NI rate activity) are given effect by treating allowances as deductions, and charges as receipts, of the actual trade (i.e. ignoring the deemed separate trade rule). Allowances and charges which relate to an NI rate activity are then treated in applying the Northern Ireland rate as forming part of the Northern Ireland profits (or losses) and any allowances and charges which relate to so much of the trade as is not NI rate activity are treated as forming part of the mainstream profits or losses. This provision does not apply to the patent and know-how codes.

'*NI rate activity*' means:

(a) a qualifying trade (see **17.46A** above) carried on by a SME (NI employer) company, except to the extent that it is an 'excluded activity';
(b) a qualifying trade, other than an 'excluded financial trade', carried on by a NIRE company to the extent that it is carried on through a Northern Ireland regional establishment of the company and does not consist of an excluded activity;
(c) the back-office activities (see **17.46A** above) of an excluded financial trade carried on by a SME (NI employer) company which has made an election for that trade to be treated as a qualifying trade;
(d) the back-office activities of an excluded financial trade carried on by a NIRE company which has made an election for that trade to be treated as a qualifying trade, to the extent that those activities are carried on through the Northern Ireland regional establishment of the company;
(e) a qualifying partnership trade (see **17.46A** above) carried on by a NI Chapter 6 firm, except to the extent that it is an excluded activity;
(f) a qualifying partnership trade, other than an 'excluded financial trade', carried on by a NI Chapter 7 firm to the extent that it is carried on through a Northern Ireland regional establishment of the partnership and does not consist of an excluded activity;
(g) the back-office activities of an excluded financial trade carried on by a NI Chapter 6 firm which has made an election for that trade to be treated as a qualifying partnership trade;
(h) the back-office activities of an excluded financial trade carried on by a NI Chapter 7 firm which has made an election for that trade to be treated as a qualifying partnership trade, to the extent that those activities are carried on through the Northern Ireland regional establishment of the partnership.

The following are '*excluded activities*':

(i) the activity of effecting or carrying out reinsurance contracts;

(ii) an activity carried on in connection with the exploration or exploitation of the sea bed, subsoil and their natural resources, in the UK sector of the continental shelf; and

(iii) an activity carried on in connection with rights to assets to be produced by activities within (ii) above or to interests in or to the benefit of such assets.

An '*excluded financial trade*' is an excluded trade (see **17.46A** above) other than an oil industry ring-fence trade or long-term insurance business.

[*CAA 2001, ss 6C–6E; CTA 2010, ss 357XF, 357XG; CTNIA 2015, ss 1,2, Sch 1 para 2; F(No 2)A 2017, Sch 7 para 24*].

Plant and machinery

[17.46C] If, as a result of the provisions at **17.46B** above, an activity of a company is treated as a separate trade, that activity is an activity separate from any other activity of the company. Similarly, if an activity of a NI Chapter 6 or Chapter 7 firm (see **17.46A** above) is treated as a separate trade for the purposes of the corporate partner calculation, that activity is, for those purposes, an activity separate from any other activity of the partnership. [*CAA 2001, s 15(2ZA)(2ZB); CTNIA 2015, Sch 1 para 4*].

For the transitional rules allocating expenditure to pools on the introduction of the Northern Ireland rate see **17.46X** below.

The following rules apply if in a chargeable period beginning after the commencement day (see **17.46A** above) a company is a SME (NI employer) company (other than as a result of an election relating to the back-office activities of a financial trade) but was neither a SME (NI employer) company nor a NIRE company (see **17.46A** above) in the previous chargeable period.

- The fact that assets which continue to be used in the chargeable period for the purposes of the trade actually carried on by the company are treated as a result of the above provisions as ceasing to be used for the purposes of a main rate activity (i.e. the company's trade except so far as it is an NI rate activity) and beginning to be used for the purposes of a NI rate activity does not give rise to a disposal event.
- If, during the chargeable period, the only qualifying activity carried on by the company is a NI rate activity, the amount of unrelieved qualifying expenditure brought forward in the main pool or special rate pool at the beginning of the period is treated as relating to plant and machinery used for the purposes of the NI rate activity.
- If, during the period, the company carries on both an NI rate activity and a main rate activity:
  - the amount of unrelieved qualifying expenditure brought forward in the main pool at the beginning of the period is apportioned on a just and reasonable basis to become a main pool relating to plant and machinery used for the purposes of the NI rate activity and a main pool relating to plant and machinery used for the purposes of the main rate activity; and
  - a similar apportionment is made of any unrelieved qualifying expenditure brought forward in the special rate pool at the beginning of the period.

The following rules apply if in a chargeable period beginning after the commencement day a company is neither a SME (NI employer) company nor a NIRE company but was a SME (NI employer) company in the previous chargeable period and continues to carry on a qualifying activity.

- The fact that assets which continue to be used in the chargeable period for the purposes of the trade actually carried on by the company are treated as ceasing to be used for the purposes of a NI rate activity and beginning to be used for the purposes of a main rate activity does not give rise to a disposal event.
- Any unrelieved qualifying expenditure which relates to plant or machinery used for the purposes of a NI rate activity which is brought forward is treated as relating to the qualifying activity which the company continues to carry on.

Similar rules apply, for the purposes of the corporate partner calculation (see **17.46B** above), to a partnership which becomes, or ceases to be, a NI Chapter 6 firm.

[*CAA 2001, ss 66B–66E; CTNIA 2015, Sch 1 para 7; F(No 2)A 2017, Sch 7 para 24*].

If a company incurs qualifying expenditure on plant or machinery partly or the purpose of a NI rate activity and partly for the purposes of a main rate activity then, for the purposes of any annual investment allowance or first-year allowance, the expenditure is apportioned between the activities on a just and reasonable basis, with regard in particular to the likely extent of use for the purpose of each activity. The apportionment is made after any reduction because the expenditure is incurred only partly for the purposes of a qualifying activity (see **5.56** above) or because of a partial depreciation subsidy (see **7.14** above). If allocated to a pool, such expenditure must be allocated to a single asset pool. If a company has to bring in a disposal value because the plant or machinery begins to be used for the purposes of a NI rate activity as well as for the purposes of a main rate activity (or vice versa), an amount equal to the disposal value is allocated as expenditure on the plant or machinery to a single asset pool. There is no disposal event where plant or machinery the expenditure on which has been allocated to a single asset pool begins to be used more for the purposes of a NI rate activity or the main rate activity. Writing-down allowances, balancing allowances and balancing charges in respect of expenditure allocated to a single asset pool under these provisions must be apportioned between the NI rate and main rate activities on a just and reasonable basis, with regard in particular to the extent of use for the purpose of each activity in the chargeable period in question. If, however:

- there is such a change of circumstances as would make it appropriate for such an apportionment for the chargeable period in which the change occurs or a subsequent period to be substantially different from that which would have been appropriate apart from the change;
- no disposal value would otherwise be brought into account in the single asset pool for the chargeable period of the change; and
- the market value of the plant and machinery at the end of the chargeable period in which the change occurs exceeds the available qualifying expenditure in the single asset pool by more than £1 million,

a disposal value must be brought into account for the chargeable period of he change and the company is treated as incurring qualifying expenditure of an amount equal to the disposal value on the provision of the plant of machinery at the beginning of the following chargeable period (and a new apportionment made for the purposes of any annual investment allowance or first-year allowance as above).

Similar rules apply to partnerships.

[*CAA 2001, ss 212ZA–212ZF; CTNIA 2015, Sch 1 para 8; F(No 2)A 2017, Sch 7 para 24*].

If a company without a Northern Ireland regional establishment (see **17.46A** above) incurs expenditure for the purposes of a trade but subsequently becomes a NIRE company, then, if the activities for the purposes of which the expenditure was incurred would have been an NI rate activity treated as a separate trade under the provisions at **17.46B** above if the company had been a NIRE company at the time it was incurred, the expenditure is treated for capital allowances purposes as incurred on the first day of the first chargeable period for which the company is a NIRE company. A similar rule applies to partnerships which become NI Chapter 7 firms for the purposes of the corporate partner calculation. [*CAA 2001, s 12(2)–(6); CTNIA 2015, Sch 1 para 3*].

See also **5.11** above for a restriction on the amount of annual investment allowance and **5.41** above for the disposal value on a sale of plant or machinery to a buyer who uses it for the purposes of a NI rate activity.

Business premises renovation

[17.46D] If, as a result of the provisions at **17.46B** above, a company or partnership is treated as carrying on two separate trades, the question of whether an allowance or charge relates to the NI rate activity or the '*main rate activity*' (i.e. activity other than the NI rate activity) is determined according to the purpose for which the qualifying building is used. If the qualifying building is used for both an NI rate and a main rate activity, allowances and charges must be apportioned on a just and reasonable basis according to the proportion of use for the purposes of the NI rate activity. [*CAA 2001, s 360Z(3)–(6); CTNIA 2015, Sch 1 para 11*].

Mineral extraction

[17.46E] If, as a result of the provisions at **17.46B** above, a company or partnership is treated as carrying on two separate trades, each of them is treated as a mineral extraction trade if the separate trades together would be so treated. [*CAA 2001, s 394(2A); CTNIA 2015, Sch 1 para 12*].

Research and development

[17.46F] If a company without a Northern Ireland regional establishment (see **17.46A** above) incurs expenditure for the purposes of a trade but subsequently becomes a NIRE company (see **17.46A** above), then, if the activities for the purposes of which the expenditure was incurred would have been an NI rate activity treated as a separate trade under the provisions at **17.46B** above if the company had been a NIRE company at the time it was incurred, the expenditure is treated for capital allowances purposes as incurred on the first day of the first chargeable period for which the company is a NIRE company. A similar rule applies to partnerships which become NI Chapter 7 firms (see **17.46A** above) for the purposes of the corporate partner calculation (see **17.46B** above). [*CAA 2001, s 439A; CTNIA 2015, Sch 1 para 14*].

Dredging

[17.46G] If, as a result of the provisions at **17.46B** above, a company or partnership is treated as carrying on two separate trades, each of them is treated as a mineral extraction trade if the separate trades together would be so treated. [*CAA 2001, s 484(2A); CTNIA 2015, Sch 1 para 16*].

Transitional rules

[17.46H] Transitional provisions apply on the entry into force of the Northern Ireland rate for any accounting period beginning, or treated as beginning (see **17.46A** above), on the commencement day (the '*transition period*'). [*CTNIA 2015, Sch 1 para 19*].

If, at the beginning of the transition period, an NI rate activity carried on by a SME (NI employer) company or a NIRE company begins to be treated as a separate qualifying activity (see **17.46C** above), no disposal event is treated as arising. The amount of unrelieved qualifying expenditure brought forward in the main pool at the beginning of the period is apportioned on a just and reasonable basis to become a main pool relating to plant and machinery used for the purposes of the NI rate activity and a main pool relating to plant and machinery used for the purposes of the main rate activity. A similar apportionment is made of any unrelieved qualifying expenditure brought forward in the special rate pool. Where expenditure is carried forward to the transition period in a single asset pool and, immediately before the start of the period, the plant or machinery is used partly for the purposes of activities that become the NI rate activity and partly for the purposes of activities that become the main rate activity, the provisions at **17.46C** above dealing with single asset pools apply. Similar rules apply for the purposes of the corporate partner calculation where an NI rate activity carried on by a NI Chapter 6 or Chapter 7 firm begins to be treated as a separate qualifying activity at the beginning of the transition period. [*CTNIA 2015, Sch 1 para 20; F(No 2)A 2017, Sch 7 para 25*].

If, at the beginning of the transition period, an NI rate activity carried on by a SME (NI employer) company or a NIRE company begins to be treated as a separate qualifying trade (see **17.46B** above) for the purposes of know-how allowances, the amount of unrelieved qualifying expenditure brought forward in any pool at the beginning of the period is apportioned on a just and reasonable basis to become a pool relating to the NI rate activity and a pool relating to the main rate activity. Similar rules apply for the purposes of the corporate partner calculation where an NI rate activity carried on by a NI Chapter 6 or Chapter 7 firm begins to be treated as a separate qualifying trade at the beginning of the transition period. [*CTNIA 2015, Sch 1 para 21; F(No 2)A 2017, Sch 7 para 25*].

Self-built, etc. assets

[17.47] In the case of buildings or works qualifying for mineral extraction allowances, references to construction in the legislation show that capital allowances are available where a person constructs an asset himself, as opposed to paying a third party to construct the asset. As regards plant or machinery, the provisions in **4.9** above specify a person 'who has incurred capital expenditure on the provision of plant or machinery'; and therefore allowances are available where capital expenditure is incurred in constructing, etc. an item of plant or machinery.

When expenditure is incurred on self-built, etc. assets, the following questions arise.

(i) Is the expenditure of a capital nature?
(ii) Is it incurred for the purpose of providing the asset?

See **1.3** above for a discussion on what constitutes capital expenditure generally.

If materials are purchased specifically for the construction of the asset, their cost will normally be capital expenditure. If they are taken from trading stock or from general stores, it might be argued that the original expenditure on them was not incurred for the purpose of providing plant or machinery; but it would be normal accountancy practice to capitalise the expenditure as part of the cost of the asset. Where materials are appropriated from trading stock for use in the construction of an asset, *ITTOIA 2005, ss 172A–172F; CTA 2009, ss 156–161* apply to treat the appropriation as if it were a sale of those items at market value.

As regards the wages of persons employed in constructing the asset (either directly or in a managerial capacity), the distinction between revenue and capital expenditure will often be difficult to make. If people are employed specifically for the construction, their remuneration will normally be capital expenditure, but if general employees are temporarily assigned to the construction, presumably their remuneration will be apportioned on a reasonable basis in accordance with general accounting practice.

Of course, where expenditure would clearly qualify as a revenue expense, it will usually be to the person's advantage to claim it as such, thus obtaining 100% tax relief in the year of construction instead of a capital allowance at a much lower rate.

Value added tax

General principles

[17.48] The treatment of the value added tax (VAT) element of capital expenditure qualifying for allowances will depend on a person's VAT status. He may be non-registered for VAT or a taxable person whose output is wholly taxable (whether at the standard rate or the zero rate) or a taxable person whose output is partly exempt. The treatment in each case is prescribed by HMRC Statement of Practice SP B1 as follows.

(a) A non-taxable person for VAT, being one whose output is wholly exempt or whose taxable supplies are below the *de minimis* limit for registration, will not be able to reclaim any input tax suffered. Such input tax therefore forms part of his expenditure for tax purposes with no distinction being made between the net cost and the VAT element. The cost of an asset for capital allowances purposes will thus be inclusive of VAT.
(b) A taxable person for VAT, being one whose supplies are wholly taxable, be they standard-rated or zero-rated, will be able to reclaim input tax suffered. Where VAT is reclaimable, it cannot also qualify for income tax or corporation tax relief. The cost of an asset for capital allowances purposes is thus exclusive of VAT. One exception to the rule is a motor car, the reclaiming of input tax on which is usually prohibited. This exception was held not to breach European Community law in *EC Commission v France*, ECJ [1998] STC 805. The cost of a car for the purposes of allowances will therefore usually be inclusive of VAT.
(c) A taxable person whose supplies are partly exempt will suffer a restriction in his recoverable VAT which will depend on the extent to which any individual item of expenditure can be attributed to non-taxable supplies. Any element of VAT which cannot be reclaimed must be attributed to the item of expenditure to which it relates. If that is an asset qualifying for allowances, its cost for the purpose of those allowances will consist of its net cost, exclusive of VAT, plus the proportion of the VAT suffered thereon which cannot be reclaimed.

Notwithstanding (c) above, partly exempt persons may sometimes attempt to deal with irrecoverable input tax by charging the total amount thereof to the profit and loss account as a single separate item. This is not correct accountancy practice; see Statement of Standard Accounting Practice No 5. For tax purposes, irrecoverable VAT attributable to capital expenditure is part of the cost of the relevant assets.

VAT capital goods scheme

[17.49] Under VAT legislation in the UK prior to 1 April 1990, no account was taken, in the calculation of recoverable input tax, of changes in the extent to which a 'capital item' was used for the making of taxable supplies. The initial use of an asset entirely for those purposes, followed by a whole or partial use in the making of exempt supplies, would not cause a clawback of input tax recoverable. Conversely, the initial use of an asset entirely in the making of exempt supplies, followed by a whole or partial use for the making of taxable supplies, would not give rise to a recovery of input tax previously denied. However, the implementation of *Article 20(2)* of the *EEC Sixth Directive* by *SI 1989 No 2355* (amending *SI 1985 No 886*) changed the position as regards certain capital items purchased, appropriated or first used after 31 March 1990. These capital items broadly consist of computers worth £50,000 or more and land and buildings worth £250,000 or more. After 2 July 1997 they also include civil engineering works and refurbishments to buildings costing £250,000 or more. After 1 January 2011 they also apply to aircraft, ships, boats and other vessels costing £50,000 or more. Adjustments will consequently be required to the original VAT input tax claimed in certain cases where there is any change in the extent to which the capital item concerned is used for the making of taxable supplies over a period of up to ten years. This will mean that the business either has to pay more VAT or will receive a repayment of VAT previously paid.

Under the existing capital allowances legislation any extra VAT paid would not have qualified for capital allowances and any VAT repaid might not be brought into account for capital allowance purposes. A Budget Press Release of 20 March 1990 issued by the Inland Revenue therefore announced a proposal that this should be remedied for extra VAT paid or repayments of VAT after 31 March 1991 (the earliest date after which any such extra payments or repayments are required to be made). As indicated in that press release, legislation was introduced in the 1991 Finance Bill and enacted as *FA 1991, s 59, Sch 14*.

Although they affect relatively few traders (Customs originally estimated that there would be no more than 15,000 VAT registered businesses which would require to make adjustments), the changes made to the capital allowances legislation are complex and lengthy. The situation is examined further below.

Outline of the VAT capital goods scheme

[17.50] When a capital asset is acquired for a consideration which includes VAT, the normal rules for claiming input tax apply (see *VATA 1994, ss 24–26*). If the asset is wholly used in making taxable supplies, input tax is recoverable in full; if used wholly in making exempt supplies or in carrying on activities other than the making of taxable supplies, none of the input tax is recoverable; and if used only partly for making taxable supplies, a proportion of the input tax may be claimed under the partial exemption rules (see *SI 1985 No 886, Regs 29–37*). Normally this is done by an initial provisional claim in the return for the prescribed VAT accounting period related to the acquisition of the capital asset, followed by an annual adjustment in the return for the first prescribed accounting period following the end of the current annual adjustment period (see below). Where subsequently in a 'period of adjustment' there is a change in the extent of the taxable use, an input tax adjustment has to be made. If taxable use increases, a further amount of input tax can be claimed and, if it decreases, some of the input tax claimed previously must be repaid.

The capital items to which the legislation applies are mentioned in **17.49** above, as is the commencement of the capital goods scheme legislation. The '*period of adjustment*' consists of five successive '*intervals*' for computers etc., aircraft and ships etc. and interests in land and buildings which have less than ten years to run when acquired. For other interests in land and buildings, the period of adjustment consists of ten successive intervals. The first interval commences, as the case may be, on acquisition etc. or first use (but not before 1 April 1990) and ends at the end of the current annual adjustment period for the purposes of the trader's etc. partial exemption computation, i.e. normally 31 March, 30 April or 31 May depending on the prescribed VAT accounting periods adopted by the trader. Subsequent intervals correspond with the annual adjustment periods for partial exemption calculations.

Where the extent to which a capital item is used for the making of taxable supplies in the second or later interval is greater or less than such use in the first interval, an adjustment amount, to be paid or claimed from HMRC, is arrived at by multiplying one-fifth or one-tenth (depending on the number of intervals involved) of the total input tax relating to the capital item initially by an adjustment percentage. That percentage is the difference (if any) between the extent, expressed as a percentage, to which the capital item is used in making taxable supplies in the first interval and the extent to which it is used in the subsequent interval in question. Where the asset is sold, or the trader deregisters for VAT, during the period of adjustment, use in the interval concerned is deemed to have continued for the whole of that interval. Taxable use in any subsequent intervals is deemed to be 100% or nil% depending on whether the item is sold on a taxable or exempt supply respectively, with the proviso that, if it is the former, the aggregate of the amounts of input tax that may be deducted in respect of those intervals cannot exceed the output tax chargeable on the taxable supply. If capital items are lost, stolen or destroyed, or cease to exist (e.g. the expiry of a lease), during the period of adjustment, no further adjustment is made for any subsequent complete intervals, whilst the adjustment for the interval in which the loss etc. takes place is calculated on the assumption that use during that interval continued for the whole of that interval.

Unless HMRC allow otherwise, the adjustment for each interval is included in the VAT return for the second prescribed accounting period following the interval to which the adjustment relates or in which a sale, loss etc. took place.

There are further provisions to cover a number of circumstances, such as a company joining or leaving a group VAT registration and when a business is transferred as a going concern. In these situations an interval will end on the day concerned and, unless the interval ending on that day is the last interval in the period of adjustment, a new one will commence on the following day. Each subsequent interval ends on successive anniversaries of that day, so that only the first such situation causes an interval to come to an end. However, if on a transfer as a going concern the transferee adopts the transferor's VAT registration number, the interval applying on the day of transfer does not end at that time but continues to the next annual adjustment date for partial exemption purposes. In all of these circumstances there is no deeming of taxable use in any remaining VAT intervals as there is above for the sale of an asset or deregistration of a trader.

The present VAT capital goods scheme legislation is contained in *SI 1995 No 2518, Regs 112–116*. See also Tolley's Value Added Tax for a detailed commentary.

General capital allowances provisions about additional VAT liabilities and rebates

[17.51] As might be expected with such complex legislation, it is necessary to understand the general outline of the effect on capital allowances of the VAT capital goods scheme before looking in detail at the specific effects for the three individual codes of allowances affected: namely, business premises renovation, plant and machinery and research and development.

'*Additional VAT liability*' and '*additional VAT rebate*', in relation to any capital expenditure, mean, respectively, an amount which a person becomes liable to pay or an amount which he becomes entitled to deduct by way of adjustment under any VAT capital items legislation in respect of input tax.

'*VAT capital items legislation*' means any Act or instrument (whenever passed or made) which provide, in relation to value added tax, for the proportion of deductible '*input tax*' (see *VATA 1994, s 24*) on an asset of a specified description to be adjusted from time to time as a result of an increase or decrease in the extent to which the person concerned uses the asset for making '*taxable supplies*' (see *VATA 1994, s 4(2)*), or taxable supplies of a specified class or description, during a specified period (the '*VAT period of adjustment*'), or otherwise for the purpose of giving effect to *Article 20(2)–(4)* of the *EEC Sixth Directive* on value added tax (see, for example, *SI 1995 No 2518, Regs 112–116*).

[*CAA 2001, ss 547, 548(2), 551*].

For capital allowance purposes, a person is treated as *incurring* an additional VAT liability, and an additional VAT rebate is treated as *made* to a person, on the last day of the period, being one of the periods making up the VAT period of adjustment applicable to the asset concerned, in which occurs the increase or decrease in use which gives rise to the liability or rebate. [*CAA 2001, s 548(1)*].

The time when, and the chargeable period in which, an additional VAT liability or additional VAT rebate *accrues* is determined as follows.

(a) Where a VAT return is made to Customs in which the liability or rebate is accounted for, the time of accrual is the last day of the period to which the return relates, and the chargeable period in which the liability/rebate is treated as accruing is the chargeable period which includes that day.
(b) If, before any such return is made, Customs assess the liability or rebate as due or repayable, the time of accrual is the day on which the assessment is made, and the chargeable period in which the liability/rebate is treated as accruing is the chargeable period which includes that day.
(c) If the additional liability or rebate has not been accounted for on a VAT return to Customs, or assessed by them, before the trade or, in the case of plant or machinery, qualifying activity, has been permanently discontinued, the time of accrual is the last day of the chargeable period in which the trade etc. is discontinued. The liability/rebate is treated as accruing in that chargeable period.

[*CAA 2001, s 549*].

It will be noted that there are two different 'times' which may be relevant in determining the capital allowance treatment of an additional VAT rebate or liability. The time in *CAA 2001, s 549* will generally be later than that in *CAA 2001, s 548*, since the VAT adjustment for each interval of the specified period is included in the VAT return for the second prescribed accounting period following the interval to which the adjustment relates.

Where an allowance or charge falls to be determined, under any capital allowance provision, by reference to a proportion only of the expenditure incurred or a proportion only of what that allowance or charge would otherwise have been, any allowance or charge in respect of an additional VAT liability or rebate is similarly apportioned. [*CAA 2001, s 550*].

Business premises renovation

[17.52] Where a person who was entitled to a business premises renovation initial allowance in respect of qualifying expenditure incurs an additional VAT liability in respect of that expenditure at a time when the qualifying building is, or is about to be, qualifying business premises, the person entitled to the relevant interest can claim an initial allowance on the amount of the liability. The allowance is 100% of the additional VAT liability and is given for the chargeable period in which it accrues (see **17.51** above). A claim for an initial allowance may require it to be reduced to a specified amount. If the allowance is made in respect of an additional VAT liability incurred after the qualifying business premises are first used or suitable for letting for business use, the amount of the allowance is written off (see **8.9** above) at the time the liability accrues (see **17.51** above). [*CAA 2001, ss 360U, 360W*].

If the person entitled to the relevant interest in relation to qualifying expenditure incurs an additional VAT liability in respect of that expenditure, the liability is treated as qualifying expenditure and is added, to the extent that no initial allowance is or can be claimed as above, to the residue of qualifying expenditure (see **8.9** above) at the time when it accrues. [*CAA 2001, s 360V*].

If an additional VAT rebate is made in respect of qualifying expenditure to the person entitled to the relevant interest, the making of the rebate is a balancing event (see **8.10** above). No balancing allowance can be given, but a balancing charge is made if the amount of the rebate exceeds the residue of qualifying expenditure immediately before the time the rebate accrues. The amount of the charge is the amount of the excess. [*CAA 2001, s 360X*].

An amount equal to an additional VAT rebate is written off the residue of qualifying expenditure at the time the rebate accrues. [*CAA 2001, s 360Y*].

Note that business premises renovation allowances are not available for expenditure incurred on or after 6 April 2017 (1 April 2017 for corporation tax purposes).

Plant and machinery

[17.53] Where a person who has incurred qualifying expenditure on plant or machinery incurs an additional VAT liability at a time when the plant or machinery is still provided for the purposes of the qualifying activity, the liability is treated as qualifying expenditure on that plant or machinery. The deemed expenditure can then be taken into account in determining the available qualifying expenditure (see **5.36** above) in the appropriate pool for the chargeable period in which the liability *accrues* (see **17.51** above). If the original expenditure was AIA qualifying expenditure (see **5.2** above), the additional VAT liability is treated as AIA qualifying expenditure incurred in the chargeable period in which it *accrues* on the same plant or machinery as the original expenditure. If the original expenditure was first-year qualifying expenditure (see **5.16** above), the additional VAT liability is treated as first-year qualifying expenditure of the same type, so that a first-year allowance arises for the chargeable period in which the liability *accrues* at the same rate as that applying to the original expenditure. An annual investment allowance or first-year allowance may be taken in respect of the whole or part of the deemed expenditure. Specific provision is made to deny annual investment allowance or a first-year allowance where, at the time the liability is incurred (see **17.51** above), the asset concerned is used for 'overseas leasing' which is not 'protected leasing' (see **6.44** onwards above). An annual investment allowance is also denied in such circumstances. [*CAA 2001, ss 235–237*].

Where an additional VAT rebate is made to a person who has incurred qualifying expenditure on plant or machinery, and that person owns the plant or machinery concerned at any time in the chargeable period in which the rebate is *made* (see **17.51** above), the amount of the rebate must be brought into account as a disposal value for the chargeable period in which the rebate *accrues* (or, under the preceding year basis, the chargeable period related to the accrual). If a disposal value has to be brought into account in respect of the plant or machinery concerned apart from this provision, the rebate is added to that value. [*CAA 2001, s 238*].

Where any additional VAT rebates have been made in respect of an item of plant or machinery, the limitation of disposal value to no more than the qualifying expenditure incurred by the person in question (see **5.41** above) is adjusted to that qualifying expenditure reduced by the aggregate amount of the rebates accruing to him in previous chargeable periods. Where the disposal value would otherwise be the amount of an additional VAT rebate (see above), it is limited to the qualifying expenditure less any disposal values brought into account as a result of any earlier event. [*CAA 2001, s 239(1)–(4)*].

If the plant or machinery was acquired as a result of a transaction or series of transactions between connected persons (see **7.2** above), the limitation on disposal value to the greatest amount of qualifying expenditure incurred by one of those persons is adjusted where an additional VAT rebate is made to any one of those persons. In arriving at the greatest amount, the qualifying expenditure of each connected person is reduced by the amount of any rebate. [*CAA 2001, s 239(5)(6)*].

Where an additional VAT liability is incurred in respect of qualifying expenditure on a short-life asset after the end of the final chargeable period for the short-life asset pool (see **5.61** above) and a balancing allowance was made for that period, then, provided that the liability was not taken into account in determining the amount of the balancing allowance, a further balancing allowance is made equal to the amount of the liability for the chargeable period in which it accrues (or, under the preceding year basis, the chargeable period related to the accrual). [*CAA 2001, s 240*].

As regards fixtures under leases (see **6.9** above), a purchaser of an existing interest in land giving consideration including a capital sum for a fixture is treated as if the fixture belonged to him. This is subject to the proviso that, for chargeable periods ending before 24 July 1996, or when the acquisition was before that date, at the time of acquisition, either no other person was entitled to allowances in respect of the fixture or, if a person was so entitled, that person brings into account a disposal value. For the purpose of ascertaining whether there has been disposal value brought into account, the making of an additional VAT rebate is ignored. [*CAA 1990, s 54(1)(c); FA 1991, Sch 14 para 10*]. See now **6.9** above.

The anti-avoidance provisions of *CAA 2001, Pt 2 Ch 17* (see **7.3–7.6** above) are modified by *CAA 2001, ss 241–246* so as to ensure that the denial of annual investment allowance and first-year allowances and the restriction on the amount of expenditure qualifying for, or the denial of, writing-down allowances in respect of any capital expenditure under a transaction within those provisions is applied equally to any additional VAT liability in respect of such expenditure. Broadly, where qualifying expenditure is restricted by reference to the market value of plant or machinery, and that market value is determined inclusive of VAT, then any additional VAT liability incurred in respect of that expenditure is ignored. Where qualifying expenditure is restricted by reference to the amount of capital expenditure incurred by the 'seller' (see **7.3** above), or a person connected with the seller, then any additional VAT liability incurred in respect of that expenditure is treated as additional capital expenditure. [*CAA 2001, ss 241–246, Sch 3 para 51; FA 2015, Sch 10 para 5*].

EXAMPLE 2

[17.54]

A Ltd is a VAT partly exempt trader which makes quarterly VAT returns to 31 March, 30 June, 30 September and 31 December. Its VAT year for the purposes of partial exemption annual adjustments is to 31 March. Its corporation tax accounting periods end on 30 June.

On 1 July 2012 it purchases and commences to use a computer the purchase price of which is £1,000,000 plus VAT of £175,000.

A Ltd decides to claim the maximum allowances available.

On 1 January 2017 the computer is sold for £150,000 plus VAT of £26,250.

The taxable VAT use made of the computer is agreed with HMRC as follows for the relevant VAT interval concerned. Also quoted is the corresponding amount of VAT not claimable initially, and amounts of additional VAT liabilities and rebates.

The capital allowances consequences are as follows.

VAT interval	Taxable %	Comment	£
1.7.12–31.3.13	48	VAT not claimable initially	91,000
1.4.13–31.3.14	22	Additional VAT liability	9,100
1.4.14–31.3.15	79	Additional VAT rebate	10,850
1.4.15–31.3.16	48	No VAT adjustment	—
1.4.16–31.3.17	16	Additional VAT liability	11,200

Short-life asset treatment is not elected for. Assume that there are no other acquisitions and disposals from the main pool, and that the unrelieved qualifying expenditure in the main pool was £50,000 immediately before the corporation tax accounting period beginning on 1 July 2012.

The capital allowance consequences are as follows.

Accounting period 1.7.12–30.6.13

Annual investment allowance is available in respect of qualifying expenditure incurred before 31 December 2012 up to a maximum of £25,000. For the accounting period a writing-down allowance at the hybrid rate of 18% is available on the unrelieved qualifying expenditure brought forward (£50,000) and the balance of the capital expenditure incurred on the computer (£1,000,000 plus £91,000 of VAT not claimable initially under SP B1 less £25,000). The writing-down allowance is £200,880 ((£50,000 + £1,066,000) × 18%) and the annual investment allowance is £25,000. The unrelieved qualifying expenditure carried forward on the main pool is £915,120.

Accounting period 1.7.13–30.6.14

Although an additional VAT liability of £9,100 is treated as *incurred* on 31 March 2014 it is not brought into account for capital allowance purposes until the corporation tax accounting period which includes the last day of the VAT accounting period relating to the VAT return in which the liability is accounted for (i.e. the chargeable period in which it *accrues*). Accordingly the writing-down allowance at 18% is £164,722 and the unrelieved qualifying expenditure carried forward is £750,398.

Accounting period 1.7.14–30.6.15

The additional VAT liability of £9,100 incurred on 31 March 2014 is taken into account in the accounting period. Annual investment allowance is available on the amount of the liability. The annual investment allowance is £9,100 and the writing-down allowance at 18% on the unrelieved qualifying expenditure brought forward of £750,398 is £135,072. The unrelieved qualifying expenditure carried forward is £615,326.

Accounting period 1.7.15–30.6.16

The additional VAT rebate of £10,850 treated as incurred on 31 March 2015 is taken into account in the accounting period. Consequently the amount of the rebate is treated as a disposal value and is deducted from the unrelieved qualifying expenditure brought forward (£615,326) to produce net unrelieved qualifying expenditure of £604,476. Thus the writing-down allowance at 18% is £108,806 and the unrelieved qualifying expenditure carried forward is £495,670.

Accounting period 1.7.16–30.6.17

There is no additional VAT liability or rebate treated as incurred or made on 31 March 2016. As the asset was sold for net proceeds of £150,000 on 1 January 2017, this amount is deducted as a disposal value from the unrelieved qualifying expenditure brought forward (£495,670) to produce net unrelieved qualifying expenditure of £345,670. The writing-down allowance at 18% is £62,221 and the unrelieved qualifying expenditure carried forward is £286,449.

The additional VAT liability of £11,200 is treated as incurred on 31 March 2017. Because the computer was not then owned by A Ltd, the liability is ignored for these purposes. However, had A Ltd had a taxable use greater than 48% in that VAT interval so that an additional VAT rebate would have been made, the position would be different. Because the computer was owned by, and the rebate would have been deemed to have been made to, A Ltd at some time in the accounting period ended 30 June 2017, the amount of the VAT rebate would have been taken into account as a disposal value. The disposal value would be brought in, in this case, for the accounting period ending on 30 June 2018, i.e. an accounting period throughout which the computer was not owned by A Ltd.

Research and development

[17.55] Where a person incurs an additional VAT liability in respect of expenditure which is qualifying expenditure for the purposes of research and development allowances, then the liability is treated as additional capital expenditure on the same research and development as the original expenditure. This does not, however, apply if the person has ceased to own the asset represented by the expenditure before the liability is incurred, or if the asset has by then been demolished or destroyed. Any allowance available as a result of the incurring of the liability is made for the chargeable period in which the allowance accrues, or if later the chargeable period in which the relevant trade is set up and commenced. Where *CAA 2001, s 438(4)* (see **11.4** above) allows the whole of a building to be treated as used for research and development where no more than one-quarter of the expenditure is referable to a part of the building consisting of a dwelling, any additional VAT liability or rebate is ignored in considering that fractional limit. [*CAA 2001, ss 438(6), 447*].

Where an additional VAT rebate is made before the asset representing qualifying expenditure is disposed of, demolished or destroyed, the amount of the rebate (assuming it does not already fall to be brought into account for industrial buildings or plant and machinery allowances purposes) is treated as a disposal value to be brought into account for the chargeable period in which the rebate accrues or, if later, the chargeable period in which the relevant trade is set up and commenced. (Under the preceding year basis, it is brought into account for the later of the chargeable period related to the accrual, and that related to the commencement of the trade.) If a disposal value would have to be brought into account for that period apart from this provision, the rebate is added to it.

Modifications are made to the rules for calculating a balancing charge (see **11.12**(ii) above) where any disposal values ('*VAT disposal values*') have been brought into account for previous chargeable periods as a result of additional VAT rebates. Any 'unclaimed allowance' is treated as reduced by the excess of the VAT disposal values over any balancing charges arising as a result of bringing into account those disposal values, and the allowance made is treated as reduced by those balancing charges.

[*CAA 2001, ss 448, 449; FA 2008, Sch 27 para 7*].

EXAMPLE 3

[17.56]

Assume that the references in *Example 2* in **17.54** above to a computer used in A Ltd's trade are replaced by references to a computer used by A Ltd in research and development related to A Ltd's trade and that the reference to qualifying expenditure of £50,000 brought forward to the accounting period beginning on 1 July 2012 is ignored. Otherwise purchase prices, dates, extents of VAT taxable use and amounts of VAT not claimable initially and amounts of VAT liabilities and rebates are as in **17.54** above.

The capital allowance consequences are as follows.

Accounting period 1.7.12–30.6.13

A 100% allowance for research and development expenditure is available in respect of the qualifying expenditure incurred on the computer (£1,000,000 plus £91,000 of VAT not claimable initially under SP B1). A deduction of £1,091,000 is therefore given.

Accounting period 1.7.13–30.6.14

Although an additional VAT liability of £9,100 is treated as incurred on 31 March 2014 it is not brought into account for capital allowance purposes until the corporation tax accounting period which includes the last day of the VAT accounting period relating to the VAT return in which the liability is accounted for (i.e. the period in which it accrues).

Accounting period 1.7.14–30.6.15

The additional VAT liability of £9,100 treated as incurred on 31 March 2014 is taken into account in the accounting period. Consequently the amount of the liability is eligible for the 100% allowance.

Accounting period 1.7.15–30.6.16

The additional VAT rebate of £10,850 treated as made on 31 March 2015 is taken into account in the accounting period. Consequently the amount of the rebate is treated as a disposal value (as this is less than the allowance made), giving rise to a balancing charge.

Accounting period 1.7.16–30.6.17

There is no additional VAT liability or rebate to be treated as incurred/made on 31 March 2016. As the asset was sold for net proceeds of £150,000 on 1 January 2017, this gives rise to a balancing charge for the accounting period. The charge is the lower of the disposal value (£150,000) less unclaimed allowances (nil) and the allowance made (£1,091,000 plus £9,100) as reduced by the previous balancing charge (£10,850).

The additional VAT liability of £11,200 is treated as incurred on 31 March 2017. Accordingly, because the asset did not then belong to A Ltd, the liability is ignored for these purposes. If A Ltd had had a taxable use greater than 48% in that VAT interval so that an additional VAT rebate would have been made, the rebate would also have been ignored.

Trusts

[17.57] In broad terms a trust is entitled to capital allowances in the same way as an individual. As the income of a trust is chargeable to income tax, *CAA 2001* applies to trustees as it applies to others within the charge to income tax. Where there is an excess of capital allowances over the income to which they relate, the excess is, under general principles, either carried forward (usually as a trading etc. loss) or set against other income of the trustees (see generally **2.35** above). There is no specific provision, even for interest in possession trusts, enabling allowances (or an excess of allowances) to be transferred to the beneficiaries and utilised against their own income.

It must be said that the tax position of trusts can be complex according to the circumstances; if the income or part of the income arising within the terms of the trust is deemed to be that of a person other than the trustees (*qua* trustees), it may follow that any capital allowances are claimable by that person.

In broad terms, authorised unit trusts are treated for capital allowances purposes as UK resident companies whilst unauthorised unit trusts are treated in the same way as trusts generally. [*ITA 2007, s 504; CTA 2010, ss 616, 617, 622*].

Tonnage tax

[17.58] A special corporation tax regime was introduced by *Finance Act 2000* enabling shipping companies which are 'qualifying companies', or groups of companies of which at least one member is a 'qualifying company', to elect for their corporation tax profits from the activities of 'qualifying ships' to be calculated by reference to the net tonnage of each of those ships, and for losses to be left out of account for corporation tax purposes. All 'qualifying companies' within a group must be taxed on the same basis. Amendments to the regime were made by *Finance Act 2005*.

A '*qualifying company*' is a company within the charge to corporation tax which operates 'qualifying ships' which are strategically and commercially managed in the UK. Certain temporary cessations from operating any 'qualifying ships' may be disregarded. Companies participating in the tonnage tax regime must also meet a minimum training obligation. '*Qualifying ships*' are, broadly, seagoing ships carrying on certain activities which are of at least 100 tons gross tonnage, but excluding fishing and factory support vessels, pleasure craft, harbour and river ferries, fixed and floating oil rigs and platforms, floating production, storage and offtake vessels, existing dedicated shuttle tankers subject to the petroleum revenue tax regime, certain dredgers, and any vessel whose main purpose is the provision of goods or services normally provided on land. *FA 2005* introduced additional requirements as to the flagging of vessels. Types of vessel may be added to or removed from the excluded categories by Treasury order. The activities in which they must be engaged are transportation by sea, the provision of marine assistance or the provision of transport for services necessarily provided at sea. They may also, to a limited extent, include certain secondary and incidental activities.

Initially, for existing qualifying companies, the *election* had to be made within twelve months from 28 July 2000, but elections can also be made at any time in the period 1 July 2005 to 31 December 2006. New qualifying companies can make an election up to twelve months after first becoming a qualifying company (or within the above periods). In the case of a group of companies, an election may be made within twelve months of a group company first becoming a qualifying company, provided that the group is not substantially the same as a group which at any earlier time had a member which was a qualifying company. The Treasury may provide further opportunities for elections by statutory instrument. Special provisions apply in relation to mergers and demergers. An election generally has effect from the beginning of the accounting period in which it is made (or, where that accounting period began before 1 January 2000, from the beginning of the following accounting period), subject to earlier or later effect in certain cases with HMRC agreement. It normally remains in effect for ten years for so long as the company (or group) qualifies and is not excluded, and (subject to the training requirements having been met) may at any time be renewed (such renewal being treated in effect as a valid new election). There is provision for exit charges on a company leaving the tonnage tax regime, and a bar on re-entry to the regime within ten years. *FA 2005* provided an opportunity for companies to withdraw from the regime by giving notice to HMRC during the period 7 April 2005 to 31 March 2006. A notice can only be given where the election was in force for the whole of the three-year period ending on 7 April 2005. Where a notice is given, the election ceases to have effect at the end of the accounting period preceding the first accounting period of the company to begin after 1 July 2005, subject to transitional provisions.

Foreign dividends from non-UK resident shipping companies are (subject to conditions) also included in the profits covered by an election, as is any loan relationship credit, exchange gain, or profit on an interest rate or currency contract which would otherwise be treated as trading income. Otherwise, investment income is excluded.

Profits within the tonnage tax regime are 'ring-fenced', with appropriate anti-avoidance measures to prevent exploitation of the regime There are similar 'ring-fence' provisions for capital allowances (see **17.59** below). No chargeable gains will arise during the currency of the election in relation to assets used for the qualifying activities.

Special provisions apply to the chartering in of qualifying ships and joint charters and to the chartering out of short-term over-capacity. There are also special rules for offshore activities in the UK sector of the continental shelf, and for group mergers and demergers.

The Treasury have made provision by regulations for *inter alia* the application of the provisions to activities carried on by a company in partnership (*SI 2000 No 2303*). HMRC have published a Statement of Practice (SP 4/2000) dealing with the practical administration of the tonnage tax regime.

[*FA 2000, s 82, Sch 22; TIOPA 2010, Sch 8 paras 56, 119; FA 2012, Sch 20 paras 18–20; FA 2014, Sch 1 para 7; SI 2005 Nos 1449, 1480; SI 2007 No 850*].

Capital allowances

[17.59] The following is a brief outline of the capital allowances scheme for companies subject to the tonnage tax. The detailed provisions are outside the scope of this book. Note that there are special provisions relating to 'offshore activities' in the UK sector of the continental shelf which are not covered here. In summary:

- a company subject to tonnage tax is not entitled to capital allowances in respect of expenditure incurred for the purposes of its tonnage tax trade, whether incurred before or after its entry into tonnage tax;
- a company's tonnage tax trade is not a trade nor other qualifying activity for the purposes of determining the company's entitlement to capital allowances;
- entry of a company into tonnage tax does not of itself give rise to any balancing charges or balancing allowances; and
- on leaving tonnage tax on the expiry of an election or on the taking effect of a withdrawal notice, a company is treated as incurring qualifying expenditure on its tonnage tax plant and machinery assets of an amount equal to the lower of cost and market value; otherwise, the company is put broadly in the position it would have been in if it had never been subject to tonnage tax.

When a company enters the tonnage tax regime, any unrelieved qualifying expenditure (including expenditure unrelieved due to the postponement of an allowance under **5.74** above) attributable to plant or machinery that is to be used wholly for the purposes of the company's tonnage tax trade is taken to a single pool (the company's '*tonnage tax pool*'). The amount to be transferred from a class pool, or the main pool, is determined by apportionment by reference to the market value of the assets in the pool immediately before entry. No allowance may be claimed in respect of any expenditure taken to the company's tonnage tax pool, but a balancing charge may arise as indicated below.

The tonnage tax pool is not increased by reason of an asset beginning to be used for the purposes of the tonnage tax trade after the company's entry into tonnage tax.

Where, whilst a company is subject to tonnage tax, an event occurs in respect of expenditure within the tonnage tax pool which would require a disposal value to be brought into account if the tonnage tax trade were a trade for capital allowance purposes (see **5.41** above), that disposal value, limited to the market value of the plant or machinery when the company entered tonnage tax, is brought into account in the tonnage tax pool. If a balancing charge arises as a result, it is reduced on a sliding scale by reference to the number of whole years the company has been subject to tonnage tax at the time of the event giving rise to the charge. A balancing charge is also reduced in certain circumstances where the plant or machinery concerned has been taken into account in calculating income under the sale of lessor provisions (see **17.30** above) as a result of a company joining a tonnage tax group.

The balancing charge is treated as arising in connection with a trade (other than the tonnage tax trade) carried on by the company, and is treated as a trading receipt for the accounting period in which it arises. There are provisions for deferring the balancing charge where the company incurs capital expenditure on qualifying ships within the period beginning one year before and ending two years after the event giving rise to the charge, and for another tonnage tax company within the same group to surrender all or part of its tonnage tax pool balance to reduce or extinguish the charge.

Where plant or machinery is used partly for the purposes of the tonnage tax trade and partly for the purposes of another qualifying activity, the normal provisions for assets used partly for non-qualifying activity purposes at **5.55** and **5.56** above apply as if the use for the purposes of the tonnage tax trade were use for purposes other than those of a qualifying activity.

Where plant or machinery used for the purposes of the tonnage tax trade which was acquired after entry into tonnage tax begins to be used for the purposes of another qualifying activity carried on by the company, the normal provisions for assets previously used outside a qualifying activity at **7.13** above apply as if the tonnage tax trade use were use outside a qualifying activity.

When a company leaves tonnage tax it will again become entitled to capital allowances in respect of plant or machinery held by it at that time and used for its tonnage tax trade. Where the company leaves on the expiry of an election or on the taking effect of a withdrawal notice, the amount of qualifying expenditure in respect of each item of plant or machinery used in the tonnage tax trade is taken to be the market value at the time of leaving or, if less, the amount of expenditure incurred on the provision of the asset that would have been qualifying expenditure had the company not been subject to tonnage tax. In any other case, for each item of plant or machinery, the amount of expenditure which would have qualified for allowances but for its use for the purposes of the tonnage tax trade is determined and that amount is written down by reference to a percentage reduction depending on the number of whole years since the expenditure was incurred, using the table set out in *The Tonnage Tax Regulations 2000 (SI 2000 No 2303)*. In the latter case, there are separate rules for expensive cars within **5.53** above and long-life assets within **5.66** above.

[*FA 2000, Sch 22 Pt IX; CAA 2001, Sch 2 para 108; FA 2012, s 24(8)(10)*].

Ship leasing

[17.60] There are special provisions applying in respect of leases of qualifying ships provided to companies within tonnage tax. Originally, the provisions applied only to finance leases, but they were extended by *FA 2003* to all leases (subject to the exceptions noted below). For these purposes, a '*lease*' means any arrangements for a ship to be leased or otherwise made available by one person to another. The provisions are broadly as follows.

(a) The lessor is not entitled to capital allowances in respect of the ship if the lease (or any transaction or series of transactions of which the lease forms part) includes provisions (other than certain types of security provided by the lessee or a third party) removing from him (or a connected person) the whole or greater part of any risk of loss arising from a failure to make payments in accordance with its terms.

(b) The lessor is not entitled to capital allowances if the lease is part of sale and lease-back arrangements (as defined).

(c) Where the lessor is entitled to capital allowances, annual investment allowance and first-year allowances are not available. Writing-down allowances are available at the main rate (currently 20% — see **5.32** above) for the first £40 million of expenditure on providing the ship, at the special rate (currently 10% — see **5.49** above) on the next £40 million, and no writing-down allowances are available on the excess. Where, for expenditure incurred on or after 1 January 2011, the ship is a long-life asset (see **5.66** above), writing-down allowances on the first £40 million of expenditure are given at the special rate. Separate class pools (the 'tonnage tax (main rate) pool' and the 'tonnage tax (special rate) pool' are established for expenditure qualifying for allowances at each rate. For accounting periods beginning before 1 April 2008, the rate for the first £40 million of expenditure was 25%, and a hybrid rate applied for periods straddling that date, calculated using the formula at **5.32** above. These rules are applied separately in relation to each ship. Where a disposal value falls to be brought into account in respect of such a ship, there are provisions for allocating that value to the separate pools. HMRC may by regulations alter the rates at which allowances are given, and the rates will change automatically as a result of the 2012 changes to the main and special rates (see **5.32** and **5.49** above).

(d) Certain leases are treated as not being long funding leases for the purposes of the provisions at **6.21** above where they would otherwise be so treated. As a result the prohibition on capital allowances for lessors under long funding leases will not apply to such leases and the lessor's entitlement to allowances will be determined under (a) to (c) above. The ship must be provided directly by the lessor to the tonnage tax company or a member of its group, and the tonnage tax company must meet conditions as to its operation and management of the ship and as to the period and rate of any sublease.

The restrictions at (c) above do not apply to leases which constitute 'ordinary charters' (as defined).

A claim for capital allowances by a lessor in respect of expenditure on the provision of a qualifying ship must be accompanied by a certificate by the lessor and the lessee stating that:

- the ship is not leased (directly or indirectly) to a company subject to tonnage tax, or
- neither (a) nor (b) above apply and, where the lease would otherwise be a long funding lease, (d) above applies.

Where circumstances change so that any matter certificated ceases to be the case, the lessor must, subject to a penalty for failure, inform HMRC within three months after the end of the chargeable period of the change.

[*FA 2000, Sch 22 Pt X; CAA 2001, Sch 2 para 108; FA 2011, ss 10(5)–(13), 57*].

Real estate investment trusts

[17.61] For accounting periods beginning on or after 1 January 2007, companies meeting the necessary conditions can elect to become real estate investment trusts. The company must be UK-resident, must not be an open-ended investment company or a close company and its ordinary share capital must be admitted to trading on a recognised stock exchange. Groups of companies are able to become group real estate investment trusts.

The 'property rental business' (as defined, and including both UK and overseas property) of such a trust is ring-fenced and treated as if it were a separate business carried on by a separate company. Profits and gains arising in respect of the business are exempt from corporation tax (although a tax charge may arise in certain tax avoidance cases). Profits of the company which are not from the tax-exempt business are chargeable to corporation tax at the main rate (currently 20%). To the extent that dividends paid by the company derive from ring-fenced profits and gains they are taxed in the hands of the recipient as property income rather than as distributions. Companies which entered the regime before 17 July 2012 had to pay an entry charge.

Companies may exit the regime at any time by notice, and may be required to do so by HMRC notice where they repeatedly fail to meet certain conditions. Exit from the regime is automatic where certain other conditions cease to be met. On entry into or exit from the regime the company's accounting period is deemed to come to an end, and a new one begins.

For capital allowances purposes, assets transferred into the tax-exempt business (and therefore treated as transferred to a separate company) on entry into the regime or otherwise are, in effect, transferred at their written-down value such that no balancing allowance or charge arises. Within the tax-exempt business, capital allowances are automatically taken into account in the calculation of the profits without the requirement for a claim under *CAA 2001, s 3* (so that, even though the profits are exempt, the assets continue to be written down). Assets ceasing to be used for the purposes of the tax-exempt business, whether on exit from the regime or otherwise, without being disposed of are transferred at their written-down value.

[*CTA 2010, ss 518–609; FA 2012, s 21, Sch 4, Sch 16 para 219; FA 2013, s 39, Sch 19; FA 2014, Sch 1 para 14; F(No 2)A 2017, Sch 4 paras 168, 169*].

For full coverage of the provisions, see *Tolley's Corporation Tax*.

18

Capital Allowances Planning — General

by
Heather Britton
of Francis Clark Tax Consultancy Limited

Introduction

[18.1] Capital allowances are a very commonly encountered aspect of the tax legislation. Whilst they will be familiar to most tax professionals, there are a number of possible allowances or reliefs that can be claimed. It is easy for these to be overlooked or misunderstood. It is important that all the available allowances and reliefs are fully considered and assessed. In respect of the available reliefs, once identified, the adviser's objectives will normally be to:

(a) claim as much tax relief as is legitimately possible, by identifying the maximum expenditure qualifying for capital allowances or related tax reliefs;
(b) claim the optimum tax relief as quickly as possible by identifying the fastest possible method of relief; and
(c) ensure the claim is technically robust and properly supported to allow the taxpayer to confidently meet the self-assessment obligations to submit an accurate and properly supported return.

The first step is identify the nature of the expenditure in terms of whether it is revenue or capital expenditure. If it is capital expenditure then does it qualify for capital allowances, and if so, the highest possible rate of tax relief needs to be assessed and claimed. In certain cases it may be appropriate to disclaim capital allowances where that avoids the wastage of personal allowances or may enable a higher rate of tax relief to be achieved in the future; or to enable losses to be utilised now (such as by means of a sideways loss claim) where losses will not be available in future. However, in considering such options, it is important to establish the rate of relief applying. If the annual investment allowance is disclaimed, then it is likely to be many years before the same amount of tax relief is achieved.

When assessing capital allowance planning options, it is important to fully establish the marginal tax rates being faced and the income tax, national insurance and benefit savings applying. The working tax credit or universal credit position needs to be taken into account as a claim for capital allowances could lead to a substantial award. A similar position can apply where a claim for allowances could prevent an individual losing entitlement to child benefit. Also the capping of loss relief in certain instances could influence a decision as to when to claim allowances.

There are a number of different types of capital allowances which can apply, often introduced by the Government to meet certain policy objectives. These all need to be assessed as part of any tax planning project and the rest of this chapter considers some planning opportunities.

The Office of Tax Simplification ('OTS') has been considering the capital allowance regime in light of their remit to consider ways of aligning corporation tax more closely with the accounts. In July 2017 their initial report recommends further work in exploring various options which include replacing capital allowances with accounts depreciation, introducing a small capital allowance exemption per item and reviewing the effectiveness and compliance process for making fixtures elections or enhanced capital allowances claims.

Are plant and machinery allowances available?

[18.2] One of the first planning points to consider is to ensure that claims for plant and machinery allowances are maximised. For such a day to day matter in tax compliance and planning, the capital allowances tax rules for plant and machinery are surprisingly complex and are often misunderstood. It is therefore essential that, as part of any tax planning exercise, the available allowances are assessed against the case law and statutory tests.

The fundamental definition of plant arose in *Yarmouth v France* CA 1887, 19 QBD 647:

> ' . . . in its ordinary sense, it includes whatever apparatus is used by a businessman for carrying on his business – not his stock-in-trade which he buys or makes for sale; but all his goods and chattels, fixed or moveable, dead or alive, which he keeps for permanent employment in his business.'

However, in practice this definition is not usually very helpful in identifying plant, so several more precise case law tests have arisen. Perhaps the most useful test resulted from the decision in *Wimpy International Ltd v Warland* CA 1988, 61TC 51 and is known as the 'premises' test. The aim is to identify whether the asset in question is part of the premises *in* which the business is carried on and performs *simply and solely* the function of housing the business (which cannot be plant), rather than apparatus *with* which the business is carried on (which may be plant). The terms 'premises' and 'setting', which are often used interchangeably, in fact have different legal meanings and are not mutually exclusive, so although the setting is generally not plant, it can sometimes be so.

In identifying the 'premises' Justice Hoffmann proposed four factors to be taken into account. They are questions of fact and degree, and not absolute hurdles, but merely *some* of the considerations (that is, there may conceivably be others):

(a) whether the item appears visually to retain a separate identity;
(b) the degree of permanence with which it has been attached to the building;
(c) whether the structure would be incomplete without it; and
(d) the extent to which it was intended to be permanent.

Determining the dividing line between the premises and business apparatus can often be tricky.

Following the definition in *Yarmouth v France* perhaps the most fundamental plant test to pass is whether the plant performs a *function* as *apparatus* in the taxpayer's business, and case law includes several instances where entire large assets have been held to be plant, even though they are also the setting. Examples include a dry dock in *CIR v Barclay Curle & Co Ltd* HL 1969, 45 TC 221 (which lifted and lowered ships for repair), a swimming pool in *Cooke v Beach Station Caravans Ltd* ChD 1974, 49 TC 514 (which attracted customers) and a silo in *Schofield v R&H Hall* CA(NI) 1974, 49 TC 538 (which handled grain).

A final test, which came to greatest prominence in *CIR v Scottish & Newcastle Breweries Ltd* HL 1982, 55 TC 252, considers whether the asset performs a *particular* function as apparatus in the context of the 'nature of the particular trade being carried on, and the relation of the expenditure to the promotion of the trade', that is, whether the asset functions as apparatus in that tax-payer's *particular* business (recognising that identical assets may be plant in one business and not in another). The issue under consideration in that case, where decorative lighting and other décor was successfully claimed as plant by an hotelier, was the providing of 'ambience'. In HMRC's view the particular business use test is 'basically the same as the functional test' (HMRC Capital Allowance Manual, CA21140).

HM Revenue & Customs' manuals provide commentary on whether caravans will qualify for capital allowances (CA22100). A caravan is plant if it does not occupy a fixed site and is regularly moved as part of normal trade usage, even if it is only moved from its summer to winter quarters. In the South West we see a large number of caravan sites and HMRC widely accept that a caravan on a holiday caravan site is plant regardless of whether it is moved.

Nowadays there are more types of units provided and the term "caravan" can cover double units delivered in two sections and then joined together and wooden lodges provided these are moveable. The definition of a caravan is from the *Caravan Sites and Control of Development Act 1960 (c.62)* ('CSCDA') or the *Caravans Act (Northern Ireland) 1963* (c.17 (N.I)). Structures which look similar but are not moveable will not qualify. HMRC only allow the wider definition to holiday caravan sites (being those licensed by the local authority under CSCDA) so care should be taken when dealing with holiday camps, leisure parks or hotels.

Caravans occupying residential sites do not qualify for capital allowances. HMRC allow special treatment to farmers (and only farmers) where capital allowances will be given on a caravan provided by a farmer to house a farm employee even if it occupies a fixed site and is used solely for residential purposes.

See **4.10–4.15** above for further consideration of the case law on the meaning of plant. See also **Appendix 1** for a list of items which may qualify as plant or machinery.

The main statutory rules that have grown out of the case law and Government policy are:

(a) expenditure incidental to the installation of plant and machinery during alterations to an existing building (see **4.16** above);

(b) demolition of plant and machinery (see **5.37** above);
(c) thermal insulation of buildings except dwellings (against loss of heat, not cold). This extended relief is treated as 'special rate' expenditure which qualifies at 8%, rather than the main rate of 18%. It should be noted that this relief is only available for thermal insulation added to an existing commercial building, and not that incurred as part of the original construction;
(d) personal security (see **4.17**(d) above) — but this only gives limited relief to individuals and partnerships (*not* companies) on security assets used to meet a 'special threat' to an *individual's personal* physical security arising by virtue of his trade, profession or vocation;
(e) integral features at a 8% writing down allowance (see **4.23** above); and
(f) computer software (see **4.19** above).

The case of *JD Wetherspoon plc v Revenue & Customs Commissioners* [2012] UKUT 42 (TCC) involved detailed consideration of what expenditure was deemed to be 'incidental' to the installation of plant and machinery. Considerable reliance was placed on there being a required 'nexus' between the installation of plant and the alteration of the building. For example in relation to tiling it was decided that if a basin was installed in an existing building a small splash-back would be incidental, but they would not accept the tiling of an entire wall (for example in a kitchen) due to its numerous purposes.

Plant and machinery allowances are not available for expenditure on the acquisition or alteration of land (see *CAA 2001, ss 22(1)(b), 24(1)*). The default starting position is that 'buildings' and 'structures' *cannot* be plant. *CAA 2001, s 21* defines a 'building' as including the following assets which are in, or are connected with, a building:

(a) walls, floors, ceilings, doors, gates, shutters, windows and stairs;
(b) mains services, and systems for water, electricity and gas;
(c) waste disposal systems;
(d) sewerage and drainage systems;
(e) shafts or other structures in which lifts, hoists, escalators and moving walkways are installed; and
(f) fire safety systems.

Section 22 defines a 'structure and other asset' as works involving the alteration of land; various civil engineering works like tunnels, bridges, embankments, cuttings, reservoirs, piers and jetties, etc.; as well as a fixed structure, other than a 'building' (as defined by *CAA 2001, s 21*).

However, to further complicate matters, *CAA 2001, ss 21, 22* are subject to *s 23*, which comprises a long list of assets that are unaffected by *ss 21–22*.

Section 23 lists many types of asset, including among others:

(a) machinery;
(b) gas and sewerage systems provided mainly to meet the particular requirements of the qualifying activity, or to serve particular plant and machinery;
(c) manufacturing or processing equipment, counters, storage and display equipment;

(d) sanitary ware;
(e) furniture and furnishings;
(f) burglar and fire alarm systems; and
(g) moveable partition walls (which are intended to be moved in the course of the qualifying activity), etc.

HMRC's view is that the *s 23* assets above are not automatically regarded as plant, but must still meet the usual tests set out by case law. However, it was the clear intention of the legislators that the assets *should* be treated as plant (provided that they are used in a relevant business activity). Consequently, most of the assets are quite clearly plant, and it should be no surprise to discover that when the case law tests are applied to them they are found to be plant (as the legislation was drafted on the basis of these case law tests).

See **4.21–4.30** above and **Chapter 19** for further discussion of plant and machinery in buildings.

Revenue and renewals expenditure

[18.3] Even if expenditure is on plant and machinery, the best form of relief is treatment as revenue expenditure. A revenue deduction is available for expenditure incurred on repairs and maintenance works (for example, during a building refurbishment project) at the rate of 100%, provided that the costs have been charged immediately to the profit and loss account. In HMRC's view, where revenue expenditure has been capitalised or 'deferred' then the tax deduction is only available when that expenditure is expensed through (that is, charged to) the profit and loss account (HMRC Business Income Manual, BIM 42215). Therefore, the tax deduction follows the depreciation rate in the accounts. Taxpayers may wish to consider expensing revenue expenditure, rather than capitalising it and deferring the tax relief, or obtaining no tax relief at all if the expenditure is not depreciated.

CAA 2001, s 33B introduced special rules in respect of repairs to integral features in a building. If the repair expenditure exceeds 50% of the current cost of replacing the entire integral feature, then that expenditure is treated as being a capital replacement (which will qualify for capital allowances). The legislation requires repair expenditure within any twelve-month period to be considered, so this can catch repairs spanning two different accounting periods, and can prove difficult to monitor. It would be advisable to keep a record of any quotes or estimates used in evaluating the 50% test, as it would be far harder to gather this information at a later date if justification were required.

The creation of a new asset for the enduring benefit of the business is capital, whereas expenditure of a less durable nature is revenue. HMRC will accept that expenditure on tangible assets with a life of less than one year is revenue (and conversely on assets with an expected life of two years or more is capital). They will also normally accept that expenditure that repeats every few years (for example: cleaning, redecoration, re-pointing brickwork, replacing roof slates, flashings or gutters and mending broken windows or doors) is revenue.

The repair of an asset includes its restoration by replacing subsidiary parts of the whole. Therefore, it is important to identify the entirety being repaired, because if the entirety is being replaced the expenditure is capital, not revenue. The leading cases in this area are *O'Grady v Bullcroft Main Collieries Ltd* KB 1932, 17 TC 93, *Samuel Jones & Co (Devondale) Ltd v CIR* CS 1951, 32 TC 513, *Conn v Robins Bros Ltd* ChD 1966, 43 TC 266 and *Brown v Burnley Football and Athletic Co Ltd* ChD 1980, 53 TC 357.

The first two cases both concerned the replacement of factory chimneys. In *Bullcroft* the chimney constituted a complete asset in itself separate from the main factory building, so its replacement was held to be capital. However, in *Samuel Jones* where the chimney was merely part of a larger building, the expenditure was treated as repairs.

In *Robins Bros* substantial repairs to a four hundred year old building were held to be revenue because the entirety was the whole building.

In the *Burnley Football* case a new football stand was constructed to replace one that had become unsafe and it was claimed that the cost was properly chargeable to repairs. However, it was found that it was the stand and not the football ground as a whole that constituted the entirety, so the expenditure on the new stand was not a repair.

The recent first tier tribunal case of *Cairnsmill Caravan Park* [2013] TC 02580 held that the replacement of the grass surface on part of a caravan park by hard-core surface was a repair as the entirety was the whole caravan park. This was supported by valuations before and after the works which suggested that no value had been added to either the area allocated to the touring caravans or to the park as an entirety. This highlights the importance of deciding the entirety of the asset when seeking to argue a revenue deduction.

Where a refurbishment or alteration project is so extensive to effectively amount to the reconstruction of the property then it cannot be revenue. However, depending on the facts, it can sometimes be possible to take a liberal interpretation of the entirety and expense substantial elements of a refurbishment scheme as revenue.

Where a subsidiary part of an entirety is replaced as a like-for-like replacement then it will be revenue. However, expenditure will generally be regarded as capital if that asset is an improvement of the one it replaced, unless it is the *nearest modern equivalent*. For example, HMRC accept that replacing single-glazed windows with double-glazed ones is allowable as a repair.

One potentially difficult area is where repairs are made to a property after it has been acquired. The two leading cases in this area are *Law Shipping Co Ltd v CIR* CS 1923, 12 TC 621 and *Odeon Associated Theatres Ltd v Jones* CA 1971, 48 TC 257.

In the *Law Shipping* case a ship was purchased in a dilapidated condition and subsequently renovated. The courts held that the need for repair was reflected in a low purchase price, and that the subsequent repair costs, to the extent that they were attributable to the period prior to acquisition, were therefore properly to be regarded as capital. On the same principle, if a taxpayer leases a property under terms which require it to be restored to a good state of repair so that it is fit for occupation, then the repairs are capital expenditure (*Jackson v Laskers Home Furnishers Ltd* ChD 1956, 37 TC 69).

In contrast, in the *Odeon Associated Theatres* case a number of cinemas were purchased during and immediately after World War II. The cinemas were in need of repair, but were nonetheless capable of use, and were in fact so used, before being repaired. When the repairs were eventually carried out it was held that the amounts expended were revenue and not capital.

Repairs to reinstate a dilapidated property are normally revenue unless:

(a) the property was not in a fit state for use in the business until the repairs had been carried out;
(b) the price paid was substantially reduced because of its dilapidated state; or
(c) on acquisition the purchaser agrees to reinstate the property to a good state of repair.

One alternative method for obtaining tax relief on replacement assets was previously achieved using the 'renewals' basis. However this form of non-statutory relief was withdrawn from April 2013.

Until April 2016 there were two other methods available for obtain tax relief for replacement expenditure:

- Despite the withdrawal of the non-statutory renewals basis, the strict statutory allowance for trade tools (under ITTOIA 2005, s 68 or CTA 2009, s 68) remained for a further three years. This allowed a deduction in calculating trading profits for expenditure on replacing or altering any implement, utensil or article used for the purposes of a trade. In a let property this could include items such as crockery or rugs, but not larger items such as carpets or freestanding cookers.
- Landlords of fully furnished residential property could elect to claim tax relief for wear and tear on furnishings at a rate of 10% of the net rent receivable.

The result of the above changes was that landlords of properties which were not fully furnished may not have achieved tax relief on the replacement of all items (e.g. white goods) for the three years to 5 April 2016.

From April 2016 the wear and tear allowance was withdrawn and replaced by a relief which enables landlords of residential dwelling houses to deduct the costs they actually incur on the replacement of furnishings, which brings us back to a logical rule and provides tax relief as expected. The deduction is available for capital expenditure on furniture, furnishings, appliances, white goods and kitchenware where the expenditure is a replacement item used for the dwelling.

The amount of the allowable deduction is:

- the cost of the new replacement item, limited to the cost of an equivalent item if it represents an improvement on the old item (beyond a reasonable modern equivalent), plus
- the incidental costs of disposing of the old item or acquiring the replacement, less

- any amounts received on the disposal of the old item.

Fixtures are not included in these new rules as they remain part of the property (e.g. bathroom sanitary ware, boilers, fitted kitchens, etc.) and any replacement would generally be deductible as a repair to the property itself.

The replacement furnishings deduction will not be available for furnished holiday lettings because capital allowances will continue to be available for both furniture and fixtures in these properties.

Annual investment allowance

[18.4] Once it is established that the expenditure is on plant and machinery and that revenue treatment is not available, then the best form of relief is through an annual investment allowance ('AIA') claim. This is because the AIA accelerates the tax relief that would otherwise be available compared to conventional writing-down allowances. However the benefit is limited to the maximum AIA for the relevant period multiplied by the taxpayer's marginal tax rate. The AIA was £500,000 from 1/6 April 2014 until 31 December 2015, before it decreased to its new 'permanent' level of £200,000. Even though the new £200,000 allowance is meant to be permanent, it is likely that this will be tinkered with in future years as it is a way of altering tax relief without impacting the main rates of corporation tax and income tax. In effect, AIA acts like a type of de minimis provision. Any additional expenditure above the maximum limit is written off under the normal capital allowances rules, at either the 18% rate or the 8% special rate.

The allowance is available to *almost* all businesses (per individual business or company group), regardless of size or legal form. This includes companies, partnerships (of which all the members are individuals), individuals, registered friendly societies and certain bodies corporate that are not companies but are within the charge to corporate tax. However, it does not include trusts or mixed partnerships (that is, those of which a company is a member, as these are not 'qualifying persons' as defined by CAA 2001, s 38A(3)). This final point was confirmed in the first-tier tribunal cases of *Hoardweel Farm Partnership v HMRC* FTT, [2012] UKFTT 402 (TC) and *Drilling Global Consultant LLP v HMRC FTT*, [2014] UKFTT 888 (TC04003).

As the AIA may be allocated flexibly, the taxpayer should allocate it to expenditure that would otherwise qualify for the lowest rates of relief (for example, in the first instance to integral features or long-life assets).

Single companies receive a single AIA (regardless of the number of trades). However, only a AIA may be allocated flexibly in any way between:

(a) groups of companies;
(b) groups of companies under common control who are 'related' to one another;
(c) other 'related' companies under common control.

A company is 'related' to another company in a financial year if one or both of the shared premises condition and the similar activities condition are met.

The similar activities condition considers whether more than 50% of the turnover derives from the same type of income (determined by reference to the 'NACE' international classification system, which divides industries into main categories such as agriculture and manufacturing).

Further restrictions are required due to devolving powers to set the tax rate to Northern Ireland and the rules for allocating AIA are considered further at *CAA 2001, s 51JA*.

It should be noted that the AIA sharing rules differ from companies which may be treated as 'associated' or 'related' for other tax purposes, including quarterly instalment payments for corporation tax or the long-life asset regime. These rules have been simplified so that, for accounting periods beginning on or after 1 April 2015, only companies in the same 51% group are taken into account.

Similar restrictions apply to 'related' unincorporated businesses under common control. However it should be noted that where an individual controls a company and has a sole trade then there is no requirement to share the AIA, regardless of whether the trades are 'related'.

See **5.11** above for full details of the operation of these restrictions.

Virtually all plant and machinery expenditure up to the AIA threshold is eligible for the 100% allowance in the period the expenditure is incurred, including fixtures and long-life assets, but excluding:

(a) cars;
(b) cases where the provision of the plant or machinery is connected with a change in the nature or conduct of the trade carried on by a person other than the person incurring the expenditure and the obtaining of an annual investment allowance is a main benefit from making the change;
(c) cases where the expenditure is 'deemed' rather than actual (for example, where it is first acquired for a non-trading purpose and only later used for the qualifying activity);
(d) gifts;
(e) plant previously used for long-funding leasing (that is, financing transactions that are not short leases as defined by *CAA 2001, s 70G*);
(f) expenditure incurred in the period when the capital allowances qualifying activity is permanently discontinued (for example in the year of incorporation of a sole trade or partnership — the recent case of *Keyl v Revenue & Customs Comrs*, [2015] UKUT 383 (TCC), highlights the importance of business transfer documentation to support the transaction, along with careful consideration of the timing of incorporation); and
(g) expenditure incurred in connection with ring fence trades (that is, oil extraction).

As the AIA may only be claimed in the chargeable period in which the expenditure is incurred, it cannot be deferred to a later period (but may be used to augment a loss carried forward). However, although it will rarely be appropriate, all or part of the AIA may be disclaimed, in which case writing-down allowances would be available for that expenditure in future periods.

Where a taxpayer has a chargeable period which is more or less than twelve months, the maximum AIA is proportionally increased or reduced. Similarly, the AIA is time-apportioned where the period overlaps a change in the level of AIA (most recently for periods straddling 1 January 2016). Where the period in question consists of entire calendar months, HMRC will accept that the calculation may be made on either a daily or monthly basis, but in other contexts, apportionments must be made according to the precise number of days.

For a chargeable period straddling the date of change in the AIA limit, the maximum allowance for the period is calculated on a time-apportioned basis. However there are complex rules which determine the maximum amount of expenditure in certain date ranges; the rules for periods in which allowances increase differ to those when the allowances decrease. These can particularly catch the unwary in relation to periods when the maximum allowances available may be far lower than expected due to the timing of expenditure. For example, areas in practice that can cause confusion include:

- The only restriction for year ends spanning the increase in April 2014, is a maximum spend of £250,000 in the period to 31 March 2014 or 5 April 2014. As a general rule of thumb, the restrictions are logical when the AIA limit increases, but unfavourable and can lead to unexpected results when the limit decreases.
- For year ends after 31 December 2015, the maximum expenditure that can be claimed from 1 January 2016 is only the pro-rata amount of £200,000 for the second part of the period. This is the same restriction as had to be tackled when the rate previously decreased to £25,000 and can catch the unwary.

For example, a business with a year end of 31 March 2016 could claim up to £425,000 of AIA in total for the year. This is calculated as £375,000 (nine months at the £500,000 level), plus £50,000 (being three months at the new £200,000 level). Any amount up to £425,000 could be incurred during the first nine months, but the key restriction is that only £50,000 could be incurred in the final three months of the year if the goal was to obtain AIA on all qualifying capital additions. Any excess would get writing down allowances at 8% or 18%. In these circumstances the optimum timing of capital spend may not be just before the year end.

See **5.4** above and Examples 1 and 2 at **5.5** and **5.6** above.

With the significant fluctuations in the level of annual investment available over the past couple of years, the date when capital expenditure is incurred has particular significance. The general rule is that expenditure is incurred when there is an unconditional obligation to pay it (see *CAA 2001, s 5(1)*). This applies even where part of the expenditure is not required to be paid until a later date. The rule is modified to a 'cash paid' basis in two important ways:

(a) where part of the expenditure is not required to be paid until more than four months after the normal unconditional obligation to pay; or
(b) if the obligation to pay is advanced before normal commercial practice in order to benefit from allowances in an earlier period.

These rules on the timing of expenditure are often overlooked, especially the need to consider payments after the year end under the above rules. For hire purchase or similar contracts, capital allowances are allowed under *CAA 2001, s 67*, which provides that:

(i) plant and machinery is treated as owned by the person who has the benefit of the contract; and
(ii) the hirer is treated as having incurred all the capital expenditure due under the contract when the asset is brought into use in the trade.

Thus, from the point of view of the hirer, capital allowances are due on all capital payments when the hire purchase contract is signed and the asset is bought into use in the trade, profession or vocation. If the asset is not in use at the year end, then capital allowances are only due on the capital element of the payments made under the contract. HMRC will often request evidence of this for substantial hire purchase acquisitions shortly before the balance sheet date.

100% First-year allowances (enhanced capital allowances)

[18.5] After considering revenue treatment and maximising the claim for the annual investment allowance then the next most favourable capital allowance to consider is 100% first-year allowances (often referred to as 'enhanced capital allowances'). These allowances are particularly useful for those businesses that have fully used their AIA entitlement and may be sought more widely now that the AIA has reduced from £500,000 to £200,000 from 1 January 2016.

Such allowances are available for certain expenditure incurred on green technologies — energy-saving plant and machinery (see **5.17** above) and environmentally beneficial plant (that is, currently water-conserving or quality-improving plant — see **5.21** above). To qualify, the assets on which the expenditure is incurred must be of a description specified by Treasury order, or meet the criteria specified by Treasury order for plant of that description, or have a certificate of energy efficiency or environmental benefit in force.

As an investment incentive to start-up and other loss-making companies (but not unincorporated businesses) they can surrender the element of their trading losses attributable to such allowances in return for a cash payment, thereby reducing the trading loss by the amount surrendered. The Capital Allowances (First Year Tax Credits) Order 2013 clarified that these tax credits will be available until 31 March 2018.

Broadly, a company which has a 'surrenderable loss' may claim a first-year tax credit (that is, a cash payment from HMRC) equal to 19% of that loss (or may use the tax credit to discharge any outstanding corporation tax liability). A company may also restrict its claim to only part of the total amount available.

The amount of the loss that may be surrendered is the smaller of:

(a) the amount of the first-year tax allowance; or

(b) the actual loss.

A loss may only be surrendered for a first year tax credit provided it has not been, or could have been, relieved elsewhere (for example against other taxable profits or group relieved).

Furthermore, the repayment is subject to a maximum limit, which is the larger of:

(a) the total amount of the company's PAYE and NIC liabilities for payment periods ending in the chargeable period; or
(b) £250,000.

It is important to note that a valid claim must be specified on the tax return and be supported by a schedule providing a list of qualifying items (including amount of expenditure and date of purchase).

A loss making company may make claims for first year tax credits under the enhanced capital allowance scheme, as well as under another scheme such as research and development tax credits. There is no prescribed order of surrender, so the company can decide on the magnitude of each claim. Despite the increase in rates from 11% to 14.5% in April 2014, the research and development tax credit rate is still lower.

Anti-avoidance applies to prevent the claiming of tax credits where arrangements have been entered into which have the claiming of a tax credit as a main purpose. Also, if a first-year tax credit is claimed and that asset is sold before the end of the 'clawback' period (ending four years after the end of the period for which the tax credit was paid), then the tax credit must be repaid to HMRC and the surrendered loss reinstated. HMRC also do not have to make a payment where the company has outstanding corporation tax, PAYE or NIC liabilities.

See further 5.28 onwards above.

The classes of energy-efficient and water-saving assets are specified on the Government's energy and water technology lists (see www.gov.uk/guidance/energy-technology-list and www.gov.uk/government/publications/water-efficient-enhanced-capital-allowances). The assets must be unused, not second-hand, and, for environmentally beneficial plant, must not be a long-life asset. Establishing entitlement to enhanced capital allowances can be a problematic and time consuming business. There are many different items of energy efficient or environmentally beneficial plant in existence. The essential planning point is therefore to review proposed expenditure at a very early stage in order to ensure that enhanced capital allowances are maximised. Technologies included on the list are reviewed and updated periodically. Changes made during 2015 include the addition of waste heat to electricity sub-technology and the removal of the packaged chillers sub-technology. 2016 changes included the addition of leak detection equipment.

Despite sounding very green, technologies such as solar photovoltaics (PV), hydro power and wind turbines are not on the qualifying Energy Technology List ('ETL') as these are energy generating rather than energy saving and therefore outside the remit of the scheme.

If only some components of a larger item of plant or machinery qualify for enhanced capital allowances, then the amount qualifying is limited to the amount specified by Treasury Order, which overrides the just and reasonable apportionment provisions that would otherwise normally apply. The direct transport and installation costs associated with the purchase of an ECA-eligible piece of equipment can also be included within the ECA claim.

Many taxpayers do not realise how difficult it sometimes is to claim the first-year allowance. For a CHP (combined heat and power) system, for example, the taxpayer must complete a lengthy self-assessment process, analysing in detail and measuring accurately the degree of energy efficiency. This can only be done by a specialist electrical engineer. Once issued with a certificate of energy efficiency, the taxpayer must in turn use it to obtain another certificate from the Secretary of State, entitling him to claim the first-year allowance on his tax return.

Certain technologies are not listed on the ETL but can be included in the claim: white light emitting diode lighting units, high efficiency lighting units, lighting controls, pipework insulation, automatic monitoring and targeting systems. Purchasers will need to obtain a statement from the manufacturer or supplier to confirm that the product supplied meets the eligibility criteria in force at the time of purchase. This can then form the basis of the supporting evidence for the tax claim.

There is a restriction to prevent 100% first-year allowances from being claimed where certain other incentives apply, namely feed-in tariffs and renewable heat incentives. This change applies from 1 April 2012 for corporation tax purposes and 6 April 2012 for income tax purposes. The taxpayer will effectively be allowed to choose which relief they claim. Should they claim the first year allowance and then later receive a tariff payment, the first year allowance will be clawed back. This withdrawal also applies to CHP systems; however this did not come into force until 1 April 2014 for corporation tax purposes and 6 April 2014 for income tax purposes. In most circumstances it will be preferable to receive the Government incentives and not claim enhanced capital allowances, even if this means tax relief for capital allowances are achieved over a longer period.

Enhanced capital allowances are also available for certain new, low emission or electric cars. The carbon dioxide limit to claim immediate tax relief was reduced from 95 g/km to 75 g/km from April 2015, and it was announced in the 2016 Budget that the threshold will further reduce to only 50 g/km from April 2018. The ECA scheme for cars has been extended by a further 3 years to 2021. From April 2018 the government also intend to reduce the threshold for the main rate of capital allowances (where 18% WDAs are claimed) from 130 g/km to 110 g/km. Carbon dioxide emission information can be obtained from the Vehicle Certification Agency at http://carfueldata.direct.gov.uk/. One important change occurred in April 2013, from which date cars acquired for leasing are not eligible for first year allowances, in line with the first year allowance rules for other assets.

As announced at Budget 2014, legislation has now been introduced to extend the deadline for 100% ECA for zero-emission goods vehicles. Previously these were only available until April 2015, but this has been extended by three years to 2018. From April 2015, a further restriction has been imposed that limits the availability of this ECA to businesses that do not also claim other state aids, such as the Government's 'plug-in van' grant.

A further first-year allowance is being introduced which is designed to support the development and installation of electric recharging equipment for electric vehicles. This is part of the increasing Government focus on promoting the wider uptake of electric vehicles. The measure provides a 100% first-year allowance for electric charge-point equipment. This measure was included in the Spring 2017 Budget and draft legislation in the Finance Bill 2017. However, this was one of the many measures which was put on hold following the last-minute calling of the 2017 General Election. The Government has indicated that they intend to introduce the proposals as intended, which would give 100% tax relief on qualifying expenditure from 23 November 2016 until 31 March 2019 or 5 April 2019.

Research and development allowances

[18.6] Research and development capital allowances are, in effect, another 100% first year allowance. They are not as uncommon and esoteric as might be imagined and the relief is by no means restricted to high-tech and pharmaceutical industries. With effort, many taxpayers have found that a potential claim has been overlooked and have been able to identify valuable research and development activities, where they previously believed none existed (for example, manufacturers, software and telecommunications industries, food and drink technology, etc.). These allowances could be particularly valuable where capital spend is in excess of the annual investment allowance now that it has decreased to £200,000 per annum.

In contrast to research and development tax credits, which are only available to companies, research and development allowances are available to 'traders' so opportunities to claim by sole traders and partnerships should not be overlooked.

For research and development allowances purposes, qualifying expenditure is capital expenditure incurred by a person on research and development directly by him or on his behalf. The phrase 'on his behalf' includes research and development sub-contracted to a third party, providing there is a close and direct link (that is, a relationship of agency or similar), which need not be contractual, between the claimant and the work undertaken (*Gaspet Ltd v Elliss* CA 1987, 60TC 91). See **11.2–11.6** above.

It is essential that the research and development must relate to the trade being undertaken by the claimant when it is carried out. For example, for various commercial reasons, a group property company may sometimes be used to hold properties occupied and used by a trading member of a group. However, where a landlord incurs expenditure on an asset to be used for research, no research and development allowances will be due because the legislation requires the existence of a trade, and a property investment business is not sufficient for this purpose. The same applies to businesses that are professions or vocations.

Research and development allowances are available for capital expenditure on all research and development facilities (for example laboratory buildings), equipment and cars. However, they are not available for:

(a) the acquisition of rights in, or arising out of, research and development;
(b) the acquisition of land, or rights in or over land; or
(c) expenditure on the provision of a dwelling, unless the dwelling part is no more than 25% of the cost of the whole building of which it is part.

Research and development has the meaning given by *ITA 2007, s 1006* and *CTA 2010, s 1138* (that is, those activities which are treated as research and development under generally accepted accounting practice). Research and development is defined under UK GAAP by FRS 102, *s 18.8* (and internationally by IAS38), which broadly distinguish research and development activity from non-research and development through the presence of an appreciable element of innovation. However, importantly the accounting definition is subordinated to extensive Department for Business, Innovation and Skills (BIS) guidelines issued on 5 March 2004, which form for all practical purposes the basis of defining research and development activities for capital allowances purposes.

The BIS guidelines define research and development as taking place when 'a project seeks to achieve an advance in science or technology', with 'the activities that directly contribute to achieving this advance in science or technology through the resolution of scientific or technological uncertainty', being research and development. Therefore, it is not enough that the supposed research and development work is innovative, or at the 'cutting edge' as is sometimes thought, but it must crucially also lead to a scientific or technological advance, as defined by the BIS guidelines.

The BIS guidelines include certain 'qualifying indirect activities' within the definition of research and development (i.e. activities that do not directly contribute to research and development, but are related to it, for example, information, maintenance and security support services). Therefore, facilities and equipment used for these purposes will also qualify for research and development allowances.

The BIS guidelines define 'science' as 'systematic study of the nature and behaviour of the physical and material universe' and 'technology' as 'the practical application of scientific principles and knowledge'.

A 'project' is defined as consisting of 'a number of activities conducted to a method or plans in order to achieve an advance in science or technology'. This means that there must be an intention to undertake research and development and a systematic project, with evidence left in the records available, rather than the research and development simply being an ad hoc or unexpected discovery.

An 'advance' means an increase in overall knowledge or capability in a field of science or technology, not just a business's own state of knowledge alone. However, it can include the adaptation of knowledge from another field of science or technology to make the advance, and may still occur if several businesses are doing similar work independently, or the work has already been done elsewhere, but the details of how are still a trade secret or not readily available.

'Scientific or technological uncertainty' exists when 'knowledge of whether something is scientifically possible or technically feasible, or how to achieve it in practice, is not readily available or deducible by a competent professional working in the field' (that is, a technical specialist). This can include turning something that has already been established as scientifically feasible into a cost-effective, reliable and reproducible process, material, device, product or service.

So, according to the BIS guidelines research and development may take place when a project seeks to:

(a) extend overall knowledge or capability in a field of science or technology;
(b) create a process, material, device, product or service which incorporates or represents an increase in overall knowledge or capability in a field of science or technology;
(c) make an appreciable improvement to an existing process, material, device, product or service through scientific or technological changes; and
(d) use science or technology to duplicate the effect of an existing process, material, device, product or service in a new or appreciably improved way.

Although it is sometimes thought research and development cannot include product development, the last three of these examples (that is, those that constitute development work and not pure research) do include work related to products and services.

A distinction must also be drawn between research and development and commercial pre-production activities which are not research and development. Research and development work starts when work to resolve a scientific uncertainty begins and it finishes when that uncertainty is resolved, or the work to resolve it ceases, or the knowledge is written-up in a usable form. So it is important to correctly identify the start and finish dates of any research and development projects.

Where capital assets are acquired with the intention of being used in both research and development and non-research and development activities then the expenditure should be apportioned between the two on a just and reasonable basis (see *CAA 2001, s 439(4)*). However, if an asset is acquired for research and development but its use later changes (for example, a building constructed to house research facilities is turned over to manufacturing after, say, one year) this does not prevent the claiming of allowances, or result in a clawback of the allowances claimed. Therefore, taxpayers may be able to maximise allowances by carefully planning the use to which a new building will be put to maximise its use for research and development, although the taxpayer should be aware that HMRC may look closely at cases where an asset ceases to be used for research a short period of time after allowances have been given. If a manufacturer with existing premises constructs a new building to carry out research and development, that building should qualify for research and development allowances. Whereas, if the production operation is moved into the new building and the old one is used for research and development, no allowances will be available. This is a particularly important planning point following the withdrawal of industrial building allowances.

Where an asset qualifying for research and development allowances is disposed of a balancing charge may arise (there is no provision for balancing allowances). However, in some cases, it may be possible to avoid the balancing charge by not selling the entire legal interest in the asset, but by granting some lesser interest, for example a long lease.

When considering potential allowances on research and development and similar rights then know-how allowances and patent allowances (see CHAPTER 12) should also be considered. For companies, there is also the potential to claim on expenditure under the intangible asset regime in *CTA 2009, Pt 8*. This favours corporate entities where intangible expenditure is contemplated. Certainly the intangible asset regime needs to be considered alongside any review of research and development expenditure.

Short-life assets

[18.7] Short-life assets are normal plant and machinery, but which are likely to be owned by a business for only a short time. They become short-life assets by formal written election to HMRC. See 5.59 onwards above.

They are designed to deal with the problem resulting from the pooling system normally applying to plant and machinery. The issue is that, unless a trade ceases, balancing allowances or charges do not generally occur. Therefore an individual plant asset may continue to attract writing-down allowances at an ever-diminishing amount long after the actual plant has been sold or scrapped. The effect of a short-life asset election is that if that short-life asset is sold or scrapped before the eighth anniversary of the end of the chargeable period in which it was acquired, this is regarded as the 'final chargeable period' for capital allowances purposes. For expenditure incurred before April 2011 the relevant cut-off used to be based on a four year rule. The disposal proceeds are then used to calculate a balancing allowance accelerating all of the remaining tax relief (or, more rarely, a balancing charge if the disposal proceeds exceed the tax written-down value at that time). If the asset is still held at the end of the 8 year period the tax written down value is transferred to the main pool.

Various assets are not eligible for short-life asset treatment. These include:

(1) cars;
(2) long-life assets, integral features or special rate pool expenditure;
(3) plant and machinery generally provided for leasing but with some exceptions;
(4) plant or machinery used only partly for the purposes of a qualifying activity;
(5) plant or machinery received as a gift, or originally provided for other purposes;

(6) plant or machinery which is subject to a 'partial depreciation subsidy' (that is, where a person receives sums towards the depreciation of the plant caused by its use that are not taken into account as income of that person, or in computing the profits or gains of any trade carried on by him); and
(7) ships.

A short-life asset election is irrevocable and must identify the assets involved, the amount of capital expenditure and the date it was incurred. Strictly speaking a short-life asset election should be made for each individual plant asset for which the treatment is intended to apply. However, in practice this is often impractical or impossible, so where a class of assets has broadly similar average lives of less than nine years HMRC will by concession accept elections referring to batches of acquisitions with the costs shown on the election as one sum. In practice, most elections are made within corporation tax computations which show sufficient detail and draw to HMRC's attention that such an election is being made. On income tax returns this may include a white space disclosure to draw such an election to HMRC's attention.

Apart from the administration involved, and those unusual circumstances where the disposal proceeds of plant exceed its written-down value when it is sold or scrapped, there is generally no downside to making a short-life asset election for plant. This is because if an asset is not sold or scrapped before the eighth anniversary of the end of the chargeable period in which it was acquired, the balance of expenditure not yet written-off simply transfers into the main pool and continues to attract writing-down allowances in the normal way. Care should be taken to ensure all fixed asset disposals are reviewed to ensure that any short-life asset disposals are identified and balancing allowances claimed.

Given that the main pool writing down allowances at 18% can take several years to achieve substantial tax relief, there is a clear planning imperative to maximise short life asset treatment for expenditure not attracting 100% annual investment or first-year allowances. These elections will be an increasingly common feature of tax computations in forthcoming years, especially for businesses exceeding the new annual investment level of £200,000 from January 2016.

Avoiding long-life asset treatment

[18.8] Once an asset has been treated as a long-life asset (see **5.66** onwards) that cannot be changed, even if it is sold to a new owner. Therefore, a second-hand purchaser may find himself bound by long-life asset treatment agreed by a former owner and this should be considered in the apportionment used on the acquisition of the assets. On the other hand where writing-down allowances have previously been given at 18% then that treatment is grandfathered, regardless of whether the asset subsequently proves to have a life of 25 years.

The long-life asset legislation does not apply to:

(a) plant or machinery fixtures in a building used wholly or mainly (that is, if at least 75% of the building is used for the exempted purpose — see HMRC Capital Allowances Manual, CA23730) as:
   (i) an office;
   (ii) a hotel;
   (iii) a retail shop or showroom (or premises of a similar character where a retail business, including repair work, is carried on);
   (iv) a dwelling-house; or
   (v) for purposes ancillary to any of the above,
(b) cars (including those which are hired out, and are generally not regarded as motor cars for capital allowances purposes — see **18.9** below) or motor cycles; or
(c) expenditure incurred before 1 January 2011 on sea-going ships (other than those used primarily for sport or recreation, or in connection with offshore mineral workings), or on the provision of a railway asset.

CAA 2001, s 99 provides that long life asset treatment does not apply where the taxpayer's total expenditure on potential long-life assets (at all sites) does not exceed £100,000 in a year (which is varied pro-rata if the period is longer or shorter and is also divided between the number of related 51% group companies). As far as is commercially practicable it is therefore better to stagger expenditure over a number of years to fall below the de minimis threshold of £100,000.

Income tax losses

[18.9] The aim of claiming capital allowances is to reduce taxable income of whatever description — usually trade profits. Most efforts are therefore made to maximise allowances — often producing a loss where there are substantial capital allowances.

In such cases it is important to appreciate the loss relief opportunities and also the possible pitfalls. This is because there are special loss relief rules for losses created by capital allowances and it is easy for these to be overlooked.

A special loss relief rule in *ITA 2007, s 120* allows a loss on a property business to be relieved against general income where it has a 'capital allowances connection', i.e. where allowances exceed balancing charges. *ITA 2007, s 122* restricts the loss relief against general income to that created by the capital allowances connection. The loss can be offset against other income of the current year or the subsequent year. This is an easy relief to miss and the self-assessment tax return also does not deal with it in a user-friendly way.

This loss relief option is not available to owners of furnished holiday lets. It is most commonly encountered in cases where a commercial building has been purchased and there are substantial capital allowances on integral fixtures — in excess of net rental income in the first period of letting.

For trading losses caused by capital allowances it is necessary to consider the restriction on leasing businesses in *ITA 2007, s 75*. This restriction is often not appreciated and can be encountered in such circumstances as boat chartering unless the owner is actively involved and meets the time commitment tests. More generally, the loss relief cap of £25,000 applies under *ITA 2007, s 74A* if the individual is involved in a 'non-active capacity'. An active capacity means spending an average of at least ten hours per week personally engaged in the activities of the trade which is carried out on a commercial basis with a view to the realisation of profits.

For 2013/14 and subsequent tax years there is a limit on the amount of income tax relief that an individual may deduct. The limit is the greater of £50,000 or 25% of their adjusted total income for the tax year. There is also an anti-avoidance rule which denies relief for tax generated losses attributable to the annual investment allowance where it arises from or in connection with 'relevant tax avoidance arrangements' entered into on or after 24 March 2010.

Transfers and successions

[18.10] The ability to transfer plant and machinery between connected businesses at written-down value is an important planning point and is commonly used. It is most usually encountered on incorporations or the restructuring of unincorporated businesses. In such cases it is possible to elect for assets to be transferred at written-down value under *CAA 2001, s 266*. See **7.17–7.19** above. By contrast, for corporate reconstructions, there is an automatic transfer at written-down value where a trade is transferred under *CTA 2010, Pt 22* so that no formal election is necessary. See **17.22–17.26** above.

For a corporate transfer under *CTA 2010, Pt 22* there is an apportionment of the allowances between the predecessor and successor companies. The position is different for a *CAA 2001, s 266* election which transfers the brought forward written-down value without any claim for annual investment allowance or writing-down allowances being possible in the period. This is an easy point to overlook in planning a business change. Where an incorporation is planned to take place at a business year end, it may be beneficial to take place after the end of the period, i.e. on the first day of the new period rather than the last day of the previous accounting period, subject to considering the other tax implications. Otherwise the former business owner is precluded from making a claim for capital allowances on plant and machinery.

From 26 February 2015, new rules were introduced to ensure that the anti-avoidance rules work as anticipated by HMRC. This change impacts on certain connected party transactions and sale and leaseback transactions and seeks to ensure that capital allowances are only obtained on the genuine cost of plant and machinery.

Further anti-avoidance rules were introduced for leasing transactions from 25 November 2015 to counter two types of avoidance. These changes prevent companies from artificially lowering the disposal value of plant and machinery for capital allowances purposes and ensure any payment received for agreements to take responsibility for tax deductible lease payments is subject to tax as income.

Capital allowances in respect of fixtures on the disposal and acquisition of a building

[18.11] Historically there was no time limit on when expenditure on plant or machinery, including fixtures, needed to be pooled. This led to expenditure on fixtures being pooled several years after the fixtures were acquired, risks of double claims and inconsistent figures used by vendor and purchaser. New rules have been introduced in *Finance Act 2012* which significantly restrict the flexibility in claiming allowances on the acquisition of a building.

The new rules, set out in *CAA 2001, s 187A*, apply to acquisitions from 6 April 2012 for income tax purposes and 1 April 2012 for corporation tax purposes of premises containing fixtures from a vendor entitled to claim allowances in respect of the historic expenditure. The initial 2012 change involved the introduction of the 'fixed value requirement', followed by the 'pooling requirement' which came into force in April 2014.

The 'fixed value requirement' applies if the vendor has claimed allowances on a fixture, then the parties of the transaction need to enter into a formal agreement to fix the value of those fixtures on sale. A failure to do so will prevent the purchaser, and any subsequent owner, from claiming any allowances in respect of those fixtures. This agreement will take the form of the existing elections under *CAA 2001, s 198 or s 199* or, where the parties do not agree, may be made by the first-tier tribunal.

The 'pooling requirement' which came into force in April 2014, has important implications for any commercial property transaction. The result is that any vendor who is entitled to make a claim for allowances in respect of fixtures, must quantify and pool their qualifying expenditure in order to enable a purchaser to claim allowances under the 'fixed value requirement'. Fortunately, due to the time delay of tax filings, there will be an opportunity for the vendor to pool the expenditure after the property has in fact been disposed of. Therefore, subject to contractual negotiations, this requirement should not significantly delay the completion of property transactions. However, it is key for purchasers to negotiate this point early otherwise their bargaining power will be jeopardised.

There is a relaxation for purchasers who are not entitled to claim an allowance, such as charities or pension funds that are not chargeable to tax, so that they are able to make a fixed value election under *CAA 2001, s 198* or *s 199* or apply to the tribunal for a determination of the fixed value, so to enable any future purchaser to claim upon those fixtures. There are also options available to obtain written statements to ensure continuity of relief to a future owner. This could potentially protect or enhance the value of their investment.

During the transitional period before the pooling requirement came into force (from April 2012 to March 2014), only fixtures on which the vendor has actually made a claim are subject to the fixed value requirement. Therefore to the extent that the vendor did not make a claim for allowances on a property disposed of between April 2012 and April 2014, the purchaser can make a claim based on the normal apportionment method (see below). This also applies where the vendor is not entitled to claim allowances, even after the pooling requirement comes into force. This may be because the vendor is not within the charge to tax (for example a charity or pension fund). Alternatively there may be historic spend on fixtures which did not qualify in the vendor's hands before the introduction of integral features in April 2008 (often referred to as 'pre-commencement integral features').

See **6.16** above and **19.4** below for further consideration of this statutory requirement.

Capital allowances buying

[18.12] There is anti-avoidance legislation in *CAA 2001, ss 212A–212S* that targets perceived avoidance, where a company is sold (or its ownership otherwise changes) at a time when the tax written-down value of its plant and machinery exceeds its balance sheet value and the main purpose, or one of the main purposes, of the change in ownership is the obtaining of a tax advantage.

This is designed to prevent the scenario where a company has made losses, such that it cannot make use of the allowances to which it is entitled, it disclaims them and the company is subsequently sold, so that it becomes part of a new group, and the company then claims the allowances in order to create or augment a loss which is then surrendered to another group company.

Where the legislation has effect, it will be necessary to compare the written-down value of each pool with the balance sheet value of the plant within that pool. The amount (if any) by which the written-down value of a pool exceeds the balance sheet value is transferred to a new pool, and future losses generated by allowances on that new pool may simply be carried forward against subsequent profits of the same trade. They may not be surrendered by way of group relief, for example. Nor is it possible to transfer a trade (even a similar one) into the loss-making company in order to generate profits against which the new pool allowances may be used.

CAA 2001, s 212B sets out the four criteria required for the restriction to apply, namely:

- a *company* carries on a qualifying activity (this previously only applied to trades, but was amended by *FA 2013, s 71*);
- a 'qualifying change' (broadly, a change of ownership) affects the company;
- the company (or partnership) has a 'relevant excess of allowances'; and
- the qualifying change meets one of the 'limiting conditions' (defined by *CAA 2001, s 212LA*).

Finance Act 2013 extended the 'limiting conditions' provisions to apply where the relevant excess is:

- £50 million or more (in any circumstances);
- £2 million to £50 million and 'not insignificant' as a proportion of the total amount or value of benefits derived; or
- Less than £2 million where the qualifying change has an 'unallowable purpose'.

An unallowable purpose is one where the main purpose, or one of the main purposes, of the 'change arrangements' (transactions or other arrangements connected with the change) is to obtain a 'relevant tax advantage'. A relevant tax advantage is defined as becoming entitled to a reduction in profits (or increase in losses) for corporation tax purposes, in consequence of a claim for capital allowances on the plant and machinery relevant to the 'excess of allowances' calculation.

See **17.17–17.19** for the detailed provisions.

HMRC set out in their Technical Note of 9 December 2009 some of the factors that they will consider when looking at the unallowable purpose test:

- the amount paid, compared to the balance sheet value;
- changes made prior to the change (e.g. attempts to isolate the 'excess of allowances' from other trading activities);
- whether the trade of the company sold is compatible with that of the acquirer (for example, a financial institution acquiring a shipping company would be more likely to attract attention than a business acquiring another in the same industry);
- the planned conduct of the business (whether the acquirer intends to run the acquired business in the long term, or a sell-off seems imminent). Although it is not explicitly stated, actual events will be strong evidence of what was planned — if the transferred business is in fact sold off within, say, six months, it may be difficult for the acquirer to argue that a sale was not intended throughout. Even then, each case will depend on the circumstances — an unexpected offer from a competitor would not indicate the 'planned conduct of the business'.

The Technical Note confirms that normal due diligence enquiring into the capital allowances status and history of a potential acquisition does not imply that obtaining the capital allowances is a 'main purpose'.

Land remediation relief

[18.13] Under *CTA 2009, Pt 14* where a company (not an individual or partnership — although a company that is a member of a partnership may claim in respect of its share of the expenditure) has acquired land in the United Kingdom for the purposes of a trade or property investment business and then incurs expenditure remediating land or buildings that were contaminated or derelict at the time of the acquisition, it may make a claim to treat that expenditure as if it were 150% of the actual amount (that is, a £15,000 tax deduction for every £10,000 of land remediation expenditure). This applies to revenue expenditure, and so allows a trading property developer to claim land remediation relief at the point of sale, but also extends to deem capital expenditure as revenue, providing that the taxpayer elects in writing within two years of the end of the relevant accounting period. See **14.3** above.

It should be noted that the legislation does *not* require the land to be owned by the company at the time the expenditure is incurred. If a company acquires land, then sells it on condition that it will clean it up, it does not matter that the clean-up expenditure is incurred after ownership has passed to the buyer.

There are some key exclusions which include that the relief is not available where the company, or a connected party, was responsible for causing the contamination (the 'polluter pays' principle), for cleaning up nuclear sites or, for landlords, where contamination is caused by the tenant.

HMRC take the view that living organisms such as plants and seeds do not normally qualify for relief as they are not 'substances' for the purposes of this legislation. However secondary legislation resulted in the removal costs of Japanese Knotweed qualifying from April 2009 as well as costs of the removal of naturally occurring arsenic and radon. It should be noted that these exceptions have been specifically allowed by secondary legislation and other, seemingly closely-related, items do not attract relief by analogy. The requirement that land is in a contaminated state at the time of acquisition does not apply to Japanese Knotweed. Therefore relief will be available where Japanese Knotweed has been introduced to a site by 'fly tipping'. Due to developments in the technologies for dealing with Japanese Knotweed, land remediation relief is no longer available where material containing knotweed is taken to landfill. Other methods, such as the use of offsite treatment centres, continue to qualify. Substantial claims can also be made in cases such as asbestos removal or removing chemicals from groundwater as the result of previous industrial activity.

Furthermore, if the 150% deduction gives rise to a loss, the company may surrender the loss and instead claim a land remediation tax credit payable to it which is equal to 16% of the loss (that is, a £2,400 cash payment from HMRC for every £10,000 of qualifying expenditure).

Where a land remediation deduction or tax credit is given for capital expenditure this will be partially clawed back on sale or a tax liability may be suffered, depending on the company's tax rate. This is because, although enhancement expenditure is normally included in the capital gains base cost, the land remediation expenditure, which is given as a trading deduction, should be excluded from the capital gains base cost on disposal.

Following an Office of Tax Simplification recommendation, the Government originally announced that it intended to abolish land remediation relief after 2012, following a period of consultation regarding the abolition of this and various other tax reliefs. Subsequent to the consultation, it was concluded that the relief should remain. Respondents to the consultation argued that removing the relief would affect the regeneration of uneconomic brown field sites. The Government decided that removal of this relief, in conjunction with the already agreed removal of the exemption from landfill tax, would risk undermining the Government's plans to support the housing and construction sectors through planning reforms and the release of large areas of publicly owned land for development.

Flat conversion allowances

[18.14] Following an Office of Tax Simplification recommendation, the Government announced that it intended to abolish flat conversion allowances. This intention did come to fruition and this relief was withdrawn by *Finance*

Act 2012 in respect of expenditure incurred on or after 1 April 2013 for corporation tax purposes and 6 April 2013 for income tax purposes. See CHAPTER 9.

Business premises renovation allowances (BPRA)

[18.15] The business premises renovation allowance scheme ended on 31 March 2017 for corporation tax purposes and 5 April 2017 for income tax purposes. Care should be taken to identify any qualifying costs incurred before the scheme was abolished. There is therefore only a limited period left in which to make BPRA claims. The allowance is given as an expense of the claimant's property investment business, trade, profession or vocation up to a maximum of €20m for each project. The taxpayer may claim the 100% initial allowance or choose to take a lesser amount, in which case any balance is subsequently relieved by a writing-down allowance of 25% per annum (straight-line). See CHAPTER 8 above.

The expenditure that qualifies is capital expenditure on, or in connection with, the conversion, renovation or repairs of qualifying buildings into qualifying business premises. *FA 2014* has clarified the scope of the expenditure that can qualify, and this is now included in legislation (*CAA 2001, s 360B*):

- building works;
- architectural or design services;
- surveying or engineering services;
- planning applications; or
- statutory fees or statutory permissions.

Additional associated but unspecified activities, such as project management services, qualify for relief, but this is limited to 5% of actual costs.

The allowance is not available for:

(a) the acquisition of land, or rights in or over land;
(b) the extension of a qualifying building, except where to provide access to or from qualifying business premises;
(c) the development of land next to a qualifying building;
(d) the provision of plant and machinery, other than fixtures (fixtures in this context are defined as integral features plus other specified general plant fixtures listed in *CAA 2001, s 360B*);
(e) the demolition of existing buildings; or
(f) property previously used, or to be used for, the following trade sectors: fishery; shipbuilding; the coal industry; synthetic fibres; the primary production of certain agricultural products; and the manufacture and marketing of products which imitate or substitute for milk/milk products. This is in order that the allowance code should not constitute state aid.

A 'qualifying building' is any building or structure which:

(a) is situated in a designated disadvantaged area when the renovation works began. There are approximately 2,000 such disadvantaged areas across the UK (see **8.4** above);

(b) was previously vacant for a year or more;
(c) had last been used for business purposes (a trade, profession or vocation) or as an office(s); and
(d) had not last been used as, or as part of, a dwelling.

The first-tier tribunal case of *Senex Investments Ltd v Revenue & Customs Comrs* [2015] UKFTT 107 (TC) considered whether the conversion of a former church into a restaurant came within the remit of being a qualifying building; the tribunal decided in favour of the taxpayer.

As explained above, the allowance is only available in certain disadvantaged areas. One of the difficulties for the adviser is spotting the availability of the allowance when it applies. It will normally be the case that those advisers operating in such disadvantaged areas will be aware of the possible availability of BPRA. Otherwise, the allowance was previously usually encountered in marketed tax favoured investment schemes designed to use the high level of tax relief against other income, although such options are now more limited following the introduction of the general anti-abuse rule (or 'GAAR') and alterations to the scheme which were made in *FA 2014* to clarify the nature of qualifying expenditure (see above).

Other changes implemented in April 2014 include:

- the period in which balancing adjustments must be made, if a balancing event occurs, is now reduced from 7 years to 5 years;
- for expenditure paid in advance, relief is withdrawn if the work is not completed within 36 months;
- care should be taken to consider the limitation on BPRA if other forms of state aid have been received (*CAA 2001, s 360L*).

One of the significant benefits of BPRA is that it is not subject to the new cap on tax reliefs for income tax purposes from 2013/14 as the relief has its own monetary cap of €20m per project, however there is now only a limited window of opportunity to claim for expenditure incurred by April 2017.

Expenditure on plant and machinery for use in designated assisted areas

[18.16] *Finance Act 2012* introduced a new first year allowance of 100% at *CAA 2001, s 45K* in respect of expenditure by companies (not individuals or partnerships) on the provision of plant and machinery for use primarily in an area which is a designated assisted area at the time the expenditure is incurred. The allowance has recently been extended by three years to an eight-year period from 1 April 2012 to 31 March 2020. Budget 2016 made a further change to ensure that 100% ECAs are available for eight years from the date they are announced. A designated assisted area has now been formalised following the passing of SI 2014/3183, the Capital Allowances (Designated Assisted Areas) Order 2014. This relief is available for designated assisted areas within Enterprise Zones.

There are five conditions for the relief which are as follows:

(A) the company must be within the charge to corporation tax,
(B) the expenditure is incurred for the purposes of a qualifying activity within *CAA 2001, s 15(1)(a)* or *(f)*,
(C) the expenditure is incurred for the purposes of:
  (a) a kind of business not previously carried on by the company,
  (b) expanding a business carried on by the company, or
  (c) starting up an activity which relates to a fundamental change in a product or production process of, or service provided by, a business carried on by the company.
(D) the machinery is unused and not second hand,
(E) the expenditure is not replacement expenditure.

A qualifying activity predominantly means a trade or a mining, transport or similar undertaking for these purposes.

Finance Act 2014 has introduced a further restriction in that condition C(c) above is only met if the amount of the expenditure exceeds the amount by which the relevant plant and machinery is depreciated in the period of three years ending immediately before the beginning of the chargeable period in which the expenditure is incurred.

Replacement expenditure means expenditure incurred on new plant or machinery intended to perform the same or similar function as other plant and machinery. However where new plant and machinery is capable and intended to perform a significant additional function (for example enhancing the productivity capability) then it can qualify for these allowances.

The relief qualifies as a State Aid under European rules and therefore contains sundry exceptions to eligible companies and is restricted to €125 million per investor or a maximum of €125 million on expenditure incurred by any person in respect of the same single investment project. For large spends in excess of the annual investment allowance, this is potentially a valuable relief for companies in areas which qualify. See further 5.23 above.

Businesses using the cash basis

Impact on tax relief for capital expenditure

[18.17] *Finance Act 2013* has introduced a new cash basis for calculating trade profits in *Chapter 5* of *ITTOIA 2005*. These optional new rules first apply for the 2013/14 tax year and are available to most sole traders and partnerships (except LLPs or those partnerships with a corporate partner), provided they are beneath the VAT registration threshold.

Capital allowances are not available under the cash basis, other than on cars. There is a choice in respect of cars — a taxpayer can either:

- claim capital allowances and running expenses (on the business use percentage) as usual; or
- claim a mileage rate of 45p per mile (25p after 10,000 miles) and claim no relief for any other expenses relating to the car.

Deductions will be available for expenditure on fixed assets used in the business which would normally qualify for capital allowances, other than cars (see above).

A deduction in the first cash basis period will be available for tax written down values carried forwards at the end of the last accounting period. Care must be taken to ensure the tax written down value of cars is excluded from this deduction (calculated on a just and reasonable basis if the car is included in a pool).

As with all new rules, attention will need to be taken to ensure that capital items are treated correctly to minimise the risk of any errors. For example, in the transitional year, ensuring that deductions are taken for pool values brought forward and identifying any assets on hire purchase in order to undertake the transitional calculations. Once in the cash basis, any proceeds from the disposal of plant and machinery need to be included in business income.

There are also further adjustments which may need to be taken into account where the non-business use of an asset increases. The legislation in *ITTOIA 2005, s 96A* requires an income adjustment to be made based on current market value. We may soon have to deal with clients leaving the cash basis either through choice (for example, if they have taken out substantial loans) or if they exceed the VAT threshold. In the first period after leaving the cash basis, some adjustments may be required to ensure that future transactions involving equipment are taxed correctly. On exiting the cash basis, this would include:

- where all assets have been purchased outright, the net impact will be nil introduced to the main pool (being the full acquisition cost introduced less a deduction for the full amount claimed under the cash basis); or
- where an asset has been bought by instalments, the net impact will be that payments yet to be made will be brought into the main pool. This will also be applicable to the capital element outstanding on a hire purchase contract.

One of the aims of introducing the cash basis was that of simplification, however the new rules appear to have instead added a further layer of complexity.

Finance Bill 2017-2019, which was published on 8 September 2017, introduces new rules in relation to the calculation of the taxable profits of unincorporated business from 6 April 2017. The changes include a simplified treatment for capital expenditure under the cash basis and the introduction of the cash basis for the calculation of taxable profits of a property business. The property cash basis is now the default position for the calculation of the profits of eligible property businesses, although the person carrying on the business may elect to use UK GAAP to calculate profits instead.

Changes to capital deductions under cash basis

The previous rules only allowed a deduction for capital expenditure where the expenditure was incurred on qualifying plant and machinery. The Finance Bill 2017-19 proposes to amend the rules in *ITTOIA 2005, s 33A* so that capital expenditure is only disallowed if it falls within the following:

- capital expenditure incurred on, or in connection with, the acquisition or disposal of a business or part of a business, or
- an item of capital expenditure incurred on or in connection with, education or training, or
- an item of a capital nature incurred on, in in connection with the provision, alteration or disposal of:
  - any asset that is not a depreciating asset (broadly speaking, those with a useful life of 20 years or more),
  - any asset not acquired or created for use on a continuing basis in a trade,
  - a car,
  - land,
  - a non-qualifying intangible asset (unless the asset has a definite, fixed life of less than 20 years)
  - a financial asset

The Finance Bill goes on to clarify that the exclusions do not prevent a deduction for a depreciating property fixture. Therefore tax relief will be available at 100% for most items of qualifying plant or fixtures. It will still be important to be aware of which items of capital expenditure are fixtures as this would be relevant in relation to a *CAA 2001, s 198* election on sale.

Extension of cash basis to property businesses

Finance Bill 2017-19 also proposes that a revised version the cash basis be extended to unincorporated property business. Therefore the default position is that such business use the cash basis going forward unless:

(a) the landlord elects not to use the simplified cash basis (within one year of the ordinary filing date), or
(b) the gross rental income (under the cash basis) exceeds £150,000, or
(c) the property business is carried on by a company, a limited liability partnership, a partnership with a corporate member or trustees, or
(d) the property is jointly owned with a spouse or civil partner and their partner elects to use the accruals basis, or
(e) business premises renovation allowances are being claimed and there is a balancing adjustment in the tax year.

The rules for the simplified cash basis for property business are very similar to those for the cash basis for trading businesses, but there are some key differences. For example, interest for property businesses will be allowed without reference to the £500 limit, but the rules do still take into account the new restrictions for tax relief for residential properties which started to be phased in during the 2017/18 tax year. A tax reducer is being phased in (at 20%) as the ability to deduct interest costs against property profits is being phased out over 4 years. Care should be taken when considering the deductibility of the costs of loans in accordance with *ITTOIA 2005, s 307C-307D*.

FRS 102 and capital allowances

[18.18] Financial Reporting Standard 102 ('FRS 102') is the new accounting standard for medium and large businesses and is applicable for accounting periods beginning on or after 1 January 2015. FRS 102 should have little impact on capital allowance claims.

FRS 102 requires that investment property is initially recognised at cost and subsequently measured at fair value in most cases. However, in contrast to old UK GAAP (SSAP 9), FRS 102 section 16 requires those fair value movements to be recognised in the profit and loss account.

The capital allowance position for fixtures within the building is based on the original cost at acquisition (or subsequent spend on refurbishment or improvements), therefore the fair value movements are not applicable for capital allowance purposes and are not subject to corporation tax. Corporation tax will become payable if the property (including fixtures) is sold for a gain on ultimate disposal, with indexation available to reduce any gain. On sale the pooling and fixed value requirements become relevant. However care should be taken when providing fixture information as the capital allowance figure is restricted to the original base cost regardless of any uplift to market value in the accounts.

Section 17 of FRS 102 regarding property, plant and equipment is broadly similar to the previous UK GAAP (FRS 15). There are some very minor differences, for example FRS 17 requires that cost is measured by reference to the present value of all future payments where the asset is acquired under terms beyond normal credit terms, and residual values are to be based on current rather than historic prices.

In some cases where 'revenue' expenditure is added to the cost of an asset, the tax follows the accounts by recognising for tax purposes the amounts reflected in the profits and loss account by way of depreciation on revenue expenditure. In cases where depreciation under section 17 of FRS 102 differs from that under FRS 15 (for example because of a revaluation of residual values), tax will follow the amount of depreciation as calculated under FRS 102.

FRS 105 and capital allowances

[18.19] For periods commencing on or after 1 January 2016 small businesses are no longer allowed to prepare their accounts in accordance with the Financial Reporting Standard for Smaller Entities ('FRSSE'). Instead such companies will need to transition to one of the new UK GAAP alternatives. For most this will mean a transition to either Financial Reporting Standard 105 ('FRS 105') or section 1A of FRS 102. Section 1A of FRS 102 is available to small entities and is aligned with FRS 102 (see above) but with reduced disclosure and presentation requirements.

Under FRS 105 investment property is initially recognised at cost and subsequently measured at cost less accumulated depreciation. If the property is held as an investment the income arising on the property (usually rental income) is brought into tax as it is recognised in the accounts. The disposal of investment property will be treated as a capital gain, with indexation calculated on a disposal by a company.

In relation to property, plant and equipment (section 12 of FRS 105) the new standard is broadly consistent with previous UK GAAP. Some of the minor differences include:

- the requirement that major spare parts are capitalised in the accounts;
- where payment is deferred beyond normal credit terms, cost is measured by reference to the cash price available at the recognition date;
- renewals accounting is not permitted – so there may be an adjustment for tax purposes made under the change of basis legislation; and
- residual values are based on current prices rather than historical prices.

As UK tax law departs from accounting standards (as depreciation and revaluations are added back and instead capital allowances are given on qualifying assets) the above accounting changes are unlikely to have a significant tax impact. If the OTS review leads to any changes to the capital allowance regime then this could make a far larger difference to the timing of tax relief.

In cases where revenue expenditure is added to the cost of the asset, tax law allows a deduction for the amounts reflected in the profit and loss account (i.e. the depreciation on the revenue element). Where depreciation under section 12 of FRS 105 differs from that under FRS 15 and the FRSSE (for example because of revaluation of residual values) tax will follow the amount as per section 12 of FRS 105.

19

Planning — Plant and Machinery in Buildings and Related Issues

by
Heather Britton
of Francis Clark Tax Consultancy Limited

Introduction

[19.1] One of the most complex areas of capital allowances concerns expenditure on properties and, in particular, the availability of allowances for plant and machinery within a building. The tax issues in connection with that and the planning opportunities that arise are the subject of this chapter. The points raised highlight the importance of the rules to properties still owned as well as for property transactions. However, in addition, it is appropriate to consider the associated issue of the goodwill relating to trade related properties as the existence (or otherwise) of such goodwill impacts on the property value that is considered for the purposes of apportioning as between qualifying expenditure for plant and machinery and non-qualifying expenditure.

Fixtures, fittings and chattels

[19.2] For capital allowances purposes a fixture is 'plant or machinery that is so installed or otherwise fixed in or to a building or other description of land as to become, in law, part of that building or land'. In English property law whether something becomes a fixture depends on:

(a) the method and degree of annexation (broadly, *how* it is fixed); and
(b) the object and purpose of annexation (broadly, *why* it is fixed).

The first test, which has historically had the greatest significance, suggests that property is prima facie a fixture if it is physically fixed or substantially connected to the land. If an asset cannot be removed without causing serious damage to some part of the land or building to which it is attached, then it is likely to be a fixture.

However, more recently, the courts have given greater prominence to the second test. This considers whether the asset's attachment to the land is meant to be a permanent and lasting improvement of the land or building (in which case it is a fixture), or whether it has been fixed on a temporary basis and merely so the asset may be used and better enjoyed as a chattel (in which case it is not a fixture).

The term fixture specifically includes any boiler or water-filled radiator installed in a building as part of a space or water heating system (see *CAA*

2001, s 173). Typical examples of fixtures include: sanitary appliances and fittings, hot water and heating installations, ventilation and air conditioning installations, electrical installations, lifts and various other kinds of assets.

In practice it can sometimes be difficult to establish whether assets are fixtures. Some examples of fixtures decided in cases are shown below. Several of these are now also 'integral features' within **19.3** below (that is, lifts, central heating equipment and boilers).

Lifts and central heating equipment.	*Stokes v Costain Property Investments Limited* CA 1984, 57 TC 688
Video door entry systems, alarm systems, boilers, crematorium cremators, swimming pool ventilation and filtration plant.	*Melluish v BMI (No 3) Limited* CA 1995, [1995] STC 964
Domestic fitted baths and taps, mirrors, towel rails, soap fittings, shower heads, fitted kitchen units and sinks (but *not* light fittings, fitted carpets, curtains, 'mock coal' gas fires and white goods).	*TSB Bank v Botham* CA 1996, (1996) 73 P & CR D1
Automatic and disabled public conveniences, bus shelters, information panels and information boards.	*JC Decaux (UK) Limited v Francis* (Sp C 84), [1996] SSCD 281

To further complicate matters, a sub-division of fixtures has arisen in practice between 'landlord's fixtures' and 'tenant's fixtures'. Most commonly tenant's fixtures comprise trade fixtures attached by a tenant for its business and which are removable during its tenancy but not after it has ended. However, once they are fixed, in law all of these assets form part of the land and belong to the landlord (unless and until the tenant chooses to exercise his power and sever them, when they revert back to being chattels). So they are still fixtures in the broadest sense. The recent case of *Peel Land & Property (Ports No 3) Ltd v TS Sheerness Limited* (2014) concluded that, whilst a tenant was, in principle, entitled to remove any tenant's fixtures, such a right can be modified or excluded by the terms of the lease. A *CAA 2001, s 198* election is only possible for fixtures (not chattels).

In circumstances where a *new* interest in land is created for a capital sum (for example, a lease is granted), the lessee is *only* able to claim capital allowances if both parties jointly elect for the fixtures to be treated as belonging to the lessee. This is only possible if the lessor would have been entitled to claim capital allowances (lessors that are not within the charge to tax, e.g. pension funds, are regarded as being within the charge to tax for this purpose). The election must be made within two years of the lease taking effect.

If a new interest in land is granted for a capital sum, but the lessor was not entitled to claim capital allowances (other than simply not being within the charge to tax) the fixtures are treated as belonging to the lessee, but *only* if no person has previously been entitled to allowances and the fixture has not been used for the purposes of a trade by the lessor or a connected person.

Whether an item is a fixture or a chattel remains important, particularly in relation to the new era of capital allowances on fixtures from April 2012, as well as remaining relevant regarding Stamp Duty Land Tax payable by a purchaser. Whilst the distinctions and rules may seem arcane, recent history has shown that such claims for allowances are easily overlooked — and the sums involved can be substantial.

See **6.2–6.17** above for the detailed provisions.

Integral features

[19.3] A reduced rate of writing down allowances of 8% applies for 'integral features' (10% prior to April 2012). This rate does not apply to expenditure incurred before 2008 as any qualifying expenditure (under the rules at that time) was normally allocated to the main pool (being the current 18% pool, which was 20% prior to April 2012). It is *not* necessary to retrospectively review expenditure in the main pool and reclassify any as integral features. Hence one of the attractions of identifying previously omitted claims for expenditure has been to achieve a higher rate of writing down allowance.

Integral features are:

(a) electrical systems (including lighting systems);
(b) cold water systems;
(c) space or water heating systems, powered systems of ventilation, air cooling or air purification (including floors or ceilings comprised in such systems);
(d) lifts, escalators and moving walkways; or
(e) external solar shading (that is, brise soleil).

HMRC have provided guidance on their interpretation of these terms. For example, an electrical system is a system for taking electrical power (including lighting) from the point of entry to the building or structure, or generation within the building or structure, and distributing it through the building or structure, as required. It does not include other building systems intended for other purposes, which may include wiring and other electrical components. For example, communication, telecommunication and surveillance systems, fire alarm systems or burglar alarm systems, will qualify as plant and machinery in the main pool.

The cost of a ducting system within a building follows the tax treatment that the ducting supports. So ducting which relates solely to the building's electrical system would be part of that system and would be included in the special rate pool, whereas ducting relating solely to a computer system would enter the main pool. Where ducting has a mixed use, the expenditure can be apportioned on a fair and reasonable basis.

Perhaps in the face of lobbying from the hospitality industry, which was hit hard by the abolition of industrial buildings allowances for qualifying hotels, the list does not include toilet or kitchen facilities because they may also be an essential piece of productive equipment for an occupier's trade (for example, in a hotel or restaurant).

Following the consultation period before the integral features regime was introduced, it was decided that a simple list approach would be adopted as the system to define integral features rather than a purposive or 'trade specific' test. Therefore electrical wiring in a building from April 2008 is treated as an integral feature regardless of whether it is to serve particular plant or machinery. Previously only plant-specific or trade-specific wiring qualified for capital allowances.

Where expenditure is incurred on the provision or replacement of an integral feature after April 2008 and it is more than 50% of the cost of replacing that entire integral feature (for example, the heating system), then the expenditure must be treated as a capital replacement, rather than a revenue expense (see *CAA 2001, s 33B*). When considering this test a 12 month window must be considered and not just an accounting period, which makes this test hard to monitor.

Where an integral feature is sold for less than its written-down value as part of a scheme or arrangement with obtaining a tax advantage being a main purpose, then the 'notional written-down value' is substituted for the actual disposal value. Anti-avoidance also exists to prevent assets which did not previously qualify for capital allowances (for example, cold water systems) being transferred to a connected person and a claim being made on the original expenditure.

There are specific rules which address intra-group transfers and provide for an election so that fixtures which qualified in the main pool of the vendor can be transferred at tax written down value to the main pool of the purchaser (and 18% WDAs claimed), instead of reclassifying some items as integral features (which would normally only attract 8% WDA).

Some integral features would not have qualified as plant before the integral features rules were introduced (for example, external solar shading, cold water systems, and parts of electrical systems like general power and lighting) and they remain non-qualifying in the hands of existing owners if the expenditure was incurred before April 2008.

It may be appropriate to review historic expenditure and ensure appropriate claims have been made, where relevant. This information will be required for any future transaction and may provide further valuable tax relief.

See **4.23** and **5.49** above for the detailed provisions.

Claiming capital allowances on expenditure on plant in buildings

[19.4] When preparing capital allowances claims for plant in buildings a combination of specialist tax and property/valuation skills is required. A purchaser's claim may be restricted by the vendor's disposal value (for example under *CAA 2001, s 185* or *s 198* (see **6.15**, **6.17** above)) and so it is important to establish through due diligence investigations the correct entitlement and basis of claim before starting any valuation or claim preparation. The precise nature of the valuation techniques involved depends on the type of project. However, understanding building costs and being able to prepare supportable cost estimates for construction work are a common feature of all capital allowances claims for plant in buildings.

Historically there was no time limit on when expenditure on plant or machinery, including fixtures, needed to be pooled and no requirement to pool to pass relief on. The historic position led to expenditure on fixtures being pooled several years after the fixtures were acquired and often made it difficult for HMRC to substantiate the true capital allowance position. The previous rules led to risks of double claiming of allowances or inconsistencies between the disposal value used by purchaser and vendor. New rules have been introduced through *FA 2012* which seek consistency in capital allowance claims and ensure that tax relief is only obtained once by all owners in total during the lifetime of a fixture in a building.

The new rules, set out in *CAA 2001, s 187A*, apply to acquisitions from 6 April 2012 for income tax purposes and 1 April 2012 for corporation tax purposes of premises containing fixtures from a vendor entitled to claim allowances in respect of the historic expenditure. The requirements of the new rules are a 'fixed value requirement', a 'disposal value statement requirement' (if required) and, from April 2014, a 'pooling requirement'.

The 'fixed value requirement' is that where the vendor of the property has claimed allowances on a fixture, then the parties to the transaction need to enter into a formal agreement to fix the value of those fixtures. A failure to do so will prevent the purchaser, and any subsequent owner, from claiming any allowances in respect of those fixtures. This agreement will take the form of the existing elections under *CAA 2001, s 198* or *s 199*. Where the parties do not agree on the fixed value a determination may be made by the first tier tribunal.

In a relaxation of the original proposals the legislation allows, in certain circumstances, for the new purchaser to obtain a written statement from a past owner which states the disposal value brought into account to satisfy the fixed value requirement. Allowances can then be claimed on the values contained in the statement. This 'disposal value statement' will apply in circumstances where the normal steps to achieve the fixed value requirement cannot be met, such as where the owner of the fixtures has ceased to carry on a qualifying activity without there being a sale at that point, requiring a deemed disposal value to be brought into account.

The 'pooling requirement' came into force from April 2014 due to transitional provisions. This may appear to be a subtle change, but has wide-reaching implications. A vendor who is entitled to make a claim for allowances in respect of fixtures must quantify and pool their qualifying expenditure in order to enable a purchaser to claim allowances under the 'fixed value requirement'. Fortunately, due to the time delay of tax filings there will be an opportunity for the vendor to pool the expenditure after the property has in fact been disposed of. Therefore, subject to contractual negotiations, this requirement should not significantly delay the completion of property transactions. However, a lack of advance planning by a purchaser on negotiating a value for fixtures prior to the exchange of contracts will result in little bargaining power.

Under the new fixtures regime the onus falls on the purchaser to prove that the fixed value requirement is satisfied; early planning is key to secure the allowance position.

There is a provision which permits a fixed value election to be made in respect of fixtures on which the vendor has claimed business premises renovation allowances, to the extent that the expenditure has not already been relieved.

There is a relaxation for purchasers who are not entitled to claim allowances, such as charities that are not chargeable to tax, so that they are able to make a fixed value election under *CAA 2001, s 198* or *s 199* or apply to the tribunal for a determination of the fixed value, so as to enable any future purchaser to claim upon those fixtures. This could potentially protect or enhance the value of their investment.

During the transitional period before the pooling requirement came into force, only fixtures on which the vendor has actually made a claim are subject to the fixed value requirement. Therefore, to the extent that the vendor did not make a claim for allowances on a property disposed of between April 2012 and April 2014, the purchaser can make a claim based on the normal apportionment method (see below). This also applies where the vendor is not entitled to claim allowances, even after the pooling requirement comes into force. This may be for example either because they are not within the charge to tax or where they are within the charge to tax but some of the expenditure is on fixtures which previously did not qualify for allowances (for example general lighting prior to April 2008). Where there are no restrictions then the claim may be made on the basis of current replacement value of the plant, which can be substantial.

See further **6.16** above.

There is still no statutory time limit for claiming plant and machinery allowances on properties currently owned (i.e. purchased prior to April 2014), but some clients still struggle to see the benefit of claiming before sale or have misconceptions on how the rules work. Many clients incorrectly assume that claiming capital allowances will increase the capital gains tax payable when they sell the property, which simply is not the case. Some clients occasionally resist because they feel that claiming capital allowances is merely a cash flow exercise because the allowances will be clawed back when the property is sold. However, most owners who pay tax would prefer to pay less tax now and seek to retain some or all of the benefit of these allowances on sale, depending on negotiations. If the property owner is in a tax paying position, then a review of the potential scope of allowances is key.

The complexity of preparing claims for new construction work can vary greatly depending on the type of project and availability of construction cost information. Where bills of quantities provide a line-by-line priced schedule of the work, then analysing the information is pretty straightforward but it is now common with design and build contracts to only have a lump sum total including the heating, plumbing and electrical elements of the project. From a tax perspective, the total spend will comprise elements of non-qualifying costs, main pool plant, integral features plant, long-life assets and expenditure qualifying for 100% first-year allowances. Costs such as sanitary appliances, fire and intruder alarms, sprinkler installations and data communication installations may all be included under a lump sum cost for building services. Without a further breakdown of this element, these general plant assets that qualify for relief at 18% or 8% can be missed completely. The early appointment of a capital allowances specialist should therefore be considered.

Skills of valuation and professional judgement are required when determining what element of preliminaries and professional fees can be included in the claim for qualifying expenditure. Preliminaries are a contractor's general cost items for management and the provision of site-based services. A pro rata allocation of these costs historically was resisted by HMRC which prefers to see an element of disallowance, arguing that certain preliminaries costs are too remote from the provision of the qualifying assets (see *JD Wetherspoon plc v HMRC* (Sp C 657, [2008] SSCD 460, and *JD Wetherspoon plc v HMRC (no 2)* FTT 2009, [2009] UK FTT 374 (TC)). In the recent Upper Tier Tax Tribunal decision: *JD Wetherspoon plc v. HMRC* UT, [2012] UKUT 42(TCC), this was said at paragraph 92:

> 'Preliminaries are, by their nature, items of overhead expenditure which cannot be, or which have not been, attributed to any single item in the building project. Some, like insurance, are inherently incapable of being so attributed. Others, like scaffolding, may be capable of specific attribution, but the time and cost involved in the process of specific attribution is often disproportionate to the amount at stake. Thus, apportionment of preliminaries between items which do, or do not, qualify for capital allowances is the only solution in relation to un-attributable preliminaries, and may be the sensible solution where attribution is uneconomic.'

Following this decision, HMRC have relaxed their approach to such apportionment claims and now take a much more pragmatic approach.

Prior to the introduction of the 'fixed value requirement' in April 2012 for expenditure on which the vendor has made a claim for allowances, in the absence of a *CAA 2001, s 198* election (see **6.17** above) or prior to the pooling requirement in April 2014 in respect of expenditure on which the vendor has made no claim, the purchaser's claim will be based on a just apportionment of the purchase price in accordance with *CAA 2001, s 562*. It is necessary to apportion the purchase price to reflect the value that each constituent part makes to the value of the whole property (*Salts v Battersby* KB 1910, [1910] 2 KB 155). Simply deducting a value for the non-qualifying assets (e.g. land) is not sufficient (*Enterprise Zone Syndicate v Inspector of Taxes* [1996] SSCD 336). HMRC (and subsequent owners of a property) are not bound by any allocation agreed between the parties and reflected in the purchase contract (*Fitton v Gilders and Heaton* ChD 1955, 36 TC 233), unless a *s 198* election is validly made.

The Valuation Office Agency's (VOA) preferred method for achieving the apportionment is known as the 'multiplier formula' and this is by far the most commonly used method in practice (see 4.21 above). This method was held to be a 'just and reasonable' method in the recent case of *Bowerswood Retirement Home Ltd v HMRC* [2015] UKFTT 94 (TC). The taxpayer unsuccessfully tried to argue that capital allowances could be claimed based on the replacement cost of an asset (in this case a swimming pool in a retirement home) which had been valued in isolation. However it was held that this was not just and reasonable as it does not treat all aspects of the building on purchase on the same basis.

When preparing claims in this way it is necessary to value the three elements of the acquisition: land, non-qualifying building and qualifying plant (further split between integral features and general plant). The valuation of building and plant is based on an assessment of what it would cost to reconstruct the property, in that location, at the date of purchase, essentially a quantity surveying exercise. As with new-build expenditure, a site survey is required. However, given the lack of any actual detailed construction drawings, specifications or costs, surveys for apportionment claims are by necessity complex and thorough because they form the entire basis for the reconstruction cost estimates on which the claim is based. The surveyor should seek to obtain an accurate measure of the internal floor area and site area, prepare a comprehensive schedule of the qualifying assets and note the general construction details of the property. Particular attention should be paid to the building's services installations since much of the qualifying plant is contained within these elements.

A detailed estimate of the reconstruction cost for the entire building is then required in a format that clearly identifies the assets that are included under each qualifying category. Where vendor's disposal value restrictions apply, the reconstruction cost estimates may need to take account of the original cost of the building when first built. When preparing claims for a property that is occupied by third party tenants it is important to ensure that only plant that belongs to the claimant (i.e. the landlord) is included in the claim. Where the property has been extensively fitted out or refurbished by a tenant it can be difficult in practice to identify what belongs to the landlord.

For the purpose of the multiplier, it is also necessary to value the land element of an acquisition. The VOA guidelines require the valuation to assume that it is a bare site with planning consent for the current use. Although no capital allowances are available for land, the application of the multiplier means that its value does affect the qualifying expenditure. Therefore, an accurate and supportable valuation is required.

Legislation exists to prevent the obtaining of a 'tax advantage', defined as the obtaining or increase of an allowance or avoiding or reducing a charge (see *CAA 2001, s 577*). Where, as part of a scheme or arrangement for obtaining a tax advantage, a taxpayer brings into account a disposal value which is less than the 'notional written-down value' of that plant (that is, assuming that all allowances that *could* have been claimed *had* been claimed), then that notional amount is substituted for the actual disposal value and neither a balancing allowance or charge may arise for the vendor, but the purchaser's claim is restricted to the actual low consideration (see *CAA 2001, s 197* and **6.17** above). However, merely electing for a low *s 198* value does not, of itself, fall to be treated as coming within *s 197*.

Disposal of an interest in a property

[19.5] A disposal value must be brought into account in respect of fixtures on cessation of a qualifying interest. This can happen under a sale, a discontinuance of trade as well as where the fixture is severed from the land. For each circumstance there is an extended table of disposal values to be applied under *CAA 2001, s 196*, (see **6.17** above). The other general disposal value rules in *CAA 2001, ss 62* and *63*, such as proceeds not to exceed initial qualifying cost and values to use upon gifts, still apply. None of the conditions contained in the new *CAA 2001, s 187A* affect the disposal value that the vendor must bring into account. Therefore if the 'fixed value requirement' has not been satisfied because no election has been made and a tribunal determination has not been requested (so that the purchasers qualifying expenditure is deemed to be nil), the vendor is still required to bring in a disposal value in accordance with *CAA 2001, s 196*. It is therefore in the interests of both parties to ensure a valid election is made on a property sale.

An unhelpful vendor cannot avoid bringing into account disposal proceeds or refusing to assist the purchaser in establishing their entitlement to make a claim. Indeed a vendor may be far worse off if no election is made and a market value disposal figure is included (whereby it is likely that all allowances on fixtures would be clawed back), compared to the security of an election whereby they could still retain significant allowances, depending on negotiation.

A disposal value is also only required for assets upon which the vendor has actually claimed capital allowances. So a vendor who is outside the charge to tax, or whose expenditure is on trading account, such as a property developer, cannot make an election. In these circumstances an apportionment is required.

Establishing disposal values can be complicated when buildings are sold because the proceeds relate to a combination of assets. Some may qualify for capital allowances, but could be chattels or fixtures that are subject to the rules contained in *CAA 2001, ss 172–204*. Additionally, many assets will not have qualified for plant and machinery allowances or the vendor may not have claimed capital allowances for all of the qualifying plant.

To deal with this, the legislation permits two methods:

(a) a just and reasonable apportionment under *CAA 2001, s 562*, or
(b) an election under *CAA 2001, s 198* or *CAA 2001, s 199* (for leases) — see **6.17** above.

The purchaser and vendor have to use the same apportionment in their returns. HMRC do not accept figures until those submitted by each party concur (HMRC Capital Allowances Manual, CA12100).

An apportionment is the default approach for all plant. This aims to reflect the value that each constituent part makes to the whole. The legislation does not specify how this has to be done so it is a specialist tax valuation exercise. Unless the property is sold at a loss or plant is scrapped, an apportionment will normally result in a full claw-back of allowances claimed. What is never permissible (irrespective of the parties' wishes), but frequently happened in practice, was simply to make an allocation in the sale and purchase agreement, without this being based on a proper apportionment, or ratified by a valid *s 198* election. Under the new rules it is no longer possible to make an allocation on this basis as an election is required in order for the purchaser to make a claim.

Where there is an attempt to set the disposal consideration under *s 198*, but all that is inserted into the contract is an apportionment clause (without a *s 198* election being made) then under the old rules HMRC can insist that a just and reasonable apportionment of the sale price be put in place (as determined by the VAO). This probably won't be the allocation that the parties wanted and could lead to allegations being made against the professional advisers concerned. Under the new rules from April 2014, this will result in the purchaser's qualifying expenditure being deemed to be nil, whilst HMRC can still require a just and reasonable apportionment for the purposes of the disposal value to be brought into account by the vendor, which is a poor result for both parties concerned. The option of doing nothing regarding elections on a commercial property transaction could lead to two dissatisfied parties.

Section 198 elections are crucial for vendors seeking to minimise any claw-back of allowances claimed. In the hope of the purchaser agreeing to this, it is normally sensible to market property by specifying in the sale particulars and heads of terms that capital allowances will be retained. The contractual objective is then to agree as low a disposal value as possible. Two commonly proposed amounts on sale are the tax written down value (thereby ensuring no balancing charge on the vendor) or £2 (representing £1 for main pool assets and £1 for integral features).

However, for purchasers the opposite applies and an election at less than the vendor's full claim for fixtures is generally inadvisable unless adequate compensation is received elsewhere in the deal. This is because without an election, most, if not all, of the capital allowances would normally automatically transfer to the purchaser under the old rules. However, vendors will inevitably push for a much lower amount, so a negotiated compromise is likely to result in a purchaser losing relief. This also opens up the option for the purchaser not to agree an election under *CAA 2001, s 198* and instead to apply to the first tier tribunal as the likely result would favour the purchaser. However, the potential benefit of this must be weighed up with the time and costs associated with going to the tribunal, as well as the impact on commercial negotiations of the deal as a whole. In any case, a purchaser may have to prepare an apportionment to value any chattels, newly qualifying integral features and fixtures for which the vendor has not claimed.

Ultimately, however, elections are a commercial matter and a purchaser may feel on balance that the loss of some capital allowances is a price worth paying to buy the property in question; the risk being that disagreement may delay or jeopardise the deal.

Section 198 elections must be made by notice to HMRC no later than two years after the completion date of the sale and purchase. A copy should accompany both parties' tax returns for the first period in which the election has effect (normally when the transaction occurred). *CAA 2001, s 201* sets out the requirements for a valid election, namely: the amount (which must be quantified when the election is made); the name of each of the persons; information sufficient to identify the plant; information sufficient to identify the 'relevant land'; particulars of the legal interest acquired, and the persons' tax references (if they have one). The legislation was amended in 2012 so that elections can be signed by non-taxpaying bodies such as pension funds and charities, and they should state that they do not have a unique tax reference on the election. This election protects the value of fixtures for a future owner should they sell the property.

One point of practical difficulty is that receivers cannot enter into such elections on behalf of either a purchaser or vendor as they are legally the agent of the defaulter. Problems can arise for capital allowance claims where a Law of Property Act (LPA) receiver is appointed by a lender in respect of a property upon which they have a charge. The LPA receiver is also not an 'affected party' for the purposes of an application to the tribunal. This can cause practical difficulties if the vendor does not co-operate and future claims may be affected. The price which the purchaser is willing to pay may be lower if allowances cannot be secured on the purchase. This area of difficulty has been brought to the attention of HMRC (via a letter from the Chartered Institute of Taxation of 18 June 2014), but HMRC's response gave no indication that they would be making any changes in the immediate future.

In terms of the amount of the election, this must not exceed the vendor's original expenditure on the fixture, or the total sale price for the entire property. It is automatically reduced if it subsequently proves too high. There is no minimum, but £1 or £2 is often proposed by hard bargaining vendors. Elections are irrevocable, so affect all future purchasers of the same fixtures, but it is possible to elect for lower amounts if that plant is later sold. Significantly, capital allowances claims (and hence disposal values) are for 'qualifying expenditure'. If plant fixtures (e.g. a hot-water system) are later stripped out, then a disposal value (e.g. scrap value or nil) must brought into account by the owner at the time and a further claim may be made for any new expenditure on a replacement system. That replacement expenditure would fall outside any pre-refurbishment election mentioning hot water because the election related to earlier qualifying expenditure (albeit on a similar asset to the replacement expenditure).

Perhaps the greatest practical difficulty relates to the obligations to provide 'information sufficient to identify the plant' and quantify the 'amount fixed'. The election should list in as much detail as possible only the fixtures upon which capital allowances have been claimed by the vendor (with amounts against each, where appropriate). This could be amalgamated at 'elemental' level (e.g. sanitary appliances, hot water system).

For most commercial property transactions, the purchaser's solicitor is likely to use the Commercial Property Standard Enquiries form ('CPSE'). The enquiries in section 32 of the CPSE cover capital allowances claimed on the building in the past. They are designed to enable the purchaser to assess the likely level of capital allowances that will be attached to the property on purchase. See 19.6 below for practical considerations for a vendor completing the questionnaire and a purchaser reviewing the responses.

If the vendor has not claimed allowances on fixtures and refuses to do so, the purchaser has no right to refer the matter to a tribunal for determination. This is because a tribunal cannot get involved until the expenditure has been pooled by the vendor.

If the vendor and purchaser do agree that the vendor will pool qualifying costs and pass some or all of their benefit on to the purchaser (via an election under

CAA 2001, s 198), then thought needs to be given to the fact that the vendor will need to be comfortable with the valuation figures being provided by a reputable source. These valuation figures will form part of their tax computation, so could be subject to an enquiry. Any third party experts will need joint approval, agreement over who is appointing them and paying for their costs, as well as the scope of their work.

From April 2014 the vendor is, in many ways, in a stronger position than in the past. The default starting point is that the purchaser cannot claim any allowances unless the vendor makes a claim. This is a reversal of the previous position, where a purchaser often preferred it if the vendor had not made a claim.

It is important that these CPSE enquiries are given adequate consideration. The contract clause on warranties and representations would apply to the replies given to these enquiries and errors could lead to a claim for damages for misrepresentation. In particular, if the vendor overlooks a previous *s 198* election such that the purchaser is denied any entitlement to allowances. For sales from April 2014 a missed claim of allowances on expenditure means that no future allowances will be available on these fixtures to any future owners. An irrevocable loss of allowances could reduce the future sale price of some properties.

Commercial Property Standard Enquiries ('CPSE') — practical issues

[19.6] The Commercial Property Standard Enquiries ('CPSE') questionnaire has been updated several times in recent years and it is important that the most up-to-date version is used. Previous versions (especially those where the capital allowance enquiry is numbered question 19 instead of question 32) are now out of date and do not include sufficient information for a post-March 2014 purchase given the new 'pooling' rules. It is essential that anyone advising on a purchase has sight of a correctly completed new questionnaire, with question 32 on capital allowances given proper consideration.

In the past many sections may have been completed with 'not applicable'; whereas now it is essential that proper information is obtained for each relevant section.

Some practical issues that often arise for a vendor in relation to completing question 32 on fixtures are:

- As question 32 on capital allowances is the last question on the form it is often not given adequate attention or time, which can cause problems or delays for the transaction. It is advisable for the capital allowance and VAT questions to be passed to the vendor's accountant or a specialist at an early stage and not left until the end.
- The information required to complete the questionnaire may not be readily available. For example, many fixed asset registers may not contain sufficient descriptions to determine whether an item is a fixture or there may be entries such as "refurbishment works 2006" where

further clarification may be required from old files. This is often encountered where new accountants are given insufficient handover information so it is key to ensure as much historic detail is obtained as possible.

- It is key to know whether any election under *CAA 2001, s 198* (or predecessor election under *CAA 1990, s 59B*) was entered into on purchase as this impacts on the value that can be passed on to the purchaser.
- Question 32 is only relevant to fixtures in the property, so responses should be limited to such items. However, vendors may also want to negotiate apportionments on other assets, such as chattels (i.e. moveable items such as furniture or computers), but this matter is outside of CPSE question 32 and the resultant agreed chattels figure is purely reflected in the contract and not part of the election under *CAA 2001, s 198*.
- It is key to understand the capital gains and income tax implications of any suggested apportionments of the purchase price. For example, if the vendor is making losses they should recognise the potential great value of capital allowances to a future owner and aim to reflect that value in the sales price.
- The fixtures rules can deem a fixture to belong to another party, such as a tenant, for the purposes of capital allowances claims. It is key that any such items are identified and not included in the list of assets qualifying for capital allowances on sale. The entitlement to claim on the fixtures remains with the tenant if the freehold reversion is sold.
- When clarifying how the property is owned, it is normally only property developers or traders that tend to hold property as stock (meaning they would not be able to claim capital allowances and an election is not possible). Most will own property as an investor/owner occupier so the remaining questions will all be relevant.
- Whether a property is capital or revenue depends on the intention of the owner when the property was purchased. If their intention was to sell it quickly or re-develop it for sale then it is likely to be stock in their hands (and capital allowances are not relevant). However, if the purchaser intends to hold the property for the longer term and earn a rental income then it is usually capital. This can be hard to judge on occasions where clients may have intentions which change over time. A starting point is to consider the "badges of trade" from case law. It is advisable to keep any documentation which supports the initial intention (e.g. correspondence and funding paperwork, projections, etc.) as it can be hard to justify at a later date.
- Most property owners will have claimed some capital allowances on fixtures, but it key to establish whether capital allowances have been fully claimed on both the original acquisition cost (noting that claims can only made for assets still in existence in the year the claim is made) and on subsequent refurbishment works.
- 'Pooling' means adding it to a tax ledger and including it in a tax return. Note that it does not matter whether an annual investment allowance or writing down allowance is made as it is indeed possible to disclaim allowances.

- When asked whether a vendor would be willing to pool any expenditure which has not yet been pooled it is key to understand that there may be fixtures on which the vendor is unable to claim, for example cold water systems in place prior to 2008. It is not possible for the vendor to pool these amounts, so this question purely relates to missed capital allowance claims. This should provide an opportunity for the vendor to consider whether there may be an opportunity to claim some further tax relief and, if so, whether they wish to retain some/all of the benefit, or whether it is not cost-effective to consider this further.
- If the vendor has not pooled their expenditure then there will be no capital allowance clawback on sale. However, where capital allowances have been claimed there will be a clawback (probably of the full allowances) if no election under *CAA 2001, s 198* is made to protect the position and retain some or all of the allowances. Doing nothing could therefore be an expensive option.
- The election under *CAA 2001, s 198* can be for any figure the parties agree provided it is not more than the qualifying expenditure pooled by the vendor, capped at the property price. HMRC have no power to insist that the election should contain a realistic or market value figure – this is entirely a matter for negotiation between the parties concerned. However, if the matter gets referred to the tribunal instead of agreeing a value themselves by election, this is likely to result in most or all of the allowances being clawed back and passed to the purchaser. It is therefore in the vendor's best interests to enter into an election after obtaining advice to understand the tax implications.
- If the vendor is a non-taxpaying entity then they will be required to know the capital allowance history of the building from July 1996, or make enquiries, if any benefit is to pass on to the purchaser. Pension trustees and charities should take collating this information seriously in order to maintain the value of their property.
- The questionnaire asks whether any assets are long-life assets or whether any other types of capital allowances have been claimed, for example Industrial Buildings Allowances, Research and Development Allowances or Business Premises Renovation Allowance. As Industrial Buildings Allowances have now been phased out (ceasing to be available in April 2011), this information may not be readily available so should be considered on the sale of properties such as factories, farms or hotels as the information may not be in the current computation.
- It is normally the seller's accountant who prepares the election under *CAA 2001 s 198*. It is advisable to get this signed at exchange, where possible.

A purchaser will receive the completed CPSE questionnaire and there are some key points and practical considerations when reviewing the information provided:

- The answers provided should give sufficient information to establish the type of claim which may be made and any restrictions as this may impact on the price the purchaser wishes to offer. Steps will be needed both before and after the sale to safeguard the ability to claim.

- The CPSE responses should be reviewed at an early stage by an experienced adviser and they can then consider whether further enquiries are necessary and consider appropriate next steps. For example, it is common for responses to say that capital allowances have been claimed on all fixtures, but is often the case that only partial claims have made, but the seller is unaware. This could be either where claims may have been made on the original purchase cost but not on subsequent improvements or where only improvement costs have been reviewed for a capital allowance claim, omitting a claim for fixtures in the original purchase cost of the building. In purchase contracts the term 'fixture and fittings' is often used when referring to chattels – and the opportunity to claim for fixtures can be overlooked. However, with some information on the property a specialist in this field could carry out a high level review for any potential gaps in the claim history.
- If possible, try to understand the tax consequences for the vendor. For example, if they are loss-making then may be far more willing to allow substantial allowances to pass to the purchaser as they may be able to absorb a balancing charge. Tax-paying vendors can be much more reluctant to negotiate! However some thought on overall apportionment, for example ensuring market value attributed to chattels in the contract, can benefit the purchaser by reducing Stamp Duty Land Tax (as SDLT is due on fixtures as they are affixed to the property, but not chattels) and also be of benefit to the vendor as this may slightly reduce their capital gain (as fixtures are included in any gain on property).
- If the responses fail to answer a question when it is relevant then this must be followed up to clarify the position. For example, where a factory, farm or hotel is purchased, it is key to understand whether there has been a previous IBA claim which will restrict plant and machinery capital allowance claims going forward.
- The vendor may provide extracts of information, for example a fixed asset register, without clarifying which items are fixtures or, indeed, on which items capital allowances have been claimed. Further information may be required to confirm the position, taking into account the cost-benefit of any extra work.
- If the vendor has not made complete capital allowance claims and initially refuses to 'pool' expenditure then this should be challenged if commercially viable to do so. It may be that they are not willing to pay for this work, but that they may allow the purchaser to incur the expense of a valuation exercise and agree to 'pool' the expense to pass it on to the purchaser. It is advisable to make the pooling of expenditure and the associated election a condition of exchange. If the seller does not pool (when they are able) then this means no capital allowances are available to the purchaser.
- If capital allowances are being considered late in the day then there is a misconception that the vendor has to pool before the transaction and some purchasers give up hope of any allowances. Waiting until nearer the date of the transaction puts the purchaser in a very weak bargaining position, so early negotiation is encouraged to ensure this part does not hold up the sale. However, eleventh-hour planning is possible. If the vendor has not claimed capital allowances but will do so in order for

the purchaser to claim, then appropriate clauses can be put in the purchase contracts to allow contracts to be exchanged, with a valuation exercise carried out and the election finalised post-transaction. If the purchaser is benefitting from the tax relief then they would normally pay the professional costs of any valuation and may be asked to cover any enquiry costs of the vendor in relation to the capital allowance figures pooled on their computation.

- A purchaser will often start off seeking allowances close to the original cost but should accept that a high value is likely to be resisted in any commercial negotiation and the outcome will depend on the bargaining power of the parties. If an election is not agreed then a purchaser can use the threat of a first-tier tribunal as a bargaining tool, as a tribunal is likely to award most of the value to the purchaser; then the vendor may be willing to share a proportion of the allowances if they are keen to sell.
- In relation to any expenditure where the vendor is unable to claim capital allowances (and they had not previously been claimed by a previous owner), which is often the case for 'pre-commencement' integral features (e.g. cold water systems and general electrics), these will fall entirely outside of any pooling or election requirement. It is up to the purchaser to value these and include an appropriate claim for these separately on their tax return. These can be substantial on a larger property and take advantage of the rules of 'just and reasonable' apportionment based on current replacement costs.
- If the previous owner could not claim allowances (e.g. a pension fund or charity) then you still need to know the capital allowance history of the building, in particular in relation to the last tax-paying entity owning the building since 24 July 1996. If a previous owner was required to bring in a disposal value then this will restrict the purchaser's claim.
- It is key that the vendor is legally bound to sign a fixtures election for the agreed figure and that the capital allowance clauses in the contract provide the necessary protection to the purchaser.

The capital allowance history for the building will be relevant in clarifying the basis of any claim. A summary of the key implications for a purchaser from April 2014 are:

Vendor's entitlement	**Did the vendor claim/pool capital allowances?**	**Purchaser's perspective**	**Commentary**
Entitled to claim	Yes - claimed	Fixed value requirement applies on purchase.	Make *CAA 2001, s 198* election or apply to first-tier tribunal.
Entitled to claim	No capital allowances expenditure pooled	Pooling required before any fixed value can be agreed.	No allowances are available to the purchaser where the vendor could have claimed unless the vendor cooperates.

Vendor's entitlement	Did the vendor claim/pool capital allowances?	Purchaser's perspective	Commentary
Vendor not entitled to claim Acquired before April 2012	N/A	Existing restrictions in *CAA 2001, s 185* apply if past owners made a claim.	It can be difficult to trace previous ownership and capital allowance history.
Vendor not entitled to claim Acquired between April 2012 and March 2014 Past owner claimed capital allowances	N/A	Fixed value requirement would have applied to the previous transaction. If the vendor and past owner can no longer make a *CAA 2001, s 198* election then the purchaser must obtain a written statement from the vendor.	Two statements are required – one from the vendor stating that it can no longer elect and one from the past owner confirming the disposal value brought into account.
Vendor not entitled to claim Acquired between April 2012 and March 2014 Past owner entitled but did not claim	N/A	Existing restrictions in *CAA 2001, s 185* apply if any past owners made a claim. No restriction if no past owner claimed from July 1996.	This requires knowledge of the ownership of the property back to July 1996, which can be hard to trace.
Vendor not entitled to claim Acquired from April 2014 Past owner claimed	N/A	Fixed value requirement applies to earlier transaction. If the vendor and past owner can no longer make an election then written statements must be obtained, as per above.	This highlights the needs for non-taxpaying entities to obtain capital allowance information on purchase and either enter into an election or obtain written statements to ensure no value is lost on the ultimate sale.
Vendor not entitled to claim Acquired from April 2014 Past owner entitled but did not claim	N/A	No allowances available to the purchaser.	Is it possible to persuade the past owner to pool in order to pass on allowances?

Once a *CAA 2001 s 198* election figure has been agreed by both parties it is key that a valid election is signed otherwise it could be set aside. This could leave the seller with an unexpected balancing charge and the purchaser unable to claim the allowances to which they thought they were entitled. It is also key to ensure this valid election is submitted to HMRC within 2 years of completion and is attached to the return appropriate to the transaction to protect the interests of both parties.

Capital contributions by landlords

[19.7] Where a landlord makes a capital contribution to the tenant's fitting out works, then the landlord may be able to make a claim for capital allowances under *CAA 2001, s 538* (see **2.9** above).

If the contract does not specify that the landlord is going to claim capital allowances on the expenditure (and apportion it accordingly) then this leaves the tenant with an argument that the contribution was a general inducement towards the tenant taking up occupation. The tenant could then seek to claim the allowances and deprive the landlord of such a claim. It is therefore important that the contract is carefully considered from a capital allowances perspective, both by the tenant and the landlord.

In addition to the capital allowances, there are also other taxes to consider especially VAT.

Capital allowances and dwellings

[19.8] Plant and machinery allowances are available to property businesses under *CAA 2001, s 17* but for ordinary property businesses are restricted from applying to expenditure 'in a dwelling-house' by *CAA 2001, s 35*. No such restriction applies to furnished holiday lettings that meet the qualifying criteria. However, if the furnished holiday lettings qualifying criteria are not met, then the restriction would apply. There is also concern expressed by HMRC over the extension of capital allowances to residential accommodation so it is worth considering this restriction further.

It should be noted that *s 35* refers to 'dwelling-house', and not 'dwelling' which is used in other parts of the Act. There is a definition of 'dwelling-house' in *CAA 2001, s 531(1)* (in relation to assured tenancy allowances) which states that it is to have 'the same meaning as in the *Rent Act 1977*'. However, the *Rent Act 1977* does not have a defined term of 'dwelling-house'. As there is no definition of 'dwelling-house' for other parts of the *Capital Allowances Act*, it must take its ordinary meaning.

HMRC Brief 45/10 revised HMRC's interpretation of dwelling house with effect from 22 October 2010. Now the guidance at HMRC Capital Allowance Manual, CA11520 states:

> 'A person's second or holiday home or accommodation used for holiday letting is a dwelling-house. A block of flats is not a dwelling-house although the individual flats within the block may be. A hospital, a prison, nursing home or hotel (run as a trade and offering services, whether by the owner-occupier or by a tenant) are not dwelling-houses.'

In addition, university accommodation consisting of clusters of individually lockable flats with shared or communal kitchen and living areas would be classified as dwelling-houses (apart from communal areas such as stairs and lifts where a building contains two or more dwelling houses), as together they provided the facilities necessary for day to day private domestic existence. Such a house or flat would be a dwelling house if occupied by a family, a group of friends or key workers, so HMRC accept that the fact that it is occupied by students is, in a sense, incidental.

The change of view had arisen as a result of HMRC's consideration of the implications of a case concerning the *Housing Act 1988* (*Uratemp Ventures Ltd. v Collins* HL 2001, [2001] UKHL 43) which found that a hotel room could be a 'dwelling-house', despite the absence of cooking facilities. There have also been suggestions by HMRC of unacceptable abuse of the capital allowances code in an attempt to secure allowances on what in HMRC's view were meant to be dwelling-houses. During the course of the consultation discussions with HMRC on the proposed changes to the furnished holiday lettings regime it became clear that there was quite a lot of head-scratching going on by HMRC more generally over dwellings. The issue for furnished holiday lettings was over the extent of the term 'dwelling'. Clearly communal swimming pools and play equipment would still qualify, but what proximity to the dwelling was permissible.

The revised HMRC interpretation is based on the case of *Gravesham Borough Council v Secretary of State for the Environment* QBD 1982, (1982) 47 P&CR 142. This case concerned the interpretation of 'dwelling-house' for the *Town and Country Planning General Development Order 1977* (since updated in 1995 to *SI 1995 No 418*).

That Order contains the following interpretations:

- 'dwelling-house' does not include a building containing one or more flats, or a flat contained within such a building; and
- 'flat' means a separate and self-contained set of premises constructed or adapted for use for the purpose of a dwelling and forming part of a building from some other part of which it is divided horizontally.

In *Gravesham* it was determined that:

> 'The Secretary of State could find that a building built under a permission for a weekend and holiday chalet, but to be used only in summer, was a dwelling-house. The distinctive characteristic of a dwelling-house is its ability to afford to those who use it the facilities required for day-to-day private domestic existence.'

However HMRC Brief 45/10 mentions the *Use Classes Order* (*SI 2010 No 653*) but does seem to stretch this by extending dwelling-house to include lockable cluster flats of up to six flats with individual bedrooms and shared kitchen facilities, or to properties occupied by students where that property is not their main residence.

Based on current legislation, capital allowance claims are possible on furnished holiday lets and certain communal parts of blocks of flats.

'Dwelling' is referred to in various parts of the Taxes Acts, including in relation to zero rating for VAT at *VATA 1994, Sch 8 group 5 note 2*, referring to a building designed to remain as, or become a dwelling. The term 'dwelling' is also used in connection with determining taxable property for the pension legislation (*FA 2004, Sch 29A paras 7–10*).

More recently the term dwelling has been used in the legislation to restrict interest relief for buy-to-let landlords to a basic rate reducer only for higher or additional rate taxpayers. The changes introduced by *Finance (No 2) Act 2015, s 24* inserted a new section into *ITTOIA 2005*. This introduces the terminology for a 'dwellings-related' loan. *ITTOIA 2005, s 272A* states that a 'dwelling house' includes 'any land occupied or enjoyed with it as garden or grounds'.

The meaning of dwelling for SDLT is set out in *FA 2003, Sch 6A para 7* and is stated to include land occupied and enjoyed with the dwelling as its garden or grounds. A similar definition is included in *FA 2003, Sch 9 para 7(6)* with reference to relief from SDLT for right to buy, shared ownership lease and certain related transactions, and in *FA 2011, Sch 22 para 7* in respect of transfers of multiple dwellings. However residential rates of SDLT only apply if the relevant land consists entirely of residential property, and the meaning of residential property in *FA 2003, s 116* includes a building used or suitable for use as, or in the process of being constructed as, or adapted for use, as a dwelling.

HMRC's current guidance on the extent of grounds to be treated as part of a residential property indicates that the capital gains tax interpretation for main residence relief is to be used. Thus where there is land around a dwelling in excess of what would be regarded as normal for *TCGA 1992, s 222*, it would appear as though HMRC would interpret the whole property as non-residential for SDLT. However, remember that *CAA 2001, s 35* refers to 'in a dwelling-house'.

When considering the scope of the restriction in the term dwelling-house, it is also worth considering the terms 'accommodation used for holiday letting' (the term used in the HMRC Capital Allowances Manual at CA11520 prior to 22 October 2010), and 'hotel'. The nearest definition to 'accommodation used for holiday letting' appears to be the definition of 'holiday accommodation' for VAT where *VATA 1994, Sch 9 group 1 item 1(e)* and *note 13* (an exclusion from VAT exemption) refers to:

> 'any accommodation in a building, hut (including a beach hut or chalet), caravan, houseboat or tent which is advertised or held out as holiday accommodation or suitable for holiday use, but excludes any accommodation within paragraph 1(d)'.

Paragraph 1(d) covers a hotel, inn, boarding house or similar establishment of sleeping accommodation or of accommodation in rooms which are provided in conjunction with sleeping accommodation or for the purpose of catering. 'Similar establishment' is further clarified in *note 9* as including premises in which there is provided furnished sleeping accommodation, whether with or without the provision of board or facilities for the preparation of food, which are used by, or held out as being suitable for use by, visitors or travellers.

The *Hotel Proprietors Act 1956* defines an hotel as: 'an establishment held out by the proprietor as offering food, drink and, if so required, sleeping accommodation, without special contract, to any traveller presenting himself who appears able and willing to pay a reasonable sum for the services and facilities provided and who is in a fit state to be received.' The *Use Classes Order* (*SI 2010 No 653*) has category C1 as: 'Hotels, boarding and guest houses where no significant element of care is provided (excludes hostels).' However, there is no reference to number of rooms or a required period of letting as there was for industrial buildings allowances.

There is currently a lack of clarity over the tax definitions of 'dwelling-house' and 'accommodation for holiday letting'. There is also scope for that confusion to spread for property tax purposes to the interpretation of 'dwelling' and 'hotel'. It would not be surprising if there was a future attempt to restrict entitlement to capital allowances on such properties (a continuation of the policy of withdrawing industrial building allowances on hotels).

Change in use of furnished holiday let

[19.9] As capital allowances are available to the owner of a commercial property held as either an investment property or to an owner who trades out of the property, a change in use does not normally impact on the capital allowance position. The impact of a disposal is considered at 19.5 above.

However, where a property qualifies as a furnished holiday let ('FHL') (the criteria which include needing to be let for at least 105 days per tax year and available for 210 days), the implications of any change in use need to be carefully considered in relation to capital allowances. Issues can arise when either the owner occupies the property themselves, it is let on a longer term basis (e.g. assured leasehold tenancy) or it is let as holiday accommodation but fails to meet the qualifying letting criteria.

As discussed above in **19.8**, capital allowances are not available in dwelling houses so a change of use could lead to a clawback of allowances or a restriction on the ability to claim.

If the owner uses the property for a number of weeks or during the "off-season" but the property meets the other qualifying FHL criteria, then the owner-occupation does not give rise to a balancing adjustment. However, capital allowances and expenses would need to be time-apportioned. If the owner moved in permanently then this would be a disposal event for capital allowances purposes and a balancing adjustment calculated based on the market value.

If an FHL owner decides to switch to long-term letting (for example to an assured leasehold tenancy) then they will cease to have a qualifying FHL property and this will be a balancing event. Again, the disposal proceeds will be equal to market value.

Another common occurrence is for an FHL owner to fail to meet the letting criteria, for example if they stop using a letting agency and struggle to market the property themselves. Up to and including the 2011/12 tax year a property only needed to be let 70 days in a tax year to qualify. Since 2012/13, some owners have struggled to meet the increased 105 day limit. There are period of grace elections possible where an owner fails to meet the conditions (having tried to do so), but these are only available for two failed years. Averaging elections may also be applicable for owners who own more than one holiday let in order to meet the relevant criteria. If the property still fails to qualify then, on the strict letter of tax law, there should be a disposal event potentially giving rise to a balancing charge. It is not possible to enter into an election under CAA 2001, s198 as there has not been a sale to a third party.

The above strict interpretation could be particularly harsh as a taxpayer could be hit with a large tax liability on a balancing charge in a tax year when they can least afford to pay it due to lower rental income. However HMRC's property income manual at PIM4120 does (on a non-statutory basis) comment that if the property only temporarily ceases to qualify then capital allowances may be continued. If the property is unlikely to qualify in the foreseeable future then a disposal value should be brought into account. Any difficulties in letting should therefore be considered during a period of grace to evaluate the options open to the taxpayer and the basis of any market value disposal. There is a risk that HMRC would seek to impose a disposal value equal to original cost on the basis that the market value of the assets has appreciated in line with the value of the property. This could lead to all (or the majority) of the allowances claimed being clawed back.

Landlord's energy saving allowance

[19.10] Under *ITTOIA 2005, s 312* and *CTA 2009, s 251* a tax deduction in computing rental income of up to £1,500 (per dwelling-house) was available to landlords who installed certain energy saving insulation to residential property. This relief expired on 31 March 2015 for corporate landlords and 5 April 2015 for individuals. See **14.2** above.

No tax deduction is available if:

(a) the insulation etc. is installed during the course of construction, that is the relief is only intended for the retro-fitting of insulation; or
(b) the business consists of the commercial letting of furnished holiday accommodation and the dwelling-house constitutes some or all of that accommodation;
(c) the person incurring the expenditure:
    (i) does not have an interest in the property; or
    (ii) is in the course of acquiring an interest in the property or a further interest.

However, confusion arises on the latter point where a person currently does not have an interest, but is trying to obtain one. A literal reading of the legislation suggests that the person would not qualify because they are in the course of acquiring an interest in the property. However, this is illogical for two reasons:

(a) that person would not qualify anyway (because they already do not have an interest in the property, so the extra wording is unnecessary); and
(b) if a person with a qualifying interest (for example, a tenant) was looking to improve their interest (for example, was acquiring the freehold) then they would no longer qualify.

Therefore, the logical conclusion is that the legislation is poorly drafted and the allowance was intended to be made available to a person with an interest, or who was looking to acquire an interest or further interest.

Furthermore, no deduction is available if the property is let under the rent-a-room scheme.

Valuation and apportionment of goodwill in trade-related properties

[19.11] An apportionment of the price paid for a business as a going concern between the underlying assets will be required for the purpose of calculating the allowances available for plant and machinery. The allocation to goodwill used to be a key point for corporates due to the ability to obtain a tax deduction for the amortisation (or writing-down) of goodwill. This favourable regime unexpectedly came to an end for goodwill acquired from 8 July 2015. This change followed an earlier clamp-down in the 2014 Autumn Statement on 3 December 2014 whereby individuals can no longer claim Entrepreneurs' Relief on goodwill transferred on incorporation to a related close company, nor can a claim be made for amortisation on goodwill relating to the individuals carrying on the business prior to incorporation. Goodwill apportionment is therefore now of more relevance when considering Stamp Duty Land Tax, given the loss of corporate tax relief on amortisation on future acquisitions.

In the past HMRC took the view that it was unlikely that there would be 'free goodwill' of any significant value in businesses carried out from trade related properties (for example public houses, hotels, petrol filling stations, cinemas, restaurants, care homes etc.) because the occupation and use of the particular, specially adapted, premises was usually essential and integral to the generation of the business income.

However on 29 January 2009, HMRC changed their view and acknowledged that when a business is sold as a going concern the sale price will reflect the combined value of the tangible assets together with the benefit of other business assets such as any contracts with customers, staff and suppliers, records of previous customers etc. Substantial value can be realised by combining the tangible and other business assets together for sale as a going concern but this enhanced value may be reduced if the assets are split and sold separately.

At the same time that HMRC announced this change of view, a Practice Note was published on the valuation aspects as to how HMRC and the VOA consider the price paid for a business as a going concern should be apportioned as between goodwill and other assets included in the sale. The Practice Note reflects the VOA view that the appropriate method of valuing this type of property is by reference to the profit making potential of the premises. This approach is not accepted by all valuers and there is continuing dispute on this.

There are implications not just for capital allowances and the intangible asset regime but also for SDLT and capital gains tax. HMRC have historically sought to distinguish between different types of goodwill and categorise it as between the following:

(1) personal — related to the skill and personality of the proprietor of the business;
(2) inherent — related to the location of the business premises; and
(3) free — related to the overall worth of the business and subdivided into:

(a) free adherent goodwill — this arises not from the location of the premises but the carrying out of a particular business for which those premises have been or are specifically adapted or licensed; and

(b) free separable goodwill — true free goodwill which is entirely separate from the business premises and can be transferred independently from them. This is most readily identified where the business has a 'name' or brand.

In HMRC's view, inherent and free adherent goodwill cannot exist independently of the real property to which they are attached. Therefore, these types of goodwill are part of the land for capital gains tax purposes.

HMRC's classification of goodwill is derived in part from the decision of the Court of Appeal in *Whiteman Smith Motor Co Ltd v Chaplin* KB 1934, [1934] 2 KB 35 which identifies four types of customers:

(i) the cat — who stays faithful to the location not the person;
(ii) the dog — who stays faithful to the person and not the location;
(iii) the rat — who is casual and is attracted to neither person nor location; and
(iv) the rabbit — who comes because it is close by and for no other reason.

Goodwill is fundamentally an accounting concept and any modern court is likely to take heed of specialist accounting opinion and GAAP. In this context, FRS 10 defines purchased goodwill as:

> ' . . . the difference between the cost of an acquired entity and the aggregate of the fair values of that entity's identifiable assets and liabilities. Positive goodwill arises when the acquisition cost exceeds the aggregate fair values of the identifiable assets and liabilities. Negative goodwill arises when the aggregate fair values of the identifiable assets and liabilities of the entity exceed the acquisition cost.'

Medium and large businesses will now be accounting for goodwill under *s 19* of FRS 102 for accounting periods commencing on or after 1 January 2015. *Section 19.22* states that:

> 'The acquirer shall, at the acquisition date:
>
> (a) recognise goodwill acquired in a business combination of an asset; and
> (b) initially measure that goodwill at its cost, being the excess of the cost of the business combination over the acquirer's interest in the net amount of the identifiable assets, liabilities and contingent liabilities . . . '

Where the goodwill is personal to the individual concerned, the HMRC view is that it cannot be transferred and so cannot form part of any apportionment. In other cases, HMRC have historically argued that the goodwill is part of the property value and cannot be separated from it. This is relevant on the value of hotels, restaurants, etc.

The approach of HMRC was not accepted by the Special Commissioner, Michael Tildersley, in the capital gains tax case of *Balloon Promotions Ltd v Wilson* [2006] SSCD 167. This case concerned franchised operations of Pizza Express and whether the franchisee had any goodwill of its own. The Special Commissioner made it clear that, '*Whiteman Smith Motor Co* was not authority for the proposition that the value of net adherent goodwill will as a matter of course be incorporated into the valuation of premises sold'.

This case is one of the reasons why HMRC decided in the end to change their valuation approach. However, there is still plenty of scope for debate. For purchasers within the charge to corporation tax where the acquisition took place before 8 July 2015 the issue is potentially very significant, especially on hotels and other high value properties. Indeed, with the abolition of industrial buildings allowances there is now more at stake as the non-qualifying proportion of buildings has increased.

Appendix 1

Items which may qualify as Plant or Machinery

This schedule is an alphabetical list of items which may qualify for plant and machinery allowances in accordance with CHAPTER 4 above. The list is not exhaustive and is taken from an original list compiled from case law (both United Kingdom and overseas), Commissioners' decisions and Inland Revenue practice by Edward P. Magrin FTII and which first appeared in '*Taxation*' magazine on 18 November 1993, pp 148–150. The authors are indebted to Mr. Magrin who has willingly given of his time and advice and has kindly granted us permission to include his list in this book. As the law develops, the list will be updated to reflect the changes.

It should be noted that even though an item may be included in this schedule, this is no guarantee that it will necessarily qualify for plant and machinery allowances, as each case has to be considered on its merits, and the actual use of the item in the trade of the taxpayer is a critical factor.

In addition, a number of the items listed below may no longer qualify where they are caught by *CAA 2001, ss 21–23* (exclusions from expenditure on plant or machinery—see **4.22** onwards above) as not all have been held to be machinery or plant by virtue of previous court decisions.

A

Acoustic treatment of e.g. room ducts (specialised installations)
Advertising signs, billboards, hoardings and roller boards
Acid chambers
Aerials
Air compressors and services
Air conditioning including ducting and vents
Air lines
Alterations to a building re: plant installation e.g. ventilating ducts
Amusement slides
Annealing ovens
Aquarium tanks
Arc and gas welding plant
Architects and professional fees related to a number of items including plant (part may qualify)
Armco barriers
Artificial manure manufacturing plant
Art works at a museum etc.

B

Bacon curing plant
Baffles
Baker's plant

Baths
Ball feeders and specialist tennis equipment
Banana ripening plant
Battery chargers
Beehives
Bitumen laminating plant
Blast furnace
Blast tunnels
Blinds, curtains, blind boxes and pelmets
Bicycle holders
Biscuit making plant
Boat shed jetties
Bobbin tamping machines
Boiler plants and auxiliaries
Boilers
Bowling alleys including ball return, tracks, gutters, pit signals and terminals
Bowser tanks
Brewing plant including pipes, condenser and expansion
Brick elevators (portable)
Brick kilns
Bullet resistant screens
Burglar alarms
Buzz bars

C

Cable TV provision and ducting
Cable, both overhead and underground
Cable car systems
Calorifiers
Cameras
Canopy—where certain conditions met e.g. serves purpose of advertising
Canteen fittings and equipment
Capital contribution to a sewerage authority in the UK
Car park illumination
Carpets and other loose floor coverings
Car wash apparatus and housing
Cash dispensers
Casting pit
Catalysts (granuals)
Cathode filling machines
Cat walks
Ceilings—false, but only when performing a function distant from setting e.g. an integral part of a ventilation or air conditioning system
Central dictation systems
Charcoal burning kilns
Checkouts
Chillers
Cleaning cradles (including tracts and anchorages)
Clock installations

Coal carbonising apparatus
Coal hulks
Coffee making machines
Compressed air plant and piping
Computers and associated attachments together with specialised flooring and ceilings
Conduit for security alarm systems
Construction costs of erecting plant on site
Contribution to plant purchased by others (certain conditions must be met)
Conveyor installations and equipment
Cooking baths
Cooking, conveying and servicing equipment
Cooler rooms
Cooling furnaces
Cooling-water systems for (i) drinking and (ii) air-conditioning
Counters and fittings
Court floors—indoor and outdoor (certain cases only)
Cradles and fire balconies (demountable)
Crane gantries and towers
Curing barns e.g. tobacco and peanuts
Cyclic reforming apparatus

D

Dam (certain situations where not made of earth)
Dark rooms (demountable)
Derricks
Designs and blueprints
Dips for sheep and cattle
Dispensers
Disposal units with all live feeds, wastes and flues
Distillery plant and brewery apparatus including casks
Distribution systems
Documents hoist and other hoists and doors
Door closers
Draglines and buckets
Drilling plant
Drop hammers
Dry dock
Dryers
Dry riser installation
Dumbwaiters
Dust extraction equipment
Dyehouse—specially designed
Dynamos

E

Electric dodgems
Electric fences

Electrically operated doors (but see '*Taxation*' magazine, 5 May 1994, p 135)
Electrically operated roller shutters
Electrical sub-stations and generators
Electrical wiring closely related to an accepted piece of plant, e.g. to smoke detectors
Electrical wiring and sockets in connection with particular trades e.g. TV shops and departments where the numbers of sockets are more than is normal for the size of the shop or department
Electronic scoring equipment
Electronic timing devices
Emergency lighting
Escalators and travelators
Excavating costs re: plant installation
Exchange losses when linked to capital expenditure
Extinguishers

F

Fairground and similar amusements
Fans
Fascia lettering
Fermentation chambers
Fire alarms
Fire blankets
Fire protections systems and sprinklers
Fires
Fire safety equipment to comply with the requirements of a fire authority
Fish farming equipment
Fish ponds at garden centres and fish farms
Fitted desks, writing tables and screens
Fixed site caravans in a motor village
Flight simulators and trainers
Floating docks, pontoons and marinas
Floodlighting
Floor covering
Flooring (demountable)
Flooring (raised but only where incorporating special features necessary for trade)
Foreign currency fluctuation relating to expenditure (in certain cases)
Forges
Freezer rooms and chambers
Furnaces

G

Gamma irradiation apparatus
Gangways
Gantries
Gas bells
Gas installations after incoming main

Gazebo in public house garden (moveable)
General control and supervisory systems
Generators
Glasshouse (if of sophisticated design with e.g. a computer system monitoring and controlling such matters as temperature, humidity, ventilation and screens)
Goods and bullion lifts and doors
Grain silos
Gramophones and juke boxes
Grill work (removable)
Gymnasium equipment

H

Hand dryers
Heating installations, fittings, pipes and radiators
Hoists
Holding bay for oxygen steelmaking installation
Hoses and hose reels
Hot water services and related plumbing
Humidification buildings (specialist)
Hydraulic elevated platforms and hoists e.g. for car parking trade
Hydraulic presses

I

Ice making apparatus
Immersion and instant water heaters
Incinerators
Installation costs re: plant
Inter-com installations
Internal signs

K

Kennels (moveable)
Kitchen equipment
Knives and lasts

L

Launches for ships
Laundry equipment and services
Letter-boxes
Lift and lift shafts
Light fittings and lamps (certain trades e.g. hotels re ambience)
Lighting protection systems
Livestock pens and cages
Loudspeakers
Lockers
Locks (certain situations)
Loose floor coverings and doormats
Loose furniture

LPG cylinders

M

Mannequin display figures
Mechanical hand dryers
Mechanical gates
Mechanical ventilation systems
Mechanical vehicle barriers
Merry-go-rounds
Mezzanine storage platforms (moveable)
Milking machinery and refrigeration storage facilities
Mining machinery
Mirrors
Model steam trains, permanent way and other equipment for carrying passengers
Moveable partitions (where required by the trade)
Murals (certain trades e.g. hotels re ambience)
Museums—items displayed

N

Name plates
Navigation apparatus (both on and offshore)

O

Offshore accommodation modules and helidecks
Oil rigs, well linings and platforms
Organic peroxides expansion cell block
Ornaments (certain trades e.g. hotels re ambience)
Outside tennis fencing
Ovens

P

Paper combining plant
Passenger lifts and doors
Payment for cancellation of options (in certain cases)
PBX
Personnel—location and call systems
Photo finish equipment
Pictures (certain trades e.g. hotels re ambience)
Pig unit (purpose built), automatic feeding etc.
Pipelines
Planetarium and space theatre domes
Plant housing (special circumstances)
Pneumatic tube conveying systems
Poles, cables, conductors and switch boards for the distribution of electricity
Polytunnels (if used only for growing plants and not a fixed structure)
Portable toilet
Portakabins, huts of a nomadic type moved from site to site (e.g. the construction industry)

Pottery—works equipment and kiln
Poultry house—specially designed
Powering barrel mills
Power cables
Power installations
Prawn farming ponds
Professional fees specially related to an item of plant acquired
Projecting signs
Protective structures closely related to accepted items of plant
Public address and piped music systems
Pulleys
Pumps
Purifiers

R

Racking, cupboards and shelving (removable)
Radar installations
Radiators
Radio, television and data transmission installations
Radio, television and data receivers
Railway track including sleepers and ballast
Refinery
Refrigeration installations and cold stores
Refrigeration plant
Refrigerated fruit juice dispensers
Refuse collecting and disposal systems (including chutes and incinerators)
Reinforcing plant
Reticulation services installed in a factory if certain conditions are met
Retorts and associated structures
Revolving mechanical doors
Rock crushing machines
Roller shutter doors
Roofing—cost of strengthening roofs to support plant such as cranes and hoists

S

Safes, night safes and enclosures
Safety equipment and screens
Salmon farming apparatus
Sanitary installations such as lavatories, urinals and pans together with pipeline fittings
Sauna and jacuzzi
Screens and fire safety curtains—cinemas
Screens in a window display (moveable)
Sculptures (certain trades e.g. hotels re ambience)
Seats
Security assets and devices
Security gates to cash loading area (removable)
Security screens and lobbies

Sewer pipes in relation to e.g. factory or a large hotel
Shafts
Showers and baths
Shutters (mechanical)
Silage storage bunkers
Silos e.g. slurry blending and mixing and cement storage
Skating surface—synthetic
Skidpans and special surface tracks
Sleeping units for workers which are portable and taken from site to site
Slicing and wrapping machines
Smelters
Smoke detectors and heat detectors
Soda water fountains
Soft furnishings
Software purchased at the same time as the hardware re a computer system
Software with a life or more than two years
Solar energy systems
Special acoustical or suspended ceilings (in certain cases)
Special buildings which cannot be used as ordinary buildings e.g. boiler house, concrete shells housing plant, wind tunnels and anechoic chambers
Special foundations or reinforced flooring for plant
Special housing around plant
Special lighting related to the trade
Splashbacks (where not part of a wholly-tiled wall or floor)
Sports stadia expenditure re a safety certificate
Spray booth
Sprinkler systems
Squash courts—directly related to certain trading activities e.g. amusement park
Staff lockers
Stage lights and scenery
Stand (racecourse and similar trades but only if certain conditions are met)
Starting gantries and stalls
Steam and other trains, permanent way and other equipment for carrying passengers or goods
Steam vats
Storage racks
Storage tanks and bins
Stoves
Stream services and condensate return systems
Strong rooms (demountable)
Strong room doors
Swimming pools directly related to certain trading activities e.g. amusement or caravan park
Switchboards
Switchgear

T

Tanks (for brine, cream etc.)

Tapestries (certain trades e.g. hotels re ambience)
Tea and coffee dispensers
Telegraph poles
Telephone booths and kiosks
Telephone equipment and conduits
Teleprinters
Telex systems
Tennis courts—directly related to certain trading activities e.g. amusement or caravan park
Testing tanks
Thermal insulation re industrial buildings
Ticket issuing and collecting machines
Toll booths
Totalisator equipment
Towel dispensers
Towel rails
Traffic control apparatus
Tramway rails
Transformers
Transportation costs of plant
Trellis
Trickle irrigation equipment in glasshouses
Trolley parks
Turnstiles
Turntables

V

Vacuum cleaning installations
Vats e.g. for cyanide
Vaults
Vents
Vibration control
Video equipment

W

WC partitions (if demountable venestra type)
Wall decor (certain trades e.g. hotels re ambience)
Wash basins including drains
Water slide and associated equipment
Water softening installations
Water tower
Water treatment and filtration
Weighbridge
Welfare facilities
Wells
Wet and dry risers
Wharves—certain situations
Winches
Wind tunnels

Windmills
Window display lighting e.g. shops
Window displays (moveable)
Window panels, lighting and sockets for a shop front
Wiring and trunking to accepted items of plant

X

X-ray apparatus

Z

Zoo cages (fixed) (see '*Taxation*' magazine, 23 March 1995, pp 599–601)

Appendix 2

Revenue & Customs Brief 3/10

GUIDANCE ON PLANT AND MACHINERY CAPITAL ALLOWANCES FOR THE PIG INDUSTRY

23 February 2010. *Revenue & Customs Brief 3/10*

BACKGROUND

Following the Government's decision to phase-out agricultural buildings allowances by April 2011, the Department for Environment, Food and Rural Affairs (DEFRA) approached HMRC to discuss the implications of this change for certain agricultural sectors that are particularly heavy investors in buildings and structures with very short economic lives. A prominent example of such a sector is the pig industry. As a result of these discussions, HMRC agreed to prepare some additional guidance, to illustrate the range of assets on which the pig industry might claim plant and machinery capital allowances (including the new £50,000 Annual Investment Allowance). This guidance is reproduced below.

THE PIG INDUSTRY — GUIDANCE ON PLANT AND MACHINERY CAPITAL ALLOWANCES (PMAS)

Introduction

This special guidance is intended to help the pig industry make claims for plant & machinery capital allowances (PMAs) by providing examples of some of the main types of expenditure that can qualify for PMAs. PMAs allow capital expenditure to be deducted from business profits. The main PMAs are:

Enhanced capital allowances (ECAs): rate 100 per cent ECAs enable a business to claim 100 per cent of its expenditure on certain energy- saving or environmentally beneficial plant & machinery (P&M) in the year the expenditure is incurred. [Some types of equipment that may be covered are mentioned below, but whether any particular item will qualify depends on whether it falls within the precise eligibility criteria. Please check the ECA website for more precise details — http://www.eca.gov.uk/.]

Annual Investment Allowance (AIA): rate 100 per cent for expenditure on P&M up to £50,000 each year. The AIA applies to both main rate (20 per cent) and 'special rate' (10 per cent) expenditure on P&M The expenditure must be incurred on or after 1 April 2008 (companies) or 6 April 2008 (sole traders & partnerships).

Temporary 40 per cent First-year allowance (FYA) for 2009–10: This extra encouragement to invest was announced by the Chancellor at Budget 2009, and applies to most expenditure on P&M incurred in the year 2009-2010 (not otherwise wholly relieved by the 100 per cent ECAs or AIA).

Writing-down allowances (WDAs) at 20 per cent or 10 per cent a year for 'main rate' or 'special rate' P&M expenditure respectively. 'Special rate' expenditure includes expenditure on the new classification of 'integral features' of a building or structure, incurred on or after 1 April 2008 (companies) or 6 April 2008 (sole traders &

partnerships). But most expenditure on P&M qualifies at the main rate of 20 per cent.

Small pools allowance: This is an alternative WDA, applying to accounting periods beginning on or after 1 April 2008 (companies) or 6 April 2008 (sole traders & partnerships), which allows the whole balance in the (10 per cent) 'special rate', and/or main (20 per cent) rate pools to be written-off at once, where the balance in either or both of those pools is £1,000 or less.

Notes

1. These PMAs apply only to capital expenditure on "plant and machinery" (P&M). This means that:

Buildings & structures

2. Although certain fixtures in buildings & structures may qualify as P&M (please see the examples that follow) — the shell of the building itself (for example, walls, floors, ceilings, doors, windows and stairs) does not generally qualify. And fixed structures (such as bridges, aqueducts, roads, hard standings and car parks) do not qualify for PMAs.

Revenue expenditure

3. Expenditure on routine maintenance and repairs normally constitutes a revenue deduction, deductible from the business's revenue account for tax purposes. As revenue, rather than capital expenditure, it cannot qualify for PMAs. However, one exception is expenditure on replacing the whole or more than 50 per cent of an 'integral feature' (such as an electrical or cold water system, heating system or lift) which, if incurred after 1/6 April 2008, is deemed to be capital expenditure in all cases, and which will generally qualify for WDAs at 10 per cent.

Double allowances

4. Double or allowances on the same amount of expenditure are not permitted. For example if:

- in the year 2009–10, a business spent (say) £75,000 on a new slurry storage system, it could claim a 100 per cent AIA on £50,000 of that cost, and a 40 per cent temporary FYA on the balance of £25,000, that is, total allowances of £50,000 + £10,000 = £60,000 in the year 2009–10. This would leave £15,000 to be written down at 20 per cent a year in 2010–11 and in later years
- a 100 per cent ECA is claimed on (say) a piece of equipment costing £100,000, then that cost is wholly relieved and an AIA may not be claimed on that same piece of equipment to give more than 100 per cent relief.

General

5. Expenditure on the provision of P&M (for example, transportation & on site installation costs) and alteration of land for the purpose only of installing P&M, can qualify for PMAs at the rate applicable to the P&M being installed. However, expenditure on works involving the alteration of land more generally do not qualify. For example, the cost of levelling land in order to provide a stable base for a heavy machine would qualify, but the cost of levelling land in order to lay a hard standing or a foundation for a building would not qualify.

Examples of P&M

1. Outdoor items

Expenditure on the following can qualify for the AIA, FYA, WDAs and, in some cases * ECAs

- Slurry storage systems, including, for example:
  - slurry storage tanks (whether above or below ground)
  - any reception pit and/or effluent tank and/or channels and pipes used in connection with the slurry storage tank
- Small scale slurry and sludge dewatering equipment (*may qualify for 100 per cent ECA)
- Rainwater harvesting and filtration equipment (*may qualify for 100 per cent ECA)
- Gutters and associated piping for carrying rain water harvested for business uses
- Sewerage systems designed to meet the particular requirements of the business
- Silos for temporary storage
- Concrete pad surrounded by low-level barriers for temporary storage of manure
- Storage tanks
- Moveable pig tents or pig arks
- See also under 'general plant & machinery' and 'cars' at 3 and 4 below for the treatment of vehicles, etc.

2. Fixtures in buildings or structures

Expenditure on the following can qualify for the AIA, FYA, WDAs and, in certain cases* ECAs. In the case of WDAs, certain fixtures attract WDAs at 20 per cent & others at 10 per cent — as shown separately at (a) and (b) below.

(a) Building features that can qualify for WDAs at 20 per cent

- Monitoring systems (including telemetry) for monitoring temperature, humidity, lighting, water and food levels
- Water meters and monitoring equipment, including flow meters and water management software (*may qualify for 100 per cent ECA)
- Computer & telecommunications systems (including their wiring or other links)
- Fire alarm, burglar alarm & surveillance systems (including their wiring or other links)
- Feed systems (whether or not automated)
- Slatted flooring areas (as internal parts of a slurry system)
- Farrowing crates
- Moveable, adjustable pen dividers
- Taps, sinks, basins and drinkers (certain water efficient taps *may qualify for 100 per cent ECA)
- Fitted bathrooms, toilets, showers, kitchens & furnishings in office and staff accommodation used in the business (certain water efficient taps, toilets and showers *may qualify for 100 per cent ECA)

(b) Building features that can qualify for WDAs at 10 per cent

- All parts of a general electrical system (whether providing mains power or a lighting system) irrespective of whether or not the system is designed to be 'trade specific'
- Certain lighting controls and Automatic Monitoring & Targeting (AMT) equipment designed to save energy, *may qualify for 100 per cent ECAs, if certified by the Department for Energy and Climate Change (DECC)

- All parts of air conditioning systems including, for example:
  - Ventilation shafts
  - ACNV (automatically controlled natural ventilation) shutters
  - Metal mesh & curtain arrangements for controlling airflow
- Cold water, hot water and heating systems, including pipes, pumps, boilers, valves, etc. (but not sinks or basins that are plumbed into the system that can qualify for WDAs at 20 per cent — see above)
- Thermal insulation added to existing buildings or structures. (Certain pipe work insulation *may qualify for 100 per cent ECA.)

3. Non-fixtures: general plant & machinery (20 per cent) apart from cars

Expenditure on the following can qualify for the AIA, FYA, WDAs and, in certain cases* ECAs.

- Any agricultural or other machinery used for the purposes of the business. For example:
  - Specialist equipment for the production, storage, handling & distribution of pig feed
  - Pig transportation crates
  - Pig weighing and handling equipment
- Lorries, vans, tractors, trailers, fork-lift trucks and other agricultural vehicles and machines
- Computers & computerised equipment
- Free-standing heaters & air conditioning units (certain radiant heaters *may qualify for ECAs)
- Office equipment & furnishings.

4. Other P&M: Cars

Expenditure on cars used for business purposes does not qualify for the AIA or temporary 40 per cent FYA, but can qualify for:

- 100 per cent FYA if the car is electrically propelled or its CO_2 emissions do not exceed 110 grams per kilometre driven (g/km)
- 20 per cent WDA if the car's CO_2 emissions exceed 110 g/km, but do not exceed 160g/km, or
- 10 per cent WDA if the car's CO_2 emissions exceed 160 g/km.

These environmentally based rules, to tie the rate of WDA to a car's CO_2 emissions, apply to expenditure on cars purchased on or after 1 April 2009 (companies) or 6 April 2009 (sole traders and partnerships).

FURTHER INFORMATION

CT VAT Reliefs Incentives & Capital Allowances Team

3rd Floor Mail Station A, 100 Parliament Street London SW1A 2BQ

Phone: 020 7147 2610 Email: joy.guthrie@hmrc.gsi.gov.uk

Notes:

PMAs: more detailed, general guidance on capital allowances is contained in HMRC's Capital Allowances Manual.

*ECAs – In all cases where 100 per cent ECAs are mentioned in this note, please check the ECA website for the precise eligibility criteria — http://www.eca.gov.uk/.

Index

U

V

W

Z